Making the Supreme Court

Making the Supreme Court

The Politics of Appointments, 1930–2020

Charles M. Cameron
Princeton University
Jonathan P. Kastellec
Princeton University

Oxford University Press is a department of the University of Oxford.
It furthers the University's objective of excellence in research, scholarship,
and education by publishing worldwide. Oxford is a registered trade mark of
Oxford University Press in the UK and in certain other countries.

Published in the United States of America by Oxford University Press
198 Madison Avenue, New York, NY 10016, United States of America.

CIP data is on file at the Library of Congress.

ISBN 978–0–19–768053–7 (hbk.)
ISBN 978–0–19–768054–4 (pbk.)

DOI: 10.1093/oso/9780197680537.001.0001
DOI: 10.1093/oso/9780197680544.001.0001

Printed by Integrated Books International, United States of America

To my students, who've taught me as much as I ever taught them.
CMC

To Katie, Jack, & Nora, for all their love and support.
JK

Contents

Acknowledgments

The ninety years from 1930 to 2020 saw stunning changes in American national politics. The politics of Supreme Court nominations changed utterly as well. When we started working together on this topic more than a decade ago, the changes that solidified into a new era were well under way. But those changes were difficult to discern at the time. They became clearer and clearer with each new vacancy on the court. As a result, what we thought might be a quick and easy book turned out to be neither, and is quite different than it would have been a decade ago. But perhaps it is more interesting.

A book of this length results in even more intellectual debts than typical. First, we thank the many co-authors we have worked with on our previously published articles on Supreme Court nominations, both together and separately: Leeann Bass, Deborah Beim, Julian Dean, Cody Gray, Jeff Lax, Michael Malecki, Lauren Mattioli, Jee Kwang Park, and Justin Phillips. The ideas from these articles all have found their way into the book, in one form or the other.

We thank several friends and colleagues who read and critiqued the manuscript in full, particularly Josh Chafetz, Tom Clark, and Nolan McCarty. We also thank reviewers at Oxford University Press and Princeton University Press for their very helpful suggestions. Several friends and colleagues read and critiqued individual chapters. Markus Prior read and thoughtfully responded to Chapters 7 and 10, and Joshua Kalla read Chapter 10 as well; we apologize for not taking all your excellent suggestions. Lewis Kornhauser, John Ferejohn, Sandy Gordon, and Anna Harvey critiqued Chapter 12 in the Law, Economics, and Politics Colloquium at NYU Law School, which resulted in substantial improvements. We have presented various chapters several times at Princeton's Center for the Study of Democratic Politics; we thank our colleagues and Princeton graduate students for many helpful suggestions over the years. Finally, many scholars offered helpful suggestions on our previously published articles on Supreme Court nominations. We thank: Chris Achen, Stephen Ansolabehere, Michael Bailey, Deborah Beim, Benjamin Bishin, Brandice Canes-Wrone, Devin Caughey, Joshua Fischman, Andrew Gelman, Virginia Gray, Andrew Guess, Alex Hirsch, Gregory Koger, George Kraus, Keith Krehbiel, Shiro Kuriwaki, Kosuke Imai, Jeff Lax, Josh Lerner, David Lewis, Michael Nelson, Tom Romer, Robert Shapiro, Chuck Shipan, Jeff Staton, Alissa Stollwerk, Yu-Sung Su, Georg Vanberg, and Alan Wiseman.

To the extent a book written by two authors over many years reads almost as if one person wrote it in a single sitting, we owe a tremendous debt to a wonderful development editor, Elaine Duncan, who read the entire book and turned our social science prose into something we hope is quite readable. (We thank econometrician extraordinaire Harry Paarsch for connecting us to Elaine.) We thank Angela Chnapko at Oxford University Press for helping us to fulfill our vision of a big book with color figures, and for helping us shepherd the manuscript through the review and production process. We also thank Alexcee Bechthold at Oxford for her timely assistance throughout the process, and Thomas Deva for excellent copy-editing. We also thank Phil and Laura Pascuzzo for designing the cover of the book. We owe a debt to Doug Arnold—in addition to his canonical work on accountability that inspired Chapter 11, Doug also helped us navigate the book publishing process. We also thank long-time acquaintance Chuck Myers for sharing his formidable expertise about academic publishing.

The amount of data collected for the analyses in this book required a veritable army of research assistants over many years, and we are grateful to all for their hard work: Chelsie Alexandre, Amna Amin, My Bui, Sena Cebeci, Annabeth Donovan, Mahishan Gnanaseharan, James Goble, Laura Huchel, Julia Ilhardt, Hillel Koslowe, Mary Kroeger, Naomi Lake, Hal Moore, Michael Pomirchy, Nina Sheridan, Ephraim Shimko, Connor Staggs, Sophie Steinman-Gordon, and Albert Wen. (We apologize if there is anyone we forgot!) Hal, Nina, and Naomi, in particular, worked tirelessly to code much of the interest group data in Chapter 5. Leeann Bass and Huchen Liu worked extensively on various data and coding projects while working as postdocs at Princeton; many of the analyses in Chapters 5, 6, 11, 12, and 13 would not exist without their efforts. Sally (Ye Lin) Hahn did the main coding for the simulation analyses that appear in Chapters 13 and 14, while Julian Dean and Tan Shanker helped us code and merge several interest group datasets. Julian also was responsible for overseeing the creation of the dataset of newspaper editorials that appears in Chapter 6. Rohnin Randles did some last-minute research assistance that greatly improved Chapter 5, and Kodiak Sauer proof-read the final manuscript. Finally, we thank Princeton University and the Center for the Study of Democratic Politics for generously funding this research support.

While much of the data in the book is newly collected, a number of scholars generously shared their data with us. We thank: Stephen Ansolabahere, Michael Bailey, Tom Clark, Lee Epstein, Thomas Hansford, Philip Edward Jones, Shiro Kuriwaki, Ben Lauderdale, Geoff Layman, Rene Lindstadt, Christine Nemacheck, Jeffrey Segal, and Chad Westerland. We also thank other scholars for making their data easily and publicly accessible, including: Sara Benesh, Adam Boche, Henry E. Brady, Traci Burch, Jeffrey Lewis, Andrew Martin, Keith Poole, Kevin Quinn, Aaron Rudkin, Ted Ruger, Kay Schlozman, Luke Sonnet, Keith Whittington, and Hye Young You. Much of the data on Supreme Court nominees in the book comes from the U.S. Supreme Court Justices Database; we thank its creators for making this data very easy to work with. Similarly, the Federal Judicial Center's fantastic database of federal judge biographies was the source of most of the data on Courts of Appeals judges. Finally, our public opinion datasets would not exist without the Roper Center's for Public Opinion Research's astounding poll archive.

Cameron thanks his friend, collaborator, and former colleague Jeff Segal for many intellectual gifts, not the least of which was an abiding interest in Supreme Court appointments. He also gratefully thanks faculty assistant extraordinaire Helene Wood, without whose help he would have missed or forgotten every other professional deadline or responsibility.

Cameron also warmly acknowledges the contribution of a group of Columbia University and Princeton University undergraduates whose honors theses and senior theses on appointment politics he had the pleasure of directing. The theses were all interesting; more than that, the imprint of some can be found in this book. Thanks to Columbia College undergraduates Pablo Amador, Raymond Amanquah, Leslie Arias, Lee Arnold, Janet Balis, Isabel Barbosa, Katherine Beasley, Tom Brady, Michelle Brown, Phil Bussey, Anthony Canale, Tom Casey, John Cerza, Allison S.Y. Chang, Sam Chi, Eugene Chen, John Patrick Collins, Dennis Comstock, Kevin Connoly, Julie Davidson, Wade Davis, Elizabeth Doherty, Alexis Donnelly, Peter Egan, Marily Farquharson, Robert Fernandez, Jack Gaeta, Robert Gaudet, Jr., Ross Gotler, Shin-Kap Han, Brian Hansen, George Hassan, Joe Hill, John Jennings, David Lee, Paul Lee, Andrea Lipton, Daneil Lorge, Mark Mandrake, Lorely Marinez, Maria Master, Jennifer Maxfiled, Steve McAnulty, Ingrid Michelsen, Stuart Miller, Doug Murphy, Paul O'Donnell, Yon Okorodudu, Sean Rogers, RaLea Sluga, Michele Smith, Jeffrey Sweat, Yin Yin Tan, Peter Torres, Alex Trias, and Phillip Winiecki. He also thanks Allison Margolin for memorable discussions about many aspects of the law. Notable Princeton undergraduates included Mikaela Weber, Ross Williams, and Daphne LeGall. He apologizes to any whose name has escaped him.

Finally, we thank the University of Chicago Press, Cambridge University Press, and Now Publishers for granting us permission to reproduce work from our published articles in the book. This includes:

- Portions of Chapter 5 appear in our 2020 article, "From Textbook Pluralism to Modern Hyper-Pluralism: Interest Groups and Supreme Court Nominations, 1930–2017," co-authored with Cody Gray and Jee-Kwang Park and published in the *Journal of Law & Courts*.
- Portions of Chapter 8 appear in our 2013 article, "Voting for Justices: Change and Continuity in Confirmation Voting 1937–2010," co-authored with Jee-Kwang Park and published in the *Journal of Politics*.
- Portions of Chapter 9 appear in our 2021 article, "Presidential Selection of Supreme Court Nominees: The Characteristics Approach," co-authored with Lauren Mattioli and published in the *Quarterly Journal of Political Science*. In addition, the discussion in the first part of Chapter 9 about move-the-median theory is drawn from our 2016 article, "Are Supreme Court Nominations a Move-the-Median Game?", published in the *American Political Science Review*.
- The voter accountability analysis in Chapter 11 is based on our 2022 article, "The Politics of Accountability in Supreme Court Nominations: Voter Recall

and Assessment of Senator Votes on Nominees," co-authored with Leeann Bass and published in *Political Science Research Methods*. In addition, the co-partisan analysis in Chapter 11 is based on Kastellec's 2015 article, "Polarizing the Electoral Connection: Partisan Representation in Supreme Court Confirmation Politics," co-authored with Jeffrey Lax, Michael Malecki, and Justin Phillips, and published in the *Journal of Politics*.

We have created a website for the book—`www.makingthesupremecourt.com`—that contains the Appendix to the book, as well as replication data and code for all the analyses that appear in the book.

PART I

WHAT HAPPENED

1
Then and Now

> He [the President] shall nominate, and by and with the Advice and Consent of the Senate, shall appoint Ambassadors, other public Ministers and Consuls, Judges of the supreme Court, and all other Officers of the United States, whose Appointments are not herein otherwise provided for, and which shall be established by Law.
>
> **—U.S. Constitution, Article II, Section 2**

On January 31, 1941, James McReynolds announced his retirement as an associate justice of the Supreme Court. McReynolds, appointed by President Woodrow Wilson in 1914, was one of the notorious "Four Horsemen," a bloc of justices who consistently voted to strike down as unconstitutional President Franklin Roosevelt's New Deal measures between 1933 and 1937. Although the court would eventually endorse the New Deal in full in 1937, McReynolds continued to oppose it until the bitter end of his tenure on the bench.

McReynolds's retirement granted Roosevelt, now in his third presidential term, his sixth Supreme Court appointment. During his first term, Roosevelt had no opportunity to alter the court's membership and end the reign of the Four Horsemen. Following his landslide re-election in 1936, Roosevelt proposed court packing—increasing the number of justices to give a favorable majority—as a way to break the logjam. While Congress soundly rejected the court packing plan, Roosevelt ultimately prevailed, as a majority of the court dropped its opposition to the New Deal that year.[1] Then, a combination of five retirements and deaths between 1937 and 1940 granted Roosevelt the opportunity to greatly reshape the court.

A few months after McReynolds' announcement, Chief Justice Charles Evans Hughes announced his retirement as well. Roosevelt now had the rare opportunity to select a new chief and simultaneously replace an associate justice. The master politician eagerly grasped the chance, converting it into a "triple play." First, he nominated sitting Justice Harlan F. Stone to replace Hughes as chief justice. Then he nominated Senator James Byrnes, a strong New Dealer who had supported court packing, to replace McReynolds. Finally, he nominated his attorney general, Robert Jackson, to replace Stone as associate justice. In one stroke, the triple play replaced 22% of the court's membership and produced a much friendlier chief justice.

Roosevelt officially submitted all three nominations to the Senate on June 12, 1941. Democrats overwhelmingly controlled the 77th Senate and saw eye-to-eye with the

Making the Supreme Court: The Politics of Appointments, 1930–2020. Charles M. Cameron and Jonathan P. Kastellec, Oxford University Press. © Oxford University Press 2023. DOI: 10.1093/oso/9780197680544.003.0001

president on judicial matters. Nevertheless, one might have expected the august body to review the three appointments with a degree of due diligence. For example, Byrnes, a power broker in the Democratic Party, had enjoyed a long and distinguished career as a House member and senator from South Carolina—but he never attended law school nor practiced at the Supreme Court Bar.[2] Such diligence would not come due, however—the Senate confirmed Byrnes on the same day it received his nomination! The Senate's reviews of Stone and Jackson were only slightly less perfunctory; unlike Byrnes, both were referred to the Senate Judiciary Committee for a hearing. But the hearing was brief, and the Senate quickly confirmed both nominees by voice vote, with not even a single dissent sounded against them. Within a span of five years, Roosevelt had appointed an astounding eight justices.[3] The court that had so famously frustrated the president would no longer pose any obstacle to his agenda.

Seventy-five years later, things looked quite different. In February 2016, Justice Antonin Scalia died suddenly while on a hunting trip. Scalia's death created an unexpected opportunity for President Barack Obama—in his last year in office—to make a third appointment to the court. The Senate had confirmed his first two appointments, Sonia Sotomayor and Elena Kagan, with minimal fuss in 2009 and 2010, respectively. But Democrats overwhelmingly controlled the Senate in those years. Although fewer than 10 Republican senators voted "yea" on either nominee, the GOP's opposition did little to impede Sotomayor and Kagan's smooth paths to confirmation.

The political landscape in 2016 was quite different, however. The 2014 midterm elections placed Republicans in control of the Senate. Within mere hours of Scalia's death, the new Senate Majority Leader, Mitch McConnell of Kentucky, threw down the gauntlet, stating in a press release that Senate Republicans had no intention of filling the vacancy before the inauguration of the next president in 2017.[4]

A month later, President Obama nominated Merrick Garland, a widely respected judge on the U.S. Court of Appeals for the D.C. Circuit, to replace Scalia. In 2009 and 2010, Obama had placed Garland on the short list of candidates for the vacant seats. But he passed over Garland in favor of Sotomayor and Kagan, purportedly to "save" him for possible future appointment under divided party government. Indeed, relative to the larger pool of potential Democratic nominees, Garland was noticeably less liberal and also somewhat older than a typical modern nominee. In fact, in 2010, Senator Orrin Hatch, a Republican and a former chair of the Senate Judiciary Committee, had urged Obama to nominate Garland to replace Justice John Paul Stevens, stating that Garland would be a "consensus nominee" and confirmed with broad bipartisan support.[5]

Six years later, however, Obama's selection of Garland met a brick wall. Under McConnell's leadership, the Senate took no action on Garland's nomination. The Judiciary Committee held no hearings, and no floor vote was ever scheduled. Though some nominees prior to the Civil War and then again during Reconstruction and the late nineteenth century were rejected quite summarily by the Senate, the tactic of refusing to take *any* action on a Supreme Court nominee appears to be unprecedented.[6] Nine months after Scalia's death and eight months after Garland's nomination, Donald Trump shockingly upset Hillary Clinton in the 2016 presidential election, thereby dooming the already slim prospects of a Garland confirmation in the lame duck period. Garland's nomination would end with no bang and barely a whimper on January 3, 2017, the day the 114th Congress officially ended.

The successful deep-sixing of Garland gave Trump the rare opportunity to enter office with a Supreme Court vacancy in hand. Trump had invoked the vacancy as a campaign issue, pledging to appoint conservative justices in Scalia's mold; he even took the unprecedented step of publicizing during the campaign a list of potential nominees from whom he would choose.[7] On January 31, 2017, Trump kept his promise. From his public list, he picked Neil Gorsuch, a judge on the Tenth Circuit Court of Appeals, to replace the conservative icon Scalia.

By all accounts, Gorsuch was highly qualified, having served on the Court of Appeals for a decade—indeed, the American Bar Association gave Gorsuch its highest rating of "well qualified." When George W. Bush nominated Gorsuch to the Tenth Circuit in 2006, Democrats joined Republicans in confirming him unanimously. Now, with the Senate in Republican hands, a smooth elevation of the president's pick to the highest court might have seemed likely. But McConnell's blockade of Garland had enraged liberal activists, groups, and voters, and many Democratic senators pledged to do everything they could to block Gorsuch's path.

The main procedural tool available to Senate Democrats was the filibuster. The 2016 elections had left Republicans with a narrow majority (52 to 48), which meant that if enough Democrats stood together, Gorsuch would not achieve the 60 votes required to overcome a filibuster. Indeed, on April 6, a cloture vote to move Gorsuch's nomination to a final vote received only 55 votes in favor, five short of the 60-vote threshold. If the process had ended there, Scalia's seat would have continued to sit vacant. But Senate rules depend upon the preferences of the majority. The next day, McConnell turned the tables on the Democrats by exercising the "nuclear option"—introducing a measure to change the cloture threshold for Supreme Court nominations to a simple majority. In 2013, Democrats had used the same tactic to quash persistent minority Republican opposition to Obama's appeals court nominees—but only for lower federal court nominations.[8] Now, a majority of Republicans voted to remove the filibuster for Supreme Court nominees as well, paving the way for Gorsuch to be confirmed the next day by a vote of 54–45.

In the end, the fact that Gorsuch, not Garland, replaced Scalia meant that the court would remain broadly conservative in its overall trajectory, rather than moving to the left for the first time in several decades.[9] In short, the policy consequences of the appointment politics of 2016 and 2017 were substantial. Moreover, the death of the filibuster for Supreme Court appointments seemed to foretell a future of extremist nominees—from both parties.

* * *

If Roosevelt and his advisors could have looked into a crystal ball and foreseen the confirmation story of 2016, they would have been astounded. The rancor and divisiveness of the politics would have reminded them of Reconstruction, the key experience of their parents' generation. What new Civil War could have triggered this partisan battle over Supreme Court appointments? Conversely, Obama and McConnell probably never spent much time studying Roosevelt's brilliant triple-play appointments of 1941. The politics of the early 1940s would have seemed as distant from their reality, and as irrelevant, as life on Mars.

What produced the sea-change in appointment politics between 1941 and 2016?[10] This question lies at the heart of this book. Answering it requires a journey through American history and politics. It also requires the tools of modern political science.

1.2 The Pelican Problem

Supreme Court appointments have rarely been subjects for works of popular culture. But there is one high-profile exception: *The Pelican Brief*, the 1992 pot-boiler novel by John Grisham, which was turned into a movie starring Julia Roberts and Denzel Washington the following year. In typical Grisham style, the plot of *The Pelican Brief* favors intrigue and action over verisimilitude. But, if you indulge us, the plot is actually instructive for our theoretical approach in this book.

In the novel, an oil developer has a project tied up in litigation by an environmental group. The case seems likely to head to the Supreme Court. If the high court rules in a liberal, pro-environment fashion, the developer stands to lose billions. So what is the poor developer to do? Ask his lawyers to write a really good brief? Fortunately for the novel's readers, a demented legal genius in the developer's law firm suggests a somewhat more aggressive litigation strategy: simultaneously assassinate two Supreme Court justices. The legal genius's elaborate calculations show that their likely replacements will alter the balance of power on the court, leading to a conservative outcome and assuring the developer and his law firm an enormous financial windfall.[11]

Of course, we do not endorse assassination as a means of advancing one's legal and financial goals. But as political scientists, we could not help but be impressed by the actions of the legal genius, who performed a social science *tour de force*. First, he understood the court so well that he could accurately predict how replacing any Supreme Court justice and changing the ideological mix on the court would affect case outcomes. Second, he understood presidential politics so well that he could accurately forecast the likely ideology of a president's nominee based on the president's ideology, the make-up of the Senate, and other relevant factors surrounding a nomination. Third, he understood the behavior of the Senate, interest groups, the media, and public opinion so well that he could accurately foresee the outcome of the confirmation process for any given Supreme Court nominee.

We call this analytical challenge "the Pelican Problem." In a nutshell, the task of solving the Pelican Problem means:

- Predict the likely ideology of a Supreme Court nominee chosen by any given president under any given circumstances;
- Forecast the outcome of the confirmation battle for any given nominee; and
- Foresee the broad policy consequences of replacing any Supreme Court justice with a new justice.

Finally, because we have rather "high church" tastes in social science, it also means:

- Use political science theory to ground the predictions and forecasts.

If one can solve the Pelican Problem, one can claim to understand the politics of Supreme Court nominations.

Can real-world political scientists follow in the footsteps of Grisham's legal genius and actually crack the Pelican Problem? Remarkably, for a time it looked like the answer was "yes." Starting in the late 1980s, political scientists created a simple, clear, and logical theory of Supreme Court appointment politics: Move-the-Median (MTM) Theory. As a social science theory, MTM is quite elegant; for any vacancy, it makes predictions about the type of nominee a president should select, whether the Senate should vote to confirm or reject a nominee, and the impact of a nominee on the court's decision making. Unfortunately, it turned out that these predictions fall short when applied to the real world of nomination politics. In a 2016 article in the *American Political Science Review*, we undertook an exhaustive review of MTM theory's predictions and arrayed them against a great deal of newly available data. We showed that, for nomination politics since 1930, MTM theory does a rather poor job of predicting the ideology of nominees, the voting decisions of individual senators, and the success and failure of nominations in the Senate.[12] These shortcomings in turn mean that the theory also does not satisfactorily predict changes in the court's decision making.[13] To be clear, our point here is not that MTM theory tells us nothing about nomination politics. But these shortcomings do mean that a satisfactory *collective explanation* of changes in Supreme Court appointment politics over time with respect to presidents, senators, and the court—as well as additional relevant actors, such as the mass public and interest groups—will have to go beyond the narrow confines of MTM theory.

So where does that leave us? Most political science books articulate a single theory and provide evidence evaluating the theory's predictions throughout the book. Ideally, one might prefer a unified theory of Supreme Court nominations that solves the Pelican Problem for the 90 years from 1930 to 2020. Such a revised theory would have to include a powerful meta-account of American political history, explaining the transformation in appointment politics over these nine decades and showing how larger changes in American politics drove the transformation.

A single unified grand narrative like this may exist. But if so, we have been unable to find it. Consequently, we pursue a different approach to history and politics. Rather than forge a single master narrative covering nine decades of history—one theory to rule them all!—we deploy multiple mechanisms. By a "mechanism," we mean a well-elaborated causally oriented account of a political phenomenon. We examine several mechanisms because different processes worked themselves out over time, intersecting and interacting in ways not really intended or foreseen by actors focused myopically on their own affairs and narrow concerns. Also, because we are committed to the social science school of methodological individualism, our mechanisms focus on human beings—presidents, senators, justices, interest groups, and voters—who have agency and goals, and make choices to advance their goals. We employ this "rational choice" approach because it usually makes intuitive sense and comports well with quantitative and qualitative data—not just roll call votes, survey responses, and election returns, but also the evidence one finds in diaries, memoirs, recorded conversations and telephone calls, oral histories, speeches, contemporary reportage, investigative journalism, and academic histories—all of which we use in this book.[14]

So, in lieu of a single unified solution to the Pelican Problem, we present what we believe is a coherent overall account of the history of Supreme Court appointment politics from 1930 to 2020. In a nutshell, we argue that the growth of federal judicial power from the 1930s onward created a multitude of politically active groups struggling to shape judicial policy. Over time, some of these groups moved beyond lobbying the court and began seeking to influence who sits on it. As a result, presidential candidates increasingly pledged to select justices who conformed to policy litmus tests (mostly for Republicans) and diversity demands (mostly for Democrats). Once in office, these presidents re-shaped the executive selection system from casual and haphazard to meticulous and effective. As a result, presidents gained the ability to deliver to the groups precisely what they had promised. The groups also transformed the public face of appointments, pushing the process from a brief and usually closed affair to a highly visible political campaign mobilizing public opinion via intensive media coverage focused on controversy. In turn, confirmation voting in the Senate gained an engaged and attentive audience, whose presence pressured senators into ideologically polarized voting. The result is a new politics of appointments biased toward selecting and placing consistent judicial ideologues on the court—and only such ideologues.

If this account is correct, the implications for the future of the U.S. Supreme Court—and for the court's place in the American political system—are profound.

1.3 A Lens on American Politics

A study of the history of Supreme Court appointments naturally draws the interest of die-hard aficionados of the court (like us). But such a study also has the potential to be much more than a chronicle of nominees and justices, a re-telling of half-remembered dramas from days gone by. It can—we claim—train a sharp lens on American government and how it functions. A multiple-mechanism history of appointment politics offers a powerful device—a laboratory of sorts—for studying the origins, evolution, and consequences of the American governmental process, and a new American politics.

1.3.1 A Separation-of-Powers Laboratory

These are bold claims! What is their basis?

First, Supreme Court nominations constitute the *same political event* occurring rather frequently and fairly regularly over an *extended period*. So they allow one to observe and measure what changes in the process and what doesn't, over time. In terms of being a regularly occurring event, Supreme Court appointments are similar to, say, elections to the U.S. House of Representatives. Unlike elections, however, every Supreme Court nomination puts America's distinctive governance system, based on the separation of powers (SOP), through its paces. The president and Congress always interact, sometimes vigorously; but interest groups, the media, and citizens can join the interbranch bargaining, all against the backdrop of judicial policymaking. Supreme Court appointment politics do not implicate the entire governmental process; federalism, for example, plays little role. However, as a device for revealing change and continuity in the performance of the SOP system, and as a venue for thinking about mechanisms and institutions, Supreme Court appointment politics shines.

Figure 1.1 interrogates our claims about "rather frequently," "fairly regularly," and "extended period." It presents a timeline of our primary 90-year period of study, 1930 to 2020. This era saw 54 Supreme Court nominations, beginning with Herbert Hoover's selection of Charles Evans Hughes as Chief Justice and ending with Donald Trump's nomination of Associate Justice Amy Coney Barrett. The nominations span nine decades, and feature the involvement of 15 presidents and 29 Senates. (A table containing information on each nominee appears in the Appendix.)

In the figure, the lower graph gives the name of each nominee and the year of nomination, the name and party of the nominating president, and whether the nomination succeeded or failed. So it is a handy overview of the whole history. The top part of the figure shows the incidence of nominations, with a thin vertical bar indicating the date of each nomination. On average, a nomination occurred about every 20 months. The figure reveals, however, that many periods saw flurries of nominations, while others witnessed "dry" spells for nominations. One five-year gap occurred after Cardozo's nomination in 1932, coinciding with Roosevelt's famous confrontation with the court. The longest dry spell occurred between 1995 and 2004. From our perspective, this unusually long hiatus is not so concerning because both presidents who served in this period, Bill Clinton and George W. Bush, made nominations. More problematic were the sparse nominations of the 1970s; not only did Jimmy Carter have no opportunity to alter the court, this period saw a dramatic growth in the number of interest groups (both generally and with respect to Supreme Court nominations). Nonetheless, on average, Supreme Court nominations

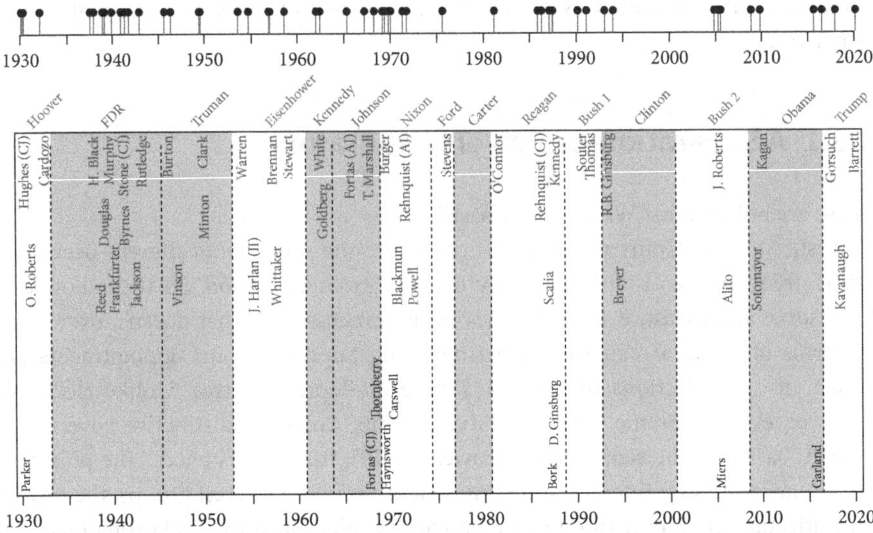

Fig. 1.1 The timeline of Supreme Court nominations, 1930–2020. The top panel shows the incidence of nominations. In the bottom panel, successful nominees are depicted at the top of the plot (in green text), while unsuccessful nominees are at the bottom of the plot. Shaded areas depict Democratic presidents, white areas denote Republican presidents, and the dotted vertical lines separate individual presidents.

occurred with sufficient frequency that we can conclude that appointment politics constitute a suitable laboratory for studying the evolution of the separation-of-powers system.

1.3.2 The New American Politics

Before entering our "separation-of-powers laboratory," it is helpful to review the big changes that transformed American politics during the last half of the twentieth century and the first decades of the twenty-first century. These changes helped drive the transformation of Supreme Court appointment politics.

There are many ways to tell a "big picture" story about the emergence of the new American politics. Our version naturally looks ahead to appointment politics, which affects what we emphasize and what we downplay. For example, war has been a huge driver of political change, but it plays little role in our story.[15] Similarly, the rise of income inequality has exerted a profound effect on American politics, but is not central to our story.[16] Finally, race and identity politics make an appearance, but they are somewhat secondary to the larger political story about changes in focus and preferences that we tell.[17] Our rendition of the "big story" focuses on five changes. They are:

1. The growth of government and the concomitant rise of a powerful judicial state;
2. The stunning proliferation of interest groups, activists, firms, and wealthy individuals vying to shape government policy, including federal judicial policy;
3. The capture of the political parties by interest groups, activists, and issue enthusiasts, leading to an astounding ideological polarization of elites;
4. The remarkable rise in the frequency of divided party government; and
5. The emergence of a new electorate, one better sorted into parties by ideology, but retaining huge disparities in political knowledge between the most- and least-engaged citizens.

Each of the five changes was important in itself. Together, they interact to create a new politics of American governance, and a new politics of Supreme Court appointments.

1.3.3 The Growth of Government and the Rise of the Judicial State

Figure 1.2 describes a revolution in American government and society. It depicts per capita federal expenditures in real terms, from 1900 to 2020.[18] In 1900 the federal government spent about $160 per person (using constant 2015 dollars). As late as 1930, the beginning of the period we study, the federal government expended only about $400 per person. The reason for the tiny numbers is simple: in practical terms the federal government did almost nothing. The military was puny, social insurance programs almost non-existent, and public improvements few and far between. But

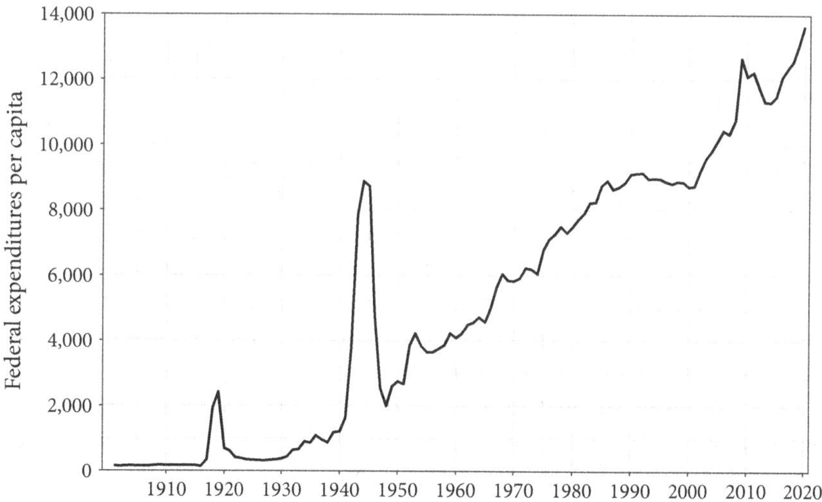

Fig. 1.2 Real Per Capita Federal Expenditures, 1900–2020, per person in 2015-constant dollars.

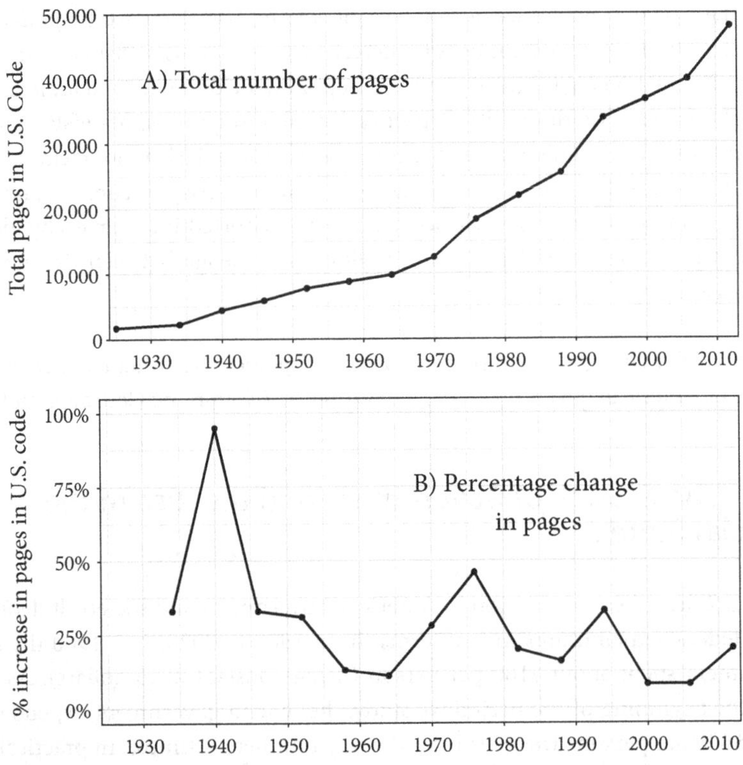

Fig. 1.3 Pages in the U.S. Code, 1925–2012. A) The total pages in the U.S. Code at each revision from 1925 forward. B) The percentage increase in pages from one revision to the next.

this situation changed dramatically, and growth in expenditures continued its upward trend even after the sharp spike generated by World War II.

Figure 1.3A displays a perhaps more subtle trend. It shows the number of pages in the U.S. Code, the omnibus compilation of federal statutory law, which provides a rough measure of the "size," or volume, of federal law.[19] As shown, the Great Depression (1929 to 1939) doubled the volume of law compiled in the U.S. Code, but that was just the beginning of a continued and ever-increasing upward trend. Figure 1.3B depicts the percentage increase in pages from one revision to the next, and shows that the change between the 1930s and 1940s was by far the largest. But also notable were surges in the 1970s and the 1990s.

This explosion in law-making translated into a tremendous increase in federal programs, all of which required funding. By 1940, the New Deal social insurance programs had almost tripled federal governmental expenditures in ten years, to about $1,200 per head. This increase involved a titanic struggle between President Roosevelt and Congress versus the Supreme Court.[20] As remarkable as the New Deal was, the next half-century saw an even more jaw-dropping change as the volume of law and

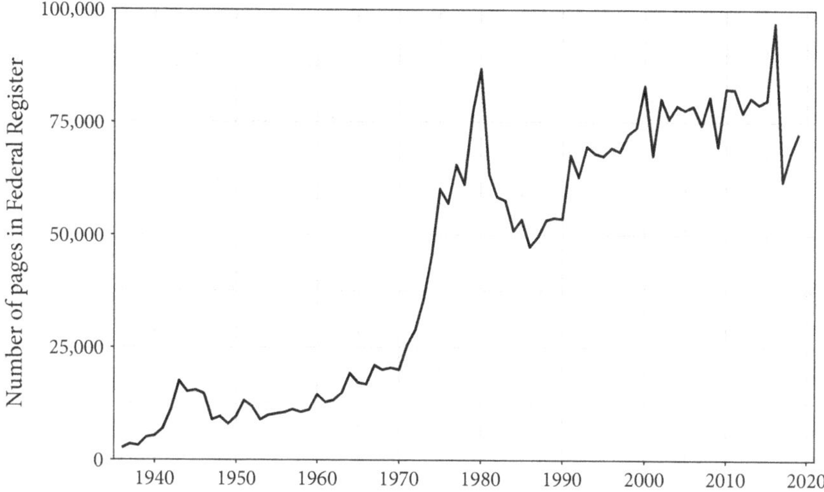

Fig. 1.4 The number of pages in the Federal Register, 1936–2019.

expenditures rose hand-in-hand. Between 1940 and 1965, the U.S. Code doubled in size and per capita real expenditures quadrupled. Between 1965 and 2010, the code nearly quintupled in size, while expenditures nearly tripled, rising to just over $12,000 per capita (in 2015 constant dollars). In other words, between 1930 and 2010 real per capita expenditures increased more than 30-fold. The volume of federal statutory law, as measured by pages in the U.S. Code, increased 15-fold. Changes of this magnitude are not evolutionary; they are *revolutionary*.

With the federal government expanding at this rapid rate, Congress turned to the executive branch to implement these new programs, thereby giving rise to the "administrative state." As a simple measure of the size of the administrative state, consider Figure 1.4, which shows the number of pages in the Federal Register, the official record for agency rules in the U.S. federal bureaucracy. The number of pages exploded in the 1970s, reflecting the new regulatory authority created by statutes passed in the 1960s and early 1970s. While the number of pages would dip in the 1980s, it has since climbed to levels roughly 30-times greater than those in the 1930s.[21]

The rise of the administrative state raises several serious constitutional questions. What restricts the agencies to actions authorized by the duly elected agent of the people, Congress? What compels bureaucrats to respect citizens' rights, and those of other people who reside in the country? The Constitution is silent on these matters, for the obvious reason that no one in 1789 anticipated the future shown in Figures 1.2–1.4.

Once the dust settled from World War II, Congress filled this constitutional gap by passing the Administrative Procedures Act of 1946, which created a formal role for courts to review the rules issued by federal agencies. Courts were to act as the guardians of the people against potential agency overreach.[22] This produced an immediate consequence that is very important for our story: a vast expansion in the responsibilities of federal courts. Bluntly, federal courts received a hunting license in all the policy arenas that federal agencies inhabit. In other words, every expansion of federal regulatory authority meant an expansion in the power of the judicial state.

But this is not all. At the same time that Congress created an administrative state, it also revised the meaning of federal citizenship. Congress, with some help from the court, created many new rights for whole classes of citizens, and many new obligations for others.[23] Examples include new rights in areas such: federal voting; equal treatment in private establishments regardless of race; freedom from sexual harassment in the workplace; freedom from age discrimination in the workplace; humane treatment for those incarcerated in state prisons; access to birth control and a fundamental right to abortion (until 2022); and many others. The federal courts play a central role in defining and enforcing these rights, which became precious possessions for many—and unwelcome burdens for others.[24]

Can we measure the expansion of federal judicial power? A simple albeit crude measure of the activity of the federal judicial state is the caseload of the federal Courts of Appeals.[25] These courts do not have discretionary dockets, unlike the U.S. Supreme Court, which chooses how many cases it hears. So the caseload in the lower courts is a better reflection of the number of legal challenges that litigants bring to federal courts. In addition, appellate cases are important cases, in the sense that litigants are willing to spend considerable time and money pursuing them.

The data on federal appellate caseload, shown in Figure 1.5, is thus informative. In 1900 the U.S. Courts of Appeals heard few cases—litigants commenced about 1,000 cases at the turn of the twentieth century. By 1930 this number had increased to about 2,500, and further increased to about 3,500 in 1940. The caseload then increased only gradually until the late 1960s and early 1970s, when it exploded. The caseload increased from about 9,000 in 1968 to about 50,000 in 2017. From 1930 to 2010,

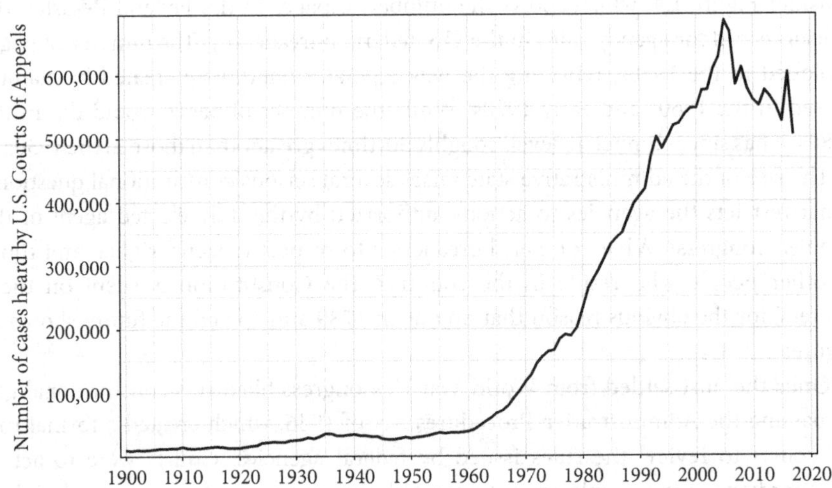

Fig. 1.5 Number of cases commenced in the U.S. Courts of Appeals, 1900–2017.

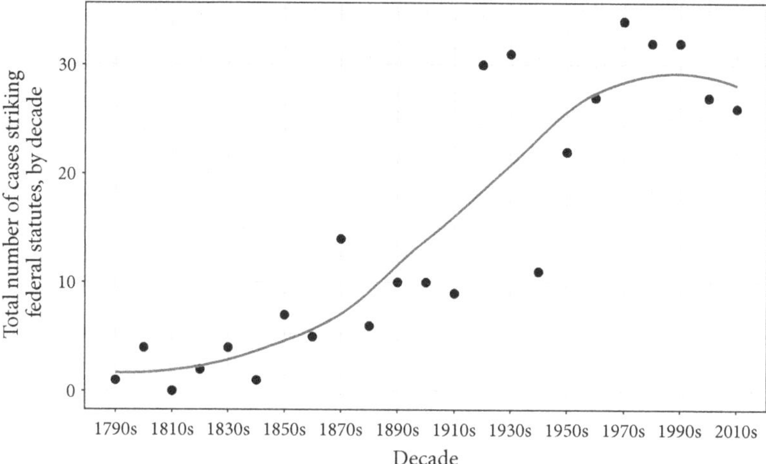

Fig. 1.6 The exercise of judicial review over time. The figure shows the number of federal statutes struck down by the Supreme Court, by decade, between 1790 and 2020. The blue line is a loess line. See note 27 for a description of these lines, which appear throughout the book.

the workload of the courts of Appeals increased 20-fold, an enormous growth in the activity and reach of the federal judiciary.

Of course, it matters not just how many cases courts hear, but what decisions they make. As a simple indicator of judicial power, consider Figure 1.6—the points show the number of federal statutes struck down by the Supreme Court, by decade, between 1790 and 2020.[26] The line (called a loess line) is the fit from a non-parametric regression, which summarizes the trend over time.[27] Early in the nation's history, the stock of federal statutes was quite small; the Supreme Court, on average, struck relatively few federal statutes as unconstitutional. As the federal government grew in size—and as the court's power increased—the number of laws struck down by the court grew markedly. In recent decades, the court has struck down about 30 federal laws per decade, or an average of three per year.[28] Of course, some of the policies overturned are more liberal statutes, and some more conservative. So which justices are doing the reviewing of statutes will matter a great deal.

In short, the last half of the twentieth century saw the rise of a new entity, a powerful and active federal judicial state that now touches the lives, and affects the livelihoods, of virtually all Americans.

1.3.4 From Pluralism to Hyper-Pluralism

In 1926, a promising graduate student at Johns Hopkins University, E. Pendleton Herring, came up with an interesting idea for his political science dissertation. Herring had noticed that Washington, D.C., was overrun with groups, stating, “The cast iron dome of the Capitol has strange magnetic powers. It is the great hive of the nation to which each busy big and little association sooner or later wings its way."[29] His dissertation, which was published in 1929 as *Group Representation Before Congress*, studied the groups and their methods. His census of Washington groups found about 500, and he guessed that there might be as many as 1,000. Imagine, 500 groups!

In the mid-1970s, the Columbia Books publishing company saw a commercial opportunity. Venders, the press, firms, congressional staff, and individuals wanted to be able to find and contact the organized groups with offices in Washington. And the groups wanted to be found. If Columbia Books compiled and sold a directory of the groups, it might be a commercial success. Hence was born *Washington Representatives*. The industrious compilers of repeated editions of the directory probably did not anticipate that future political scientists would pore over their work, sometimes even turning it into data.[30] Such compilations were made in the years 1981, 1991, 2001, 2006, and 2011.

The simplest use of the directory is just to count the number of organizations with offices in Washington. Figure 1.7 displays the number of unique groups from the Washington Representatives Study in the publication years; for reference, we also include Herring's estimate from 1929. The figure shows an explosion in the number of groups, with a 30-fold increase between 1929 and 2011.

When he reviewed Herring's book for the *American Political Science Review* in 1929, Peter Odegard (1929, 470), another future star in the profession, stressed the continuity of Herring's Washington with that of previous generations. "There may

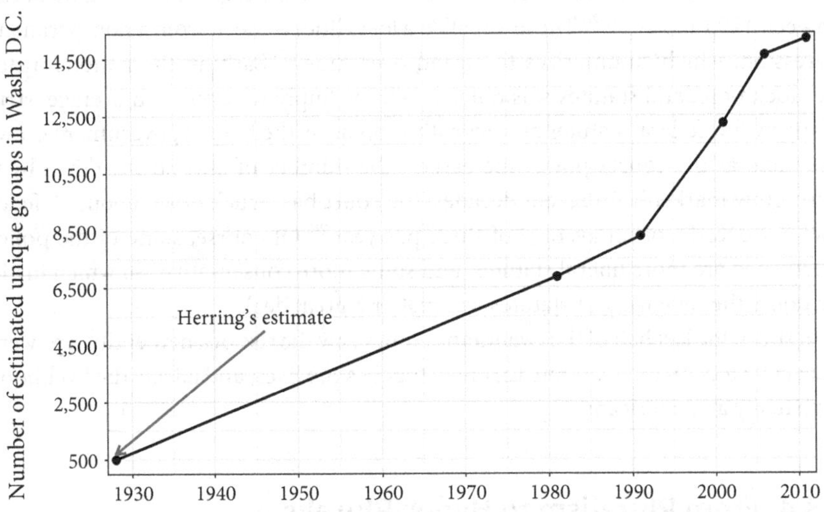

Fig. 1.7 The growth of unique groups from the Washington Representatives Study, 1929–2011. The first point shows Herring's estimate of 500 groups in 1929. The later points show the estimates from the various iterations of the Washington Representatives Study.

have been fewer organized minorities in the old days; there may have been less lobbying; but it is a difference in degree, not in kind," he declared. But Figure 1.7 shows a change in the size of the Washington, D.C. interest group universe between 1930 and 2020 that goes beyond a difference in degree. As Stalin supposedly quipped, "Quantity has a quality all its own." The American polity has transitioned from pluralism to something different, which we call hyper-pluralism.[31]

The explanation for the emergence of hyper-pluralism is fairly straightforward. When the federal government did almost nothing, there was little point in lobbying it—and few people did. A somewhat bigger and more active federal government offered somewhat better returns on time and effort invested in influence peddling, so more groups came. And when the federal government became a leviathan, throngs of groups, associations, firms, wealthy individuals, and professionals set up shop on the Potomac, seeking a piece of the action—or protection from it. Today, no cause is too obscure, nor seemingly too vile; every conceivable interest that can pay has its advocate in the nation's capital.[32]

So too with the judicial state. Judicial lobbying at the Supreme Court comes in the form of so-called amicus briefs submitted by interested groups, firms, and state and local governments. These "friends of the court" advance arguments favoring one side or the other in a given case, and one or several judicial policies over others. Submitting amicus briefs is certainly "lobbying." But it is a genteel version compared to what goes on in Congress or state legislatures, where lobbyists can legally make nominal "campaign contributions" that open doors and grease the legislative skids.

Figure 1.8 shows the increase of judicial lobbying over time.[33] The dashed line shows the number of amicus briefs filed in each Supreme Court term between 1917

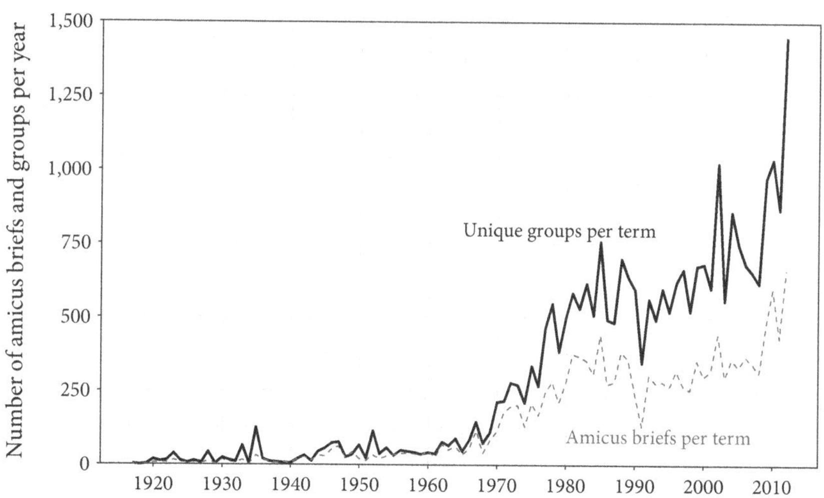

Fig. 1.8 Lobbyists before the U.S. Supreme Court, 1917–2012. The figure shows the number of briefs and the number of unique groups signing onto briefs per term of the United States Supreme Court.

and 2012. The solid line shows the number of unique groups signing onto briefs in each term; this line is higher because multiple groups may sign on to a single brief.

As shown, the number of annual briefs did not change much between 1917 and about 1970, averaging about 25 or so per term. But then, the number of briefs exploded during the 1970s, reaching a new plateau in the mid-1980s of about 350 per term, a 14-fold increase. Growth resumed in the 2000s; between 2005 and 2012 the average number of briefs per term was 450. All told, by this measure, judicial lobbying increased about 40-fold between 1930 and 2012, with almost all the growth occurring since about 1970. A similar pattern appears in the number of unique groups signing briefs; that number increased 60-fold, from 24 in 1930 to nearly 1,500 in 2012.

In short, more than just Mr. Smith went to Washington. The formerly sleepy little town now fairly swarms with Herring's "bees." Eagle eyes monitor every congressional bill, every regulation, every federal court case. At every turn, paid supplicants besiege members of Congress, the managers of the administrative state, and the black-robed rulers of the judicial state. Indeed, the advocates sometimes write the bills, provide language for the regulations, and pen parts of the legal opinions.[34]

Would it not seem strange if the supplicants did not conclude that better results might follow from not just lobbying government officials, but actually changing the decision makers themselves?

1.3.5 The Polarization of Political Elites

The previous subsection documented the dramatic increase in lobbying by interest groups, issue enthusiasts, firms, and wealthy individuals to influence decisions and even change decision makers. We now address the fascinating outgrowth of those efforts: polarization of America's political class into two sides with wildly divergent views.

Measures of such polarization have become central material in the scholarly study of American politics, in part because they raise interesting and critical questions. One such measure, presented in Figure 1.9, is something of a triumph of modern political science, based on the pioneering work of Keith Poole and Howard Rosenthal (1997). Here's what they did. First, use every recorded roll call vote in Senate history to derive the ideological "ideal point" of every senator who ever served, using sophisticated scaling methods derived from psychometrics. In doing so, take care that the scores are comparable over time. The famous scores that result, the so-called NOMINATE scores, run from −1 (for an extreme liberal) to +1 (for an extreme conservative). Next, in each senate, find the ideological score of the "average" Republican and the "average" Democrat, where average means the median member of the party—the member whose score divides the party membership exactly in half, so one-half has a higher score and one-half a lower one. What is the difference in the party medians? This is the data displayed in the figure, for the Senate from 1867, which marks both the end of the Civil War and the emergence of the Republican and Democratic parties

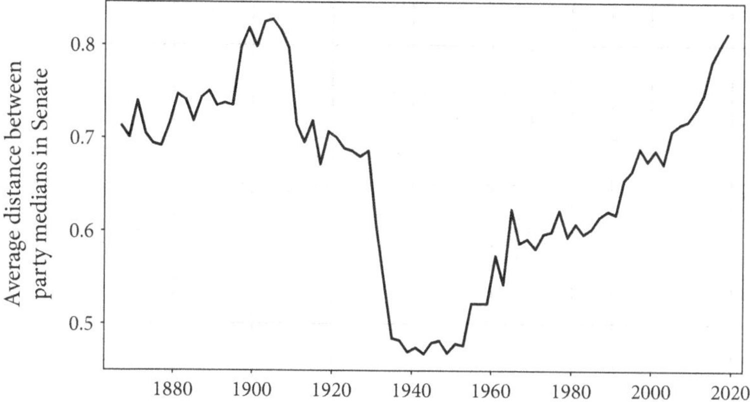

Fig. 1.9 Ideological Polarization in the U.S. Senate, 1867–2020. The figure shows the difference in ideology scores of the median Republican senator and median Democratic senator, using first-dimension NOMINATE scores.

as the mainstays of American politics, to 2020. The difference in average scores provides a measure of party polarization—probably the best such measure we are likely to get.[35]

Figure 1.9 is not just a technological marvel, but it also raises several intriguing substantive questions about why we see such peaks and valleys in party polarization. If we focus on the 1870s, for example, party polarization is hardly surprising following a civil war with three-quarters of a million battle deaths. Similarly, party polarization in the 1880s and 1890s is no mystery. Mass urbanization, industrialization, immigration, wild economic booms and busts, and gigantic disparities in wealth wrenched the fabric of American society. In both cases, party polarization reflected significant divisions in society.

But the dramatic rise in polarization since about 1980 is more puzzling. While many scholars and commentators have offered explanations for this puzzle, most do not stand up to scrutiny. For example, some suggested gerrymandering was the culprit; others pointed to changes in congressional procedures. We know the gerrymandering hypothesis doesn't hold water because polarization patterns are similar in the House (with gerrymandering) and the Senate (no gerrymandering). Likewise, congressional procedure cannot be the answer because we know most state legislatures also polarized.[36] The correct explanation has to be something stretching across the entire country and reaching from the top to the bottom in American politics.

A further puzzle is that American political elites polarized starting in about 1980 *while the public showed no such movement*—at least not initially. Careful studies of public opinion data find no comparable mass polarization in the 1980s and 1990s, excepting a few issues like abortion and affirmative action.[37] As we discuss below, the public has now begun to display the same kind of polarization, but elites clearly polarized first, in the virtual absence of ideological polarization in the mass electorate.[38] So the question remains: why did party polarization happen absent social polarization?

Political scientists and political historians have begun to connect the dots. The evidence points to the *party system itself*. This finding would not have surprised an earlier generation of scholars, like V. O. Key (1942) and E. E. Schattschneider (1942), who placed political parties at the center of American politics. That generation of political scientists would have turned immediately to the party system as the polarizing force.[39] To a younger generation of political scientists, however, trained to see the political parties as "weak," antiquated, moribund, and virtually irrelevant, the parties seemed like the least-likely suspects. The story that is emerging is surprising to many and remains controversial.

The story goes something like this. The parties familiar to Key and Schattschneider were local and state organizations run by professional politicians as businesses. The "owner-operators" of the parties were rent-seekers who made politics pay. They had no interest in ideology *per se*. The rise of an American middle-class in the late nineteenth century created businessmen and voters who found the rent-seeking machines financially burdensome and morally repugnant. Their antipathy set off one of the great reform battles in American history.[40] Over time, the reformers prevailed almost everywhere and put the parties out of the rent-seeking business.

With rent-seeking vanquished, middle-class reformers lost interest in the parties. But the parties did not go away. Though grievously wounded, they remained the main vehicle for selecting candidates for elected office. As such, they eventually drew the attention of a new cast of characters, neither Boss Tweed-style rent-seekers nor Teddy Roosevelt-style reformers. The new actors were "amateur Democrats" on one side and "suburban warriors" on the other—in other words, the same sort of ideologically motivated activists who filled the ranks of the proliferating social groups of the 1970s.[41]

The political scientist James Q. Wilson summarized his observations from fieldwork among the amateur Democrats in the early 1960s:

> The amateur believes that political parties ought to be programmatic, internally democratic, and largely free of reliance on material incentives such as patronage. A programmatic party would offer a real policy alternative to the opposition party. A vote for the party would be as much, or more, a deliberate vote for a clear and specific set of proposals, linked by a common point of view or philosophy of government, as it would be a vote for a set of leaders. The programmatic basis of one party would, to some extent, compel an expression of purpose by the opposing party and thus lead to the realignment of both parties nationally, with liberals in one and conservatives in the other (Wilson 1962, 16–17).

The "amateur Democrats" slowly took over the local, state, and finally national parties on the Democratic side.[42] Something similar happened in the Republican Party, especially after the Goldwater debacle of 1964. As they took control of the parties, the well-intentioned activists became "the polarizers," in the apt phrase of political historian Sam Rosenfeld (2017).

This story is hardly complete. It may still seem surprising that party activists could have so dramatic an impact on members of Congress, state legislatures, governors, even city councils. After all, candidates still have to get elected. And the general public does not share the hardened convictions and passionate enthusiasms of the polarizers. Brilliant fieldwork by Bawn et al. (2023) documents how the polarizers work in practice to control the selection of House candidates. Even in the parties' somewhat debilitated state, party leaders work relentlessly to find and advance ideological champions. Party activists, affiliated groups, firms, and wealthy individuals support the champions and enable them to run professional, competitive campaigns. In addition, moderates considering a candidacy are deterred from running by the levels of existing polarization.[43] At the end of the day, voters can only choose between what is offered to them; they can't vote for people who aren't on the ballot. And if the people deciding who gets on the ballot are the polarizers, they will happily trade away popularity in order to gain extremity, and still often prevail at the ballot box.[44]

This is but a sketch of a complex story. The story continues to unfold, with the recent unraveling of the traditional Republican coalition. But, the bottom line is clear, at least for our purposes: beginning in the late 1970s or early 1980s, America's political class polarized. It is now deeply polarized, with the two sides committed to wildly divergent goals.

1.3.6 The Resurgence of Divided Party Government

Polarized elites by themselves do not imply a crisis in governance. California, for example, has deeply polarized political elites.[45] But the state government passes laws and pursues a relatively coherent set of priorities, for good or for ill. It can do so because the liberal party controls every lever of power worth controlling while the conservative party is an impotent rump. The mirror image prevails in Kansas, which, until recently, was effectively a one-party state controlled by the conservative party.[46] Changes in state policy, which have been dramatic, reflected changes in the strength of different factions within the Republican Party.

The situation at the national level resembles neither California nor Kansas because neither the liberal nor the conservative party reliably controls all the levers of power all the time. Instead, divided party government often prevails, meaning one ideologically extreme and coherent party controls part of the government, while the other equally extreme but coherent party controls another part. Under the American constitutional design, this is a prescription for conflict and gridlock.

Figure 1.10 presents the basic story, focusing on control of the presidency and the Senate (since the House plays no role in confirmation politics). The "rug" (i.e. hash marks) at zero denotes a Congress in which one party controlled both the Senate and presidency; the rug at one indicates a Congress in which different parties controlled the Senate and presidency. The loess lines indicates the local probability of divided party control of the Senate and presidency.

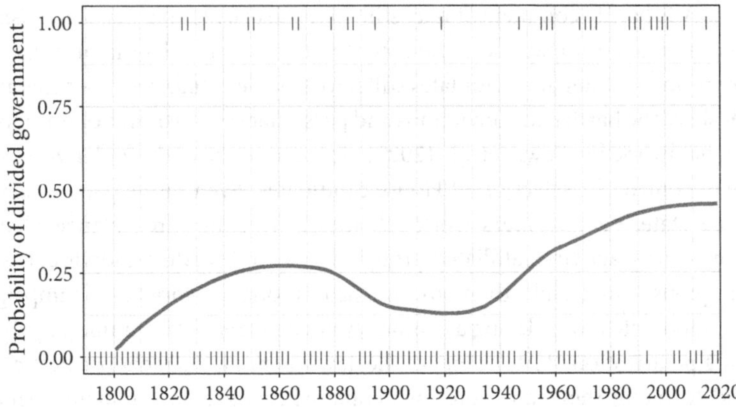

Fig. 1.10 The probability of divided party control of the Senate and the presidency from 1789 to 2020. The rugs indicate occurrences of unified (bottom) and divided (top) government. The blue line is a loess line.

As shown in the figure, divided control of the presidency and Senate has been a regular occurrence throughout American history, though never the dominant pattern. A rarity early in the Republic, divided party control increased in frequency and rose to a modest height prior to the Civil War and during Reconstruction (about 25% or so, for divided Senate-presidency control).[47] The probability of divided party control of the Senate and presidency then fell dramatically for the next half-century. This period saw leading political scientists formulate (fanciful) theories of "realigning elections" leading to long bouts of one-party control of government.[48] Starting in the late 1940s, however, divided party government rose from the grave. And with a vengeance! Today we live in the greatest era of divided party government in American history. At present, the probability of split party control of the Senate and presidency is almost 50%.

What lies behind the undulations in the graph? One factor is the geographic distribution of party members, which may make it possible or even probable for one party to control the presidency (which hinges on the Electoral College) while the other controls the Senate (or House). At various times in American history, the geographic distribution of the parties intersected with America's strange electoral system to create frequent divided party government.[49] That is the situation today.

A second factor is also important, particularly when the parties are programmatic, distinct, extreme, and distant from many voters. This factor involves the thermostatic quality of "public mood."[50] Public mood refers to the public's general tendency toward liberalism and conservatism. When one party controls the government and enacts policies, public mood shifts away from it. This famously occurs at midterm elections but is more pervasive than that. It is almost as if Americans lean against the winds blowing from the extremist parties.

In the American separation-of-powers system, the combination of extreme parties and divided party government is explosive. The combination leads to presidential impeachments, legislative gridlock, aggressive use of presidential executive orders, congressional sabotage of the executive—and failed or near-failed Supreme Court nominations.

1.3.7 Ideologically Sorted, Informationally Bifurcated

In 1964, Philip Converse wrote a revolutionary study of the American electorate, an analysis that remains required reading in graduate programs more than half a century later. Converse's article summarized and codified what political scientists and social psychologists had learned from the polling revolution of the 1950s and early 1960s. His study extended over 75 pages but we can emphasize two important takeaways for our purposes.

The first is that most Americans did not follow politics closely and knew astoundingly little; they could not correctly answer the most elementary questions about civics, and they were often somewhat confused about which issues went with which, in terms of political ideology as defined by elites. Converse said these voters showed little "ideological constraint."[51] A few citizens, however, knew a huge amount about politics and issues. Some of these citizens may have had professional reasons to acquire political information. Generally, though, they were simply people who found politics fun and engaging.

The second important takeaway involves the link between partisanship and political ideology. In the 1950s and early 1960s, the Republican Party included Northeastern liberals, Western conservatives, and Midwestern moderates. Similarly, the Democratic Party included Northern liberals, Southern conservatives, and Western moderates. Thus, the political parties of the 1950s and early 1960s were "big tent" parties that attracted many different kinds of people. As a result, in terms of voter identification with the parties, both parties out-numbered self-declared Independents. Figure 1.11, which is based on Figure 2.7 in Fiorina (2017), shows the percentage of self-identified Democrats (both strong and weak), Republicans (both strong and weak), and Independents, based on the quadrennial American National Election Survey between 1952 and 2020. Since 1972, the percentage of Independents has either rivaled or outpaced the percentage of Democrats, which in turn have always been larger than the percentage of Republicans.

How should one apply the lessons of Converse today? First, it is simply not the case that knowledge about politics is distributed randomly across the population. Rather, as one might expect, the extent to which people follow politics and are knowledgeable correlates with education, news consumption, and whether a person identifies with either the Democratic or Republican party (versus Independents). Moreover, citizens who have more extreme ideology (i.e. those who are increasingly liberal or conservative, relative to moderates) are also more likely to be politically informed.[52]

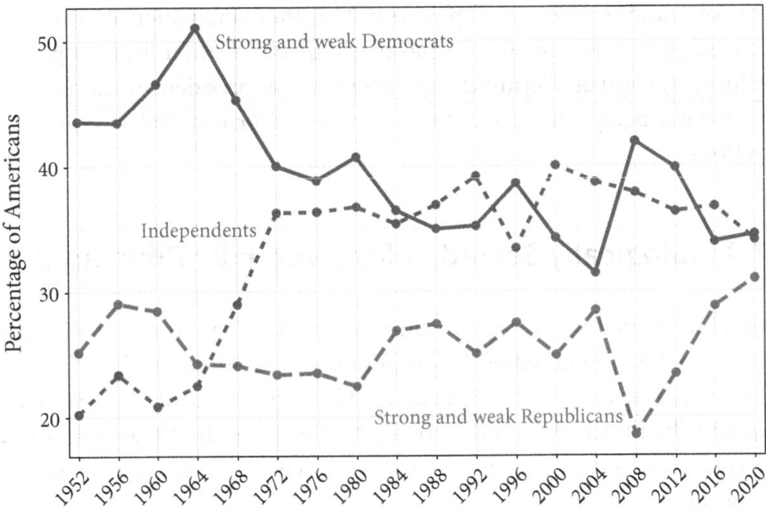

Fig. 1.11 Changes in self-identified party identification, 1952–2020. Percentages based on the ANES' 7-point party identification scale. "Strong" and "weak" responses are coded as partisans, while "Independent Democrat," "Independent Independent," and "Independent Republican" responses are coded as Independents.

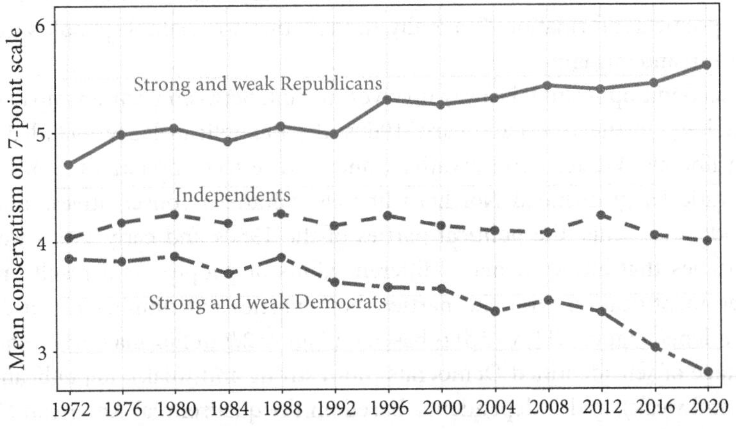

Fig. 1.12 Ideology and partisanship, 1972–2020. The lines show the mean ideology on a 7-point scale (from liberal to conservative) broken down by partisanship.

These facts affect the politics of accountability in Supreme Court nominations. In Chapter 11, we show that these factors now predict whether Americans know how their senators voted on Supreme Court nominees.

Second, the relationship between partisanship and political ideology has changed dramatically, as seen in Figure 1.12. For each ANES survey from 1972 to 2020, we coded the ideology of respondents, as measured by the standard 7-point scale, which runs from more liberal to more conservative.[53] We then calculated the mean ideology score broken down by partisanship for each year. Not surprisingly, the figure shows a clear ordering with Republicans always more conservative on average than Independents, who in turn are more conservative then Democrats. In the 1970s, the differences were not so great; the difference between Democrats and Republicans in 1972, for example, is only about 1 point, on average, on the 7-point scale. But the figure reveals the clear emergence over time of a high degree of overlap between party and ideology, with Republicans identifying increasingly as conservative and Democrats identifying increasingly as liberal. Meanwhile, the reported ideology of Independents has been stable over time.

Not surprisingly, political scientists have spilled considerable ink over exactly how the transformation happened. Did the heterogeneous people calling themselves Democrats convert to liberalism? Did the heterogeneous people who called themselves Republicans convert to conservatism? Or, did conservative Democrats switch to the Republican Party, liberal Republicans switch to the Democratic Party, while people in-between tended to become Independents? The latter possibility, sometimes called "the partisan sort," seems more consistent with the data.[54] An important implication is that Americans have not transformed fully into two partisan camps. Recall from Figure 1.11 that Independents now constitute as large a camp as either of the two parties. However, the two groups of well-sorted partisans lie very far from one another ideologically. Perhaps not surprisingly, their members increasingly detest one another.[55] Moreover, because partisanship, ideology, race, education, and class are linked more tightly, some analysts see a rise in identity politics and affective polarization, in which partisan divisions transcend mere policy differences.[56]

The new realities of the mass public has important implications for the job of senators, and therefore for the politics of Supreme Court nominations. Senators have always engaged in high-profile position-taking and obsequious pandering to popular views.[57] However, the changes in the electorate elevate the importance of these activities, and modify how they operate. On many issues, senators may see little reason to represent moderates, who mostly don't pay attention or don't much care. But same-party partisans present a very different audience. These voters care intensely about some issues, follow high-profile events in Washington, know how their senators voted in major controversies, they sometimes contribute time and money to campaigns, and—most critically—many participate in primaries. Bucking mobilized, in-party partisans can abruptly end a political career. Consequently, it mostly does not happen.

1.4 The Politics of Supreme Court Appointments

A laboratory for studying the evolution of the SOP system would hold little interest if nothing changed. One could study the system, but time, sequence, and feedback would matter little. However, dramatic changes mark Supreme Court appointments politics over our 90-year period. These changes reflect the larger changes in American politics.

1.4.1 The Process

Let's begin with an overview of the modern process of Supreme Court appointments. Figure 1.13 lays it out schematically. The figure is not formalist—it reflects what actually occurs, though in somewhat stylized fashion. In the figure, key decisions or actions by players are indicated by boxes. The actors are in bold type. The solid lines connecting boxes represent a time line, so there is a sequence of actions. The dashed line reflects feedback from earlier actions. The six phases of the process are the following:

Setting the Stage describes what occurs before a vacancy on the court even takes place. Presidents, of course, have the final say in who gets nominated. But our account emphasizes the decision by groups and activists to enter the realm of appointment politics in the first place and then have a say in who gets nominated and confirmed.

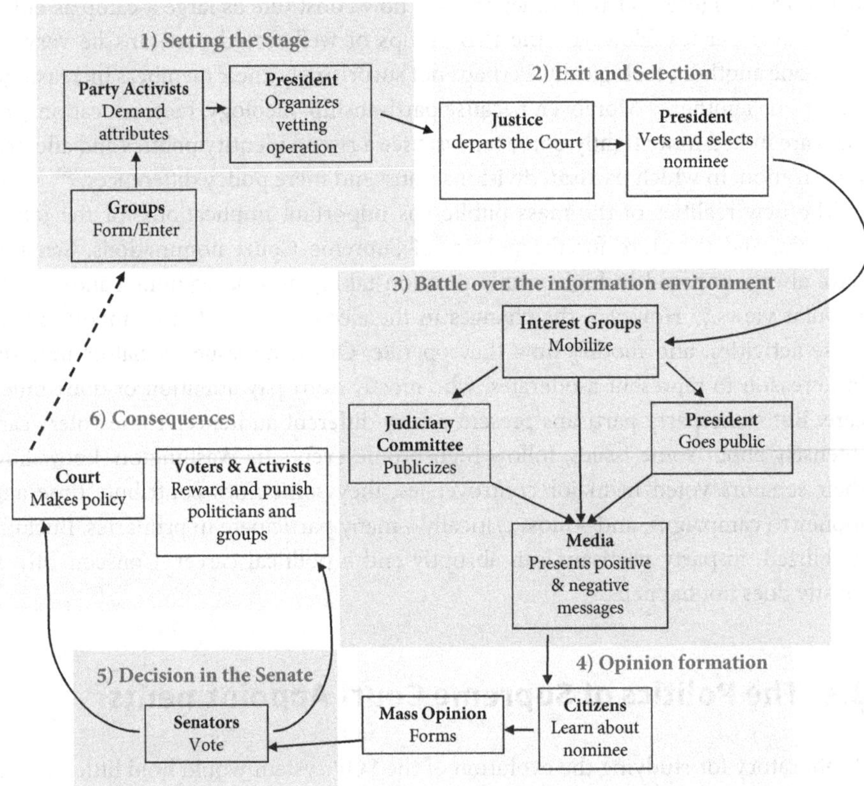

Fig. 1.13 The Supreme Court appointments process—a dynamic view.

Once they do, the activists carry their passionate convictions about the need for judicial change into the presidential primaries and into the party convention. They seek to influence the choice of presidential nominee; they also often leave their fingerprints on the party platform in the form of demands (i.e. "litmus tests") on future nominees. While many scholars of American politics see party platforms as meaningless guff or campaign blather written by the candidate himself, we see the platforms as "accountability contracts" between the presidential nominee and the policy activists who control or influence the party. They are a statement of demands and expectations that the president (if elected) ignores at his peril, at least if he wishes to remain in the good graces of the activists whose contributions of time, money, and effort are essential for a successful campaign.

Once elected, the president assembles a managerial team and organizes the White House. The people he chooses, and the procedures he puts in place, will determine what his policy priorities actually are in practice. As the mantra goes, "personnel is policy"—but so is organization and procedure. The president's people and procedures strongly affect what he can accomplish in office. One part of the White House operation may be a judicial selection operation aimed at fulfilling the president's obligations under his accountability contract with party activists. The judicial selection operatives (whether inside the White House or in the Justice Department) will be tasked with identifying, screening, and vetting candidates to fill anticipated vacancies in the judicial state, including the high court. The team will often assemble a preliminary "short list" of potential nominees in the event of a vacancy.

The early work pays off in Stage 2, *Exit and Selection*, which is triggered by the exit of a justice from the court, either by death or retirement. The president will review the short list, or assemble one if none has been readied. He may order or engage in additional vetting. Then, he will make his choice.

Stage 3, *The Battle over the Information Environment*, begins with the president's announcement of the nominee. Interest groups may mobilize, organizing protests, demonstrations, and letter-writing. Sometimes they, or wealthy individuals, will mount paid media campaigns. The hearings in the Judiciary Committee become a natural focus for media attention. The appearance and grilling of the nominee is a modern high point. In addition, the president may mount his own media campaign by "going public" in support of the nomination. Scandals often play a large role in media coverage, which may be intense or may be sparse, depending on the overall visibility of the nomination.

Stage 4, *Opinion Formation*, is an immediate consequence of media coverage. If the nomination remains obscure, the public will hardly notice the event at all and opinion will remain inchoate. But if the coverage is intense, the public may actually notice the nomination and form opinions about whether the nominee should be confirmed.

Stage 5 is the *Decision in the Senate*. In some cases, the battle over the information environment may damage the nominee so badly that the president withdraws the nomination. But this is rare. More typically, the nomination moves to the Senate for a vote. If the Senate rejects the nominee, the president selects another nominee, and the process resumes. But more typically the Senate confirms the nominee.

Stage 6, *Consequences*, reflects the fact confirmation does not end the process, as appointments to the court have several consequences (as the legal genius in *The Pelican Brief* appreciated so well). The policy impact of the nominee on the court may be large or small, and may be predictable and anticipated or erratic and unexpected. But while the appointment of a single justice only rarely shifts the direction of the court, the confirmation of several like-minded justices can have dramatic effects. In turn, policy outputs can bring political consequences—the population of the groups may change, and activists may change in response to the court's actions. This population shift is an example of what political scientists call "policy feedback." Here, the entry of new groups and activists feeds back into Stage 1, *Setting the Stage*—for the next nomination or series of nominations. And so the cycle continues.

1.4.2 The Changes

Figure 1.13 describes the nomination process as it exists today. If we compare that process with the one familiar to Herbert Hoover, Franklin Roosevelt, Harry Truman, or Dwight Eisenhower, what is different? Table 1.1 summarizes the differences, highlighting 12 attributes of appointment politics. The table identifies the chapter(s) in which we cover the respective topics; the attributes are listed in roughly the chronological order they appear in the book. The 12 changes are summarized below; this subsection also provides a roadmap to the book by identifying the chapters covering each change. Finally, the endnotes in this section discuss how our approach both fits into and is distinguishable from the existing literature on Supreme Court nominations, where relevant.

Party & Activist Interest in the Court

In our telling, the demands of party activists and party-affiliated interest groups loom large. The reason is, those demands force the president to change how he finds nominees and who he selects from among the short-listed candidates. In the early period, party activists rarely cared about the court and asked for nothing from the president. Today, party activists and party-affiliated groups care intensely about the court, and insist that the president deliver a nominee who meets the demands laid out in party platforms. The rising influence of party-affiliated groups may be the single most important change in the process, because so much else follows.[58]

In Chapter 2, we present a systematic overview of the two parties' judicial agendas, based on new evidence on the party platforms from 1928 to 2020 and the parties' stands on the Supreme Court and judicial nominations. In particular, we document the parties' focus on particular "hot-button" Supreme Court cases and issue areas. We also scrutinize policy requirements for Supreme Court nominees—that is, "litmus tests"—as well as calls for diverse and high-quality nominees. The result is the first

Table 1.1 Supreme Court Appointment Politics, 1930–2020: The attributes of nomination politics, then and now. The chapter column summarizes the chapter(s) in which a given attribute is examined.

Attribute	Then	Now	Chapter
Party & Activist Interest in the Court	Almost non-existent	Systematic and pervasive	2
Presidential Vetting	Casual, little formal process	Careful, formalized, meticulous	3
Nominee Characteristics	Often cronies, politicos, patronage nominees	Legal technicians with extensive track records	4, 9
Interest Group Mobilization	Rare, modest in scope	Routine, coordinated, sometimes massive	5
Media Coverage	Perfunctory absent scandals	At least moderate, often intense	6
Presidents Going Public	Rare, reactive	Routine, prospective	6
Senate Hearings	Non-existent or desultory	Intense, media-oriented	7
Public Opinion	Opinion formation rare	Opinion formation frequent, heavily polarized by party	7, 10
Senate Voting	Many voice votes, rarely polarized	Conflictual and partisan	8, 11
Voter Electoral Response	Non-existent	Measurable retrospective voting	11
Appointee Behavior on Court	Occasionally erratic	Very predictable, high policy reliability	12
Exits from the Court	Little evidence of strategic retirements	Some recent strategic retirements—more likely going forward	13

systematic overview of the parties' judicial agendas. Next, by examining delegates to the national conventions, we present suggestive evidence that evaluates the sources of these agendas. The chapter demonstrates that, before 1970, both parties had only limited and sporadic interest in the Supreme Court. However, while both expanded their Supreme Court agendas in the early 1970s, starting in the 1990s the Republican Party became much more focused on the court than the Democratic Party. The GOP also became much more demanding of the policy stances of judicial nominees, while Democrats placed greater emphasis on diversity and quality. The result today is a striking asymmetry between the parties in their approaches to the Supreme Court.

Presidential Vetting

As a result of pressure from party activists and affiliated groups, presidential vetting and selection procedures changed dramatically. In Chapter 3, we trace the evolution of the selection and vetting process over almost a century. Nominee selection started as a small, lightly staffed, under-institutionalized, and often erratic endeavor. Over time, it grew into a large, professionally staffed, systematic, and bureaucratized machine run out of the White House; indeed presidents today employ a virtual law firm embedded in the White House that generally conducts thorough and diligent reviews of potential nominees.

Our review of the history identifies three distinct organizational modes of selecting nominees: no delegation, external delegation, and internal delegation. A simple framework explains the president's organizational preference. Critical are the president's interest in judicial policy, and the availability and location of specialized expertise in the form of a legal policy elite. The chapter documents the growth of professionalization and institutional sophistication in selection and vetting, with the result that modern nominees are all highly qualified individuals with predictable opinions on policy questions.[59]

Nominee Characteristics

Changes in presidential vetting produced dramatic changes in judicial selection, as the characteristics of Roosevelt's and Truman's nominees were extraordinarily different from those of Obama and Trump. Cronies and politicos were replaced by nickel-plated legal technicians. We explore these changes in the nominees in Chapters 4 and 9.

First, in Chapter 4, we systematically describe changes in the characteristics of every nominee between 1930 and 2020, as well as those of candidates the presidents considered but did not ultimately select—that is, the "short list." We first focus on the major considerations for nomination politics today: ideology, qualifications, diversity, and age. We then consider religion and geography. We show a significant transformation from 1930 to 2020 in both the characteristics among the men (and now women) who have been considered for the court and in the nominees themselves. All told, even as the justices have become more ideologically polarized in the modern period, on every other dimension (except diversity), the court has become more homogenous. Today, a justice is very likely to be: a former judge on the Courts of Appeals; in their mid-50s; from the East Coast; a graduate of Harvard, Yale, or Columbia; and Catholic or Jewish. Noticeably absent are practicing politicians (such as Earl Warren), who used to be common on the court. This narrowing affects both who sits on the Supreme Court and the manner in which they make decisions.

In contrast to the descriptive approach in Chapter 4, in Chapter 9 we develop and test a new theory of presidential selection of nominees, the "characteristics approach." The key idea is that a Supreme Court nominee is a bundle of characteristics, and it is those characteristics that presidents value rather than the nominee *per se*. We focus on four of the characteristics discussed in Chapter 4: ideology, policy reliability, race, and gender. At various times and to various degrees, presidents value these characteristics. But beyond a minimal level, none comes for free. If presidents desire characteristics, they must "pay" for them by searching for nominees, vetting them carefully, and perhaps overcoming political opposition. For each characteristic, presidents must weigh benefits against costs. We then marshal a variety of empirical evidence in support of the characteristics theory, which results in two important findings. First, presidents care deeply about the characteristics of their nominees. Second, other changes in the process (such as the role of interest groups in helping vet potential nominees) mean the "cost" of obtaining these characteristics declined dramatically over the past decades, which helps explains the much more professionalized nominees that we regularly see today.

Interest Group Mobilization

As we noted above, interest groups emerge as a prime mover in the political transformation. Using an original dataset of newspaper reporting, Chapter 5 examines the growth and changes in interest group participation in the nomination process. First, we document a sizable increase in interest group activity over time. From 1930 to 1970, there was relatively little mobilization, with zero groups mobilizing in many nominations. After 1970, and in particular after Robert Bork's nomination in 1987, mobilization became routine for most nominees, with many groups participating in confirmation politics. Second, while past mobilization largely focused on opposition to a nominee, today groups mobilize about equally on both sides. Third, the calculus of interest groups appears to have changed significantly over time, with a shift from "opportunistic mobilization" based on a nominee's qualifications to more routine mobilization more heavily influenced by a nominee's ideological extremity. The data also reveal significant shifts in both the types of groups that routinely mobilize and the tactics they employ. Finally, the mobilizers appear to be quite polarized and many groups on the right are distant ideologically from those on the left (e.g. the Judicial Crisis Network and Demand Justice). In sum, our results illustrate how the interest group environment in Supreme Court nominations moved from a relatively sparse ecology characterized by occasional, generally opportunistic mobilization that focused on traditional forms of lobbying, to a dense ecology characterized by routine, intense, highly ideological, and very visible contention. The explosion of group participation in nominations accords perfectly with the general trend in American politics toward hyper-pluralism that we described earlier.[60]

Media Coverage

As nominations changed from usually sleepy affairs to high-stakes battles royale, media coverage of nominations changed accordingly. In Chapter 6, we examine these changes using original datasets of newspaper reporting (i.e. "hard news"), broadcast, and cable television coverage, as well as editorials, about every nominee from 1930 to 2020. We find that most nominations from 1930 to around 1960 received very little media attention. Hard news coverage of a nominee tended to focus on the nominee's background/biography, judicial philosophy, and economic issues, in accordance with the high salience national issues of the day. Occasionally, a scandal or controversy attracted media attention. Newspaper editorials, providing the views of media elites, generally supported nominees and the president; outright opposition to nominees was rare. Importantly, these editorials focused on the qualifications of a nominee as the key evaluative criterion, rather than on ideological considerations.

Beginning in the 1960s, the court became more involved in social issues, and the national political agenda shifted toward such issues. Nominations increased in duration, and the volume of media coverage increased concomitantly. Public hearings before the Senate Judiciary Committee became standard for every nominee, providing focal points for each nomination. Hard news coverage shifted toward a focus on contentious social issues like civil rights, the death penalty, and (especially) abortion. When a nominee scandal occurred, the media significantly increased their coverage of that nominee. Elite media opinion increasingly polarized along ideological lines over time. The cumulative effect of these changes on media coverage has been huge. Some early nominations were practically invisible in the media. Today, coverage is always substantial and sometimes extraordinary.[61]

Presidents Going Public

In addition to presidential changes in the selection process, presidents have also become much more actively involved in the media fray. In the past, they would rarely "go public" over nominees. Today presidents routinely use the "bully pulpit" as part of the nomination campaign—we document this rise in Chapter 6, as well as the effect of going public on the amount of media coverage of a nomination.

Senate Hearings

In the early period, the Judiciary Committee sometimes skipped hearings altogether. When they were held, the hearings were usually brief and pro-forma. As nominations became media circuses, the hearings changed into theatrical platforms where senators grandstand for their constituents, posturing for the cameras by flinging constitutional law "gotcha" questions at the nominee, or heaping him or her with fulsome praise. Scandals add an additional fillip. We do not devote much time in the book to the hearings, as they have been extensively studied by previous scholars.[62] However, in Chapter 7, we examine whether the hearings seem to change public opinion about nominees.

Public Opinion

The broader changes in media coverage coincided with dramatic changes in public opinion on Supreme Court nominees. We examine these changes in public opinion in Chapters 7 and 10.

Chapter 7 provides the most comprehensive look at public opinion on Supreme Court nominees to date. Using a dataset of every available public poll between 1930 and 2020 that asked the public their views on a Supreme Court nominee, we show that polling on nominees did not become commonplace until the 1980s. When polling did exist, many people had no opinion, and those who did generally favored nominees absent some scandal. We demonstrate that high-quality nominees and those that display path-breaking diversity traits receive a boost in public opinion. Most dramatically, though, in the twenty-first century public opinion on nominees has become sharply polarized by party, as citizens who identify with the president's party are likely to support a nominee and members of the opposite party are likely to oppose a nominee. This polarization bodes poorly for a return to the "normal" nomination politics of the mid-twentieth century. The chapter also examines so-called "campaign effects"—e.g. did hearings and scandals affect public opinion? Except for the Bork nomination, campaign effects were usually modest. However, scandal did have a palpable impact in the Kavanaugh and Thomas nominations, but this effect was mediated by citizens' party affiliation. All told, the chapter provides the most comprehensive look at public opinion on Supreme Court nominees to date.

In Chapter 10, we develop a theory of public opinion that seeks to disentangle policy evaluation from partisan evaluation. In particular, we create a new theoretical framework for studying individual level answers to the standard "approve"/"disapprove"/"don't know" question for assessing approval of nominees; the framework draws on modern choice theory and cognitive science and simultaneously incorporates information, evaluations, and an explicit theory of the survey response. We show that citizens are capable of evaluating the ideology of nominees. In turn, because of the increased extremity of nominees over time, ideological assessments play a larger role in the calculus of citizens than before. At the same time, partisan attachments have also increased, meaning both party and ideology play key roles in shaping public approval and disapproval of nominees. Finally, there is a substantial gap in utility for nominees between presidential co-partisans, on the one hand, and Independents and out-partisans on the other. The former are well served by presidential selection of ideologically extreme nominees, but the others much less so.

Senate Voting and Voter Electoral Response

The climax of the nomination process is the decision in the Senate, which we examine in Chapters 8 and 11.

Chapter 8 describes changes in Senate voting on nominees over time, back to 1789. First, we show that contentiousness in the Senate—by which we mean the levels of opposition to a nominee—has ebbed and flowed over time. However, the modern period has seen the peak in contentiousness. In earlier eras, confirmation votes were often voice votes or nearly unanimous roll call votes. Today, Senate votes on nominees are always roll call votes, with the voting nearly perfectly breaking down upon party lines. We also show that ideological distance between senators and the nominee is now a much better predictor of a vote against confirmation than it used to be.

Chapter 11 seeks to explain these changes by linking senators' voting decisions to their constituents, using the logic of accountability. In the past, because most nominations were not very visible, most voters either did not know of or care about most nominees. This, in turn, meant that senators did not have to worry much about their votes on nominees from an electoral perspective.[63] Over time, as nominations became more visible and contentious, more voters became informed about nominations, and their opinions began to break down more along party lines. We also show that recent confirmation votes cause changes in voter support of senators. In sum, the fact that public opinion on nominees is heavily polarized by party, combined with the fact that voters hold senators accountable for their confirmation votes, helps explain the dramatic shift to near party-line voting on nominees that we have witnessed this century.

Appointee Behavior on the Court

As we discussed above, the changes in the nomination politics do not end with confirmation. Perhaps the most important consequence is changes in the voting behavior of confirmed justices, which we examine in Chapter 12. We show that in the past justices selected on the basis of patronage or cronyism would often prove independent or at least erratic on the court. And, even if not erratic, voting in early periods was much more heterogeneous across "party lines." Today, justices are selected for ideological fealty, and their voting behavior is much more predictable. The result is a "judicial partisan sort," leading to ideologically polarized blocs on the court.[64]

We also connect the voting behavior of justices back to the changes in party platforms and presidential selection that we documented in earlier chapters. We show that justices selected with litmus tests in mind do deliver on those implicit guarantees, and that better-vetted nominees vote more reliably. We then show that as the court's composition veers left or right, case disposition and the content of majority opinions follow. As in the executive branch, "personnel is policy" on the Supreme Court.

All in all, changes in the selection process have produced a very different Supreme Court than the one that existed even 50 years ago.

Exits from the Court

Finally, when and why justices exit the court is potentially significant—whether justices deliberately time their exits to help a like-minded president choose their successors. The historical evidence for strategic departures is mixed at best.[65] In the book, we do not directly examine changes in retirements across time. However, in Chapter 13, we conduct simulations of the future ideological trajectory of the court that examine how a greater likelihood of strategic retirements going forward would affect future ideological trajectory of the court.

Summary

One can summarize these changes to nomination politics rather succinctly: a casual, amateur, and erratic process, accountable to no one, has become an organized, professionalized, predictable process that is accountable to highly engaged interests. Collectively, the changes summarized in Table 1.1 amount to a revolution in Supreme

Court appointment politics, a revolution that reflected the larger changes in American politics.

1.5 How to Read This Book

Making the Supreme Court has three parts. Part I, *What Happened*, details the history of Supreme Court appointments in the twentieth and early twenty-first centuries. Part II, *Why It Happened*, digs into the Pelican Problem by examining the mechanisms driving the history. Part III, *How It Matters, and What the Future Holds*, explores the consequences of appointment politics, another part of the Pelican Problem, as well as possible paths the court might take; it also examines potential reforms for the selection and retention of justices.

The result is a very long book that perhaps not everyone will want to read cover to cover (though we hope you do!). If not, we suggest five different ways to "read" it, depending on your interests.

1. **A Social Science History of Supreme Court Appointments (Chapters 2–8)** *What Happened* is a self-contained history of Supreme Court appointment politics from 1930 to 2020. Its seven chapters are fact-oriented but not a chronology. Rather, they follow the sequence laid out in Figure 1.13, moving from Setting the Stage, to Exit and Selection, to the Battle over the Information Environment, to Opinion Formation, and finally to Decision in the Senate. These chapters document the unlikely transformation of a sleepy, low-conflict process into the site for some of the biggest brawls in contemporary American politics.
2. **A Study of Political Parties and Interest Groups (Chapters 2, 5, and 12)** Interest groups emerge as a prime mover in the transformation of appointment politics. Chapters 2 and 5 develop three themes: an explosion in the number of groups, big changes in who they were, and shifts in what they did. Chapter 5 focuses on their participation in nomination campaigns. Chapter 2 traces their impact on the political parties, judicial agendas, which (we argue) become the judicial agendas of presidents. Here, partisan asymmetry stands out. Finally, Chapter 12 shows how the changes in the party agendas led to more reliable justices being selected—in particular, justices who would carry out the parties' new "litmus tests" for nominees.
3. **A Study of Presidents, Politicization, and Institutional Design (Chapters 3, 4, and 9)** Modern presidents try to manage federal administrative agencies by filling the agencies' top ranks with team-playing political appointees, a technique political scientists call "politicization."[66] Chapters 3, 4, and 9 show how presidents brought politicization to the Supreme Court. Chapter 9 explores the presidential logic of judicial politicization; it develops and tests a new theory. Pursuing its logic, presidents re-organized their process for selecting

nominees (Chapter 3). They also dramatically altered whom they considered and the type of person they chose (Chapter 4).

4. **A Study of Public Opinion and Democratic Accountability (Chapters 6, 7, 8, 10, and 11)** Supreme Court appointments now involve a full-throated political campaign waged over every vacancy, albeit an unusual one. Rather than two candidates competing for the ballot of a swing voter, two sides compete for public opinion and the votes of senators—votes for which citizens may (and sometimes do) hold their representatives accountable. While nominations differ from typical campaigns, many of the same fundamental questions about public opinion and democratic accountability still arise. Chapters 6 (media coverage of nominees), 7 and 10 (public opinion), and 8 and 11 (senators' voting decisions and electoral accountability) provide the first historical analysis of these unique political campaigns, as well as the nature of public opinion on nominees and its consequences for senators.
5. **A Study of the Supreme Court (Chapters 4, 12–14)** *Making the Supreme Court* is about appointment politics, but inevitably about the Supreme Court too. Chapters 4, 12, and 13 study how appointment politics altered the composition of the court, how the court's composition affected its decisions, and what the future may hold for the court. Finally, Chapter 14 discusses how Americans should evaluate the tradeoffs in reforming the Founders' 230-year-old selection and retention system for Supreme Court justices.

We offer a final word about "how to read this book." In 1959, British scientist and novelist C. P. Snow penned a short book about the mutual incomprehension between "the two cultures" of natural science and the humanities. Snow's two cultures have come to the social sciences as well, and with a vengeance. In *Making the Supreme Court*, we try to bridge the chasm between social scientists and sophisticated generalists in two ways. First, the history in Part I is accessible to anyone with a tolerance for graphs and data displays. Part I is serious social science history but, we hope, readily comprehensible to the curious. Ultimately, however, the deep "why" and "so what" questions of Parts II and III demand heavier artillery than simple graphs. So there we deploy the game theory, structural estimation, instrumental variables, simulations, and other methods demanded by some very tough nuts to crack. We refer readers interested in the more technical details to the online Appendix (and sometimes to our published academic journal articles). In addition, citations to and discussion of relevant studies and literatures mainly appear in the notes (as well as in the Appendix). Nonetheless, some of what remains will challenge even sophisticated readers. We hope the importance of the questions, and the interest of the answers, warrant the effort.

Finally, in addition to what you read in these pages, we have created a website for the book—`www.makingthesupremecourt.com`—that contains the supplemental Appendix, which reports additional analyses and discussions in several chapters. The website also houses all the data used in the book, including:[67]

- Data on party and presidential interest in the Court, including the use of "litmus tests" for Supreme Court nominees (Chapter 2).
- Data on the type of selection process employed by the president (Chapter 3).
- Data on the background characteristics of Supreme Court nominees, and those who made the president's "short list" (Chapters 4 and 9).
- Data on interest group participation in Supreme Court confirmation battles (Chapters 5).
- Data on media coverage of Supreme Court nominees (Chapter 6).
- Data on public opinion of nominees (Chapters 7, 10, and 11).
- Data on Senate roll call voting on Supreme Court nominees (Chapters 8 and 11).
- Data on Supreme Court decision making as a function of changes in appointment politics (Chapter 12).
- Simulated data on the future ideological composition of the court (Chapters 13 and 14).

We hope this data will prove useful to scholars of Supreme Court nominations for years to come.

2

The Party Demands

Party Agendas for the Supreme Court

In 1973, the Supreme Court handed down its landmark decision in *Roe v. Wade*.[1] The decision, which ruled unconstitutional most existing state-level restrictions on abortion, effectively nationalized the issue. Whereas before *Roe* states were generally free to establish abortion restrictions without constraints, states now had to meet the minimal standards established by the trimester framework set forth in Justice Blackmun's majority opinion.[2]

Today, support for abortion rights is heavily polarized, with Republicans much more likely to take a pro-life stance compared to Democrats.[3] And, when the Supreme Court overturned *Roe* in 2022, the debate over abortion rights reached even greater heights.[4] Yet, when *Roe* was decided in 1973, support and opposition to abortion was not well sorted along party lines. Many Republican elected officials supported the right to an abortion, in line with the party's base of support among mainline Protestants, while many Democratic officials allied with Catholic opposition to abortion rights. Among the public, attitudes did not display a clear partisan divide; if anything, Democratic identifiers were less likely to hold a pro-choice position than Republican identifiers.[5]

It is an overstatement that *Roe* emerged out of nowhere and instantaneously reordered American politics, as is sometimes claimed.[6] The fault lines in the abortion debate began to emerge in the decade before the *Roe* decision, with anti-abortion forces mobilizing well before 1973.[7] Indeed, in *Roe*'s wake, the parties grappled with responses to the landmark decision, as evidenced by their respective platforms in the 1976 presidential race. The Democratic platform equivocated on the issue:

> We fully recognize the religious and ethical nature of the concerns which many Americans have on the subject of abortion. We feel, however, that it is undesirable to attempt to amend the U.S. Constitution to overturn the Supreme Court decision in this area.

Similarly, the Republican platform acknowledged the complexity of the party's response to *Roe*:

> The question of abortion is one of the most difficult and controversial of our time.... There are those in our Party who favor complete support for the Supreme

Making the Supreme Court: The Politics of Appointments, 1930–2020. Charles M. Cameron and Jonathan P. Kastellec, Oxford University Press. © Oxford University Press 2023. DOI: 10.1093/oso/9780197680544.003.0002

> Court decision which permits abortion on demand. There are others who share sincere convictions that the Supreme Court's decision must be changed by a constitutional amendment prohibiting all abortions. . . . We protest the Supreme Court's intrusion into the family structure through its denial of the parents' obligation and right to guide their minor children. The Republican Party favors a continuance of the public dialogue on abortion and supports the efforts of those who seek enactment of a constitutional amendment to restore protection of the right to life for unborn children.

As it turned out, abortion played little role in the outcome of the 1976 presidential election.[8] Yet the issue would soon prove consequential in the 1980 Republican primary campaign, due in large part to organized interests (such as Jerry Falwell's group, the Moral Majority) pushing a pro-life position. As policy historian Daniel Williams (2011, 533) relates:

> By the end of the Carter administration, rising abortion rates and concerns about sexual promiscuity prompted evangelical pastors and televangelists, such as [Falwell], to begin speaking out on the issue and to create a national political coalition that made opposition to abortion a central theme. Ronald Reagan capitalized on this newfound concern over abortion by meeting with right-to-life activists in New Hampshire before the 1980 presidential primary and by continuing to advocate a constitutional amendment that would ban all abortions except those that were necessary to save a mother's life. As party moderates drifted toward George H.W. Bush, Howard Baker, John Anderson, or other contenders for the nomination, Christian Right activists lined up behind Reagan, and they cited the abortion issue, along with other "moral" causes, as their reason for doing so.

The 1980 Republican platform retained the language seeking a constitutional amendment to overturn *Roe*. But the party went further, tying the issue of abortion to a promise to appoint particular types of judges: "We will work for the appointment of judges at all levels of the judiciary who respect traditional family values and the sanctity of innocent human life." This *litmus test* for judges (a term we define below) marked the first promise by the Republican party to appoint Supreme Court justices who would take a pro-life stance. It would be far from the last: *every* Republican platform between 1980 and 2020 included such a test. Democrats, meanwhile, increasingly became identified as the party of abortion rights, pushed in part by both women's rights groups and pro-choice groups. Four years later, the Democratic Party issued a parallel litmus test, stating that its presidential nominee would appoint justices who would protect the "fundamental right of a woman to reproductive freedom," a test that would be repeated in several subsequent Democratic platforms.

The evolution of public opinion on abortion is well-tilled ground in the broader literature about party coalitions and party change.[9] For our purposes, however, this transformation illustrates *how changes in party demands and interests translate into preferences over who should sit on the Supreme Court*. These changes, in turn, are often driven by particular Supreme Court cases that "launch" an issue into the national political realm, as *Roe* did. What exactly does this process look like?

We will examine the full interplay among the court and its policies, interest groups, parties, and presidents, in Sections II and III of this book. But before we can get there, in this chapter we lay some groundwork examining the party platforms over time and their stands on the Supreme Court and judicial nominations. Our first goal is to establish the parties' agendas for the Supreme Court. In particular, we document when the parties—as well as presidential nominees in their acceptance speeches—focus on particular "hot-button" Supreme Court cases and issue areas. We also scrutinize policy requirements for Supreme Court nominees—that is, "litmus tests"—as well as calls for nominee diversity and nominees of high quality. The result is the first systematic overview of the parties' *judicial agendas*. Next, by examining delegates to the national conventions, we present suggestive evidence that evaluates the source of these judicial agendas. Finally, later in the book we show that the parties' judicial agendas predict the type of nominees presidents select, as well as the voting behavior of justices.

As Ronald Reagan's emphasis on his opposition to *Roe* in 1980 illustrates, a presidential candidate can influence his party's platform. But presidents may have interests in the court that are somewhat distinct from those of the larger party. We capture both types of interest by coding presidential acceptance speeches at the quadrennial nomination conventions. All together, the data offer a wide-ranging and novel view of how party and presidential demands about the Supreme Court have changed over time.

To summarize the key results of this chapter, before 1970, both parties displayed only limited and sporadic interest in the Supreme Court. However, both expanded their Supreme Court agendas in the early 1970s. Starting in the early 1990s the Republican Party became much more focused on the court than were the Democrats. The GOP also became much more demanding of the policy stances of judicial nominees. Democrats, on the other hand, emphasized judicial diversity and quality much more frequently than did Republicans. The result was a striking asymmetry between the parties in their approaches to the Supreme Court, over a decades-long period.

2.2 Party Platforms and Party Agendas: Theoretical Foundations

As the evolution of the abortion issue illustrates, changes in party coalitions can profoundly affect preferences over who sits on the Supreme Court. Yet, most studies of federal judicial appointments tend to treat the appointment and confirmation processes in relative isolation from broader developments in American politics. To be sure, leading studies of selection and confirmation emphasize potential partisan conflict between the president and the Senate.[10] Yet, the underlying source of this conflict is usually black-boxed, and assumed to be captured by a simple ideological distance. Alternatively, qualitative accounts of the selection process often emphasize idiosyncratic differences among presidents, rather than tethering presidents' goals to the larger goals of their political party.[11]

An important and notable exception to these tendencies is the work of Nancy Scherer. Her 2005 book *Scoring Points* studies the transformation in lower court appointment politics over the course of the second half of the twentieth century. She finds humdrum patronage politics prior to the late 1960s, but then a fiery politicization of lower court appointments sparked by issue activists. Today's appointment activists, she argues, favor a take-no-prisoners politics, and senators and the president cater to them. She connects these preferences of the activists to the larger presidential and party goals in judicial selection.

Scherer's insight connecting appointment politics to the larger party system accords neatly with the recent re-discovery of political parties by American political scientists. Following in the footsteps of Gerring's (2001) classic study of party ideologies since the early nineteenth century, this new line of research uses the party platforms and presidential acceptance speeches to investigate asymmetries between the parties, as well as issue emergence, activist coalitions and cross-coalition bargains, and voters' ideological alignment with the parties. In treating party platforms as data, American political scientists now follow in the footsteps of scholars of European democracies who have long adopted this approach.[12]

But there is a conceptual issue here. Much of the empirical research using party platforms simply assumes that the platforms are meaningful documents. For example, Gerring's use of platforms and speeches to gauge party ideology assumes sincerity and (as he discusses) substantive meaning. Similarly, Grossman and Hopkins (2016) use party platforms to contrast the two parties' ideologies. Levendusky (2009) uses party platforms and acceptance speeches to identify party positions on issues in order to compare the congruence of voters' personal ideologies and their partisanship. This procedure implicitly assumes that party platforms accurately reflect real and important differences in party positions—that is, that they substantively mean something.[13]

In this chapter, we similarly assume that the parties' stances on the Supreme Court and appointment politics are meaningful. But is this assumption reasonable? Despite the extensive empirical work utilizing party platforms, theories of party platforms remain surprisingly inchoate. However, three broad possibilities present themselves. These theoretical frameworks have very different implications for the origins of party agendas (as instantiated in the platforms) and, in turn, for how the party agendas for subsequent governmental performance. Two of the frameworks are compatible with the recent work on party platforms. But only one appears likely in view of the findings.

We label the three possibilities (1) campaign rhetoric, (2) Downsian platforms, and (3) coalition contracts.

Campaign Rhetoric

This framework might also be called the "folk theory" of campaign platforms—it follows the man-in-the-street's cynical view that politicians will say anything to get elected, and then do anything to stay in office. This framework views party platforms not only as cheap talk, but as almost entirely meaningless cheap talk. If this view is correct, then a study of party platforms is mostly a study of ephemeral pandering within particular election cycles. This cynical view of party platforms is hardly limited to ordinary citizens. For example, famed political scientist E. E. Schattschneider declared in *Party Government*, "party platforms are fatuities. They persuade no one, deceive no one, and enlighten no one."[14]

If this view is correct, then a study of party platforms is probably pointless. In fact, the empirical evidence from the last 80 years of American national party platforms shows this cynical view to be incorrect. According to Pomper's (1967) study of platforms from 1944 to 1964, "Rhetoric is limited. Evaluations of past performance concentrate on the incumbent party's policies. Pledges of future action are relatively specific, particularly those promises of distributive benefits." In this telling, platforms are sincere documents composed by engaged partisans who take policy seriously. Moreover, research shows that platforms have actual consequences for the winning party. In a recent review essay, Petry and Collette (2009) examined nine studies of how U.S. party platforms were implemented after a winning presidential campaign. Across all the studies, the average percentage of promises fulfilled was 67%, ranging from a low of 50% to a high of 80%. Overall, then, the platforms do seem to mean something.

Downsian Platforms

A very different understanding of the platforms emerges from the long tradition of spatial theory in political science, often called Downsian theory, due to the impact of Anthony Downs' influential 1957 book, *An Economic Theory of Democracy*. In this approach, the parties compete for votes by each announcing a position on a left-right issue dimension or, perhaps, a point in a multi-dimensional issue space. The platforms thus state each party's position in the issue space and voters choose between them prospectively.

But a similar question arises in this framework: what binds winning officials to the party platform? If the answer is "nothing" then the Downsian Platform framework essentially devolves to the campaign rhetoric theory—platforms are just cheap talk. Many spatial models evade this question by simply assuming that campaign positions bind the candidates once elected. Positive political theorists James Snyder and Michael Ting (2002) offer one mechanism that could bind elected officials to party platforms: party reputations with voters. An alternative could rely on retrospective voting, but with voters evaluating incumbents based not on their policy performance *per se* but on whether they kept their campaign promises. However, we do not know of any theoretical models that take promise-performance gaps seriously; most accountability models assume voters are concerned solely with policy performance or political skill, rather than campaign truthfulness *per se*.[15]

A further complication arises from the informational demands placed on voters in the Downsian platform framework. Actual platforms are quite detailed documents, elaborating positions in a great many areas, including some quite obscure ones—such as Supreme Court cases. Only a metaphorical handful of voters would actually read, understand, and evaluate such complex documents. To be sure, presidential acceptance speeches are shorter and are watched by millions of Americans; but, as we note later, the sheer number of policy items that comes out of the platforms is much larger than what emerges from acceptance speeches. So, simply on a *prima facie* basis, viewing the platforms as binding, prospective Downsian spatial positions seems doubtful.[16]

Coalition Contracts

What theoretical framework would make the multifarious, extremely detailed policy prescriptions of the platforms meaningful documents? One answer links well with the current reappraisal of the parties, especially the so-called "UCLA School." In a nutshell, the UCLA approach holds that parties are coalitions of high-demanding interest groups who select candidates whose views accord with their own, and do so largely unconstrained by the public's policy preferences.[17]

Platforms play no theoretical role in the UCLA-style conception of parties. Rather, the theory emphasizes "adverse selection"—the theory holds that party elites select a candidate who actually shares their views. So, the candidate will likely try to enforce them once in office. Alternatively, one can view the party platforms as (1) instantiating the policy bargains and compromises struck between issue activists within the party, and then (2) providing an *accountability contract* between the governing coalition within each party and the candidate selected by the party. The contract's implicit enforcement clauses involve sanctions at the next election: if the president violates the contract by adopting positions at variance with those favored by the party's governing coalition, the president may face withdrawal of funds and labor by activists, a primary challenge, or other sanctions from party activists. Call this account of the party platform the "coalition contract" approach.[18]

The coalition contract approach provides a theoretical account supporting the quantitative promise-performance studies of platforms. It is also compatible with some detailed historical studies. For example, Schickler (2016) shows the rise of factions within the Democratic party on the issue of race. Essentially, between the 1940s and 1960s northern party activists and officials moved to a desegregation position while southern Democratic Party activists and officials did not. During this period, the party's national position reflected the balance of power between the two regional factions. This power balance favored the Southern position until the mid-1960s. However, when civil rights became a more prominent national issue due to the increased strength of the civil rights movement, the balance of power between the factions shifted, resulting in a new position in the national Democratic Party platform.

An obvious question for the coalition contract framework involves the electability of the candidates. At present, the UCLA School essentially assumes the problem away by viewing voters as almost totally non-policy-minded.[19] Hence, in this view, party activists are nearly completely free to impose a favored contract on the candidate even if it deviates significantly from the preferences of the median voter. An alternative and seemingly more reasonable version would adopt something closer to the so-called Calvert-Wittman position: party activists are somewhat constrained in the contract they can impose on the candidate due to the electoral liabilities of extremist contracts.[20] But true-believer activists are quite willing to run a risk of defeat in the election in order to garner possible policy gains from a more attractive contract in the event of victory.[21] Under either interpretation, however, party platforms actually mean something. Another major question concerns contract enforcement: do party elites/activists actually sanction presidential contract-breakers? Can popular presidents evade party sanctions from policy betrayals, or perhaps even shift the activists to other positions? These are interesting questions, but answering them is beyond the scope of this book.[22] Instead, we (like the other empirical researchers using the platforms) simply assume something like the coalition contract framework. We now delineate the terms of the party contracts with respect to the Supreme Court.

2.3 The Parties' Agendas for Supreme Court Nominees

To see how presidential candidates and parties prioritize the Supreme Court within their larger agendas, we examined the texts of the Republican Party and Democratic Party platforms, as well as the acceptance speeches of the presidential candidates, between 1928 and 2020 (we ignore third party candidates).[23] Together the platforms and speeches provide clear statements of the party's agenda every four years.[24]

We read each platform and acceptance speech to identify mentions of the Supreme Court and statements about Supreme Court nominations. To assure we did not overlook relevant statements, we also searched the documents using obvious key words (e.g., Supreme Court, nomination, nominee, judge, court, law, and so on). Importantly, we focused solely on statements that *directly implicated the Supreme Court*. While a more ambitious effort would attempt to code the entire "judicial agenda" of each party—for instance, general references to abortion, rather than those made in the context of Supreme Court decisions or confirmations—we concluded that such an approach would introduce too much subjective judgment about categorizations. So we opted for the less ambitious but more reliable method of focusing solely on Supreme Court-related statements. Finally, because the platforms are much longer than the speeches, the vast majority of information comes from the former.

For each document, we coded the following information.

2.3.1 Cases

Platforms and speeches often referenced a particular Supreme Court case, either explicitly or implicitly. For example, in 1956, two years after the court decided *Brown v. Board of Education*,[25] the Democratic platform stated:

> Recent decisions of the Supreme Court of the United States relating to segregation in publicly supported schools and elsewhere have brought consequences of vast importance to our Nation as a whole and especially to communities directly affected. We reject all proposals for the use of force to interfere with the orderly determination of these matters by the courts. The Democratic Party emphatically reaffirms its support of the historic principle that ours is a government of laws and not of men; it recognizes the Supreme Court of the United States as one of the three Constitutional and coordinate branches of the Federal Government, superior to and separate from any political party, the decisions of which are part of the law of the land. We condemn the efforts of the Republican Party to make it appear that this tribunal is a part of the Republican Party.

For each case mentioned, we identified the key political issue in the case (e.g., "desegregation"), as well as whether the document endorsed the decision, criticized it, or was neutral. Because the party or president regarded these cases as sufficiently important to warrant mention, we call them "hot-button cases."

2.3.2 Appointments

We recorded every statement related to the appointment of Supreme Court justices. For example, the 1968 Republican platform stated:

> Public confidence in an independent judiciary is absolutely essential to the maintenance of law and order. We advocate application of the highest standards in making appointments to the courts, and we pledge a determined effort to rebuild and enhance public respect for the Supreme Court and all other courts in the United States.

Within the general category of appointments, we coded the following information:

Policy Litmus Tests

Does an appointment statement specify a "litmus" test for the party's future Supreme Court nominee? We define a litmus test as referencing a particular policy position that a Supreme Court nominee must be highly likely to adopt if confirmed. We include both explicit and implicit litmus tests. For example, here is an explicit anti-abortion litmus test from the 1996 Republican platform: "We support the appointment of judges who respect traditional family values and the sanctity of innocent human life." An example of an implicit test comes from the 1972 Republican platform: "Appointed judges whose respect for the rights of the accused is balanced by an appreciation of the legitimate needs of law enforcement." This statement implicitly endorses judges who are strong on "law-and-order."

For every litmus test, we coded the issue referenced in the test—most were very straightforward. For example, we code all references to crime as "law and order" concerns. Other issues could be readily inferred. For example, Republican pro-life litmus tests often mention support for "family values." However, the meaning of "family values" is never defined, and the two statements go hand-in-hand, so we collapse "support family values" into "oppose abortion." Likewise, the 2000 Democratic platform refers approvingly to the "right to privacy"; we treat this as a pro-choice litmus test and fold it into the abortion category.

Ideological Requirements for Nominees

In some instances, a statement did not meet the threshold for a litmus test, but nevertheless establishes an ideological frame for appointments.[26] For example, consider this statement from the 1984 Republican platform:

> We commend the President for appointing federal judges committed to the rights of law-abiding citizens and traditional family values. We share the public's dissatisfaction with an elitist and unresponsive federal judiciary. If our legal institutions are to regain respect, they must respect the people's legitimate interests in a stable, orderly society. In his second term, President Reagan will continue to appoint Supreme Court and other federal judges who share our commitment to judicial restraint.

We denote such statements as "ideological requirements."

Quality

In many cases a document will invoked a desire for qualified judges, and we coded all such statements. For example, the 1984 Democratic platform pledged: "It is essential to recruit people of high integrity, outstanding competence, and high quality of judgment to serve in our nation's judiciary."

Diversity

Finally, we coded whether a document expressed a desire for increasing the racial or gender diversity of the Supreme Court. For instance, the 1980 Democratic platform stated:

> One of President Carter's highest priorities has been to increase significantly the number of women, Blacks, Hispanics and other minorities in the federal government. That has been done. More women, Blacks and Hispanics have been appointed to federal judgeships during the Carter Administration than during all

> previous Administrations in history. Of the 39 women federal judges, 35 have been Carter appointees; of the 38 Black federal judges, 19 have been Carter appointees; of the 14 Hispanic judges, 5 have been Carter appointees. This record must be continued. The Democratic Party is committed to continue and strengthen the policy of appointing more women and minorities to federal positions at all levels including the Supreme Court.

In addition, the parties occasionally supported diversity more generally. For example, the 1996 Democratic Platform stated, "The president and vice president remain committed to an administration that looks like America, and we are proud of the administration's extraordinary judicial appointments—they are both more diverse and more qualified than any previous administration." We coded such statements as falling under "general diversity."

While straightforward, these data provide us with rich insights into the changes in the parties' agendas for the Supreme Court. Taken together, the first three kinds of statements—hot-button cases, litmus tests, and ideology demands—demarcate the party's overall interest in Supreme Court nominees and Supreme Court policy. We consider these three categories in turn and then fashion an overall index of party interest in Supreme Court policy.

A Note about Party Factions and Southern Democrats

A final point deserves mention. By relying on party platforms as an indicator of party interest in the court, our approach will privilege issues, demands, and cases on which the parties are generally aligned. Because we view the platforms as akin to coalition contracts, it makes sense to examine areas of broad agreement. This approach, however, downplays instances where significant heterogeneity exists *within* a party coalition and only a subset of the party cares intensely about the courts. The prime example of such a split in our period of study was when Southern Democrats fiercely opposed the decision in *Brown v. Board of Education*. This opposition led to the publication of the "Southern Manifesto" in 1956, in which about 100 representatives and senators attacked the court's decision in *Brown* as an abuse of judicial power that illegitimately curtailed the power of Southern States.[27] This split between Southern and Northern Democrats led to a rather anodyne mention of *Brown* in the 1956 Democrat platform, quoted above.

We return to the role of race in splitting the party coalitions with respect to the courts in Chapter 8. For now it suffices to note that the Southern Democrats' post-*Brown* emphasis on the court was primarily *defensive* with respect to appointments. Southern Democrats criticized many of the court's decisions and voted against several nominees in the 1950s and 1960s that they viewed as racially liberal, but this opposition did not translate into an increased emphasis on *judicial selection* (at least at the Supreme Court level) as a means to address the court's perceived waywardness.[28] Accordingly, we argue that focusing on platforms and acceptance speeches to understand party interest in the court is a sensible approach.

2.3.3 Hot-Button Cases and Their Topics

We begin by examining hot-button cases cited by the parties. In the platforms, the parties frequently denounce "bad" Supreme Court decisions, often going so far as to call for their reversal. For example, recent Democratic Party platforms called for the reversal of the *Citizens United*[29] campaign finance decision, while Republican Party platforms after 1973 routinely called for overturning *Roe v. Wade.* Sometimes, however, the parties hail "good" Supreme Court decisions. For instance, the 1996 Republican platform enthusiastically supported the anti-union decision in *Communications Workers v. Beck.*[30] In addition, both parties' platforms often praised *Brown v. Board of Education.*

Figure 2.1 displays case mentions over time by case topic and party mentioning the case topic. (Note that neither party's platform or acceptance speech from 1928 and 1932 contains any mentions of the Supreme Court or appointments whatsoever; accordingly, to enhance the clarity of the figures in this section, we begin the data displays in 1936.) Thus, each red block in the top half of the figure indicates a

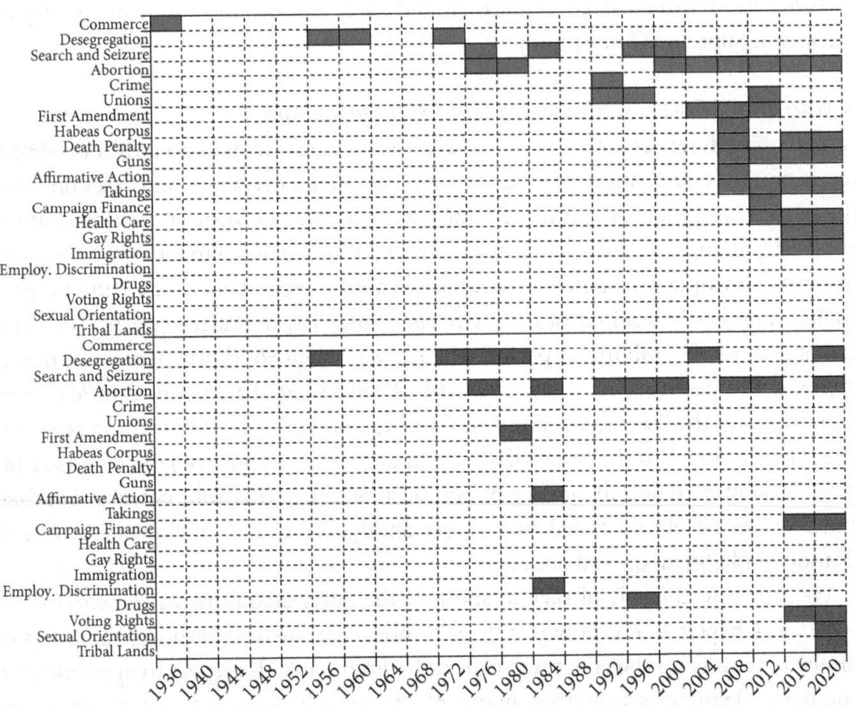

Fig. 2.1 Party mentions of Supreme Court cases, by topic and by party, 1936–2020. The red boxes (top) indicate Republican mentions, while the blue boxes (bottom) indicate Democratic mentions. Of the 21 issues discussed across the platforms, some were only discussed by one party; the empty rows in the figure mean a given party never mentioned a given issue.

Table 2.1 Mentions of Supreme Court cases, by case subject and party, 1936–2000.

Issue	Democrats	Republicans	Total
Abortion	9	12	21
Desegregation	6	3	9
First Amendment	1	5	6
Campaign Finance	3	1	4
Gay Rights	0	4	4
Guns	0	4	4
Search and Seizure	0	4	4
Takings	0	4	4
Death Penalty	0	3	3
Health Care	0	3	3
Unions	0	3	3
Affirmative Action	1	1	2
Immigration	0	2	2
Voting Rights	2	0	2
Commerce	0	1	1
Crime	0	1	1
Drugs	1	0	1
Employment Discrimination	1	0	1
Habeas Corpus	0	1	1
Sexual Orientation	1	0	1
Tribal Lands	1	0	1

Republican Party mention of a case in the corresponding topical area. The blue blocks display the same information for Democratic Party platforms.

The figure shows that mentions of Supreme Court cases in party platforms or acceptance speeches were very rare before the early to mid-1970s. Alf Landon's 1936 Republican acceptance speech mentioned an agricultural price support case in passing. In 1956, both party platforms mentioned *Brown*, the Republicans favorably (as they did again in their 1960 platform). But, as we discussed previously, the Democrats were more circumspect; that platform stopped well short of endorsing school desegregation, but decried calls for violence and recognized the authority of the Supreme Court. These were the only mentions of Supreme Court cases in party platforms and acceptance speeches over the four decades from 1928 to 1968.

The 1970s saw a dramatic change. First with the 1972 Democratic platform, and then with the 1976 Republican platform, the parties began to address Supreme Court cases. As shown in Figure 2.1, both parties invoked Supreme Court cases in every subsequent platform, except in 1988. However, which cases were invoked and why differed dramatically between the two parties.

Table 2.1 examines these asymmetries by displaying the frequencies of the different topics and their relative importance to the parties. Abortion cases received more mentions in the party platforms than cases in any other topic area. In addition, abortion was discussed somewhat more frequently in the Republican platforms than Democratic ones (the ratio of mentions is 1.25:1). The parties took opposing stances, with Republican platforms uniformly denouncing the Supreme Court's decisions supporting abortion rights and the Democratic platforms always hailing them.

The second most frequently mentioned type of case were the desegregation cases, particularly *Brown*. Besides the ambivalent 1956 Democratic mention, both parties have lauded the decision. Interestingly, Democratic platforms mentioned *Brown* much more frequently than Republican ones, with a ratio of 2.5:1.

First amendment cases were the third most frequently mentioned category of cases. Most of these are Republican mentions that focus on religious liberty issues. The sole Democratic mention of a First Amendment case denounced a ruling that weakened protections for the press.

For most of the remaining case types, they are typically cited by one party or the other, but not both. One exception, however, is campaign finance (Republicans have lauded the Supreme Court's blows to campaign finance regulation, Democrats have denounced them). The Republican Party has frequently cited topics such as search and seizure (denouncing the court's exclusionary rule), unions (supporting decisions that place obstacles on union organizing), government takings of private property (opposing decisions that enable support for local government takings), gun ownership (supporting the court's anti-gun control rulings), health care (opposing the court's rulings upholding the Affordable Care Act), gay rights (opposing the court's support for gay marriage), and the death penalty (opposing Court limitations on the use of the death penalty).

In contrast, the Democratic Party has discussed many fewer topics; it has tended to focus on voting rights (opposing the court's overturning several parts of the Voting Rights Act), employment discrimination (opposing the court's limits on enforcement of employment discrimination), and drugs (supporting a case allowing drug testing of athletes).

Summary

Overall, four patterns stand out in the case-mention data. First, with few exceptions, the party platforms did not mention hot-button cases until the early to mid-1970s. Of course, there were plenty of controversial Supreme Court cases between 1928 and 1972, notably those striking down key components of the New Deal between 1933 and 1936. Yet the party professionals and elected officials who dominated the platform committees chose not to highlight them in the platforms. Even the 1968 Republican Party platform, which imposed a law-and-order litmus test on nominees, did not mention specific Warren Court cases. In contrast, later platform committees, often including many more activists, invoked specific cases much more frequently.

Second, the Republican Party has been much more focused on specific Supreme Court cases than the Democratic Party. In Figure 2.1 there are 68 boxes filled in—that is, 68 unique combinations of years and case mentions by party (allowing for the fact that in some years both parties mentioned the same case). Of these 68, 44 (65%) were Republican mentions, while only 24 (35%) were Democratic.

Third, the parties have been interested in different kinds of cases. "Social issue" topics loomed large for Republicans, particularly after about 2004. Abortion was the pre-eminent topic for case mentions for both parties, but many of the other Republican mentions involve religious liberty, gay rights, guns, and crime. In contrast, aside from abortion, Democratic mentions generally eschewed social issues in favor of "diversity" issues like desegregation, employment discrimination, and voting rights. The contrasting perspectives appear to reflect the interests of high demanding coalition partners in the parties, as well as their very different understandings of the Supreme Court's proper role in society.

Finally, the timing of mentions often reflects the topicality of recent hot-button Court actions; after a few years, mentions of these cases may fade. But some cases moved beyond hot-button status to become totems or emblems for particular issues of perennial concern. Most notably, *Brown* became a symbol of diversity and virtue in Democratic platforms, while *Roe* became an iconic flashpoint in Republican platforms.

2.3.4 Specific Policy Litmus Tests

We next turn to specific policy litmus tests imposed by the parties. In the past, presidents often denied that they would impose specific policy litmus tests on Supreme Court nominees. For example, while campaigning in 1999, George W. Bush stated the following when asked whether he would appoint justices who would overturn *Roe v. Wade*: "There is no litmus test except for whether or not judges will strictly interpret the Constitution."[31] Like many norms related to Supreme Court confirmations, this one evaporated. In 2016, for example, both presidential candidates dropped any pretense of avoiding litmus tests. On the campaign trail, Donald Trump invoked the recent death of Justice Scalia and explicitly said he would appoint justices opposed to abortion rights and in favor of gun rights. Hillary Clinton, meanwhile, stated she would "have a bunch of litmus tests," including abortion and guns but also campaign finance and gay rights.[32] In 2020, Joe Biden, while running for the Democratic nomination, stated, "A litmus test on abortion relates to a fundamental value in the Constitution. A woman does have a right to choose."[33]

Figure 2.2 depicts the issues on which parties imposed litmus tests from 1936 to 2020. For convenience, we consider "ideological requirements for nominees" (defined above) as overall liberal or conservative litmus tests and pool them together in a single category. Prior to 1968, policy litmus tests were absent from platforms and convention speeches; they may have been seen as outside the bounds of normal American politics. Richard Nixon introduced litmus tests with his focus on law and order, which the Republican party pursued on and off in subsequent years. After 1968, Republican Party platforms frequently stated explicit policy requirements for acceptable appointees to the Supreme Court; Democratic platforms did so as well, though somewhat less often.

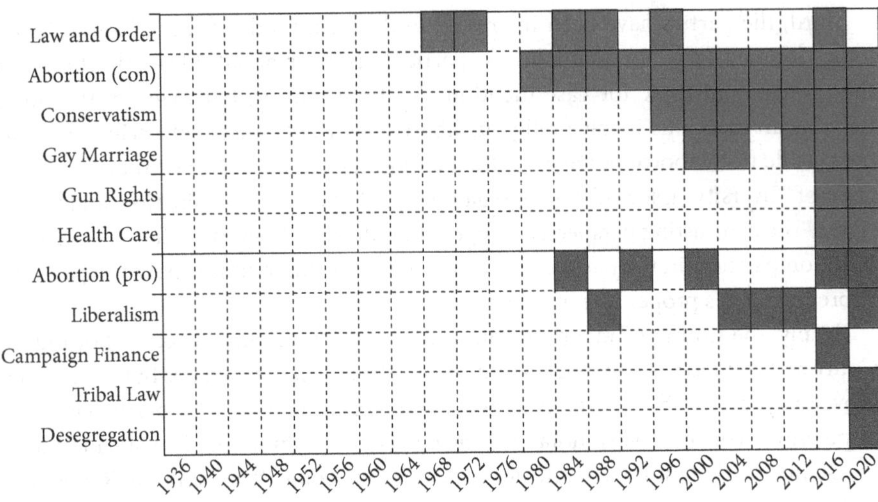

Fig. 2.2 Litmus tests, 1936–2020. The red boxes (top) indicate Republican mentions, while the blue boxes (bottom) indicate Democratic mentions.

Republican litmus tests have focused on three main issues: law and order, abortion, and general conservatism. Beginning in 1980, every Republican platform imposed an "abortion/family values" litmus test on judicial appointments to the Supreme Court. In every year since 1996, Republicans have insisted on general conservatism in their nominees. For instance, the 2016 Republican platform stated: "We, therefore, support the appointment of justices and judges who respect the constitutional limits on their power and respect the authority of the states to decide such fundamental social questions." Finally, in 2012, the Republican Party agenda added opposition to the Affordable Care Act as a policy requirement for nominees, and in 2016, support for gun ownership.

The imposition of policy requirements for nominees in Democratic Party platforms was less focused and more sporadic. In only a handful of years did the Democrats demand judicial conformity to a policy agenda, with that infrequent demand restricted to abortion rights litmus tests in 1984, 1992, 2000, 2016, and 2020. In 2016, the Democrats added one new litmus test, support for restrictions on campaign finance (which was based on opposition to the hot-button case *Citizens United*). Then, in 2020, the Democrats explicitly made desegregation a litmus test for the first time (although mentions of this issue in other contexts have been frequent on both sides since 1956). Finally, since 1984 Democrats have often insisted on general liberalism in their nominees. For example, the 2012 Democratic platform stated: "Moving forward, we will continue to nominate and confirm judges who are men and women of unquestionable talent and character and will always demonstrate their faithfulness to our law and our Constitution and bring with them a sense of how American society works and how the American people live."[34]

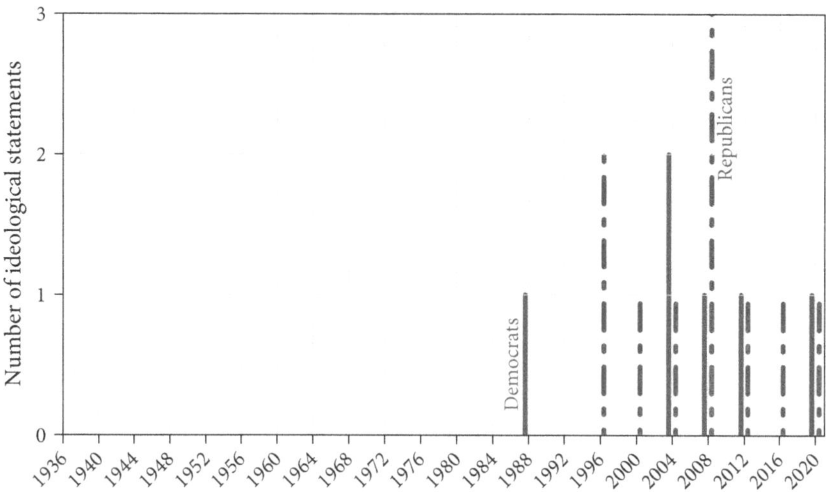

Fig. 2.3 Ideological statements, 1936–2020. The dashed (red) lines depict Republican mentions, while the solid (blue) lines depict Democratic mentions.

2.3.5 General Ideological Demands

In addition to specific policy positions, as we noted above, the parties have sometimes adopted language advocating a more general ideological orientation for nominees. To give another example, the 1988 Democratic Platform stated:

> We believe that we honor our multicultural heritage by assuring equal access to government services, employment, housing, business enterprise and education to every citizen regardless of race, sex, national origin, religion, age, handicapping condition or sexual orientation; that these rights are without exception too precious to be jeopardized by Federal Judges and Justice Department officials chosen during the past years—by a political party increasingly monolithic both racially and culturally—more for their unenlightened ideological views than for their respect for the rule of law.

Figure 2.3 depicts a lineplot of the number of ideological statements by party, over time. The overall number of such statements is smaller compared to case mentions and litmus tests, but the basic pattern is the same. The parties did not make ideological statements until later years, and the Republican Party generally made them more often than the Democratic Party.

2.3.6 Index of Party Interest in Supreme Court Policy

What does this combined data tell us? We can calculate a simple measure of party interest in Supreme Court policy by aggregating the three components. Specifically,

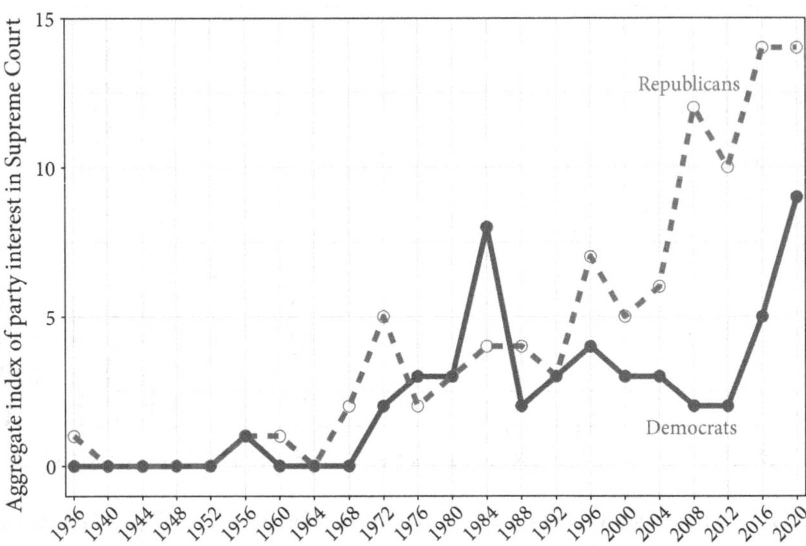

Fig. 2.4 Aggregate index of party interest in the Supreme Court, 1936–2020.

for each party-year combination, we sum the number of paragraphs in the party platforms and presidential acceptance speeches that invoke hot-button cases, litmus tests, or ideological requirements for nominees. (We exclude quality and diversity statements, which we address below.)

Figure 2.4 depicts these indices over time. The aggregate data show very little presidential and party interest in the court before the 1960s.[35] But perhaps even more importantly, the figure reveals a clear asymmetry beginning in the 1990s. Republican interest in the Supreme Court increased dramatically around then through 2020, while Democratic interest was fairly flat until 2012, before increasing in 2016 and then again in 2020 (but still remaining below Republican interest in both years). We return shortly to the importance of this asymmetry.

2.3.7 Diversity Promises and Calls for Quality

Ideology, of course, is not everything. Both parties and presidents have often shown interest in promoting high-quality judges and in increasing the diversity of the federal bench. To examine these concerns, Figure 2.5 documents the number of diversity and quality statements over time, by party. As with ideology, the parties made no mention of these concerns until the late 1960s and early 1970s. But since then, a sharp reverse asymmetry appears: the Democratic Party emphasized diversity and quality far more than Republicans. Strikingly, the Republican Party never highlighted racial diversity among federal judges in its platform, although it did mention gender diversity in 1972, 1984, and 1988.

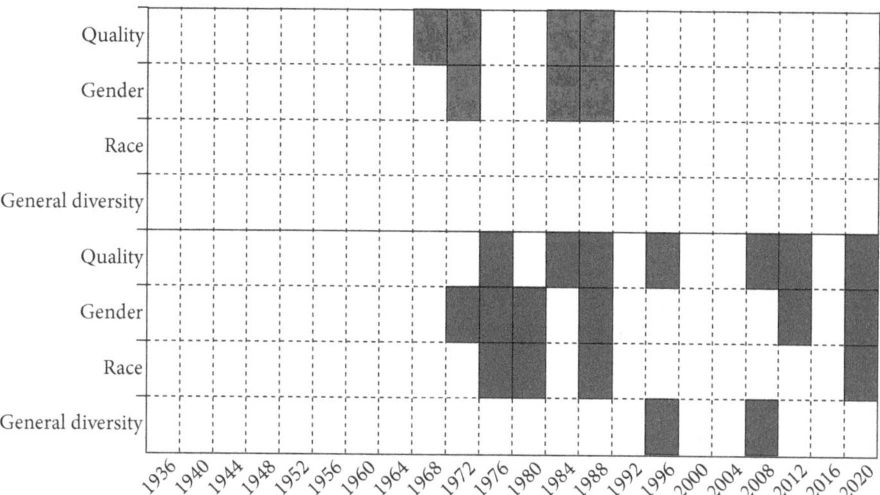

Fig. 2.5 Diversity and quality statements by party, 1936–2020. The red boxes (top) indicate Republican mentions, while the blue boxes (bottom) indicate Democratic mentions.

The Democrats' focus on diversity rather than ideology, combined with their lesser interest in the courts, meant that they were playing "catch up" to the Republicans in fully appreciating the policy importance of federal courts. This asymmetry persisted even as late as the 2020 party conventions for Donald Trump and Joe Biden. (The conventions were held before Justice Ruth Bader Ginsburg died in September 2020, but the Garland-to-Gorsuch conversion in 2016–2017 and the contentious fight over Justice Kavanaugh's appointment in 2018 were still quite relevant.) Continuing his emphasis on judicial appointments begun in 2016, President Trump stated in his acceptance speech: "By the end of my first term, we will have approved more than 300 federal judges, including two great new Supreme Court Justices." Other speakers at the convention lauded Trump's success in transforming the judiciary during his term. Conversely, Democrats paid very little attention to the federal courts at their convention. Biden did not mention judges a single time in his acceptance speech. This lack of interest—in sharp contrast to the Republican focus on the courts—provoked consternation among liberal interest groups.[36]

However, once in office, Biden did appoint a record number of federal judges, with the most confirmed of any president though March 1 of his second year in office. And, consistent with the Democratic Party's emphasis on diversity, Biden also appointed a record-number of minority women to the federal bench, including his 2022 selection of Ketanji Brown Jackson to replace Justice Stephen Breyer on the Supreme Court.[37]

The reverse asymmetries on ideology and quality/diversity that the platform data documents reflects broader patterns in party asymmetry, as documented by political scientists Matt Grossman and David Hopkins. They note, "While the Democratic Party is fundamentally a group coalition," the Republican Party can be most accurately characterized as the vehicle for an "ideological movement."[38] From this perspective, it makes perfect sense that the parties have responded differently in crafting their judicial agendas. Republican activists have tended to emphasize ideological commitments and policy. Democrats, while not oblivious to such commitments, have pushed for greater inclusion of women and racial minorities on the federal bench in general and on the Supreme Court specifically.

2.4 Explaining the Party Positions: Evidence from Convention Delegates Survey

What explains the content of the party platforms? Pinpointing specific mechanisms through which ideas emerge onto party platforms is a tricky exercise, because we can directly observe only the final product. Accordingly, the discussion and evidence we present in this section are at best suggestive—but we hope informative.

In the previous section we showed that interest in the Supreme Court was basically non-existent until the *Brown* decision of 1954; even then, little discussion of the court took place until the late 1960s. The parties' growing interest in the Supreme Court seemingly went hand-in-hand with organized interest groups' heightened attention to the court, a theme that we return to in detail in Chapter 5. As Scherer (2005) notes, proliferating activists on both sides came to see the Supreme Court as important for their policy goals.[39] According to Scherer, the issue activists responded strongly to landmark judicial decisions of the 1960s and 1970s, both in opposition and support, and focus on judicial nominations followed naturally. Critically, at the same time the interest group landscape changed, the party reforms of the 1970s drove largely non-ideological party professionals from the field. These reforms essentially turned over party governance and goals to the issue activists.[40] At present, the activists command organizational and financial resources essential for successful campaigns, with the president and senators willing and eager to do their bidding. If issue activists are primarily responsible for pushing the parties' toward their respective agendas, this would be entirely consistent with the UCLA School's argument that the parties function as coalitions of high demanding interest groups.

To investigate the influence of issue activists on the parties' judicial agendas, we turn to survey data of delegates to various meetings of the Democratic and Republican national convention. The data series, known as the Convention Delegate Study [CDS] Series, covers every convention that met from 1972 to 2004, with the exceptions of 1976 and 1996.[41] The surveys are unique in that they provide regularly occurring snapshots on the views not just of party identifiers (the "masses"), but of party activists—those sufficiently engaged with the party that they attend the national convention as a delegate. Scholars have used the surveys to great effect to study changes in the views of party activists over time.[42]

Ideally we would have access to data that measured activists' views from the period before the parties showed much interest in the Supreme Court. Unfortunately, such data does not appear to exist. In addition, to connect the views of activists to changes in the platforms, we need sufficient temporal coverage on the same issue to examine changes over time. One of the very few issues with this coverage is abortion, which has been the most salient recurring issue in Supreme Court confirmation politics.

Our analysis proceeds on two tracks. First, we document changes in the views of Democratic and Republican convention delegates over time. This analysis essentially replicates Carmines and Woods (2002), and shows that views have polarized heavily by party over time.[43] Second, we show that a significant amount of the variation correlates with an increase in the number of delegates saying they belong to an abortion-related group: these delegates have more extreme views on the abortion issue than delegates who do not belong to such a group. To the best of our knowledge, this analysis is the first to leverage the group membership questions from the CDS data to study changes in the views of party activists. This evidence does not prove that an influx of abortion activists at the highest rungs of the parties *caused* the emergence of abortion litmus tests for Supreme Court nominees, but the evidence is certainly consistent with such an effect.

Abortion Preferences and Group Membership over Time

The CDS asked delegates about their preferences on abortion policy in every year of the survey. While the question wording varied slightly over time (see the Appendix for complete question wordings), preferences were always measured using a four-point scale, ranging from most conservative to most liberal. For every year, we calculated the mean response to the abortion question, broken down by party—Figure 2.6A shows these results. In 1972, the year before *Roe* was decided, Republican and Democratic delegates differed little in their average abortion views. Even in 1980, the partisan differences were still fairly slight. After that, however, opinion steadily polarized, with Democratic delegates far more likely to state a liberal position on abortion than Republican delegates.[44]

Delegates in general are, of course, a self-selected group of party activists. But even within this set of high demanders, certain members may care more intensely about a particular issue than others. It is these members, we conjecture, who push the party to adopt particular stances on a platform. To capture these "super demanders," we use questions in the CDS that ask delegates about their membership in a variety of organizations or associations. Beginning in 1980, the CDS asked respondents whether they were members of an abortion-specific group—Figure 2.6B depicts the proportion of delegates who said they belong to an abortion group, by party.[45] The graph shows a striking increase from the first time the question was asked in 1980; by 1992, 30% of Republicans and 45% of Democrats said they belonged to an abortion-related group. Presumably the increase would have been even more striking had this data existed in 1972.

Moreover, if we examine the interaction of group membership and opinion on abortion, Figure 2.7 clearly shows that these group members had more extreme views than non-group members. In every year, Democratic abortion-group members had

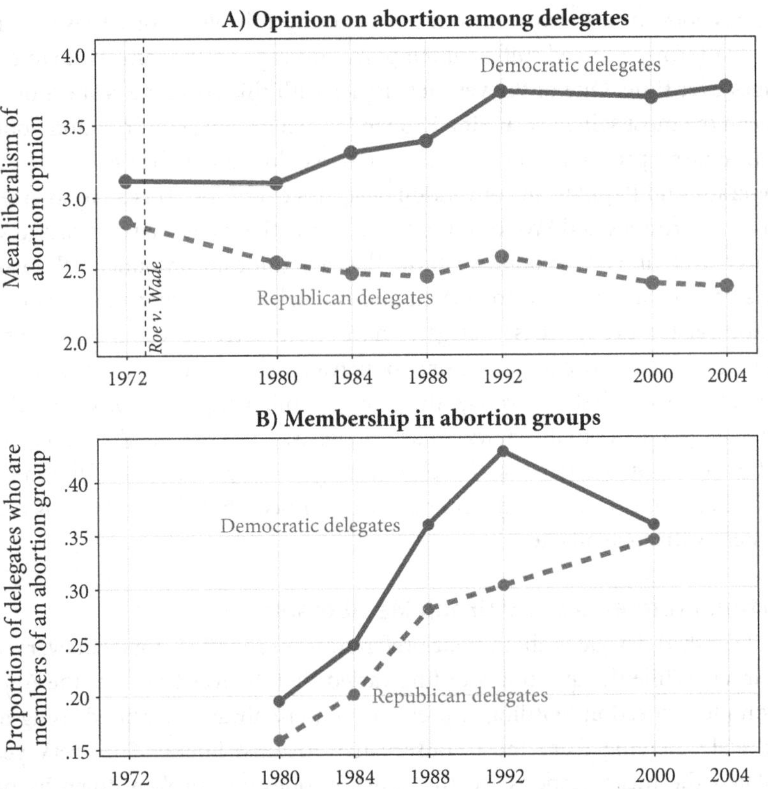

Fig. 2.6 Abortion opinion and membership among convention delegates. A) Abortion preferences among convention delegates, 1972–2004. B) Proportion of delegates saying they belong to an abortion group.

more liberal abortion views than Democratic non-group members, and Republican group members more conservative views than Republican non-group members. Thus, the "super demanders" drove a significant portion of the polarization among party activists over time.[46]

What difference did the growth of abortion-group members, combined with the extremity of their views, have on the content of the party platforms? Both a quantitative and qualitative evaluation of changes in the party platforms with respect to abortion does suggest that such a connection is quite plausible.

As we noted in the introduction to the chapter, early Republican ambiguity on abortion quickly turned to a solidly pro-life position. Figure 2.2 showed that every Republican platform between 1980 and 2016 contained a litmus test for a pro-life position by any Supreme Court nominee. In addition, as Williams (2011, 533) notes, even though Republican members of Congress abandoned their attempts to pass a constitutional amendment overturning *Roe* in the 1980s, every Republican platform from 1980 to 2012 called for a "human life" amendment. Finally, later

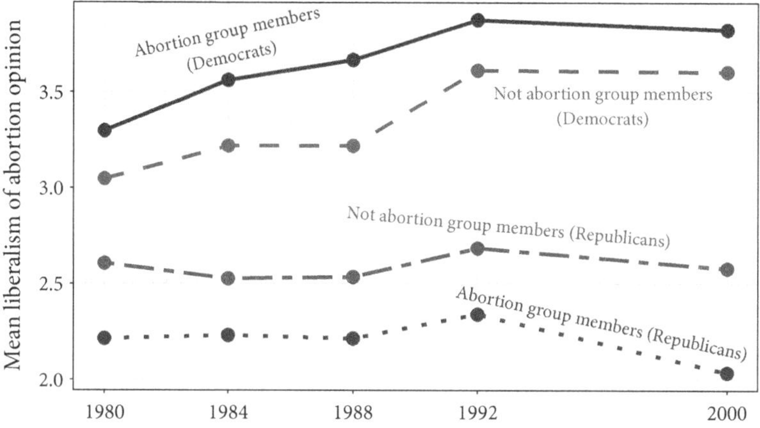

Fig. 2.7 Abortion preferences among convention delegates, broken down by group- and non-group members, 1972–2004.

platforms would extend their discussion of abortion to include disapproval of the Supreme Court's 1999 decision striking down restrictions on so-called "partial-birth" abortion,[47] as well as provisions in the Affordable Care Act increasing access to abortions.

The Democratic move toward abortion rights was less linear. Figure 2.2 showed that the party platforms only sometimes included abortion litmus tests. While the 1976 and 1980 platforms opposed any constitutional amendment to overturn *Roe*, the 1984 and 1988 platforms actually eschewed the word "abortion" in favor of "fundamental right of a woman to reproductive freedom." Nevertheless, every Democratic platform since 1988 has steadfastly advanced a pro-choice position; the 1996 platform, for example, stated that "The Democratic Party stands behind the right of every woman to choose, consistent with *Roe v. Wade*, and regardless of ability to pay." Subsequent platforms would defend the relevant provisions of the Affordable Care Act and urged repeal of the federal law barring federal funding for abortion services.

In sum, abortion emerged as an issue in the 1970s, but one in which the parties were not sorted ideologically. Organized interests and party activists took stands and mobilized forces in a manner that gradually induced ideological sorting on the issue. The CDS data reveal that activists in both parties were increasingly likely to be members of abortion-related groups, and these members had more extreme views than non-group members. As the polarization of activists increased, the party platforms reflected these divisions, with early ambiguity giving way to forceful and opposing stances. This shift, of course, would play out in the selection and confirmation of every Supreme Court nominee chosen after 1980.

Delegate Diversity

Can the composition of the party delegates also cast light on the asymmetric emphasis on judicial diversity, as documented above? Again our approach is only suggestive

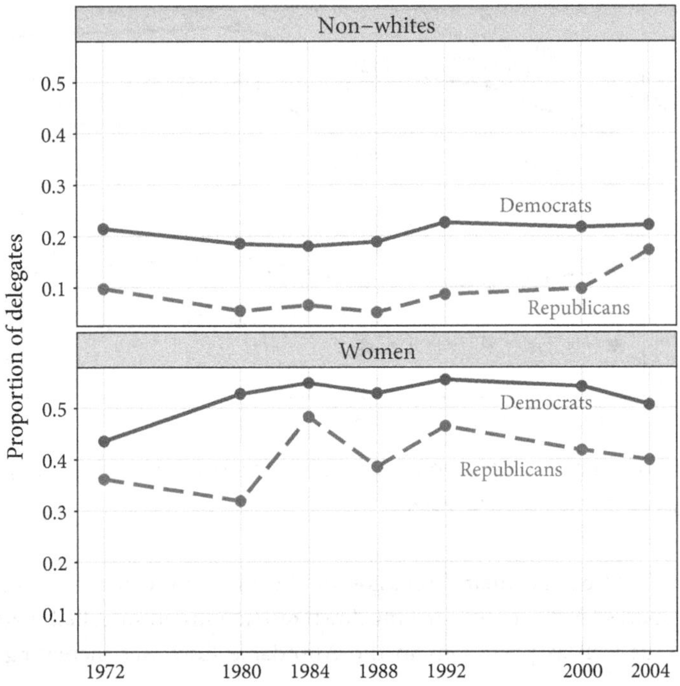

Fig. 2.8 Proportion of non-white and women delegates to the party conventions, by party, 1972–2004.

but quite straightforward. For each party convention in years with CDS surveys, we calculated the proportion of women and non-white delegates—the results are presented in Figure 2.8. The differences between the two parties is perhaps less dramatic than one might expect, given the differences in the broader party coalitions in recent decades. And although the levels of non-white delegates among Democrats was always relatively low from 1972 to 2004, never exceeding 25%, in every year the proportion of women and non-white delegates among Democrats exceeded that of Republicans. Thus it is perhaps not surprising that Democratic platforms emphasized judicial diversity more than Republican ones.

2.5 Conclusion

> The various leaders, activists, and interest group leaders who seek to influence presidential nominations are more than a collection of individual actors; they meet the standard definition of political parties. They are, in other words, a broad coalition aiming to control not only the presidency, but also Congress, the Supreme Court, governorships, state legislatures, city councils and county boards, and every other locus of political power in the United States (Cohen et al. 2008, 6).

This crisp assertion illustrates well the UCLA School's understanding of political parties as coalitions of high-demanding interest groups with specific policy agendas who try to select candidates likely to prove loyal servitors once in office. To this we add the notion of coalition contracts: the policy statements in national party platforms are not meaningless, but rather provide a concrete and consequential blueprint for a presidency. Empirical scholarship consistently shows that presidents take their campaign promises very seriously and strive diligently to implement them once in office. The quotation also highlights the breadth of interest group coalition ambitions, extending far beyond the presidency to other sites as well, including the Supreme Court of the United States. In this sense, the parties' focus on the Supreme Court—and the justices' subsequent voting behavior—offers a manageable case study of the coalition contract framework.

The coalition contract approach sets the stage for several later parts of the book. While in this chapter we folded the goals of presidents into those of their party, at the end of the day the president makes the decision of whom to nominate to the court. In Chapter 9, we show that the parties' judicial agendas predict the type of nominee a president selects, particularly the nominee's overall characteristics, including ideology, policy reliability, and diversity.[48] Then, in Chapter 12, we examine what is perhaps the fundamental question of the coalition contract framework: do presidents meet the terms of the contract by appointing justices who actually vote in accordance with the parties' judicial agendas?

But, before that point, we first examine how presidents organized their processes for selecting Supreme Court nominees, for it makes little difference what type of nominees presidents wanted if they couldn't reliably find them. We then document the types of individuals presidents considered for the court during our period of study. We turn to these tasks in the next two chapters.

3 Selecting How to Select

Presidents and Organizational Design

In the early 1960s, Princeton political scientist Walter Murphy interviewed Supreme Court Justice William O. Douglas at considerable length. One topic of discussion was President Harry Truman's 1949 selection of Sherman ("Shay") Minton to replace Justice Rutledge. Douglas told this tale:

> Shay Minton knew Truman. Shay Minton had been in the Senate. He was a member of the Truman Committee in the Senate and he was a member of the Truman Subcommittee. And that Subcommittee was composed of Truman, Minton and Harold Burton. There may have been others also. But those three were the chief members and they went around the country investigating war efforts, manufacturers, and so on.... Truman and Minton became very, very close friends. Sherman Minton in those days had his full health. He was very vigorous, active. He liked to take a drink. He enjoyed smoking-room stories. It was conventional for, sort of a standing joke, for Minton once they got their bags at the airport on coming to a new town, to turn to Truman and say, "Harry, shall we go to the hotel and check our bags or go straight to the whorehouse?" This was rough and tumble warmhearted, wonderful Shay Minton, who had a very keen bawdy sense of humor, greatly loved by everybody who knew him, one of my very, very close friends for many, many years. And when there was a vacancy on the court, Shay Minton, who was then on the Court of Appeals in the Second Circuit, got on a train or a plane, came to Washington, walked into the White House and said, "Harry, I want that job on the Supreme Court." And Harry said, "Okay, I'll give it to you." It's just as simple as that.[1]

This story illustrates one example of *how* presidents choose nominees, *who* they choose, and *why*. For Truman picking Minton, the how, the who, and the why could not have been more straightforward: do it on your own, pick a crony, please yourself. But for most presidents, it is hardly "as simple as that."

In this chapter and the next, we address the how and the who of presidential nominee selection; we defer the tricky why question until Chapter 9. We begin by tracing the evolution of presidents' selection and vetting process over almost a century. The nominee selection started as a small, lightly staffed, under-institutionalized and often erratic endeavor. But it grew into a large, professionally staffed, systematic,

Making the Supreme Court: The Politics of Appointments, 1930–2020. Charles M. Cameron and Jonathan P. Kastellec, Oxford University Press. © Oxford University Press 2023. DOI: 10.1093/oso/9780197680544.003.0003

and bureaucratized machine—albeit one sometimes resisted and undermined by the president himself. To a remarkable degree, this story is, in miniature, the story of the modern presidency itself.

As explained in greater detail below, our review of the history identifies three distinct organizational modes for selecting nominees: no delegation, external delegation, and internal delegation. We explain presidents' organizational choices by focusing on the interplay of two variables: first, the president's interest in judicial policy (documented in Chapter 2), and second, the availability and location of specialized resources in the form of a legal policy elite. For presidents interested in the Supreme Court, the emergence of these expert resources, first in the Department of Justice and then in the White House, professionalized the selection and vetting process. To gauge professionalism, we propose two measures: the length of the president's short list of potential nominees and the speed of the selection process. We argue that very brief short lists (especially one-nominee lists or "singletons") and lengthy searches suggest a lack of preparation—although overly hasty selection processes may arise through cronyism.

A caveat for the chapter is warranted: studying presidential procedural choice is harder than studying the output of the procedures, the selected nominees. For one thing, finding details on individual selection processes can be difficult. For some nominees, we can get a good sense of the process, thanks to interviews, records and memoranda, diaries, memoirs, and oral histories—many painstakingly assembled or mined by energetic scholars and talented journalists. But in other cases, the historical record is extremely thin—no official records, no interviews of the participants (who are now deceased), and little or no contemporary journalism—so the process remains blurry. This problem is worse for obscure nominees than for celebrated or controversial ones. For example, journalists and scholars wrote extensively about Robert Bork's failed nomination in 1987. But few paid attention to Elena Kagan's smooth confirmation in 2010. Likewise, Hoover's selection of judicial phenomenon Benjamin Cardozo stimulated two excellent studies, but the same president's pick of legal functionary Owen Roberts left scholars cold.[2]

Second, there are really only a few decisions to study. Presidents do not make separate, independent design choices for each nomination. Rather, they tend to set up a process and stick with it, or just modify it somewhat—President George W. Bush's wild swing between two very different selection modes (discussed below) is quite unusual. So, from Warren G. Harding to Donald Trump, we do not have hundreds of decisions to analyze (if we use the short lists of final candidates), or even 50 or so (if we focus on the nominees themselves).[3] Instead, we have only 16 observations—one selection mode for each president from Harding to Trump (except Carter, who never made an appointment)—with a few second thoughts or modifications by presidents who made multiple appointments. As a result, this chapter relies more on qualitative history—in particular, brief portraits of different selection and vetting operations—than on statistical tests and data displays.

3.2 Procedural Design: Presidential Interest, Executive Resources

We begin by returning to Truman's selection of Minton—what are we to make of this story? Perhaps its picture of an ultra-personalistic, crony-based appointment appealed to Douglas who, as a young New Dealer, had been a poker buddy and drinking companion of Roosevelt.[4] His friend then plucked him from the relative obscurity of the Securities and Exchange Commission to place him on the Supreme Court when he was just 40. It's possible then that Minton's story as related by Douglas simply validates Douglas' own story, and therefore may be apocryphal. On the other hand, David Yalof's (2001) careful review of documents in the Truman Library found no evidence that Truman ever considered anyone for the appointment other than his long-time friend Minton. Yalof concludes that Truman consulted no one and simply made his own choice. Likewise, the oral history of Justice Tom Clark—Truman's attorney general during his previous selections—broadly supports Douglas' account as well.[5]

But other presidents used very different processes. Consider President Gerald Ford's 1975 selection of John Paul Stevens to replace Douglas.[6] Taking office in the wake of the Watergate scandal, Ford decided to clean house at the Department of Justice—to "de-Nixonize" it, as described by historian Douglas Brinkley, with two of Nixon's former attorneys general facing trial and conviction. Ford brought in Edward H. Levi as attorney general—a noted legal scholar and author, former dean of the University of Chicago Law School, and then president of the University of Chicago.

Ford charged Levi with de-politicizing the Justice Department and restoring its integrity after the Nixon scandals, and after considerable arm twisting, Levi acquiesced. To underscore the break with his disgraced predecessor, Ford took a hands-off approach to the pending vacancy on the court and delegated the selection job to his superbly qualified attorney general. Though Ford met periodically with Levi, generally in tandem with the new White House legal counsel (Phillip Buchen), it was Levi who identified the candidates, did the vetting, and wrote the briefing memos for the President. Perhaps not surprisingly, Levi knew the top candidates well—one, Robert Bork, was Levi's former student, and another, John Paul Stevens, was a long-time acquaintance and colleague at the Chicago Law School. In fact, Stevens had listed Levi as a reference when he applied for a federal judgeship. In the end, adhering to Levi's advice, Ford selected his top candidate, Stevens.[7]

Ford's general approach in this instance—delegating a task to a highly knowledgeable and trusted subordinate in the relevant agency, with some supervision—is a standard design choice for modern presidents trying to manage the federal bureaucracy.[8] The scale of the federal government and the mammoth job of the presidency leave them little option. Nonetheless, presidents sometimes decide to go in the opposite direction, centralizing decisions rather than delegating them. In such a case, presidents dedicate substantial White House resources to this important task.[9]

Consider, for example, the process used by President George W. Bush in 2005 to fill the vacancy created by the retirement of Sandra Day O'Connor.[10] In this case, both the White House and the Department of Justice undertook extensive screening and vetting operations in advance of the vacancy; in fact, White House staffers began assembling short lists of potential nominees immediately after Bush took office in 2001. The White House group involved Vice President Dick Cheney, the president's top political advisor Karl Rove, and the White House Legal Counsel and long-time Bush family factotum Harriet Miers, as well as members of her staff. The Department of Justice group included the Attorney General, Alberto Gonzales, who had previously been the White House Legal Counsel. Among both groups, the name of one contender, John Roberts, drew particular attention. Roberts had served as a top lawyer in the Reagan and George H.W. Bush administrations, appeared before the Supreme Court in high-profile cases, was twice nominated (and once confirmed) to the D.C. Circuit Court of Appeals, and was a long-time member of the Federalist Society, the influential conservative legal organization. Both the attorney general and the high-level White House group interviewed him personally. Ultimately, rigorous winnowing of potential nominees by the White House group—including legal experts' careful study of opinions and writings, along with personal interviews and FBI background checks—led to a final short list of nine. Few of the short list candidates were friends, advisors, long-time political allies, or even personal acquaintances of the president. The final stage, a one-on-one interview with Bush, led to the selection of Roberts.

This process appears careful, systematic, painstaking, thoughtful, and above all, *rational*. The administration marshaled an abundance of high-quality talent, skillfully coordinating staffers who served the president's interest by presenting clear and thoughtful options. This process is miles away from Truman's apparently haphazard and capricious cronyism. It is also much more institutionalized, complex, and professionalized than Ford's simple delegation to Attorney General Levi.

So, the evolution of the selection process from Hoover to Bush looks like a story of administrative rationality triumphing over personal eccentricity, favoritism, and bad judgment in some cases (on the one hand), and bare-bones delegation (on the other). But: just two months after selecting Roberts, Bush engineered a debacle by nominating Harriet Miers to fill the second vacancy on the court. This bizarre event occurred when the president and his chief of staff became desperate to nominate a woman to fill Sandra Day O'Connor's seat (following William Rehnquist's death in September 2005, Bush switched Roberts' nomination to replace Rehnquist, leaving O'Connor's seat still vacant). But the two failed to identify a strong female Republican candidate in the federal judiciary, and instead turned to the familiar figure of Miers. Unfortunately, White House political operatives remained silent about the likely response to this unusual move—no one wanted to say no to the president.[11] Bush's crony pick led to an embarrassing withdrawal of the nominee in the face of opposition from the president's own party and allied interest groups, who doubted Miers' commitment to the goals of the conservative legal movement.

At this point, readers may be scratching their head in puzzlement (we have as well!). Are there patterns and logic in how presidents devise procedures to select Supreme Court nominees? Or is it all idiosyncratic, improvised, random, path dependent?

3.2.1 A (Sketch) Theory of Presidential Procedural Choice

The presidency is not like a Fortune 500 corporation or an agency like the Department of Defense. These organizations have a largely fixed organizational structure, standard operating procedures, and long-term personnel pre-dating the arrival of the latest CEO or Secretary, and long out-lasting her brief tenure. But in the White House, each new president confronts a blank slate. There is no standing White House civil service, no secretariat, no permanent employees.[12] With few exceptions, no statute specifies the nature or extent of White House offices or divisions.[13] Almost incredibly, each new president must build his own White House organization and procedures from scratch.

Speaking to a group of lawyers, former White House Legal Counsel Bernie Nussbaum (2002) painted a vivid picture of this dilemma as he experienced it in the opening days of the Clinton Administration:

> To envision what it was like, imagine entering your law firm one day in November and being told that by mid-January, everybody would be gone. Every partner, every associate, every paralegal, every secretary, every messenger, every meaningful file, would be gone. But you had to see to it that the firm would be fully operational, that it would be prepared to hear crises on a daily basis, with an entirely new team of professionals and staff. That's what it was like.... It was like walking into my office and having everybody gone. Everybody gone, there's nobody there. But the matters are there, more than ever. The cases are there, the telephone is ringing all the time, there's crisis after crisis, and you have to deal with that.

Of course, there is some institutional memory. Old hands from prior administrations eagerly share advice or volunteer to serve again. Earlier executive orders and presidential directives create a legacy. Consequently, valuable organizational innovations, like the press secretary, the White House chief of staff, and the White House legal counsel, accumulate and repeat from administration to administration. In addition, all presidents face similar tasks: how to craft a legislative program, lobby Congress, supervise agency policy making, or manage sudden crises. These activities demand design decisions, and one sees presidents making similar choices about organization and procedures for similar activities. Political scientists have thought creatively about how presidents do this.[14]

One recurring activity that demands organizational and procedural choices from the president is—of course!—identifying, vetting, and selecting nominees to the U.S.

Supreme Court. One would expect the general logic of presidential design choices to apply here, and we claim it does.

To be sure, we are not the first to study presidential procedural choices about judicial nominees. In chapter 5 of her path-breaking book, Christine Nemacheck (2008) analyzes the procedural choices behind about 40 nominees. Our approach is in the same vein but differs both theoretically and methodologically. The key theoretical variables in our framework are presidential interest in the courts and the extent of executive resources. Nemacheck, on the other hand, focuses on growing institutionalization, partisan differences across Republican and Democratic administrations, and divided versus unified government. In addition, Nemacheck characterizes the choice over procedures as a principal-agent problem, with conflict between a principal (the president) and agents (his vetters). In contrast, our reading of the history suggests a "team" approach in which the main players within administrations generally hold shared goals about nominees. Hence, we see presidents as CEOs trying to efficiently manage firm resources, including his own time and effort, in pursuit of common goals.[15]

As alluded to above, our review of the historical materials reveals three major design options. The first option is the *no delegation* process. Here, the president runs the process himself. He may talk to aides, senators, and friends around the country, but he keeps his cards close to his vest. We saw this decision mode at work with Truman, who seems to have used it for all his Supreme Court appointments, as did Roosevelt and Johnson.

The second design option is *external delegation*, well illustrated in Ford's pick of John Paul Stevens. Here, the president turns over the search and vetting process to a knowledgeable, trusted individual or entity *outside* the White House, typically the attorney general and his staff of experts (at least after the mid-1950s). Of course, the final decision remains with the president. Perhaps the most extreme and ingenious example of this design was that employed by President Warren G. Harding. In essence, the Republican Harding turned over the whole process to William Howard Taft, the former Republican president and then chief justice. What Taft recommended, Harding did. Although this example is extreme, other presidents have employed the external delegation mode as well; President Eisenhower's selection process (discussed below) is a prominent instance.

The third design option is *internal delegation*, the most organizationally complex and resource intensive option. Bush's pick of John Roberts illustrates this option. Here, the White House legal counsel operates as a project manager of sorts, perhaps supervised by the White House chief of staff. The legal counsel uses staff from his or her own office and the White House more broadly, but also draws on, coordinates with, or even directs the attorney general and the Department of Justice's Office of Legal Counsel. In some cases, like in the Clinton and Trump Administrations, the insiders may call on help from outsiders. The involvement of the president may be limited, but in the end he makes the final pick.

Table 3.1 Presidential choice of procedure for selecting and vetting Supreme Court nominees. Using historical accounts, we identify 19 selection modes governing the choice of 59 nominees by 16 presidents from 1921 to 2020.

No delegation (25 nominations)
Harding (Taft) Hoover (Hughes (Chief Justice), Parker, Roberts, Cardozo) F. D. Roosevelt (Black, Reed, Frankfurter, Douglas, Murphy, Stone (Chief Justice), Byrnes, Jackson, Rutledge) Truman (Burton, Vinson, Clark, Minton) Kennedy (Goldberg) Johnson (Fortas, Marshall, Fortas (Chief Justice), Thornberry) G. W. Bush (Miers)
External delegation (15 nominations)
Harding (Sutherland, Butler, Sanford) Eisenhower (Warren, Harlan, Brennan, Whittaker, Stewart) Kennedy (White) Ford (Stevens) Reagan (O'Connor, Rehnquist (Chief Justice), Scalia, Bork, D. Ginsburg)
Internal delegation (19 nominations)
Nixon (Burger, Haynsworth, Carswell, Blackman, Powell, Rehnquist (Associate Justice)) Reagan (Kennedy) G. H. W. Bush (Souter, Thomas) Clinton (Ruth Bader Ginsburg, Breyer) G. W. Bush (Roberts, Alito) Obama (Sotomayor, Kagan, Garland) Trump (Gorsuch, Kavanaugh, Barrett)

These three organizational modes are ideal types, and exact boundaries may be hard to delineate in practice. For example, how much presidential involvement turns a White House-led operation into a no delegation process? When the president and the attorney general pick together, is this no delegation or a team? Nonetheless, based on the available historical materials, we can map—with varying degrees of certainty—each president's selection procedure into the ideal types. Table 3.1 displays our classification, some of which may be contestable. But taking them broadly at face value, what determines the president's choice among the three design options?

Three patterns stand out. First, *presidents switched from the no delegation process to other procedural modes over time.* Aside from the Miers anomaly under George W. Bush, Lyndon Johnson was the last president to opt for the no delegation mode. In some sense, this trend is hardly surprising. In the early period, presidents had to do the job themselves for the simple reason that no one else was available (excepting Harding's delegation to Chief Justice Taft following his appointment to the Supreme Court). Later, as resources grew in the Justice Department and the White House, presidents could and did shift the work to others, not only to unburden themselves but to get a better result.

Second, *presidents delegated to the Department of Justice mostly in the middle of the time period we study*. In this era, a president who wanted to shift the burden of work from himself had only one way to do so, because only the Department of Justice had the skilled operatives to do the job; the White House Counsel's Office typically consisted of a single individual. But after the mid-1950s, the Office of Legal Counsel in the Justice Department could deploy a dozen or more highly skilled lawyers to work on selection and vetting.

Third, *the internal delegation process emerged fairly late but quickly became the standard mode for modern presidents*. Nixon appears to be the institutional innovator (as he was in many other regards), struggling to direct resources in both the White House and the Department of Justice to help with selection and vetting. Two factors seem plausible in driving the move to centralization. First, presidential interest in Supreme Court policy grew as Nixon and later presidents recognized its potential for real political gains and seized the opportunity. Second, the institutionalization of the White House Counsel's Office (described below) enabled a modern president interested in judicial policy to command a sizable in-house law firm to direct and coordinate activities of the attorney general and the Department of Justice. This resource-rich option is organizationally complex, but given skilled managers at the White House, it allows for highly professional selection and vetting like that in the Roberts nomination.

Figure 3.1 captures the logic of this argument. With low levels of executive resources, the president has little choice but to do the work himself. With intermediate levels of resources and low-to-moderate interest, the president favors delegation, especially external delegation. With high levels of resources and moderate-to-high interest, internal delegation emerges as the preferred option. Intermediate cases are less clear—for example, intermediate resources and high interest, or high resources and low presidential interest.

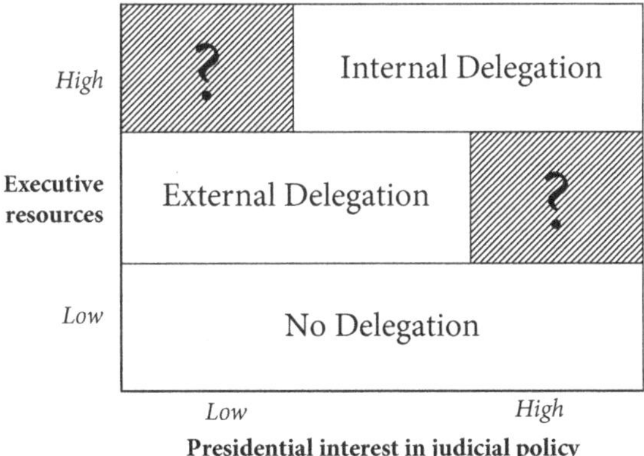

Fig. 3.1 Presidential choice of selection procedures: the roles of interest and resources.

We could recast this logic into the form of a formal game-theoretic model of procedural choice. But several models are equally plausible *ex ante* and neither the statistical evidence nor the qualitative historical record are sufficient to favor one. So we curtail our theory building at this point. However, one important fact from the historical record is relevant for existing political science frameworks used to study delegation and centralization: the "ally principle" is not particularly important here. This principle holds that presidents are more likely to delegate to entities who share their policy goals.[16] But in almost all cases, the attorney general and the White House counsel shared the president's policy goals for the Supreme Court; thus, presidents faced no trade off between bias and expertise in their procedural choice.[17] Rather, the more important consideration seems to have been an efficient deployment of available resources at reasonable cost to the president.

Because the growth of specialized executive branch resources is so important in our account, we turn now to that history.

3.3 The Growth of a Legal Policy Elite

The cast of characters involved in the selection process has changed dramatically over time. Early on, the president and often the attorney general were the key players. Over the last century, though, the White House and executive establishment expanded dramatically, with the creation of new offices for the proliferating specialists. An important development was the emergence within the administrative state of sophisticated, ideologically engaged lawyers—a legal policy elite—eager to help the president select men and women for the bench.

The legal policy elite's primary task is to determine and implement legal policy for a president and administration.[18] But the growth of the legal elite also allowed presidents to shift the burden of selecting and vetting Supreme Court nominees onto them, as this group of super-lawyers—invariably super-politicized lawyers—is the ideal staff to conduct a meticulous selection and vetting process. These individuals have the ability and motivation to identify potential nominees, scour every line of their judicial opinions, pour over confidential executive branch memos, master academic writings, and comb through speeches seeking explicit markers of ideological fidelity or subtle hints of doctrinal deviationism, review their tax records for "issues," and interrogate physicians, friends, and family to uncover hidden health problems. However, not every president chose to use this available resource. Indeed, as late as the Clinton White House, the president supplemented his own staff with private law firms in Washington to help identify and vet Supreme Court nominees.[19] President Trump famously delegated the crafting of his initial short lists to the Federalist Society.[20] Still, from Eisenhower forward, the legal elite typically played an increasingly large and often critical role.

The legal policy elite have appeared in two key sites: the Department of Justice and the White House. As the Department of Justice institutionalized over time, the Office of Legal Counsel (OLC)—whose head is essentially the attorney general's lawyer—became the key locus of its policy elite.[21] At the White House, this is primarily the office of counsel to the president (the White House legal counsel).[22] Although the personnel in the two sites have worked amicably hand-in-hand on most issues, on occasion they have clashed sharply about some policy issues.[23]

3.3.1 The Justice Department

The Judiciary Act of 1789 established the Office of the Attorney General, who was to represent the federal government in lawsuits before the Supreme Court and provide legal advice to the president. From a modern perspective, the attorney general initially combined the roles of solicitor general (who argues the administration's cases before the Supreme Court) and the White House legal counsel.

The OLC's role with respect to the attorney general has shifted over time. Following a Department of Justice reorganization in 1933, then Attorney General Homer Cummings tasked a new assistant solicitor general to assist him in his role as legal advisor to the president.[24] At one point this group was dubbed the Executive Adjudications Division, reflecting its role in settling legal disputes between federal agencies. In 1953, Attorney General Herbert Brownell, Jr., renamed the bureau the Office of Legal Counsel. In its early period, the office apparently mostly drafted opinions for the attorney general, but today OLC attorneys perform a broader range of functions. They draft the attorney general's formal opinions, render informal opinions and legal advice to governmental agencies, review all executive orders and proclamations, resolve legal disputes between agencies in the executive branch and within the Department of Justice, make veto recommendations to the president about passed legislation, and carry out special assignments as directed by the attorney general.[25] At times, they also perform the systematic and painstaking review of potential Supreme Court nominees. In the Obama Administration, the OLC employed about 25 attorneys (37 staff total), a number which had remained more-or-less constant since the early 1970s.[26]

The modern OLC has been described as heavily politicized.[27] This does not mean that the OLC is staffed by campaign operatives or party hacks of the type sometimes employed in agencies like the Department of Education or FEMA.[28] But it is certainly true the modern OLC's leadership and short-term attorneys are highly skilled, extremely committed partisans and ideologues. In the words of one of the OLC's more famous alumni, Chief Justice William Rehnquist, "the plain fact of the matter is that any president, and any attorney general wants his immediate underlings to be not only competent attorneys, but to be politically and philosophically attuned to the policies of the administration."[29] In addition to Chief Justice Rehnquist, Justice Scalia, and Justice Alito, many federal appellate judges, Solicitors General, White House legal counsels, and prominent law professors have served as OLC attorneys.[30]

To get a better feel for the legal policy elite and the type of person who becomes head of the OLC, consider the case of Rehnquist.[31] After graduating Phi Beta Kappa from Stanford with a BA and MA in Political Science, and after briefly attending Harvard as a doctoral student, he returned to Stanford for a law degree. There he served as editor-in-chief of the *Law Review* and earned the top grades in his class. Although already a committed conservative, he clerked for Associate Justice Robert Jackson, then moved to Arizona and joined a law firm closely connected to the Goldwater political machine. In Phoenix he became active in Republican party circles, including supervising "ballot security" for the Arizona Republican machine—in other words, challenging the literacy of black and Latino voters at the polls. He opposed school desegregation in Arizona and, according to his biographer, persuaded Goldwater to oppose the Civil Rights Act of 1964. He served as a strategist and speechwriter in Goldwater's 1964 campaign, After Goldwater's disastrous defeat, Rehnquist worked with Nixon-affiliate Richard Kleindienst to re-build the Arizona Republican Party—Kleindienst was the state party chairman while Rehnquist was the party's general counsel. After Nixon won Arizona in 1968, the president-elect rewarded Kleindienst with the number two job in the Department of Justice, working for Nixon's close friend, former law partner, and ex-campaign manager, John Mitchell, the new attorney general. Kleindienst recommended Rehnquist to Mitchell as a top legal talent and conservative stalwart. The two hit it off, and at age 44 Rehnquist became the head of the OLC.

We could trace a similar lineage for a typical Democratic OLC head. The point is that by about 1970 the Justice Department staff members most likely to be involved in selecting Supreme Court nominees exemplified a type of person entirely characteristic of modern Washington: the "techno-pol," a substantively skilled, ideologically committed, highly partisan political appointee.

3.3.2 The White House

The White House is the second site of the legal policy elite, for two reasons. First, as overall presidential staff increased in size, presidents innovated by creating essentially an in-house law firm for the president, the White House Counsel's Office. Second, the head of the "law firm," the White House counsel, could then organize and run the selection process for the president.

Growth of Presidential Staff

Even during the Civil War, Abraham Lincoln had to devote hours to picking postmasters for small towns across the country, largely because there was no one else to do the work—he had only three aides. Grover Cleveland would answer the telephone at the White House himself; Woodrow Wilson typically typed his own letters; and Herbert Hoover had but eight aides.[32] So too, presidents like Taft, Coolidge, Hoover, and Roosevelt had to labor over Supreme Court nominee selection themselves—as mentioned above, Harding sub-contracted the job to the chief justice. Senators and notables across the country would lobby the president personally, writing letters,

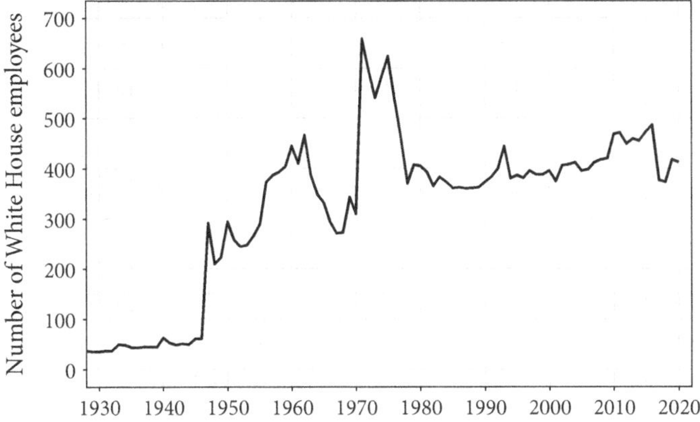

Fig. 3.2 The growth of staff in the White House, 1924–2020. Until 1993, the data come from the Statistical Abstract of the United States; after that, from Annual Reports to Congress on White House Staff.

sending telegrams, or speaking face-to-face—after all, how else would the president learn of deserving candidates for the court?

Things have changed. The Brownlow Report of 1937 famously declared, "The president needs help"—and he got it. In 1939, Congress provided statutory authority for a Roosevelt executive order that created the Executive Office of the President (EOP), added some new staff, and moved the Bureau of the Budget from Treasury to the EOP.[33] The modern presidency began to take shape. Today, the president commands a centralized executive staff numbering in the thousands, and a White House workforce usually numbering four to five hundred.[34]

Figure 3.2 displays the growth in size of the White House staff from 1924 to 2020. Whereas White House staff numbered fewer than 50 individuals in the 1920s, they now number around 400 (following a peak of above 600 in the 1970s). The contemporary president has abundant staff; indeed, the president has become "the presidency," a sizable and formidable bureaucratic entity itself. From our perspective, the growth *within* the White House of its own legal policy elite has been a particularly important development.

The White House Legal Counsel

Franklin Roosevelt created the position of White House legal counsel in 1943, reportedly because he was irritated by the slow pace of legal work from the Department of Justice.[35] However, his first White House counsel, Samuel Rosenman, did almost no legal work, functioning instead as a speech writer, occasional domestic policy advisor, and political fire-fighter.[36] His title was honorific—Rosenman had been a state judge in New York before joining the administration. In any event, he seems not to have been involved in any of Roosevelt's Supreme Court nominations.[37] Most of the White House legal counsels in the Truman, Eisenhower, Kennedy, and Johnson administrations operated in a similar mode.[38]

The watershed figure who created the modern office beginning in 1970 was—somewhat ominously—Nixon's White House counsel John Dean. Dean was eventually disbarred and served prison time for his role in organizing and abetting the Watergate cover-up, but before his downfall Dean established an office with three other lawyers that focused primarily on legal matters. He assisted in three Supreme Court nominations—the tail end of the Carswell fiasco, plus the Powell and Rehnquist nominations, in which he was a key player—before Nixon fired him for cooperating with the Watergate investigation in 1973. Despite Dean's unhappy end, his organizational innovation stuck. By the mid-1980s the office had eight to ten lawyers, growing to 40 by the end of the Obama administration.[39] At the beginning of the Trump administration, the office comprised 26 attorneys, including eight partners from major law firms, eight former lawyers for the Department of Justice or other federal agencies, 16 former law clerks including seven Supreme Court clerks, and nine former Hill staffers.[40] In short, the White House now boasts a mid-sized, and quite high-powered, law firm embedded within it.

Much of the work of these lawyers has nothing to do with the Supreme Court, and instead concerns advice to the executive branch regarding compliance with ethics rules, conflict of interest rules, and financial disclosure and related matters. They also advise White House aides on their legal authority and its limits. In the post-9/11 era, in which terrorism, national security, and law became deeply entangled, some of the attorneys typically engage in "lawfare," the law of national security.

In recent presidencies, the office has become more heavily involved in judicial selection. Procedurally, several modern administrations established a judicial selection committee, chaired by the White House legal counsel. In the estimation of several presidential scholars, "the selection process has shifted from being centered in the Justice Department to being firmly ensconced in the White House, albeit with the status of the attorney general always a factor."[41] The Roberts selection process, described earlier, exemplifies this development. And, despite its often eccentric procedures, the Trump Administration followed suit; White House Counsel Don McGahn devoted a great deal of effort to selecting federal judges at all levels, and, as a member of the Federalist Society himself, reportedly worked closely with its vice president, Leonard Leo.[42]

Finally, members of another group of staffers occasionally play a role in judicial selection. Presidents invariably have an inner core of policy-oriented super-staffers, advisors whose careers are closely intertwined with the person in the Oval Office.[43] Their greatest loyalty lies to the master they serve rather than a professional network or ideological clique. Examples include Eisenhower and his brother Milton, as well as Ike's powerful Chief of Staff Sherman Adams; Kennedy and half a dozen aides like McGeorge Bundy and Ted Sorensen; Nixon and John Mitchell, H. R. Haldeman, and John Ehrlichman; Carter and Hamilton Jordan and Jody Powell; Clinton and Hillary Clinton; Obama and David Axelrod, Valerie Jarret, and Susan Rice; and Trump and his daughter Ivanka and son-in-law Jared Kushner. These aides effectively form the president's Praetorian Guard. Despite their pervasive involvement in White House policy making, direct involvement in nominee selection is rare, unless one of the super-staffers also functions as a legal policy elite. For example, Nixon super-staffer John Ehrlichman was White House legal counsel for most of 1969, and hence was heavily involved in the Burger nomination and the Haynsworth imbroglio. Likewise, Reagan installed his trusted friend and advisor Ed Meese as attorney general so he naturally became involved in judicial selection. Finally, if the process run by the legal elite seems to be going awry, generalist super-staffers may intervene to protect the president's interests. The late Reagan process (discussed in the Appendix) provides an illustration.

3.4 The Growth of Professionalism

A prominent theme in the president's management of Supreme Court nominations is the growth of professionalism over time. We propose two markers to gauge an alleged increase in presidential professionalism: first, the length of the president's short list of potential nominees, and second, the duration between the receipt of an impending vacancy and the announcement of a nominee.

3.4.1 The Short List

An important feature of the nomination process is the *short list*, the final list of candidates the president selects from. A thoughtful, highly groomed short list goes hand-in-hand with institutionalized, professional vetting. What have short lists looked like historically? Fortunately, by scouring the presidential libraries and other sources, Christine Nemacheck (2008) was able to reconstruct the short lists in every nomination from 1930 to 2005. We have updated her data to include all nominations through 2020 (see the Appendix for further details). Thus, we can see exactly who was under active consideration for each vacancy. In this chapter we focus on the *length* of the short lists, as a marker of the institutionalization of the search process. In Chapter 4, we examine who was on the lists and what they looked like; in Chapter 9 we explain why presidents short-listed the type of people they did.

First, a prior question arises: are the short lists sincere, or are they just political theater, something thrown together purely for public consumption? If the latter, then neither the length nor the composition of the short lists is very informative. The historical records finds some instances of presidents deliberately leaking names during the selection process to gauge public responses to a given individual, but rarely did they release the actual short list.[44] So, in our view, these lists are sincere.[45]

Figure 3.3 displays the length of each short list from 1930 to 2020, and reveals some interesting patterns.[46] First, consider lengthy short lists, those with 10 or more names. In the first half of the time series (to the left of the dashed vertical line), lengthy short lists were rare, occurring only three times in the 32 nominations (9%) between 1930

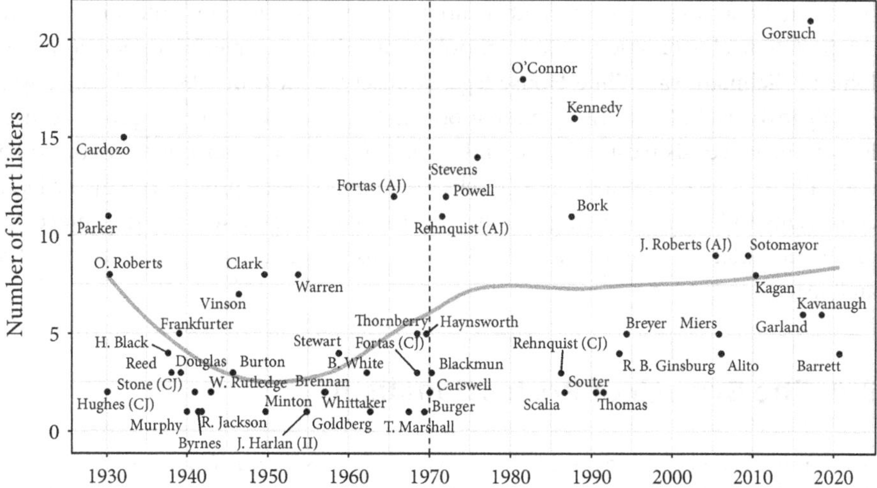

Fig. 3.3 The size of the short list over time. The vertical line separates the time series into two periods where short lists tended to be much longer after 1970 compared to before. The blue line is a loess line.

and 1970 (Hughes to Blackmun). In the second half of the series, lengthy short lists became much more common, occurring seven times in the 21 nominations (33%) between 1971 and 2020. The increase in size thus coincided with the White House staff becoming larger and more specialized.

Now consider short lists with but one name, "singleton" short lists. The historical record shows that singleton short lists are often a marker of a crony, patronage, or tactical political appointment. In the first half of the time series, eight nominations (25%) involved singleton short lists. By contrast, in the second half of the time series, short lists always included more than one name.

Finally, consider the average number of individuals on the short list, or the length of the list. The mean short list length in the whole time series is 5.7 names. In the early period, the mean length was 4.0 names. In the later period, the short list length more than doubled, to 8.2, a difference that is statistically significant.[47] So, on average short lists became longer after the transformation of the White House Counsel's Office.

These are just simple descriptive statistics, but in combination with the historical record, they are consistent with a structural break following John Dean's re-imagining of the role of the White House legal counsel. The break point seems to correspond with the Powell nomination; earlier lists were shorter and singletons occurred regularly, whereas from Powell on, the lists got longer—sometimes much longer—and singletons disappeared. In summary, the length of the short lists is compatible with increased presidential interest, more resources, and greater organizational complexity and effectiveness.

3.4.2 Thinking It Over: The Duration of the Selection Process

The second marker of professionalism is the length of time between a "go" signal—a public or private notification to the president of an impending departure—and the announcement of a nominee. If the White House is running smoothly, much of the basic selection and vetting work will already have been done, and selection can occur quickly. But if the White House is a shambles, and the Justice Department leaderless, under-staffed, or disorganized—then the administration will be caught flat-footed, and the selection process may be protracted. To be sure, this marker is hardly infallible; for example, Truman's crony nomination of Sherman Minton took less than a week. So a dearth of professionalism need not translate automatically into an extended delay between the vacancy and an announcement. Still, a well-oiled White House/Department of Justice selection machine should quickly produce a well-vetted nominee.

One obvious difficulty for outside observers is determining the exact date of the go signal. Some are quite clear, as in the case of Antonin Scalia's sudden death. Others can be less obvious, as when a justice confides in the president before publicly announcing retirement. Fortunately, dedicated civil servants at the Congressional Research Service have pored over historical materials to identify the likely dates of go signals, whether public or private.[48] In most cases there was no early warning. Even when justices did notify the president, the advance warning was usually brief. Still, early warning might have given the president a head start on the selection process.

Figure 3.4 displays the time in days between the go signal and the president's announcement of a replacement. Overall, the average duration was 33 days, with a standard deviation of 43. The loess line suggests that durations decreased over time (if somewhat modestly). The mean duration before John Dean transformed the White House legal counsel's office in 1970 was 44 days, compared to 19 days after this point, a statistically significant difference. In addition, a closer look at the figure reveals a clear outlier in the later period: the shambolic Clinton nomination of Ruth Bader Ginsburg. As we discuss below, this nomination occurred early in the Clinton administration, after an inept transition and with a barely functional White House organization. Omitting Ginsburg's nomination, the mean in the later period falls to 15 days, or one-third of the mean duration in the pre-1970 period.[49]

3.5 Portraits of the Process

Earlier we described examples of the no delegation, external delegation, and internal delegation decision modes. A closer look at the history affords insights on presidents' choices over procedures, and how the different procedures worked in practice. (Also, the material is fun for presidency buffs!)

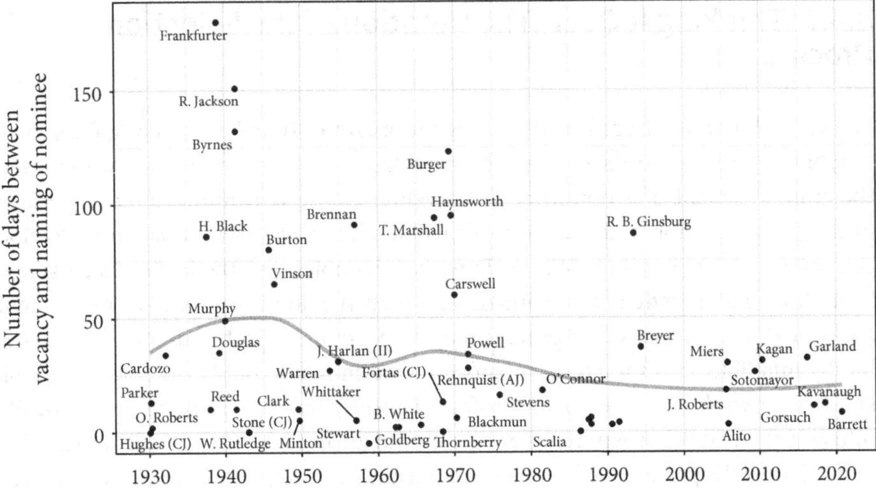

Fig. 3.4 The duration of each selection process. For each nominee, the graph shows the number of days between when the president was first informed of the pending vacancy and the eventual naming of a nominee. The blue line is a loess line.

In the interests of space, we eschew strict chronology but instead group the selection decisions by category, and discuss two or three presidential processes per category. Discussions of the other nominee selections in our time frame appear in the Appendix.

3.5.1 No Delegation

Herbert Hoover: No Delegation by Default

Herbert Hoover made four nominations to the Supreme Court: Charles Evans Hughes for chief justice, John J. Parker (a failed nomination) and Owen Roberts (all in 1930), and Benjamin Cardozo (1932).[50]

By our measures, Hoover displayed very little interest in the Supreme Court; this is perhaps not surprising, given that he faced the crisis of the Great Depression. In fact, the data show his interest as among the lowest of any president studied. Such modest attention suggests he may have been eager to delegate an unwanted chore to expert allies. But he had virtually no opportunity to do so, as there was no OLC in the Department of Justice, no White House counsel, and very few White House staff of any kind. Moreover, Chief Justice Taft—who had been so helpful to Harding—was extremely ill by the time Hoover entered the White House, and died soon after. Facing this dearth of help, Hoover was personally involved in selecting nominees, generally working in tandem with his attorney general, William Mitchell, an experienced figure in Washington legal circles. Hoover's searches were typically brief and rather cursory, with the exception of the process that selected the celebrated jurist Benjamin Cardozo.

Take, for example, the Hughes nomination. In his noted biography of Justice Stone, Alpheus Mason reports that Mitchell became convinced in 1930 that Taft's declining health would soon require the naming of a replacement.[51] There were two obvious candidates for the chief justiceship: Justice Harlan Fiske Stone, a close friend and confidant of the new president, and Hughes, a former justice who had resigned in 1916 to become the Republican Party's nominee for president. Hughes, a conservative lion of the Republican Party, prominent New York corporate lawyer and notable Hoover supporter, was thus not only highly qualified but also politically prominent. Taft resigned from the court on February 3, and Hoover nominated Hughes less than five hours later. Hoover's no delegation process produced a short list of only two candidates and an extremely brief search duration.

Franklin D. Roosevelt: The Ringmaster at Work

Franklin D. Roosevelt appointed a remarkable nine justices; only George Washington, who selected the court's first set of justices, nominated more. Roosevelt's nominees were: Hugo Black (1937), Stanley Reed (1938), Felix Frankfurter (1939), William Douglas (1939), Frank Murphy (1940); Harlan Stone for chief justice, James Byrnes, and Robert Jackson (all in 1941); and finally Wiley Rutledge (1943). This remarkable run likely transformed the court even more than Roosevelt's 1937 court packing plan would have. So profound were the changes that by the late 1940s, Roosevelt's first nominee, Hugo Black, was the senior member of the court.

Roosevelt's selection process is surprisingly thinly documented, with a few exceptions. But the available evidence paints an entirely consistent picture: across all nine nominees, Roosevelt ran the process himself. Sometimes he consulted with his attorney general (particularly for the early nominees), in order to generate lists of names and discuss them. Advocates of various candidates would lobby him—for example, Felix Frankfurter and his surrogates at times became irritating with orchestrated "mentioning" campaigns among the president's friends and acquaintances. There was no vetting in the modern sense. The president simply kept his own counsel, made his own decisions, and announced them both to the nominee and the public according to his own script. At least for the first five nominees, ideology loomed large: Roosevelt only wanted "thumping evangelical New Dealers," and he got them. Procedurally, the move from Harding to Roosevelt is mostly a story of continuity in methods.

3.5.2 External Delegation

Earlier we discussed an externally delegated operation in Ford's empowerment of Attorney General Edward Levi. Other presidents have also opted for this design, including Eisenhower and Reagan (for most of his nominees).

Dwight D. Eisenhower: Politicized Delegation

In his eight years as president, Dwight Eisenhower selected five justices: Earl Warren for Chief Justice (1953), John Marshall Harlan (1954), William Brennan (1956),

Charles Whittaker (1957), and Potter Stewart (1958). Only two of these—Harlan and Stewart—can be scored as solid Republican judicial successes. Yet none are flagrant crony picks of the Truman variety. How could the normally hyper-competent Eisenhower compile such a record? The answer lies in his peculiar selection process.

Eisenhower had little interest in the Supreme Court, with good reason: at the height of the Cold War, his challenges lay primarily in international affairs. Nor did he pretend to have any expertise in judicial matters. As a long-time Washington hand and "political" general, Eisenhower had a sophisticated understanding of D.C. politics.[52] But his political experience was spotty. For example, he knew little about the intricacies of Republican Party machine politics or the arcana of party conventions with their horse-trading, smoke-filled rooms, and procedural bickering. For that, he needed help. As one might expect from one of the great military managers of the twentieth century, the former general sought out capable people with the expertise he lacked, and delegated to them, albeit with clear supervision. In this case, he turned to perhaps the most skilled and experienced Republican political operative of his generation, Herbert Brownell.

Brownell was a prominent player in New York Republican Party political circles. A graduate of Yale Law School, he started practicing corporate law in New York in 1927.[53] In 1931 he entered the New York State Assembly as a Republican reformer representing part of Manhattan's Greenwich Village. He subsequently aligned with Thomas Dewey, who was first a crusading district attorney and prosecutor, then governor of New York, then failed Republican presidential nominee in 1944 and 1948. Brownell served as Dewey's campaign manager in both losing campaigns, in the process mastering the intricacies of Republican Party machine politics and convention maneuvering. In 1951 and 1952, Brownell joined a small group of Republican Party notables trying to persuade Dwight Eisenhower, then the first military head of NATO, to run for president in 1952. Famously, Eisenhower summoned Brownell to a secret meeting in which the campaign maven spent 10 hours leading the political novice through the intricacies of what it would take to win the Republican nomination and then the general election; shortly thereafter, Ike threw his hat in the ring. Because of Brownell's ties to the losing Dewey campaigns, he was not named Ike's official campaign manager, but in practice he was in charge. After the victory, Eisenhower offered Brownell the (new) position of White House chief of staff; Brownell declined, but accepted the second offer, to become attorney general.

Perhaps not surprisingly, Eisenhower delegated selection of Supreme Court justices to his trusted and experienced attorney general. Memos show that, while Eisenhower often expressed general criteria for appointments, Brownell was largely in charge. Perhaps not surprisingly given his background, Brownell usually recommended nominees with at least one eye on politics, and sometimes both.[54]

Take, for example, one of the more consequential appointments in the court's history: the selection of Earl Warren to become chief justice in 1953. Long-standing rumors hold that the chief justiceship was given to the California governor as a quid-pro-quo for not opposing Eisenhower at the Republican national convention in 1952 (Warren, a favorite son of California, reportedly held his block of votes in neutral). A second rumor suggests that Eisenhower simply moved to eliminate his most prominent rival as leader of the "new Republicans" by placing him in a job in which he could no longer act as a partisan leader. A third, offered by Justice Douglas in the Murphy interviews and attributed by Douglas to Warren himself, holds that the appointment was a maneuver by Vice President Richard Nixon to wrest control of the California Republican Party from Warren. The truth will probably never be known for sure. What is clear is that Eisenhower promised Warren the first available opening on the court, and then stuck to the deal. In fact, Brownell drew up a list of possible alternatives and he and the president discussed them. But the actual deliberation was rather desultory as Eisenhower's apparent political obligation to Warren proved to be the trump card.[55]

Ronald Reagan: Contested Delegation

Ronald Reagan made six Supreme Court nominations: Sandra O'Connor (1981), William Rehnquist (chief justice) and Antonin Scalia for associate justice (both 1986), Robert Bork (1987), Douglas Ginsburg (1987), and finally Anthony Kennedy (1987). The Reagan Administration emerges as a transition period in which two organizational mechanisms for selecting nominees vied for ascendancy. At first, external delegation to the Department of Justice prevailed—a rather natural mode of operation for the president, who favored a hands-off management style. Moreover, from 1985 on, the Department of Justice was in the hands of his long-time friend and advisor, Edwin Meese. At the same time, however, the White House Counsel's Office continued to grow in size and influence. Absent clear direction from the president, these two centers of legal expertise jostled for influence.

We score the O'Connor nomination as delegation. We do so as well with the Rehnquist-Scalia pair, though one can view the procedure as a kind of subdued "team of rivals" approach involving the Department of Justice and the White House legal counsel. The Bork and Ginsburg picks were driven by the Department of Justice over White House reservations. But the egregious failure of these two nominations opened the door to a new mode of selection, and the internal White House-dominated team prevailed for the compromise selection of Kennedy. We summarize the first four nominations below.

The O'Connor nomination was relatively straightforward.[56] In an effort to shore up his support among women during the 1980 presidential campaign, Reagan publicly pledged to nominate the first woman to the Supreme Court. When Potter Stewart retired in 1981, Reagan turned to his attorney general, William French Smith, to identify good female candidates. The search, directed by Smith's advisor Kenneth Starr, led to an acquaintance of Smith's, Sandra Day O'Connor. Fred Fielding, the White House legal counsel, tried somewhat ineffectually to weigh in, but had little impact. When Reagan and O'Connor hit it off personally, the process was over.

The paired selection process for Rehnquist and Scalia in 1986 fell to the new attorney general, Ed Meese.[57] Appointed in 1985, Meese brought a harder-edged ideological tenor to the department coupled with a determination to reshape the federal judiciary. Meese quickly re-staffed the Department of Justice with conservative true-believers and organized them into a working group to vet potential Supreme Court nominees. The Department of Justice group, including the head of the Office of Legal Counsel and the head of the Civil Rights Division, homed in on Antonin Scalia and Robert Bork as the purest of ideological paladins; Justice Rehnquist also drew their praise.

When Chief Justice Warren Burger announced his retirement in 1986, the Department of Justice group had its short list ready. Nonetheless, Peter Wallison, the White House legal counsel, insisted on canvassing and vetting potential nominees himself (among the White House vetters was a young attorney named John Roberts), but came up with largely the same names. Final meetings with Meese, Wallison, White House Chief of Staff Don Regan, and the president resulted in the Rehnquist-Scalia pair.

When Justice Lewis Powell retired the following year, the Meese-led Department of Justice was poised and ready with their preferred selection: the previous runner-up, conservative lightning rod Robert Bork. But the strategic landscape had shifted dramatically. First, and most importantly, the Democrats had taken the Senate in the 1986 midterm election. Second, the Iran-Contra scandal had weakened Reagan's popularity, leading to a housecleaning at the White House and both a new chief of staff, James Baker, and a new White House legal counsel, A. B. Culvahouse. Pragmatists rather than strict ideologues, they warned about the Senate response to Bork. But both were just finding their feet and not in a position to challenge the Bork enthusiasts at the Department of Justice. Disaster soon followed.

Following Bork's defeat in the Senate, the Department of Justice team proposed another conservative ideologue, Douglas Ginsburg. The White House group again protested, somewhat more vigorously this time, favoring smooth confirmation of a somewhat less conservative nominee. Yet again Reagan sided with Meese and the Department of Justice.[58] Again Reagan chose poorly, as repeated scandals, including allegations of marijuana use by Ginsburg, forced the administration to withdraw his nomination. This failure led Reagan to pursue an internal White House-led delegation process for the final selection of Kennedy, who was easily confirmed by the Senate.

3.5.3 Internal Delegation

Several examples illustrate the internal delegation mode.

George H.W. Bush: Pragmatism Gone Awry

George H.W. Bush was a more conventional kind of conservative than Reagan and his circle, and so were most of his immediate advisors. As pragmatic conservatives, they (aside from White House Legal Counsel C. Boyden Gray) did not look on Supreme Court nominations as transformational acts to—in the words of Robert Bork—halt the "tempting of America," stop its "slouching to Gomorrah," to end its slide into

"American decline," block "the legal assault on American values," or prevent the United States from becoming "a country I don't recognize."[59] Instead, their goal was more modest: place solid conservatives on the court in the face of a Senate held 55-45 by Democrats, while avoiding another Bork-like debacle. In fact, although Bush assembled a smoothly operating White House-led selection team, the Bush process produced one nominee who was far from a solid conservative and another whose nomination exploded into lurid controversy. Partly this was bad luck. But it also reflected contradictions at the heart of the Bush selection operation.

Immediately after Bush's inauguration, new Attorney General Richard Thornburgh ordered Department of Justice staffers to prepare dossiers on prime Supreme Court candidates. When William Brennan decided to retire in 1990 after a minor stroke, staffers were able to place a well-prepared briefing book in the president's hands in less than 24 hours. Bush, Gray, Thornburgh, and White House Chief of Staff John Sununu then began winnowing the candidates.

Almost immediately, things began to go awry. After eliminating various candidates, the group focused on David Souter. A Vermonter, Souter had a fervent advocate in Sununu, a former governor of that state and Souter's long-time acquaintance. Because most of his judicial service had been on the Vermont state court, Souter had never taken positions on many contentious constitutional issues, including abortion. Later talk of Souter as a "stealth" nominee was somewhat overblown; in hindsight, there were clear indications that he had always been the kind of moderate, northeastern-style Republican on its way to extinction in the party. But his judicial track record was relatively sparse. This lack of provocative positions struck the White House pragmatists as a major asset, and Sununu solemnly assured the president that, despite the absence of verifiable evidence, Souter was a solid, reliable conservative. The Department of Justice vetters found no reasons to believe otherwise. Taking Sununu at his word, Bush sent Souter's name forward within three days of Brennan's announcement. The Senate easily confirmed Souter, meeting at least one of Bush's goals.

Nevertheless, Souter's subsequent performance on the court offered bitter weeds to judicial conservatives of the crusading stripe: within a few years "No more Souters!" became a watchword among Federalist Society activists.

Bush was afforded a second opportunity to fill a court vacancy the following year, when Thurgood Marshall, in physical and mental decline, gave up waiting for a Democrat to take back the White House and announced his retirement from the court.[60] The Bush selection team again reviewed its options, focusing on racial minority candidates to replace the trailblazing Marshall. Gray, the extremely conservative White House counsel, strongly pushed the candidacy of Clarence Thomas, a young Black conservative who Bush had recently appointed to the D.C. Circuit as a grooming opportunity. The 42-year-old Thomas possessed relatively little judicial experience and had not been extensively vetted. But he was a fervent movement conservative as well as a devout Catholic. Thornburgh suggested a review of possible conservative Latino candidates as well, but none had even as much experience as

Thomas. After his team consulted interest groups, Bush followed Gray's recommendation and settled quickly on Thomas, making the announcement only three days after Marshall's decision to step down. Thomas went on to weather an exceedingly stormy confirmation process in the face of charges of sexual harassment by a former employee, Anita Hill. After narrowly gaining confirmation, Thomas went on to become one of the court's most reliably conservative members.

Despite the seeming professionalism of the Bush selection process, the rocky results underscore the tension between desiring non-controversial nominees versus ideologically reliable extremists. The former approach favors candidates who have avoided strong positions; the latter almost demands an extensive track record of ideological fealty. The cry "No more Souters" is essentially a demand for commitment to specific judicial policy positions, regardless of the opposition generated. In addition, the Thomas example underscores the difficulty of finding and vetting strong candidates without a deep "bench" of potential nominees, as well as the risks of a quick and superficial vetting process.

Bill Clinton: White House Chaos

Just 58 days into his first term, Bill Clinton faced an unexpected windfall: a seat to fill on the U.S. Supreme Court. The vacancy opened in March 1993 when Byron White submitted his resignation letter to the president, having served 31 years on the high court.

What followed was "disorganized and messy," in stark contrast to the crisp Bush 41 process.[61] The next 87 days were a chaotic scramble with a poorly organized White House, staffed mostly with Washington neophytes—some well out of their depth—rushing distractedly from one controversy to another, such as whether to allow gay Americans to serve in the military. The Senate had only just confirmed Clinton's Attorney General, Janet Reno, an outsider with no Washington experience or personal ties to the president—two previous attempts to fill the top job at Justice had been derailed by "Nannygate" scandals. This organizational chaos left the brilliant but indecisive president dithering over a list of political celebrities rather than hard-core jurists, seeking a splashy "big personality" for the court. General purpose staffers frequently weighed in during interminable midnight meetings, but not in the incisive "we must protect the president" style of Reagan's seasoned pro, Howard Baker. Rather, some staffers enabled Clinton's worst ink-seeking instincts, while others just muddied the waters. Finally, a lucky, late-in-the-day intervention by White House Counsel Bernie Nussbaum finally led Clinton to Ruth Bader Ginsburg, with whom the president quickly established a warm rapport. But this selection came only after the longest selection process since the early Nixon Administration. Unsurprisingly, no subsequent president has followed this model, and with good reason.

Trump: Internal Delegation with Outsourcing

As with almost everything in his presidency, Donald Trump did things differently in selecting his three Supreme Court nominees: Neil Gorsuch (2017), Brett Kavanaugh (2018), and Amy Coney Barrett (2020).

During the 2016 campaign, Trump had to convince conservatives that he was "one of them," given his previous liberal positions on issues like abortion, as well as his overall political idiosyncrasies. Together with his main campaign lawyer and future White House Counsel Don McGahn, Trump seized on the issue of judicial appointments as a way to convey his conservative *bona fides*. McGahn realized that drawing on the resources of the Federalist Society would be a good way to accomplish this goal. According to David Kaplan:

> When he [joined] the campaign, McGahn insisted on being in charge of judicial nominations, subject to Trump's final say. The candidate agreed. But though McGahn was among the best election law experts in the country, he wasn't versed in constitutional law generally. Nor did he participate in the Great Mentioner parlor game of identifying who might be obvious candidates for the court. So he assigned the task of finding names to Leonard Leo, a leader of the Federalist Society—an influential conservative legal group funded by wealthy businesspeople like Charles and David Koch.[62]

With Leo's assistance, Trump became the first presidential candidate to release a short list of potential nominees *before* entering the White House, primarily to show conservatives and evangelical Christian interest groups his willingness to nominate judges they favored.[63] And, in fact, the lists used in the Gorsuch and Kavanaugh nominations closely resembled the campaign lists.

Trump was gifted an immediate vacancy upon taking office, thanks to Mitch McConnell's blockade of Garland in 2016. Trump effectively delegated the search for a nominee—which began during the transition between Election Day and the inauguration—to a team of close advisers, led by McGahn. Journalist Ruth Marcus noted the extreme centralization of the McGahn operation. "In a more traditional administration, the attorney general would have at least played a key advisory role, certainly on Supreme Court nominations. But Jeff Sessions [Trump's first attorney general] had been excluded from the start from judicial selection," leaving McGahn as the main overseer.[64]

This process thus appeared to track the classic internal delegation story. However, Leo also took an active role in the search process, interviewing leading contenders for the nomination.[65] In this sense, the process combined internal delegation with a degree of *outsourcing* to the Federalist Society, a hallmark of the Trump administration's approach to nominations at every level of the federal judiciary.[66] McGahn himself joked about the outsourcing. "Our opponents of judicial nominees frequently claim the president has outsourced his selection of judges," McGahn told a Federalist Society gathering in 2017. "That is completely false. I've been a member of the Federalist Society since law school. Still am. So, frankly, it seems like it's been in-sourced."[67]

The combination of internal delegation with some outsourcing worked well for Trump in his three selections. As David Kaplan argues with respect to the selection of Gorsuch, "Trump's relative lack of involvement—in contrast to how other presidents handled Court selections—worked to his benefit, even if accidentally. By leaving the process in competent hands . . . he ended up with a concrete accomplishment."[68] Of course, today's extreme polarization (which we document in Chapter 8) meant that none of Trump's nominations would be completely smooth. Gorsuch's confirmation required the Senate Republican majority to exercise the "nuclear option" to reduce the cloture threshold on a Supreme Court nominee to 50 votes. The nomination of Brett Kavanaugh nearly foundered after a high school acquaintance of the nominee, Christine Blasey Ford, alleged that he had sexually assaulted her when they were teenagers. But both were eventually confirmed.[69] Finally, when Ruth Bader Ginsburg died in September 2020, Trump very quickly selected Amy Coney Barrett—who had been on the short list to replace Kennedy. The Republican-controlled Senate quickly confirmed Barrett before Election Day.

At the time we write, all indications suggest that Gorsuch, Kavanaugh, and Barrett will prove reliable conservative votes on the court for decades to come.[70] In sum, Trump's combination of internal delegation with outsourcing to a highly organized conservative network successfully transformed the federal judiciary, even as his bid for re-election went down to defeat.[71]

3.6 Conclusion

For most of the twentieth century, presidents cared about the Supreme Court only infrequently. Today, the structure of the party coalitions assures that presidents do care—particularly Republican presidents. In addition, at one time the executive branch contained few people who had the skill, time, or inclination to undertake informed and scrupulous vetting of Supreme Court nominees. Now, such resources are abundant, not only in the Justice Department but, critically, in the White House itself. Republican presidents can call on even more expert assistance from highly organized and richly funded networks of conservative legal scholars like The Federalist Society. The combination of greater interest and more resources revolutionized the procedures for selecting and vetting nominees.

One result of this procedural revolution is increased professionalism, at least as measured by the simple indicators we employed. But another result is a dramatic transformation in the type of person selected. An agenda-driven, professionalized, institutionally sophisticated, and abundantly resourced process produces very different nominees than does a crony-oriented, amateurish, desultory, and thinly staffed process. So let's turn from the procedural revolution to the fruits of that transformation: the nominees themselves.

4
The Candidates for the Court and the Nominees

In 1971, the resignations of Justices Hugo Black and John M. Harlan six days apart handed President Richard Nixon the rare opportunity to fill a double vacancy on the court. Discussing a strategy for selecting his two nominees, Nixon held the following conversation with his friend and confidant, Attorney General John Mitchell:

MITCHELL: So, then, we may have a double play here, and of course what you do in the northern slot might very well help what you do in the southern slot, and vice versa.
NIXON: Well, even then, I don't want a liberal.
MITCHELL: Oh no, no.
NIXON: I don't want a liberal.
MITCHELL: Absolutely not.
NIXON: I just feel so strongly about that. I mean, when I think what the busing decisions have done to the South, and what it could do with *de facto* busing.
MITCHELL: I agree.
NIXON: And forced integration of housing, I just feel that if the last thing we do, we have got to have exerted—.
MITCHELL: You would be going back on the commitments that you made during your presidential campaign.
NIXON: Now can I ask you this? This is just to play an awful long shot. Is there a woman, yet? That would be a hell of a thing if we could do it.
MITCHELL: I think there is, if there's a woman that's credible within an age limit. There's a couple of them, as you know, up in years.
NIXON: They're old?
MITCHELL: It would be very hard for [senators] to vote against a woman.
NIXON: Oh, hell yes.[1]

In this vivid (if somewhat coarse) discussion, Nixon illustrates the attributes that presidents weigh when selecting a nominee to further a specific agenda. First, and of primary importance to Nixon, was *ideology*: his nominees had to be conservative. More than that, he demanded specific policy stances on certain issues; in other words, he applied *policy litmus tests*. One such test involved a recent Supreme Court case allowing federal judges to impose busing to remedy school segregation—a case later

Making the Supreme Court: The Politics of Appointments, 1930–2020. Charles M. Cameron and Jonathan P. Kastellec, Oxford University Press. © Oxford University Press 2023. DOI: 10.1093/oso/9780197680544.003.0004

indirectly alluded to in the 1972 Republican Party platform's attack on forced busing.[2] In addition, Mitchell reminded Nixon of the law-and-order litmus test that he had announced in the 1968 campaign.[3]

Next, and perhaps surprisingly, Nixon was also concerned with *diversity*. He was enthusiastic about appointing a woman nominee, both because he would be the first president to do so and because he believed it would reduce the likelihood of defeat in the Senate. Third, Nixon and Mitchell viewed *qualifications* as a *sine qua non*. Any nominee had to be "credible," apparently meaning well-credentialed and experienced. Fourth, Nixon and Mitchell were concerned with *age*. The nominee (male or female) could not be too "up in years," which would mean a shorter term on the court.[4] Finally, Mitchell noted the *geographic balance* on the court, especially between the North and the South. Although the discussion is not lengthy on this point, it stemmed from Nixon's infamous "Southern strategy" aimed at wooing Southern whites away from the Democratic Party.

An actual recording of a president engaged in selecting a Supreme Court nominee is a remarkable artifact.[5] However, traces of similar conversations involving other presidents exist. For example, in an entry in his personal diary, Attorney General Homer Cummings relates a 1937 conversation with Franklin Roosevelt during the process that eventually led to the selection of Hugo Black that year, in which the two discussed nominee attributes such as geography, qualifications, and, most importantly for Roosevelt, someone who supported the New Deal.[6]

The main considerations raised in the Nixon-Mitchell colloquy—ideology, policy commitments, race and gender diversity, qualifications, and age—today are central in presidential selection of Supreme Court nominees. Yet some presidents have made decisions on quite idiosyncratic grounds (recall Justice Douglas' story of the Minton selection), and the emphasis on other factors waxes and wanes over time. For example, diversity is a relatively recent consideration, while two other factors that used to be important—geographic balance and religion—have fallen out of favor.

In this chapter, we examine the characteristics of the candidates the presidents considered for the court—that is, those who made the short list for a given vacancy—as well as the actual nominees.[7] We focus first on the major considerations highlighted in the Nixon-Mitchell dialogue: ideology, qualifications, professional experience, diversity, and age. We then consider religion and geography. The data show a remarkable transformation from 1930 to 2020 in the characteristics of the men (and now women) considered for the court—that is, on presidents' short lists—and even more so for the actual nominees. All told, even as the justices became distinctly polarized ideologically, on every other dimension (except diversity), they became homogeneous legal technicians.

4.2 Ideology

From the perspective of modern-day appointments, a nominee's ideology is usually the key consideration for presidents, senators, and interest groups. Yet, as we saw in

Chapter 2, the court's importance to the parties and presidents changed dramatically over time. Not surprisingly, the extent to which presidents emphasized ideology in their selection of nominees also changed.

Measuring the ideology of nominees and justices is a recurring difficulty for scholars of judicial politics. For our purposes here, no single "perfect" measure exists, so we rely on multiple measures. Because we are interested in the ideologies of both nominees and short listers, and not just the justices, we cannot rely on measures based on voting in Supreme Court cases for the obvious reason that such measures do not exist for short-listers who were not nominated or nominees who were not confirmed.

Fortunately, Nemacheck (2008) ingeniously constructed an inferential measure of ideology based on the average DW-NOMINATE of a candidate's co-partisan members of her home state congressional delegation (the Appendix for this chapter provides details).[8] We call this measure the *State Partisan Representative* score, or SPR score. For nominees, we also employ the NOMINATE-Scaled Perceptions (NSP) scores developed in Cameron and Park (2009). These scores project the well-known "Segal-Cover" (1989) scores based on the content of contemporary newspaper editorials, into DW-NOMINATE space. Cameron and Park (2009) show that the NSP scores do a reasonable job predicting the subsequent voting on the court. Importantly, both the SPR and NSP measures exist for nominees who were not confirmed.

These two measures provide different but complementary ways to assess the ideology of short listers and nominees. (As noted below, the two measures tell basically the same story about nominees.) Of course, some measurement error is inevitable, and making valid comparisons across time using ideal-point estimates is quite tricky.[9] But here we are more interested in broad temporal trends over time, and not in the exact ideal point of any particular individual, and we are confident that these measures reflect the changing presidential emphasis on particular nominee characteristics over time.

4.2.1 The Nominees

Beginning with the nominees themselves, Figure 4.1 displays the NSP measure for all nominees from 1930 to 2020. Democratic appointees appear in blue text, Republican appointees in red text, with separate loess lines for each. These lines can be thought of as the over-time moving average of nominee ideology, within each party.

Figure 4.1 reveals that, not surprisingly, Democratic presidents have always tended to appoint more liberal nominees than Republican presidents. However, the degree of separation has varied considerably—until the 1960s, there was often sizable ideological overlap between appointees of each party. In 1941, for example, Roosevelt, a Democrat, promoted Associate Justice Harlan Stone to chief justice; President Coolidge, a Republican, had originally placed Stone on the court in 1925, and while Stone was firmly in the court's liberal bloc, his reputation was that of an ideological moderate. Similarly, Republican Presidents Truman and Eisenhower appointed

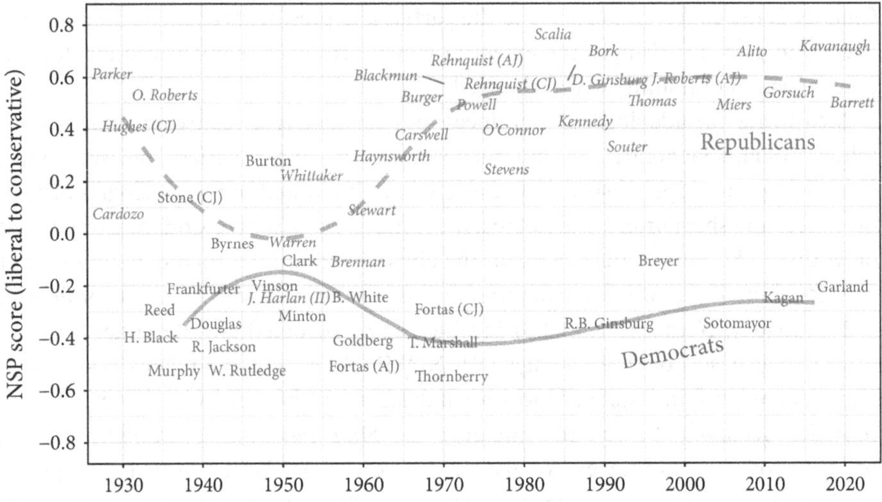

Fig. 4.1 The ideology of Supreme Court nominees from 1930 to 2020, according to the NSP measure. Republican nominees are in red italics, Democratic nominees in blue regular font. The lines are loess lines.

several individuals perceived as moderates, such as Burton, Warren, and Brennan. Thus, there was clear partisan overlap in the middle of the twentieth century.

Appointments since then tell a very different story. Beginning with the appointments of Lyndon Johnson, ideological overlap ended: Republican presidents reliably chose nominees perceived as conservative, and Democratic presidents reliably chose nominees perceived as liberal.[10] This polarization across the parties mirrors the political polarization of American elites since the 1970s, as discussed in Chapter 1.

How do the 90 years on display in Figure 4.1 compare with the complete history of Supreme Court nominees?[11] Unfortunately, the ideology measures extend back only to 1930. However, as a second-best option, Figure 4.2 shows the incidence of "cross-party" appointments—the selection of a nominee not a member of the president's party—from 1789 to 2020.[12] The hash marks at the bottom of the plot depicts the incidence of same-party nominees, while the names at the top indicate a cross-party nominee. The loess line can be thought of as the probability of a cross-party nomination at any given point in time.

Figure 4.2 shows that cross-party nominations first occurred in the mid-nineteenth century, but became most common between 1900 and 1950. In that period, there was a roughly 20% chance of the president going outside his own party to pick a justice. Since then, however, the probability has fallen steadily to zero; the last cross-party appointments were made by Richard Nixon.[13]

4.2.2 The Short Listers

Next, we can examine the ideology of individuals on presidents' short lists for vacant seats, in order to understand changes in presidential emphasis on ideology over time.

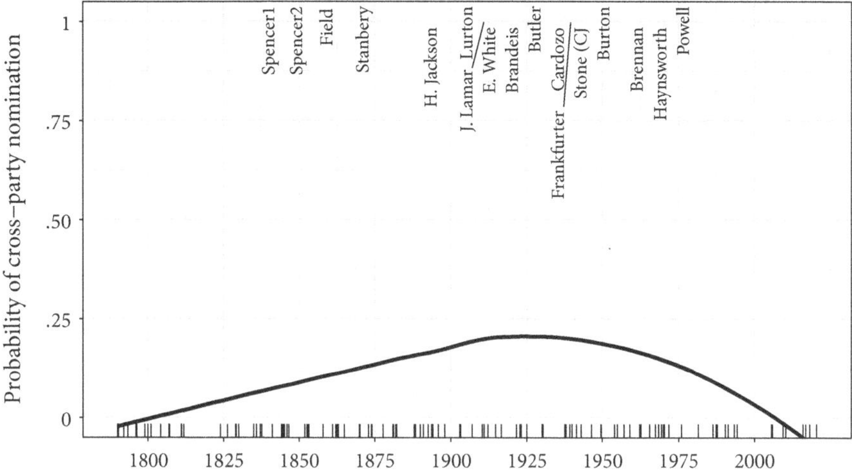

Fig. 4.2 The incidence of cross-party nominations, 1789–2020. The named nominees at the top were appointed by presidents of a different party.

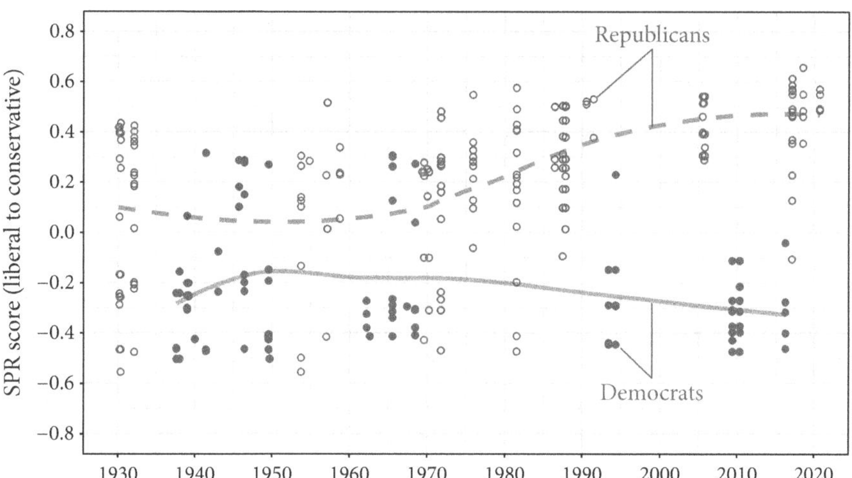

Fig. 4.3 The ideology of short listers, 1930–2020, according to the SPR score. The red (open) points depict short listers considered by Republican presidents, while the blue (solid) points indicate the short listers of Democratic presidents. The lines depict respective loess regression lines by party of the president.

Figure 4.3 shows the ideology of short listers from 1930 to 2020 using the SPR score. The red points indicate short listers considered by Republican presidents, while the blue points depict those of Democratic presidents. The lines depict respective loess regression lines: blue for Democrats and red for Republicans. The figure shows that as with nominees, the ideology of short listers showed a large degree of ideological overlap in the middle of the twentieth century, followed by a steady partisan separation.

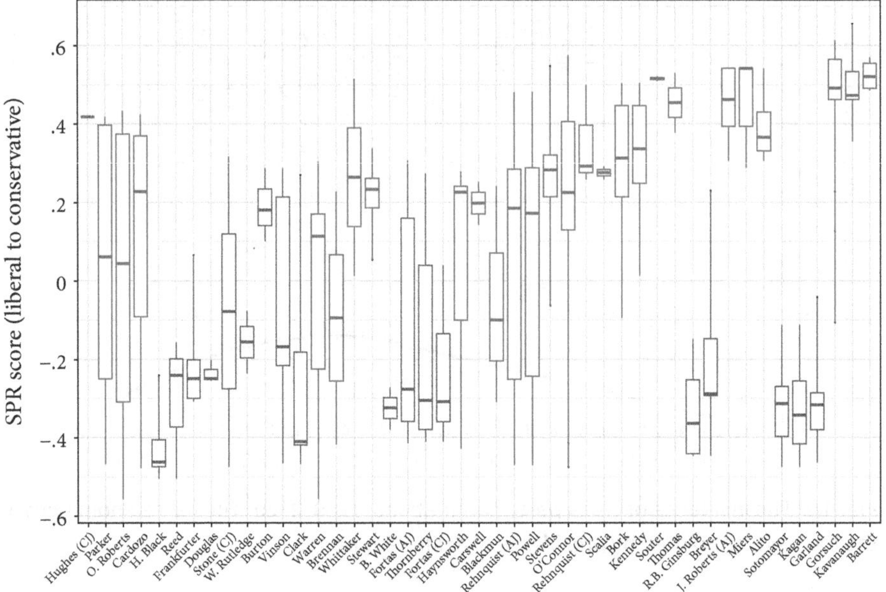

Fig. 4.4 The variation in ideology of short listers, 1930–2020, according to the SPR measure. Republican nominations are in red, Democratic nominations in blue. For each nomination, the boxes comprise the 25% and 75% quartiles, while the horizontal line in each box depicts the median. The thin vertical lines extend to the minimum and maximum values.

One way to directly examine the range of ideologies each president considered is to look at "within-selection" variation. For each nomination (as defined by the eventual nominee), Figure 4.4 presents a boxplot that summarizes the distribution of candidate ideologies on the respective short lists. (We remove "singleton" nominations where the short list was of size one, since they contain no variation.) Because several short lists include only a few individuals, we extend the vertical line of the boxplot to the minimum and maximum values of the distributions. Although the figure reveals lots of variation, notably the *centers* of the distributions for more recent nominees are much tighter than in previous years. Thus, over time presidents have come to consider a narrower range of ideology when considering candidates for a vacancy.

4.3 Experience and Policy Reliability

The shift toward more ideologically extreme justices occurred concomitantly with a shift in the type of person who became a justice. By 2020, the Supreme Court was a body of experienced judges with all but one (Kagan) coming directly from the U.S. Courts of Appeals.[14] But this was not always so.

The prior experience and background of short listers and nominees can be parsed in many ways. Ultimately, our goal is to measure the plausible *policy reliability* of a would-be justice, since this quantity emerges as central in the theory of presidential selection we develop and test in Chapter 9.[15] Accordingly, we focus on several variables that (we suggest) plausibly indicate how reliable a nominee will be, in advancing the president's policy goals on the Supreme Court, as discussed shortly. These are:

- **Politician**: Was a candidate ever an elected politician?
- **Executive administrator**: Did a candidate have any experience working in an executive branch agency (at the state or federal level)?
- **Federal judge**: Was the candidate a federal judge?
- **Executive branch lawyer**: Did a candidate have experience working as a lawyer in an executive branch agency?
- **Top law school**: Did a candidate attend a "top-14" law school?[16]

Figure 4.5 shows how candidates' background changed from 1930 to 2020. Each panel depicts a given category (we define "Super Tech" shortly). The "rugs" in the top and bottom of each panel show instances where a candidate either fell into a given category (top) or did not (bottom). The green (solid) lines depict a loess line for nominees only, while the purple (dashed) lines depict a loess line for short listers only. The two lines thus summarize mutually exclusive sets of individuals. The x-axis represents time, while the y-axis depicts the probability that type of individual appeared at a given point in time.

Figure 4.5 reveals several striking patterns, both across time and between nominees versus short listers. Early on, presidents often nominated elected politicians, including Hugo Black, James Byrnes, and Earl Warren, but then gradually shifted away from doing so. Since 1981, the only nominee with experience as a politician was Harriet Miers, who served for two years on the Dallas City Council. Likewise, very few elected officials even made it to the short lists after the 1980s. Similarly, executive administrators were formerly favored by presidents; nominees in the "middle period" of 1950–1970 often served as politically appointed administrators, but since then the presence of administrators on both the short list and among nominees declined precipitously.

Together, we can dub politicians and politically appointed administrators as "politicos." So prevalent were politicos in mid-century that in 1946 the editorial board of the (conservative leaning) *Chicago Tribune* blasted Truman's nomination of Fred Vinson—who, in addition to sitting on the D.C. Circuit for a number of years, had also served in Congress and in several executive branch positions in the Roosevelt and Truman administrations, including Secretary of the Treasury:

> It does not follow from the fact that most of these men rose thru [sic] politics that all of them are without legal insight and learning. It does follow, however, that the

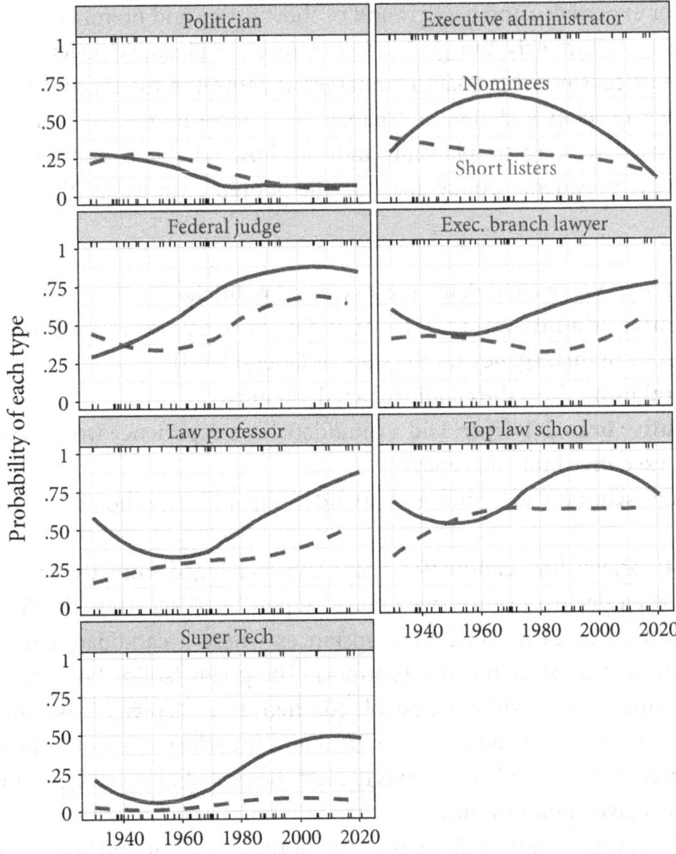

Fig. 4.5 The changing nature of candidates' professional backgrounds, 1930–2020. The "rugs" in each panel show instances where a candidate fell into a given category (top) or did not (bottom). The green lines depict a loess line for *nominees* only, while the purple lines depict a loess line for *short listers* only (thus, the two lines summarize mutually exclusive sets of candidates). The y-axis depicts the probability of that type of candidate at a given point in time.

> court is overweighted with Democrats, with New Dealers, and with former office holders. It does not fairly reflect the political division of the country in which close to half of the people are Republicans and by no means all of the rest are New Dealers. There is room on the court for men selected primarily for legal learning and judicial experience rather than political service. (*Chicago Tribune* 1946)

A half-century later, the *Tribune* editorialists would see their wish fulfilled—once so prominent on the short lists, politicos receive virtually no consideration for a seat on the court today.

Who has taken their place? Beginning in the 1970s, the characteristics of short listers shifted noticeably, and those of nominees even more so. First, federal judges became more likely to make the short list and even more likely to be nominated. Second, over time nominees—and only nominees, not short listers—were much more likely to have served as an executive branch lawyer, to have been a law professor, and to have attended a top law school. The trends for short listers, on the other hand, were rather stable (though Figure 4.5 shows an increase in executive branch lawyers among short listers in recent years). Taken together, this shift in desired experience points to a new kind of nominee: the highly skilled *legal technician*. Federal judges, particularly those on the Courts of Appeals, are obviously immersed in the law. In addition, given the policy-making discretion of their courts, federal judges can indicate their future reliability through their decision making. So can individuals who have served in the executive branch as lawyers and legal policy makers—often in the Justice Department but also in the White House itself. They leave a trail of confidential memos and candid conversations about the hot button legal issues of the day, all of which can be mined to determine their policy reliability. Finally, attending a top law school and serving as a law professor provide further signals of legal acumen.

Indeed, over time the new kind of nominee displayed the signature of what can be called a *legal Super Tech*: the "superfecta" of federal judge, executive branch legal policy maker, law professor, and top law school graduate. The last panel in Figure 4.5 shows a striking rise in such Super Tech nominations in recent decades; however, there has been no corresponding percentage increase in Super Techs among short listers. This divergence shows that, on at least this dimension, presidents did not draw randomly from the short lists, but rather winnowed them in search of nominees with a distinctive profile.

To give a concrete example of how executive branch experience translates into reliability, consider the career trajectory of Samuel Alito. In 1985, Alito was an attorney in the Reagan Solicitor General's office, and sought a promotion to become assistant attorney general. In response to an inquiry from the president's appointments office, Alito wrote: "Most recently, it has been an honor and source of personal satisfaction for me to serve in the office of the Solicitor General during President Reagan's administration and to help advance legal positions in which I personally believe very strongly. I am particularly proud of my contributions in recent cases in which the government has argued that racial and ethnic quotas should not be allowed and that the Constitution does not protect a right to abortion." Alito got that promotion. Then, in 1990, President George H.W. Bush appointed him to the 3rd Circuit Court of Appeals. Fifteen years later, President George W. Bush elevated Alito to the Supreme Court. In 2022, events came full circle—Alito wrote the majority opinion in *Dobbs v. Jackson Women's Health Organization* overturning *Roe v. Wade*.[17]

We can further parse these changes by examining whether and where nominees attended law school, not simply whether they attended a top-14 law school. Figure 4.6A focuses just on nominees, in order to extend our perspective back to 1789; it displays rug plots with loess lines for four categories of attendance—no law school training; a law school not in the "Top 14"; a Top 14 school; or Harvard, Yale, or Columbia (a super-elite subset of the Top 14 category).[18] The figure shows

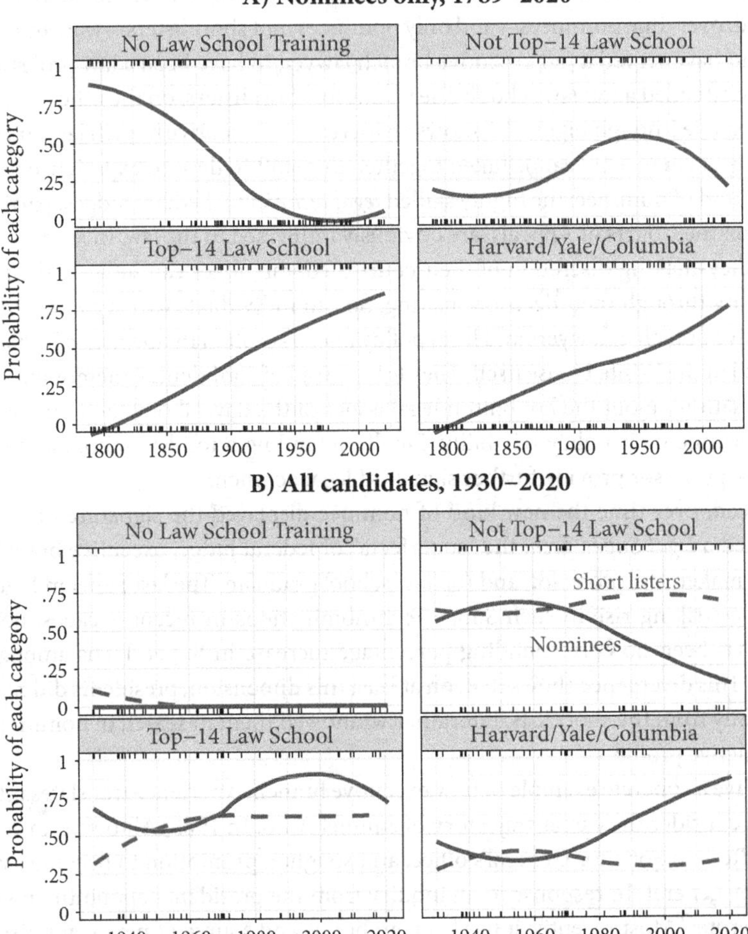

Fig. 4.6 The changing law school experience for A) just nominees, from 1789 to 2020; and B) for all candidates from 1930 to 2020. The rugs in each panel show instances where a candidate fell into a given category (top) or did not (bottom). The green lines show loess lines for nominees only, the purple lines for short listers.

that early in the court's history, most nominees had no formal law school training. This fact is less surprising than it seems, as legal training remained in its infancy; Harvard Law School, for example, was founded only in 1817.[19] Instead, the standard route to a legal career was apprenticeship. But as law schools institutionalized, the apprenticeship route went into eclipse, and the last Supreme Court nominee without a law school degree was James Byrnes in 1941, a politico. Concomitantly, presidents increasingly drew their Supreme Court nominees from top law schools—Harvard, Yale, and Columbia in particular. Twenty-three nominees have had Harvard Law degrees, with 10 each from Columbia and Yale. No other law school counts more than three nominees among its alumni.

Figure 4.6B compares the patterns of law school attendance for both nominees and short listers from 1930 to 2020. As with nominees, those with no law school training very quickly dropped off short lists altogether. However, the other three panels show interesting differences across nominees and short listers. The rate at which graduates of law schools outside the Top 14 make the short list has remained basically unchanged since 1930. From 1930 to about 1970, presidents increasingly considered short listers from top law schools, but that propensity then leveled off. Likewise, the rate of short listers from Harvard, Yale, and Columbia has remained flat since 1930. Yet, when it comes to actually selecting nominees, presidents increasingly were drawn to individuals with degrees from top law schools—now they almost exclusively select graduates of the "Big 3," with very few exceptions.[20]

The data in this section raise an obvious question: what explains the rise of the Super Techs? Notably, the trend coincides with the institutionalization of a professionalized vetting process in the Justice Department and White House, as discussed in Chapter 3, replacing the often haphazard processes employed by previous presidents. In our view, the driving force behind the rise of the legal Super Techs and the institutionalization of the vetting process was one and the same: the desire to find ideologically reliable nominees, including ones likely to pass policy litmus tests.[21]

4.4 Racial and Gender Diversity

Like most American institutions, the United States Supreme Court has been monolithically white and male throughout most of its history. Not until 1967 was the first minority justice, Thurgood Marshall, appointed to the court. Fourteen years later, Sandra Day O'Connor became the first female justice. Overall, at the time we write, and including the 2022 confirmation of Kentanji Brown Jackson (who does not appear in our data), of the 115 justices who sat on the court in U.S. history, 107 have been white men. Justices Marshall, O'Connor, Thomas, Ginsburg, Sotomayor, Kagan, Barrett, and Jackson are the exceptions; Harriet Miers is the lone failed nominee who was not a white man.

In Chapter 9, we further examine changes in presidential demand for diversity on the court. For now, Figure 4.7 depicts the diversity of the short listers and the nominees from 1930 to 2020. Unsurprisingly, short list diversity increased substantially over time. No woman or racial minority made a short list until after 1960, but presidents have increasingly included them since then. However, white males still make up a large proportion of short listers. Interestingly, and in contrast to the pattern with candidate reliability, the trends for short listers and nominees moved on parallel tracks. But even today, a Supreme Court nominee will still more likely than not be a white male.

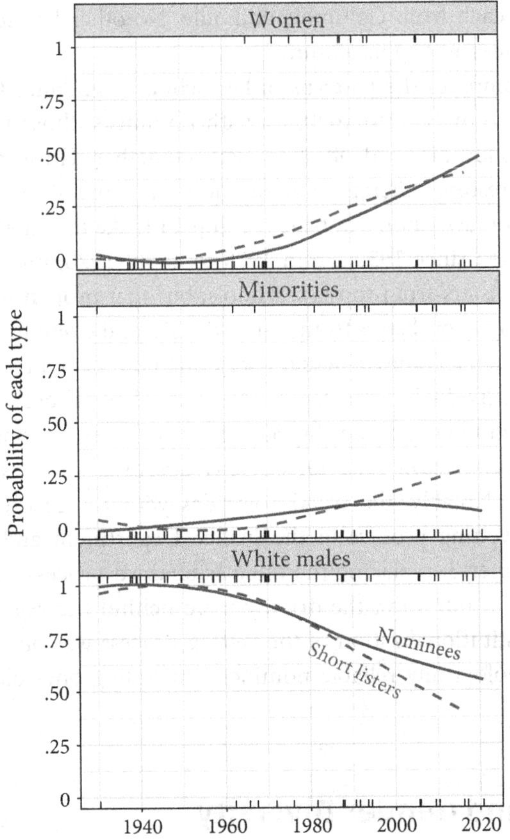

Fig. 4.7 The race and gender of short listers and nominees, 1930–2020. The rugs in each panel show instances where a candidate fell into a given category (top) or did not (bottom). The green lines show loess lines for nominees only, the purple lines for short listers.

4.5 Age

Recall Nixon's conversation with Mitchell expressing concern about the age of potential short listers: "I think there is, if there's a woman that's credible within an age limit. There's a couple of them, as you know, up in years." This concern illustrates what we would describe as the conventional wisdom: when it comes to Supreme Court nominees, the younger the better. As it turns out, things are not that simple.

The top graph in Figure 4.8 depicts the age of every nominee from 1790 to 2020.[22] The loess line reveals that the average age actually increased over the course of the nineteenth century before leveling off. Overall, average age declined slightly since 1900, but the average age of a nominee remained in the low to mid-50s.[23]

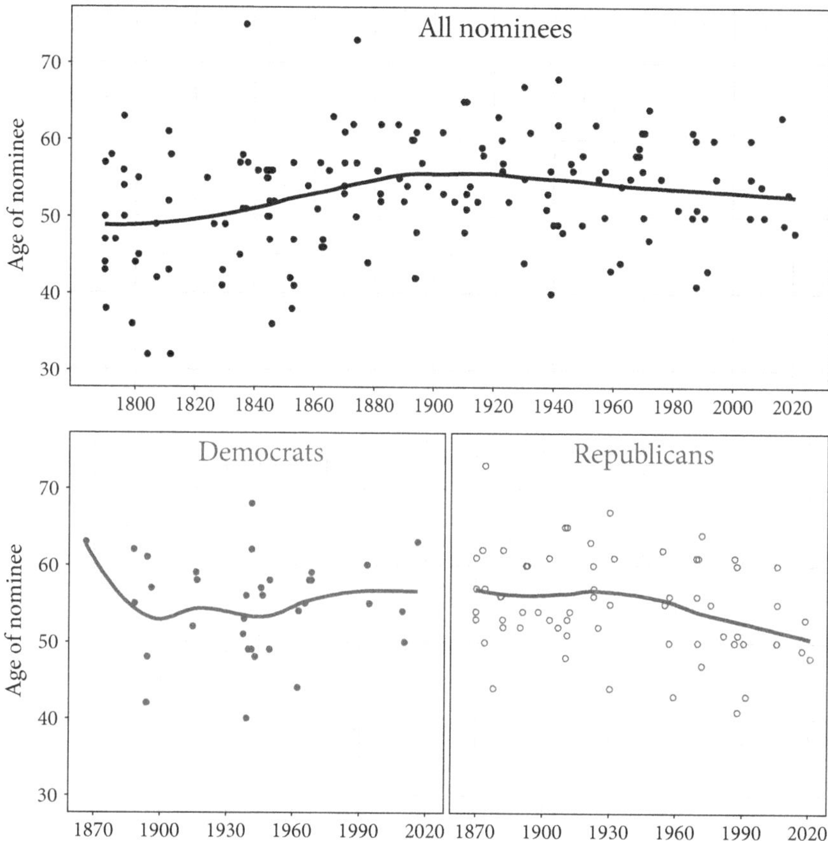

Fig. 4.8 Top) The age of all nominees, 1789–2020. Bottom) The age of nominees by party, 1866–2020.

Examining all nominees may mask party-specific changes. The bottom graphs in Figure 4.8 distinguish between nominees of Democratic and Republican presidents since 1866, the beginning of the modern two-party political system. Indeed, while the average age of Democratic appointees increased slightly since 1900, the average age of Republican appointees declined somewhat in recent years (from about 56 years old around 1900 to 52 today).

Changes in the mean, however, are less dramatic than changes in the *variance* of the age of Supreme Court nominees over time. For every 20-year interval from 1789 to today, we calculated the standard deviation of the age of nominees in that period. The results are presented in the top graph in Figure 4.9. The figure shows a steep drop in the standard deviation from 1800 to 1900, a fairly flat trend in the twentieth century, and a subsequent decline this century. The bottom graph in Figure 4.9 repeats this

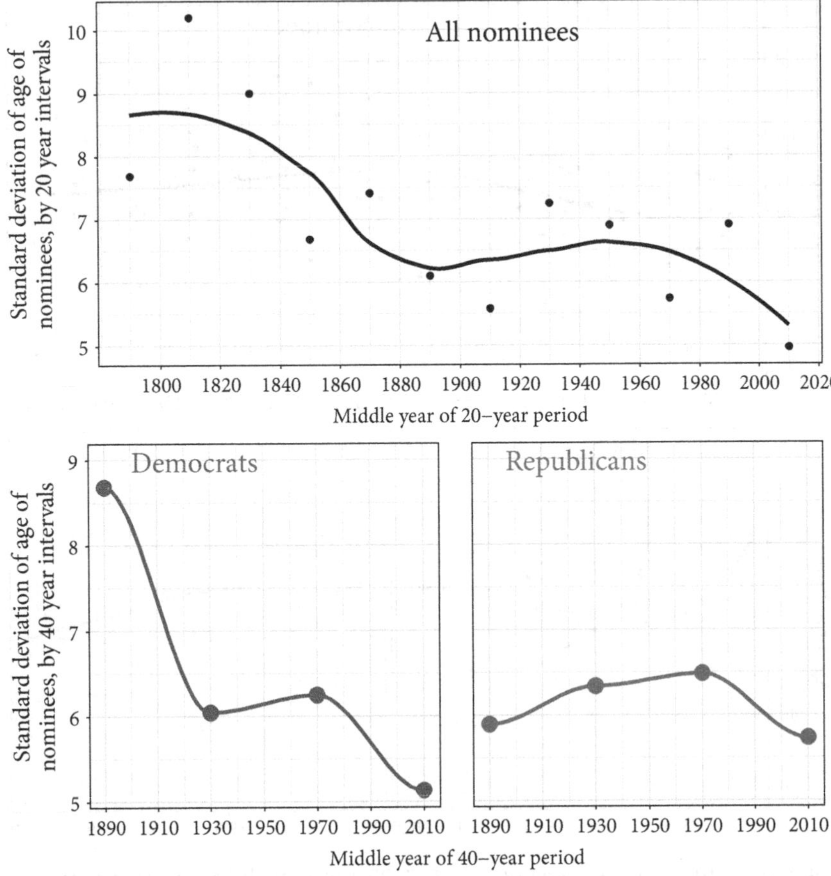

Fig. 4.9 Top) The standard deviation of nominee age, calculated at 20-year intervals, 1789–2020. Bottom) The standard deviation of nominee age, by party, calculated at 40-year intervals, 1866–2020.

analysis separately by party from 1866 to 2020 (using 40-year intervals, since there are fewer observations when we subset by party). Interestingly, the decline in variance was concentrated among Democratic appointees (though much of the overall decline occurred before the party-specific data starts in 1866).

The data indicate that presidents "truncated" the age distribution of entering justices. They now avoid older nominees who cannot expect long careers on the bench in expectation. Caleb Cushing, for example, was 73 when President Grant nominated him in 1874. But presidents also increasingly pass over nominees who are "very young." As examples, Joseph Story was 32 when President Madison appointed him in 1812, while William O. Douglas was 40 when Roosevelt appointed him in 1939. Today, potential nominees of such a young age likely have not reached professional prominence or established the impeccable track records needed for policy reliability.

4.6 Religion

As President Trump made his selection to replace Justice Kennedy in 2018, his final four short listers (Brett Kavanaugh, Amy Coney Barrett, Thomas Hardiman, and Amul Thapar) differed from one another in important ways, yet all shared one outstanding characteristic: their Catholic faith. Kavanaugh's confirmation boosted the number of Catholic justices to six, joining three Jewish justices.[24] Two years later, Trump selected Barrett, who is also Catholic, to replace Ruth Bader Ginsburg, who was Jewish, increasing the number of Catholic justices to seven.

How unprecedented was the religious composition of the 2020 Court? The U.S. Supreme Court Justices Database tallies the religious affiliation of nearly every justice appointed to the court since 1789. We divide the justices into three groups: Protestants, Catholics, and Jews.[25] For each "strong" natural court from 1789 to 2020 (that is, those in which every seat is filled), we calculated the number of justices belonging to each group. Figure 4.10 shows the results: the purple boxes depict Protestants; the green boxes show Catholics; and the blue boxes in the upper right-hand corner depict Jewish justices.[26] The x-axis indicates the starting year of each natural court; because natural courts are of uneven length, the axis is not scaled perfectly to time.

The graph makes clear that until the twentieth century, Supreme Court justices were almost exclusively Protestant. Only four Catholic nominees served before 1900, and no Jews served until Louis Brandeis' selection in 1916. Indeed, Jewish and Catholic nominations were so rare that a norm of the "Catholic seat" and "Jewish seat" developed, in which presidents would replace an outgoing member of the respective religions with a nominee of the same faith.[27] This can be seen in the top part of Figure 4.10, in the middle of the twentieth century. Since then, the shift toward Catholic and Jewish justices became quite pronounced.

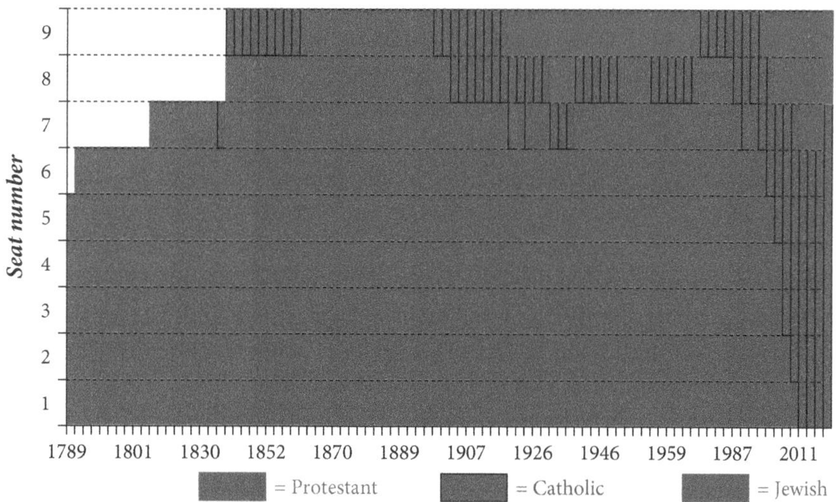

Fig. 4.10 The religion of Supreme Court nominees, 1789–2020, by natural courts.

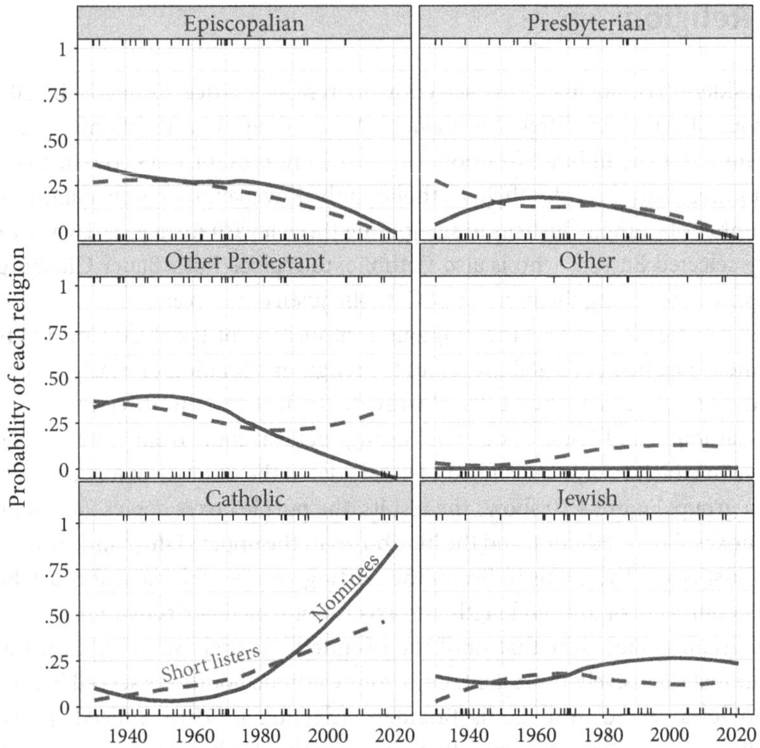

Fig. 4.11 The religion of short listers and nominees, 1930–2020. The rugs in each panel show instances where a candidate fell into a given category (top) or did not (bottom). The green lines show loess lines for nominees only, the purple lines for short listers.

Interestingly, the short listers display a similar change. Figure 4.11 depicts the religious affiliation of short listers and nominees from 1930 to 2020. Here we separate Protestants into Episcopalians, Presbyterians, and other Protestants; we also add a residual "other category" for individuals outside the five main categories. The short listers display a rise in both Jewish and (especially) Catholic individuals whom presidents considered since 1930. In addition, the top right panel shows that other varieties of Protestants have made it onto recent short lists, but were not selected.

One way to gauge the significance of the shift toward Catholic and Jewish nominees is to compare the distributions seen in Figures 4.10 and 4.11 to the overall distribution of faiths among the American public. Figure 4.12 depicts annual self-reported religious affiliation among Americans from 1948 to 2019.[28] The graph shows that by 2020 Protestants no longer comprised a majority of Americans, although they remained a plurality by a wide margin. Meanwhile, the proportion of Catholics and Jews had remained basically flat for decades—as of 2020 Jews comprised about 2% of Americans and Catholics about 23%. These latter two groups were thus heavily

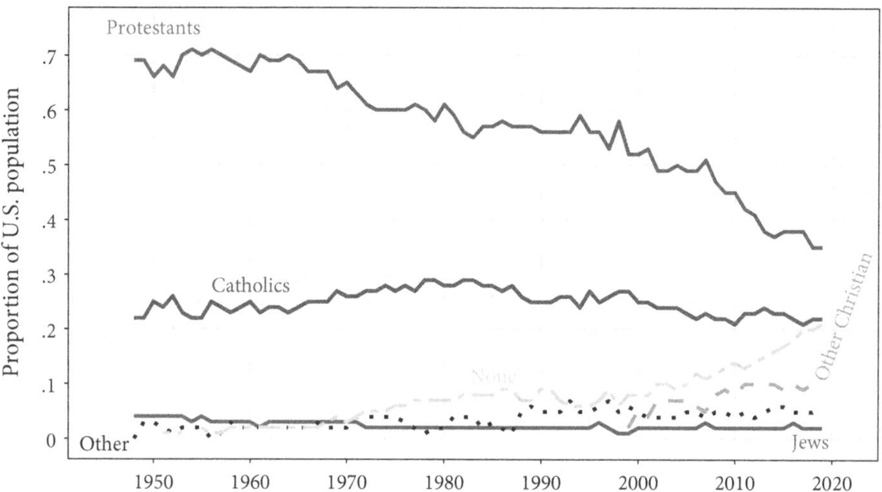

Fig. 4.12 The religious distribution of the U.S. population, 1948–2019.

over-represented on the Supreme Court in 2020 while Protestants were quite under-represented.[29]

4.7 Geography

In 1932, President Hoover appointed to the Supreme Court Benjamin Cardozo, then the Chief Judge of the New York Court of Appeals (that state's highest court). The *Chicago Tribune*'s (1932) editorial board deplored this choice:

> If the senate confirms [Cardozo], as there is reason to believe it will and no reason to protest that it should not, New York will have given four of the justices to the present bench. Massachusetts and Pennsylvania supply two and three come from the west. Thus three eastern states contribute two-thirds of the justices and the New York bench and bar as nearly half as can be.
>
> There is, of course, not even an implied reason why the places on the Supreme bench should require predominant sectional qualifications. It is also true that the geographical consideration has not been ignored at all times. Although the folk changes which occur between parallels of latitude and meridians of longitude are not great in the American people, there are such changes. There are diversities east and west and north and south—political, social, temperamental and traditional. There has been some political regard for these diversities in composing the Supreme Court and they have had consequences.

As this argument illustrates, the idea of "geographic balance" was often prominent or at times even at the forefront in the discussions of the court.[30] Indeed, for the first 120 years of the court's existence, and particularly before 1869, geography was baked into the justices' duties, as each would "ride circuit" to hear appeals from a designated geographic area. Even after this practice ended, presidents often emphasized geographic diversity for electoral reasons—recall John Mitchell telling Nixon that "what you do in the northern slot might very well help what you do in the southern slot" as the two discussed the twin vacancies in 1971.

How has geographic diversity on the court changed over time? Similar to our analysis of religious diversity, we group the justices by natural court, and measure their state of residence when appointed (see the Appendix for details). Based on nominees' home states, we place them into one of five regions: New England, Mid-Atlantic, Midwest, South, and West. Figure 4.13 shows these results, and reveals considerable geographic diversity on the court over time. Presidents never systematically excluded individuals from any region (accounting for the westward expansion of states in the nineteenth century and early twentieth century). However, the last three decades in the figure display a steady shift toward justices from the East Coast (New England or Mid-Atlantic). The only exceptions were Justices Kennedy, Gorsuch, and Barrett, who hailed from California, Colorado, and Indiana, respectively. The result was a 2020 court that (at least superficially) exhibited what Justice Kagan labeled a "coastal perspective."[31]

Figure 4.14 compares regional affiliations of nominees to short listers in the post-1930 period. This comparison makes the East Coast shift even more pronounced. The graph shows considerable geographic diversity among the short listers—each of the five regions had about a 20% probability of contributing a short lister, with some notable temporal variation. Yet in selecting the actual nominee, presidents came to largely eschew short listers from everywhere but the Mid-Atlantic corridor.

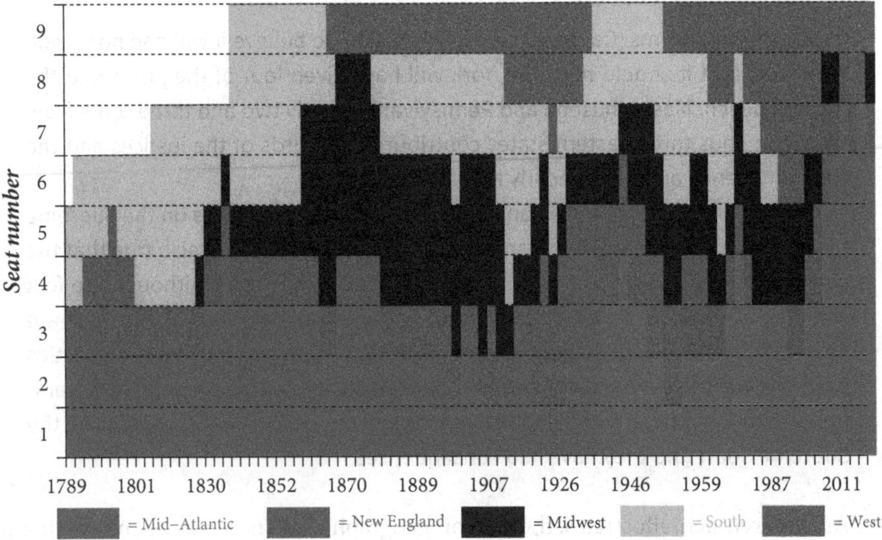

Fig. 4.13 The regional affiliation of Supreme Court justices, 1789–2020, by natural courts.

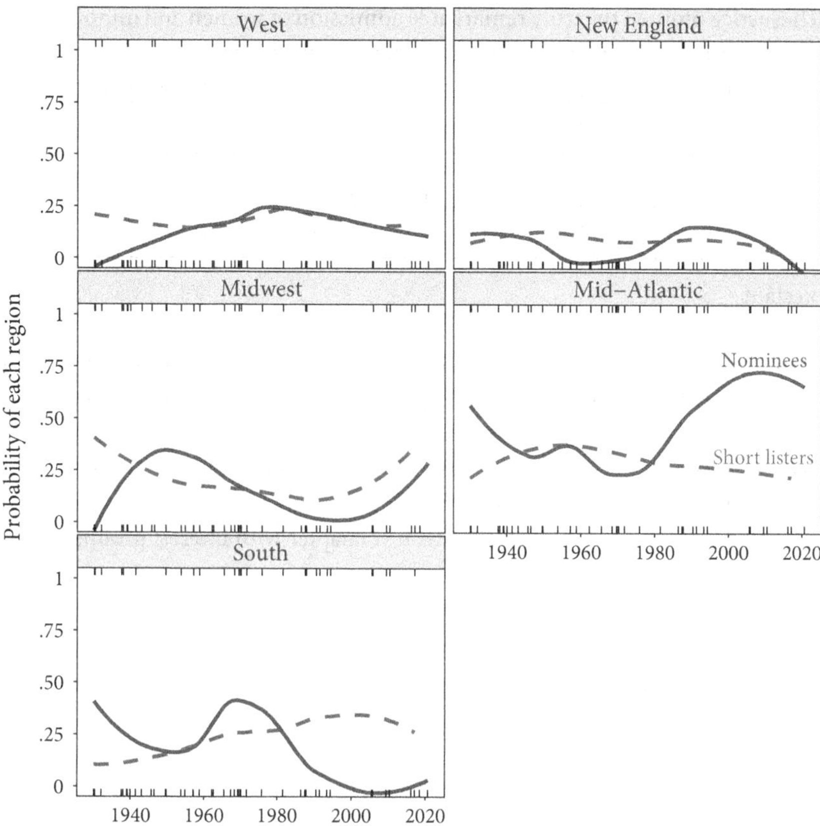

Fig. 4.14 The regional affiliation of Supreme Court short listers and nominees, 1930–2020. The rugs in each panel show instances where a candidate fell into a given category (top) or did not (bottom). The green lines show loess lines for nominees only, the purple lines for short listers.

4.8 Conclusion

Justice Scalia, in one of his characteristically withering dissents, addressed the make-up of the 2015 court:

> Take, for example, this Court, which consists of only nine men and women, all of them successful lawyers who studied at Harvard or Yale Law School. Four of the nine are natives of New York City. Eight of them grew up in east- and west-coast States. Only one hails from the vast expanse in-between. Not a single Southwesterner or even, to tell the truth, a genuine Westerner (California does not count). Not a single evangelical Christian (a group that comprises about one quarter of Americans), or even a Protestant of any denomination.[32]

The justice omitted the truly remarkable admission of women and minorities to the court's historically all-white and all-male ranks. But otherwise, his depiction neatly summarized the end result of an extraordinary transformation in who sits on the court. By the first decades of the twenty-first century, a justice was very likely to be: a former judge on the Courts of Appeals; in their mid-50s; from the East Coast; a graduate of Harvard, Yale, or Columbia; and Catholic or Jewish. In contrast, justices in the mid-twentieth century looked very different: often politicos, sometimes educated in non-elite schools, from all across the country, both older and younger, and mostly Protestant.

Notably, it is *not* the case that twenty-first-century presidents ignored individuals with profiles other than that catalogued by Justice Scalia. The presidential short lists fairly bulged with other kinds of people. But at the time of the final decision, modern presidents preferred justices cut from a narrow cloth. Why this happened—and what the consequences are for the court—are subjects of later chapters. But first we turn our attention to other actors who became increasingly interested in Supreme Court nominations over time, beginning in the next chapter with interest groups.

5
Interest Groups

On June 26, 1987, Justice Lewis Powell announced his impending retirement from the Supreme Court. The resignation of Powell, then the "swing" justice on the Court, gave President Reagan the opportunity to shift the court's ideological balance well to the right. As we discussed in Chapter 3, Reagan's Department of Justice team, led by Attorney General Ed Meese, quickly pushed the president to select Robert Bork to replace Powell.

As news of this choice spread, liberal interest groups prepared for a bruising confirmation battle. Two days after Powell's retirement, Ralph Neas, the executive director of the Leadership Conference on Civil Rights (LCCR), a coalition of civil rights groups, said, "The Bork nomination, or that of anyone who would jeopardize the civil rights accomplishments of the past 30 years, would most likely precipitate the most controversial legislative battle of the Reagan years."[1] Reagan, of course, nominated Bork, and the battle was joined. Mark Gitenstein, chief of staff for Senator Joe Biden, who was then the chair of the Judiciary Committee, had a ringside seat to Bork's nomination. In his vivid account, Gitenstein (1992, 112) notes that interest groups opposed to Bork developed a new tactic:

> Early in the effort to organize the anti-Bork coalition, the key strategists of the LCCR determined that they would do something they had never done before in one of these nomination struggles. They would turn to sophisticated national polling and focus groups, the high-tech wizardry of modern election campaigns. A national poll could help strategists understand how a large statistically random group of Americans felt about the various issues in the Bork fight. A focus group could go one step farther. A focus group is a carefully selected unit of voters who are exposed, through a moderator, to a variety of arguments to determine which arguments are the most powerful and why.

These efforts paid off handsomely, as Bork's nomination went down to defeat on the floor of the Senate a few months later.

From today's perspective, the immediate mobilization against Bork is unsurprising. For example, in 2018 the Judicial Crisis Network, a conservative advocacy group, spent millions of dollars on media "buys" to help confirm Justice Anthony Kennedy's successor *before* Kennedy announced his retirement in June of that year.[2] Yet, from the perspective of 50 years ago, the timing, extent of mobilization, and tactics seems astounding. How did we get here?

Making the Supreme Court: The Politics of Appointments, 1930–2020. Charles M. Cameron and Jonathan P. Kastellec, Oxford University Press. © Oxford University Press 2023. DOI: 10.1093/oso/9780197680544.003.0005

Though infrequent in earlier eras, interest group involvement in Supreme Court nominations is not a new phenomenon. For example, the Grange, an agricultural interest group, played a role in the wild nomination of railroad attorney Stanley Matthews in 1881.[3] During the political donnybrook sparked by Woodrow Wilson's nomination of Progressive lawyer Louis Brandeis in 1916, individuals connected to railroad commissions, newspapers, manufacturers, and unions participated actively, although typically as individuals rather than group representatives. Herbert Hoover's 1930 nominee John J. Parker famously sparked opposition by the American Federation of Labor (AFL) and the fledgling National Association for the Advancement of Colored People (NAACP), apparently contributing to Parker's rejection by the Senate.[4] But many other nominations in this period drew no group interest. For example, Danelski's detailed case study of Pierce Butler's confirmation in 1922 found very little group involvement, despite a degree of controversy over his Catholicism.[5] These examples show long-standing, though at best intermittent, involvement of interest groups in Supreme Court nomination politics prior to 1930.

What do political scientists know systematically about interest group involvement in Supreme Court nominations? In the Appendix, we discuss several outstanding studies of interest group participation in Supreme Court nominations. These studies feature in-depth analysis of, for example, lobbying strategies in a handful of nominations. Some report on surveys of interest groups, while others study interest group involvement in multiple nominations but focus on participation in the hearings. This chapter is more synoptic and covers nearly a century of nominations from a multitude of perspectives.[6]

In particular, using an original database of newspaper reportage, we construct a systematic, historically oriented portrait of group participation in Supreme Court nomination politics from 1930 to 2020.[7] Combining this new and expansive data set with other sources, we document changes in the following:

- The levels of mobilization, both for and against a nominee;
- The types of interest groups that mobilized;
- The size and composition of liberal and conservative mobilizers;
- The tactics employed by the groups;
- The timing of group participation during the nomination process;
- The birth year and length of time until first mobilization among groups who participated in multiple nominations;
- The prior involvement of mobilizing groups as amici curiae before the Supreme Court.

In addition, we document:

- The ideologies of repeat mobilizers and their extraordinary ideological polarization;
- The absence of ideological moderates among the repeat mobilizers;
- The changing relationship between nominee-group ideological distance and mobilization over time.

The result is not only the most detailed picture of interest group involvement in Supreme Court nominations over an extended period of time, it is also one of the most complete portraits of interest group participation in any recurring political event in American political history.

The data reveal a sizable increase in interest group activity over time. Little mobilization occurred between 1930 and 1970, with many nominations attracting no interest. After 1970, and in particular after Robert Bork's nomination in 1987, mobilization became routine for most nominees, with many groups participating. Early on, most mobilization involved opposition to a nominee, but today occurs about equally on both sides. We also find that the calculus of interest groups appears to have changed significantly over time, with a shift from "opportunistic mobilization" based on a nominee's qualifications, to routine mobilization more heavily influenced by the ideological extremity of the nominee.

In addition, the data reveal significant shifts in both the *types* of groups that routinely mobilize and the *tactics* mobilized groups employ. On the left, labor unions and core civil rights groups dominated the earlier period, but today public interest/citizen groups and "identity" groups (in particular, pro-choice organizations) now comprise the majority of participating groups. On the right, in the earlier period, the few conservative groups that existed and mobilized tended to be from the "Old Right"—groups that combined libertarian economics with ethno-nationalism and isolationism.[8] Today, conservative interest groups that mobilize during Supreme Court nominations tend to focus on specific policies that are emphasized by the conservative legal movement, such as abortion and gun rights. We also find a universal shift among all types of groups from more traditional "inside" tactics like lobbying to the heavy use of "outside" and "grassroots" tactics. Thus, the overall density and scope of mobilization has changed dramatically over the nine-decade period we study. Finally, we show the ideological distribution of interest groups who participate in multiple nominations is polarized, with very few moderate groups.

Taken together, our results show that interest group participation in Supreme Court nominations moved from occasional and generally opportunistic mobilization that focused on traditional forms of lobbying to more routine, intense, highly ideological and very visible contention. In a nutshell, the politics of Supreme Court confirmations moved from the *textbook pluralism* of Herring (1929), Truman (1951), Key (1942), Schattschneider (1960), and Dahl (1961) to something quite different: what we call *hyper-pluralism*.

5.2 A Portrait of the Groups and Their Behavior

To construct a consistent and reliable data source over time, we follow scholars of social movements and "contentious politics," and use newspaper coverage to measure interest group mobilization and actions over time.[9] Specifically, we conducted a content analysis of all articles in the *New York Times* and the *Los Angeles Times* that reported on interest group activity during Supreme Court nominations, from 1930 to 2020.

Using Proquest's historical newspaper electronic archive, we first identified every story from each paper that discussed a nominee, searching between the announcement of a new nominee and when the nomination officially ended (i.e. either in confirmation, defeat, or withdrawal). We then read the articles to identify whether they mentioned any interest group involvement. If so, we coded the story in detail. All told, the data reveals that interest groups mobilized during 41 of the 54 nominations in this period, with 368 unique interest groups participating.[10] In the stories with mentions of group participation, we identified each group, whether it supported or opposed the nominee, its tactics or actions, and the timing of the actions. Some stories reporting interest group activity did not specify the identity of the groups—e.g. "environmental groups" or "anti-abortion groups." In our reckoning, these stories contribute to the counts of stories reporting interest group activity and to counts of different types of tactics, but do not contribute to the counts of interest groups themselves, which are based on an identification of specific groups. In addition, we classified each group into substantive and ideological categories, described below. We also compiled organizational profiles of each group, mostly from Internet searches but also the scholarly literature. All told, the data paints a vivid and detailed portrait of interest group mobilization in Supreme Court nominations from 1930 to 2020.

Before turning to the descriptions of the groups and their activities, Table 5.1 highlights an important distinction among the groups. For each group, we counted

Table 5.1 The frequency of mobilization across interest groups. The table depicts the number of groups that mobilized in the given number of nominations in the first column; e.g. 256 groups participated in only a single nomination.

Number of nominations participated in	Number of Groups
1	256
2	50
3	26
4	6
5	6
6	5
7	5
8	6
10	1
11	1
12	1
13	1
15	1
16	1
17	2
18	1

the number of nominations in which it participated between 1930 and 2020. The table depicts the distribution of participation rates, and it shows that the majority of groups (256, to be exact, or 69% of all groups) mobilized in one and only one nomination. Some of these "one-shotters" were serious on-going groups but others were ephemeral—for example, "Italian-Americans for Alito." In contrast, a smaller number of "repeat players" mobilized across multiple nominations. When we present data on levels of mobilization, the type of groups that mobilized, group tactics, and so on, we present data on *all* the mobilizing groups, because the participation of both one-shotters and repeat players determined the texture of interest group mobilization in a nomination. However, when we address the origins of groups, their prior involvement as lobbyists before the Supreme Court, and their finely textured ideological orientation, we focus on the repeat players who form the backbone of serious appointment activists (we will interchangeably refer to these groups as "repeat players" or "repeat mobilizers").

5.2.1 Levels of Mobilization

We begin by examining level of mobilization. For each nominee, we calculated the number of unique groups participating in the confirmation process. The data is displayed in Figure 5.1A, and reveals a clear change over time. The number of groups that mobilized in the 29 nominations from Charles Evans Hughes to Warren Burger (1930–1969) was typically small; indeed, nearly half (13) of these nominations witnessed zero mobilization, with the mean level at three groups in this period. The controversial nomination of Clement Haynsworth (1969) marked a shift to higher levels of mobilization. From 1969 to 1986, the year in which President Reagan elevated William Rehnquist to Chief Justice and appointed Antonin Scalia as an associate justice, the mean number of groups that mobilized was 10. Figure 5.1A shows that the level of mobilization during the Bork nomination was—and remains—unprecedented, with more than 80 groups taking part. After Bork, the levels of mobilization fluctuated, with the nominations of Thomas, Roberts, and Kavanaugh triggering a large number of groups. The mean number of groups in the 1987 to 2020 period was 33 (30 if Bork is excluded).

Mobilization can occur on both sides of a nomination fight. Figure 5.1B disaggregates the data into the number of groups in support and in opposition to the nominee. Until very recently, mobilization against a nominee was typically larger than mobilization in support. Indeed, the latter is a relatively recent phenomenon, and hardly existed until the Bork nomination. However, in recent nominations, the levels of support and opposition virtually equalized. This equalization may reflect presidents' growing sophistication in directing what are essentially political campaigns on behalf of their nominees.

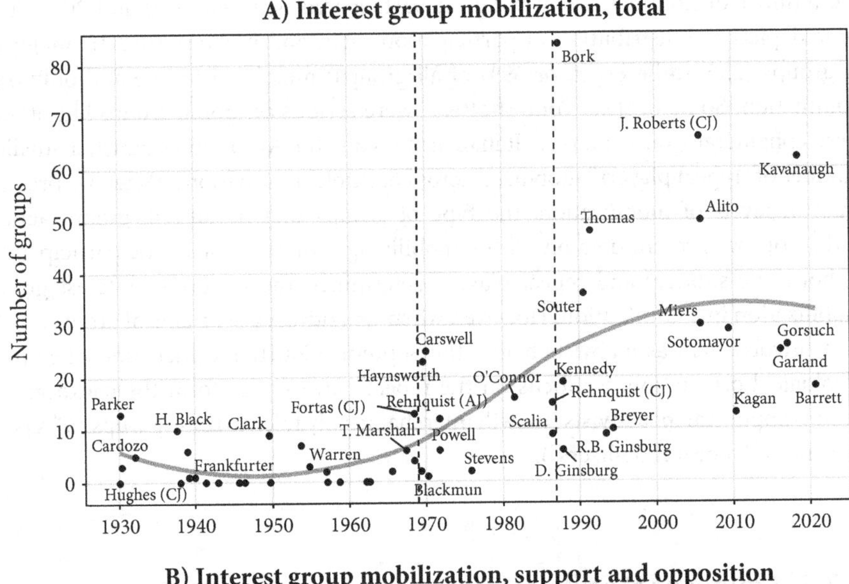

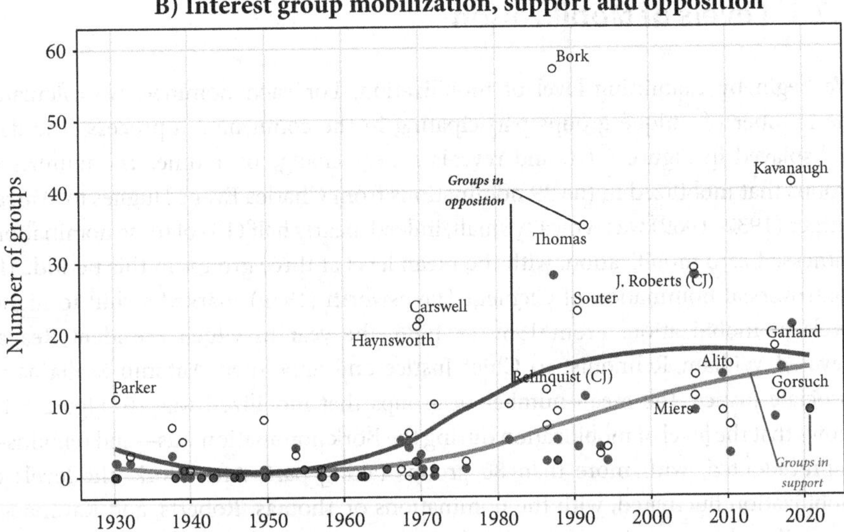

Fig. 5.1 A) Total interest group mobilization over time. The vertical dashed lines at 1969 and 1987 demarcate what appear to be three distinct eras in mobilization. B) Mobilization broken down by support (green points and green line) and opposition (black points and black line). We label nominees for whom at least 10 groups mobilized in opposition. The lines are loess lines.

5.2.2 Who Participated: The Changing Nature of the Groups

Beyond the sheer increase in mobilization shown in Figure 5.1, the identity and types of groups changed dramatically. The left column in Table 5.2 shows the most active groups (in descending order) that mobilized across the entire 90-year period, while the right column breaks down the data into the three eras indicated in Figure 5.1: 1930–1969, 1969–1987, and 1987–2020. The numbers in parentheses depict the number of nominations in which each group mobilized during that time period. Over the entire period, the most frequent participants were liberal groups such as the NAACP, NARAL (the National Abortion Rights Action League), and People for the American Way—as well as the AFL-CIO federation of unions.[11]

Perhaps more illuminating, however, is the transformation in the types of groups seen in the bottom three panels of Table 5.2. The five most frequently appearing groups in the early period were the AFL-CIO, a core industrial union; the NAACP; and the Association of the Bar of the City of New York; the Liberty Lobby, a conservative anti-communist and nativist group with connections to the "Old Right"; and the Socialist Party (although all of this group's mobilization came in the 1930s). In the middle period, the most prominent groups were the AFL-CIO, the Leadership Conference on Civil Rights (LCCR), and the NAACP. Finally, the third period saw the rise of liberal groups focused on social issues and identity politics, as well as conservative groups that focused extensively on nominations (such as the Judicial Confirmation Network and the Federalist Society) and those that focus on social issues, particularly abortion (such as the National Right to Life Committee). All told, the nature of mobilized groups shifted dramatically, from industrial unions, core civil rights groups, and Old Right groups in earlier eras to public interest/citizen groups, "identity" groups and social policy groups today.

To classify the groups more systematically, we build on earlier efforts by interest group scholars, who often classify groups based on the policy areas in which they operate or the constituencies they represent.[12] We do the same; the categories include, for example, groups involved in environmental and health politics, as well as abortion and gay rights. Using this micro-level taxonomy as a starting point, we then aggregated certain categories in order to generalize about larger collections of similar organizations.[13]

Based on this classification, Figure 5.2 displays the changes in mobilization of particular types of groups. For each nominee, Figure 5.2A shows the number of labor, civil rights, and abortion groups that mobilized—these are the types of groups that have been most active in nomination politics. Labor groups were active over the entire period, but their mobilization rates declined in the twenty-first century. Civil rights groups also have a long history of involvement, although their mobilization peaked in the contentious Clarence Thomas nomination. Finally, the increase in the number of abortion groups indicates the primacy of that issue in recent years. Taken together, the three loess lines show sequential "peaks" in mobilization for labor, civil rights, and abortion groups, respectively.

Table 5.2 Lists of the ten active groups, first across the entire time period, then in each era. The groups appear in descending order of total mobilization; the numbers in parentheses depict the number of nominees the groups mobilized for in each period.

All
NAACP (18)
NARAL (17)
People for the American Way (17)
AFL-CIO (16)
LCCR (15)
NOW (13)
ACLU (12)
Alliance for Justice (11)
National Right to Life Committee (10)
Judicial Confirmation Network (9)
American Conservative Union (8)
Concerned Women for America (8)
Family Research Council (8)
Federalist Society (8)
Americans for Democratic Action (7)

Hughes to Burger (1930–1969)
AFL-CIO (6)
NAACP (4)
Association of the Bar of the City of New York (3)
Liberty Lobby (3)
Socialist Party (3)
American Airlines Lobbyist (2)
American Trial Lawyers Association (2)
Anti-Saloon League (2)
Lawyer's Committee on Supreme Court Nominations (2)
United Automobile Workers (2)
United Mine Workers (2)

Haynsworth to Scalia (1969–1986)
AFL-CIO (6)
LCCR (6)
NAACP (6)
National Womens Political Caucus (5)
NOW (5)
ACLU (4)
Americans for Democratic Action (4)
National Bar Association (4)
NARAL (3)
National Urban League (3)
United Automobile Workers (3)

Bork to Barrett (1987–2020)
People for the American Way (15)
NARAL (14)
Alliance for Justice (11)
LCCR (9)
National Right to Life Committee (9)
ACLU (8)
American Conservative Union (8)
Family Research Council (8)
Judicial Confirmation Network (8)
NAACP (8)
National Womens Law Center (8)
NOW (8)
Concerned Women for America (7)
Federalist Society (7)
Heritage Foundation (7)

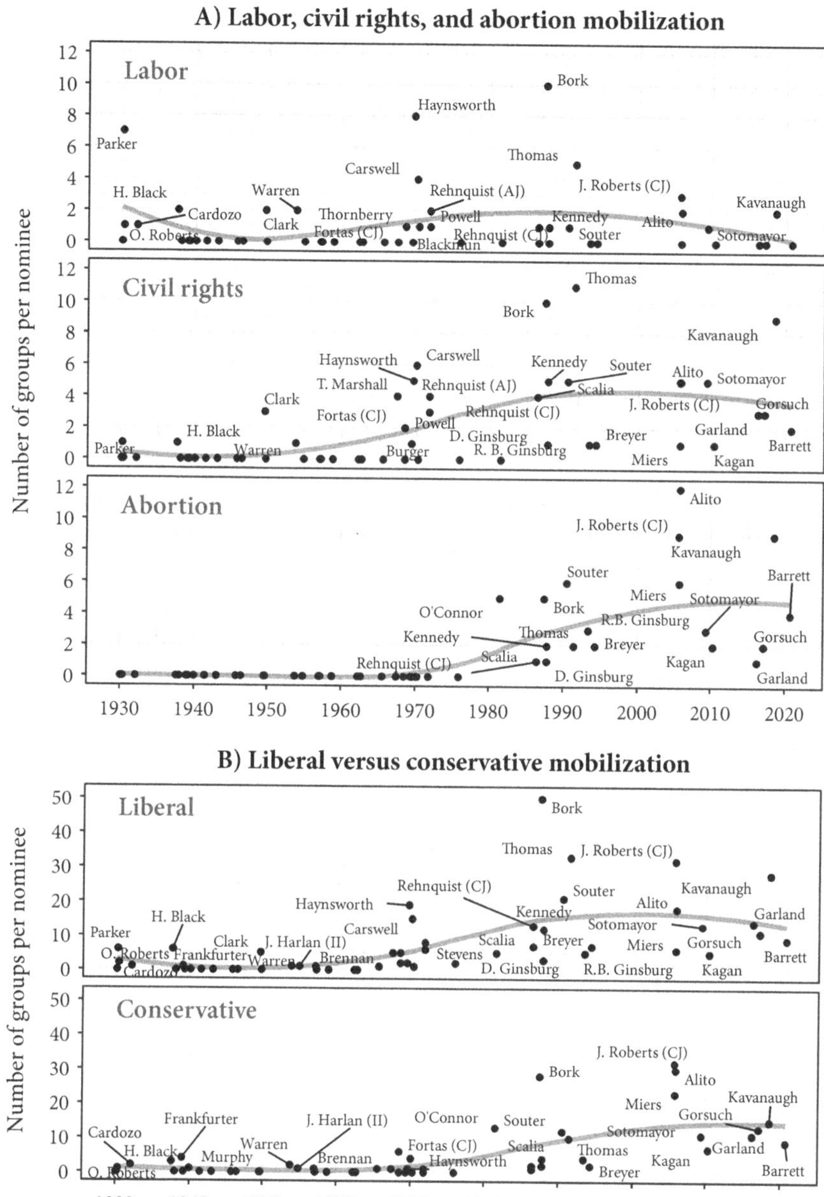

Fig. 5.2 The shifting composition of interest groups. A) The number of groups mobilized in three categories: labor, civil rights, and abortion. B) Mobilization by liberal and conservative groups.

In addition to characterizing groups by policy areas, it is also possible to classify many groups on the ideological spectrum as either liberal or conservative. To classify all the mobilizers, including the one-shotters, we first use a hand-coded classification scheme in which we code each group as liberal or conservative. For the most part, this is very straightforward: for example, active abortion groups include liberal organizations such as NOW and NARAL and conservative groups like the National Right to Life Committee. (Shortly, we will examine more sophisticated ideal point estimates for the repeat mobilizers.)

Figure 5.2B depicts the trends in mobilization by liberal and conservative groups; note the scale of the y-axis is different from Figure 5.2A. This figure shows that groups in both ideological camps have become more active over time. But conservative mobilization lagged behind liberal mobilization, only catching up in nominations in the twenty-first century. This pattern is consistent with the rise of the conservative legal movement in the 1980s as a counter-reaction to the dominance of the liberal legal movement in the law—as documented superbly by Teles (2008)—and the conservative legal movement's subsequent emphasis on stocking the federal bench with reliable conservatives.

It is also useful to categorize groups by their broader purposes. For every interest group that appears in our data, we placed them in the following categories:

- Corporations/businesses (e.g. the National Federation of Independent Business);
- Groups that are organized at the state or local level (e.g. the New York Civic League);
- Occupational groups (e.g. the AFL-CIO);
- Identity groups (e.g. The Women's Legal Defense Fund);
- Public interest/citizens groups (e.g. the ACLU);
- A residual category ("other") for groups that fall outside these categories (e.g. the Anti-Saloon League).

Note that we allow groups to fall into multiple categories if appropriate.

Although professional and occupational groups have always outnumbered other organized interests in the larger pressure group universe, citizen groups now represent a larger proportion of national lobbying organizations in existence than ever before. According to interest group scholar Jack Walker (1991), citizen groups emerged at roughly twice the rate of occupational groups in the two decades following 1965. Walker (1991, 39) attributes this rise to a number of causes, including the growth of a large, educated middle class, the emergence of new sources of political patronage such as foundations willing to subsidize political organizations, and the steady expansion of the power and responsibility of the federal government. We refer to this distribution of different types of groups as the "interest group ecology."

Figure 5.3 examines the shift in the ecology of the mobilizers over time, and shows that the patterns reported in Walker's analysis of the interest group community at

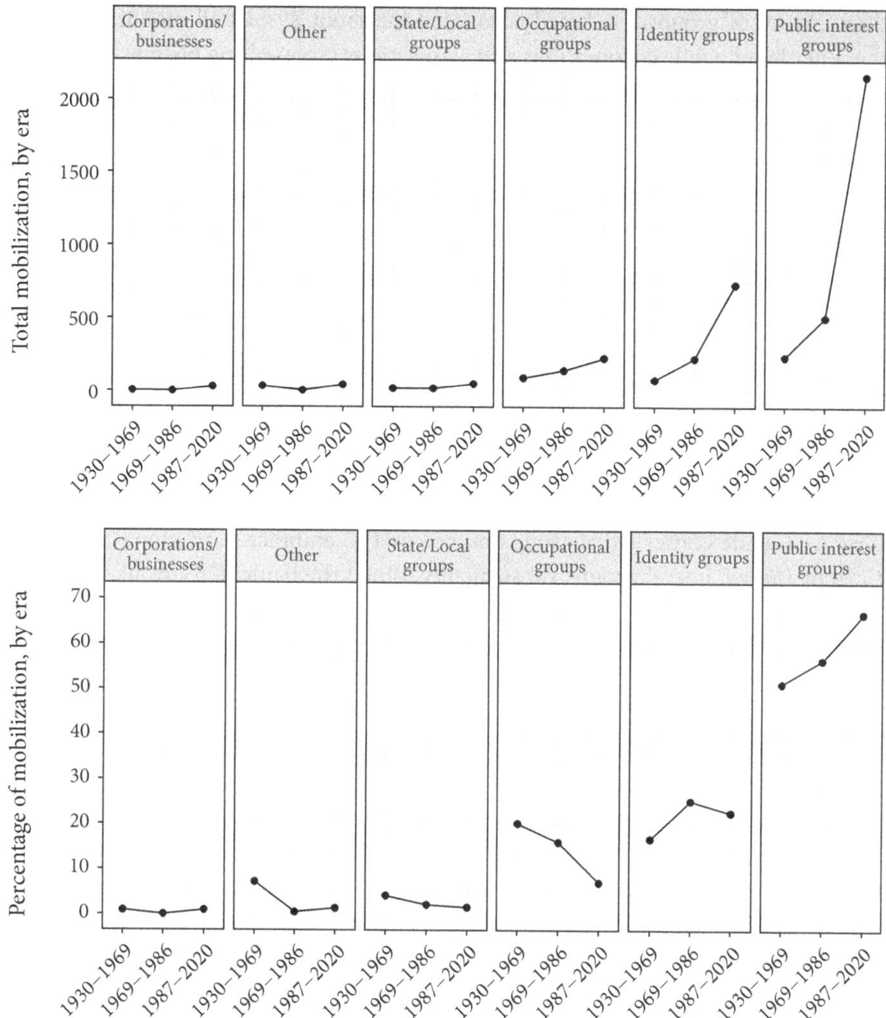

Fig. 5.3 Changes in interest group ecology over time.

large also hold for Supreme Court nominations. Each graph breaks down mobilization by group type and by the three eras of mobilization. In the top graph, the y-axis depicts the *total* amount of mobilization in each period for a given class of groups. For example, in the 1930–1969 period, a total of 93 occupational groups mobilized. Changes in the top graph across time also reflect the larger overall increase in mobilization over time. To normalize the data by era, the y-axis in the bottom graph depicts the total amount of mobilization for a given class/era pair, divided by the total amount of all mobilization in that era.

Examining the patterns across group types, Figure 5.3 shows a striking increase in mobilization by identity and public/citizen interest groups; in the 1987–2020 period, these classes of groups combined accounted for about 89% of all mobilization. On the other hand, while corporations and associations representing businesses actively lobby the Supreme Court by filing amicus briefs, we find very little involvement by these groups in the confirmation process (in stark contrast to the early involvement of labor unions)—for example, only in 1991 did the U.S. Chamber of Commerce issue its first formal statement regarding a nominee (in support of Clarence Thomas). Given these changes in the interest group ecology, it is perhaps not surprising that modern confirmation fights tend to focus heavily on hot-button social issues like abortion rights, and not on economic issues.

Finally, a recent trend worth noting is the rise of "dark money" groups, such as the conservative groups Judicial Crisis Network (JCN) and Americans for Prosperity (both of which appear in our data). Enabled by the Supreme Court's decision in *Citizens United*, these groups raise large amounts of money from wealthy individuals who can remain anonymous legally. For example, the Judicial Crisis Network focuses on expensive media campaigns using paid advertisements in the states of key senators. And while conservative groups moved first to embrace dark money following *Citizens United*, liberal groups subsequently joined the battle. Groups like Demand Justice spent huge sums of dark money in their unsuccessful effort to defeat Brett Kavanaugh's nomination in 2018.[14]

5.2.3 Choice of Tactics and Timing

Next, we examine how the interest groups' choice of tactics changed over time. Scholarly accounts of interest group lobbying generally differentiate between two types of advocacy. *Inside advocacy* involves direct personal access and contact with legislators; for example, contacting a member of Congress personally, testifying in a congressional hearing, or contributing to a member's campaign. *Outside advocacy* entails mobilizing citizens outside the policy-making community in order to put pressure on public officials inside the policy-making community; for example, speaking with the press or running an advertising campaign. Finally, although similar in spirit to outside advocacy, we can also distinguish *grassroots* advocacy, in which groups directly mobilize the public itself to participate; for example, via a demonstration or letter-writing campaign.

For every interest group action discussed in the articles, we coded the type of tactic the newspaper reported, as well as whether it was best described as inside, outside, or grassroots advocacy (or a residual category of "other").[15] Figure 5.4 shows the breakdown of tactics over time; the top panel depicts counts of each type, while the bottom panel normalizes the counts by the total amount of advocacy in each period. The figure shows a dramatic change in the choice of tactics over time. First, in the 1930 to 1969 era, interest groups relied primarily on inside advocacy (about 57% of the tactics employed in this era). The two most common inside lobbying tactics were sending a letter to members of Congress and testifying before the Judiciary

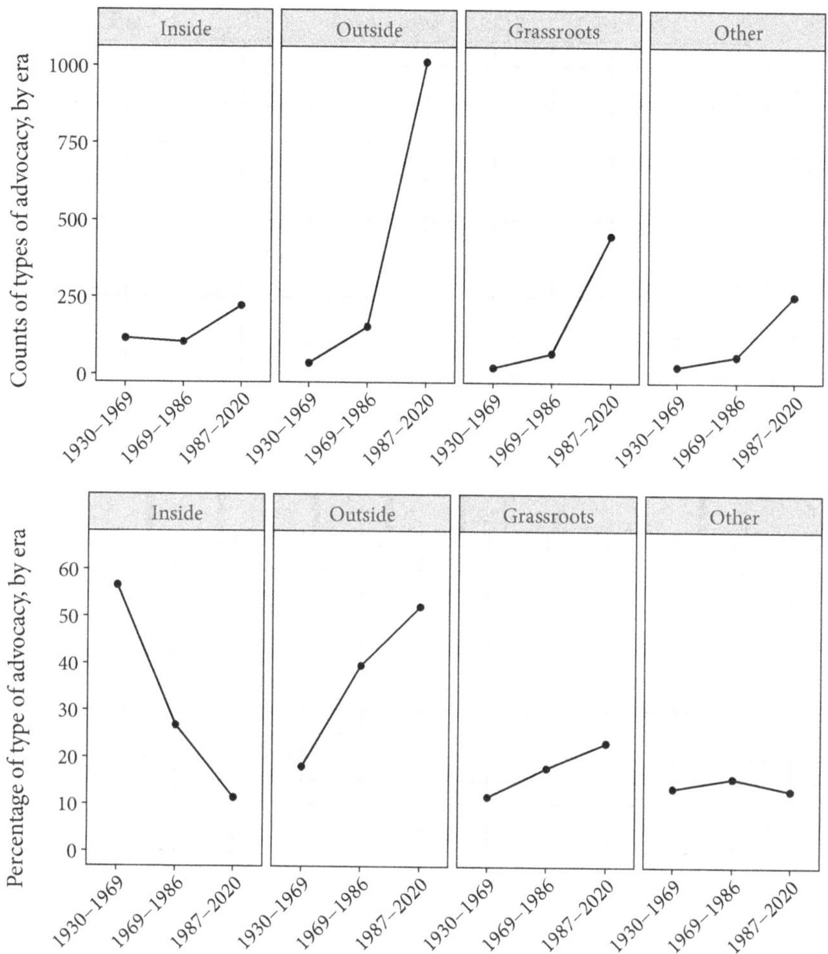

Fig. 5.4 Changes in interest group tactics over time. In the top graph, the y-axis depicts the *total* amount of mobilization in each period, for a given class of groups. In the bottom graph, the y-axis depicts the total amount of mobilization for a given class/era pair, divided by the total amount of all mobilization in that era.

Committee in formal hearings on the nomination, which together comprised about 40% of all tactics. While outside advocacy accounted for only 18% of the lobbying activity in this time period, contact with the press was the third most prevalent tactic, comprising 14% of overall activity.

The ratio of inside lobbying to outside lobbying reversed in the second era of 1969 to 1986. In this period, outside advocacy accounted for 40% of the tactics employed by interest groups, while grassroots activities comprised 18%. Press contact was the most prevalent lobbying tactic utilized by interest groups (32% of overall activity), while testifying before Congress remained the second most utilized tactic (19%).

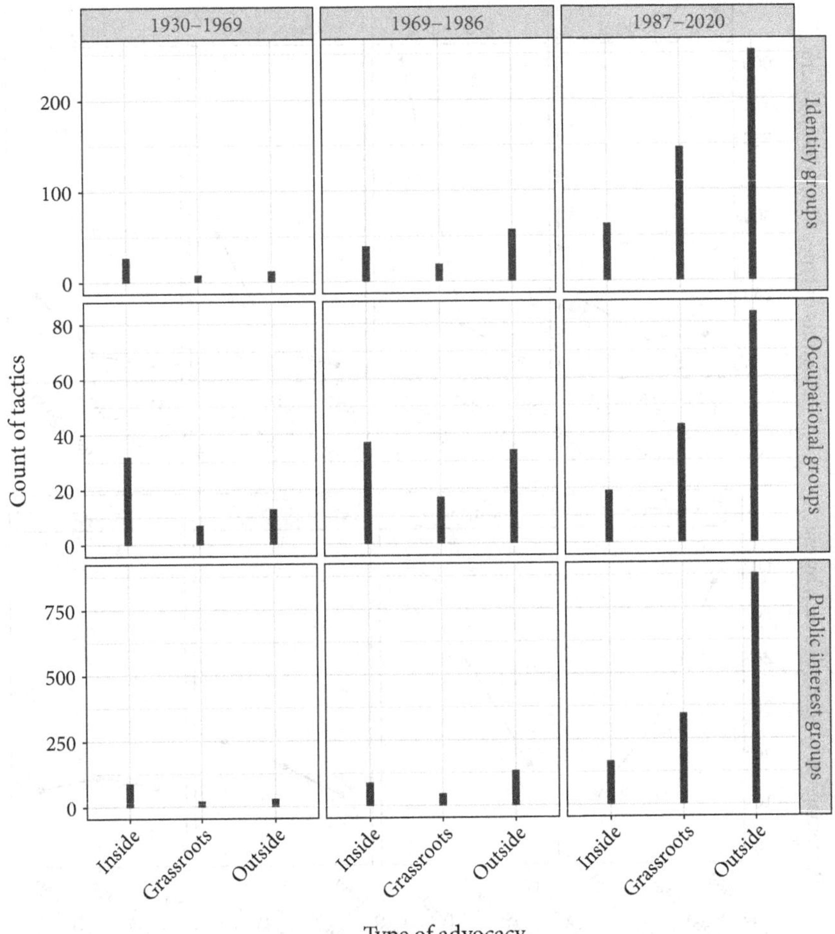

Fig. 5.5 Changes in advocacy over time, by class of groups. For each panel, the y-axes (which differ across the panels) depict the distribution of the total count of tactics (inside/grassroots/outside) chosen by the given group type/era combination indicated at the top of each panel.

Finally, in the final era of 1987 to 2020, the shift from inside tactics to outside and grassroots tactics became nearly wholesale. Outside lobbying accounted for 52% of the tactics employed, with direct press contact representing the most utilized tactic, comprising 36% of all activity. In this period, grassroots lobbying comprised 23% of all tactics, with inside advocacy comprising only 11%.

One possibility is that the shift from inside to outside tactics simply reflected the changing composition of the groups over time (discussed above). Figure 5.5 examines this possibility, and rejects it. Focusing on the three most prominent classes of groups—identity groups, occupational groups, and public interest (citizen groups)—each panel displays the distribution of advocacy (inside/grassroots/advocacy) for a given class in each period. (Note the y-axes vary in each panel.) The figure indicates a very similar pattern in changes in tactics across the group types. In the early period, inside tactics prevailed; the middle period saw a roughly equal mix of all three tactics; finally, in the third period, outside and grassroots tactics became the most popular tactics for all types of group. Thus, it seems clear that factors common to all groups, such as the relative costs of the tactics or their relative political returns to the groups, drove the changes in tactics, and not the changing composition of groups.

The Timing of Mobilization

Another strategic choice interest groups must make is *when* to mobilize. Liberal groups, for example, famously mobilized against Robert Bork immediately after his nomination, rather than waiting to lobby closer to the Senate's vote.[16] For each activity mentioned in the newspaper data, we coded the date of the activity during the nominee's timeline, dividing activities into three periods: before, during, or after the Judiciary Committee hearings on the nominee.

Figure 5.6 depicts the timing of mobilization in two ways. The top panel breaks down mobilization for each nominee; in each stacked bar, the darker portion depicts the proportion of mobilization that occurred in the pre-hearing period; the middle gray bar depicts mobilization during the hearing; and the lighter bar shows mobilization after the hearing. The bottom panel aggregates the data by grouping mobilization into the three eras and displaying the distribution of timing within each era.

Figure 5.6 shows that until recently, the timing of mobilization occurred fairly evenly across the nomination period. In some cases, such as the controversial nomination of Fortas to become chief justice in 1968, most of the mobilization occurred during the hearings. In others, such as the Haynsworth nomination, mobilization occurred after the hearing. However, a very different picture emerges in more recent nominations. Beginning with the nomination of Justice O'Connor in 1981, the bulk of mobilization occurred *prior* to the hearing. In the 1987–2020 period, 74% of mobilization occurred before the hearing, compared to 44% in the earlier two periods. This pattern reflects the emergence of full-blown nomination campaigns, with interest groups ready to mobilize right off the bat.

Summary of Tactics and Timing

We suspect that these shifts in tactics and timing reflect larger shifts in confirmation politics. During the early era, confirmation hearings were important opportunities for senators to learn about the nominee and either form or solidify their views. Accordingly, the interest groups mobilized primarily around the hearing itself as the principal venue to lobby Congress and spread the groups' messages. As the battles over Supreme Court nominations became more ideologically charged, the hearings transformed into staged performances featuring legalistic "gotcha" questions and bland or even evasive answers, with senators posturing for their constituents. Absent a scandal or some noteworthy revelations about the nominee, the hearings provided scant edification for anyone.[17] Indeed, the new groups that entered politics during the

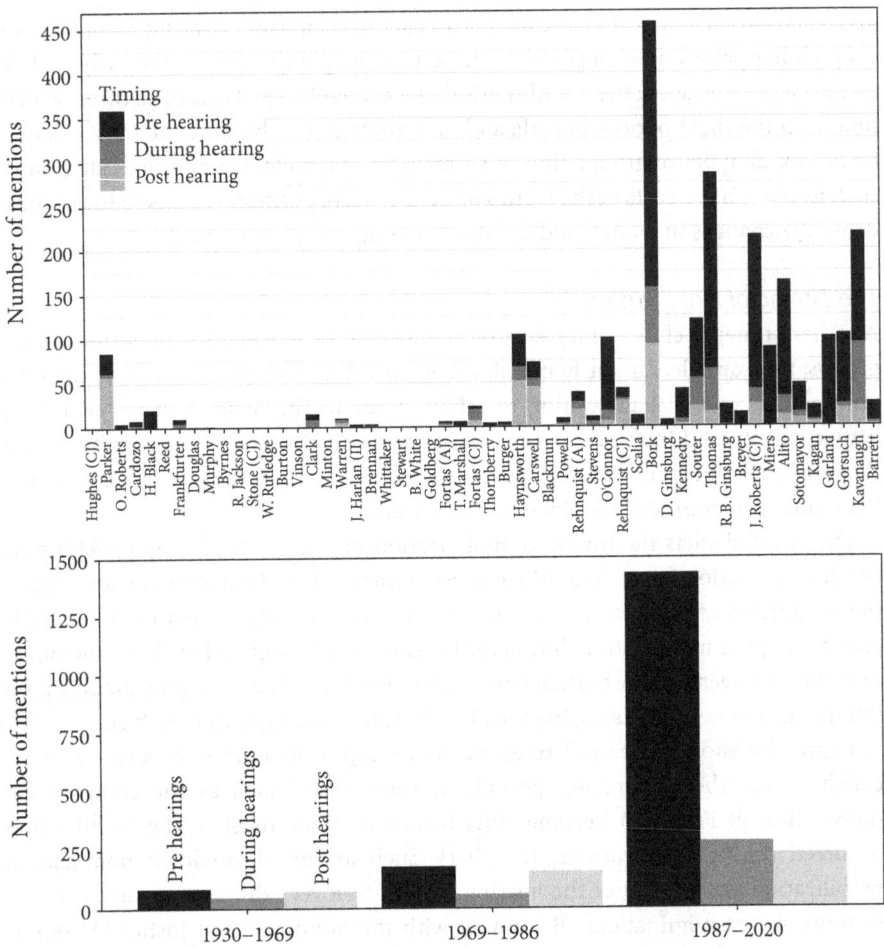

Fig. 5.6 Changes in the within-nomination timing of interest group mobilization over time. The top panel breaks down mobilization for each nominee. For each stacked bar, the darker portion depicts the proportion of mobilization that occurred in the pre-hearing period; the middle gray bar mobilization during the hearing; and the lighter bar mobilization after the hearing. The bottom panel groups mobilization into the three eras and displaying the distribution of timing within each era.

1970s, and then became engaged in nomination politics, took a different approach than their predecessors. They began to treat nominations as political campaigns, waged from the moment a vacancy emerged on the court. The hearings remained a centerpiece for the campaign, but the bulk of the action occurred in the run-up to that increasingly kabuki-like political theater. Thus, in the modern era interest group mobilization occurred earlier and revolved around framing the nominee through calculated messaging disseminated in the popular press.

5.3 Eras of Formation and Activation

The mobilization and participation data indicate a massive increase in interest group activity over time, with a changing cast of characters. While useful, we can go much farther and map out exactly when groups came into existence and when they began to participate in nominations. Did the same groups just participate more (or less) over time, was there a slow and steady accretion of groups, or were there distinct waves of formation and activation into nominations politics? In answering these questions, and for the rest of the chapter, we turn our attention to the repeat mobilizers. By definition, one-shotters' interest in nomination politics is ephemeral, whereas the repeat mobilizers are the groups sufficiently invested to participate in at least two nominations (and often many more).

5.3.1 Birth Years

To help understand the formation of these groups, for each repeat player, we collected the "birth year" of the organization—the year in which it was founded.[18] Figure 5.7A depicts a histogram of these birth years, and shows that a small number of participating groups began in the nineteenth century, including the National Education Association, the National Rifle Association, the American Bar Association, the AFL, and the Anti-Saloon League. But these groups are the rare exception; most were created later. In fact, from 1930 until 1970, the count of groups created each decade varied from one to five. However, the number of new groups exploded in the 1970s, reaching some 31. In fact, the count of group births in that one decade exceeds the total count in the preceding four decades. Following the 1970s, and through the 2000s, the number of new groups leveled off, with around eight new groups per decade, on average. Finally, the 2010s only saw the emergence of two new groups who would become repeat mobilizers.

Figures 5.7B and 5.7C show the birth years of liberal and conservative groups, respectively (using the same basic coding we used for Figure 5.2B). Comparing the two figures show that more liberal groups formed earlier; only 14 conservative groups formed before 1970, compared to 34 liberal groups. However, while the number of both types of groups increased in the 1970s, conservative groups in particular skyrocketed, with 17 new groups in that decade, compared to 12 new liberal groups. Thus, as we saw with mobilization, the formation of conservative groups who would eventually participate in nomination politics lagged behind liberal groups. But the conservative groups eventually caught up in numbers and achieved parity with their liberal counterparts.

5.3.2 Activation Years

While the birth of mobilizing groups is important to document, a related but distinct phenomenon is each group's "activation date"—the year of the nomination in which

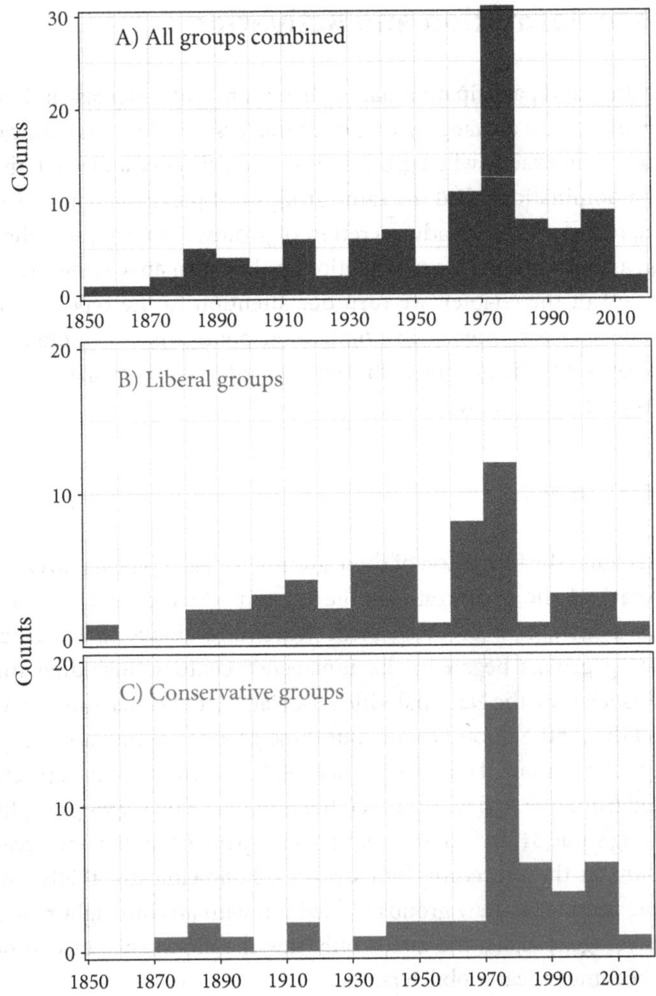

Fig. 5.7 The distribution of birth years for A) all groups combined; B) liberal groups; and C) conservative groups.

they first mobilized. Figure 5.8 depicts the distribution of activation dates; this differs somewhat from the distribution of birth years seen in Figure 5.7. In particular, Figure 5.8 indicates three activation decades—the 1960s, the 1980s, and the 2000s—in which many groups began their participation in Supreme Court nominations. By far the largest of these was the 1980s, followed by the 2000s and the 1960s.

What explains this discrepancy between birth years and activation years? In essence, potential participating groups accumulate over time as new groups form. But many of these groups do not participate immediately in Supreme Court nominations. Instead, a large accumulation of groups suddenly jump into nomination politics in specific periods.

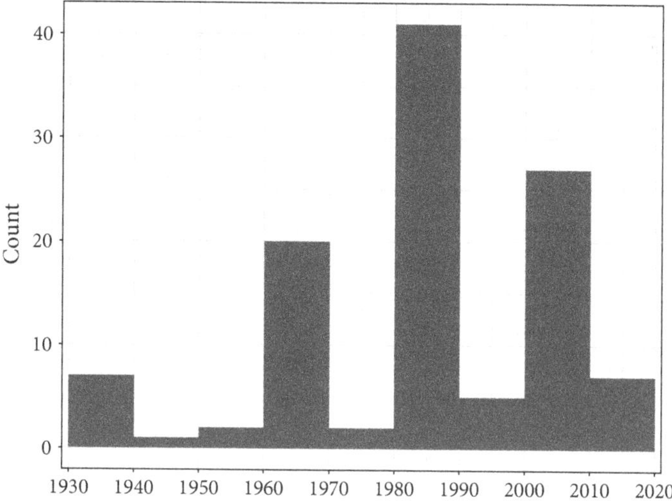

Fig. 5.8 The distribution of "activation" years—the year of first mobilization—for all repeat mobilizing groups.

We can identify the historically important "attractor" or initiating nominations that provoked a significant amount of activation. In descending order, the top attractor nominations were the Bork nomination of 1987, the Haynsworth/Carswell nominations of 1969 and 1970 (combining the two fast-paced events into one episode), and the Roberts/Miers/Alito nominations of 2005, again treating these as a single event. The Bork nomination brought into play primarily liberal groups, those created in the 1970s wave. The Haynsworth/Carswell event mobilized the liberal groups that had slowly accumulated over a period of decades. But the Roberts-Miers-Alito event brought onto the scene many conservative groups, mobilized to support the nominees. These included many groups created in the conservative wave of the 1980s.

5.3.3 Gestation

Next, if we put the birth years and activation years together, we can examine each group's "gestation period"—the interval between a group's birth and its activation date. Figure 5.9 displays the variation in gestation periods. The x-axis in the figure captures time.[19] The groups themselves are listed on the y-axis, in chronological order of formation; we list every other group to make the names more legible. For each group, the blue lines indicate the years in which the group was in existence (i.e. from birth to either 2020 or the year a group "died"). The triangles on the group timelines indicate the years of nominations in which the group mobilized. Finally, the three vertical lines indicate the nomination years that sparked the most activation: Haynsworth and Carswell (1969), Bork (1987), and Roberts-Miers-Alito (2005).

Figure 5.9 reveals many groups whose gestation period was brief; this can be seen comparing the distance between the beginning of the group's timeline and the left-most triangle on the timeline. These groups presumably were formed for nominations activism—e.g. Judicial Confirmation Network and the Alliance for Justice—while others saw this activity as an important part of their organizational mission; e.g. the National Women's Political Caucus and the National Organization of Women.

Figure 5.9 also reveals extremely long gestation periods for some groups. For example, the National Urban League, an African-American civil rights group, formed in 1910 but entered nominations politics only with the Marshall nomination in 1967. The American Federation of State, County and Municipal Employees (AFSCE), the largest public sector union in the United States, formed in 1932 but entered nomination politics only at the Bork nomination in 1987. Finally, the American

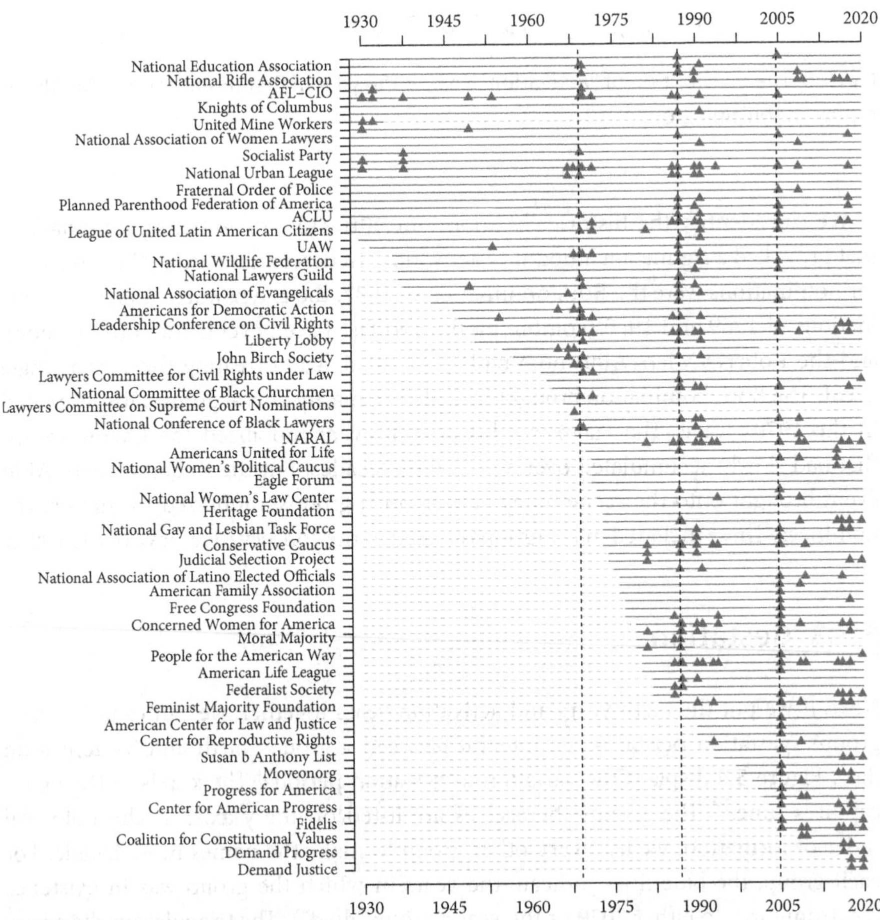

Fig. 5.9 The timeline of interest group formation and participation among repeat mobilizers. The blue lines indicate the years in which the group was in existence, while the red triangles depict nomination years in which a group mobilized.

Conservative Union formed in 1964 but sat out nomination politics until it answered the Reagan Administration's call-to-arms over the Bork nomination in 1987.[20]

5.3.4 Activation by Judicial Lobbyists versus Non-lobbyists

The variation in gestation periods suggests that groups choose to enter nomination politics for a variety of reasons. Explaining when groups undertake a new activity like Supreme Court appointment politics could be the subject of its own book. But we can use data from amicus briefs to conduct a simple analysis and classify mobilization groups based on their orientation with respect to the courts. Recall from Chapter 1 that amicus briefs are memos filed by interest groups with the Supreme Court that seek to persuade the justices to vote in the groups' preferred directions. Hansford, Depaoli, and Canelo (2021) collected data on amicus briefs filed with the Supreme Court between the 1953 and 2013 terms. They then estimated ideal points for every group that signed on to at least 10 briefs in that interval. We will examine these ideal points shortly, but for now denote these groups "amicus groups"—akin to our repeat mobilizers, they are groups that have been relatively active in trying to lobby the court via amicus briefs. We then merged our data with theirs to determine which mobilizer groups were frequent amici and which were not. If a repeat mobilizer who was also an amicus group filed an amicus brief *concurrently or before* it first mobilized on a Supreme Court nomination, we label the group "judicially oriented" at its activation—in other words, such groups chose to lobby the court directly before turning to nomination politics. In contrast, we label repeat mobilizers who had not filed an amicus brief at the time of their first nomination mobilization as "non-judicially oriented."

Using this classification, we find that 51 (or 46%) of the repeat mobilizers were judicially oriented groups at the time of their activation into appointment politics. However, this simple percentage masks a dramatic difference between the two types of groups. Consider all the amicus groups in the Hansford data as the universe of potential judicially oriented mobilizers. Of the roughly 550 such groups, 41 eventually became repeat mobilizers, or about 74 groups per 1,000. While this rate might seem absolutely low, it reflects the fact many groups who lobby the court on highly specific cases—e.g. business groups—choose not to enter into nomination politics. However, as a point of comparison, define the potential universe of all non-judicially oriented groups as all the groups ever listed in the Washington Representatives Study; this is about 40,000 groups.[21] Now consider the 57 repeat mobilizers who entered nomination politics as non-judicially oriented. While in absolute terms, this number is slightly higher than the number of judicially oriented groups (51), in proportional terms, the rate of potential non-judicially oriented groups becoming mobilizing groups is only about 57/45000, or 1.2 groups per 1,000. In other words, *the rate of entry into nomination politics by judicially oriented groups was about 60 times higher than that for non-judicially oriented groups.*

It is perhaps not surprising that groups with such a substantial interest in Supreme Court policy that they frequently lobbied the court were far more likely to become repeat mobilizers than groups without such an interest. Still, the relative magnitudes are remarkable. For the judicially oriented mobilizers, a major part of their story can be summarized as, "we came to lobby the Supreme Court, but stayed to fight over its composition."

5.4 Ideology, Ideological Polarization, and Mobilization

Our final set of analyses examine the role of ideology—both for interest groups and nominees—in predicting mobilization. As discussed above, Hansford, Depaoli, and Canelo (2021) developed ideal points for repeat amicus groups. After merging our data of repeat mobilizers with theirs, we created ideal points for all the repeat mobilizing groups. To estimate scores for the groups who do not overlap—i.e. groups who are repeat mobilizers but not frequent participants in lobbying the court—we use the DIME scores based on campaign contributions to connect the groups across the two datasets.[22] We can thus place all repeat mobilizer groups in the Hansford et al. amici ideological space; in addition, Hansford et al. estimated ideal points for justices in this same space, which allows for comparison between the ideology of justices and groups.

Figure 5.10 displays the distribution of ideological scores for all the repeat mobilizers. The bottom rug shows the individual estimates for each group, while the blue density line summarizes the distribution. We label a few well-known groups for reference. The top rug depicts the estimated ideal points of the justices; we also label a few justices for reference.

The most important takeaway from Figure 5.10 is that the repeat mobilizers were highly polarized. The distribution of ideal points has two modes, one on the left and one on the right. The left mode occurs at an ideological point somewhat to the left of the NAACP and well to the left of any justice serving between 1952 and 2013, except the extremely liberal William Douglas. The mode on the right occurs at about the ideological position of Justice Antonin Scalia, and is just slightly less conservative than the very conservative Judicial Confirmation Network. In short, not only are the two distinctive groups of mobilizers quite far from each other, they are very liberal and very conservative.

As a consequence, moderate groups were few and far between. Although the zero mark on the scale has no special meaning, examination of the lower rug shows a dearth of groups more conservative than the AFL-CIO and less conservative than the Log Cabin Republicans, a moderately conservative group dedicated to advancing LGBT-rights. This portion of the ideological space is about the range that includes Justices Sotomayor, Kagan, Breyer, and O'Connor.

Finally, the distribution has a very long left-hand tail. The left-hand mode occurs at about the ideology of the NAACP but it extends quite far left, including groups well

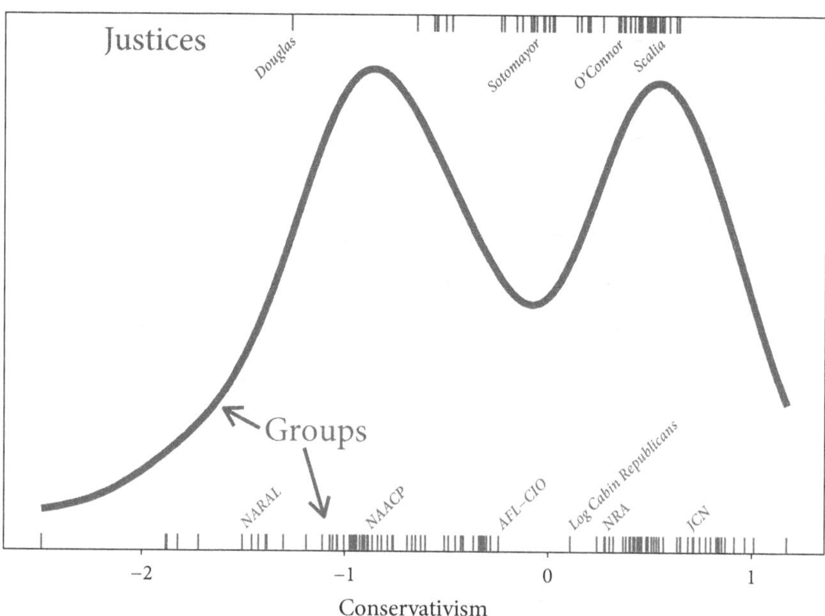

Fig. 5.10 The distribution of ideology of repeat players. The bottom rug and density plot summarize the ideology of the repeat mobilizers; the top rug depicts the ideology of the justices for reference.

to the left of NARAL. The right side of the distribution does not include such a group of ultra-extreme conservatives. Although such groups exist, apparently they declined to participate in nomination politics.

5.4.1 Predicting Mobilization

With the ideal point estimates of the repeat players in hand, for our final analysis in the chapter we statistically model when groups choose to mobilize on Supreme Court nominees. To do so, we leverage the theoretical foundation laid by studies of roll call voting on Supreme Court nominees, in particular the model developed in Cameron, Cover, and Segal (1990). That model, as well as much subsequent work shows that senators are more likely to oppose nominees who are more ideologically distant, as well as those lacking in legal qualifications, or "quality."[23] We use these variables to uncover whether interest group mobilization displays similar tendencies.

To understand the relationship between ideology, nominee quality, and mobilization, we conducted a regression analysis in which the dependent variable is whether a repeat player mobilized for a given nomination or not.[24] For distance, we combine the Hansford scores with the NSP scores of nominees (discussed in Chapter 4) to create an estimate of how far each group is from a nominee; we also allow the predictive

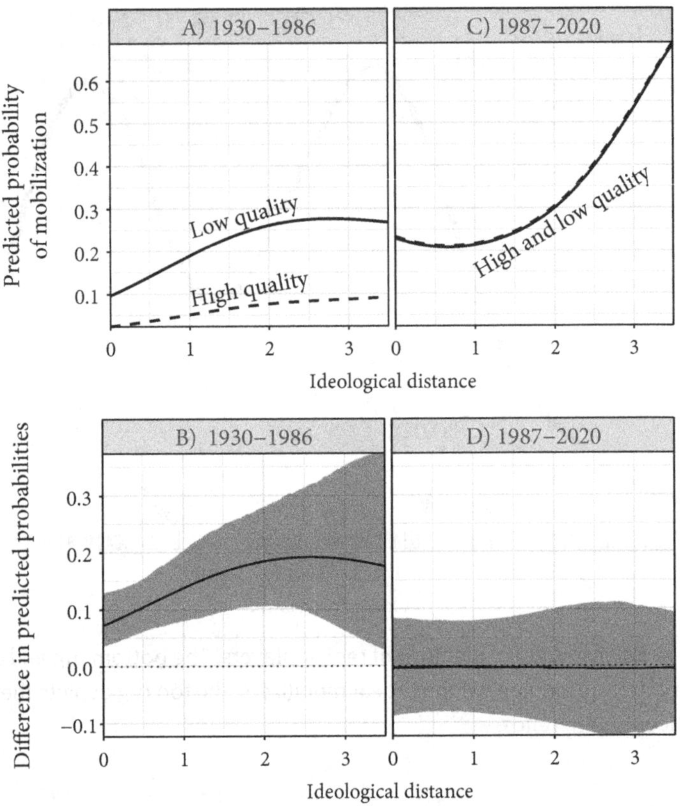

Fig. 5.11 Predicted mobilization as a function of ideological distance between nominees and groups and nominee quality, before and after the 1987 nomination of Robert Bork. Panels A and C shows the predicted probability of mobilization as distance and quality vary, while Panels B and D show the difference between the two lines in the respective top plots; the shaded areas depict 95% confidence intervals. Quality had a significant predictive effect in the early period, but not late.

effect of distance to be non-linear by including squared distance as well. For quality, we use a standard measure based on content analysis of newspaper editorials.[25] The measure mixes perceptions of the nominee's qualifications and adverse shocks from scandals. Finally, to allow for possible changes in the calculus of group mobilization over time, we allow the predictive effect of distance and quality to vary before and after the watershed nomination of Robert Bork in 1987.

Figure 5.11 depicts the predicted probability of mobilization as distance and quality varies, in both the pre- and post-Bork period (with Bork included in the latter); these are based on simulations of the regression models shown in the Appendix. We allow distance to vary continuously; for quality, we dichotomize the predictions across "low" and "high" levels of quality.[26] Figure 5.11A shows the predicted probability of mobilization in the pre-Bork era; two patterns stands out. First, the relationship between distance and mobilization is somewhat modest, particularly for high-quality nominees—the likelihood of mobilization does increase as the distance between a group and the nominee increases, but even for very distant nominees, the predicted probability of mobilization is always less than 30%. In contrast, there is clear difference for quality; lower-quality nominees are much more likely to be accompanied by mobilization, at any level of ideological distance. Figure 5.11B depicts the difference between the high- and low-quality predictions, along with the 95% confidence interval of the difference, which is always statistically larger than zero.

The post-Bork column in Figure 5.11 tells precisely the opposite story. In the post-Bork period, there is a strong and substantively large relationship between ideological distance, as seen in Figure 5.11C. Moving from the smallest distance to the greatest distance predicts an increase in mobilization from a predicted probability of about .2 to above .6. In contrast, changes in nominee quality have no predictive effect in the later period; the two lines are nearly on top of one another; as a result the differences in Figure 5.11D are never different from zero. Finally, note that the intercept was much higher in the later period, consistent with the aggregate data presented earlier in the chapter. For any nominee, no matter their ideology or quality levels, the predicted probability of mobilization was always greater in the later period than in the earlier period.

These models are sparse, and so the conclusions we draw from them must be tentative. Nevertheless, the regression results, combined with the data on the changes in tactics, suggest that prior to the mid-1980s, groups seemingly mobilized *opportunistically*: intense mobilization occurred only when opponents could exploit an adverse shock to the nominee's perceived quality, for example, in response to a scandal. As time went on, perceived nominee quality diminished in importance, but a nominee's ideological extremity became an increasingly important predictor of mobilization.

5.5 Conclusion

The intense involvement of interest groups in contemporary Supreme Court nominations is strikingly obvious even to casual observers. The data in this chapter show that this intensity is a relatively recent development and takes very different forms than before. The interest groups changed from a small number—primarily liberal groups—infrequently mobilizing, to a diverse array of liberal and conservative groups often mobilizing. In earlier periods, the few mobilizers used somewhat restrained inside-oriented tactics, focused on the hearings. In the modern era, the mobilizers—often identity politics and public interest groups—employ outside tactics and grassroots activity amounting to a political campaign. In addition, the universe of repeat players is both highly ideologically polarized and quite ideologically extreme. In contrast, few ideologically moderate groups participate.

Although we have focused on interest group involvement in Supreme Court appointments, similar patterns are evident in lower court appointments as well. In the Appendix, we review several creative and insightful studies of this venue. Broadly speaking, the same increase in group involvement took place, as well as the shift from inside to outside tactics, with greater involvement by identity and public-interest groups. However, the failure of a lower court appointment typically results from delay rather than outright rejection. One sees similar patterns in group involvement in appointments to politically sensitive independent agencies, including the Federal Elections Commission and the National Labor Relations Board.

The sea change in group participation in Supreme Court nominations is important in its own right, but it also stands as a case study in American interest group politics more generally. In particular, the portrait of interest group involvement in appointment politics from 1930 to the mid-1960s illustrates a world of *pluralism*. This political theory was the central organizing framework for several generations of scholars, leading lights of their day such as Robert Dahl, V. O. Key, David Truman, Pendleton Herring, and E. E. Schattschneider. The essential idea was that a relatively small number of organized interests—farmers, labor, business, consumers—would play a somewhat restrained tug-of-war over public policy. The result would reflect the respective strengths of the groups but would often approximate a relatively consensus notion of the public interest. In contrast, the new world of interest groups and appointment politics is textbook pluralism on steroids—many more groups, tougher tactics, ideologically polarized, and sometimes leading to winner-take-all outcomes. This kind of politics demands a new appellation: *hyper-pluralism*.

Some evidence suggests hyper-pluralism characterizes a great deal of contemporary American government, modified somewhat across policy domains but recognizably the same phenomenon. For example, case studies of major congressional legislation, like the Affordable Care Act or the Dodd-Frank banking legislation, show a scale and scope of interest group involvement that might have shocked the classical pluralists of the 1950s and early 1960s.[27] In Chapter 1, we alluded to the explosion in Supreme Court lobbying via amicus briefs. Regulations and major acts of the administrative state also routinely attract jaw-dropping levels of interest group mobilization.[28] Organized interests routinely maneuver behind the scenes to select candidates for House races.[29]

In the concluding chapter, we further discuss the implications of the emergence of hyper-pluralism for both understanding the new politics of Supreme Court nominations and American politics more broadly. But our immediate task in the next three chapters is to trace the immediate downstream impact of hyper-pluralism in Supreme Court appointments. We examine first the media (Chapter 6), then public opinion (Chapter 7), and finally voting in the Senate (Chapter 8). The latter half of the book explores the logic and consequences of a politics in which the engaged are relatively extreme and the political elites who care deeply about the Supreme Court are highly polarized.

6
The Media

Co-authored with Leeann Bass and Julian Dean

On June 27, 1991, Justice Thurgood Marshall announced his retirement from the Supreme Court. Marshall, the legendary civil rights lawyer and the first African-American justice, presumably would have preferred to wait for a Democratic president to appoint his successor. Declining health, however, led him to leave office during President George H.W. Bush's tenure.[1]

Marshall's retirement gave Bush the opportunity to make his second appointment in as many years. As we discussed in Chapter 3, Bush and his selection team focused their search on minority candidates to replace the trailblazing Marshall, ultimately settling on Clarence Thomas, an African-American. Thomas' main career experience had been heading the Equal Employment Opportunity Commission in the 1980s, before Bush appointed him to the D.C. Circuit Court of Appeals in 1990. Thomas' scant judicial experience, combined with his solidly conservative views, promised a somewhat rocky path to confirmation in the Democratic-controlled Senate. Indeed, the Senate Judiciary Committee split 7-7 on his nomination, which sent it to the Senate floor without a recommendation. Nevertheless, Thomas' confirmation seemed fairly certain as of early October, with several Democratic senators pledging their support.[2]

Things changed dramatically on October 6 when Nina Totenberg, the Supreme Court reporter for National Public Radio, broke the news that Anita Hill, a former employee of Thomas, had accused him of sexual harassment. The revelation transformed Thomas' nomination into a full-fledged donnybrook. The Judiciary Committee held a second round of hearings, with an estimated 20 million Americans watching, in which Hill and Thomas give competing accounts of their actions and Thomas denied Hill's graphic accounts of sexual harassment.[3] Ultimately, the Senate confirmed Thomas by a vote of 52-48, the smallest margin of victory for a Supreme Court nominee in more than 100 years. This modern-day record would hold until 2018, when Brett Kavanaugh was confirmed by a two-vote margin under eerily similar circumstances—an allegation of sexual misconduct followed by extremely high-profile hearings in which he and his accuser (Christine Blasey Ford) offered diametrically opposed accounts.

While the Thomas and Kavanaugh nominations are outliers in the extent of their public attention, they nevertheless illustrate the broader shift in Supreme Court nominations from largely "private" affairs in which most key events were conducted

Making the Supreme Court: The Politics of Appointments, 1930–2020. Charles M. Cameron and Jonathan P. Kastellec, Oxford University Press. © Oxford University Press 2023. DOI: 10.1093/oso/9780197680544.003.0006

behind closed doors to highly public affairs in which nominations play out before the eyes of the American people. For example, whereas Senate Judiciary Hearings had not been previously televised, today they are made-for-TV events in which senators from the president's party seek to bolster nominees, while senators from the out-party attack them.[4] In this chapter we examine changes over time in the key institution publicizing these events: the media.

To study these changes, we present an extensive longitudinal analysis of media coverage of Supreme Court nominees, situating this analysis within changes in media coverage of politics more generally. Whereas in 1930 the media environment consisted largely of regionally focused newspapers, today countless media sources—from nationally distributed newspapers to both broadcast and cable television channels to Internet-based social media platforms and news sites—cover American politics and Supreme Court nominations. The effect of these changes in the media landscape on American politics more broadly has been well documented.[5] In particular, while Americans used to share the same sources of news coverage, the fragmentation of the overall media market in recent decades means that partisan messages are much more available to citizens, should they seek them out; this shift has significant implications for political knowledge, public opinion, political expression, and popular engagement.[6]

To study changes in media coverage of nominees, we collected original data of newspaper reporting (i.e. "hard news"), broadcast television coverage, and cable television coverage about every nominee from 1930 to 2020, as well as an original database of editorials on these nominees from 13 newspapers. Using these new measures, we assess how both the quantity and tone of coverage has changed over time.[7] In line with our findings in earlier chapters, we find substantial differences over time with respect to media coverage of nominees. Most nominations between 1930 and 1960 received very little media attention. Hard news coverage of a nominee tended to focus on the nominee's background/biography, judicial philosophy, and sometimes economic issues. Occasionally a scandal or nominee controversy attracted media attention.[8] Newspaper editorials—the views of media elites—generally supported nominees or deferred to the president, and outright opposition was rare. Importantly, these editorials evaluated nominees primarily on their qualifications, not their ideologies.

Beginning in the 1960s, the Court became more involved in social issues, reflecting broader shifts in the national political agenda.[9] The duration of nominations increased, and the volume of media coverage increased concomitantly. Public hearings before the Senate Judiciary Committee became standard, providing focal points for each nomination.[10] Hard news coverage shifted toward contentious social issues like civil rights, the death penalty, and abortion. When a scandal occurred, the media significantly increased their coverage of that nominee. Elite media opinion increasingly polarized along ideological lines over time, editorials focused more on a nominee's ideology than on legal qualifications for the Court. Finally, the rise of cable news meant that members of the viewing public who were interested in partisan messages on nominees could readily find them on Fox News or MSNBC. All in all, the sleepy nominations of yesteryear have transformed into all-out, high stakes political fights—in the modern era, the confirmation will be televised.

6.2 Newspaper and Television Coverage of Nominations

To study media coverage over 90 years, we collected a wealth of new data on national newspapers, broadcast television, and cable television. We chose these media because they are the most widely consumed sources of news in the United States over the time period studied. Despite newspaper industry turmoil in recent decades, nationally distributed newspapers remain widely read, either in print or online, and provide much original reporting.[11] Similarly, television remains Americans' foremost source of news, despite the rise of the Internet and social media as news sources.[12] And even though broadcast television newscasts have lost viewership in recent years, the broadcast news audience still exceeds that of cable.[13] Cable news, however, is consumed by those most interested in and attentive to politics, providing highly visible and accessible forums for ideologically based coverage.[14] Given data availability, we can document the volume and content of news from these three types of news sources for relatively long time series: 1930 to 2020 for newspapers, 1969 to 2020 for broadcast television, and 1990 to 2020 for cable television.

Newspapers

We collected the universe of straight news reporting from the *Los Angeles Times* and the *New York Times* on each nominee. To account for newspapers' one-day lag in coverage of events, we define the nomination period as spanning from the announcement of the nominee until the day after the nomination ended (via a confirmation vote in the Senate, withdrawal, or expiration). In addition, for each paper, we excluded editorials and op-eds (we return to editorials below). All told, the data include 3,881 newspaper articles on nominees.

Broadcast Television

We collected ABC, CBS, and NBC news and special events coverage (including televised announcements of Supreme Court nominations) starting with Clement Haynsworth's nomination in 1969 (the first year in which broadcast data is available). We obtained the number of broadcast telecasts mentioning each nominee from 1969 to the 1980s from the Vanderbilt Television News Archive. Beginning with the 1980s, full-text transcripts of news and special events coverage are available from LexisNexis and Factiva (starting with Sandra Day O'Connor's nomination in 1981 for ABC, and David Souter's nomination in 1990 for CBS and NBC). All told, the data include 1,139 broadcast telecasts on nominees.

Cable Television

CNN was the first cable news channel, founded in 1980, with Fox News and MSNBC following in 1996. Data on CNN coverage is available after 1990—we collected transcripts of CNN shows mentioning the nominations of Clarence Thomas, Ruth Bader Ginsburg, and Stephen Breyer, and added Fox News and MSNBC transcripts starting with John Roberts in 2005.[15] All told, the data include 2,313 cable telecasts on nominees.[16]

6.2.1 Frequency of Coverage over Time

We begin our analysis with a straightforward question: how has the frequency of coverage changed over time? Figure 6.1 depicts the number of articles written or telecasts aired, per nominee. Figure 6.1A shows that prior to Abe Fortas' nomination to be chief justice in 1968, nominations generally received little overall newspaper coverage. The first 26 nominations in our study averaged only about 21 articles per

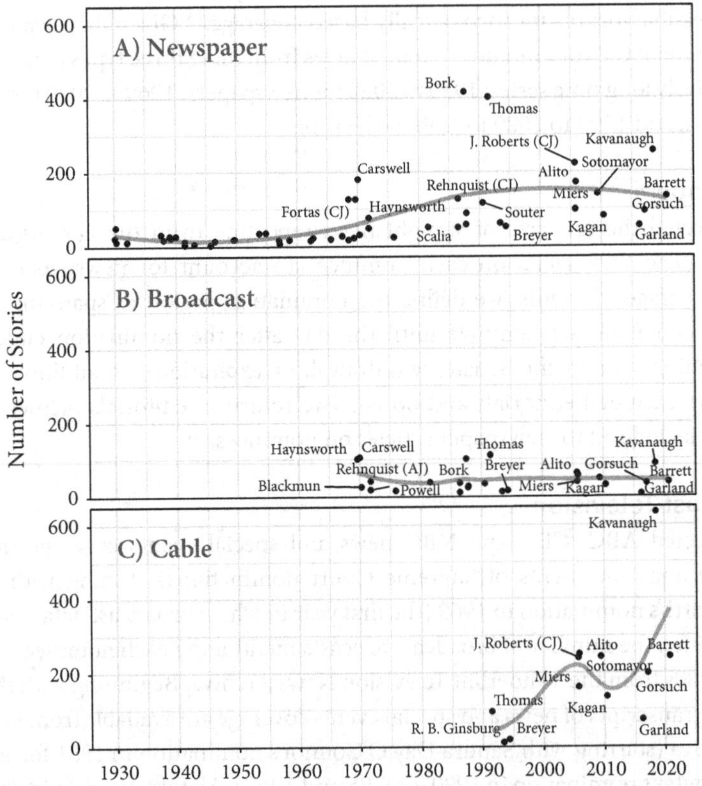

Fig. 6.1 Media coverage by nominee and type of news source. The graphs plot the number of articles or telecasts per nominee. The blue lines are loess lines.

nomination. Those nominees above one standard deviation of the mean either faced controversy (John Parker, Hugo Black) or were recess appointments (Earl Warren and John Harlan). In contrast, after 1968, the *New York Times* and *Los Angeles Times* published an average of 120 articles per nomination. The only nominees above one standard deviation of the mean were Robert Bork, who was defeated in 1987 after a lengthy battle in the Senate, John Roberts, who was nominated to Chief Justice after a period of 11 years without a nomination to the Court, and Clarence Thomas and Brett Kavanaugh, both of whom were accused during the confirmation process of past sexual misconduct.

Turning to television coverage, Figure 6.1B shows that the average number of broadcast telecasts from 1969 to 2020 was 46, with no clear trends over time. Again Haynsworth, Carswell, Bork, Thomas, and Kavanaugh received higher amounts of coverage. Finally, Figure 6.1C examines cable coverage and shows that CNN provided far more coverage to Thomas (96 telecasts) than to Ruth Bader Ginsburg and Stephen Breyer combined (12 and 20 telecasts, respectively). For the period in which all three cable channels existed, the average number of telecasts was 243. Kavanaugh's nomination received the most coverage by far (635 telecasts), followed by Sotomayor (243 telecasts), Alito (251 telecasts), and John Roberts (241 telecasts).

Overall, Figure 6.1 reveals a secular growth in media coverage, though considerable heterogeneity across nominees exists, and, not surprisingly, higher salience nominees attracted more coverage. However, Figure 6.1 does not account for the fact that the average *duration* of Supreme Court nominations increased over time.[17] Longer durations, of course, allow for more total media coverage, all things equal. Table 6.1 provides the average length of nomination periods across time. We divide the data into three eras: (1) 1930 to 1954, before public Judiciary Committee hearings were standard practice for every nominee; (2) 1955 to 1980, in which there were public, but non-televised, hearings for all nominees; and (3) 1981 to 2020, the "modern era" of nominations, with all hearings televised. In the middle period, nominations lasted an average of 63 days, or about nine weeks (this drops to seven weeks if we exclude the recess appointments of Harlan, Stewart, and Brennan). For the third

Table 6.1 Mean length of nominations in days, by period. The last column depicts nominees excluded for the respective calculations because they are outliers (in either direction); see text for more details.

	All nominees	Excluding nominees	Excluded nominees
Pre-mandatory hearings (1930–1954)	22 (3 weeks)	15 (2 weeks)	Warren
Hearings for all nominees (1955–1980)	63 (9 weeks)	48 (7 weeks)	Harlan, Stewart, Brennan
Televised hearings (1981–2020)	85 (12 weeks)	80 (11 weeks)	D. Ginsburg, Miers, Garland

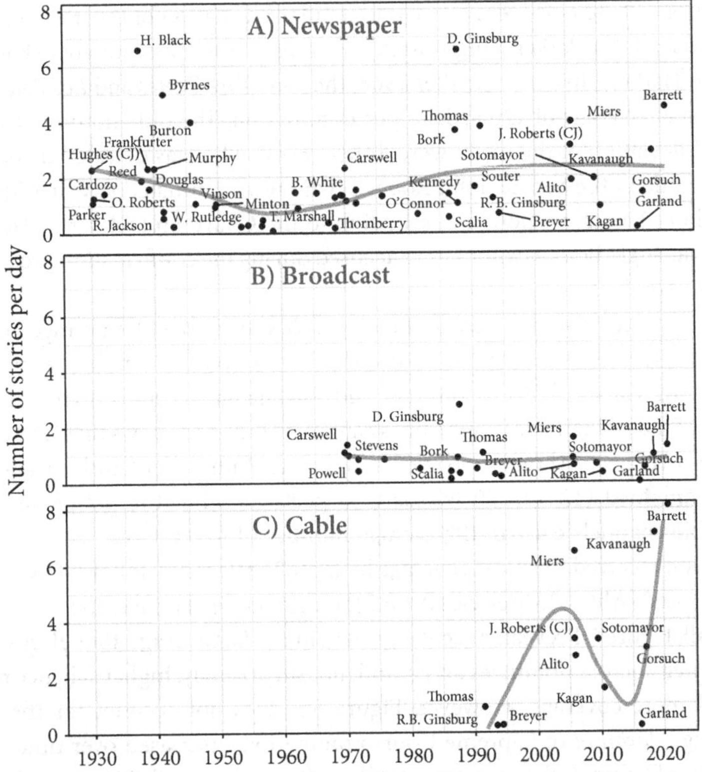

Fig. 6.2 Total number of news stories for each nominee, divided by number of days in the nomination period.

period, nominations lasted an average of 85 days, or approximately 12 weeks (the very short nomination durations of Douglas Ginsburg and Miers, who withdrew after nine and 25 days, respectively, are cancelled out by the nine-months-long nomination of Merrick Garland in 2016).

Figure 6.2 presents the number of stories *per day* for each nomination. The number of newspaper stories per day was relatively high early on due to the short length of nominations (for example, Black, Byrnes, and Burton were all confirmed very quickly). As the length of nominations began to increase, the number of stories per day decreased. This trend remained relatively stable through the Bork nomination in 1987, when the number of stories per day increased. Indeed, the recent growth in stories per day demonstrates the transformation of Supreme Court nominations into sustained media events. Whereas in the early period both the *New York Times* and the *Los Angeles Times* might run, on average, one story combined about a nominee every other day for two or three weeks, more recently each paper published an average of about one story each, per day. Moreover, the longer durations of nominations in the modern period means that this coverage is more sustained, reflecting the importance of nominations on the national political agenda in recent years.

Turning to television, per-day broadcast television coverage of nominations has remained relatively stable since 1969. On average, the three networks combined have aired less than one telecast per day between them that mentioned a nominee during this time (Douglas Ginsburg and Harriet Miers are the exceptions, both of whom had very short nomination periods before withdrawing). Finally, average levels of modern cable television coverage have consistently exceeded the broadcast rate, with Miers, Kavanaugh, and Barrett receiving particularly high rates of coverage.

6.2.2 The Structure of Coverage

Supreme Court nominations—especially in the modern period—typically follow a carefully choreographed sequence of events. As such, the media has a template to follow for each new nomination. For television news, the announcement of the nominee and the Judiciary Committee hearings provide key visuals and soundbites of the nominee. Although newspapers are not as constrained by the need for visuals, key events in each nomination often provide new developments on which to report.

Figure 6.3 illustrates the coverage "rhythm" of a typical nomination. For each nominee, we calculated the weekly number of stories (combining print, broadcast, and cable). To account for differences in total coverage across nominees, we normalize these weekly counts by dividing by the total number of stories for each nominee. For visual clarity, we only show the nominees from 1970 onwards (we exclude the very brief nominations of Douglas Ginsburg and Harriet Miers). In addition, we truncate the x-axis at 17 weeks in order to allow for easier comparisons across nominees; this only affects a few nominees with very long nomination periods. Finally, the blue lines indicate the week before the nominee's initial hearing before the Senate Judiciary Committee (if they had one), while the green lines indicate the week before a scandal first emerges (if one does).

The figure displays the typical media pattern. Coverage spikes when the nominee is first announced, drops off for a few weeks, and then picks up again once the hearings begin and/or a scandal emerges. For very controversial nominees (like Thomas and Kavanaugh), coverage remains high through the end of the nomination period.

Another important possible driver of reporting is when the president attempts to influence the volume of coverage of a nominee outside of these scheduled events by "going public" on the nomination—namely making public remarks or speeches about the nominee. We collected data on every presidential public statement on each nominee from 1930 to 2020 during the nomination period.[18] Figure 6.4 depicts the total number of going public presidential sentences delivered on each nominee from 1930 to 2020. Before the 1960s, presidents rarely went public over their Supreme Court nominees. Presidents Johnson and Nixon did go public for some of their nominees (notably Thurgood Marshall, Clement Haynsworth, and Harold Carswell). But the administration of Ronald Reagan marked a watershed, as Reagan

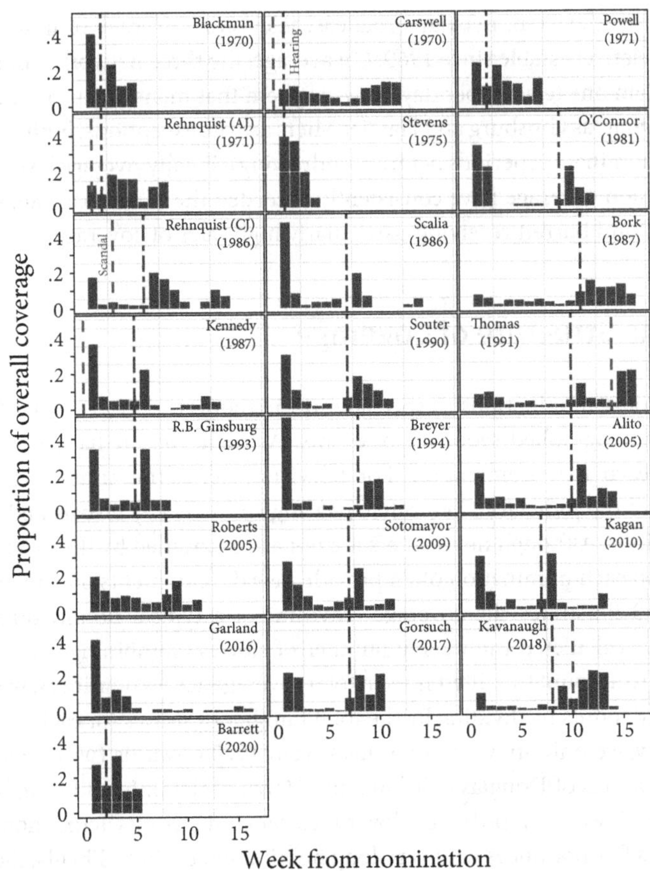

Fig. 6.3 Counts of media coverage, within nominations. The bars present weekly counts of coverage, combining print, broadcast, and cable, as percentage of the total amount of coverage for a given nominee. The x-axis depicts the week of the nomination. The blue lines indicate the week before the nominee's initial hearing before the Senate Judiciary Committee, while the green lines indicate the week before a scandal first emerges.

routinely and vigorously went public in support of his nominees, particularly Robert Bork. Subsequent presidents have followed suit—if not to the extent of the Bork nomination—by going public over their nominees at levels that typically met or exceeded all pre-Reagan efforts. Since Bork, the nominations of Clarence Thomas, Merrick Garland, and Brent Kavanaugh have seen the largest amount of going public by their nominating presidents.

To test the extent to which news coverage follows key events and/or the president's decision to go public, we estimated regressions on the count of stories per day for each type of news source (defined as an article for newspapers and a telecast for broadcast and cable television), the details of which can be found in the Appendix. We

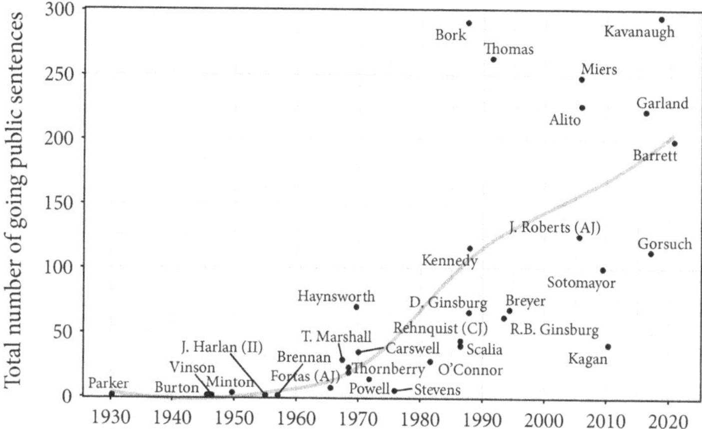

Fig. 6.4 "Going public" on Supreme Court nominees. The points show the total number of sentences made by presidents on each Supreme Court nominee from 1930 to 2020.

found that the announcement of the nominee, hearing days, days when the nominee is voted on by the Senate or withdraws, and the president going public, are all associated with statistically significant increases in coverage. The predictive effect is largest for the announcement, with approximately four to eight more stories being published or broadcast about the announcement compared to a non-announcement day. The results for scandals are somewhat ambiguous, but the emergence of a scandal does seem to shift the salience of a nomination, with the media more likely to publish stories after than before the scandal. All told, we find that the quantity of media coverage follows a well-established pattern and structure, based on the key events in the "lifespan" of a nomination.

6.2.3 Topics of Coverage

While the *quantity* of coverage about Supreme Court nominees is certainly important, we also wish to understand changes in the *quality* of coverage over the past 90 years. We tackle this question in several ways, beginning with an analysis of how the topics discussed during media coverage of Supreme Court nominations changed over time. To do so, we focus solely on newspaper coverage, since it is available over the complete 1930–2020 period.

Top Phrases

We begin with a simple analysis that examines the most frequent words or phrases used in the newspaper coverage (see the Appendix for details). The results are presented in Figure 6.5. The top phrases for each nominee are presented in descending order of frequency. We color code the phrases by category, highlighting economic issues in blue, social issues in purple, and ethical issues/scandal in red.

Hughes (CJ)	Parker	O. Roberts	Cardozo	H. Black	Reed	Frankfurter	Douglas	Murphy	Stone (CJ)
eligible for retirement	yellow dog contract(s)	favorable report	chief judge	majority leader	full committee	judiciary subcmte	rate of change	press conference	exercise of power
property rights	organized labor	full committee	white hair	public hearings	able lawyer	lame duck	business and finance	civil liberties	average age
public service	human rights	oil cases	great judge	court bill	general counsel	committee members	stock exchanges	average age	constitutional interpretation
public utilities	labor union	constitutional amendment	great appointment	full pay	important cases	public hearings	public service	judiciary subcommittee	legislative branches
human rights	public policy	legal qualifications	associate judge	retirement act	gold clause	national committee	government service	automobile plants	own sense
natural resources	floor leader	criminal cases	lawyers and laymen	immediate confirmation	income tax	administrative law	close friend	labor disputes	unconstitutional exercise
economic questions	peaceful persuasion	early confirmation	small thin man	hour bill	lower courts	civil liberties	economic problems	prompt confirmation	associate justices
vested right	roll call	public utilities		mail contracts	distinguished career	law school	cattle train	long robes	only check
common people	administration forces	oil lease cases		labor leaders	better man	full committee	administrative government	great discretion	own exercise
economic views	contract case	dry leaders		conference committee		public utilities	business organization	anti-trust	full membership

R. Jackson	Vinson	Minton	Warren	J. Harlan (II)	Brennan	Whittaker	Stewart	B. White	Goldberg
criminal libel	former law partner	court packing bill	civil rights	public schools	recess appointment	high school	recess appt(s)	attorney general	secretary of labor
yacht basin	news conference	news conference	racial segregation	full bench	investig. of communism	recess appointment	school segregation	law clerk	general counsel
general counsel	majority opinion	executive session	judicial oath	world government	judicial training	law firm	recess judicial appointments	individual rights	labor management
big business	war crimes	administrative assistant	full committee	school segregation	separation of church	judicial training	admiralty law	football player	labor movement
radio broadcast	judicial policy	party man	conference room	special session	public hearing	law school	maritime law	professional football	labor law
voice vote	coal miners		right hand	racial segregation	judicial oath	office boy	judicial oath	high regard	former law partner
judiciary subcommittee	conservative side		free world	full court	matters of law		formal nomination	law practice	organized labor
full membership	close cases		free inquiry	segregation cases	former member		cum laude	intellectual force	labor leaders
	best possible man		free investigation	judicial experience	salem witch hunts		critical questions	corporation law	full committee
	coal case		faithful experiment	lower court	international communism		constitutional oath	character experience	labor secretary

Fortas (AJ)	T. Marshall	Fortas (CJ)	Thornberry	Burger	Haynsworth	Carswell	Blackmun	Powell	Rehnquist (AJ)
law firm(s)	civil rights	news conference	lame duck	law and order	civil rights	civil rights	death penalty	civil rights	civil rights
law enforcement	solicitor general	separation of powers	old friend(s)	strict constructionist	conflict of interest	district judge(s)	civil rights	judicial philosophy	attorney general
criminal law	criminal law	lame duck	separation of powers	criminal law	chief judge	white supremacy	capital punishment	law and order	right wing
press secretary	right thing	law school	poll tax	law school	news conference	news conference	strict constructionist	former president	law clerk
earliest possible moment	right man	civil rights	majority leader	civil rights	judicial ethics	voting rights	civil liberties	blind trust	civil liberties
civil rights	right time	committee chairman	minority leader	code of ethics	ethical standards	recommittal motion	lower court	bar association	judicial philosophy
assistant professor	right place	law and order	committee members	criminal justice	vending machine company	golf club	judicial philosophy	peace forces	law and order
law office	qualified by training	majority leader	committee chairman	family foundation	textile company	country club	net worth	criminal law	legal counsel
government service	self incrimination	minority leader	press conference	adversary system	financial interest	strict constructionist	cases involving companies	legal profession	other nominee
amateur violinist	attorney general	committee members	civil rights	financial reporting	press conference	civil rights lawyers	confirmation hearings	civil liberties	public accommodations

Stevens	O'Connor	Rehnquist (CJ)	Scalia	Bork	D. Ginsburg	Kennedy	Souter	Thomas	R.B. Ginsburg
death penalty	first woman	civil rights	civil rights	civil rights	appeals court	civil rights	confirm. hearing(s)	sexual harassment	appeals court
sex discrimination	confirmation hearings	affirmative action	affirmative action	appeals court	cable television	appeals court	abortion rights	civil rights	abortion rights
law school	equal rights amendmen	confirmation hearings	appeals court	confirmation hearings	drug use	confirmation hearings	civil rights	affirmative action	right to abortion
capital punishment	abortion groups	appeals court	confirmation hearings	special prosecutor	marijuana use	abortion rights	attorney general	natural law	death penalty
appeals court	majority leader	racial preferences	law professor	law professor	use of marijuana	judicial philosophy	affirmative action	law professor	law professor
civil rights	social issues	attorney general	judicial restraint	judicial restraint	civil rights	affirmative action	right to abortion	confirmation hearings	civil rights
confirmation hearings	death penalty	law clerk	attorney general	law school	law professor	confirmation process	right to privacy	law school	confirmation hearings
fair trial	abortion issue	family members	abortion issue	equal protection	law school	chief of staff	rights groups	confirmation process	law school
search and seizure	law firm	law professor	libel suits	chief of staff	antitrust division	constitutional law	appeals court	news conference	equal protection
antitrust law	news conference	committee members	conservative views	interest groups	chief of staff	highest rating	abortion issue	committee members	constitutional right

Breyer	J. Roberts (CJ)	Miers	Alito	Sotomayor	Kagan	Garland	Gorsuch	Kavanaugh	Barrett
confirm. hearing(s)	solicitor general	abortion rights	abortion rights	appeals court	confirm. hearing(s)	next president	appeals court	high school	health care
death penalty	confirm. hearing(s)	law firm	appeals court	confirmation hearings	solicitor general	appeals court	simple majority	sexual assault	confirm. hearing(s)
chief counsel	civil rights	chief of staff	confirmation hearings	affirmative action	law school	majority leader	nuclear option	confirmation hearing(s)	abortion rights
chief judge	abortion rights	confirmation hearings	attorney general	law professor	law professor	chief judge	confirmation hearing	sexual misconduct	appeals court
appeals court	appeals court	law school	civil rights	abortion rights	gun rights	lame duck	executive branch	abortion rights	conservative majority
civil rights	right to privacy	judicial philosophy	law professor	district attorney	appeals court	presidential election	majority leader	confirmation process	law professor
confirmation process	law professor	appeals court	liberal groups	death penalty	military recruiters	confirmation hearings	law professor	appeals court	confirmation process
law professor	attorney general	constitutional law	right to abortion	civil rights	domestic policy	conservative groups	travel ban	sexual harassment	health care law
pollution cases	affirmative action	social conservatives	swing vote	white firefighters	high school	confirmation vote	majority vote	staff secretary	majority leader
federal judges	gay rights	executive privilege	solicitor general	gun rights	judicial experience	liberal groups	attorney general	law professor	presidential election

Fig. 6.5 Top adjective/noun and noun/noun phrases in newspaper articles mentioning each nominee. Phrases written in a larger font size appear more frequently. Font color indicates whether the phrase falls into one of the following issue categories: economic policy issues (blue), social policy issues (purple), or ethical issues/scandal (red). Phrases in the remaining categories are in black (nominee background, judicial philosophy, internal court relations, executive/congressional politics, and miscellaneous). Clark, Byrnes, Burton, and Rutledge are not shown due to the small

In general, phrases about the nominees' backgrounds and judicial philosophies appear throughout the time series, as do phrases related to executive and congressional politics. Phrases related to internal court politics and issues are more common in earlier nominations. Phrases related to scandals appear idiosyncratically, but can be prominent in media coverage of nominees when they do occur. For example, the top phrases for Haynsworth include six phrases about conflict of interest allegations, and Kavanaugh's top phrases include four phrases concerning the details of the sexual misconduct allegations leveled against him.

Perhaps the most striking shift apparent in these simple phrases is the disappearance of economic issues from discourse about nominees, and the corresponding rise of social issues in media coverage. At least one phrase concerning economic policy appears in 12 of the first 22 nominations in our data (Hughes through Goldberg). Economic issues do not appear in the top phrases of any nominee after the 1975 nomination of John Paul Stevens, who was an expert in antitrust law. Starting in the Warren Court years (1953–1969), phrases related to civil rights, civil liberties, segregation, affirmative action, criminal justice, gender discrimination, capital punishment, and abortion appear more frequently. The newspapers' focus on these issues appears to reflect the current national political agenda often because either the court had ruled on a subject or was viewed as likely to do so.[19] For example, phrases related to criminal justice appear in several nominations in the 1960s and 1970s, a period of rising crime—but do not appear thereafter. Phrases related to abortion begin appearing with the nomination of O'Connor in 1981—recall from Chapter 2 that this is right around when the fight over abortion took national prominence—and are among the top phrases in 11 of the 19 nominations from O'Connor through Barrett.

Topic Models

We now turn to a more systematic analysis of how the topics covered during Supreme Court nominations varied over time. For 49 of the 54 nominees between 1930 and 2020, we estimated separate structural topic models based on coverage in the *New York Times* and *Los Angeles Times*—see the Appendix for details.[20] This process produced estimates of the following content categories:

- *Background*: biographical sketches of the nominee (where the nominee is from, family, early life, education, interests and hobbies), discussions of his/her career or previous job which do not focus on ideology or partisanship, non-ideological speeches or appearances by the nominee.
- *Conflict*: debate, opposition, or partisan fight in the Senate; discussions of the possible failure or withdrawal of the nomination.
- *Cronyism*: friendship or personal ties between the president and the nominee.
- *Docket*: the current Supreme Court docket, or caseload.
- *Ethics*: ethical concerns (usually failure to recuse from a case) or financial disclosures which may affect the nominee's impartiality.
- *Hearings*: hearings of the Senate Judiciary Committee.

- *Ideology*: the nominee's ideology, personal beliefs, partisanship, or judicial philosophy; discussion of a nominee's political work indicating a particular ideological persuasion; discussions of a nominee's lower court opinions addressing controversial issues.
- *Personnel*: discussions of a nominee replacing the outgoing justice, the makeup of the court (non-ideological, i.e. usually in reference to age or geography).
- *Procedural updates*: routine information on the progress of the nomination, including the announcement, scheduling of courtesy calls, hearings, or votes.
- *Scandal*: discussions of a nominee's scandal.
- *Selection*: the president's rationale or the process used for selecting the nominee.

Figure 6.6 depicts the proportion of coverage over time, in each of the content categories. Several content categories appeared infrequently, including cronyism, the court's docket, ethics, and the presence of a scandal. These categories generally arose from idiosyncratic circumstances in a few nominations. For example, cronyism only emerged as a distinct topic in the nominations of Minton, a friend of President Truman, and the two nominations of Abe Fortas, President Johnson's close confidant. After Fortas resigned from the court in 1969 following accusations of improperly accepting outside income, ethical issues (mainly related to financial disclosures) emerged as a distinct topic for several nominees, including Burger, Haynsworth, Blackmun, Powell, Douglas Ginsburg, Breyer, and Alito. Next, the current court's docket was heavily discussed only in three nominations: Warren, John Harlan II (because *Brown v. Board of Education* had recently been decided), and Rehnquist's elevation from associate justice to chief justice. Finally, scandal emerged as a distinct topic for Fortas (for chief justice), Carswell, both Rehnquist nominations, Douglas Ginsburg, Thomas, and Kavanaugh.

Background, conflict, and selection appear throughout the 1930 to 2020 period at relatively stable levels. Hearings emerge as a distinct topic only for part of that time. In the early period, hearings did not take place for every nominee, and in the later period, discussions of ideology and scandals may have overtaken routine hearings coverage. Similarly, routine matters of personnel and procedural updates were commonly covered early on, but appeared less frequently as distinct topics over time. Finally, and perhaps most importantly, ideology is covered throughout the time period under study, but increasingly so over time.

We can dig deeper into the data to examine how the ideological focus of newspaper coverage has changed over time. For each ideology topic, we classify the topic as either covering "general ideology" (i.e. more general discussion of the nominee's liberalism or conservatism) or specific ideological subjects, such as abortion. Figure 6.7 presents the results of this analysis. Here we use individual nominees on the x-axis: the solid black bars show the proportion of general ideology coverage. If no such bars exist for a nominee, this means that there was no general ideology topic in their coverage. The open boxes (with purple borders) show the proportion of any specific ideology coverage, with issues labeled in the boxes. An open box stacked on top of a black bar

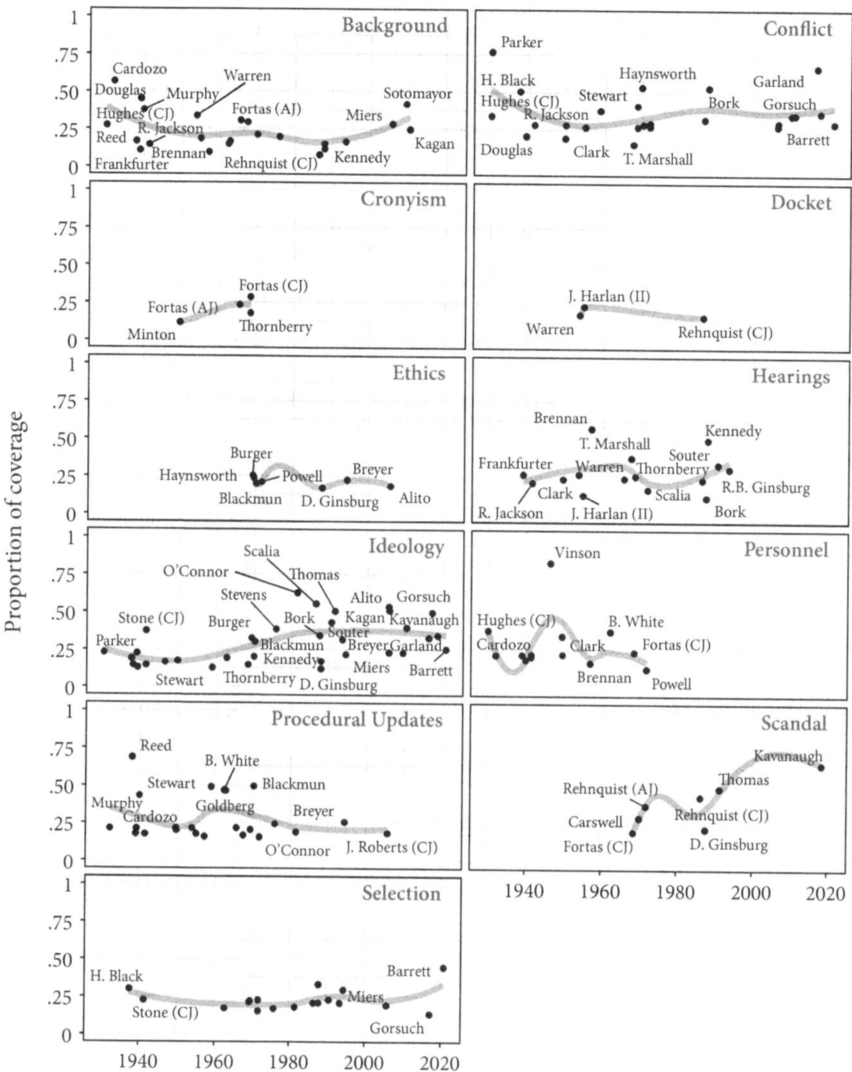

Fig. 6.6 Topic content for newspaper coverage of nominees. Each panel depicts the proportion of coverage dedicated to that topic-category (the topic-categories are mutually exclusive, and for each nominee the proportions across the panels sum to one). The blue lines are loess lines.

means that coverage on both general and specific ideology topics. Finally, nominees with red points at the bottom featured no ideology topics.

Figure 6.7 shows the proportion of newspaper coverage about specific issues and reiterates the increasing focus on ideology displayed in Figure 6.6. Aside from the single emergence of labor politics in the failed nomination of John Parker in 1930, before the late 1960s, any ideological coverage of a nominee—when it existed—was

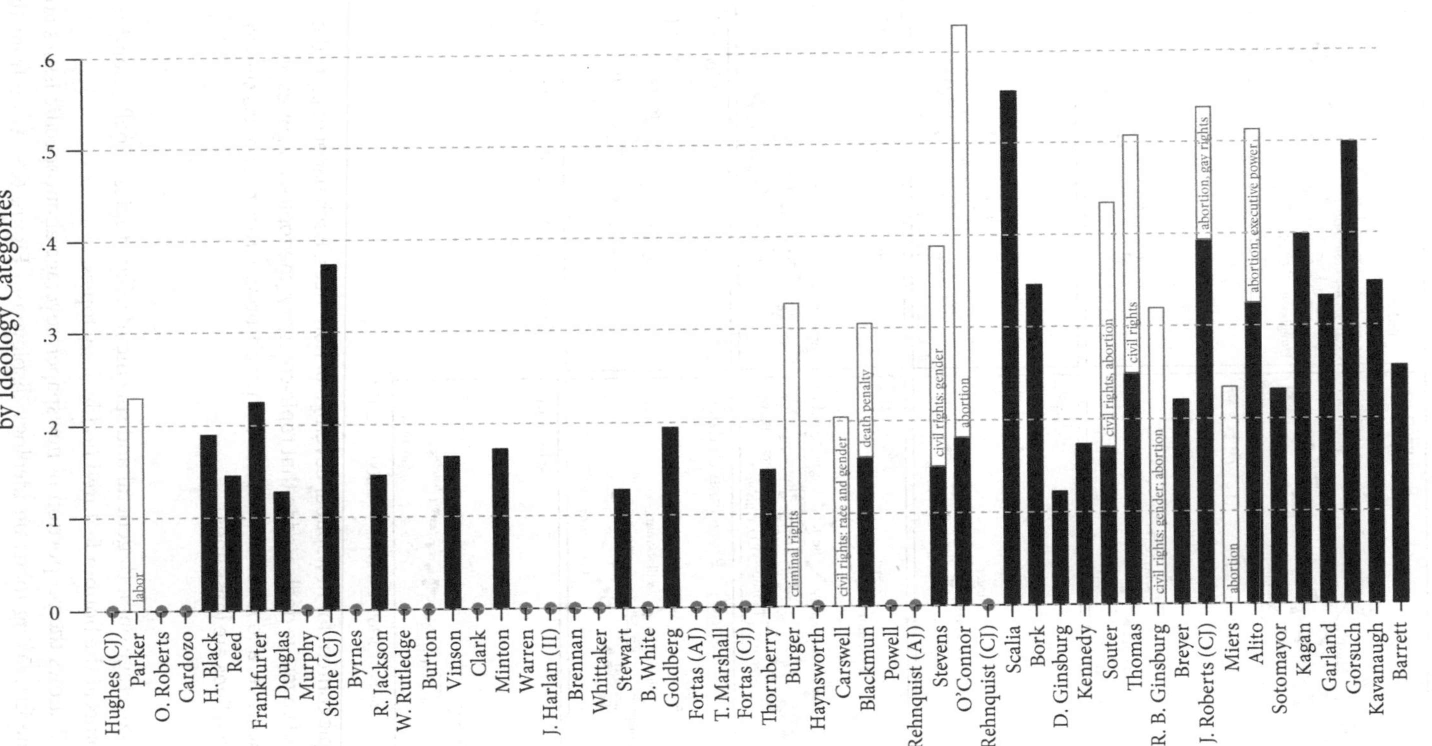

Fig. 6.7 Ideological topics in newspaper coverage of nominees, 1930–2020. See text for details.

general. Starting in the late 1960, coverage of the nominees' views on specific issues occurred more frequently—e.g. criminal rights (Burger 1969), civil rights (Carswell 1970), the death penalty (Blackmun 1970), and race and gender (Stevens 1975). After *Roe v. Wade* was decided in 1973, abortion commonly appeared as its own topic, starting with the nomination in 1981 of the first female justice, Sandra Day O'Connor. Other ideological issues discussed in more recent years include civil rights (Souter (1990), Thomas (1991), and Ruth Bader Ginsburg (1993)); gay rights (John Roberts 2005), and executive power (Alito 2005). Given this increasing newspaper focus on specific, controversial issues, it would not be surprising if the public viewed both nominees and the court as an institution in more ideological terms over time.

Indeed, one consequence of the rise of ideology in modern-day Supreme Court nomination politics is the common observation that nominations have become "politicized." The usual thrust of this critique is that nominations tend to reflect the "low politics" of normal partisan battles, rather than the high-minded (and idealized) politics that a legal institution is supposed to embody.[21] Our topic analysis can help assess whether this perceived growing politicization of Supreme Court nominations has been reflected in newspaper coverage. To examine this, we grouped the content categories into three areas: ethics and scandal, politicized, and routine. "Politicized" categories are those that reveal partisan or policy cleavages among the key players in the nomination process: conflict, cronyism, and ideology. "Routine" categories are those that would occur during the course of nomination, regardless of whether it was contentious or politicized: background, docket, hearings, personnel, procedural updates, and selection.

In Figure 6.8, each panel shows the respective proportion of newspaper coverage in each category, by nominee. The results are straightforward. The top panel shows a clear rise over time in the rate of "politicized" topics appearing in nominee coverage, especially since the late 1980s. In contrast, "routine" coverage of nominees has diminished quite dramatically since the 1960s. Finally, whereas no nominees fell into the ethics and scandal reporting categories until Fortas' chief justice nomination in 1968, several later nominations show a substantial proportion of coverage on allegations of impropriety.

6.2.4 Cable News Coverage: The Kavanaugh Nomination

As we documented in Figure 6.1, cable news coverage of Supreme Court nominees is now a mainstay of media coverage of nominations. But the 2018 nomination of Brett Kavanaugh truly stands out in terms of the quantity of cable news coverage, far eclipsing any previous nominee. In some sense, the Kavanaugh nomination was the "perfect storm" for an explosion of cable coverage: the exit of the median justice (Anthony Kennedy), a controversial president, a narrowly divided Senate—and then, in September, the sudden emergence of allegations by Christine Blasey Ford that Kavanaugh sexually assaulted her when they were teenagers. With this wealth of

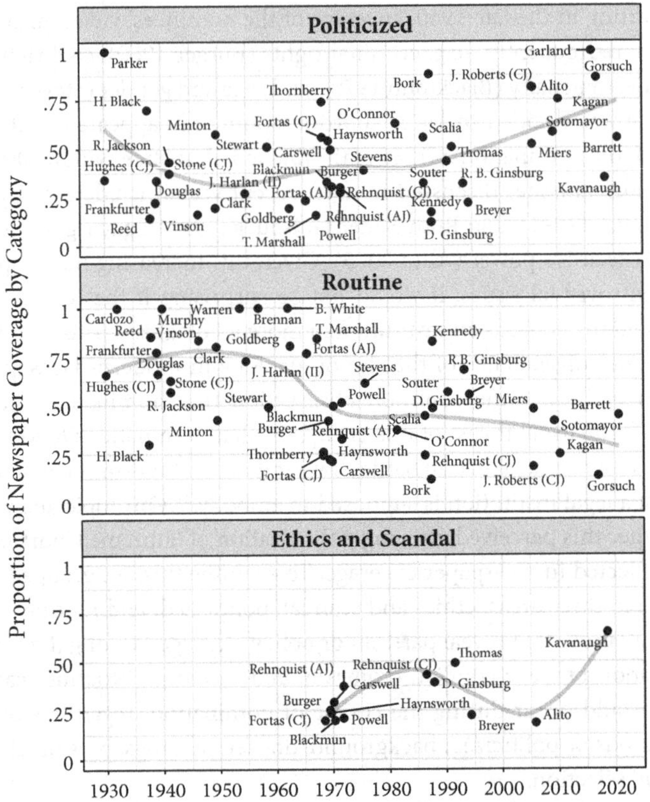

Fig. 6.8 The evolution of "politicized" coverage. The panels depict the proportion of newspaper coverage per nominee that falls into the categories of "politicized," "routine," and "ethics and scandal" coverage. See text for further details.

news to digest and expound upon, the cable channels went all-in on covering the nomination.

In this section, we home in on this particular nomination to better understand how the current partisan polarization on nominations is both reflected in cable coverage—and how it reflects back to the viewers who choose to consume such coverage. We demonstrate this polarization by analyzing the types of individuals speaking about the nomination on Fox, MSNBC, and CNN. On a given channel, how much of the information disseminated is being delivered from an ideological point of view?

To answer this question, we collected data on every individual who spoke about Kavanaugh on all three channels; this includes both program hosts (such as Sean Hannity or Anderson Cooper) and their guests. Our unit of analysis is speaker-appearance: each person who spoke during a show discussing Kavanaugh is an observation (we include speakers only from the specific portions of programs that discussed the nomination).[22] All told, we coded 854 unique individuals, 84 of whom

Table 6.2 Proportion of cable news speaker appearances by ideological affiliation, for each channel.

	Liberal	Unknown/unaffiliated	Conservative
MSNBC	0.56	0.37	0.07
CNN	0.20	0.64	0.16
Fox News	0.12	0.31	0.57

appeared on more than one channel; there were 386 distinct speakers on Fox, 284 speakers on MSNBC, and 279 speakers on CNN.

For each speaker, we coded their "ideological affiliation" as conservative, liberal, or unknown/unaffiliated (see the Appendix for detailed coding rules). Table 6.2 depicts the difference in speaker appearances by ideological affiliation across the three channels. The results are intuitive but nonetheless illuminating. CNN, the more mainstream cable channel that typically plays its politics down the middle, did not generally feature ideologues: the significant majority of speakers were in the unknown/unaffiliated category, with 20% liberal and 16% conservatives.

This pattern is reversed for Fox News and MSNBC. On Fox, 57% of speakers were conservatives, compared to about 31% unaffiliated/unknown and 12% liberal. So, for example, viewers of Sean Hannity's show on September 26, 2018, heard him describe the allegations against Kavanaugh as one of the "ugliest smear campaigns in history."[23] The patterns are symmetric for MSNBC—56% of its speakers were liberal, 37% unaffiliated/unknown, and 7% conservative. For example, viewers of Rachel Maddow's show on September 20, 2018, heard her argue that Kavanaugh could still be charged and jailed for his alleged assault of Ford, even after being confirmed to the Supreme Court.[24] In short, viewers of the two networks were receiving radically different messages about the Kavanaugh nomination.

In the Appendix we present additional data about the types of speakers and interest group representatives that appeared on cable television during the Kavanaugh nomination. Those findings are consistent with the overall polarization of the nomination process feeding into the information environment—at least among those Americans who choose to consume "partisan" cable news. CNN viewers, on the other hand, received much more "down the middle" coverage. We discuss the potential implications of this polarization of partisan cable news in the conclusion to this chapter.

6.3 Newspaper Editorials

So far in this chapter, we have focused mainly on news reporting on Supreme Court nominees (though cable coverage often straddles the line between news and opinion). But it is also useful to evaluate changes in elite opinion over time. To do so, we collected editorials about each nominee written by the editorial boards of 13

Table 6.3 Ideological categorizations of editorial boards for the 13 newspapers from which we collected editorials.

Liberal	Moderate	Conservative
Los Angeles Times	*Christian Science Monitor*	*Arizona Republic*
Nashville Tennessean	*New Orleans Times-Picayune*	*Chicago Tribune*
New York Times	*Oregonian*	*Cincinnati Enquirer*
St. Louis Post-Dispatch		*Richmond Times-Dispatch*
Washington Post		*Wall Street Journal*

newspapers. Editorials are important in both leading and reflecting public opinion on local and national issues, including Supreme Court nominations.[25] In addition, editorials can sometimes lead to significant changes in public opinion.[26] Table 6.3 lists the 13 papers and their general ideological affiliations, based on which party the editorial boards tend to endorse in presidential races. We collected 1,625 editorials in total.[27]

6.3.1 Changes in Quantity over Time

Figure 6.9A shows the total number of editorials written about each nominee by all 13 newspapers combined. As with trends in the frequency of news articles, the total number of editorials generally increased over time, but certain nominations received much more interest than others. Figure 6.9B accounts for the increasing duration of nominations by dividing the number of editorials by the duration, in days, of each nomination. Interestingly, there is no real trend in the normalized rate; the number of editorials per day (bottom panel) does not increase. However, even if only one of the 13 papers wrote an editorial every other day about a nominee (0.5 editorials per day), that is still a considerable amount of elite media discussion.

6.3.2 Editorial "Votes" on Nominees

Of course, of more interest than the number of editorials is what they say. We consider how each editorial board would "vote" on each nomination if it were a senator. Our approach here is similar in spirit to that of Ho and Quinn (2008), who code editorial opinions on Supreme Court decisions, treating these editorials as votes on the same cases the court hears. This strategy allows them to develop ideal point estimates for several newspapers' editorial boards.

We read all editorials written about each nominee by each newspaper and coded whether the newspaper approved of, disapproved of, or took no stand on the confirmation of the nominee. Editorials coded as approving nominees explicitly urged confirmation, supported the choice of the president, or said the nominee would do

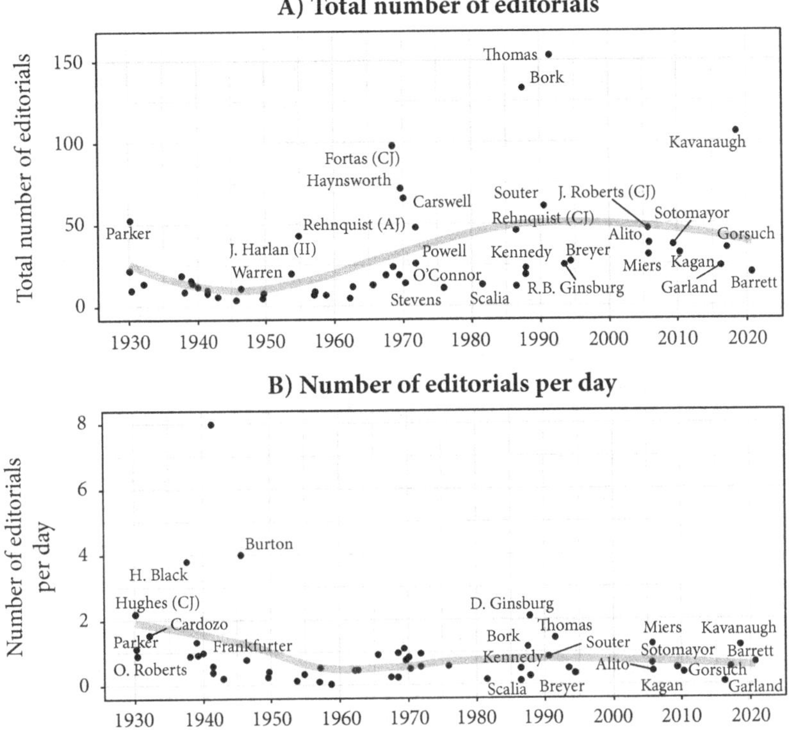

Fig. 6.9 A) Total number of editorials per nominee; B) number of editorials divided by number of days each nomination lasted. The lines are loess lines.

well on the court. Editorials coded as disapproving votes advocated that senators vote against the nominee, or said the nominee was not fit to join the court or would be harmful to the court or country. If an editorial did not state an opinion or provide enough information to discern its stance, the editorial was coded as neutral.[28]

Figure 6.10 illustrates the editorial board votes for each nominee. For clarity, we break down the papers by whether they fall into the liberal, moderate, or conservative camp; we also place "time" on the y-axis in order to make the comparisons across nominees easier. Green squares indicate approving votes and red squares disapproving votes; gray squares indicate that the paper wrote about the nominee but did not take a stand, while white squares mean that the paper did not editorialize about that nominee.

As seen, not every newspaper writes about each nominee, as is indicated by the prevalence of the white squares. In the early period, for example, many nominations were low salience or were quite short in duration, providing little opportunity or incentives for editorial boards to weigh in. Looking down the "columns" of the plot shows approval votes and neutral votes as the most common, but the number of disapproval votes over the entire period was certainly not trivial.

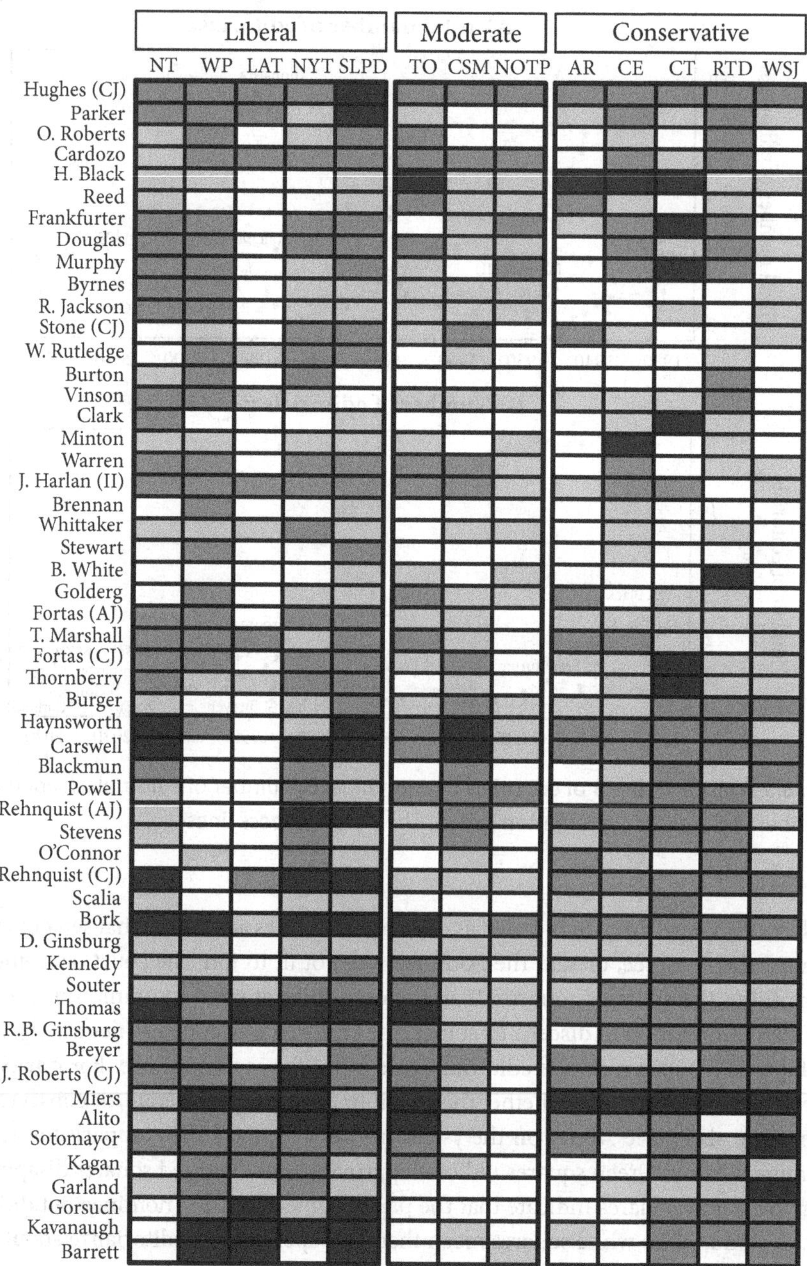

Fig. 6.10 'Votes" by each newspaper according to nominee (rows) and newspaper ideology (columns). Each square represents a nominee-newspaper pair. Green squares mean approving votes, while red squares disapproving votes. Gray squares indicate that the paper wrote about the nominee but did not take a stand, while white boxes mean zero editorials about that nominee.

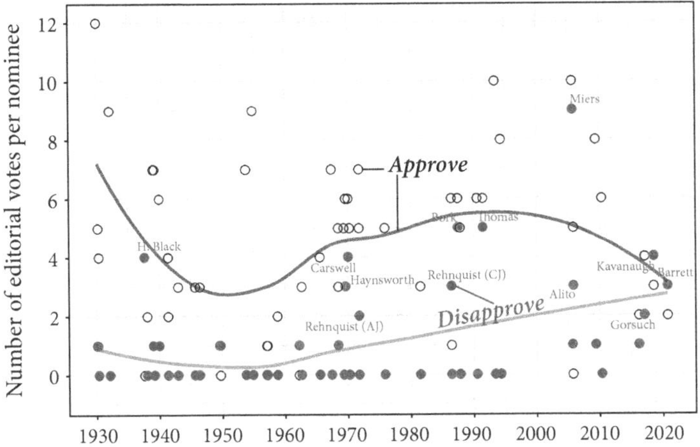

Fig. 6.11 Number of approving "votes" and disapproving "votes" by editorial boards for each nominee. We label disapproval for nominees who received at least two such votes.

Figure 6.11 examines just approving and disapproving votes, showing the total overall number of each per nominee across all 13 newspapers. The black points show approval votes, while the red points show disapproval votes. For clarity, we only label disapproval for nominees who received at least two such votes. Overall, editorial board disapprovals are relatively rare, but their frequency has increased in recent years. Nominees with more than two disapproval votes generally either suffered a scandal (e.g. Black, Carswell, Thomas, Kavanaugh) or experienced a particularly contentious nomination (Bork and Miers). The rise in the number of disapproving votes in recent decades means that the overall flow of elite opinion on Supreme Court nominees has become more polarized, consistent with broader trends in media coverage of American politics.

This polarization becomes even more evident by comparing the relationship of the partisan/ideological alignment of the editorial boards to the president's party. Specifically, we collapse ideology and partisanship and code a paper as "copartisan" if it is aligned with the president (e.g. the president is a Democrat and an editorial board has a liberal perspective). Conversely, we code a paper as "counter-partisan" if its ideology is opposed to that of the president. "Moderate" papers are assumed to be neither aligned nor opposed to the president.

Figure 6.12 depicts the trends in the proportion of approval votes, neutral votes, and disapproval votes across time, broken down by the ideological valence of the editorial boards (across the rows). We label the disapproval votes of any nominee who received at least two such votes. Not surprisingly, copartisan editoral boards have always tended to approve of the president's nominees, except for a dip in the 1950s and 1960s, which was matched by an increase in neutral stances.[29] Conversely, counter-partisan editorial boards have become more likely to disapprove and less likely to approve of nominees. For example, in 2018, Brett Kavanaugh received 100%

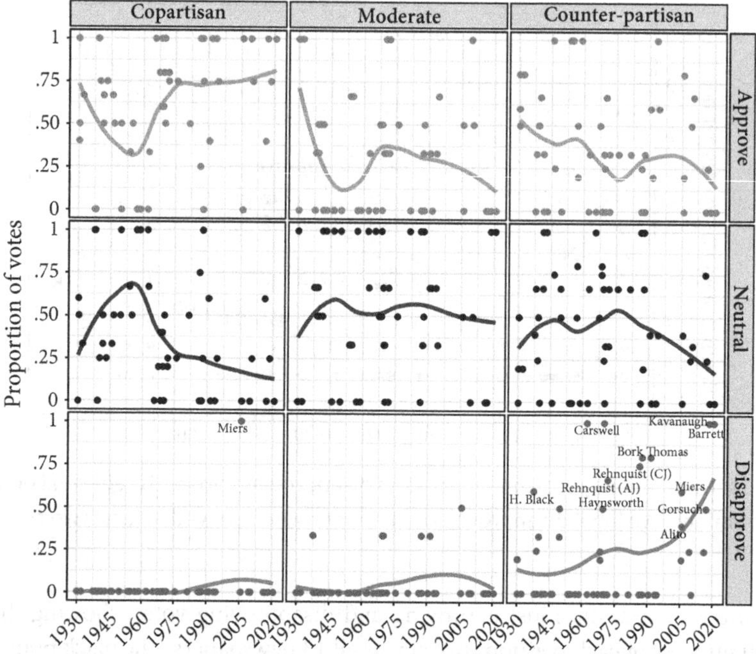

Fig. 6.12 Proportion of approving, neutral, and disapproving "votes" for each nominee according to the editorial board's partisan agreement with the appointing president. The columns depict the partisan/ideological orientation of the newspapers, while the rows show the proportion of approving, neutral, and disapproving votes, respectively. For disapproval, we label nominees who received at least two such votes.

disapproving editorials from counter-partisan (i.e. liberal) editorial boards. Although this was the first such occurrence in nearly 50 years, it occurred again two years later for Amy Coney Barrett. Finally, moderate editorial boards consistently support or stay neutral toward nominees over time, very rarely opposing nominees (only Black, Haynsworth, Carswell, Bork, Thomas, Miers, and Alito received disapproving votes from moderate papers). This analysis further shows the increasing ideological polarization in elite messaging, depending on elites' ideological alignment with the president.

6.3.3 Ideology and Quality

Turning to our final analysis, one way to understand the increase in the politicization of news coverage over time is to break down assessments of nominees into two categories: ideology and legal quality. In an "idealized" version of Supreme Court nomination politics, nominees would be judged solely by their legal qualifications, not by "political" considerations that are unworthy of the highest court in the land.

This standard is often reflected in editorial assessments of nominees. For instance, in voicing their approval of Felix Frankfurter's confirmation in 1939, the *New York Times* editorial board praised his legal qualifications.

> Mr. Frankfurter goes to the high bench because, and only because, his character, his genius and his learning made him the inevitable choice for the place. If political considerations had prevailed a dozen other men might have been preferred. If sectional considerations had figured the place would have gone to some candidate west of the Mississippi River. But Mr. Frankfurter's good qualities outshone all other candidacies and all other arguments. The good fortune, it was clear, was not so much his as his country's.

By contrast, in 2017, the *Times*' editorial board conceded that Neil Gorsuch was "clearly qualified" for the Court, but ideology motivated their bottom-line assessment:

> There's also no question [Gorsuch] would be a conservative vote on many of the most pressing issues facing the court, including abortion and reproductive rights, gay rights, religious liberty, gun-safety legislation, protections for workers and the environment, the flood of private money into political campaigns and more. Despite his insistence that he would approach every case with an open mind, his record strongly suggests he would rule the way Republicans would like in most, if not all, cases. Over three or four decades on the court, he would help push the law further to the right in many areas.

To examine changes in these types of quality-versus-ideology assessments over time, we read all the *New York Times* editorials in our dataset and created a dictionary of words and phrases associated with assessments of a nominee's quality or her ideology.[30] For example, quality-related words include "ability," "credential," and "intellectual," while ideology-related words include "abortion" and "liberalism." We then applied this dictionary to all the *Times*' editorials in our data set; for each, we thus have the count of ideology-focused words and the count of quality-related words for each nominee.

Figure 6.13 depicts the ratio of ideology-to-quality words—specifically the log count of ideology-focused words to the log count of quality-related words—for each nominee. The temporal pattern is quite clear. Early on, quality words far exceeded ideology words. Over time, the proportion of ideology assessments in editorials increased, reaching rough parity with quality words in the 1980s. Interestingly, even as late as the 1990s, the collective editorial assessments of Ruth Bader Ginsburg and Stephen Breyer still emphasized quality more than ideology. Since then, ideological assessments have easily outnumbered quality assessments for most nominees. The two exceptions are Harriet Miers, who was widely perceived as under-qualified for the court and ultimately was forced to withdraw, and Brett Kavanaugh, who was accused

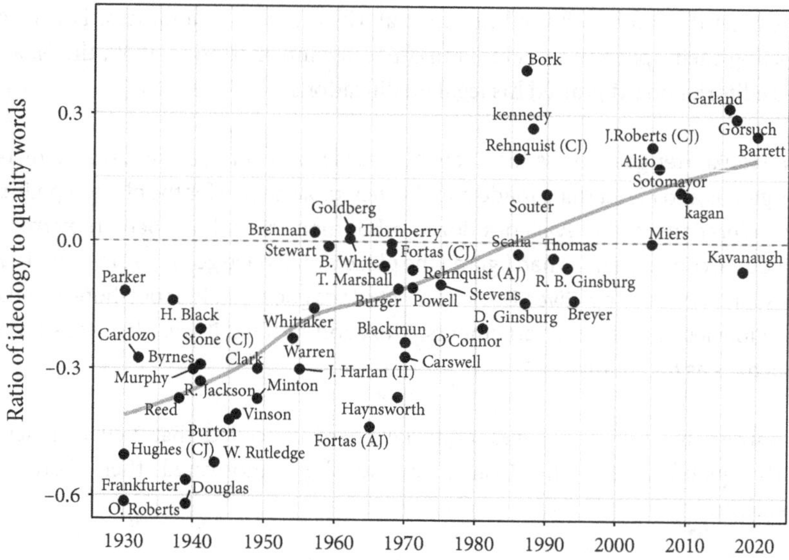

Fig. 6.13 The ratio of ideology versus quality words in editorials on Supreme Court nominees, 1930–2020. The graph compares the log count of ideology-related words to the log count of quality-related words. The blue line is a loess line.

of sexual misconduct.[31] In some sense these exceptions prove the rule: only unusual circumstances will shift the focus of media coverage to drift away from emphasizing ideological considerations.[32]

6.4 Conclusion

In many ways, the changes in media coverage documented here parallel those in interest group mobilization shown in Chapter 5. Early on, most nominations were sleepy affairs that featured infrequent mobilization by a small number of groups attempting to influence senators behind closed doors. The data reveal a shift in the 1970s from this world of textbook pluralism to "hyper-pluralism," characterized by numerous groups mobilizing much more frequently, and using outside tactics to support or oppose confirmation.

The media story is of a piece. During the 1930s television coverage itself did not exist, so only newspapers and the radio might cover a Supreme Court nominee.[33] Newspapers did cover nominees, but the typically short duration of nominations allowed little information to reach the public. In addition, hard news coverage rarely focused on the ideology of the nominees, and only then in general terms. Editorial boards likewise tended to focus on the nominees' legal quality; moreover, elite messaging was quite homogeneous, with most nominees receiving broad support from newspapers across the ideological spectrum.

Over time this landscape slowly but surely transformed into the one so visible today in every Supreme Court nomination. Coverage increased, both in the number of newspaper stories and the advent of broadcast and cable news. Coverage polarized, with entities like Fox News and MSNBC promoting their respective conservative and liberal views on the news. The nominees' ideology, particularly their stances on controversial social issues like abortion, became hot topics, while more routine or previously popular issues like business and the economy faded into the background. Coverage of nominee ethics and scandals also increased. Finally, elite messages became more polarized. Editorial board disapproval became increasingly common, with positions driven by the newspaper's ideological alignment with the nominating president.

An interesting but somewhat speculative topic is how these trends in nominee coverage interacted with changes in public consumption of different media sources. How changes in the media environment affect American politics is central in political scientist Markus Prior's (2007) landmark work on political knowledge and the media. As Prior documents, first radio and then broadcast television were widely available, so people were exposed to political news regardless of their level of interest or knowledge. But with the advent of cable television after about 1980, sources of news coverage exploded, as did sources of entertainment. As a result, people with little interest could avoid political news, while those more engaged could receive an abundance of information, often with a partisan slant. In the case of Supreme Court nominees, our data show that early broadcast television portrayed nominees in non-ideological terms, when they covered them at all, much as newspapers had previously. Further media fragmentation in the cable television era coincided with a dramatic change in coverage of nominees across the board, with a greater emphasis on nominee ideology and their stands on divisive social issues.

It would be strange indeed if the changes in media content, as well as exposure to and choice of different media sources, had no impact on public opinion. Unfortunately, we are unable to determine the distinct impacts of each factor on public opinion, or how the two interact.[34] Still, we can track the broad changes in public opinion on Supreme Court nominees over time, a task to which we turn in Chapter 7.

7
Public Opinion

In July 1990, Justice William Brennan announced his intention to resign from the Supreme Court. Brennan, one of the court's most storied liberals, almost certainly wanted to hold his seat until a Democrat could name his replacement. But like Justices Marshall and Ginsburg after him, the 84-year-old Brennan found his chance for a triumphant "strategic exit" foiled by ill health and the vagaries of presidential elections. It would fall to Republican President George H.W. Bush to select the successor to the liberal lion.

For his first nominee to a seat on the high court, Bush chose David Souter. As we discussed in Chapter 3, Souter enjoyed the backing of White House Chief of Staff John Sununu, who as governor of New Hampshire had appointed him to the state's highest court. Bush appointed Souter to the U.S. Court of Appeals for the First Circuit just a few months before Brennan's announcement, adding him to the Republicans' bench of potential nominees. Sununu and other backers in the White House favored the low-key judge, who had never expressed any controversial views and who lived a life of near monastic asceticism. The contrast between Souter and the flamboyant Robert Bork seemed perfect to Sununu and Bush—an ideal way to side-step the controversy that had brought an embarrassing defeat to the Reagan White House.[1] In the absence of any "red meat" on the nominee, the media dubbed Souter the "stealth nominee."[2]

Souter never generated much controversy. While he would go on to support abortion rights during his tenure (thereby enraging conservatives), he was perceived at the time as likely in the anti-abortion camp; as we saw in Chapter 5, pro-choice groups mobilized against him. Nevertheless, media outlets found the nomination a sleepy affair—Souter's nomination received less coverage than any other in the post-1980 period. Public opinion polls showed that most Americans found the nominee a cypher. At the same time, opinion holders mostly liked what they saw. In a *NBC News/Wall Street Journal* poll taken in mid-September (right in the middle of his Senate Judiciary Committee hearings), 32% of Americans favored his confirmation, while only 5% opposed it—but fully 58% said they "still need[ed] to know more about him" before making a decision. This was one of only five public polls taken between the announcement in late July and the confirmation vote in early October.[3] Notably, the partisan division in opinion was relatively modest. Of Republican identifiers with an opinion about Souter, 93% supported his confirmation. But so did 75% of Democratic identifiers with an opinion. Perhaps unsurprisingly given this state of affairs, the Senate easily confirmed the taciturn Souter, in a vote of 90-9. The stealth strategy had worked.

Making the Supreme Court: The Politics of Appointments, 1930–2020. Charles M. Cameron and Jonathan P. Kastellec, Oxford University Press. © Oxford University Press 2023. DOI: 10.1093/oso/9780197680544.003.0007

Twenty-eight years later, President Trump nominated Brett Kavanaugh to replace Anthony Kennedy, then the median justice on the court. The world of Supreme Court appointment politics had changed dramatically, and the media coverage and opinion dynamics of the Kavanaugh nomination were worlds apart from the Souter story. Media coverage of Kavanaugh's nomination began immediately and intensely. And, within mere *days* of the nomination, 78% of respondents in a Gallup poll had formed an opinion on Kavanaugh's confirmation. Of this 78%, support for Kavanaugh was nearly evenly split, with 53% supporting confirmation and 47% opposed. By the time the Senate voted on Kavanaugh's nomination in early October 2018, he had endured a lurid scandal arising from allegations by Christine Blasey Ford that he had sexually assaulted her when they were teenagers. This scandal produced a huge surge of media coverage, as Ford's allegations led to a second hearing before the Senate Judiciary Committee, similar to the two-hearing process that unfolded during the Thomas nomination of 1991. In both cases, the second hearing captivated the public's attention.

Due to the significance of Kavanaugh's nomination, the media and polling companies undertook more than 40 public polls from the announcement to the Senate vote. In a *CNN* poll taken just before the vote, 92% of Americans had an opinion on whether he should be confirmed. Overall, more Americans actually opposed his nomination than supported it (the splits were 41% in favor, 51% opposed, 8% no opinion). While opinion changed little during Souter's nomination, Kavanaugh's overall approval declined markedly following the Ford allegations. Moreover, unlike with Souter, support for Kavanaugh was highly polarized by party, with 90% of Republicans supporting him, compared to only 11% of Democrats. In fact, Republican support for Kavanaugh actually rose after the scandal hit. The subsequent roll call vote reflected this partisan split. Kavanaugh eked out confirmation on a near party-line vote of 50–48, the closest vote in modern Supreme Court appointment history.

* * *

Public opinion about Supreme Court nominees does *not* culminate in a referendum or some other form of direct democracy. The Constitution expressly reserves the final decision for the Senate, not the people. Nonetheless, a kind of pseudo-referendum does occur, as the public makes up its mind about the nominee. The Souter and Kavanaugh nominations illustrate important themes about nominees and the court of public opinion.

First, *media coverage matters*, both for opinion holding and evaluations. Absent much news about the stealth nominee, many citizens never formed opinions about Souter. In contrast, most citizens did form opinions about the heavily covered Kavanaugh. Second, *the popularity of nominees can vary widely*, based on the attributes of the nominees. We see this in the impact of scandal on public opinion toward Judge Kavanaugh. In addition, we show that the public thinks more highly of nominees who display path-breaking diversity traits. Third, *partisanship affects evaluations*, especially for controversial nominees. The differential response of

Democrats and Republicans to the Kavanaugh revelations vividly illustrate this point. Finally, *the nomination campaigns can matter*. While little changed during the Souter nomination, opinions did change during that of Kavanaugh. As we will see, in a few cases opinion change was significant.

In this chapter, we explore these themes using the most comprehensive set of public opinion data on Supreme Court nominations ever assembled. (As we note in the Appendix, the scholarly literature on public opinion and Supreme Court nominees is surprisingly thin.) Our emphasis here is descriptive, uncovering basic facts and revealing straight-forward patterns. We do not explore the underlying causal mechanisms in any detail; we defer consideration of those until Chapter 10. Here, we focus on the main currents in public opinion on Supreme Court nominees over the past nine decades.

7.2 The Public Opinion Data

The beginning of our period of study (1930) roughly coincides with the dawn of public opinion polling in America.[4] We sought to gather data on every public opinion poll from 1930 to 2020 that asked about the confirmation of a nominee. In this chapter, unless otherwise noted we employ only polls conducted during the *nomination period* of each nominee, which we define as the interval between the day of nomination and the day of confirmation. For nominees who were not confirmed, we use the date of their withdrawal or defeat on the Senate floor as the end of their nomination period.

Our main set of analyses involves responses to questions that directly ask whether the respondent favors the confirmation of the nominee. We collected different question wordings that address this. For example: "Do you think the U.S. Senate should or should not confirm Alito's nomination to the Supreme Court?" or "Do you strongly support, somewhat support, somewhat oppose, or strongly oppose John Roberts' serving as the next Chief Justice of the Supreme Court, or do you not know enough about him to say?" For every poll, we categorized responses as "supporting confirmation" (or "approving" of the nominee), "opposing confirmation" (or "disapproving of the nominee"), or "don't know." (As will become clear, we are substantively interested in don't know responses and the evolution of opinion holding over the course of individual nominations.)

We collected two types of survey data. First, whenever the individual-level data from a given poll was available, we collected that data and coded the responses as well as other relevant variables (e.g. party identification and demographic variables). There are many polls for which only "topline data" is available; this means we know the aggregate responses—for example, the percentage of respondents answering yes/no/don't know to a question about nominee support—but the individual-level responses are not available. We collected this data as well for use in the aggregate analyses that appear below. In addition, we are also interested in the aggregate distribution of public opinion by party identification. In some instances (mostly in recent years), Roper provides toplines broken down by party identification; if so, we collected it. To augment this data, we used the individual-level data to create distributions by partisan identification. We then merged these two sources to create a single aggregate dataset of opinion broken down by party identification.[5] In sum, in the individual level-data, we have nearly 300,000 respondents, who span 153 unique polls. When we include the polls with only topline data, the aggregate data includes 298 unique polls.

In addition to the differences between the individual-level data and the aggregate data, for some analyses we focus on the opinion of all Americans, and for others we focus only on those with an opinion (that is, excluding those who answer don't know or refuse to offer an opinion). As a result, tracking the source and nature of data is a little challenging in this chapter. To compensate, throughout the chapter we go into detail where needed to make the source of data clear.

7.3 Visible and Invisible Nominees

We begin our analysis with a simple question: how many polls were taken in each nomination between 1930 and 2020? Figure 7.1 depicts the number of polls per nominee (we label nominees with at least one poll). The first poll about a Supreme Court nominee involved Hugo Black in 1937, when Gallup polled Americans about whether the just-confirmed Black should resign following further revelations of his previously reported past membership in the Ku Klux Klan.[6] Two years later, Gallup polled Americans about the nomination of Felix Frankfurter. Although media

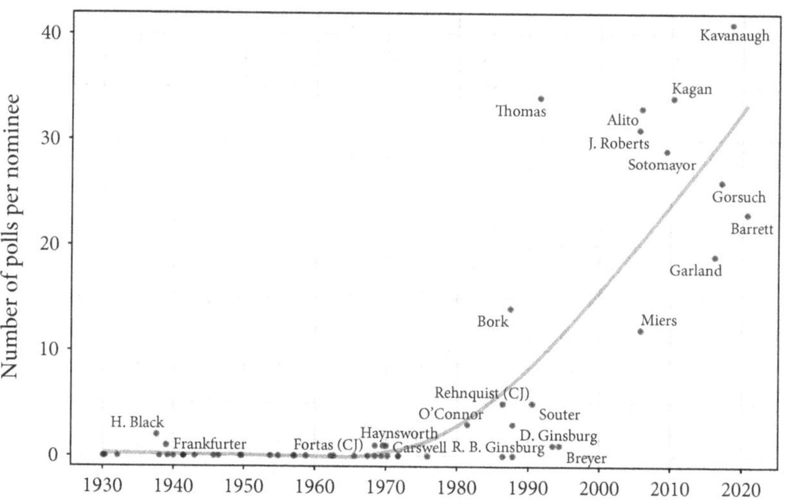

Fig. 7.1 The number of polls for Supreme Court nominees, 1930–2020. Nominees with at least one poll are labeled. The blue line is a loess line.

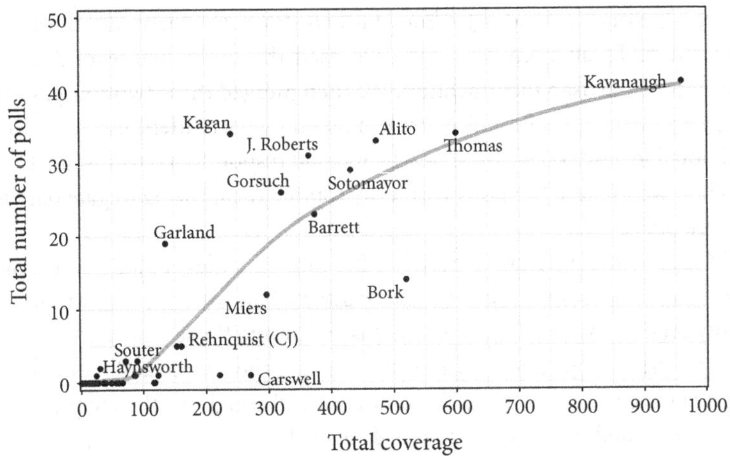

Fig. 7.2 The relationship between the incidence of polling and media coverage of nominees. The x-axis depicts the total coverage on each nominee; this is the aggregate of nominee-level data on newspaper, broadcast, and cable coverage described in Chapter 6. The y-axis depicts the total number of polls for each nominee, based on our data collection. We label the nominees whose total coverage exceeds 200 or who had at least five polls taken. The blue line is a loess line.

coverage of the nomination was light, Frankfurter's liberalism and Jewish faith stoked controversy on the far right; some remarkably colorful characters testified at his confirmation hearings. The controversy may have sparked Gallup's interest.

Figure 7.1 shows that the Black and Frankfurter polls were exceptional. Nearly three decades and 20 nominations would pass before the next poll of a Supreme Court nominee: Abe Fortas in his doomed bid for chief justice in 1968. Following that, the incidence of polling increased but remained irregular. Neither Scalia's nomination in 1986 nor Kennedy's nomination one year later featured a single public poll. Those aside, every nominee from O'Connor in 1981 forward received at least one poll. It is difficult to imagine a future nomination that would not generate public opinion polling.

What explains this variation? The media coverage data discussed in Chapter 6 showed that most nominees prior to Fortas were nearly invisible to the public. The data reveal some media attention for the rejected nominee Parker in 1930, Warren in 1953, and Harlan in 1955 (the latter reflecting Southern fury following the Supreme Court's 1954 decision in *Brown v. Board of Education*, which we discuss in detail in the next chapter). But prior to 1968, the media data reveal nominations as essentially "no news." Then, from Burger (1969) to Scalia (1986), they were "sometimes news." From Bork (1987) on, Supreme Court nominations were "almost always news"—and sometimes top news.

Early in our study period, technology was new, polls were difficult to conduct and relatively expensive, and few sophisticated consumers wanted them. Hence, polls were reserved for matters that paying clients such as newspapers found compelling. By contrast, the later study period reflects nearly continuous polling on a wide range of subjects.[7] The near-complete absence of polling on nominees before the late 1960s, and the somewhat sporadic incidence of polling through the 1970s, strongly suggests that polling tracked newsworthiness.

The data support this conjecture. Figure 7.2 examines the relationship between media coverage and number of polls. The x-axis shows total media coverage (newspaper, broadcast, and cable) for each nominee, as described in Chapter 6. The y-axis depicts the total number of polls for each nominee, based on our data collection. The correlation is quite high (.87). To be sure, some news stories are based on a poll commissioned by a news organization, and other confounders certainly exist as well. So one should be cautious of imputing causality to this strong correlation. But both intuition and the data suggest that polls and newsworthiness went hand-in-hand.[8]

7.4 Opinion Holding

We now turn to what the polling data actually tells us about nomination politics. We start with the simple question of what explains variation in opinion holding over time for nominees. The levels of opinion holding—that is, the extent to which the public has *any opinion* on a nominee indicates the overall salience of a nomination.

Note that in this section and the next, in order to capture citizens' final impressions of nominees, we subset the data to include only up to the last five polls in the nomination. For most nominees, all or most of these polls are close in time to the end date of the nomination. For nominees with fewer than five polls overall, this aggregation captures opinion holding further away from the end of the nomination.[9] We label this data subset the "last five polls" data.[10]

We begin our examination of opinion holding with the aggregate data. Figure 7.3 depicts the percentage of respondents who expressed an opinion—either approval or disapproval—on a given nominee in the last five polls; that is, the points depict 100 minus the percentage of people who don't offer an opinion or say don't know. For convenience, we show only the 22 nominees with polling data. Interestingly, little change in levels of opinion holding over time stands out. Of course, the level of aggregation is high and the figure ignores factors such as variation in question wording, which we incorporate shortly. However, opinion holding increased somewhat since the 1990s.

Some nominees stand out as enigmas to the public, with many respondents unable or unwilling to express an opinion. The prime example was indeed the stealth nominee David Souter in 1990; less than half of respondents held an opinion about whether he should be confirmed or not. Similarly, the confirmation of William Rehnquist as chief justice in 1986 saw only about 50% of survey respondents offering an opinion. Felix Frankfurter in 1939, one of the rare polled nominees in the early period, also produced many non-evaluations, as did Merrick Garland in 2016.

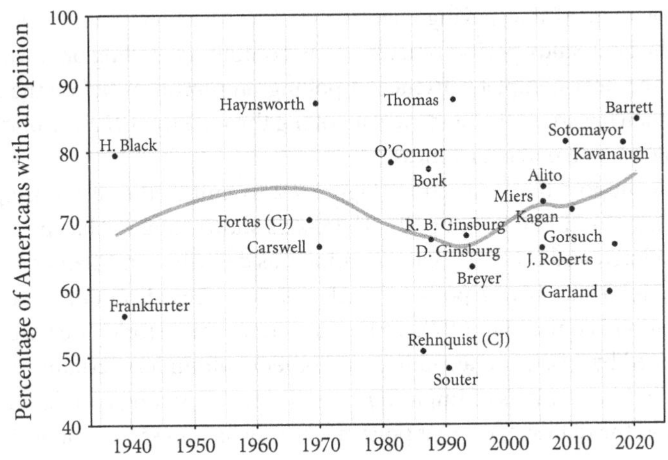

Fig. 7.3 Opinion holding using the last five polls data. The points depict the percent of Americans with an opinion on the nominee (either approve or disapprove). The blue line is a loess line.

In contrast, several nominees generated high levels of opinion holding. The prime example is Clarence Thomas in 1991, whose nomination was rocked by accusations by Anita Hill that Thomas, her former boss, had sexually harassed her. The Senate re-opened hearings, and the ensuing spectacle was beamed into the nation's homes via live television. By the end of the process, almost 90% of poll respondents had an opinion on Thomas' confirmation. A second standout was Clement Haynsworth in 1969. Coming at one of the most racially charged moments in modern American history, the accusations of racial bias leveled against the southern judge seemed to touch a public nerve. Almost 90% of respondents offered an opinion about his confirmation. Other examples of high levels of opinion holding include the nominations of Hugo Black, Robert Bork, Samuel Alito, and Brett Kavanaugh, all individuals whose nominations featured allegations of both ideological extremity and some degree of impropriety.

Just as polling frequency correlates highly with media coverage, so do levels of opinion holding. Figure 7.4 depicts the relationship between the two; the x-axis shows the measure of total media coverage, while the y-axis indicates the level of opinion holding (i.e. the same measure as in Figure 7.3). While coverage and opinion holding do not covary as strongly as does coverage and polling, the two still display a strong positive relationship. Opinion holding definitely increases with the level of coverage per nominee (the correlation is .5).[11]

A natural next question is, what explains variation in opinion holding? While we defer an extended, theoretically grounded answer until Chapter 10, in the Appendix we present simple regressions using both individual and aggregate data. These examine the relationship between opinion holding and the amount of coverage, the presence of a scandal, and path-breaking diversity traits for a nominee (i.e. if the

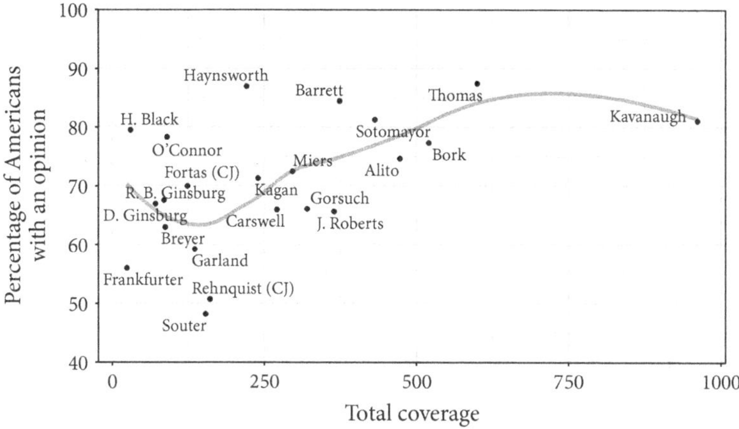

Fig. 7.4 Aggregate opinion holding versus total media coverage.

nominee was female or non-white, or both). Generally speaking, we find positive relationships for each of these predictors; the strongest association involves path-breaking nominees. At the individual-level, question wording matters a great deal: respondents are much more likely (about 38 percentage points) to say "don't know" when the question explicitly presents that as an option. Additionally, higher levels of education correlate with higher levels of opinion holding; the same pattern holds with age. With respect to race, Blacks and Hispanics are less likely to hold opinions than whites. The results for gender are not statistically distinguishable from zero.

Summary of Opinion Holding

In sum, opinion holding about Supreme Court nominees appears sensible and straightforward. At the aggregate level, media coverage, polling, and opinion holding moved together in intuitive ways. The result was considerable variation in which nominees were visible to the public and which were comparatively "stealthy." The latter often failed to elicit opinion holding. In contrast, vivid, path-breaking, and newsworthy nominees—whether for positive or negative reasons—did induce opinions. Finally, at the individual level, opinion holding varied among respondents depending on their age and education. This finding is entirely consistent with standard scholarship on the public and political knowledge.[12]

7.5 Popularity and Unpopularity

We now shift from examining opinion holding to examining the public's approval and disapproval of nominees, searching for strong patterns in the data. We begin by identifying the most and least popular nominees. We then examine whether factors such as nominee scandals and perceived "low quality" correlate with lower public esteem, and by contrast, whether path-breaking diversity apparently boosts popular approval.

7.5.1 Popularity, Unpopularity, and Net Popularity

Figure 7.5 provides basic data on the popularity and unpopularity of the 22 nominees with polling data. The figure indicates the percentage of Americans who approved of confirmation, opposed confirmation, or said they didn't know or were uncertain, using the aggregate last five polls data. The figure shows that the most popular nominee (with about 70% approval) was Sandra Day O'Connor, the first female justice.

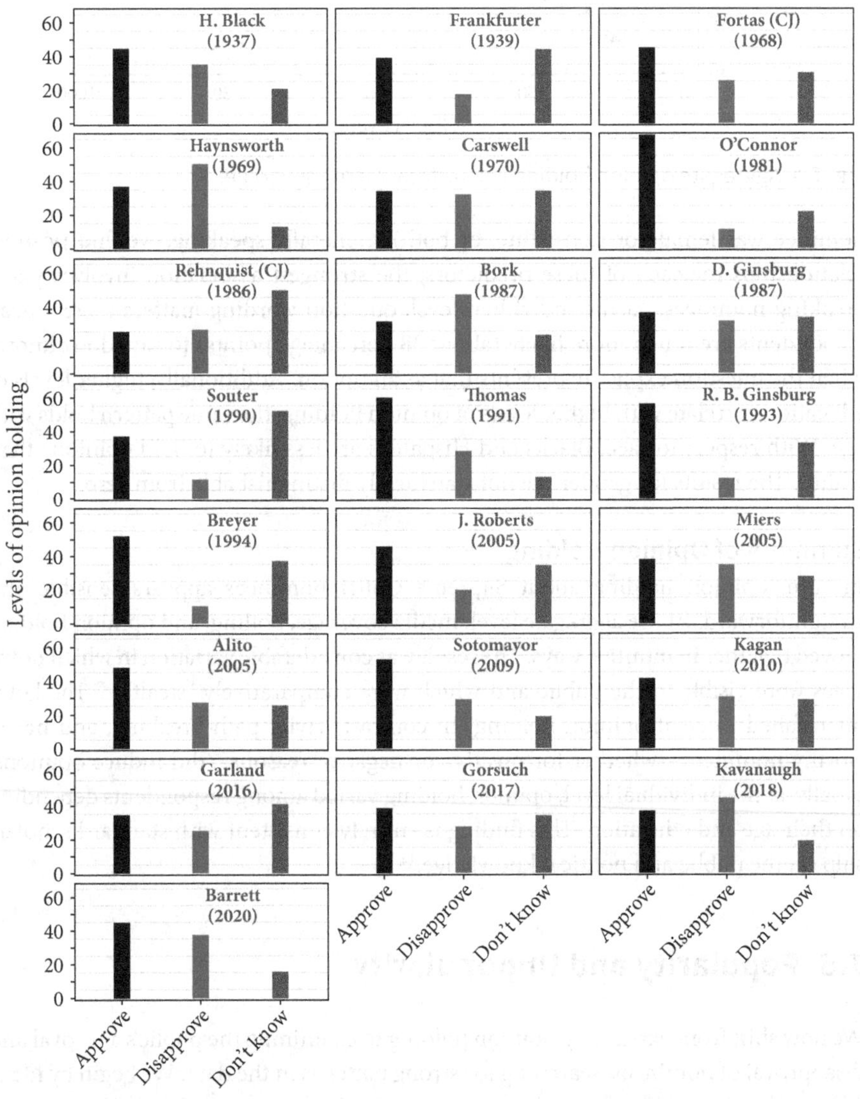

Fig. 7.5 Summarizing the popularity of nominees, using the last five polls data. For each nominee, the bars depict the percentage of respondents saying they approve, disapprove, and "don't know," respectively.

Perhaps surprisingly, the second most popular nominee was Clarence Thomas, whose approval rating approached 60%. Also notably popular was Ruth Bader Ginsburg, the brilliant litigator whose pre-confirmation work advanced women's rights.

The most unpopular nominee was Clement Haynsworth in 1969, with 50% of respondents opposed. The accusations of racial bias apparently registered with the public a year after the massive urban unrest that followed the tragic assassination of Martin Luther King, Jr. The second most unpopular nominee was Robert Bork in 1987. The nomination of the conservative lightening rod sparked heated accusations of ideological extremism. The third most unpopular nominee was Brett Kavanaugh (2018).[13]

Several nominees were characterized by high levels of *both* support and opposition, with few non-opinions. Standouts include Black, Haynsworth, Bork, Kavanaugh, and Barrett. Conversely, many nominees saw a large percentage of respondents unable or unwilling to offer an evaluation. These included Rehnquist for chief justice, as well as Carswell, Douglas Ginsburg, Harriet Miers, Elena Kagan, Merrick Garland, and Neil Gorsuch. Several of these nominees were withdrawn from consideration.

Figure 7.6 examines net popularity, which gives a snapshot of the nominee's overall popularity. Using the same data as shown in Figure 7.5, Figure 7.6 shows, for each nominee, the difference between the percentage of respondents in support and those opposed (for this figure, we place the nominees themselves on the x-axis). Nominees whose net support was less than 0 (indicated by the dashed red line) were "under water" in the sea of public opinion. Only four nominees—Haynsworth, Bork, Rehnquist, and Kavanaugh—achieved this ignominy.

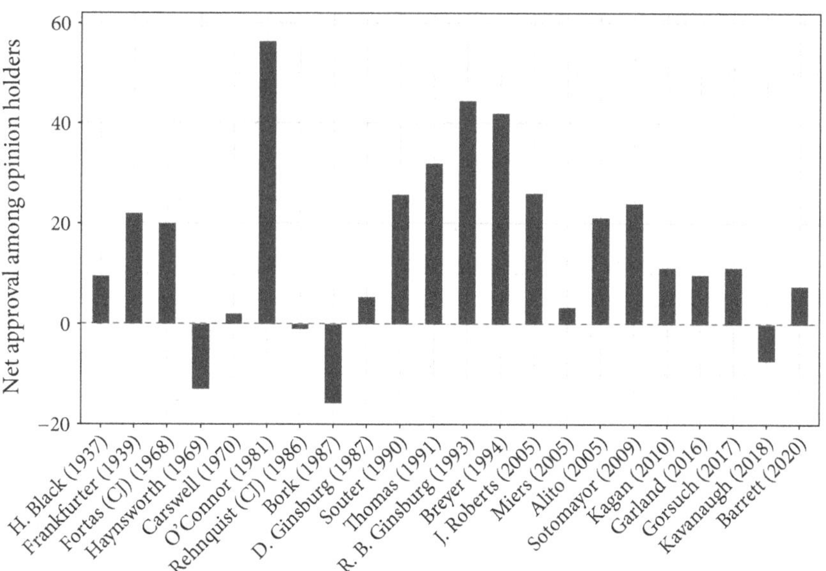

Fig. 7.6 Net approval among opinion holders, using the last five polls data.

Figure 7.6 also shows that, broadly speaking, net approval declined over time—especially if one focuses on nominees in the twenty-first century. For the nominations of John Roberts (2005), Samuel Alito (2005), and Sonia Sotomayor (2009), net approval exceeded 20 percentage points. The five nominees after them, however, saw much tighter margins, with Kavanaugh underwater. Importantly, absolute approval for most of these nominees did not decrease dramatically; recall from Figure 7.5 that nominees like Roberts, Alito, Sotomayor, and Kagan all enjoyed healthy approval ratings toward the end of their nominations. Rather, disapproval of nominees was typically much higher in later years, thereby depressing net approval over time.

7.5.2 Popularity and Nominee Attributes

These findings raise obvious questions about how attributes like perceived nominee quality or extremism affect popularity. We will examine these in more detail in Chapter 10, but discuss some simple patterns here.

We begin with Figure 7.7, which depicts the relationship between perceived nominee quality and net approval of nominees (as shown in Figure 7.6). We should note that the most commonly employed measure of perceived "nominee quality" is derived from content analysis of contemporaneous newspaper editorials. In other words, it tries to capture what the press said about the nominee's "quality" during the nomination.[14] As we noted in note 15 in Chapter 4, this measure sometimes conflates nominees with poor professional qualifications, such as Harriet Miers, with highly qualified nominees besmirched by scandal, such as Douglas Ginsburg and Brett Kavanaugh.

Figure 7.7 shows a generally positive and intuitive relationship between perceived nominee quality and net public approval of nominees, particularly at the higher range of the perceived qualifications measure. Three outliers stand out. Thomas and Breyer enjoyed high net approval relative to their middling quality scores, while Bork received less public esteem than his high-quality score might have suggested.

Finally, the high approval ratings of Sandra Day O'Connor, Clarence Thomas, Ruth Bader Ginsburg, and Sonia Sotomayor seem to suggest a public approval "bonus" for nominees with path-breaking diversity attributes (unfortunately, we have no polls from Thurgood Marshall's 1967 confirmation).[15] The net approval for the seven non-white/female nominees with polling data was 26 points, compared to 11 points for the white male nominees with polling data.

7.5.3 Differences in Partisan Response

We now turn to an extremely prominent feature of citizen evaluations of nominees: *differential partisan response*, by which we mean the difference in levels of support among Democratic and Republican partisans in the mass public. We again employ the last five polls data, but now aggregate the results by party identification.[16] To

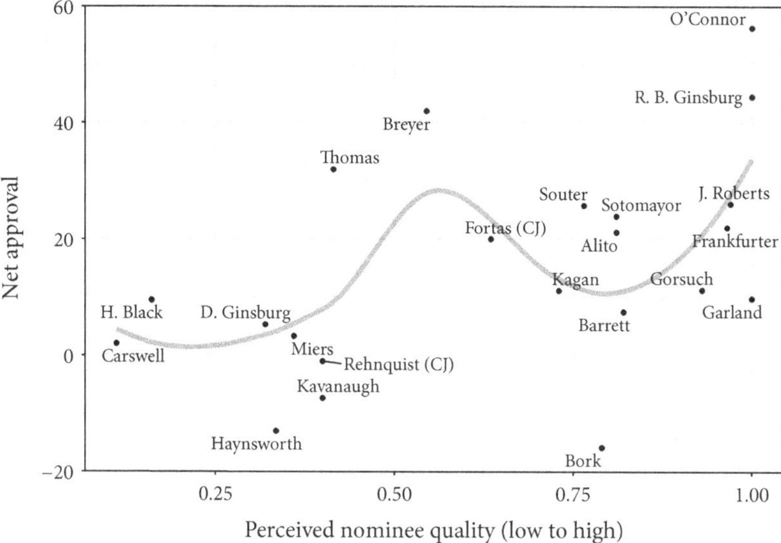

Fig. 7.7 Net approval versus perceived nominee quality. Net approval is the same measure shown in Figure 7.6. Perceived nominee quality is based on a content analysis of newspaper editorials on each nominee. The blue line is a loess line.

make the results easier to interpret, we divide the partisan response according to the party of the appointing president. This creates three groups: co-partisans of the president, independents, and out-party identifiers (whom we label "out-partisans"). One would naturally expect support for a nominee to be highest among co-partisans and lowest among out-partisans. The more interesting question involves changes in differential partisan response over time. This implies focusing on approval in each group among those with an opinion. So, within each group, we divide approval by the sum of approval plus disapproval, excluding don't knows. The temporal patterns are very similar if we include respondents who say "don't know."

Figure 7.8 presents the results.[17] The top panel shows average support by partisan groups in the 18 nominations with sufficient polling data—here the lines connect the observations within each partisan group. The bottom panel depicts the *difference* between in-party and out-party support for each nominee—here the line is a loess that summarizes the trend in the difference. The bottom panel thus provides a simple and intuitive measure of partisan differences in evaluation of Supreme Court nominees, from 1970 to 2020, some 50 years.

The patterns in Figure 7.8 could not be starker. In the twentieth century, partisan differentials were small. The Carswell nomination showed some differential, with about 65% of (in-party) Republicans supporting his ultimately doomed nomination, compared to only about 35% of Democrats. However, 12 years later, Sandra Day O'Connor enjoyed unique and near-universal support among all three groups, an astonishing feat from the perspective of today's nomination politics. Notably, Democratic elites declined to rally against the moderately conservative trailblazer, and

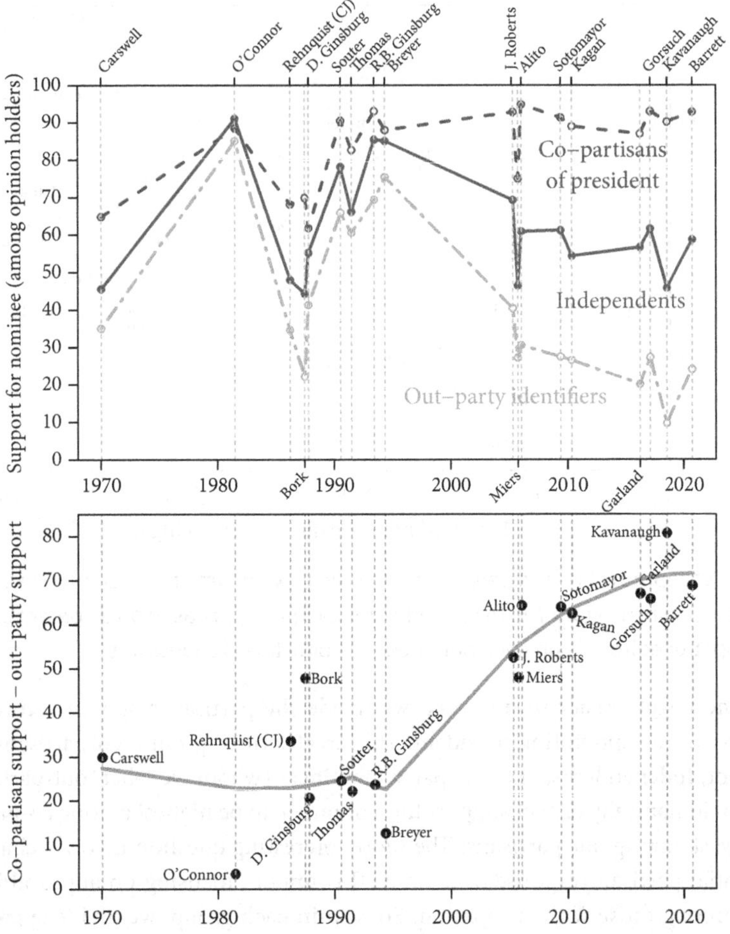

Fig. 7.8 Top) Public support for nominees among co-partisans of the president, Independents, and out-partisans from 1970 to 2020. Bottom) The difference between co-partisan and out-partisan support; the line is a loess line.

she was confirmed by a vote of 99-0. Partisan differences for Rehnquist and Bork were comparable to Carswell's, but then declined slightly for nominees through the 1990s, reaching a low with Breyer in 1994. Notably, every nominee in the 1990s (two Republicans and two Democrats) received majority support from out-partisans.

The turn of the twenty-first century, however, brought a dramatic change. Beginning with John Roberts' nomination in 2005, out-party support dropped precipitously. Clearly, something truly remarkable occurred in public evaluations between the nominations of Stephen Breyer (1994) and John Roberts (2005). The pattern intensified in the nominations that followed. Partisan differences reached truly spectacular levels in 2018, when more than 90% of Republicans supported Kavanaugh's nomination but fewer than 10% of Democrats did. Although the partisan differential declined somewhat at Barrett's nomination in 2020, it still exceeded that for every other nominee except Kavanaugh.

Notably, in the top panel in Figure 7.8 co-partisan support for nominees often "maxed out" at or close to 100%. As a result of this ceiling in out-party support, increases in the partisan differential reflected increases in opposition among out-partisans. (As shown in the figure, the average support ratings from Independents also dropped dramatically this century, compared to the 1990s.)

What should one conclude from Figure 7.8? One tempting interpretation is that the public became drunk on partisanship, as invoked the famous Twitter meme of political scientist Brendan Nyhan, "Partisanship is a hell of a drug." This interpretation is not only possible, it may even be correct—but not necessarily. These patterns might also reflect a change in the ideology of nominees, combined with the correct perception of these changes by the public. In addition, better sorting of Americans into partisan camps may well play a role.[18] We will more carefully examine in Chapter 10 the micro-foundations of public opinion on nominees. For now it suffices to say that levels of differential partisan response on the order of 80 percentage points bode poorly for a return to the "normal" nomination politics of the mid-twentieth century.[19]

7.6 The Nomination Campaigns: High Impact or Low?

Up to this point, we have taken a static perspective and focused on late stage public opinion. But nominations are dynamic events, with multiple stages between the announcement and the end of the nomination. In this sense, nominations resemble political campaigns, with the president and his supporters mobilizing to assist the nominee's confirmation and opponents mobilizing to block it. What patterns emerge in these interesting political campaigns?

Beginning in the 1980s—and especially after 2005—polling became so frequent that we can detect changes in public opinion over the course of the nomination campaigns—if any changes are there. In this section, we take advantage of the proliferating polls to hunt for obvious campaign effects. We study the 13 nomination campaigns that drew at least five polls: the campaigns for William Rehnquist, Robert Bork, David Souter, Clarence Thomas, John Roberts, Harriet Miers, Samuel Alito, Sonia Sotomayor, Elena Kagan, Merrick Garland, Neil Gorsuch, Brett Kavanaugh, and Amy Coney Barrett.[20] These nominees, of course, are all relatively recent—unfortunate, but that is where the polling was.

We focus on three broad questions. First, did opinion holding, nominee support, nominee opposition, and net support change much from early to late in the campaign? In other words, did the campaign change public opinion? Second, did these differences vary by partisanship? Third, which nominees "won" and "lost" their hearings, in terms of movement in opinion following the hearings?

Although it seems intuitive that campaigns shift public opinion, it is worth noting that the scholarly literature on "campaign effects" has found only modest effects (we review the studies in detail in the Appendix). Indeed, early landmark studies produced the famous "minimal effects" finding: presidential campaigns did not affect voters very strongly. Either opinions changed little, or they were based more on factors such as ideology and partisanship. More recently, better data and more sophisticated methods have found some campaign effects, such as the noted "post-convention bounce" in presidential races. Our search for a "post-hearings bounce" takes inspiration from this work. But for present purposes, the take-away point from the scholarly literature is clear: because nomination campaigns have modest effects on public opinion, at best, any clear effects are noteworthy.

7.6.1 Early to Late: Minimal Effects?

We begin with a simple figure that nevertheless contains a lot of information. Figure 7.9 presents a within-nomination over-time analysis of opinion among the 13 nominees. For visual clarity, we present only loess lines that summarize the three time series for each nomination.[21] The black lines depict the percent of respondents saying they approve of the nominee; the red (small-dash) line depicts the percentage disapproving; and the purple (long-dash) line depicts the percentage saying they don't know or are uncertain. The x-axis depicts the number of days between the start of the nomination and the date of the poll.[22] To enable comparisons across nominees, we fix the scale of the x-axes such that each spans the start of the nomination to about 100 days out.[23] In addition, we show the date of the nominee's initial hearing, if one occurred, before the Senate Judiciary Committee (the blue vertical lines) and the date of a nominee's scandal breaking, if one occurred (the green vertical lines).

First, focus on the purple lines connoting the don't know responses, and compare the levels early in the campaign to those late in the campaign. In only one case, the extremely lengthy Garland nomination, did the percentage of don't knows increase. In three cases (Roberts, Gorsuch, and Barrett) it remained virtually unmoved. But in all other cases, the percentage of don't knows fell; in three cases, it fell dramatically—Bork and Thomas stand out for really substantial decreases, but the decrease for Kavanaugh is also large. In these media intensive nominations featuring striking and sometimes salacious controversy, many citizens without initial opinions came to hold them. In some sense, this pattern in don't knows is what one might expect. But the general downward trend, with some dramatic drops, represents a notable campaign effect. In most recent nominations, the majority of the public makes up its mind (one way or the other) by the end of the campaign.

Next compare the early and late responses in the black lines connoting the percentage of the public that supports confirmation. In only one case does the trend line move down very much, again in the anomalously lengthy Garland nomination. In several cases, support hardly budges from the early polls to the late ones, including the Gorsuch, Kavanaugh, and Barrett nominations. In all other cases, support increases over time. However, the increase is noticeable only for the Alito, Sotomayor, and

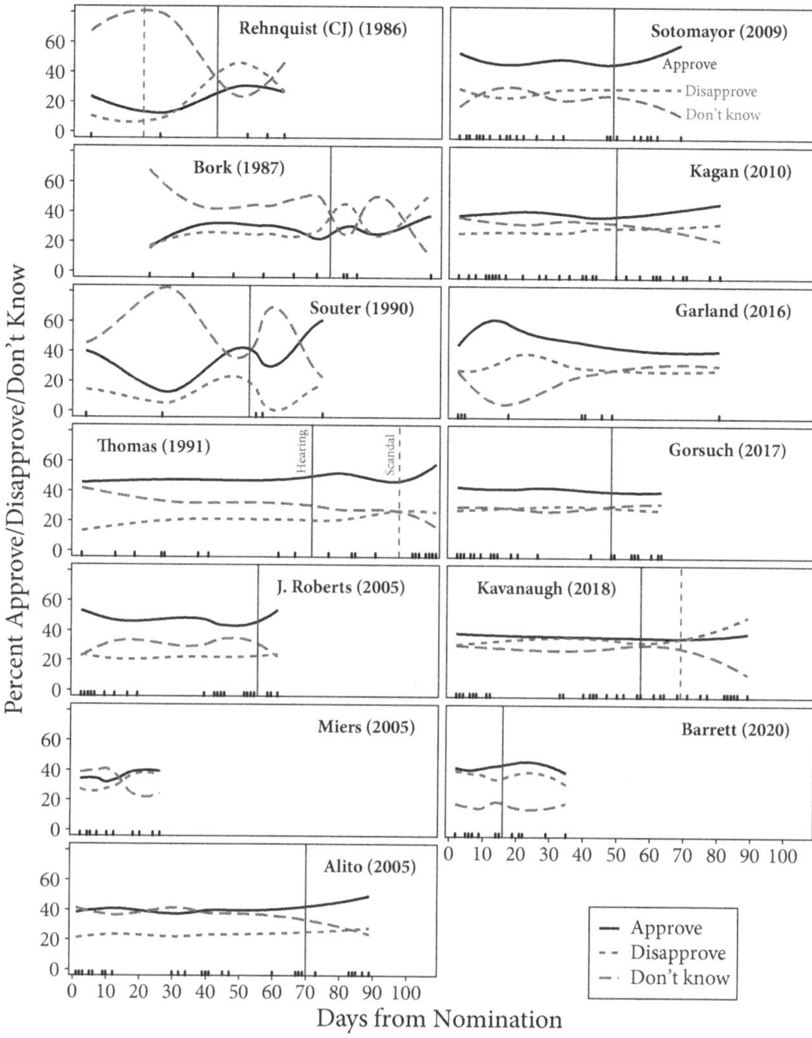

Fig. 7.9 Within-nomination temporal variation in public opinion. The loess lines summarize the time series of support, opposition, and don't know for 13 nominees with sufficient numbers of polls. The blue (solid) vertical line depicts the date of the nominee's hearing (if one occurred), while the green (dashed) vertical lines depict the date when scandals emerged (if one occurred). The rugs indicate the dates polls were taken.

Kagan nominations. In these cases, the increases came late, suggesting a favorable "bounce" from the hearings (we return to these cases in the next section). In sum, support for the nominee tended to remain relatively flat from early to late in the campaign, with a modest upward trend.

Finally, the red disapprove trend lines show that in only two cases does opposition decrease—the unusual Garland case and the Barrett nomination. In several cases, opposition hardly changed from early to late—for example, in the Roberts, Sotomayor, and Gorsuch nominations. In the remaining cases, opposition trended upward, with dramatic increases in opposition in the Bork and Kavanaugh cases.

A final quantity of interest is *net support* (support minus opposition, or the distance between the black and red bar in the figure). Because both support and opposition tend to trend upward over the course of the campaign, in many cases net support hardly budged. Examples include Thomas, Roberts, Alito, Kagan, and Gorsuch. In a few cases, net support surged late in the campaign, suggesting success in the hearings. Sotomayor stands out in this regard. However, the most dramatic change in net support occurred during the Bork campaign, with modestly positive net support rather early in the campaign turning into a substantial deficit by its end. The change reflected the relatively flat support but surging opposition. It is hard not to attribute this change to the revolutionary campaign mounted against Bork by mobilizing interest groups (see Chapter 5). Also notable is the flip from positive to negative net support during the Kavanaugh nomination, also due to late surging opposition following the dramatic accusations of sexual assault.

It is easy to over-interpret trend lines, which can be sensitive to small changes in estimation. Accordingly, we turn to comparisons of more tightly aggregated data: averages from polls in the first 30 days of the campaign (which we call "early"), with those from the last 30 days (which we call "late"). Because of either campaign brevity (in the case of Miers and Barrett) or lack of polling data, we are left with usable data from nine nominees: Bork, Souter, Thomas, John Roberts, Alito, Sotomayor, Kagan, Gorsuch, and Kavanaugh.

Figure 7.10 summarizes the overall difference between early and late opinion holding. The left graph pools the aggregate data for the nine nominees. The x-axis breaks down aggregate opinion into approval of the nominee, disapproval, and don't know. For each of these, the gray bars depict the mean level of opinion in the early period, while the black bars depict the later periods. Intuitively, the average levels of no opinion holding decrease from early to late period. In the aggregate, the conversion of no opinion into opinion must shift into either approval or disapproval. The figure shows that approval levels tend to increase slightly, while disapproval increases somewhat more dramatically.

Aggregating across all the nominees can mask some interesting variation, so the right panel presents this information separately for the nine nominees, moving down the graph in chronological order. While most of the nominees showed small changes across the campaign, two nominees stand out, for different reasons. First, the Souter nomination is unique in that the public maintained high levels of don't knows both early and late, with almost no movement across the campaign. Conversely, Robert Bork started off quite unknown, with nearly 80% of respondents holding no opinion in the early period. Bork's approval levels actually increased quite significantly over time, rising from about 10% to about 40%. But, unfortunately for his supporters, his disapproval increased much more dramatically, plunging him underwater in popularity as the nomination came to an end. Indeed, Bork is the only nominee (in

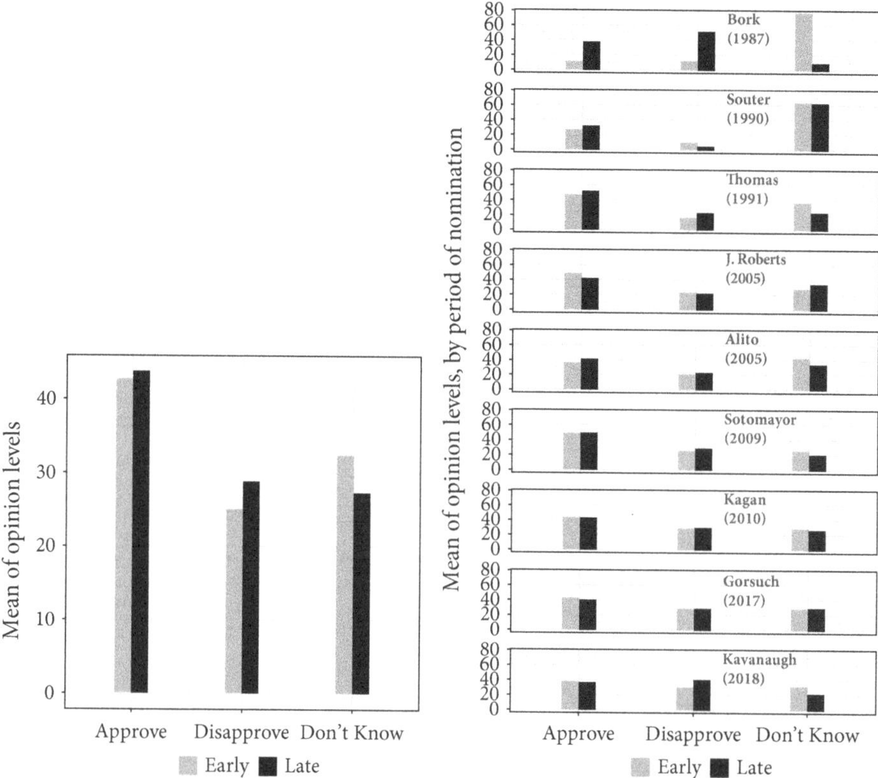

Fig. 7.10 Early versus late opinion content, for nine recent nominees. Each bar depicts the average opinion level in the relevant period. The left graph pools the nominees together.

our polling data) who clearly "lost" his nomination campaign in the court of public opinion. We suggest in later chapters that such a loss translates into danger in the Senate. Both the Republican Party and conservative legal analysts would learn from this loss, and would refuse to be out-mobilized in the future.[24]

7.6.2 Partisanship and Campaign Effects

Given the jaw-dropping partisan differences in final evaluations of nominees discussed above, an obvious question is: does partisanship interact with campaign effects? To address this question, we calculated the mean levels of support by party identification in each poll for the 13 nominees shown in Figure 7.9; there are three Democratic appointees among these nominees: Sotomayor, Kagan, and Garland. Again we label these in-party support, independent support, and out-party support, based on the party of the appointing president. As with the analysis in Figure 7.8, since

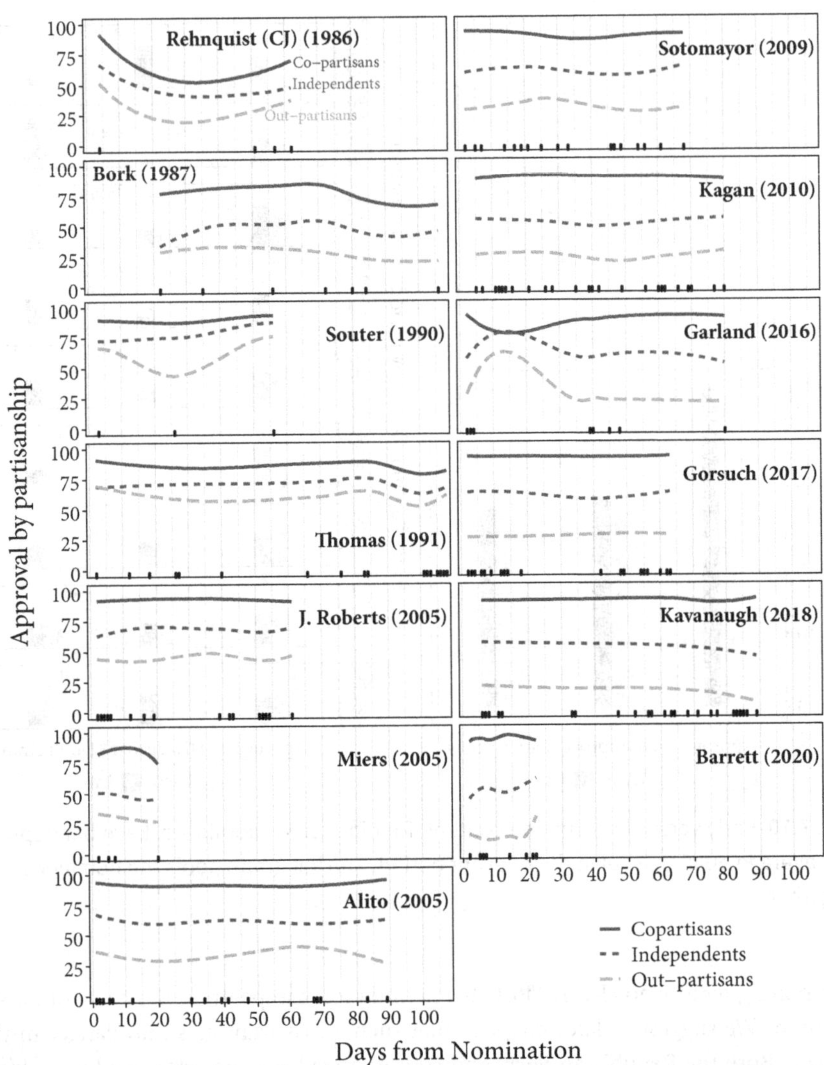

Fig. 7.11 Within-nomination temporal variation in approval, by partisanship, for 13 nominees. The loess lines summarize the time series of support, by party. The green (solid) lines, the purple (small-dashed) lines, and the orange (long-dash) lines depict in-party, Independent, and out-party support, respectively. The rugs indicate the dates polls were taken.

our interest here is in opinions, we focus on approval in each group among those with an opinion.

The results are shown in Figure 7.11. Again we summarize trends using multiple loess lines—the green lines, the purple lines, and the orange lines depict co-partisan, Independent, and out-partisan support, respectively. The graph shows stark partisan differences in opinion for most nominees (of course these are only recent nominees).

The *ordering* of levels of support is almost always in-party/independents/out-party. Moreover, this ordering holds at any given point in the campaigns.

But the *dynamics* of partisan difference are also notable—for their stability. One might imagine that partisans who begin somewhat uncertain about the nominee then move to a more polarized evaluation over time. In fact, one can see Republicans becoming more supportive of Bork over time, and both Republicans and Democrats becoming more polarized in the Alito nomination (a small increase) and more substantially in the Kavanaugh nomination (all three nominees were Republican). But in general, one sees remarkable stability in partisan evaluations: they immediately diverge and maintain about the same level of difference over the nomination. The trend lines just don't move much. Examples of partisan stability include the Roberts, Kagan, Garland, Gorsuch, and Barrett nominations. The obvious inference is that citizens make immediate judgments about the nominee based on their partisanship, and revise this inference only in the face of substantial and dramatic new information, as occurred in the Bork and Kavanaugh nominations. We examine the mechanisms behind this pattern in Chapter 10.

Again, we can aggregate the data toward the tails of the nomination period to overcome the limitations of relying on the loess lines to depict trends. As above, we contrast averages from polls in the first 30 days of the campaign to polls from the last 30 days. Figure 7.12 depicts the average movement in opinion from early to late, broken down by partisanship. The left column shows the average level of approval, the middle column the average level of disapproval, and the right column shows average levels of don't know. (Note that because we are including all respondents here, the levels of approval and disapproval will be smaller than we observed in Figure 7.11, which examined approval among opinion holders.) Each panel shows the change from early to late. Within each panel, the green lines, the purple lines, and the orange lines depict in-party, Independent, and out-party support, respectively, moving from early to late.

As before, Figure 7.12 reveals two clear patterns. First, on average, opinion simply does not move very much within the course of most nominations, a "minimal effects" finding. But, there were exceptions to minimal effects: the Bork, Thomas, and Kavanaugh nominations. Second, when opinion does change, all the partisan groups tend to move together, even as the extent of change differs across the groups.[25] Again the Kavanaugh nomination was a clear exception: approval among Republicans remained steadfast throughout his nomination, while approval among Democrats declined markedly toward the end of his nomination.

7.6.3 Do the Hearings Matter? What about Scandals?

Like election campaigns, modern-day Supreme Court nominations have a typical rhythm. In the initial phase, the president announces the nominees, the two sides mobilize to support or oppose the nominee, and the nominee meets with crucial

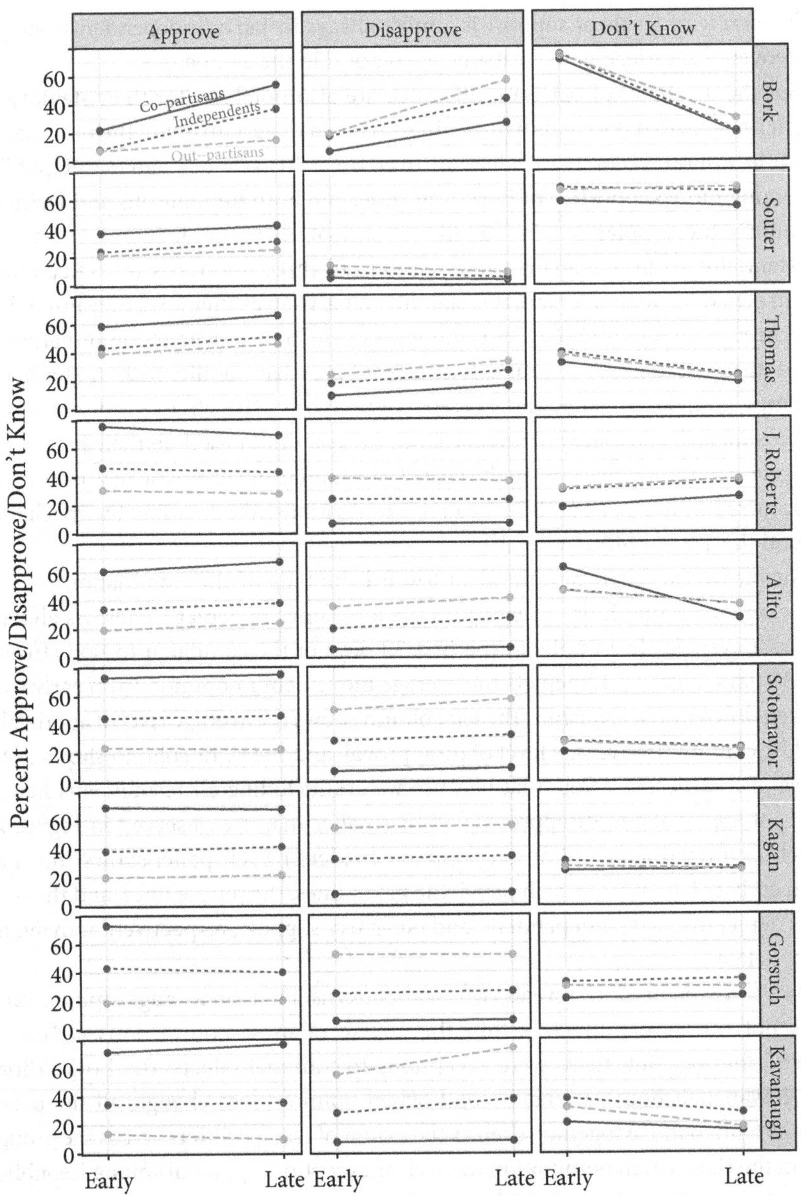

Fig. 7.12 Early versus late opinion content by partisanship, for nine recent nominees.

senators (typically those on the Judiciary Committee). As shown in the previous chapter, after the initial announcement, two other events tend to draw heavy media coverage. The first is routine and occurs for nearly every modern nominee (the exceptions were Miers and Garland): the Judiciary Committee hearings. The second is rarer, but perhaps more consequential: when a nominee faces a public scandal that threatens to derail their confirmation. If campaign effects are more than minimal, the hearings and/or scandals are almost certainly the place to find them.

We begin by focusing on routine hearings. Ideally, abundant polling data would allow a regression discontinuity style analysis comparing public opinion just before and just after the hearings. Unfortunately, we lack sufficient data, particularly pre-hearing polls. We pursue a second best strategy, using more aggregation. We retain the nominees who had at least one poll 20 days before the start of the hearings and one poll after the start of the hearings. This yields nine nominees. Then, we compare the averages of the approve, disapprove, and don't know responses in the pre- and post-periods.[26]

Figure 7.13 presents the results. The left graph pools across all nominees, while the right panel displays the results for the individual nominees, moving down in chronological order. Bork's nomination stands out. Following his widely panned hearings, Bork's approval actually rose—but his disapproval rose even more. Relatedly, as discussed above, the hearings had a seemingly dramatic effect on opinion holding, with the level of don't knows dropping from 50% to 21%.

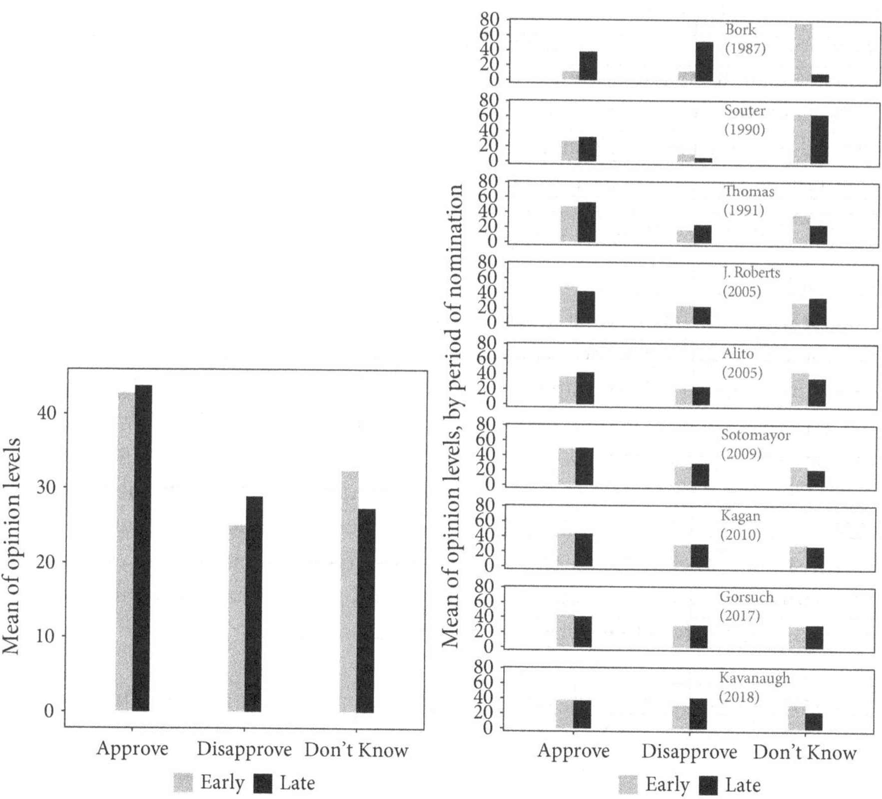

Fig. 7.13 Public opinion on nominees in the 20 days before and after the Senate Judiciary Committee's routine hearings. The left graph pools the nominees together.

But for the remaining nominees, the results are... hum-drum. Across all nine cases, approval increased slightly (from 40% to 45%), as did disapproval (from 29% to 32%). Conversely, the level of don't knows declined somewhat from (30% to 24%). In the Appendix we analyze approval by partisan groups; the data reveal initial divergence with little movement across the hearings—with Bork being the perpetual exception.

In our view, *any* campaign effects are noteworthy. The small changes in approval before and after the hearings do suggest that the public pays at least some attention to either the hearings themselves or (more likely) the media's coverage of the hearings. But usually there is little to see. Nominees and their handlers learned the lesson of the Bork nomination, and now prepare assiduously. Consequently, little of controversy is said at the hearings.

But scandals may prove an exception. Several nominations with polling data featured scandals. Two scandal-plagued nominations—Thomas and Kavanaugh—generated sufficient polls to conduct meaningful campaign-style analyses. Even though these scandals were among the most high profile ever to befall a Supreme Court nominee, they are nonetheless important case studies. The arc of the Thomas and Kavanaugh nominations were quite similar (almost eerily so, in fact). Both nominees were advanced by a Republican president. Both nominees were somewhat controversial to begin with—Thomas due to his lack of legal experience and Kavanaugh due to his replacement of the median justice—but their confirmations seemed assured, following their relatively smooth initial hearings before the Judiciary Committee. (The vote margin for Kavanaugh would surely have been narrow, due to increased party polarization in the Senate and the slender Republican majority.) Then, out of nowhere, both nominations were rocked by accusations of sexual misconduct.

Following the allegations, both nominations moved into the danger zone. Democrats, joined by some Republicans, called for further investigation. In both cases, the Judiciary Committee held a second and extremely dramatic hearing. On national television, the nominees and their accusers testified, with millions of Americans transfixed by the spectacle. Following the second hearings, the nominations quickly moved to the Senate floor. And, amidst a great outcry on both sides, each was narrowly confirmed (52-48 for Thomas and 50-48 for Kavanaugh).

The similar timelines in the two cases allow us to conduct a structured examination of whether and how public opinion changed in the face of each scandal. We divide each nomination into four periods.

- *Pre-initial hearing.* First, we capture public opinion before the initial Judiciary Committee hearing. To focus on later stage opinion, we only retain polls conducted fewer than 15 days before the initial hearing.
- *Pre-scandal.* This period comprises both the initial hearing and the days after the hearing but before the scandal broke.

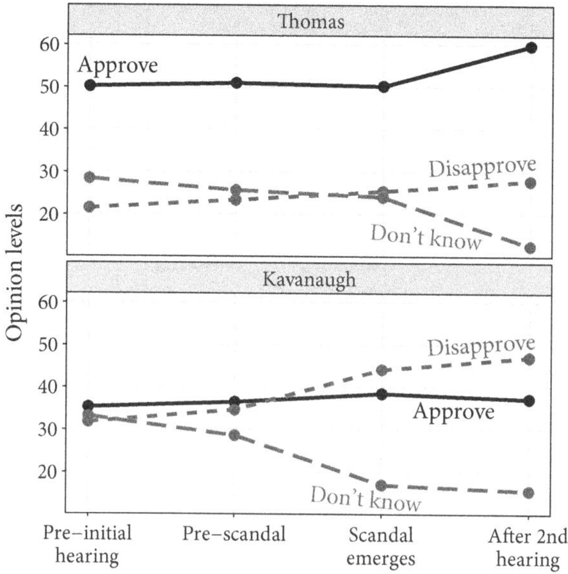

Fig. 7.14 Opinion movement in the Thomas and Kavanaugh nominations. See text for details on the coding of the periods.

- *Scandal emerges.* This period begins the day the allegations became public and continues to the date of the second hearing.
- *After second hearing.* This period starts with the second hearing and continues through the day of the floor vote.[27]

The polls were spaced irregularly over time. Accordingly, within each period, we calculate the mean of the relevant opinion categories.

Figure 7.14 depicts the levels of approval, disapproval, and don't knows among all Americans, across the two nominations. Consistent with the earlier analyses, we see very little opinion movement in the first two stages, which include the initial, routine hearings. But the picture changes dramatically in the post-scandal phase.

For the Thomas nomination, opinion moved little when the scandal broke; disapproval inched upward and don't knows inched downward. However, following the prime-time second round of hearings, Thomas' approval ratings' actually *increased* considerably, by about 10 percentage points. This boost more than offset the slight uptick in disapproval after the hearings. In this sense, Thomas "won" his tense battle in the hearing room. Indeed, one study suggests his relatively high approval ratings probably made the difference in the confirmation vote, by solidifying his support among Southern Democratic senators.[28]

A dramatically different picture emerges in the Kavanaugh nomination. The Ford allegations led to a decided boost in Kavanaugh's disapproval rating. Accompanying this was an almost mirror decline in don't knows, compatible with a direct shift

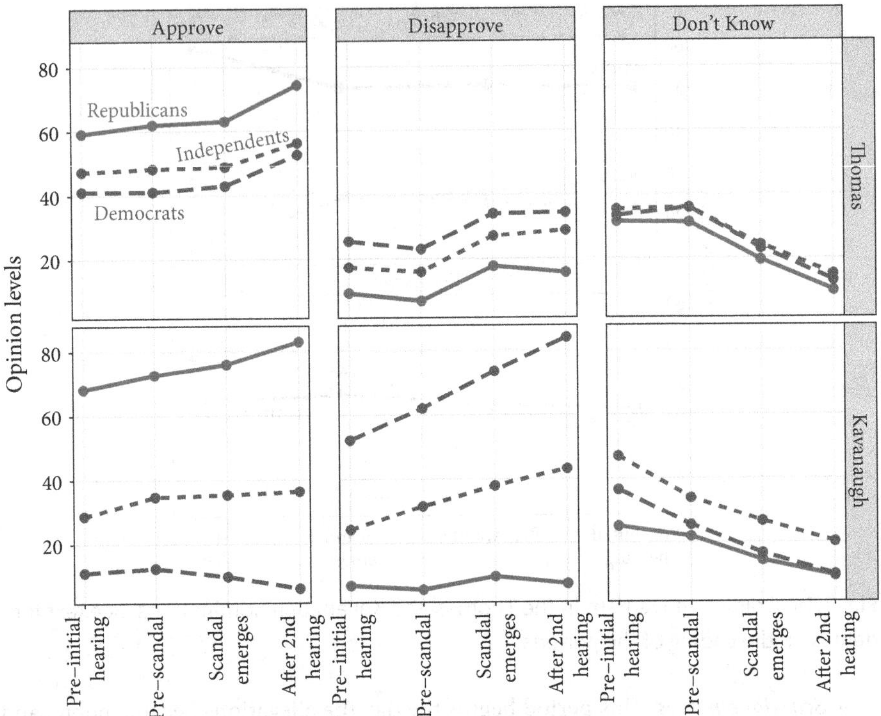

Fig. 7.15 Opinion movement in the Thomas and Kavanaugh nominations, by party. See text for details on coding of periods.

from one camp to the other.[29] This trend continued following the second round of hearings, leaving the judge underwater in popularity as the floor vote approached. Kavanaugh thus "lost" his campaign battle in the court of public opinion even as he survived confirmation.

Figure 7.15 shifts the focus to partisan opinion during the Thomas and Kavanaugh nominations. Since Republic presidents nominated both, we label party directly and employ the traditional red/purple/blue coding scheme. The results on display are perhaps even more striking.

In the Thomas nomination, partisan opinion *moved nearly in lockstep* across the phases of his nomination. Remarkably from the perspective of today's heightened partisan polarization, Thomas' favorability among Democrats (and Independents) increased essentially the same amount as among Republicans, following the second hearings. Similarly, the increase in disapproval among Republicans following the Hill allegations mirrored that among Democrats. Finally, the pattern of don't knows is indistinguishable across partisan groups during the nomination. In short, the Thomas nomination was largely a story of partisan parallel publics.

The Kavanaugh nomination tells a completely different tale. In the pre-scandal phase, public opinion polarized heavily, though a sizable portion of don't knows remained in the population. In the scandal phase, approval among Democrats shrank from its already low baseline, while disapproval skyrocketed to 80%. Conversely, Republican approval for Kavanaugh increased substantially following the break of the scandal and the second hearing, while Republican disapproval remained at very low levels.[30] This steadfast approval among the Republican public surely bolstered the nominee's support among Republican senators. In short, the data suggest that in the sordid spectacle of "he said, she said," Democrats overwhelmingly believed Ford, Republicans overwhelmingly believed Kavanaugh, and Independents followed the Democrats but more tepidly.

Few general lessons can emerge from two extraordinary cases. But they do demonstrate that when a scandal befalls a modern-day Supreme Court nominee, the public cares, is capable of processing new information, and may update their approval or disapproval of the nominee accordingly, perhaps even in surprising directions.

7.7 Conclusion

When Supreme Court nominations changed from quiet, closed door, sedate affairs into bruising, bare-knuckle brawls, public opinion—as revealed by polls—changed as well.

First, of course, pollsters conducted more polls. Prior to the nomination of Sandra Day O'Connor, polls were rare and reserved almost exclusively for high-visibility nominations. After O'Connor, polling became fairly routine, and by the Roberts nomination in 2005 so frequent that we can sometimes study the dynamics of opinion change during the nomination campaigns itself.

Second, and hardly surprisingly, opinion holding among the general public moved from probably rare—we can only guess because polls were so infrequent—to quite prevalent. Plausibly, increased media coverage drove this change.

Third, the public popularity of nominees varied widely. Much of the variation reflected seemingly sensible responses to the attributes of the nominees, for example, whether they were accused of scandalous behavior, or whether their race or gender made them trail blazers of diversity. But sometime between the nominations of Stephen Breyer in 1994 and John Roberts in 2005, a partisan transformation occurred, a transformation that became more and more pronounced in later years. The evaluations of co-partisans of the nominating president and the evaluations of out-party citizens sharply diverged. The difference between the two reached astounding levels in the second decade of the twenty-first century—as high as 80 percentage points.

Finally, something more than "minimal" campaign effects can occur between a nomination's end and beginning. The most prominent campaign effect is an increase in opinion holding, apparently driven by cumulative media coverage. Contrary to what is perhaps the conventional wisdom, most *routine* confirmation hearings did not result in significant opinion shifts—with the notable exception of the Bork nomination. The liberal interest groups that launched a carefully coordinated, skillful, and largely one-sided campaign against Bork's nomination triumphed in the court of public opinion.[31] Though most routine hearings generated minimal effects, the extraordinary scandals and second hearings during the Thomas and Kavanaugh nominations led to rather dramatic changes in opinion—in favor of Thomas and against Kavanaugh. The difference between the two cases nicely illustrates the shift toward polarized party opinion between the 1990s and the contemporary era of Supreme Court nominations.

The findings in this chapter, particularly about the exploding differences in partisan responses to nominees, raise serious questions. What lies behind this disturbing trend? Is differential partisan response a story about partisan polarization among the public? Or is it a story about changes in the nominees, as they became both more extreme and more reliably extreme? Perhaps it is some combination of the two? Probing these questions requires different data and different methods than those used in this descriptive chapter. We return to them in Chapter 10. But first we conclude Part I by examining the arena where the changes in nomination politics were most visible: the United States Senate.

8
Decision in the Senate

On July 1, 1795, President George Washington signed a temporary commission making John Rutledge the new chief justice of the Supreme Court. The recess appointment arose because the Senate was out of session, but based on Rutledge's background, Washington had little doubt that he would eventually be confirmed.[1] In 1789, Rutledge had been one of five initial associate justices selected by Washington, and the Senate unanimously confirmed him. He was highly qualified; he chaired the South Carolina delegation to the First Continental Congress in 1774, later served as governor of South Carolina, and helped draft the Constitution in 1787. Indeed, Washington had considered Rutledge for chief in 1789, but chose John Jay instead. In 1791, two years after his first appointment, Rutledge resigned this position to become chief justice of the South Carolina Court of Common Pleas. But when John Jay resigned in 1795, Rutledge expressed his interest to Washington in succeeding Jay as chief justice.

One day after Rutledge's recess appointment, the Washington Administration (coincidentally) made public the terms of the Jay Treaty with Great Britain, which addressed several lingering issues between the two countries following the Revolutionary War. The treaty immediately triggered controversy along the country's newly formed party lines. The Federalists, led by Alexander Hamilton, supported the treaty, while Democratic-Republicans, led by Thomas Jefferson, opposed it.

Unwisely, as it would turn out, Rutledge criticized the terms of the treaty in a meeting in South Carolina in mid-July.[2] News of Rutledge's speech slowly spread, and treaty opponents latched onto his criticism. Although the Senate had already ratified the treaty in June, and Washington would sign it in August, leading Federalists denounced Rutledge and vowed to oppose his confirmation as chief justice. Alexander Hamilton labeled him insane, and Federalist-backed papers launched a vituperative campaign of personal attacks against the nominee. On December 15, the Federalist-controlled Senate rejected Rutledge's nomination by a vote of 14-10, making him the first Supreme Court nominee to be defeated on the Senate floor.

Nearly two centuries later, President Ronald Reagan nominated Antonin Scalia to take the seat left vacant by Justice William Rehnquist's elevation to chief justice. At the time of the nomination, Scalia was a well-known conservative judge and legal thinker, having served for many years as a law professor at the University of Chicago before being appointed to the powerful D.C. Circuit Court in 1982. Although he lacked the "paper trail" that helped doom Robert Bork's nomination a year later, it was eminently predictable that Scalia would be a reliable conservative vote on the Supreme Court.

Making the Supreme Court: The Politics of Appointments, 1930–2020. Charles M. Cameron and Jonathan P. Kastellec, Oxford University Press. DOI: 10.1093/oso/9780197680544.003.0008

Yet—almost unbelievably in hindsight—Scalia was confirmed by a 98-0 vote and went on to become one of the most famous and influential conservative justices in the court's history.[3]

The contrasting fates of Rutledge and Scalia illustrate two phenomena that have always been at play in Supreme Court confirmation politics. The first is *contentious nominations*—nominations that are either blocked before reaching the floor of the Senate or result in a significantly divided roll call vote. Such nominations are nearly as old as the country itself. The second is *consensus nominations*—nominees with broad support from both parties. A majority of nominations since the founding have been of this type.

In this chapter, we examine the Senate's role in confirming or rejecting Supreme Court nominees. As we document in the Appendix, the Senate's role in Supreme Court nomination is the part of the process that has probably received the most attention from political scientists. With that in mind, our goal in this descriptive chapter is to lay the groundwork for explaining changes in roll call voting over time in Chapter 11; there we focus on changes in the relationship between senators and their constituents as the main driver of the shifts in roll call voting in the 1930 to 2020 period. In this chapter we focus on the two main factors in understanding confirmation outcomes and variation in roll call votes: party and ideology. We begin by examining failure and success over time going back to 1789, showing that the failure rate for nominees has varied significantly over time. We first focus on party control as the main explanation for outcomes, and show that confirmation successes have been much more likely under unified government than divided government.

We then shift our focus to ideology, and discuss two eras where divisions over race split one of the parties. In particular, we examine how Southern Democrats' fury over the court's landmark 1954 decision in *Brown v. Board of Education* injected racial politics into mid-twentieth-century nominations. We then show that over time these divisions over race were folded into the main liberal-conservative fault lines in American politics. As this happened, and as nominees themselves became more extreme, the ideological distance between nominees and senators of the party opposite of the president—i.e. the out-party—increased dramatically. In addition, we show that senators appeared to increasingly weigh ideological distance in their voting decisions. As a result, while until recently most nominees could generally count on significant support from out-party senators, those days are over, and roll call votes on Supreme Court nominees are now nearly straight party-line affairs. Unless something dramatic changes in nomination politics, the era of consensus nominations is over. In its place is the new normal of highly contentious politics.

8.2 Failure and Success over Time

From 1789 to 2020, presidents named 146 unique individuals to sit on the U.S. Supreme Court.[4] Including recess appointments, there were 178 unique appointments in this period; in most cases (and unlike Rutledge), justices who took the bench via a recess appointment went on to be officially confirmed to their seats. Excluding the 13 recess appointments, there were 165 nominations to the court. Of these 165, four nominations "died" for purely procedural reasons.[5] Of the remaining 161, 127 were confirmed.[6]

That leaves 34 nominees from 1789 to 2020 whose nominations truly failed. Of these, 10 were withdrawn due to Senate opposition. Of the remaining 24, 12 were rejected via a roll call vote, while the other 12 nominations were defeated indirectly; that is, the Senate either tabled the nomination, postponed it, or simply took no action (as with Merrick Garland). Following Whittington (2006), we define "failure" as a nominee who wished to serve but was not confirmed; thus, we pool nominations that were withdrawn with those that were directly or indirectly blocked by the Senate. That leaves us with 127 confirmation successes (including those who declined to serve on the court) and 34 failures from 1789 to 2020, yielding a success rate of 79% and a failure rate of 21%.

Figure 8.1 summarizes the trends in confirmation outcomes and roll call voting over this period. Figure 8.1A shows the rate of confirmation success versus failure; the "rugs" depict successful (top) and unsuccessful (bottom) nominations, while the line shows the probability of a nominee confirmation over time. Early on, nominees were usually confirmed, the rejection of Rutledge notwithstanding. This trend diminished in the mid-nineteenth century, during which several nominations failed, including four of President John Tyler's five nominees. While sporadic failures occurred later in the nineteenth century, by the twentieth century a very high likelihood of confirmation resumed. Remarkably, between 1894 and 1968, there was only a single confirmation failure—John Parker in 1930. After that, the confirmation rate declined steadily, if gradually, with six failures between 1968 and 2020. All in all, while the probability of confirmation success never dropped below 50%, Figure 8.1 shows significant ebbs and flows over time.

Success or failure, however, reveals only part of the story about confirmation politics. Examining roll call votes on nominees provides much more information about the depth of support for nominees over time. Figure 8.1B depicts the proportion of yea votes for every nominee that received a roll call vote in the Senate. We treat voice votes as unanimous support for the nominee, and we label nominees who received at least one nay vote. Consistent with the confirmation rate, nominees in the late eighteenth century and early nineteenth century generally received high levels of support. The middle of the nineteenth century saw many failures and close calls, followed by a return to broader support around the turn of the twentieth century. Finally, even as the confirmation rate has remained relatively high over the last few decades, Figure 8.1B shows that roll call votes have become increasingly contentious—particularly for nominees in the twenty-first century. John Roberts received 78% yea votes in 2005; none of the six nominees (through 2020) who reached the floor after Roberts (through 2020) received more than 70%. And none of President Trump's three nominees (Gorsuch, Kavanaugh, and Barrett) received more than 55%

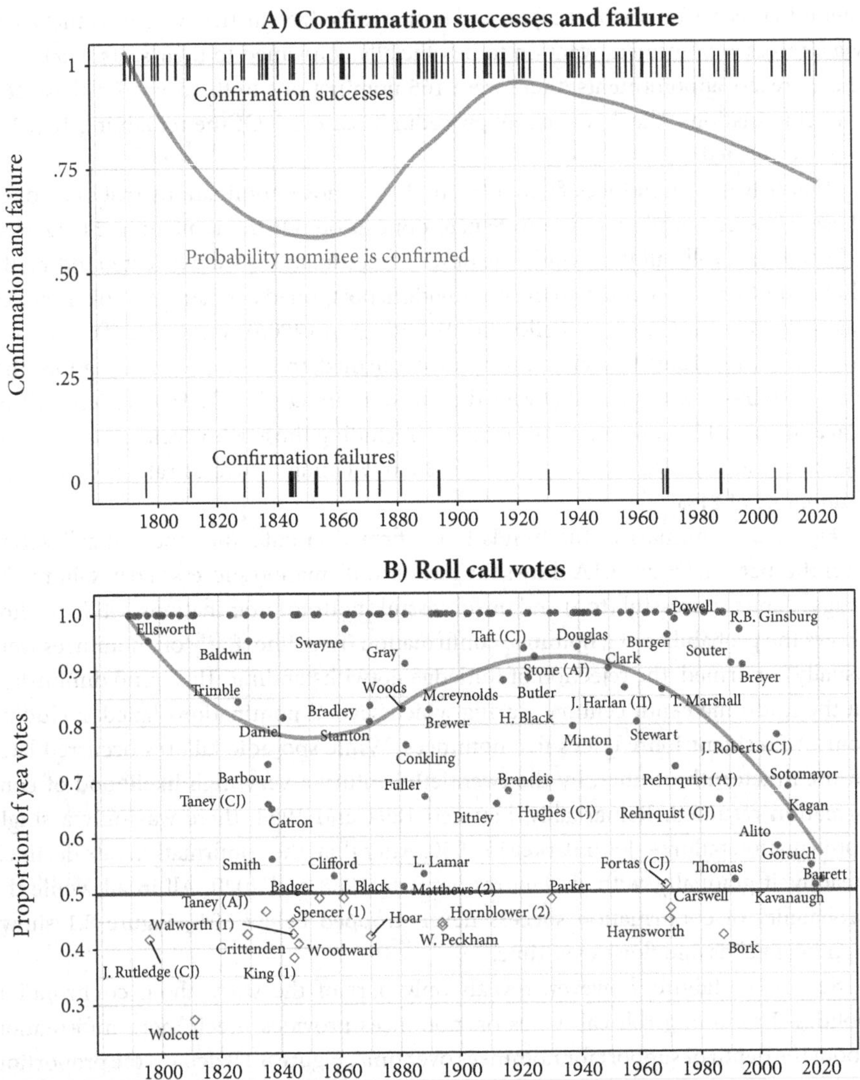

Fig. 8.1 A) The success rate of nominations, 1789–2020. The rugs depict specific instances of confirmation successes (top) and failures (bottom). B) The proportion of yea votes 1789–2020 for nominees with roll call votes or voice votes. We label nominees who received at least one nay vote. The green circles depict confirmed nominees, and the red diamonds show rejected nominees. The lines are loess lines.

support. Thus, it seems we have entered an unprecedented era with respect to Senate voting on nominees.[7]

As a final indicator of this new era, we examine voice votes in the Senate over time on Supreme Court nominees. In a voice vote, individual roll call votes are not recorded; rather, the present senators as a whole say either "yea" or "nay" in unison.

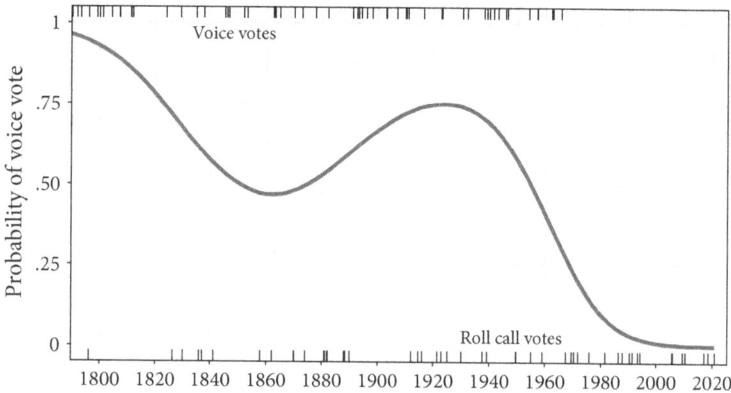

Fig. 8.2 The incidence of voice votes for Supreme Court nominees, 1789–2020. The rugs indicate voice votes (top) and full roll call votes (bottom); the loess line depicts the likelihood of a voice vote over time.

Voice votes are generally used for uncontroversial bills or confirmations, as their upshot is that no senators record their opposition. Figure 8.2 depicts the likelihood of a voice vote on nominees over time. As indicated by the loess line, this trend generally tracks with the proportion of yea votes over time. Notably, the last voice vote to confirm a nominee occurred in 1965, with Abe Fortas' appointment to associate justice. Today, it is nearly impossible to imagine a nominee in the modern era being confirmed without a roll call vote.

8.2.1 The Role of Senate Control and Nomination Timing

What explains this variation in confirmation outcomes and senatorial support for nominees? We begin with the most important historical factor for the likelihood of confirmation success—and what in fact may determine in the future with near certainty whether a nominee is confirmed or not: partisan control of the Senate.

In many respects, confirmation politics resembles legislative politics more broadly. Except in highly unusual cases, presidents can count on significant support from senators of the same party ("in-party support"). Subsequently, the fate of a nomination turns on both the *extent* of opposition from senators not of the president's party—whom we denote the "out-party"—and the *size* of the out-party; that is, whether there exists unified or divided government (defined strictly by party control of the Senate, relative to the president).

Table 8.1 presents a breakdown of confirmation successes versus failures from 1789 to 2020 (using the same definition of failure as in Figure 8.1). The left panel examines outcomes by Senate control—it shows, first, the vast majority of nominations came under unified government: 131 out of 160 in total (82%). Second, while unified government has not guaranteed a confirmation success, the likelihood of failure

Table 8.1 Confirmation outcomes by unified versus divided government (left), and the timing of nominations (right). The numbers in parentheses are column proportions.

Senate Control			Timing of Nomination		
	Unified	Divided		Before 4th Year	4th Year or Lame Duck
Success	109 (.82)	18 (.62)	Success	101 (.84)	26 (.63)
Failure	23 (.18)	11 (.38)	Failure	19 (.16)	15 (.37)
Total	132	29	Total	120	41

has been much higher during divided government—38%, compared to 18% during unified government.

Another key variable in confirmation success has been nomination *timing*, as the Senate may be less eager to confirm a president's nominee as either an election or the inauguration of a new president approaches. This was especially true of nineteenth-century nominations. As Whittington (2006) documents, nominees often failed then when named by "lame duck" presidents during divided government—that is, nominations between election day and the swearing in of a new president.[8] Even presidents in the fourth year of their term who are not technically yet lame ducks may face greater skepticism about their nominees; nominations made by such presidents are less likely to result in confirmation than those made in the first three years of a term.[9]

The right crosstab in Table 8.1 shows the relationship between confirmation success and nomination timing: whether an appointment was made in the first three years of a president's term, or in either an election year or a lame duck period. The pattern here is nearly identical to that seen with Senate control; election-year and lame duck nominees were more likely than not to result in confirmation, but the likelihood of failure was still quite higher than for nominations made earlier in a president's term.[10]

8.2.2 Party Control and Roll Call Margins

Confirmation outcomes, of course, only capture raw success or failure. Examining the proportion of yea votes by party affiliation provides a more nuanced look at how Senate partisanship can lead to different types of roll call margins. Figure 8.3 presents a scatterplot that shows the proportion of yea votes from both in-party and out-party senators for each nominee who reached the floor of the Senate (including voice votes). We jitter the points, which helps illustrate the clustering of nominees in the top-right corner with unanimous support from both groups of senators. Nominees who were either confirmed or received at least 50% in-party support are indicated with solid black dots (and named); nominees who were not confirmed or received less than 50% of in-party support are named, as are all nominees after 2000.

The graph reveals four distinct nomination "regimes." The top-right quadrant comprises "consensus nominations"—those for whom at least 50% of senators in both

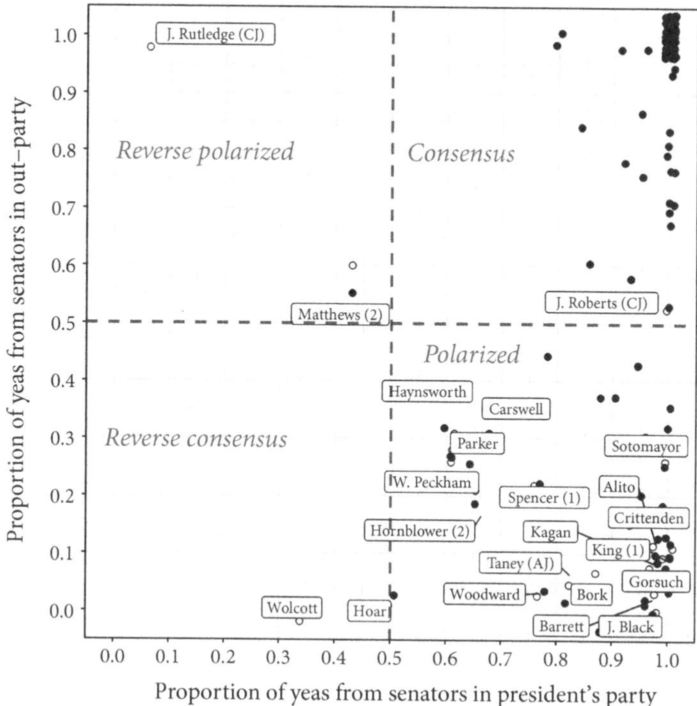

Fig. 8.3 Support for nominees by partisanship of senators. The points are jittered. Nominees who were not confirmed, who received less than 50% of in-party support, or who were appointed after 2000 labeled by name and depicted with open circles: a number after a nominee name applies to individuals who were nominated multiple times for the same position.

the in-party and out-party supported the nominee. The solid majority of nominees fall into this regime; of the 141 nominees who reached the floor between 1789 and 2020, 102 (71%) were consensus nominees. By contrast, nominees in the bottom-right quadrant constitute "polarized nominations"—those for whom a majority of the president's party supports the nominee while a majority of the out-party opposes. This category comprises 35 nominations, or 25%.

The final two categories capture very unusual situations. In the top-left quadrant, a majority of the in-party opposes the nominee while a majority of the out-party supports him or her. This "reverse polarized" scenario only happened twice. The first was Rutledge's defeat in 1795; the second was Stanley Matthews' renomination in 1881 by President Garfield. Matthews was confirmed by a vote of 24-23, in the only instance in which a nominee survived opposition from the majority of the president's party.[11] Finally, the bottom-left corner indicates "reverse consensus" nominees, in which a majority of both parties vote to reject. This scenario only happened twice: Alexander Wolcott (1811) and Ebenezer Hoar (1869). (To be sure, looking only at nominees who reached the floor of the Senate creates some selection bias; additional

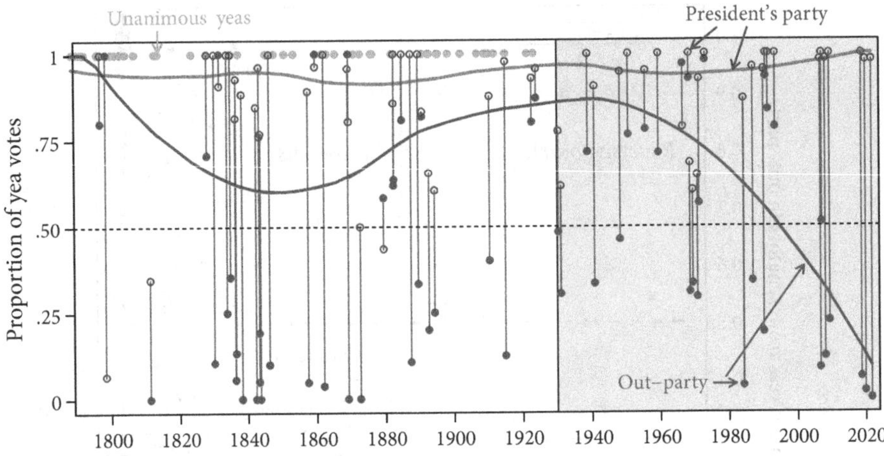

Fig. 8.4 Proportion of yea votes, by senators of the president's party (purple dots) and of the out-party (green dots). The orange dots depict nominees who received unanimous yeas from both parties (including voice votes). The green and purple lines summarize the trends in in-party and out-party support, respectively, while the gray lines connect in-party and out-party approval (among the non-unanimous nominees).

nominees probably would have fallen into the reverse polarized and reverse consensus regions had their nominations actually advanced to a floor vote.)

Given the overall changes in the confirmation rate and roll call voting seen in Figure 8.1, it would not be surprising if the likelihood of polarized confirmations changed over time. Figure 8.4 depicts the proportion of yea votes from 1789 to 2020, broken down by senators in the president's party (green dots) and the out-party (purple dots). While complex, this plot neatly summarizes a great deal of historical information; we return to it several times in this chapter, as well as in Chapter 11. In the figure, the orange points show nominees who received universal support (including voice votes). The green dots show the president's party, while the purple dots show out-party support; the lines of the same color show the trends for each. The gray vertical lines depict the difference in approval between senators of the president's party and the out-party. Finally, the shaded region depicts the 1930 to 2020 period.

As we saw above, the middle of the nineteenth century witnessed several contentious nominations; unsurprisingly, many of these featured high degrees of in-party support and significant out-party opposition. Importantly, however, the out-party opposition was *not* systematic in this period; many consensus nominations took place, and many of the polarized nominations were lame duck nominees. Indeed, the loess line shows that the moving average of out-party support never dropped below 50% in the nineteenth century. Consensus increased during the post-Civil War period. To be sure, the out-party opposed several nominees, but most nominees received bipartisan support (and, when they did not, they also received opposition from senators in the president's party).

Things have changed dramatically since then. We will examine the 1930 to 2020 period in greater detail below. For now, it suffices to note that since the middle of the twentieth century, the trend in out-party voting has moved from general support to universal opposition. Since the nomination of John Roberts in 2005, every nominee who reached the Senate floor received unanimous or nearly unanimous support from the president's party, but only a handful of yea votes (if any) from the out-party. As a result, every nominee after Roberts has fallen into the polarized category, as seen in Figure 8.3.[12]

8.3 Ideology and Racial Politics in 1930–2020 Nominations

While party obviously plays an important role in nomination politics, focusing only on the partisanship of senators ignores the heterogeneity that exists both across *and* within parties. To better understand preference diversity and how it affects political outcomes, political scientists often focus on the role of ideology in structuring politics.

8.3.1 Ideology: Concept and Measurement

What exactly do we (and most political scientists) mean when we invoke the concept of ideology? Here is one dictionary definition: "A systematic scheme of ideas, usually relating to politics, economics, or society and forming the basis of action or policy; a set of beliefs governing conduct."[13] The invocation of "scheme" and "set" is important—ideology concerns the connection and consistency of beliefs across issues or domains, not simply with regard to a single issue.

As we discussed in Chapter 1, Philip Converse launched the study of ideological consistency among voters with his seminal 1964 article, "The Nature of Belief Systems in Mass Publics." As McCarty (2019, 16) summarizes:

> *Ideological consistency* is the propensity of a voter to have either all liberal, all moderate, or all conservative views. Since [Converse's seminal work], this phenomenon is also called *belief constraint*, which Converse defines as "the success we would have in predicting, given initial knowledge that an individual holds certain further ideas and a specified attitude, that he holds certain further ideas and attitudes." For example, if we could predict a person's position on tax cuts from her position on free trade or from that on gay rights, we'd say that those beliefs exhibit constraint and that the voter is ideologically consistent (emphasis in original).

Converse's exploration of ideological consistency and the nature of ideological beliefs in the mass public has spawned thousands of articles since 1964, and we continue in that tradition in Chapter 10. But we can also apply the notions of ideology and ideological consistency to political elites—in particular, legislators (although presidents and nominees will soon enter the picture as well). For instance, take Mitch McConnell, who, during his time as Senate Majority Leader, helped usher conservative judges onto the federal judiciary under Republican presidents and who did his best to impede confirmation of more liberal judges under Democratic presidents. McConnell is clearly politically "conservative"—what this means is that across several issues (gun rights, abortion, taxes), McConnell takes positions that are broadly consistent when compared with how other politicians tend to vote on these issues. Conversely, Senator Elizabeth Warren is clearly liberal because she holds the opposite positions, which again are connected in this larger political context. It is then natural to say that McConnell and Warren are "ideologically distant," given the divergence in their preferences.

But how to measure elite ideology beyond "we know it when we see it?" While inferring ideology of the mass public from survey data is somewhat fraught, such data is nevertheless plentiful (as we noted in Chapter 7), and it is plausible that most citizens respond to questions somewhat truthfully. For political elites, however, survey data is much less useful. First, it's much more difficult to survey elites, so we don't have a wealth of historical polling data going back to the 1980s, unlike public opinion polls. And even if we did, the assumption of truthful responses to questions about political preferences is heroic when it comes to strategic politicians who seek re-election.[14]

Accordingly, the dominant way to estimate the ideology of legislators is to use roll call votes—in particular, to "scale" a set of legislators using a statistical model that analyzes a set of roll call votes. The scaling procedure produces a set of numerical estimates about legislators that results in what Poole (2005, 1) calls a "spatial map," which allows one to summarize the underlying politics of the legislature. Scaling is statistically complex and can be done in many ways, but the most widely used scores are the so-called NOMINATE scores, which were developed by Keith Poole and Howard Rosenthal. Importantly, while scholars (including us!) often imply that NOMINATE scores directly measure ideology, this is not so; rather, NOMINATE (and all ideal point estimates, for that matter) provide a *summary* of how individual legislators vote in comparison to other legislators. It is up to the analyst (and the reader) to interpret the scores and connect them to ideology and ideological consistency. Finally, it is important to note that the partisanship of legislators plays no role in the estimation of ideal points—the scaling procedure doesn't know whether a given legislator is a "D" or "R." Rather, based on the results, the analyst compares how the set of ideal points may differ both across and within parties to make substantive judgements about the spatial map.

8.3.2 Roll Call Voting and Dimensionality: The Changing Role of Race

The first step in interpreting a scaling procedure process is usually to examine *dimensionality*—the number of dimensions (or "axes," in spatial terms) needed to adequately describe the roll call voting behavior at issue.[15] Based on their underlying assumptions, different scaling procedures produce different numbers of dimensions; the NOMINATE procedure produces scores in two dimensions. But, as Poole and Rosenthal (1997, 5) note, for most of American history, a single dimension—the standard "left-right" continuum—well captures the ideological positioning of members of Congress.

Occasionally, however, a second dimension is needed to capture voting behavior in Congress. This generally occurs when some senators vote in a systematically different way on an issue (or issues) than the senators with whom they ordinarily vote together. Poole and Rosenthal found that such differences occurred in two periods; in both, the politics of race split (at least) one of the parties in an unusual way (race, of course, has always been a critical issue in American politics). The first period was in the 1830s and 1840s, when debates over slavery intensified in Congress. These concerns disrupted the normal left-right differences between members of the Whig and Democratic parties, which related primarily to economic issues; on issues related to slavery, geographic region would often trump party.[16]

The second period was the mid-twentieth century, when civil rights for African-Americans took center stage in American politics. Following the New Deal, the question of civil rights split the Democratic coalition; Northern Democrats and Southern Democrats broadly agreed on liberal economic values, but differed sharply on race. Southern Democrats were much more likely to oppose civil rights legislation, such as a federal ban on lynching. The result was a quasi-three-party system comprising Republicans, Northern Democrats, and Southern Democrats.[17]

Returning to Figure 8.4, those two eras stand out, though for different reasons. The period from 1830 to 1840 was the first era of sustained, although not constant, polarized nominations. Conversely, while the middle of the twentieth century was one of overall consensus with respect to nominations, several nominees provoked unusual amounts of *in-party opposition*.

Figure 8.5 presents roll call data on the 26 nominees between 1930 and 2020 who received a roll call vote and at least two nay votes. Each panel displays senators' estimated ideal points in the two dimensional DW-NOMINATE space—Northern Democrats are indicated by "D," Southern Democrats by "S," and Republicans by "R." Upper case letters denote yea votes, while italicized lower case letters denote nay votes. The x-axis is the primary, economic/party based dimension; senators who are more liberal fall to the left side of this continuum, and more conservative to the right. The y-axis is the secondary, race/geographic related dimension; more racially conservative senators fall toward the top of this dimension—note that the estimated ideal points of almost all Southern Democrats are more conservative on the second dimension. Also shown is the estimated cutting line that best separates yeas and nays for the roll call vote on each nominee—in other words, this line produces the fewest number of classification mistakes in predicting that senators on one side of the line will vote for the nominee, and senators on the other side of the line will not.[18] When the cutting line is more vertical, the first dimension is doing most of the work, because dividing senators along the x-axis (the economic dimension) classifies most votes correctly. Conversely, as the cutting line becomes more horizontal, the second dimension (race

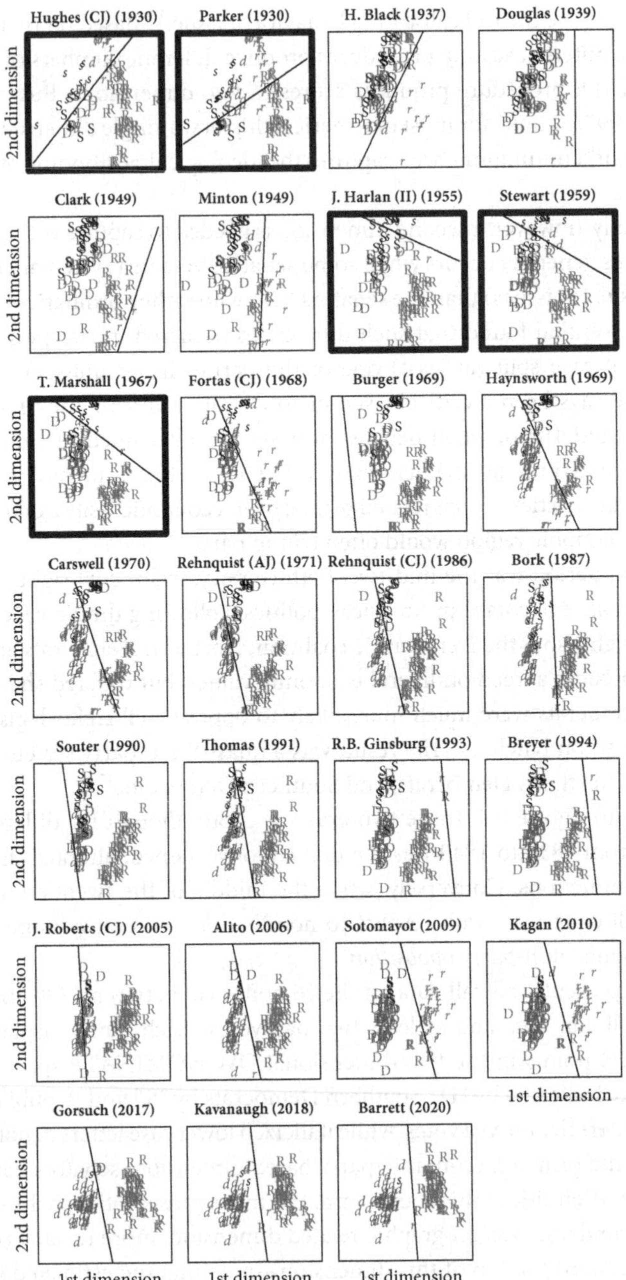

Fig. 8.5 Cutting lines in NOMINATE space. Each plot displays senators' estimated ideal points in the two dimensional DW-NOMINATE space. The x-axis is the primary, economic dimension; the y-axis is the secondary, geographic/race related dimension. Shown is the estimated cutting line for the roll call vote; i.e. the line that best separates yeas and nays. "D," "S," and "R" denote Northern Democratic, Southern Democratic, and Republican senators, respectively; italicized lower case letters denote nay votes. The nominees with solid black boxes depict those in which the second dimension was prominent.

and/or geography) also comes into play. At the extreme, a perfectly horizontal line would mean the second dimension splits the senators and the first dimension offers no additional information.

The first two nominations in Figure 8.5—Charles Evan Hughes' appointment as Chief Justice and John Parker's failed nomination as associate justice—occurred in 1930. Interestingly, for both nominees the second dimension was relevant, with cutting lines that significantly divided both parties. Hughes was confirmed by a vote of 52-26. According to Abraham (2008, 157), "conservative Southerners opposed him because they viewed him as too city-bred . . . to support national versus states' rights when the chips were down." At the same time, a coalition of more progressive Democrats and Republicans disapproved of Hughes' ties to the business community. Parker faced intense opposition from the NAACP due to disparaging statements he had made as a gubernatorial candidate about African-Americans' participation in the political process. Unsurprisingly, then, the second dimension helps predict opposition to his confirmation. In particular, many Republican senators with sizable Black constituencies broke with President Hoover and voted to reject Parker.[19] In the end, Parker was defeated by a vote of 39 to 41, one of the closest votes on a Supreme Court nominee in American history.

Race was not the sole factor in Parker's defeat—organized labor also mobilized against him over what it perceived as an anti-labor decision that Parker had made as a circuit court judge. Nevertheless, the intense battle over Parker might have augured a sustained role for racial considerations in future issues. But this did not happen. As seen in Figure 8.5, the cutting lines are nearly vertical for all of Roosevelt and Truman's nominees, with yeas and nays separated primarily along the first dimension. To be sure, the figure excludes the many Roosevelt and Truman nominees who were confirmed by voice vote and thus did not receive a roll call vote—but recall such nominees are by definition consensus nominees. Thus, between Parker's defeat in 1930 and the court's 1954 decision in *Brown v. Board of Education*, racial politics played no direct and observable role in roll call voting on Supreme Court nominations.[20]

In an interesting paper, Caughey (2007) examines why race played a minor role in Supreme Court nominations in the 1930s and 1940s. The puzzle is that during this period, Southern senators used the filibuster to block a host of legislative measures designed to undermine the Jim Crow system of segregation and discrimination in the South. Yet, at the same time the Southern Democrats voiced no meaningful opposition to the nominees of Roosevelt, Truman, and Eisenhower—until the court decided *Brown* in 1954—despite the fact that these appointees generally favored civil rights. "In short," Caughey argues, "Southern members of Congress zealously defended white supremacy on all institutional fronts except the federal judiciary, where the fatal breach [i.e. the decision in *Brown*] ultimately occurred."

Caughey posits two explanations for this seeming paradox. First, even though Southern senators strongly objected to the civil rights liberalism of the post-New Deal nominees, they appreciated their economic liberalism. Second, confirming these nominees allowed Southern Democrats to shift blame onto the court for general civil liberties and rights advancements that they did not favor, but which were necessary to preserve the Democratic coalition, such as protections for labor unions rights.

According to Caughey, this equilibrium gradually broke down during the 1940s, as the Supreme Court made several decisions that targeted Jim Crow, such as invalidating the white primary in 1944.[21] The court's decision in 1954 to reverse *Plessy v. Ferguson* in *Brown* culminated this process. While a majority of Americans supported *Brown*, Southern whites were overwhelmingly opposed, and the decision sparked furious outrage in many parts of the South.[22] As we discussed in Chapter 2, *Brown* incited an enormous backlash amongst Southern Democrats in Congress, leading to the publication of the Southern Manifesto denouncing the court.

Thus, *Brown* firmly thrust the judiciary into the debate over civil rights, which in turn meant that issues of race would no longer remain on the back-burner of nomination politics.[23] When Eisenhower nominated John Harlan II in 1955, the nominee faced immediate opposition from many Southern senators, who attacked him as both "ultra-liberal" and hostile to the South.[24] Returning to Figure 8.5, we see that the cutting line for his roll call vote is decidedly diagonal, with the second dimension playing a large role in separating the yeas from nays. A similar pattern emerges for Justice Stewart's nomination in 1959 and Thurgood Marshall's nomination in 1967. For all three nominees, Southern Democrats were much more likely to vote nay than were Northern Democrats and Republicans; note the cluster of "*s*" symbols at the top of each plot, which is the conservative wing on the second dimension. The second dimension also shows some influence in the Haynsworth and Carswell nominations in 1970—not surprisingly, given their role in Nixon's "Southern strategy."[25]

The role of race changed after 1970, when the cutting lines for all nominees became much more vertical and the first dimension dominated voting. This accords with general trends in American politics. As Poole and Rosenthal (1997, 111) note, after passage of the Civil Rights Act of 1964 and the Voting Rights Act of 1965, preferences over civil rights issues increasingly were folded into the first dimension—these landmark bills transformed the constituency of the Democratic Party in the South.[26] Eventually, as the Southern realignment in American politics occurred, the preferences of Northern Democrats and Southern Democrats converged, contributing to the polarized parties that we see today.

Table 8.2 summarizes the transformation seen in Figure 8.5 in a less elegant but perhaps clearer manner. For each nominee who reached the Senate floor between 1930 and 2020, the table shows both the number of senators from each of the "three parties"—Republicans, Southern Democrats, and non-Southern Democrats—and the proportion of yea votes among each group. We bold nominees for whom the difference in approval rates between Southern Democrats and non-Southern Democrats was at least 10 percentage points.

Two patterns stand out from Table 8.2. First, while the biggest differences in nominee approval has been *across* the two parties, those nominations that split the

Table 8.2 Summary of roll call voting among Republicans, non-southern Democrats, and Southern Democrats, 1930 to 2020. Bolded nominees indicate at least a 10-percentage point difference in approval between Southern and non-southern Democrats.

Nominee	Year	President party	Number of Republicans	Republican percent yeas	Number of Non-southern Democrats	Non-southern Democrat percent yeas	Number of Southern Democrats	Southern Democrat percent yeas
Hughes (CJ)	1930	Republican	57	0.78	17	0.50	22	0.39
Parker	1930	Republican	57	0.59	17	0.24	22	0.41
O. Roberts	1930	Republican	57	1.00	17	1.00	22	1.00
Cardozo	1932	Republican	49	1.00	23	1.00	24	1.00
H. Black	1937	Democrat	18	0.31	54	0.86	23	1.00
Reed	1938	Democrat	18	1.00	54	1.00	24	1.00
Frankfurter	1939	Democrat	25	1.00	47	1.00	24	1.00
Douglas	1939	Democrat	25	0.76	47	1.00	24	1.00
Murphy	1940	Democrat	25	1.00	47	1.00	24	1.00
Byrnes	1941	Democrat	29	1.00	43	1.00	24	1.00
R. Jackson	1941	Democrat	29	1.00	43	1.00	24	1.00
Stone (CJ)	1941	Democrat	29	1.00	43	1.00	22	1.00
W. Rutledge	1943	Democrat	39	1.00	34	1.00	23	1.00
Burton	1945	Democrat	41	1.00	32	1.00	23	1.00
Vinson	1946	Democrat	40	1.00	34	1.00	22	1.00
Clark	1949	Democrat	43	0.77	29	1.00	24	1.00
Minton	1949	Democrat	43	0.47	29	0.91	24	1.00
Warren	1954	Republican	48	1.00	25	1.00	23	1.00
J. Harlan (II)	1955	Republican	47	0.96	25	1.00	24	0.55
Brennan	1957	Republican	47	1.00	27	1.00	22	1.00
Whittaker	1957	Republican	47	1.00	27	1.00	22	1.00
Stewart	1959	Republican	34	1.00	42	0.95	22	0.32
B. White	1962	Democrat	36	1.00	43	1.00	21	1.00
Goldberg	1962	Democrat	36	1.00	43	1.00	21	1.00
Fortas (AJ)	1965	Democrat	32	1.00	48	1.00	20	1.00

continued

Table 8.2 *Continued*

Nominee	Year	President party	Number of Republicans	Republican percent yeas	Number of Non-southern Democrats	Non-southern Democrat percent yeas	Number of Southern Democrats	Southern Democrat percent yeas
T. Marshall	1967	Democrat	36	0.97	45	0.98	19	0.28
Fortas (CJ)	1968	Democrat	37	0.28	44	0.80	19	0.22
Burger	1969	Republican	43	1.00	40	0.92	17	1.00
Haynsworth	1969	Republican	43	0.60	40	0.12	17	0.82
Carswell	1970	Republican	43	0.69	40	0.10	17	0.76
Blackmun	1970	Republican	43	1.00	40	1.00	17	1.00
Powell	1971	Republican	45	1.00	39	1.00	16	0.94
Rehnquist (AJ)	1971	Republican	45	0.93	39	0.42	16	0.88
Stevens	1975	Republican	38	1.00	45	1.00	17	1.00
O'Connor	1981	Republican	53	1.00	33	1.00	14	1.00
Rehnquist (CJ)	1986	Republican	53	0.96	33	0.12	14	0.86
Scalia	1986	Republican	53	1.00	33	1.00	14	1.00
Bork	1987	Republican	46	0.87	36	0.00	18	0.11
Kennedy	1988	Republican	46	1.00	36	1.00	18	1.00
Souter	1990	Republican	45	1.00	39	0.77	16	1.00
Thomas	1991	Republican	43	0.95	41	0.10	16	0.44
R.B. Ginsburg	1993	Democrat	44	0.93	43	1.00	13	1.00
Breyer	1994	Democrat	44	0.79	43	1.00	13	1.00
J. Roberts (CJ)	2005	Republican	55	1.00	41	0.46	4	1.00
Alito	2006	Republican	55	0.98	41	0.10	4	0.00
Sotomayor	2009	Democrat	40	0.23	55	1.00	5	1.00
Kagan	2010	Democrat	41	0.12	54	0.98	5	1.00
Gorsuch	2017	Republican	52	1.00	47	0.06	1	0.00
Kavanaugh	2018	Republican	51	0.98	47	0.02	2	0.00
Barrett	2020	Republican	53	0.98	46	0.00	1	0.00

coalitions almost all came before the early 1970s. Second, this trend accompanied the overall decline in the *number* of Southern Democratic senators. The parties undertook the process of sorting over the next few decades, with Southern Democrats gradually replaced by Republicans. But even as late as 1991, in an inverse of the post-*Brown* dynamics, Clarence Thomas' confirmation barely made it over the line thanks to support from several Southern Democrats.[27] But the parties are now very well sorted, and the handful of Southern Democratic senators who served post-2005 voted like Northern Democrats.[28] The result is the pattern of polarization we see today in roll call voting, with approval of the president's nominee now falling nearly perfectly along party lines.

8.4 The Importance of Ideological Distance

Clearly both partisanship and ideology matter in predicting confirmation outcomes and roll call votes—at least at a very broad level. But what predicts whether a senator is likely to support or oppose a given nominee? To provide a more nuanced answer to this question, we turn to the model of roll call voting introduced and tested in Cameron, Cover, and Segal (1990) [hereafter CCS]. While the model allows for several factors (which we discuss below), the core idea is straightforward: senators prefer nominees who are closer ideologically to them than farther, and so the likelihood of a yea vote for a nominee decreases in the ideological distance between the senator and the nominee, all things equal.[29] As we discuss in the Appendix, the CCS finding that senators are more likely to vote for nominees who are closer to them ideologically has been replicated and extended many times.

Defining "ideological distance" can be tricky when politics operates in multiple dimensions. But the upshot of the arc of American politics in general and the politics of Supreme Court nominations in particular is that all in all the main liberal-conservative dimension captures most ideological conflict among American elites.[30] How then has the distribution of ideological distance on the primary dimension between senators and nominees changed over time, particularly if we focus on 1930 to 2020?

Recall from Chapter 1 that the levels of party polarization in Congress have reached sky-high levels. In practice, this means that the average Democratic senator is now much farther ideologically (based on their roll call voting patterns) from the average Republican senator than in the past. Also, we showed in Chapter 4 that the ideology of *nominees* has polarized as well, with the average Democratic nominee now much more likely to be farther from the average Republican senator, and vice versa, than was the case in the past.[31]

Taken together, these changes mean that out-party senators will be much farther away ideologically from nominees than formerly, a change depicted in Figure 8.6. For each nominee, we separately calculate the absolute value of the ideological difference between the nominee and the average ideology of in-party and the out-party senators. To measure nominee ideology, we use the NSP measure introduced in Chapter 4.

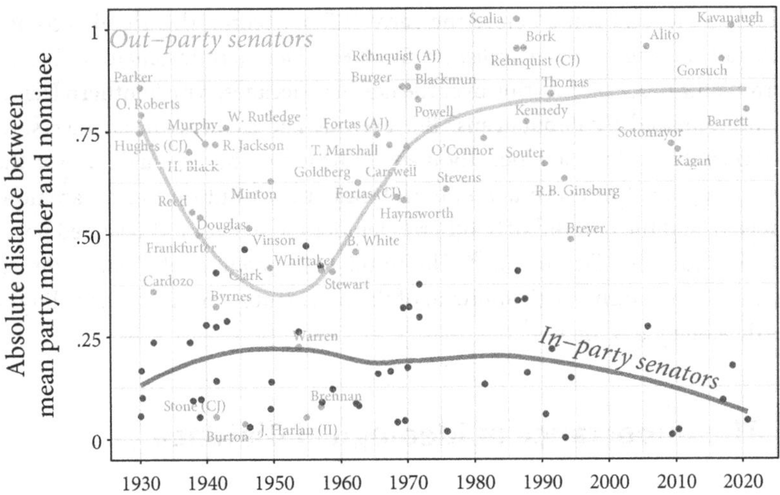

Fig. 8.6 Ideological distance between nominees and senators. The orange points (and nominee names) depict the absolute value of the distance between the nominee, as measured by the NSP score, and the average member of the out-party, while the green points do the same for in-party senators. The lines are loess lines.

For senators, we use the mean first-dimension NOMINATE scores of Democrats and Republicans in a given Senate.

Figure 8.6 shows for in-party senators, nominees tend to be close to the center of the president's party (with some variation over time). The situation is quite different for out-party senators. Although the distance between the average out-party senator and nominees declined during the low polarization period of the mid-twentieth century, it increased dramatically after that.[32] Given these changes, the emergence of routine contentious votes on nominees is perhaps not surprising.

8.4.1 Modeling Individual Roll Call Votes

As a final analysis, we statistically model individual roll call votes, incorporating additional factors beyond ideological distance that predict roll call voting on nominees. Importantly, these models cannot establish causal relationships. Rather they help describe changes in voting patterns over time, using a few variables that successfully predict voting.

In addition to ideological distance, Cameron, Cover, and Segal identified the legal qualifications of the nominee as a key predictor of voting. The idea here is that, all things equal, senators prefer better-qualified justices.[33] Next, following the analysis in Chapter 5, we account for interest group involvement in a given nomination. We operationalize this measure by using the total number of groups that mobilized in opposition to each nominee, based on our measures in Chapter 5. The intuition is that such mobilization may polarize voting, leading to more nay votes.[34] Finally, in addition to ideological distance, we also control for whether a senator is a co-partisan of the president.[35] The result is a very parsimonious model of individual votes. The results of the regression analysis can be found in the Appendix. By conventional standards, the model fits the data very well. Here we focus on the substantive implications of the model.

First, we examine whether the relationship between ideological distance and voting on nominees has changed over time. Given the increased distance between senators and nominees, even if senators placed a constant weight on ideology in their voting decisions, we would still expect to see increased nay votes among out-party senators over time, since the average distance between them and the nominee has increased. But it's also possible that ideological distance became an even greater predictor of voting over time. We examine this question in statistical detail in the Appendix, and show that, in fact, it does appear that senators seem to place more weight on ideology than they previously did, further increasing levels of polarized voting.[36]

Figure 8.7 summarizes these changes. For simplicity, as we did in Chapter 5, we use Robert Bork's confirmation vote in 1987 as a breakpoint to divide 1930 to 2020 into "early" and "late" periods.[37] Each panel in Figure 8.7 shows the predicted probability of voting yea (on the y-axis) as function of ideological distance between the senator and nominee (on the x-axis). The black lines show the probability for the pre-Bork era, the red lines for the post-Bork era. To illustrate how legal qualifications affect the baseline likelihood of more yea votes, we set quality to "low," "medium," and "high," respectively, in the three panels.[38]

All three panels show a strong shift in the relationship between distance and voting as the slopes on the post-Bork lines are much steeper. Although ideologically distant nominees had a decent chance of receiving a yea vote in the pre-Bork period, that

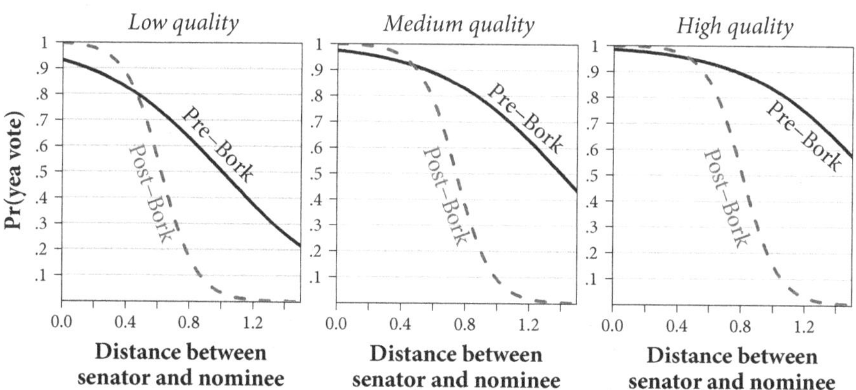

Fig. 8.7 The changing relationship between ideological distance and roll call voting over time. The panels show the predicted probability of voting yea in the pre- and post-Bork period, as nominee quality varies from low to high.

probability is minimal in the post-Bork period. And, while the intercept increases as a nominee's legal qualifications increase, we still see the shift in slopes over time across all three qualification levels. Thus, in more recent confirmations, ideologically distant senators are more likely to vote against a nominee (controlling for other factors) than they used to be.

This change provokes a counter-factual question: how might today's confirmation politics look if senators (and nominees) had not become polarized? We can investigate this and similar questions related to the other predictors of confirmation voting using different counter-factual scenarios, and how they might have altered the path of contentious votes over time. We emphasize that these scenarios explore the performance of a descriptive model, and thus are best seen more as thought experiments than tightly identified counterfactuals.[39] Table 8.3 displays the results of these simulations. Column (3) shows the actual proportion of nay votes each nominee received, while the last four columns show the predicted proportion of nay votes for each nominee under different counterfactual scenarios.

Column (4) asks what would have happened if—all else unchanged—the Senate remained unpolarized, thereby keeping nominees and senators much closer together ideologically. More specifically, the scenario assumes the relatively non-polarized 83rd Senate of 1954 had been in place for all nominations. This Senate was composed of 47 Democrats, 48 Republicans, and one Independent, a remarkably even partisan balance. Moreover, the ideal points of the senators (in the first dimension) followed a unimodal distribution—a sharp contrast to the present-day bimodal distribution. In the pre-1967 period, the model suggests that if the Senate in 1937 had not been so dominated by Democrats, opposition to the extremely liberal, scandal-plagued Hugo Black might have been even greater. But the changes in the 1967 to 2020 period are even more dramatic. A non-polarized, evenly balanced Senate suggests the probable confirmations of Haynsworth, Carswell, and Bork, a less contentious confirmation for Thomas, and a relatively routine confirmation for Rehnquist to become chief justice.

The second simulation, presented in Column (5), keeps all else the same but for each nominee substitutes the ideology of a moderate nominee (that of Chief Justice Stone). The "moderate nominee" scenario implies dramatic changes in both periods. The model suggests none of the nominations prior to the *Brown v. Board of Education*—with the exception of John Parker in 1930—would have been contentious, with only Hughes, Vinson, and Minton receiving nay votes. In later years, all nominees would be easily confirmed.

The third simulation, presented in Column (6), assumes interest groups had never become involved in Supreme Court nominations. This scenario implies little change in the pre-1967 period, which reflects the dearth of interest group mobilization in that era. In the 1967 to 2020 period, however, the simulation implies larger changes. Estimated nay votes drop by at least 20 percentage points for the nominations of Haynsworth, Carswell, Bork, Clarence Thomas, and Roberts.

The final column in Table 8.3 puts all three simulations together: no interest group activity, a non-polarized Senate, and a moderate nominee. Under this scenario, the

Table 8.3 Actual nay votes and predictions of the percentage of nay votes, by nominee, under various counterfactual scenarios. See text for details.

Nominee	Year	Actual Prop. of Nays	Non-polarized Senate	Moderate nominee	No groups	All 3 Combined
Hughes (CJ)	1930	0.35	0.12	0.02	0.27	0.02
Parker	1930	0.52	0.43	0.32	0.18	0.02
O. Roberts	1930	0.00	0.00	0.00	0.00	0.00
Cardozo	1932	0.00	0.00	0.00	0.00	0.00
H. Black	1937	0.21	0.29	0.00	0.08	0.02
Reed	1938	0.00	0.00	0.00	0.00	0.00
Frankfurter	1939	0.00	0.00	0.00	0.00	0.00
Douglas	1939	0.05	0.02	0.00	0.01	0.01
Murphy	1940	0.00	0.00	0.00	0.00	0.00
Byrnes	1941	0.00	0.00	0.00	0.00	0.00
R. Jackson	1941	0.00	0.00	0.00	0.00	0.00
Stone (CJ)	1941	0.00	0.00	0.00	0.00	0.00
W. Rutledge	1943	0.00	0.00	0.00	0.00	0.00
Burton	1945	0.00	0.00	0.00	0.00	0.00
Vinson	1946	0.00	0.00	0.01	0.00	0.00
Clark	1949	0.09	0.00	0.00	0.01	0.01
Minton	1949	0.25	0.06	0.02	0.18	0.03
Warren	1953	0.00	0.00	0.00	0.00	0.00
J. Harlan (II)	1954	0.13	0.33	0.00	0.10	0.00
Brennan	1957	0.00	0.00	0.00	0.00	0.00
Whittaker	1957	0.00	0.00	0.00	0.00	0.00
Stewart	1958	0.18	0.17	0.15	0.15	0.11
B. White	1962	0.00	0.00	0.00	0.00	0.00
Goldberg	1962	0.00	0.00	0.00	0.00	0.00
Fortas (AJ)	1965	0.00	0.00	0.00	0.00	0.00
T. Marshall	1967	0.16	0.18	0.00	0.11	0.00
Fortas (CJ)	1968	0.51	0.26	0.09	0.35	0.03
Burger	1969	0.03	0.03	0.00	0.00	0.00
Haynsworth	1969	0.55	0.33	0.01	0.33	0.01
Carswell	1970	0.53	0.10	0.01	0.29	0.01
Blackmun	1970	0.00	0.01	0.00	0.00	0.00
Powell	1971	0.01	0.02	0.00	0.00	0.00
Rehnquist (AJ)	1971	0.28	0.11	0.00	0.21	0.01
Stevens	1975	0.00	0.00	0.00	0.00	0.00
O'Connor	1981	0.00	0.01	0.00	0.00	0.00
Rehnquist (CJ)	1986	0.33	0.17	0.00	0.28	0.01
Scalia	1986	0.00	0.02	0.00	0.00	0.00
Bork	1987	0.58	0.31	0.00	0.05	0.01
Kennedy	1987	0.00	0.01	0.00	0.00	0.00
Souter	1990	0.09	0.03	0.00	0.00	0.01
Thomas	1991	0.48	0.17	0.00	0.22	0.01
R.B. Ginsburg	1993	0.03	0.00	0.00	0.01	0.01
Breyer	1994	0.09	0.00	0.00	0.03	0.01
J. Roberts (CJ)	2005	0.22	0.10	0.00	0.00	0.00
Alito	2005	0.42	0.19	0.00	0.38	0.01
Sotomayor	2009	0.31	0.06	0.00	0.28	0.02
Kagan	2010	0.37	0.08	0.02	0.37	0.03
Gorsuch	2017	0.45	0.19	0.03	0.44	0.02
Kavanaugh	2018	0.49	0.29	0.03	0.39	0.01
Barrett	2020	0.48	0.23	0.10	0.46	0.02

model predicts that Supreme Court nominations would be strikingly free of contentiousness, with even the most recent nominees getting upwards of 95% support.

8.5 Conclusion

Like the other facets of the confirmation process we have examined, the nature of roll call voting on Supreme Court nominees changed dramatically over time, and in particular over the last eight decades. Routine voice votes have given way to near party-line roll call votes; senators from the out-party now almost uniformly vote against the president's nominee. This fact is arguably the most important one for understanding confirmation politics in the Senate today. In addition, ideological considerations seem to play an even greater role in senators' voting on nominees. Given today's polarized parties with little ideological overlap across the parties, the consequences of these changes in Senate voting for the future of the court are profound—in particular, it is possible that nominees will only be confirmed during periods of unified government, with long vacancies possible during divided government. We examine this possibility in Chapters 13. And, in Chapter 11, we return to Senate voting and seek to explain in greater detail why the motivations and incentives for senators with respect to voting on Supreme Court nominees changed so dramatically over time.

This marks the end of Part I of the book. We have now presented exhaustive descriptive accounts of the parties' demands for courts; presidential selection processes; the changing nature of the candidates and nominees; the rise of interest groups in the confirmation processes; the changing landscape of media coverage; shifts in public opinion surrounding nominees; and, finally, changes in the Senate's evaluation of nominees. Yet, we have only indirectly tackled the bigger question of *why* these transformations occurred. We shift to the crucial why questions in Part II of the book.

PART II
WHY IT HAPPENED

9
The Logic of Presidential Selection

Co-authored with Lauren Mattioli

In Chapter 3 we described *how* presidents selected Supreme Court nominees, tracing the evolution of the selection and vetting process over the course of 15 presidencies since 1930. In Chapter 4 we described *who* presidents considered on the short lists and ultimately chose. But we said very little about *why*—why did presidents make the choices they did?

To answer this question, we develop, test, and use a new theory of how presidents pick individuals for high positions in government—cabinet officials, members of regulatory commissions and international bodies, ambassadors, and of course justices of the Supreme Court.[1] So, this chapter is a study in a relatively new field, "personnel politics" or "public sector personnel economics," offering new perspectives on traditional questions in public administration.[2] We call the new theory the "characteristics approach" to public sector appointees. Its fundamental insight is that top political appointees are bundles of characteristics, and it is those characteristics that elected political executives like presidents, governors, or mayors value, not the person *per se*.

Why is a new theory necessary? Presidential selection of Supreme Court nominees has been well studied in political science. In particular, as we discussed in Chapter 1, in the 1980s and 1990s, political scientists developed a theory—move-the-median (MTM) theory—that united both presidential selection and Senate voting. The core idea of MTM theory is simple but elegant: under certain assumptions about preferences and the structure of voting, the key attribute of a body is the ideological location of its "swing" or median member. Therefore, the politics of appointments to the body should turn on altering (or preserving) the ideology of the median member—"moving the median."

In the context of the Supreme Court, MTM theory posits that the court's policy output corresponds exactly to the preferences of the median justice. Thus, the expected policy impact of a nominee in moving the median will drive a president's choice of nominee, as well as each senator's voting decision. So the theory suggests that a senator should vote against a nominee who moves the court's new median justice farther from the senator's chosen ideology relative to the status quo. And if this is true for a majority of senators, the Senate should reject the nominee. In turn, the president should nominate a confirmable individual who would move the location of the new median justice as close as possible to the president's own ideal point. This means that, when facing an ideologically distant Senate, the president should be constrained in his

Making the Supreme Court: The Politics of Appointments, 1930–2020. Charles M. Cameron and Jonathan P. Kastellec, Oxford University Press. © Oxford University Press 2023. DOI: 10.1093/oso/9780197680544.003.0009

choice of confirmable nominee—which then limits the ideological range of nominees that will be confirmed to the Supreme Court.

MTM theory was first formulated and applied to Supreme Court nominations in the late 1980s in a pair of unpublished papers by Peter Lemieux and Charles Stewart.[3] Subsequently, several scholars expanded upon the theory and tested it against data.[4] Unfortunately, as documented in Cameron and Kastellec (2016*b*), MTM theory does a rather poor job of predicting the ideology of nominees, and so falls short as a unified theory of presidential selection. That article showed that MTM-theory also does a poor job of explaining the voting decisions of individual senators, and hence the success and failure of nominations in the Senate. These failures help motivate our theoretical and empirical investigations of the Senate in Chapter 11.

What motivates the characteristics theory is the fact that while MTM theory falls short of capturing why presidents nominate who they do and how senators respond, it falls short in an *extremely interesting way*. First, presidents sometimes nominated individuals who moved the median *away* from the president's ideal policy! However, such blunders occurred between 1930 and 1960, and then stopped. Second, and more commonly, presidents nominated individuals who were more extreme than predicted by the theory, given the location of the Senate median. Moreover, we showed that these nominees were usually confirmed, meaning that senators often voted for nominees the theory predicts they should have voted against (and thus the Senate confirmed many nominees the theory predicts should have been rejected). Thus, the president has been far less constrained in his choice of nominees than MTM theory would predict.[5]

These empirical shortcomings of MTM-theory suggest that while ideology is certainly a key component of any theory of presidential selection, a good theory needs to incorporate additional factors into what presidents want from their nominees.[6] In MTM-theory, only ideology matters, and its role is quite stark: the president only cares about moving the median of the Court as far as possible, subject to the constraint of Senate confirmation. No room is left for presidents (or senators) to care about any other attribute of a nominee.

That's where the characteristics theory comes in. In particular, we focus on three characteristics highlighted in Chapter 4: ideology, policy reliability, and ascriptive or diversity traits (namely, race and gender). At various times and to various degrees, presidents value these characteristics in Supreme Court nominees. But beyond a minimal level, no characteristic comes for free. If presidents desire specific characteristics, they must "pay" for them by searching for nominees, vetting them carefully, and perhaps overcoming political opposition, as we saw in the portraits of the selection process in Chapter 3. For each characteristic, presidents must weigh benefits against costs.

Pursuing this simple idea, we imagine a president assembling a nominee by "purchasing" nominee characteristics, then "selling" those characteristics and the appointee's work product to interest groups and the public for political gain. This framework allows us to derive explicit presidential demand functions for nominee ideology, policy reliability, and diversity. It also allows a precise characterization of when presidents opt for a carefully considered nominee and when a casually vetted one.

This new approach to presidential appointments may seem slightly outlandish at first glance. Do presidents really assemble Supreme Court nominees by bolting attributes together, like Dr. Frankenstein and his poor creature? Literally they do not, of course. But the characteristics approach simply assumes that each relevant characteristic carries both costs and benefits. Each characteristic of a Supreme Court nominee, for example, has a political value to the president, and a political or effort-cost to acquire. The president's demand for the specific attributes indicates how much he "buys" given the costs and benefits.

The new theory requires new data on the characteristics of the short listers and the nominees. Chapter 4 displayed some of the data. But we need even more; in particular, measures of the costs of obtaining nominee attributes. We also need data on what we call "default" characteristics (the levels presidents can acquire essentially for free). To gauge these measures, we focus on the makeup of the U.S. Courts of Appeals. We review this data shortly, much of which is interesting in and of itself.

How well does the characteristics approach perform when tested against data on short listers and nominees? As one might expect given the relatively small number of vacancies, the roughness of the measures, the willfulness of presidents, and the ever-present role of contingency, the theory doesn't work perfectly—but it performs pretty well. The data are consistent with many of the theory's predictions (though not all), and the predictions from the estimated functions track the historic data reasonably well.

First, presidential interest in the court increased substantially over time, a trend that we attribute to party demands. Simultaneously, the difficulty of finding ideologically reliable candidates decreased, especially for Republican presidents, who gradually built a strong "farm team" in the lower federal courts. Hence, the ratio of benefits to costs for ideology increased dramatically. As a result, the level of ideological conformity presidents demanded increased dramatically. So did the degree of policy reliability they demanded. As predicted, presidents choose more ideologically extreme nominees when the ideological center of the court is more distant from the president's ideal point. Less obviously, success in moving the center of the court undercut this incentive. Turning to ascriptive diversity among short-listed candidates and nominees, the story is similar. Increases in diversity followed from greater presidential interest, plus the growing supply of female and minority judges on the lower courts. The asymmetry we saw in party interest in diversity in Chapter 2 also emerges here. The number of non-white-males on the Republican farm team was relatively low, a pattern that goes hand-in-hand with the Republican's lack of emphasis on diversity in their platforms. By contrast, the Democratic farm team featured many more female and minority judges; this goes hand-in-hand with the much greater interest in diversity we saw in the Democrats' platforms. Overall, these empirical findings demonstrate how very simple ideas can help explain the dramatic changes in who presidents selected for the Supreme Court over the last nine decades.

9.2 The Characteristics Approach to Presidential Appointments

Private sector employers value employee characteristics like productivity, honesty, diligence, and loyalty, and they hire subordinates in order to get them. Public sector employers also value employee characteristics. But the traits valued by top elected executives like the president may be rather different from those prized in the private sector.

Recall from Chapter 4 the colloquy between President Richard Nixon and his attorney general, John Mitchell, discussing the type of nominee they wanted for two open Supreme Court seats. Nixon and Mitchell forthrightly discussed nominee ideology and nominee conformity to specific policy litmus tests. They also discussed qualifications, gender, and age. They evaluated individuals in terms of these characteristics. It is clear Nixon valued those specific characteristics, not the individuals *per se*.

The characteristics approach formalizes the political logic evident in the Nixon-Mitchell dialogue. As social science theory, the approach owes much to classic papers in demand theory, especially Becker (1965), Lancaster (1966), and Gorman (1980), as well as the neoclassical theory of the firm. The basic idea in those papers is simple, even intuitive. As applied to food, for example, it suggests that people order (say) a salad because they value its tastiness and nutrition. They value the salad itself only because of these attributes. This is the approach we take to presidential selection of Supreme Court nominees.

9.2.1 What's a Nominee?

The characteristics approach views nominees as a bundle of three characteristics: ideology, policy reliability, and ascriptive diversity-oriented traits, specifically race and gender (in earlier eras, the nominee's state or region was also important but no longer). In Chapter 4, we reviewed the historical record on the characteristics of short-list candidates and nominees. Let's connect that discussion to the theory.

Ideology

Recall the Nemacheck measure of ideology introduced in Chapter 4. That measure assumed an individual's ideology is reasonably well captured by a number on a one-dimensional left-right scale (in practice, the NOMINATE scale from congressional and presidential studies).

The characteristics approach starts with this standard way of thinking about ideology for nominees but adds two wrinkles. First, it assumes the ideology of a nominee is a random variable with a mean and a variance.[7] Moreover, the mean may be decomposed into two parts: first, a "default" level of ideology that a president may obtain "for free." This level is important because a president must nominate someone, even if the president cares nothing about Supreme Court policy. One may think of the default level as the expected value from a random draw from the pool of possible nominees—the president can obtain this value on average without any selection or vetting effort at all. But, the president may want to go beyond the default level and obtain "more" ideology—i.e. he can "purchase" more ideology with time and effort. Thus, total nominee ideology equals the sum of the "free" default level plus the purchased level.

The characteristics approach distinguishes two decisions. The first is whether to obtain any additional ideology at all, or whether to opt for just the default level. The second is the level of ideology that the president purchases above and beyond the default level, if any. Each unit of extra ideology creates a "cost" for the president, which we conceive of as search, vetting, and confirmation costs.

Policy Reliability

In Chapter 4, we reviewed the professional experience of nominees and short-list candidates since 1930. The idea was to use candidate backgrounds to indicate which individuals were more likely to be reliable justices in terms of the president's policy goals for the Supreme Court. Here, the theory treats policy reliability as a characteristic that a president values because he values policy. For a risk-averse president, the expected value of a nominee decreases if the nominee's ideology is highly variable—that is, if the justice will be unreliable.[8] In other words, the variance of a nominee's ideology is assumed to be inversely related to the nominee's reliability score. By "purchasing" more reliability, the president can shrink the variance of the nominee's ideology and hence improve the nominee's expected value.

As with ideology, the theory breaks an individual's policy reliability score into two components, the default level—which the president can obtain with little or no effort—and an extra component, which can only be obtained through the exertion of selection and vetting effort. Again, the characteristics approach distinguishes two decisions: whether to opt just for the default level of policy reliability, and if not, how much more to obtain. Each unit of extra policy reliability costs the president some amount in search and vetting costs.

Diversity Traits

In Chapter 4, we also reviewed the ascriptive characteristics of nominees, particularly race and gender. The characteristics approach's treatment of diversity parallels that of ideology and policy reliability. In line with the actual history of Supreme Court nominations until quite recently, we assume that the "default" selection is a white male. Nominees who are female, non-white, or both, receive a higher "diversity score."[9]

As with ideology and quality, the president can obtain the default level of diversity traits for free, but additional amounts of diversity traits require the expenditure of time and effort to secure. The two together constitute the observed level in a nominee. The characteristics approach considers whether the president opts for a white male or someone else. Moving from a white male to a non-white-male imposes search and vetting costs.

In sum, a nominee is the bundle $n(\hat{x}, \hat{q}, \hat{y})$ where $\hat{x}$ denotes the nominee's mean ideology score, $\hat{q}$ denotes the nominee's policy reliability score (related to the variance of the nominee's ideology), and $\hat{y}$ denotes the presence or absence of a diversity trait (female and/or non-white).

9.2.2 How Presidents Value Nominee Characteristics

The theory must specify how presidents value nominee characteristics. A very general formulation is fine for theory qua theory, but we desire regression models in Section 5 that flow seamlessly from the theory.[10] To do so, we require a specific utility function, not just a general one. In Cameron et al. (2019) we built a presidential utility function step by step, and we refer interested readers to the extended discussion there. Here, we just reproduce the function and explain the logic behind it.

We employ the following expected utility function for the president:

$$Eu(\cdot) = -\pi^x(p - (a\bar{x} + b\hat{x}))^2 - \frac{b^2\pi^2}{\hat{q}} + \pi^y \log(c\bar{y} + d\hat{y}) - w^x x - w^q q - w^y y \quad (1)$$

where π^x is the president's per-unit political benefit from nominee ideology; p is the president's most preferred ideology for the court as a whole; $\bar{x}$ is the average ideology of the court without the nominee; π^y is the president's per unit political benefit from court diversity; $\bar{y}$ is the average level of diversity on the court without the nominee; and w^x, w^q, and w^y are the per-unit costs of acquiring additional nominee ideology, reliability, and diversity (respectively) above the no-effort default levels. The terms a through d are parameters. Thus, the first few terms in the function capture the nominee's political benefits to the president while the last three indicate the costs needed to acquire nominee characteristics. So, the function simply displays the nominee's net political benefits to the president.

In our view, only one part of Equation 1 is particularly contentious, and that is its treatment of how an incoming nominee's ideology affects the court's policy outputs. There are two key assumptions. First, presidents value nominee ideology to the extent, and only to the extent, it has an impact on the policies the court creates. Otherwise, presidents don't care. Hence, nominees who move the court's policies closer to the president's ideological ideal are more highly valued than those who don't. Second, we assume that the average ideology of the justices on the court reasonably approximates the ideology of Supreme Court majority opinions. An incoming nominee alters expected policy by altering the average.

This approach, while unusual, reflects recent work applying modern bargaining theory to the procedures used on high American appellate courts like the U.S. Supreme Court. The new work indicates that the ideology of the median justice is critical in determining case dispositions (in other words, whether the "liberal" litigant or the "conservative" one prevails in the case). But the *policy content* of a majority opinion tends to reflect the ideological center of the majority coalition in the case.[11] If this is true, every new justice can affect policy in the cases in which she is in the majority coalition, even if the justice has no impact on the identity of the court's median justice. Because the average policy content of majority opinions reflects the mix of cases with liberal dispositions and conservative ones, and that mix tends to reflect the average ideology of the justices, the average ideology on the court may approximate the policies created on average in majority opinions.[12] (We return to some of these points in Chapter 12 when we examine how new justices created new courts that in turn created new policies.)

Equation 1 assumes that the addition of a more-liberal-than-average justice drags the average policy content of majority opinions somewhat in a liberal direction (the parameters a and b indicate how much, at the margin). Conversely, the confirmation of a more-conservative-than-average justice drags the average policy content of majority opinions somewhat in a conservative direction. As the average content of majority opinions approaches the president's ideal point, the value of a further move toward the ideal point decreases.

Equation 1's treatment of diversity is somewhat similar: the president values diversity, but at a declining rate with respect to the total number of female and/or non-white justices on the court. Finally, the value of policy reliability reflects its impact on reducing the variance of justice ideology; we refer readers to Cameron et al. (2019) for the technical details.

9.2.3 Presidential Demand for Nominee Characteristics: Empirical Predictions

Equation 1 indicates how presidents value nominee characteristics, but it does not indicate how much of each characteristic the president will purchase. Rather, the selected level of a characteristic reflects the president's effort to maximize his net political benefit from the characteristic, indicated in Equation 1.

Fortunately, given Equation 1 it is easy to derive explicit functions indicating exactly how much of each characteristic the president will select under different circumstances. We empirically estimate these three "demand functions" in Section 5. We refer interested readers to Cameron et al. (2019) for the derivation of the demand functions from the expected utility function. Here we present one demand function, then summarize the empirical predictions across all three.

Presidential demand for nominee ideology is given by:

$$x = \begin{cases} x^* & \text{if } x^* > 0 \\ 0 & \text{if } x^* \leq 0 \end{cases} \quad \text{where } x^* = \frac{1}{b}p - \frac{1}{2b^2}\frac{w^x}{\pi^x} - \frac{a}{b}\bar{x} - x^0 \qquad (2)$$

All the notation is the same as earlier except for x^0 which indicates the default level of ideology that presidents can obtain without exerting any effort.

Equation 2 indicates that the president will choose additional ideology (x) above the default if his desired level is above zero; if not, he will opt for the default level of nominee ideology. We can think of x as a left-censored latent variable, where we only observe the values of x^* if it exceeds a threshold. (This structure suggests an empirical Tobit model, a point we return to below.) If x^* is positive, then the demand function leads to the following empirical predictions (via inspection). The selected level of ideology above the default level (assuming the president is conservative and more conservative than the average justice) is:

- *increasing* in presidential ideology (p)—as the president become more conservative, he chooses a more conservative nominee;
- *decreasing* in the cost of ideology (w^x)—if finding conservative judges is hard, the president demands less conservatism;
- *increasing* in the president's interest in the court (π^x);
- *decreasing* in the conservatism of the eight-member court ($\bar{x}$)—the president demands less ideology as the court moves toward him;
- *decreasing* in the default level of ideology (x^0)—as the default level is more conservative, a conservative president demands less additional conservatism in the nominee.

Although Equation 2 is somewhat opaque, the empirical predictions are largely intuitive.

The other two demand functions have their own distinctive but similar form and lead to specific empirical predictions. Table 9.1 gathers the empirical predictions formally derived from the theory, some 44 in all. In the empirical analysis, we simplify somewhat and focus on about a dozen of the more important predictions, using both the short lists and selected nominees. Even this effort is quite ambitious given the paucity of the data.[13]

A subtlety is that the table displays predictions when presidential demand for a characteristic is sufficiently high that the president will exert effort to go beyond the default level. Suppose the president's demand for the characteristic isn't that high. Equation (2) and the other two demand equations provide a great deal of information about the threshold, which we can estimate empirically. The predictions about the level of the threshold are exactly the same as in Table 9.1 but take the opposite sign. For example, suppose the default level of ideology (x^0) increases. Then the predicted threshold for demanding additional conservatism rises. Hence, the number of empirical predictions of the theory is actually twice the number indicated in Table 9.1.

The demand functions require data even beyond that in Chapter 4, to which we now turn.

Table 9.1 Summary of comparative statics from the characteristics theory. Effects are for signed ideology (negative is liberal, positive is conservative). "+" indicates a predicted positive relationship, "–" indicates a predicted negative relationship, and "0" indicates a predicted relationship of zero.

	Effect on demand for:			
Increase in:	**Ideology (Conservative President)**	**Ideology (Liberal President)**	**Policy Reliability**	**Diversity**
Ideological variables				
President's ideology (p)	+	+	0	0
Benefits from ideology (π^x)	+	–	+	0
Cost of finding ideology (w^x)	–	+	0	0
Default level of ideology (x^0)	–	–	0	0
Extant court's ideology ($\overline{x}$)	–	–	0	0
Policy Reliability variables				
Cost of finding policy reliability (w^q)	0	0	–	0
Default level of policy reliability (q^0)	0	0	–	0
Diversity variables				
Benefits from diversity (π^y)	0	0	0	+
Cost of finding diversity (w^y)	0	0	0	–
Default level of diversity (y^0)	0	0	0	–
Extant court's diversity ($\overline{y}$)	0	0	0	–

9.3 The President's Policy Interest in the Court

The characteristics approach requires a measure of the president's political interest in Supreme Court policy. We combine two variables to measure this interest. First, we treat the president as an extension of his party, and its interest in the court. Accordingly, we return to our analysis of the party platforms and presidential convention speeches from Chapter 2. There we developed an aggregate index of each party's interest in the court, based on the number of hot-button cases, litmus tests, or ideological requirements for nominees invoked in a given year's platform.

Presidents, of course, may have different interests in the court from the larger party. And, whereas the platform and acceptance speeches are measured only at four-year intervals, there exists year-to-year variation in presidential interest. We thus employ a more granular measure of presidential interest: public rhetoric regarding Supreme Court policy.[14] We assume the president allocates more rhetoric to issues that he considers important. In particular, we assume the president displays greater interest in Supreme Court policy making when he voluntarily allocates more of his total rhetorical agenda to Supreme Court policy rather than other topics. The "voluntary" element is important, since often the president's rhetoric is reactive, for example, in response to questions put to him in press conferences. We employ data measuring

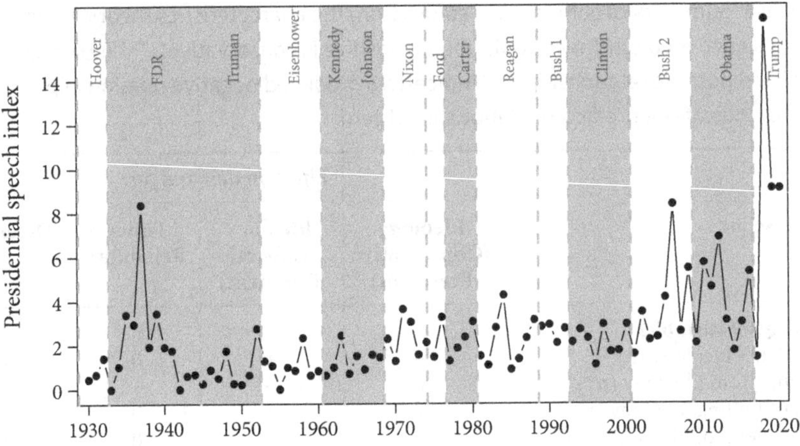

Fig. 9.1 Presidential interest in Supreme Court policy, 1930–2020. The measure is the percentage of the president's rhetoric in each year that is both voluntary and directed at Supreme Court policy.

the share of the president's rhetoric in which he voluntarily speaks on Supreme Court policy.[15]

Figure 9.1 displays the rhetoric-based measure of the president's interest in Supreme Court policy over time.[16] (Shaded regions indicate Democratic presidents.) Variation within presidential administrations is often substantial. Most dramatically Franklin Roosevelt's policy interest scores range from the highest in the observed time frame in 1937 during his confrontation with the Supreme Court over New Deal legislation, down to a score of zero from 1942–1944 (the war years). On the other hand, some presidents persist at relatively high levels of interest (George H.W. Bush) or relatively low ones (Lyndon B. Johnson) throughout their administrations. We observe a slight upward trend in voluntary rhetoric about Supreme Court policy making from the late 1960s to the present day, as well as the persistence of rhetoric even in years when no nomination occurred.[17]

The characteristics theory posits a single measure of presidential interest in Supreme Court policy. To accomplish this, we conducted a principal components analysis of the platform/convention-based measure and the presidential rhetoric measure, and employ the first principal component.[18] The resulting variable, which we call "presidential interest," looks very similar to the presidential speeches measure seen in Figure 9.1.

9.4 The President's "Farm Team"

Under the characteristics approach, presidents (unlike the rest of us!) can get a free lunch: the all-default nominee. If a president desires such a nominee, he can acquire one with very little expenditure of time and effort. But to obtain more than the default level of attributes—someone who moves the court dramatically, someone with rock-solid policy reliability, or someone who boosts the court's gender and racial diversity—the president must work to find and vet short-list candidates and then exert effort to confirm the chosen one.

If the characteristics approach is to gain any empirical traction, we must measure both the changing level of default attributes and the costs of finding someone better than the default. At some level, it would be ideal if we could identify and measure the entire universe of potential Supreme Court nominees. Unfortunately, we can't do that. No one can. The problem is the potential pool from which a president can draw is amazingly broad, extremely ill-defined, and almost totally amorphous. Consider: Franklin Roosevelt nominated someone whose highest judicial qualification was serving as the judge in an Alabama traffic court! (We refer to Hugo Black—who, to be fair, was a super-liberal senator and close ally of Roosevelt at the time of his selection.) Identifying such a broad universe of potential nominees is a fool's errand. What we can do, though, is identify a good proxy for the universe of viable candidates. The features of our proxy group should plausibly track those in the real universe of nominees. For our proxy group, we use the judges of the U.S. Courts of Appeals.

Modern presidents draw their Supreme Court nominees almost exclusively from the Courts of Appeals.[19] But, even in the era when presidents made more heterogeneous choices, we believe that the Courts of Appeals represent a reasonable proxy for the larger pool of characteristics available to the president. Indeed, we show that the overall characteristics of Courts of Appeals judges have changed in ways that parallel the broader changes seen in the president's selection process.[20] In essence, we conceptualize the Courts of Appeals as the president's "farm team." We borrow the term from sports, particularly baseball. At the top of the pyramid of baseball leagues in the United States sit major league teams. Each major league team contracts with a number of minor league teams that play in hierarchical leagues (Class A, Double-A, and Triple-A, in increasing order of skill). A key role of the minor league teams is to serve as the farm team by grooming younger players to play in the major league.[21] Before players enter the major league, their last stop is usually the AAA team for a given franchise—just as the last stop for Supreme Court nominees before they join the high court is often the Courts of Appeals.

9.4.1 The Size of the Farm Team

One important question for any president is the size of the farm team. For some measures below, we conceptualize the farm team as comprising the entire Courts of Appeals. For others, we use the president's *copartisan judges*.[22] It is thus helpful to visualize the size of each.

Figure 9.2 depicts the number of active judges on the Courts of Appeals from 1891 (the inception of the modern-day circuit courts) to 2020. At the turn of the

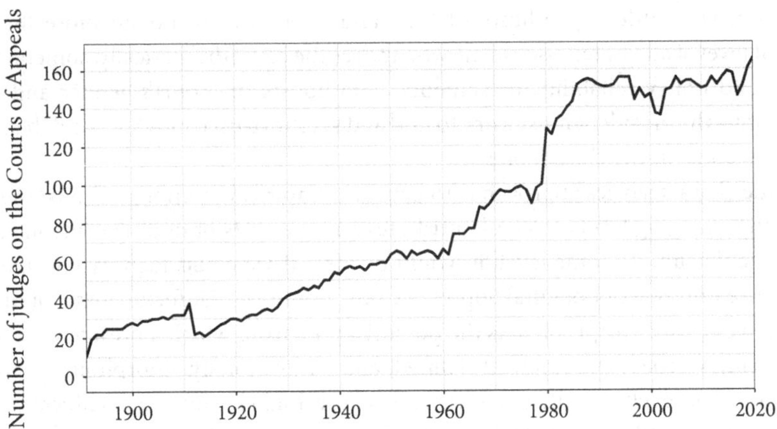

Fig. 9.2 The number of active judges on the Courts of Appeals from 1891 to 2020.

twentieth century, the Courts of Appeals were quite small (as was the federal judiciary overall), with fewer than 40 active judges. Over time, that number gradually but consistently increased, largely to keep up with the courts' increasing caseload. In the 1970s and 1980s, however, the number jumped significantly, driven in large part by two expansions. First, a unified Democratic Congress in 1978 handed President Carter 35 new seats to fill; as we document shortly, Carter used this opportunity to dramatically increase the diversity of the federal bench. Six years later, a Democratic House joined a Republican Senate to give President Reagan 24 additional judgeships. Since then, the number of active judges has hovered between 140 and 160.[23]

Federal judges, of course, are appointed by presidents, and the mix of judges appointed by Democrats and Republicans will vary over time. Figure 9.3 separately depicts the number of Democratic and Republican appointees on the Courts of Appeals from 1930 to 2020. The shaded regions depict eras of Democratic control of the White House, while non-shaded regions feature Republican presidents. The partisan distribution of the Courts of Appeals naturally follows the cycle of partisan control of the presidency. For example, there were only 13 Democratic-appointed judges when Roosevelt came into office in 1933, compared to 33 Republican appointees. Two subsequent decades of Democratic control saw those numbers switch to 57 and 10, respectively, in 1952. Similarly, the appointments of Presidents Reagan and George H.W. Bush brought a steep increase in the proportion of Republican appointees on the bench.

Importantly, the increase in the size of the farm team coincides with the rise in presidential interest in the court. For instance, after coming into office in 1953 following 20 years of Democratic White House control, President Eisenhower was handed a pool of only *nine* Republican judges on the Courts of Appeals. This shallow pool would have posed a big problem for any president who prioritized the courts and judicial selection. But Eisenhower was not such a president, as evidenced by his selection of Earl Warren and William Brennan, with both choices reflecting electoral

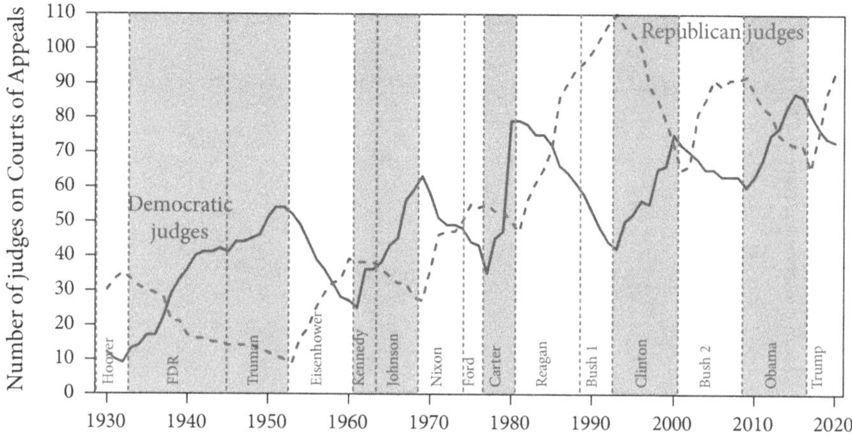

Fig. 9.3 The number of active Democratic-appointed and Republican-appointed judges on the Courts of Appeals, 1930–2020.

considerations, as we discussed in Chapter 3.[24] By contrast, 40 years later, President Clinton took office after 12 years of Republican control, but nevertheless had a pool of 55 Democratic appointees to work with in 1993, the year he nominated Ruth Bader Ginsburg. In general, given the overall increase in the size of the lower federal courts, presidents today—who have much greater interest in the courts compared to their distant predecessors—will still have a much larger copartisan farm team, even after a period of White House control by the other party.[25]

9.4.2 Ideology

Returning to the characteristics theory itself, to operationalize the default level of ideology, we follow a standard approach in the judicial politics literature and develop a NOMINATE score for every active judge on the Courts of Appeals. Specifically, for each judge, we calculated the DW-NOMINATE equivalent of the Giles-Hettinger-Pepper scores, which are based on the ideology of a judge's appointing president and/or home-state senators (Giles, Hettinger, and Peppers 2001).[26] As with NOMINATE, the scale runs from more liberal (negative numbers) to more conservative (positive numbers.)

For each year from 1930 to 2020, we calculated the mean ideology score for all judges on the Courts of Appeals, as well as separately for Democratic and Republican appointees; these results are shown in Figure 9.4. The overall mean tracks control of the White House, becoming more conservative in periods of Republican control, and vice versa. Interestingly, mean ideology by partisanship is fairly flat over time, though it has moved somewhat toward the extremes (more so for Republicans).

Which measure should we use to operationalize the default level of ideology? We opt for the overall mean, rather than the mean among the president's copartisan

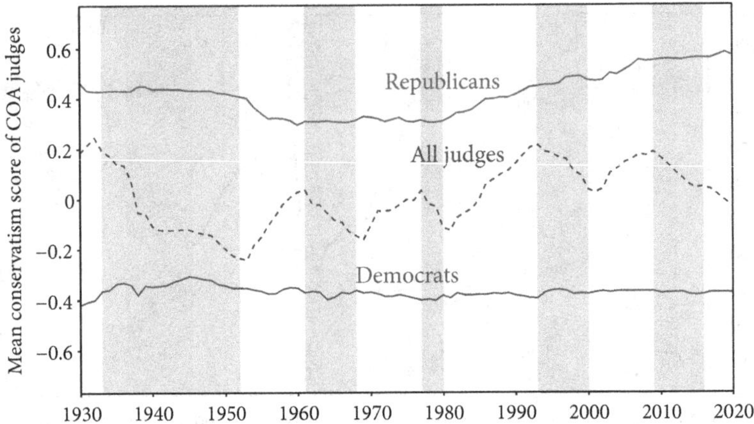

Fig. 9.4 The mean ideology of active judges on the Courts of Appeals from 1930 to 2020, for all judges and for Democratic and Republican appointees separately. Shaded regions depict eras of Democratic control of the White House. The figure shows the average of the judge-level ideal points, which are the DW-NOMINATE equivalent of the Giles-Hettinger-Pepper scores; the latter are based on the ideology of a judge's appointing president and/or home-state senators.

judges, for two reasons—one conceptual, one practical. Conceptually, notable examples in U.S. history exist of presidents making "cross-party" appointments to the court when they did not have much interest in the ideological output of the court—for instance, Eisenhower's appointment of William Brennan or Truman's appointment of Harold Burton. Thus, the idea is that if a president randomly selects a nominee, the overall mean would be the nominee's expected ideology (recall the president can acquire this amount of ideology for free). From a practical standpoint, we attempted to use the co-partisan measure; when we did so, the procedure by which we calculated the purchased level of ideology (described shortly) resulted in a large majority of observations being censored, which did not allow for enough variation to implement our regressions. We thus opt for the overall mean measure.

9.4.3 Policy Reliability

A key insight of the characteristics theory is that presidents care not solely about a justice's ideology *per se*, but also the ability to translate that ideology into effective policy making. That's where nominee policy reliability comes in. Thus, in thinking about the farm team, a president will consider not only the default ideology he is likely to get without putting forth any effort, but also the default level of reliability.

In Chapter 4, we showed that the background and experience of Supreme Court nominees changed dramatically over time. Early in our period of study, nominees were much more likely to be politicians or executive administrators. But over time, these "politicos" gave way to legal "Super Techs" with experience both in working in the executive branch and on the federal bench. This shift, in turn, was coincident with presidents instituting more formal oversight and vetting procedures when selecting nominees.

To quantify this shift, for each candidate, we construct an index, the Policy Reliability Index (PRI), using the biographical data; this measure corresponds to the actual level of reliability in the characteristics theory. We define the PRI as $PRI = \sum_i \rho_i$, where ρ_i indicates the four attributes conducive to establishing policy reliability: service as a federal judge, executive branch lawyer, law professor, and attendance at a top law school. "Politicos" like Black and Byrnes score low on the measure, while legal Super Techs like John Roberts and Brett Kavanaugh score highest.

To develop a measure of the default level of reliability, we adopt a parallel approach with respect to the Courts of Appeals. Specifically, we take the categories that we developed in Chapter 4 to describe nominees and short-list candidates, and apply them to judges of the Courts of Appeals. For every active judge on the Courts of Appeals from 1930 to 2020, we coded whether they attended a top-14 law school, whether they were a law professor before joining the bench, and whether they served as an executive branch lawyer. Panels (A)–(C) in Figure 9.5 depict the aggregate number of judges who had each of the three experience characteristics, broken down by party. Panel (D) indicates the number of judges who had any of the three characteristics. In line with the trends in nominee characteristics seen in Chapter 4, the figure shows the secular increases in all three experience characteristics over time.

From these measures, we create a measure of the default level of reliability. For each year, we define an index that is parallel to the PRI for candidates. First, because we are working with the pool of federal judges, every judge starts with a score of 1. Then for each of the three experience measures held by a given judge, we add the value 1. Each judge then has a score of 1 to 4. We define the default level of reliability as the mean rate of reliability among all Courts of Appeals judges.[27]

9.4.4 Diversity

In Chapter 4, we documented a striking increase in the number of candidates on presidents' short lists who were either female or non-white, or both. In addition, while there have only been eight justices who were not white males, all were appointed after 1966.

To find out whether these changes track shifts in farm team diversity, we coded the race and gender of every active Courts of Appeals judge. Figure 9.6 summarizes the overall diversity of the circuit courts, broken down by party. The left panel depicts the number of female judges, the middle panel depicts the number of minority judges, and the right panel depicts the number of non-white-males (the categories are thus overlapping).

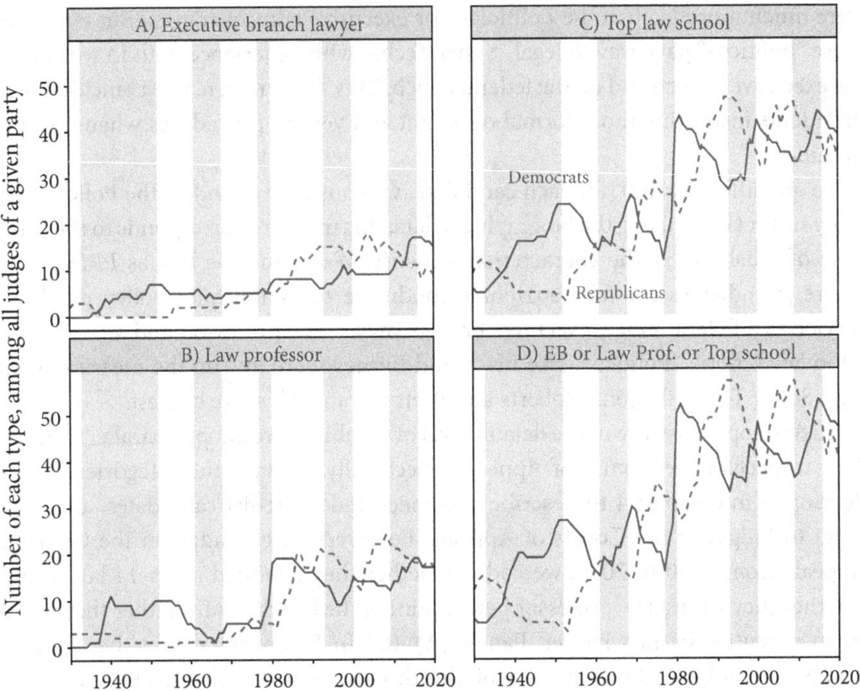

Fig. 9.5 The reliability characteristics of Courts of Appeals judges, 1930 to 2020. The solid (blue) line depicts Democratic judges, while the dotted (red) line depicts Republican judges. Shaded regions depict eras of Democratic control of the White House.

The patterns in Figure 9.6 are stark. Until the 1970s, the Courts of Appeals were nearly universally the dominion of white males. Since then, presidents from both parties have placed both women and minorities on the bench in significant numbers. However, the increases have been larger on the Democratic side. The differences in the farm teams when it comes to diversity both across time and across parties have significant implications for the cost to the president of finding a diverse nominee. Early on, the costs were effectively infinite, as there were almost no non-white-males to choose from. Now there are many, but much more so on the Democratic side.

9.5 Does It Work? Taking the Theory to Data

We now test each of the predictions about the ideology, policy reliability, and diversity of nominees and short-list candidates.

9.5.1 Testing the Demand for Ideology

Above we defined the default level of ideology available to the president. Recall that the total level of nominee ideology equals the sum of the "free" level plus the

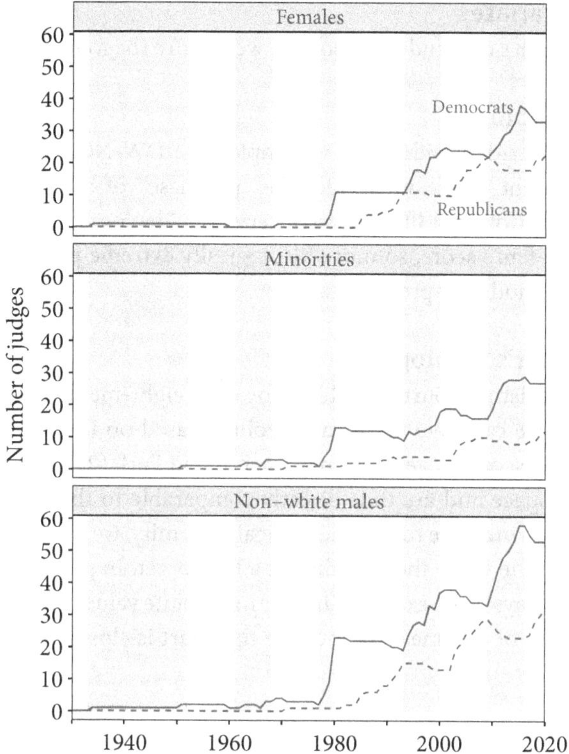

Fig. 9.6 The number of female and minority judges on the Courts of Appeals, 1930–2020.

"purchased" level. For the total level of nominee ideology, we use the inferential measure developed by Nemacheck (2008). With these measures in hand, we can develop an estimate of the purchased level of ideology that accounts for the censoring implied by the demand for ideology. Specifically, for Republican presidents, let the purchased level equal 0 if a candidate is (weakly) less conservative than the default level of ideology. The same is true for Democratic presidents when a candidate is (weakly) less liberal than the default level of ideology. Conversely, if the president is a Republican and the purchased level is more conservative than the default level, then the amount of purchased (or additional ideology) equals the difference between the total level of a candidate's ideology and the "free" default level. Similarly, if the president is a Democrat and the purchased level is more liberal than the default level, then the amount of purchased (or additional) ideology equals the difference between the total level of a candidate's ideology and the default level. Thus, our measure of purchased ideology is always non-negative and is increasing in the ideological *extremism* of the candidates and nominees (for both liberals and conservatives). The censored nature of our measure indicates the applicability of a left-censored Tobit model, and thus we employ Tobit models to estimate the demand for ideology.

Additional Covariates

To test the president's demand for ideology, we require the following measures:

Presidential Ideology

To measure the president's ideology, we employ the DW-NOMINATE score of the appointing president. Since we model the "purchase" of additional ideology (as opposed to straightforward liberal-to-conservative ideology), we take the absolute value of the president's score, so more ideologically extreme presidents have higher scores than more moderate presidents.

The Extant Court's Ideology

To measure the existing court's ideology, for each eight-member court at the time of each vacancy, we calculate the mean ideology based on the NOMINATE-Scaled Perceptions (NSP) scores developed in Cameron and Park (2009). These scores exist in NOMINATE space and are thus directly comparable to the president's ideology score. To make this measure reflect ideological extremity, we multiply the mean NSP score by negative one when the president is a Democrat. In practice, the ideology of the president is always more extreme (higher in absolute value) than the overall court; thus, higher values of this measure indicate the court is closer to the president, and vice versa.

The Costs of Purchasing Additional Ideology

We employ two different measures to proxy for the president's cost of purchasing additional ideology. First, we conceptualize the costs in terms of the president's *search costs*, given positive demand: how easy or difficult is it to find a candidate of the desired ideology? To capture this, we assume the president's search costs are decreasing in the number of co-partisan judges on the Courts of Appeals (as determined by the party of the appointing president)—see Figure 9.3 above. The number of judges has increased for both parties over time as the size of the federal judiciary has grown, but even within eras there is significant variation based on the periods of partisan control of the White House. Specifically, we measure costs as $\frac{1}{\text{the number of co-partisans}}$; thus, costs are *decreasing* in the number of co-partisan judges on the bench.

Second, we conceptualize the cost of purchasing ideology in terms of the president's *political costs*: how easy or hard will it be to get an ideologically extreme nominee through the Senate? To capture this, we measure the proportion of senators who are of the president's party. Similar to the first operationalization, we measure this variable as $\frac{1}{\text{percent of co-partisan senators}}$, so costs are *decreasing* in the proportion of the Senate controlled by the president's party.

The Ratio of Costs to Benefits

Finally, we construct a measure we call the *cost-benefit ratio*. This simply equals our measures of costs divided by the measure of presidential interest, which captures the benefits to the president. We construct this ratio separately for both measures of costs.

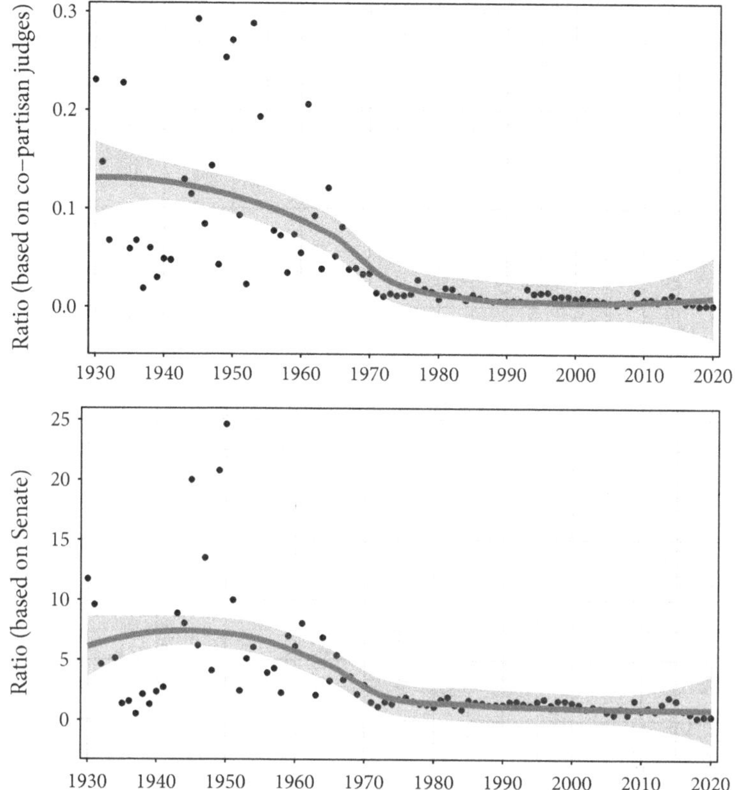

Fig. 9.7 The cost-benefit ratio for presidential demand of ideology, based on the number of co-partisan judges on the Courts of Appeals (top) and the proportion of Senate controlled by the president's party (bottom). The lines are loess lines.

For each measure of costs, the predicted sign on the ratio is negative. Figure 9.7 depicts the cost-benefit ratio for both measures; it shows a clear decrease in the cost-benefit ratio over time.

Regression Results

Table 9.2 presents eight Tobit models. The dependent variable in each is our measure of the additional amount of ideology chosen by the president; the censoring point is at zero. Models (1)–(4) employ the measure of costs based on the number of co-partisans on the Courts of Appeals, while models (5)–(8) employ the Senate-based measure. Models (1), (2), (5), and (6) include all candidates,[28] while Models (3), (4), (7), and (8) include only nominees.[29] The odd-number models present bivariate regressions where the cost-benefit ratio is the only predictor. As predicted by the theory, the coefficient is negative in each model; it is also statistically distinguishable from zero. Thus, there exists a significant bivariate connection between the ratio of costs to benefits and the presidential choice of additional ideology.

Table 9.2 Tobit regression models of the president's demand for ideology. σ gives the estimated standard error of the regression. "ALL" = all candidates, while "NOMS" = nominees only. $^{*}p < .05$

	(1)	(2)	(3)	(4)	(5)	(6)	(7)	(8)
Cost-benefit ratio	−1.021*	−0.791*	−0.778*	−0.389	−0.020*	−0.014*	−0.019*	−0.011
	(0.290)	(0.266)	(0.358)	(0.360)	(0.007)	(0.007)	(0.006)	(0.006)
| President |		0.412*		0.595*		0.384*		0.532*
		(0.170)		(0.221)		(0.171)		(0.218)
Mean of extant court		−0.344*		−0.499*		−0.257*		−0.444*
		(0.111)		(0.134)		(0.101)		(0.137)
Default ideology		−0.108		0.038		−0.068		0.036
		(0.220)		(0.207)		(0.214)		(0.204)
Intercept	0.304*	0.116	0.337*	0.072	0.319*	0.128	0.364*	0.114
	(0.027)	(0.094)	(0.035)	(0.115)	(0.029)	(0.099)	(0.035)	(0.113)
σ	0.215*	0.206*	0.206*	0.179*	0.212*	0.206*	0.197*	0.176*
	(.304)	(.012)	(.021)	(.019)	(.012)	(.012)	(.020)	(.019)
Sample	ALL	ALL	NOMS	NOMS	ALL	ALL	NOMS	NOMS
N	304	304	55	55	304	304	55	55
# of censored observations	59	59	7	7	59	59	7	7
Cost measure?		*Courts of Appeals judges*				*Senate opposition*		

The even-number models add as predictors the ideology of the president, the ideology of the extant court, and the default level of ideology. In each model, the coefficient on the cost-benefit ratio remains negative; however, it is measured somewhat imprecisely in some of the models. All told, the models provide suggestive evidence that presidents take into account the costs and benefits of choosing additional ideology—in particular, the ratio is predictive of which individuals make the short list.

Turning to the remaining covariates, more ideologically extreme presidents demand more ideology, which is intuitive. Next, the coefficient on the default level of ideology is always statistically indistinguishable from zero—the demand for ideology does not seem to vary systematically with changes in the baseline level of ideology, *ceteris paribus*. In addition, the coefficient on the overall ideology of the court is negative and statistically significant. Recall that this variable is scaled such that lower values mean the court is further from the president, and vice versa. Thus, as predicted by the theory, presidents choose less ideology when the court is closer to them. This coefficient has the interpretation of the ratio of the president's weight on the ideology of the extant court to the president's weight on the ideology of the nominee. If the estimated ratio were zero, it would suggest the president placed no weight on the ideology of the court. Instead, the estimated coefficient is statistically different from zero, suggesting presidential interest in the ideological makeup of the court. But the ratio itself ranges from about $\frac{1}{4}$ to $\frac{1}{2}$, implying much greater weight on nominee ideology *per se* than would be true if the president cared only about the mean ideology of the court (which would imply a ratio of about 8).

9.5.2 Testing the Demand for Reliability

Above we defined the default level of policy reliability available to the president. Recall that the total level of reliability equals the sum of the "free" level plus the "purchased" level. For the total level, we use the background and experience measure developed in Chapter 4. We can then define the purchased level of reliability using a similar procedure to that used for ideology—reliability, however, is strictly non-negative so we do not need to account for the "flipped" measures for liberal presidents. Let the purchased level equal zero if the total measure is less than or equal to the default measure of reliability; thus, we assume that if a candidate is (weakly) less reliable than the default level of reliability, the president has purchased no additional reliability. Conversely, if the total measure is greater than the default level, than the purchased level equals the difference between the total level of a candidate's reliability and the "free" default level. Thus, our measure of the purchased level of reliability is always non-negative, and it is increasing in the reliability of candidates (for both liberals and conservatives). As with ideology, the censored nature of the purchased reliability measure calls for a left-censored Tobit model.

Table 9.3 Tobit regressions of the president's demand for reliability. σ gives the estimated standard error of the regression. "ALL" = all short list candidates, while "NOMS" = nominees only. $^{*}p < .05$

	(1)	(2)	(3)	(4)
Benefit-cost ratio	0.038*	0.078*	0.025*	0.092*
	(0.012)	(0.027)	(0.013)	(0.033)
Baseline reliability			0.700	−0.924
			(0.609)	(1.212)
Intercept	−0.025	0.108	−1.145	1.612
	(0.131)	(0.257)	(1.048)	(1.986)
σ	0.966	1.016	0.967	1.011
	(0.053)	(0.118)	(0.053)	(0.118)
Sample	ALL	NOMS	ALL	NOMS
N	304	55	304	55
# of censored observations	110	14	110	14

Additional Covariates

Recall that demand for reliability is increasing in the president's interest in the Supreme Court. To measure presidential interest, we employ the combined measure based on the party platforms, convention speeches, and presidential rhetoric discussed above in Section 9.3. To measure the cost of reliability we again use the inverse of the number of co-partisans on the Courts of Appeals. Our assumption is that as the number of ideologically aligned compatriots on the bench increases, the cost of finding a reliable legal technician, or possibly a Super Tech, decreases. The theory also predicts that demand for reliability is increasing in the square root of interest in the courts over the cost of finding reliability; we create this measure and call it "the benefit-cost ratio." Thus, as the number of co-partisans increases, the cost of reliability decreases, and the overall ratio increases, leading to the prediction that reliability should be increasing in co-partisans. Finally, we also include the baseline level of reliability as a predictor.

Regression Results

Table 9.3 presents four Tobit regression models of candidate reliability. In each model the dependent variable is our measure of additional reliability purchased, with the censoring point at zero. Models (1) and (3) include all candidates (short listers and nominees), while Models (2) and (4) include only nominees.

Models (1) and (2) are bivariate regressions in which the benefit-cost ratio is the only covariate. As predicted by the theory, the coefficient is positive and significant—presidents choose more reliability as the cost-weighted benefits of doing so increase. Note, however, the magnitude of the coefficient in the nominee-only model is about twice the size of the coefficient in the model with all candidates. Models (3) and (4) add the baseline level of reliability as a predictor. Again, we see the same pattern: the benefit-cost ratio remains positive and significant, but is much larger in the model with just nominees (Model 4). Finally, in neither Model (3) nor Model (4) is the coefficient on baseline reliability statistically significant.

The differing magnitudes when we compare all candidates to just nominees are perhaps not surprising, in light of the differences in background characteristics over time seen in Figure 4.5 on page 94. The benefit-cost ratio predicts the president's choice of reliability when he ultimately makes a nomination, but seems to have much less influence on who makes the short list in the first instance. This divergence is noteworthy, as it means that the candidates who eventually become justices have greater professional qualifications and hence higher policy reliability.

9.5.3 Testing the President's Demand for Diversity

Finally, we examine the theory's predictions with respect to the president's demand for racial and gender diversity on the Supreme Court. Recall from Chapter 4 that we collected the race and gender of every candidate on the short lists (and thus every nominee) from 1930 to 2020. Unsurprisingly, the diversity of the short lists has increased substantially over time. No woman or minority made a short list until after 1960. Since then, their presence has steadily increased over time. White males, however, still make up a large proportion of candidates. Interestingly, and in contrast to the pattern with reliability, the trends for short listers and nominees have moved on parallel tracks.

Implementing the tests about diversity is simpler, compared to the tests about ideology and reliability. To operationalize the president's demand for diversity, in theory one could suppose that diversity is increasing in the number of dimensions on which a candidates differs from the "typical" candidate—that is, a white male. In practice, there have only been four unique candidates who were female *and* a minority, which makes an intersectional approach infeasible. Accordingly, we take the simpler step of assuming that purchased diversity equals 1 whenever the candidate is a female or minority, and 0 otherwise. This simplification means we can employ logistic regression models.

To measure the president's interest in diversity, we use the platform-based measure developed in Chapter 2. There we showed that neither party invoked diversity before 1972. Since then, Democrats have tended to stress racial and gender diversity more often, though Republicans have mentioned diversity occasionally. Note that while the index exceeds 1 for Democrats in a few years, these never occur during a Democratic presidency, and so in practice the president's interest in diversity is a binary variable.

To proxy for the "cost" of locating nominees who are not white males, we again draw on the Courts of Appeals. We assume the cost of finding diversity equals 1 divided by the number of co-partisan judges who are not white males.[30] As seen in Figure 9.6 above, the data indicate that the cost of diversity was very high prior to about 1960 but fell dramatically thereafter. However, Republican presidents continued to face high costs until more recently.

Table 9.4 Logistics regressions of the demand for diversity. "ALL" = all candidates, while "NOMS" = nominees only. $^*p < .05$

	(1)	(2)	(3)	(4)
Benefit-cost ratio	0.085*	0.161	0.068*	0.136
	(0.016)	(0.092)	(0.022)	(0.083)
Diversity of extant court			6.123*	3.680
			(1.296)	(2.645)
Intercept	−1.563*	−2.259*	−2.860*	−2.866*
	(0.235)	(0.477)	(0.324)	(0.733)
Sample	ALL	NOMS	ALL	NOMS
N	304	55	304	55

Returning to the theory, the demand for diversity is increasing in the ratio of presidential interest in diversity over the cost of finding diverse attributes in nominees—we define this as the *benefit-cost ratio* for diversity. Thus, as the number of co-partisan non-white-male judges on the Courts of Appeals increases, the cost decreases, and thus the overall ratio increases, leading to a prediction that the demand for diversity should be increasing in the number of co-partisan judges who are not white males.

For baseline diversity, we make the simplifying assumption that the baseline nominee is a white male. Because this is effectively the same as assuming the default level is zero, this term is not included in our regression specifications. Finally, to measure the diversity level of the extant court, we take the number of justices who are not white males on the extant court at the time of a vacancy and divide by 8.

Regression Results

Table 9.4 presents four logistic regressions estimating the president's demand for diversity. Models (1) and (2) are bivariate regressions in which the benefit-cost ratio is the only covariate. Model 1 includes all candidates, while Model 2 includes only nominees. As predicted by the theory, the coefficient is positive—presidents are more likely to consider female and/or minority candidates as the cost-weighted benefits of doing so increase. Note that the magnitude of the coefficient in the nominee-only model is double that of the coefficient in the all-candidate model; however, the latter is measured much more precisely (there have only been eight nominees to the court who were not white males, so there is little variation to work with in the nominee-only regressions).

Models (3) and (4) add the mean diversity level of the court as a covariate. The coefficients on the benefit-cost ratio remain the same. Surprisingly, however, the coefficient on the diversity of the extant court is positive in Model (3), perhaps suggesting that the level of diversity on the court has never approached a sufficient level to generate diminishing returns from further diversity (this coefficient is not significant in Model 4).

9.6 Understanding Changes in Selection Politics

The regression analyses are important, but they are necessarily a bit stilted. Fortunately, the characteristics setup allows us to move beyond interpreting the sign and significance of the regression models to use them to answer substantive questions about the politics of selection. Indeed, the models lend themselves to numerous questions; in the interest of space we focus on the rise of ideological nominees and pose counterfactuals about how changes over time have influenced president's emphasis on diversity.[31]

9.6.1 The Rise of Ideological Nominees

One question the empirical approach allows us to pursue is this: how has the latent probability (based on the Tobit specification) that a president purchased additional ideology and did not simply opt for the "default level" of ideology changed over time? To answer this question, we employ Model (2) in Table 9.2 to estimate this predicted probability for the short-list candidates; a probability of zero means the president almost certainly opted for the default, while a probability close to 1 indicates near certainty that the president purchased additional ideology.[32]

These estimates are depicted in Figure 9.8, and show that an important change in appointment politics over the last nine decades was the disappearance of default candidates for the Supreme Court and the rise of what we might call "ideological agenda" candidates. Notably, the figure reveals a significant drop in the later years of Roosevelt's administration and for Truman; indeed several of Truman's candidates are estimated to have had about a 50% chance of being a default nominee with respect to ideology. These estimates are consistent with his overall lack of interest in the court and with the court's ideological proximity to him, following 12 years of Democratic

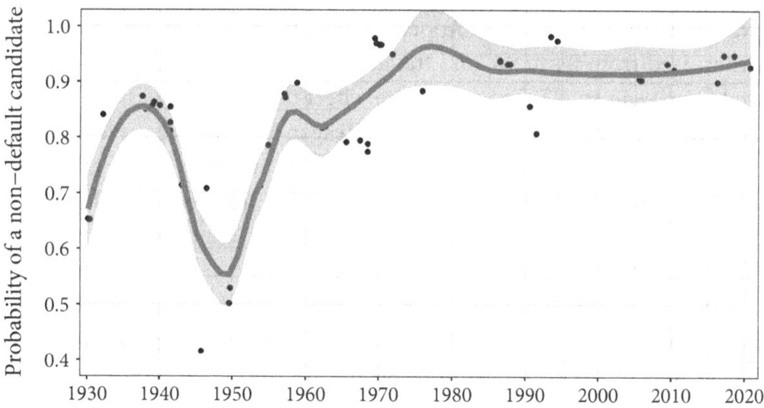

Fig. 9.8 The predicted probability of a non-default ideological candidate, 1930 to 2020. The line is a loess line.

appointments to the court. However, after 1970 almost all nominees had about a 90% chance of being an ideological agenda nominee. Given the rise in presidential interest in the court and the relative reduction in search costs due to the growth of the federal judiciary, it is difficult to imagine a scenario in the near future in which the president chooses only the default level of ideology.

9.6.2 The Importance of Seeding the Lower Courts

As we discussed earlier, participants in the nomination process often discuss the importance of "creating a pipeline" or "building a farm team" in the U.S. Courts of Appeals. This dynamic has been most notable on the Republican side, where Republican presidents have worked in tandem with the conservative legal movement (the Federalist Society in particular) to stock the Courts of Appeals with reliably conservative judges who make good candidates for the Supreme Court.[33] The characteristics model allows us to analyze this insight rigorously, both from the perspective of presidents seeking ideology and those seeking diversity.

With respect to ideology, the theory identifies three distinct effects from "seeding" the circuit courts with ideologically favorable judges; two lead to more ideologically proximate picks, the third leads to less proximate ones. The first effect, the direct effect, comes from simply moving the ideology of the default nominee. The second effect, the cost effect, reflects the decrease in search costs that results from the president being able to increase the number of co-partisan judges on the Courts of Appeals over the course of his tenure. The third effect, the offset effect, constitutes a decrease in purchased ideology because the default nominee moves closer to the president (that is, changes in default ideology stimulate somewhat offsetting changes in overall ideology). How big are these effects substantively?

To explore this question we consider the decade between 1981 and 1991. In this period two Republican presidents (Reagan and George H.W. Bush) appointed many conservatives to the U.S. Courts of Appeals. Over this span, the number of Republican judges increased from 44 to 96, and the ideology of the average circuit court judge increased from −.11 to .23. To evaluate the effect of these changes, we first calculate the additional level of ideology chosen by Reagan in 1981 (again using Model (2) in Table 9.2), based on his actual benefit-cost ratio in 1981. To do this, we set the president's interest, the mean of the court, and the president's ideal point at their average values in the 1981–1992 period. We estimate that Reagan in 1981 would have chosen .32 [.23, .41] additional units of ideology, for a total ideology of .18 [.09, .27]. We then simulate Bush's choice of additional ideology in 1991, changing only the ratio (to reflect the decrease in costs due to the appointment of more lower court judges) and the default ideology. This simulation estimates that Bush chose a comparable amount of additional ideology (.27, [.20, .33]) as Reagan did in 1981; however, because of the increase in default ideology, the estimate of purchased ideology for Bush rises to .41 [.34, .47]. The .22 difference in predicted overall ideology is statistically significant [.09, .36] and substantively large. Thus, the model suggests that the combined offset effect and cost effect yielded little difference in additional ideology. However, changing the default level of ideology in "the farm team" during the 1980s translated into a substantial conservative shift in the short list.

The presence of a farm team is also important for diversity in the president's short list candidates and nominees. Early in our period of study, presidential interest in diversity on the court was virtually non-existent; not surprisingly, few women and minorities were appointed to the Courts of Appeals. But, as interest in diversity rose, presidents were then hamstrung by the lack of representation on the lower courts.

Indeed, the difficulty of finding ideologically compatible nominees other than white males is a recurring theme in nomination selections, at least since the Nixon Administration. As we saw, Nixon expressed a strong interest in finding a woman candidate for a seat on the Supreme Court in 1971. While he would have preferred a circuit court judge, at that time only two women were federal judges and both had been appointed by Democratic presidents. Mildred Lillie, a California Superior Court judge, drew Nixon's attention as both a conservative and a woman, but she was deemed not qualified by the American Bar Association. Ultimately, Nixon failed to find a suitable woman to nominate.

In contrast, at the time of Ronald Reagan's nomination of Sandra Day O'Connor, Republican presidents had appointed 15 seated federal judges who were not white males. Though Reagan reached out to a woman who was not a federal judge, the change in the federal judiciary since Nixon's time—from 0 to 15 seated non-white-male co-partisans—illustrates his lower search costs compared to Nixon. Yet, even 25 years later, President George W. Bush still faced sizable search costs—one interpretation of his failed nomination of Harriet Miers in 2005 is that Bush was eager to appoint a woman to replace O'Connor, yet had difficulty finding a well-qualified one who met his other appointment goals.[34]

We can use our regression models of diversity to estimate how much search costs bind presidents. First, we return to Nixon, and, using Model (2) in Table 9.4, ask what is the probability he would nominate a woman or minority candidate in 1971.[35] Based on the benefit-cost ratio in 1971, we estimate that Nixon had .08 [.03, .20] probability of nominating a non-white-male candidate. What if Nixon had faced the reduced costs that George W. Bush faced in 2005 (the year he made his selections to the court)? We estimate that the probability of a diverse Nixon appointee would have increased to .20 [.06, .48]. (This difference of .11 has a 95% confidence interval of [−.01, .36].) These simulations help illustrate how the diversity of the farm team can either enable or frustrate a president who is seeking to increase the diversity of the Supreme Court.

9.7 Conclusion

Announcing his selection in 2017 of Neil Gorsuch to replace Justice Scalia, President Trump said, "I have always felt that after the defense of our nation, the most important decision a president of the United States can make is the appointment of a Supreme Court justice." This sentiment approaches conventional wisdom today. But the extent to which presidents have acted as if they believed this is true has varied significantly over the course of American history. In this chapter we developed a theory that helps explain much of the variation in presidential selection from 1930 to the present day. Rather than conceiving of selection as a purely ideological game involving a power struggle between the president and the Senate, the characteristics approach reconceives nominees as bundles of characteristics that are valued by presidents and that can be "purchased" through effort or at a political price.

The models provide several substantive insights about the politics of Supreme Court appointments since 1930. First, we demonstrated the importance of the nexus between who sits on the lower courts (particularly the Courts of Appeals) and who becomes a candidate for a seat on the Supreme Court. Building a good "farm team" of co-partisan judges in the U.S. Courts of Appeal is vital, as it reaps benefits down the road in terms of justices appointed. In addition, the model illuminates the remarkable transformation from "politico" nominees to "Super Techs," and the secular growth of female and minority candidates for the Supreme Court. The transformative impact of heightened presidential interest in the court also stands out as particularly important.[36] The characteristics approach helps explain some apparent puzzles in presidential selection. Cameron and Kastellec (2016*b*) documented numerous "own goals" by the president: nominees who are ideologically opposite to the president. From the perspective of both move-the-median theory and modern-day nomination politics, such "mistakes" by the president are inconceivable. However, all of the own goals occurred before 1960. Why is that significant? From the perspective of the characteristics theory, presidential interest in the court in earlier eras was significantly lower, and the costs of finding ideologically reliable judges were much higher. Thus, it is not surprising that presidents often made idiosyncratic choices, such as President Truman nominating Harold Burton because he *wanted* a Republican judge on the court.[37] In contrast, presidents from both parties now care intensely about the policy output of the court, and the cost of purchasing ideology and reliability has declined dramatically. It is thus not surprising that the last selection "mistake" (President George H.W. Bush's nomination of Souter) to be confirmed was more than 30 years ago—the failed nomination of Harriet Miers in 2005 due to *intra*-party opposition is the exception that proves the rule.

While the theory and data in this chapter are intricate, the ultimate substantive upshot is quite straightforward. Presidents now care deeply about selecting Supreme Court justices, and the pool of potential reliable nominees is now quite deep on both sides. It is difficult to imagine a return to the days when presidents treated selection as a casual and unimportant task. This means that nominees are now highly reliable ideologues. How does the American public respond to such nominees? We turn to this question in the next chapter.

10 What the Public Wanted

In Chapter 7, we showed that few nominations prior to 1980 saw much polling, and many saw none. But an increase in the frequency of polling marched hand-in-hand with greater public interest in Supreme Court nominations. Today, opinion holding about nominees is common and extensively measured. The aggregate data show that public evaluations of the nominees changed dramatically over time. The president's co-partisans now express nearly universal support for nominees while members of the out-party express nearly universal opposition. This pattern emerged in the twenty-first century.

What accounts for the dramatic change in how the public responds to Supreme Court nominees? More deeply, what did citizens want, and what explains their response to what they got? In Chapter 7, we restricted ourselves to describing poll results. Here we switch squarely to explanation. In doing so, we hope to illuminate important changes in nomination politics. But more than that, we engage with one of the principal debates in contemporary political science, a debate about how citizens form opinions and take political action.

A tale of three respondents

In Chapter 7 we introduced our "megapoll" of individual-level responses, comprising nearly 300,000 responses from 21 unique nominees. Out of these 300,000, consider three in particular. First, in July 2009, "Jane Doe" answered a public opinion poll, fielded by YouGov.[1] The poll asked Jane a series of questions about the nomination of Sonia Sotomayor and also about herself. Jane was a Democrat, Black, and had a high school degree. With respect to Sotomayor, Jane perceived that President Obama's nominee had a political orientation or ideology; moreover, Jane was able to specify what that ideology probably was. On a 5-point scale ranging from −2 (very liberal) to +2 (very conservative), Jane scored Sotomayor as −2, very liberal. Sotomayor's NSP score was −.30 (on a −1 to 1 scale), so this seems a fairly reasonable perception. Jane also was willing to indicate her own political orientation on the same left-right scale: she said her own ideology was −1 (liberal). Jane thus perceived herself as ideologically close to the nominee. The survey also asked Jane her perception of Sotomayor's quality or qualifications to serve on the court. Jane responded that Sotomayor, a circuit court judge who had graduated from Princeton and Yale Law, was highly qualified. Finally, the survey asked Jane whether she supported confirmation, opposed confirmation, or was unsure or didn't know. Jane said that she supported confirmation.

Making the Supreme Court: The Politics of Appointments, 1930–2020. Charles M. Cameron and Jonathan P. Kastellec, Oxford University Press. © Oxford University Press 2023. DOI: 10.1093/oso/9780197680544.003.0010

Also answering the survey was "Jim Loe." Jim indicated that he was a Republican, white, and had a college education. He too perceived Sotomayor as very liberal. But, unlike Jane, Jim said his own ideology was very conservative, thus placing him far from Sotomayor ideologically. He also did not view the nominee as qualified to serve on the Supreme Court. Perhaps unsurprisingly given these perceptions, Jim said he opposed the confirmation of Sotomayor.

Finally, "Peter Flow" said that he was an Independent, white, and had some college education. His perception of Sotomayor was that she was a moderate (0 on the 5-point scale); he also placed his own ideology as 0, dead center in the scale. When asked whether he supported Sotomayor's confirmation, Peter responded that he was undecided.

What are we to make of these survey responses? Were their ultimate judgments on confirmation driven primarily by their partisan identity, with their perceptions of nominee ideology and qualifications little more than motivated reasoning supporting a foregone conclusion? Or do their responses suggest fairly sensible or even (one might say) "rational" appraisals given their perceptions and values? Alternatively, might the truth lie somewhere between those two poles?

Partisan Intoxication or a Rational Public?

In asking these questions, we join a central debate in contemporary political science. On one side is a venerable intellectual tradition stretching back to classics like Campbell et al. (1960) and Converse (1964), and including more recently Achen and Bartels (2016) and Mason (2018), that is extremely skeptical about the ability and motivation of ordinary citizens to engage in meaningful evaluation of politics. Rather, it views citizens as primarily partisan automata, or sometimes as irrationally short-sighted slot machines. Boosting this skepticism is the apparently greater partisan polarization of the electorate—if citizen evaluations of policies and politicians mostly reflect group identification or "brains on partisanship," what remains but an endless kabuki play of partisan warfare?

On the other side is a dissenting tradition that sees citizens as, if not fully rational, at least somewhat sensible, either individually or in the aggregate, in their evaluation of and response to public policy, politicians, and political life. Recent studies using massive high-quality survey data and/or experimental manipulations appear to support the revisionist view—at least to revisionists.[2] Adopting nomenclature from the advocates themselves, one might call the first school the "Realist" camp and the second the "Rationalist" one.

How can the Realist and Rationalist schools be so far apart, since both take empirical evidence so seriously? Realists tend to dismiss citizens' stated policy preferences as the product of projection or motivated reasoning ("If my side is in favor of policy X, then so am I").[3] At the same time, Realists are vague about the exact details of a theory of projection and its boundary conditions. So it is hard to know *a priori* when it should apply, when it shouldn't, and how much. Rationalists see the Realist neglect of policy evaluations as extremely consequential, leading to substantial omitted variable bias.[4] On this account, the evidence of extreme partisan intoxication is mostly a statistical artifact from mis-specified regressions and poorly constructed survey questions.

We cannot definitively adjudicate between the Realist and Rationalist schools—doing so would require crystal clear theories and experimental or near-experimental quality data. But we do claim that citizen evaluations of Supreme Court nominees provide a useful and interesting laboratory for exploring the two perspectives. To do so, we formulate an explicit theory of citizen appraisal of Supreme Court nominees. Although our theory is tailored to nomination politics, it is much more general in scope. For example, it fits neatly with citizen approval or disapproval of the president's job performance. It could also be extended to address expressed vote intention in two candidate races. We use the theory and the survey data to identify what the public wanted, why, and how it responded to what it got.

The chapter is organized as follows. Section 10.2 presents an overview of our theory of citizen evaluation of Supreme Court nominees, the Learning-Thinking-Acting (LTA) Framework. The LTA Framework leads to what we call the workhorse regressions, explicitly relating nominee evaluations and cognitive information processing costs to answers on surveys. Section 10.3 takes an intermediate step toward understanding citizen desires by examining citizen perceptions of nominee ideology, a critical piece of the puzzle. We quantify partisan perceptual "bias" about nominee ideology. Section 10.4 turns to survey responses. We estimate the workhorse regressions across multiple nominations to uncover the substantive impact of partisanship and perceived ideological distance to the nominee on the probabilities of expressing support, opposition, or uncertainty about nominee confirmation.

Section 10.5 departs from traditional survey analysis by moving from survey answers to the underlying utility of citizens for nominees, a move made possible by the LTA Framework. We define the partisan gap in nominee evaluations as the difference in the utilities for nominees between Democratic and Republican citizens. We then measure how the partisan gap grew over time. We identify two drivers of this gap: an increase in the direct impact of partisan affiliation or opposition, and a huge increase in the ideological distance between out-party members and nominees. The latter reflects the astounding partisan sort of citizens over the past four decades, in which liberals became Democrats and conservatives became Republicans. With measures of both in hand, we provide a nominee-by-nominee accounting of the partisan gap. We find that both the direct partisan effect and ideological evaluations contributed to the partisan gap, typically in the ratio of about 2:1 party to ideology. The result of these shifts in partisan evaluations, combined with presidents selecting relatively more extreme nominees over time, is that presidential co-partisans were well served by the selection of such nominees—but others much less so.

10.2 Thinking about Citizens Thinking: The LTA Framework

If we are to go beyond a description of polls, we need to be clear about how people evaluate Supreme Court nominees, how they answer survey questions, and how the two are linked. We provide a novel theory of these phenomena, based upon recent ideas in modern choice analysis, cognitive science, and behavioral economics. We call it the Learning-Thinking-Acting (or LTA) Framework. Figure 10.1 provides an overview; the Appendix provides details.[5]

In the figure, boxes connote variables and arrows indicate putative causal impacts or at least predictable empirical correlations. Variables with dashed boundaries indicate latent variables. Some dependent variables contain an equation number; these are keyed to specific equations in the text. Bolded equation numbers indicate a relationship to be estimated empirically. Some arrows have names, because they indicate relationships of major theoretical interest. Examples are partisan perceptual "bias," partisan affiliation, policy evaluation, and risk aversion.

As the dashed boundary boxes in Figure 10.1 show, the LTA Framework has three components: a *Learning* component, a *Thinking* or cognitive component, and an *Acting* or behavioral component. The Learning component examines how reported

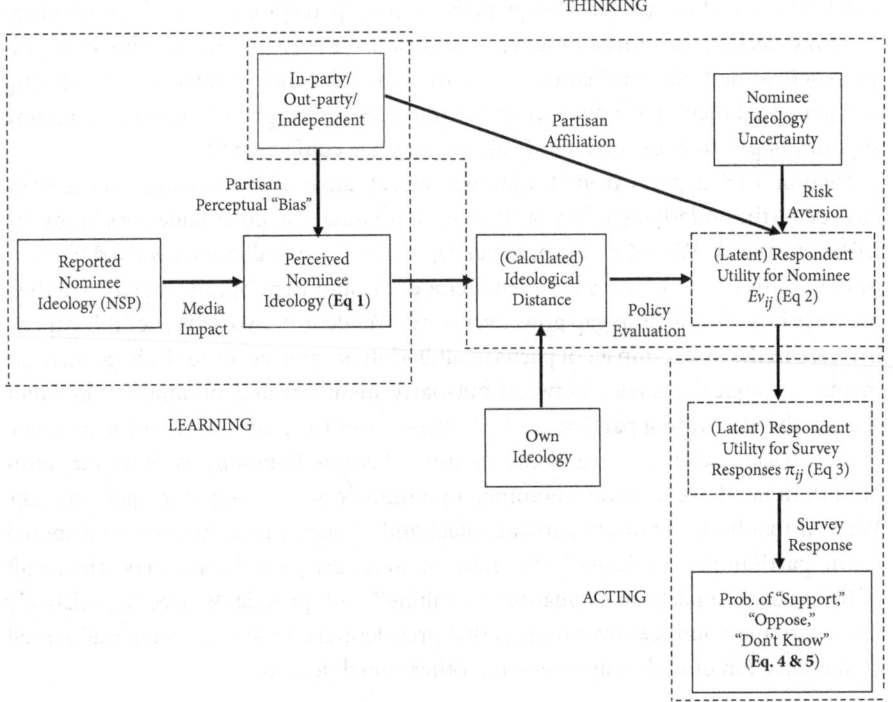

Fig. 10.1 Overview of theoretical framework for citizen evaluation of nominees.

news about nominee ideology combines with respondents' partisan relationship to the nominating president, to determine perceptions of the nominee's likely political orientation or ideology. The Learning component is deliberately ambiguous about the exact microfoundations of perceived nominee ideology, which are best explored with experimental data.[6] But even if the data do not reveal the exact micro-foundations for partisan bias, we can gauge average magnitudes by estimating variations of the simple regression equation:

$$\overline{x}_{ij} = a_0 + a_1 NSP_j + a_2 Democrat_{ij} + a_3 Republican_{ij} \tag{1}$$

Here, $\overline{x}_{ij}$ indicates citizen *i*'s perception of nominee *j*'s most likely ideological position on a left-right scale.[7] The variable NSP_j is a measure of the nominee's ideology as discussed in contemporary newspaper editorials (see Chapter 4), while the remaining two variables are indicator variables for the citizen's party affiliation (Independents are the omitted category). The coefficients a_2 and a_3 thus measure partisan "bias" in perceptions of nominee ideology.

The Thinking component of the LTA Framework focuses on how citizens appraise nominees. We assume citizens value a nominee based on the nominee's attributes. As shown in the figure, perceived nominee ideology enters this component via an ideological distance between the nominee and the respondent. The resulting *policy evaluation* is one component of the overall evaluation of the nominee, but only one. The respondent's partisan relationship to the nominating president may also directly affect the nominee appraisal, via direct *partisan affiliation*, as shown by the indicated pathway in Figure 10.1. This pathway may involve visceral emotion as much as calculation. In the framework, risk aversion from uncertainty about the nominee's ideology may also play a role (so may other nominee traits like race or gender). Empirically, any of these factors could dominate the evaluation of the nominee. We interpret the Realist school as asserting that the partisan evaluation pathway dominates citizen appraisal of nominees, while the Rationalist school would maintain a large role for policy evaluation.

We are explicit about citizen evaluations of attributes, and employ a valence-quadratic loss framework.[8] In the Appendix, we derive citizen *i*'s expected valuation of nominee *j*:

$$Ev_{ij} = a_0 + a_1 q_{ij} + a_2 p_{ij} + a_3 out_{ij} - a_4 (y_i - \overline{x}_{ij})^2 - a_5 \sigma^2_{v_{ij}} \tag{2}$$

where q_{ij} is citizen *i*'s perception of nominee *j*'s qualifications or quality as a justice, p_{ij} indicates a presidential copartisan, out_{ij} indicates the opposite party affiliation, the quadratic loss function indicates the expected policy value of the nominee to the citizen (whose own ideological placement is given by y_i), and $\sigma^2_{v_{ij}}$ is the citizen's uncertainty about the value of the nominee.

We hope to cast light on the Realist and Rationalist claims by examining empirical estimates of the coefficients a_2, a_3, and a_4 and measuring perceived ideological distances, and thus, the impact of partisan affiliation and policy evaluation on citizens' expected utility for a nominee. Of course, a citizen's expected utility for a nominee is a *latent* variable (hence, the dashed box in the figure). Pollsters cannot attach a "happiness meter" to a citizen and directly measure utility, however much they might wish to. Instead, an analyst must infer utility from survey answers.

Here is where the third component of the LTA Framework, the Acting or behavioral part, does service; it is also the theory's most novel feature.[9] This component indicates how latent utility for the nominee translates into observable behavior. In this case, the observable behavior is not a vote or a campaign contribution but instead an answer to the survey question, *Do you support confirmation of Nominee X, oppose confirmation, or are uncertain or don't know?* In a modern choice theoretic framework, each possible survey response has a value to the respondent (note the latent variable "Respondent utility for survey responses" in Figure 10.1)—the respondent simply chooses the best answer. So the key question really is, what is your theory of the survey response, in Zaller and Feldman's (1992) famous phrase? A well-formulated theory will allow one to back out the coefficients in Equation 2.

In our theory, respondents gain an expressive benefit from affiliation with, or repudiation of, the nominee. This expressive benefit is precisely Ev_{ij} from affiliation and $-Ev_{ij}$ from repudiation. However, acquiring the benefit is not costless. A definitive affiliation or repudiation requires thought about a likely unfamiliar and possibly uncongenial matter.[10] We take this cognitive processing cost to be precisely $\sigma^2_{v_{ij}}$, the respondent's uncertainty about the value of the nominee. A "don't know" answer brings no expressive benefit but avoids the mental strain required by the other answers.

The latent utilities of the three survey answers are thus

$$\pi_{ij}(r_{ij}; Ev_{ij}, \sigma_{v_{ij}}) = \begin{cases} Ev_{ij} - \sigma^2_{v_{ij}} + \epsilon_{1ij} \text{ if } r_{ij} = 1 \\ 0 + \epsilon_{0ij} \text{ if } r_{ij} = 0 \\ -Ev_{ij} - \sigma^2_{v_{ij}} + \epsilon_{-1ij} \text{ if } r_{ij} = -1 \end{cases} \quad (3)$$

where $r_{ij} = 1$ connotes the survey response "I support confirmation," $r_{ij} = 0$ connotes the survey response "I don't know," and $r_{ij} = -1$ connotes the survey response "I oppose confirmation." We assume a respondent selects the answer that affords her the greatest net satisfaction. The three other terms in Equation 3, of the form $\epsilon_{a_{ij}}$, are random shocks to each answer, idiosyncratic to each respondent, that capture all unmeasured factors affecting costs and benefits of an answer for a respondent. These shocks turn Equation 3 into a random utility model, in which we can meaningfully address the probability of a particular answer.[11] Standard assumptions about these error terms lead directly to a plain-vanilla multinomial logit regression model.

In the Appendix, we derive the two parts of this multinomial logit model. The first is the log-odds support regression and the second is the log-odds opposition regression:

$$\ln \frac{P(1)}{P0} = a_0 + a_1 q_{ij} + a_2 p_{ij} + a_3 out_{ij} + a_4 (y_i - \bar{x}_{ij})^2 + a_5 \sigma^2_{x_{ij}} + a_6 (\sigma^2_{x_{ij}})^2 + a_7 \sigma^2_{x_{ij}} (y_i - \bar{x}_{ij})^2 \quad (4)$$

$$\ln \frac{P(-1)}{P0} = b_0 + b_1 q_{ij} + b_2 p_{ij} + b_3 out_{ij} + b_4 (y_i - \bar{x}_{ij})^2 + b_5 \sigma^2_{x_{ij}} + b_6 (\sigma^2_{x_{ij}})^2 + b_7 \sigma^2_{x_{ij}} (y_i - \bar{x}_{ij})^2 \quad (5)$$

Equations 4 and 5 are the workhorse empirical models in this chapter. Using them, in Section 4 we study the probabilities of the answers "Support," "Oppose," and "Don't know," as partisanship and ideology vary.

Note that *the coefficients* a_0 *to* a_5 *are exactly the same coefficients in Equation 2*, the latent utility equation. And, the coefficients b_0 to b_5 are those same coefficients, times negative one. So, estimation of the workhorse regression equations recovers the key parameters needed to evaluate the Realist and Rationalist schools in the arena of nominations politics. With them, we can analyze the sources of the skyrocketing partisan polarization in evaluation of Supreme Court nominees. And, we can do so using estimates of citizen utility for nominees rather than revealed answer probabilities. As Zaller and Feldman noted, answering questions is not the same thing as revealing preferences. But with the right questions and a well-formulated theory of the survey response, we can use survey answers to estimate respondent preferences for Supreme Court nominees and what changes evaluations over time.

10.3 Citizen Perceptions of Nominee Ideology

We begin our empirical analysis by examining the Learning portion of our theoretical framework. We ask whether citizens perceive differences between liberal and conservative nominees and how partisanship affects these perceptions.

For data, we return to the public opinion "megapoll" of individual-level responses that we examined in Chapter 7. In that chapter, we did not examine ideology at all. A large proportion of polls did ask respondents about their *own* ideology, and we will employ these self-placements shortly. But here we focus on a smaller subset of polls that also asked respondents about how they perceived the ideology of *nominees*. For example, a September 1987 poll about the nomination of Robert Bork asked respondents: "Based on what you know or have heard, how would you describe Bork's views on most issues: would you say he is very liberal, liberal, moderate, conservative, or very conservative, or is that something you don't have an opinion on?"

Unfortunately, pollsters did not ask questions like this very often. And, even when they did, they usually offered respondents only three possible nominee placements (i.e. liberal, moderate, and conservative), rather than five, as in the Bork question, or a continuum. Accordingly we analyze both the 3-point responses and the 5-point responses, sometimes collapsing the latter into the former in order to maximize sample size (i.e. we collapse the very liberal and very conservative answers in the 5-point questions to just liberal and conservative). The 5-point scale provides more nuanced information, but such data is available for only five nominations (and for only one Democratic nominee). The 3-point data are coarser, but exist for 10 nominations, including four Democratic nominees. Overall, the dataset includes 18,763 answers on the 3-point scale, and 11,424 answers on the 5-point scale. Figures 10.2 and 10.3 below indicate which nominees are included in the surveys with the 3-point and 5-point responses.

In Section 4, we use respondents' ideological self-placements and ideological nominee-placements to analyze citizen evaluation of nominees. A potentially serious issue arises from respondents' failure to provide a nominee placement. Specifically, 28% of respondents to the 3-point question did not provide their perceptions of the nominee's ideology, while 32% of respondents to the 5-point question did not offer a perceived placement. Our theory of the survey response suggests that such people could offer some placement if sufficiently motivated, but they find the question extremely cognitively burdensome and prefer to duck it in the survey setting. However, another possibility is that the people who refuse to place nominees differ in some truly fundamental way from those willing to do so. For example, they may reject a left-right understanding of politics. Or they may be absolutely incapable of conceiving of Supreme Court nominees as political. If this were true, the patterns evident among nominee-placers would not extend to non-placers—the estimates would suffer from selection bias.

In the Appendix, we show that factors such as education do in fact predict willingness to place nominees on an ideology scale. As one would expect, the non-placers tend to be people with low knowledge about or interest in politics. However, we also conduct a missing data imputation analysis that suggests that nominee-placers and nominee non-placers tend to evaluate nominees in broadly similar ways. With this proviso, let us examine how citizens perceive nominee ideologies.

10.3.1 The Basis of Perceptions

Figure 10.2 depicts the distribution of the respondents perception of nominee ideology, for each nominee, using the 5-point scale. For clarity, we place the lone Democratic appointee (Sotomayor) at the bottom of the plot; the four Republican appointees are ordered chronologically. The bars depict the proportion of responses in each category, where the total number of responses for a given nominee is the denominator.

At the very least, we would expect the public to ascertain that Republican nominees (Bork, Douglas Ginsburg, Gorsuch, and Kavanaugh) tend to be conservative and that Democratic nominees tend to be liberal—and they do. The majority of the public viewed each Republican nominee as either conservative or very conservative; a non-trivial but still fairly small percentage of the public saw these nominees as moderate, while fewer than 10% combined saw them as either liberal or very

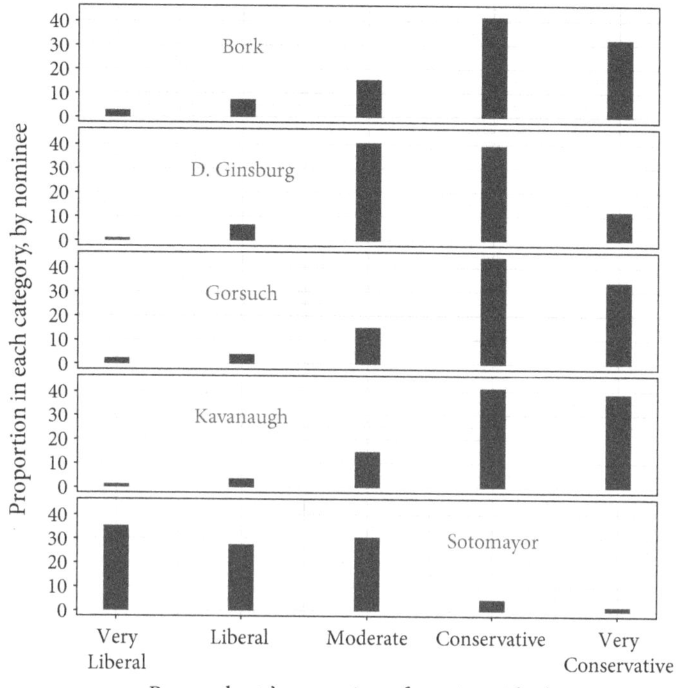

Fig. 10.2 Respondents' perception of nominee ideology, using the 5-point ideology scale. We place the lone Democratic appointee (Sotomayor) at the bottom of the plot; the four Republican appointees are ordered chronologically. The bars depict the proportion of responses in each category, where the total number of responses for a given nominee is the denominator.

liberal.[12] For Sotomayor, a sizable proportion of Americans viewed her as moderate, but the plurality category was very liberal, and very few people perceived her as conservative.

Figure 10.3 repeats this analysis, this time using the 3-point scale of respondents' perceived ideology of nominees. Again, we order by Republicans first, and then chronologically. While we see the same basic patterns, the additional nominations reveal some interesting variation both within and across the party of the appointing president. Among Republican nominees, John Roberts and Samuel Alito were viewed as much more moderate than Gorsuch and Kavanaugh. Among Democratic nominees, Ruth Bader Ginsburg and Merrick Garland were also seen as more moderate compared to Sonia Sotomayor and Elena Kagan. (Shortly we provide a quantitative analysis employing a measure of nominees' ideology.)

Figure 10.3 suggests that overall, Democratic nominees tend to be seen as more moderate compared to Republican nominees. Figure 10.4 confirms this possibility more systematically by pooling responses for Republican nominees and Democratic nominees separately. The figure shows that more than 60% of respondents viewed

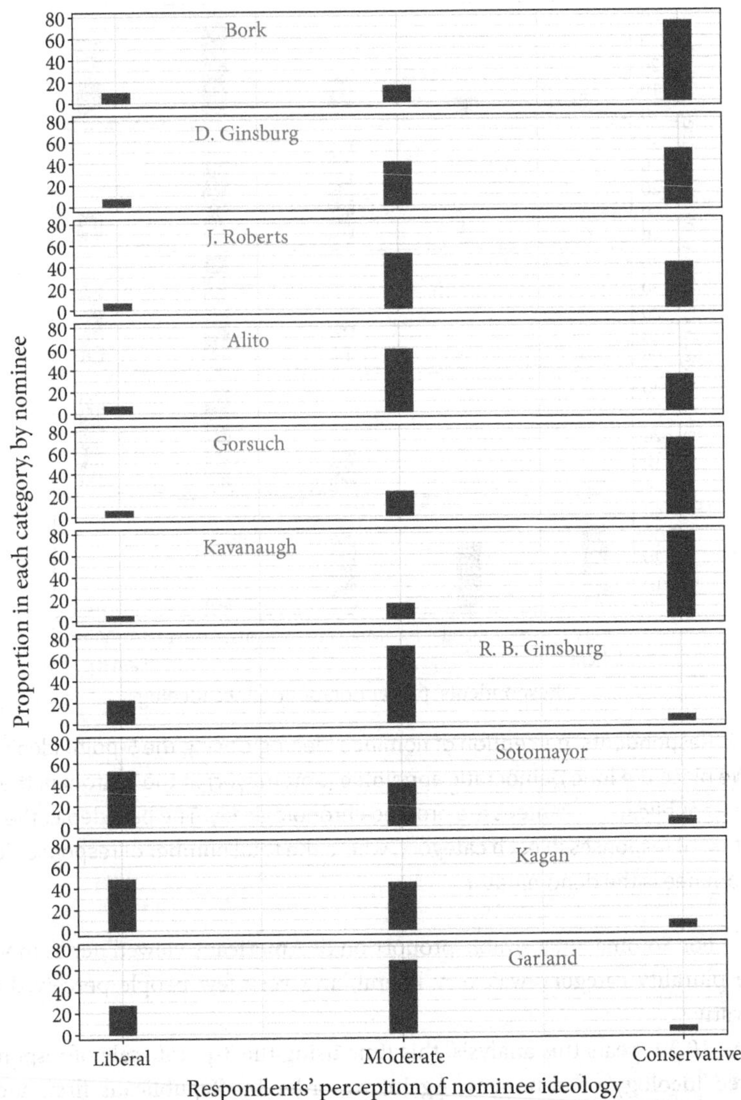

Fig. 10.3 Respondents' perception of nominee ideology, using the 3-point ideology scale. We order by Republicans first, and then chronologically.

Republican nominees as conservative, compared to only about 25% who viewed them as moderate. Conversely, equal proportions of respondents (about 45%) saw Democratic appointees as moderate or liberal. Below we show that this asymmetry can in part be explained by the fact that recent Republican nominees have in fact been more ideologically extreme than Democratic nominees (as discussed in Chapter 4). Nonetheless, the contrast in public perception of Democratic and Republican nominees is quite striking.

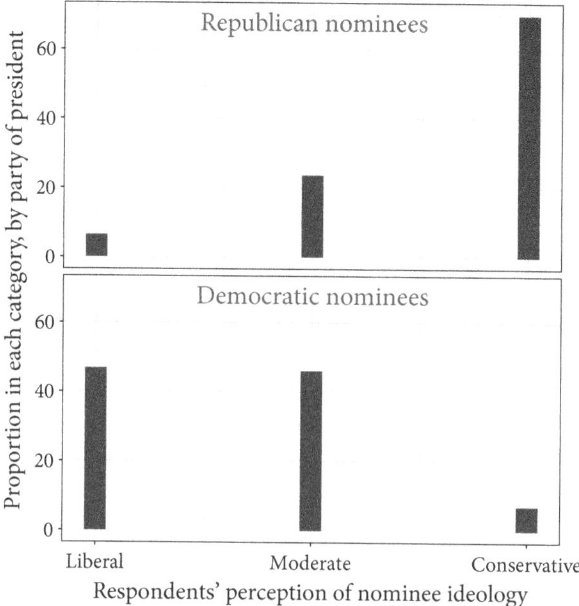

Fig. 10.4 Comparing respondents' perception of nominee ideology, by party of the appointing president.

10.3.2 Partisan Impact: Ideology versus Party

In Chapter 7 we showed that members of the president's party are much more likely to support a nominee than are members of the out-party, especially for twenty-first-century nominees. Here we examine whether there is a "partisan bias" in perceived nominee ideology. Figure 10.5 breaks down citizen perception by party identification. We employ the 5-point scale here to take advantage of the granularity in perceptions.[13] The left column shows the distribution of responses for Democratic identifiers, the middle column for Independents, and the right column for Republicans. Again, the distributions are normalized within each nominee-party pair; for example, the top-left panel depicts the proportion of Democrats who viewed Bork as very liberal, liberal, moderate, conservative, or very conservative.

The figure suggests a considerable degree of shared perceptions across respondents irrespective of their partisanship. Most citizens, both Democrat and Republican, tend to view the three Republican nominees as generally conservative and the one Democratic nominee as broadly liberal. This is true of Independents as well, who tend to be less informed than partisans.

However, there are some subtle and quite interesting differences across Democratic and Republican identifiers. First, consider Republican respondents—notice that for Republican nominees, many more Republican respondents viewed the nominee as "conservative" rather than "very conservative." This is true even for nominees

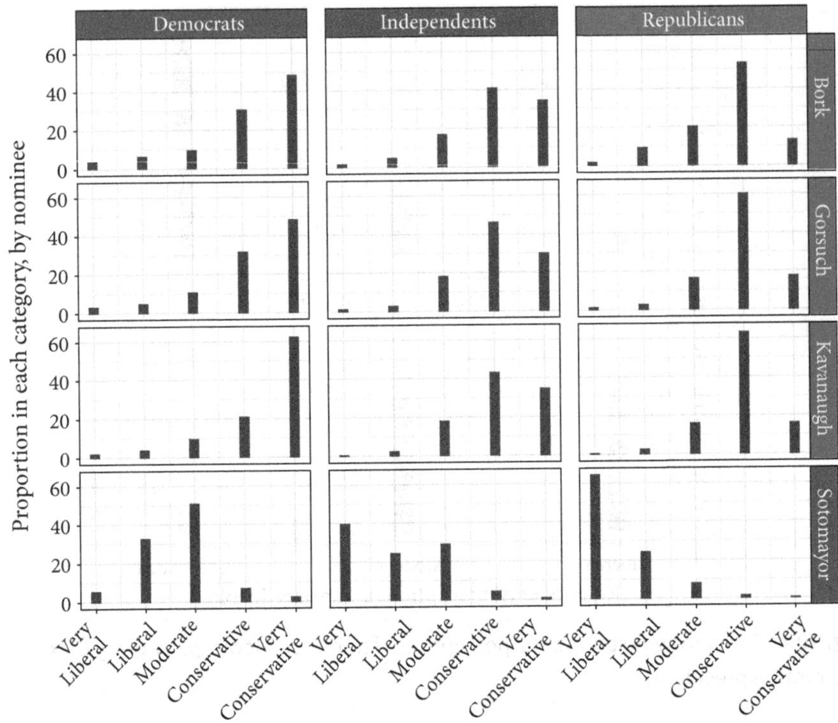

Fig. 10.5 Citizen perception of nominee ideology, broken down by party identification. The distributions are normalized within each nominee-party pair.

such as Bork, Gorsuch, and Kavanaugh, whom sophisticated observers would see as very conservative. In contrast, Democratic identifiers (shown in the top row in the figure) displayed the opposite tendency: they were much more likely to classify the Republican appointees as very conservative rather than conservative.

Now consider Sotomayor, the sole Democratic appointee in Figure 10.5. Notice again the highly asymmetrical pattern—Democratic identifiers were most likely to classify her as a moderate, with very few seeing her as "very liberal." Conversely, more than 60% of Republican identifiers viewed Sotomayor as very liberal, with the percent classifying her as liberal or moderate declining rapidly.

This asymmetry suggests the existence of a degree of partisan bias in evaluations, with out-partisans more likely to view nominees as extreme, compared to the perceptions of both in-partisans and Independents. To explore this pattern systematically, we turn to a regression analysis. In particular, we investigate the respective impacts of reported nominee ideology and respondent partisan affiliation on perceived nominee ideology.

Table 10.1 presents four regression models, each of which are variants of Equation 1. In each model, the dependent variable is respondents' perception of

Table 10.1 OLS regression models of respondent perception of nominee ideology.

	3-point ideology		5-point ideology	
	(1)	(2)	(3)	(4)
NSP score	1.12*	1.13*	2.09*	2.10*
	(0.01)	(0.01)	(0.02)	(0.02)
Democrat	0.16*	0.15*	0.34*	0.34*
	(0.01)	(0.01)	(0.02)	(0.02)
Republican	−0.15*	−0.16*	−0.25*	−0.26*
	(0.01)	(0.01)	(0.02)	(0.02)
Constant	−0.08*	−0.19*	−0.31*	−0.70*
	(0.01)	(0.03)	(0.02)	(0.05)
N	18,730	18,249	11,391	11,186
Controls?	No	Yes	No	Yes
R^2	0.44	0.44	0.47	0.48

nominee ideology; the first two regressions use the 3-point scale while the second two use the 5-point scale. In each model, a key predictor is the nominees' NSP score; recall that these scores project the Segal-Cover editorial assessment measures into DW-NOMINATE space, such that each nominee has a score that ranges from more liberal to more conservative. The other main predictors are whether the respondent was a Democrat or a Republican, with Independents serving as the reference category. Models (2) and (4) also include demographic controls.[14]

The results are quite consistent across the four models. Higher NSP scores—that is, more conservative nominees—are associated with perceptions of a more conservative nominee. In addition, we also find that Democrats tend to perceive nominees as more conservative and Republicans tend to perceive nominees are more liberal, relative to Independents (and hence each other, via transitivity). Substantively, this means that Democrats tend to see liberal nominees as somewhat more moderate and conservative nominees as more conservative, than do Independents. Conversely, Republicans tend to see conservative nominees as somewhat more moderate, and liberal nominees as more liberal, than do Independents. When we take into account the difference in scales between the 3-point and 5-point measures, the substantive magnitude of the coefficients in Table 10.1 are quite comparable across the two measures.

These results show that both party and ideology matter in citizen perception of nominee ideology. But, which effect matters more? One way to assess the relative weights on both is to generate predicted ideological placements for specific nominees. Figure 10.6 presents predicted ideological locations for Sotomayor and Kavanaugh, broken down by partisan identification, based on their actual NSP scores, which are -.30 for Sotomayor and .67 for Kavanaugh. To do so, we use Model (1) from Table 10.1. While the 3-point ideological perception measure is not literally in the same space as NSP, it has the same scale (-1 to 1), and thus allows for an easy evaluation of partisan differences.

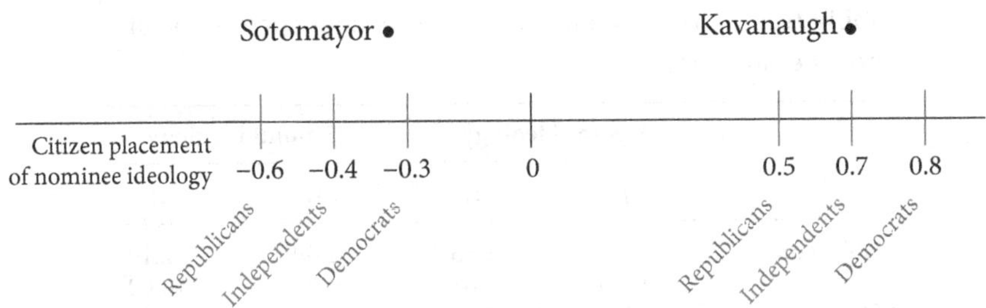

Fig. 10.6 Predicted ideological placements for Sotomayor and Kavanaugh, based on Model (1) in Table 10.1. The points for Sotomayor and Kavanaugh depict their respective ideal points, based on the NSP scores.

Figure 10.6 shows how partisanship predicts citizen assessments of nominee ideology. Consistent with the descriptive evidence above, the statistical model predicts that Republicans are more likely to view Sotomayor as more liberal (and hence more extreme) than Independents, while Democrats are more likely to view her as less liberal (and thus less extreme). The story flips for Kavanaugh. Democrats are likely to view him as more extreme (and indeed, close to the edge of the ideology scale), while Republicans are likely to view him as less conservative.

Notice, however, that the magnitude of these partisan differences is swamped by the overall gap in ideological placements of the two nominees—one liberal, one conservative. In other words, the *between-nominee* gaps in assessments for Sotomayor and Kagan are much larger than the *within-nominees* gaps across partisan groups. More specifically, within a given nominee, the difference between how Democrats and Republicans assess her ideology is .3, or 15% of the overall ideological scale. Conversely, the gap between how Democrats assess Sotomayor and Republicans assess Kavanaugh is .8, or 40% of the scale.

Thus, all told, while we see clear evidence of a degree of partisan bias in citizens' perceptions of nominee ideology, the major take-away is that perceptions rather sensibly track the substantial gap in ideology between Democratic and Republican appointees in modern Supreme Court appointments.

10.4 Answering Surveys: "Approve, Disapprove, Don't know"

We now examine the drivers of citizens' expressed support or opposition to nominees by estimating the workhorse regressions described in Section 10.2. Recall that the workhorse specification is a multinomial logit in which the dependent variable is whether the respondent indicated support for confirmation of the nominee, opposition to confirmation, or uncertainty (that is, don't know, uncertain, or no opinion). For all models in this section, the don't know responses serve as the base category.

As detailed in Equations 4 and 5, the predictors in the workhorse regression are as follows: the citizen's perception of nominee quality, whether the citizen is a member of the president's party or the out-party (with Independents the reference group), the ideological distance between the citizen and the nominee, the citizen's uncertainty about the nominee (based on uncertainty about nominee ideology) and an interaction between uncertainty about the nominee's ideology and ideological distance.

There are inherent limitations in moving from theory to data. First, for an individual-level measure of perceived nominee quality, we use a survey question in which respondents were asked whether they believed the nominee was either qualified or not qualified to serve on the Supreme Court. The theory envisions individuals who form independent beliefs about the nominee's quality or qualifications, which then affect the overall appraisal of the nominee. In reality, the response to the question likely reflects the respondent's overall evaluation of the nominee. Accordingly, we present regressions with and without this measure.

Second, the theory includes a measure of uncertainty about the nominee related to uncertainty about nominee attributes. Unfortunately, we have no direct way to measure respondent uncertainty about nominee attributes.[15] As a second-best option, we simply use respondent higher education as a proxy for holding more information and thus having less uncertainty. Specifically, we use a four-level measure of education (less than high school, high school, some college, and college grad) and invert it such that higher numbers mean less education and thus more uncertainty.

Finally, we note that the interaction term is not substantively interesting in and of itself. But we include it to remain faithful to the derivation of the theory, which affords a logically consistent way to estimate and interpret the main effects of interest (i.e. ideological distance and partisanship).[16]

10.4.1 Estimating the Workhorse Regressions

Table 10.2 presents four multinomial logit models. The top part of the table uses the 3-point ideology measures while the bottom part uses the 5-point measures. For each model, we present the support and oppose equations in side-by-side columns to allow comparisons of coefficients within models. Models (1) and (2) include perceived quality while Models (3) and (4) exclude it. Each model includes nominee fixed effects.

The results broadly accord with the theoretical model's predictions. Unsurprisingly, citizens who view the nominee as qualified were more likely to voice support for the nominee and less likely to indicate opposition. Turning to partisanship, copartisans of the president were more likely to announce support for confirmation and less likely to announce opposition, than to say don't know. For out-partisans, the coefficient in the support equation in Models (1) and (3) is negative, as expected, but is insignificant in the oppose equations in these models. However, out-party is a strong predictor itself of viewing the nominee as not qualified; when we exclude the quality measure in Models (2) and (4), out-party significantly predicts expressions of opposition.

Table 10.2 The workhorse regressions. Each model is a multinomial logit. Each model includes nominee fixed effects.

	3-point ideology			
	(1)		(2)	
	Support	Oppose	Support	Oppose
Nominee qualified	1.67*	−2.46*	–	–
	(0.16)	(0.13)		
President's party	1.09*	−0.63*	1.16*	−0.69*
	(0.12)	(0.15)	(0.06)	(0.08)
Out-party	−0.62*	0.06	−0.69*	0.30*
	(0.11)	(0.11)	(0.06)	(0.06)
Ideological distance	−0.58*	0.28*	−0.54*	0.23*
	(0.07)	(0.07)	(0.04)	(0.04)
Uncertainty	−0.18*	−0.18*	−0.52*	−0.38*
	(0.07)	(0.08)	(0.03)	(0.04)
Ideological distance × uncertainty	0.09*	0.02	0.16*	0.10*
	(0.03)	(0.03)	(0.02)	(0.02)
Constant	1.84*	4.70*	3.10*	2.03*
	(0.30)	(0.30)	(0.21)	(0.22)
N	9,624		17,816	
	5-point ideology			
	(3)		(4)	
	Support	Oppose	Support	Oppose
Nominee qualified	1.56*	−2.44*	–	–
	(0.17)	(0.14)		
President's party	1.14*	−0.36*	1.19*	−0.51*
	(0.14)	(0.17)	(0.07)	(0.10)
Out-party	−0.76*	0.00	−0.75*	0.28*
	(0.11)	(0.12)	(0.07)	(0.07)
Ideological distance	−0.28*	0.15*	−0.32*	0.14*
	(0.03)	(0.03)	(0.03)	(0.02)
Uncertainty	−0.08	−0.08	−0.55*	−0.35*
	(0.07)	(0.08)	(0.04)	(0.04)
Ideological distance × uncertainty	0.05*	−0.00	0.10*	0.04*
	(0.02)	(0.01)	(0.01)	(0.01)
Constant	1.74*	4.49*	3.20*	2.23*
	(0.31)	(0.31)	(0.16)	(0.17)
N	8,347		11,859	

Next, as predicted, greater ideological distance between the citizen and the nominee decreases the likelihood of expressing support and increases the likelihood of voicing opposition.[17] Finally, as expected, the proxy for greater uncertainty generally decreases the likelihood of respondents offering either a support or oppose opinion; in other words, those who have more certainty are less likely to say don't know. All in all, given the limitations of the data, Table 10.2 provides considerable support for the theory of the survey response.

Next, it is straightforward to use these results to generate the predicted probabilities of the three responses. To do so, we use the same specification as in Model (4), which uses the more nuanced 5-point scale, except that we exclude the nominee fixed effects to prevent the intercepts being an arbitrary function of the excluded nominee.[18] We then generate predicted probabilities of support, opposition, and don't know, for every integer value in the range of quadratic distance.[19] (Recall that using the 5-point scale, the distance measure goes from 0 (closest) to 4 (farthest); the quadratic distance scale thus goes from 0 to 16). We generate separate probabilities for presidential co-partisans, out-partisans, and Independents. For each, we set uncertainty to its mean value (which is around 2).

Figure 10.7 shows these predicted probabilities. The purple lines depict the probability of a don't know response, while the black lines show the probability of support and the red lines show the probability of opposition.

Two substantive points stand out in the figure. First, regardless of respondent partisanship, *ideological distance sensibly and strongly predicts expressions of support and opposition.* Perceived ideological proximity to a nominee is associated with a much greater likelihood of an expressed support for confirmation, and a decreased likelihood of expressed opposition. For example, for a co-partisan, moving 0 to 4 on the distance scale predicts a decrease in the probability of a support announcement from about .92 to .71.[20]

Second, *partisanship also matters.* To see this, focus on the intercepts of the support and opposition curves across the three panels. Notice that the intercepts move in a "staircase" fashion from left to right. For the support curves, the intercept for each curve decreases significantly with the movement from co-partisan to independent to out-party. Conversely, the intercepts for oppose curves increase considerably moving

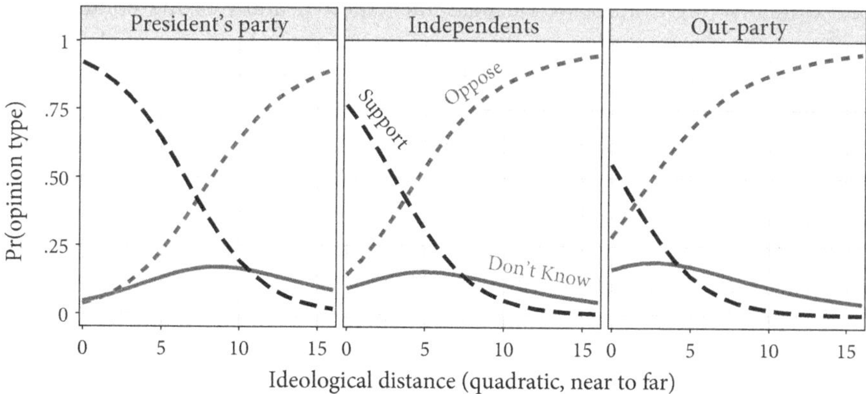

Fig. 10.7 The predicted probability of support, opposition, and don't know, by partisanship and ideological distance. Estimates based on the specification used in Model (4) in Table 10.2, except that nominee fixed effects are not included.

from left to right. This means that if a citizen is (for example) a member of the out-party who nevertheless views the nominee as quite close ideologically, the probability of announced opposition is still quite sizable, about .3. That probability then rises quickly as perceived ideological distance increases.

10.5 The Partisan Gap in Evaluations

These partisan differences align nicely with the evidence on party polarization we presented in Chapter 7—today, members of the president's party are now much more likely to support nominees while members of the out-party are much more likely to oppose than in decades past. In this section, we use the analytical lens of the LTA Framework to examine and analyze the rise of this partisan gap.

10.5.1 Defining the Partisan Gap

Let's begin by defining the partisan gap (PG) as the difference in *average expected value* of the nominee between presidential co-partisans and presidential out-partisans: $PG_j = EV_{in_j} - EV_{out_j}$. Because the theoretical framework laid out in Section 10.2 allows us to calculate respondents' expected values for nominees, we can measure the partisan gap in any nomination for which we have the appropriate data. We argue that defining the partisan gap in terms of utility, rather than answers to survey questions *per se*, focuses attention squarely on the object of interest. The unit of measure is arbitrary ("utils"), but it is comparable within and across nominees.

Figure 10.8 illustrates the idea of the partisan gap, using the 2017 nomination of Neil Gorsuch, a Republican appointee, as an example. To do so, we ran the workhorse regression using only the observations from his nomination.[21] Based on the workhorse regressions, we calculate the expected utility of the nominee. The theory posits a single value for this quantity, but the values calculated from the support and oppose regression typically vary somewhat, reflecting noisy data and random variation in the coefficients.[22] We present both measures of expected value, for Democrats, Independents, and Republicans.[23] To make the measures move in the same direction, we multiply the expected value based on the opposition equation by −1. The two tell the same basic story. The figure displays a box plot for the six combinations of party and oppose/support, with the solid horizontal line depicting the median value in a given distribution.

The figure shows an intuitive monotonic pattern of increasing utility for Gorsuch, moving from Democrats to Independents to Republicans. The partisan gap is the difference in median expected utility between Republicans and Democrats. Using the median values, as shown in Figure 10.8, the expected value for Democrats (using the support equation-based measure) is −.6, compared to 2.0 for Republicans, creating a partisan gap of about 1.4 utils. Using the oppose equation-based measure

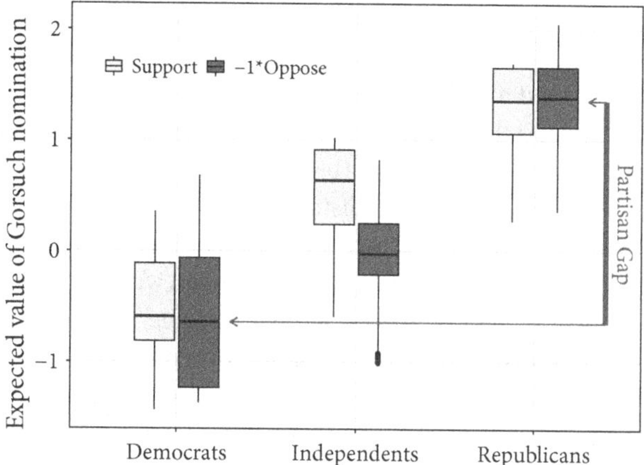

Fig. 10.8 Illustrating the partisan gap, using the expected utility for the 2017 nomination of Neil Gorsuch. For each combination of support/opposition and party, the figure depicts a boxplot summarizing the distribution of expected values across respondents of each party affiliation, with the solid horizontal lines depicting the median value.

indicates an expected value for Gorsuch of about about 1.4 for Republicans and −.6 for Democrats, again yielding a partisan gap of about 2 utils. Thus, we observe a large partisan gap in evaluations of Gorsuch.

10.5.2 The Partisan Gap from O'Connor to Barrett

To document the partisan gap over time, for as many nominees as possible, we must first confront a missing data issue. As we noted above, survey questions asking respondents to place nominees on an ideological scale only exist for 10 nominees, even if we focus on the more widely used 3-point ideology measure. Examining only these 10 nominees (only three of whom were confirmed before 2000) simply does not provide enough data to meaningfully study change over time.

To overcome this obstacle, we use the imputation analysis discussed in the Appendix as the basis for a similar imputation procedure here. Specifically, using all the observations for which respondents were asked to place the nominee (using the 3-point measure), we regress that measure on the NSP score of the nominee, the respondent's party, and our usual suite of demographic variables. From this regression, we then generate predicted values that we can apply to *all* observations (except the relatively small percentage of observations that have missing data on any of these predictors). This procedure expands the set of usable nominees to 15, including the "early" (in public opinion terms) nominations of Sandra Day O'Connor in 1981 and William Rehnquist in 1986 (to become Chief Justice).

This predicted measure is continuous on the $[-1,1]$ scale of the 3-point perceptions measure. While the actual measure is discrete, we choose to use the continuous predictor so as not to exacerbate any measurement error that may result from the prediction regression. With the imputed perceptions measure in hand, we can then construct a new imputed distance measure that equals the squared distance between imputed perceptions and the respondent's *self-placement* of ideology. The correlation between the actual distance measure (based on observations for which we have nominee placement) and the imputed distance measure is .80.

With this measure in hand, we turn to the quantities of interest, the expected values for nominees. To calculate these expected values, we employ the measurement tool of the workhorse regressions. We note that in Table 10.2 we were interested in how citizens generally answer the evaluation question on surveys, and hence did not account for time in those models. But here we are specifically interested in changes over time, particularly in estimated expected valuations of nominees.

Accordingly, using the imputed distance, we conduct *separate* regressions for every nominee for which we have the necessary data.[24] Then, for each nominee, we generate the expected value of the nominee, using both the support and oppose equations, in the same manner that we did in the Kavanaugh example. More directly, these values are the relevant "benefit" or expected value portion of the linear predictor that emerges from the workhorse regression, as applied to each nominee.

The results of this analysis are presented in Figure 10.9. (Note that for the rest of the chapter we scale nominees themselves on the x-axis, since the time frame we are working with is relatively short—1981 to 2020.) The left panel shows the expected values calculated from the support equations, while the right panel displays the expected values calculated using the oppose equations (we again multiply these values by negative one to make the two panels directly comparable). We present separate lines for co-partisans of the presidents, Independents, and out-partisans. For each nominee, we take the mean expected value among the three partisan groups (again, the units themselves are not of substantive interest, but they are directly comparable within and across nominees). For both, we can see lots of idiosyncratic variation across nominees. For example, as we saw in Chapter 7, Sandra Day O'Connor enjoyed nearly universal approval among the public, which is reflected in the fact that there is almost no difference by party in the expected value, based on either support or oppose.[25] David Souter, by contrast, had a uniformly low expected value in the support panel, reflecting in part the fact that a majority of Americans had no opinion on his nomination. But if we average over these idiosyncrasies, it appears that the partisan gap in expected value (based on both support-based and opposition-based measurement) has increased over time.

Figure 10.10 illustrates this pattern more directly. For each nominee, we measure the partisan gap by calculating the absolute value of the difference between the co-partisan and out-partisan lines in Figure 10.9, for both measures. This is the same procedure we employed in the Gorsuch example, except here it is based on the mean expected value by party group rather than the median (both measures of central tendency lead to the same story). Figure 10.10 shows that the partisan gap in expected value has increased dramatically over time. The contrast between O'Connor

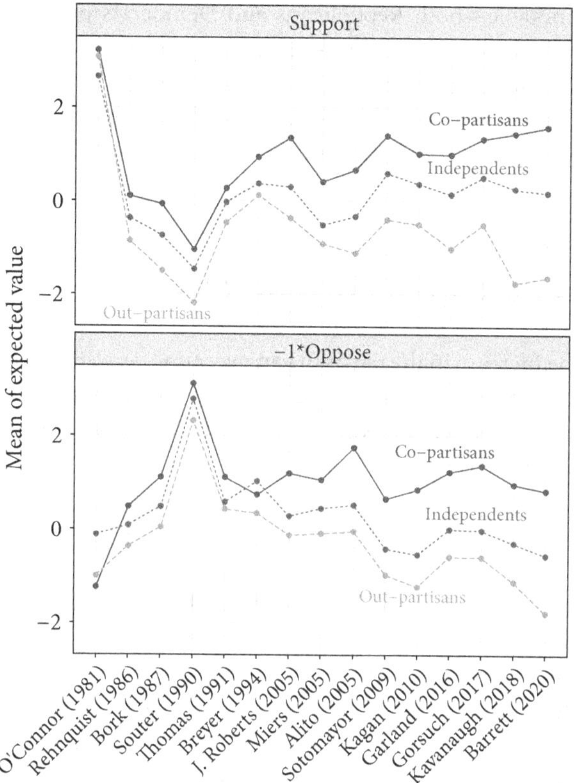

Fig. 10.9 Expected values from separate regressions for each nominee, by party of the president. The values from the oppose equation are multiplied by negative 1.

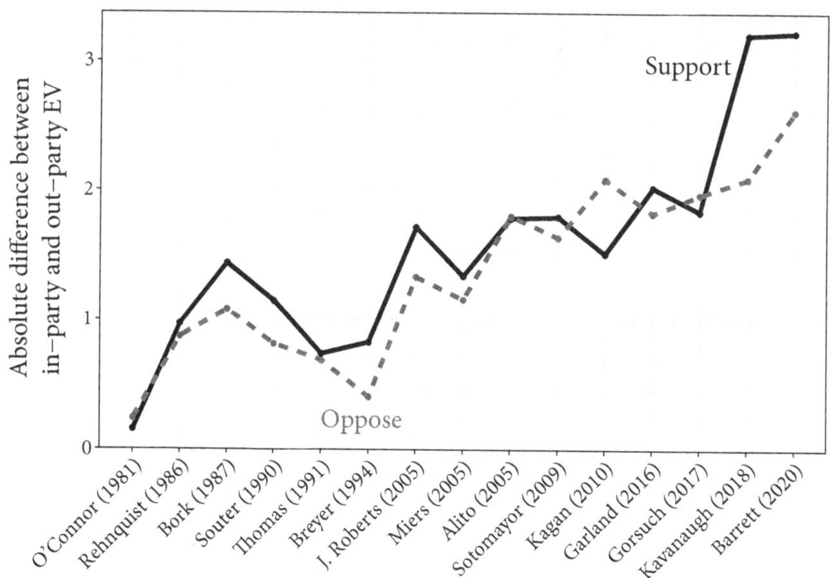

Fig. 10.10 The growing partisan gap in the expected value of supporting and opposing the nominee.

and Barrett is notable—both Republicans and Democrats prized the trail-blazing, moderately conservative O'Connor, and did so almost equally (see Figure 10.9). Hence, our measure of the partisan gap in her nomination is the smallest in all of the 15 nominations we can study. In contrast, while Republicans valued Barrett very highly, Democrats did not. Indeed, her nomination shows the largest partisan gap in all the nominations we can study.

10.5.3 Why the Gap and Why the Change?

What caused the increase in the partisan gap over time, as we measure it? Because we have an explicit measurement model, we can parse the gap and evaluate the changes, attributing them to distinct components. In particular, recall the utility function for citizen appraisal of nominees:

$$Ev_{ij} = a_0 + a_1 q_{ij} + a_2 p_{ij} - a_3 out_{ij} - a_4(y_i - \bar{x}_{ij})^2 - a_5 \sigma_{v_{ij}}$$

The equation indicates how five variables affect the expected values of nominees. In a given nomination, the partisan gap reflects the differential impact of those variables on Democrats and Republicans. However, changes in the partisan gap over time could occur in two distinct ways: either the values of *coefficients* may change over time, or the values of *variables* may change over time. (Of course, both could change.) For the coefficients, a key suspect must be the net impact in the value of partisan affiliation between co-partisans and out-party members, $a_2 - a_3$.[26] If this difference increased, it would boost the partisan gap. But another suspect is changes in the evaluative weight accorded to ideological distance, a_4—if this increased, it would magnify the partisan gap between party members even if the ideological distance between citizens and nominees (i.e. policy distance in the theory) did not. For variables, the key change must be the average ideological distance of Republicans to nominees versus Democrats to nominees. These distances depend in turn on ideological self-placements by party members, and on ideological placements of nominees. Thus, if party members become more extreme, the partisan gap would increase. Likewise, if nominees became more extreme, the gap would also increase.

Thus, we have four suspects for the increase in partisan gap over time:

1. Change in the net impact of partisan affiliations, $a_2 - a_3$;
2. Change in the impact of ideological distance, a_4;
3. Change in average ideological distances $(x_{ij} - y_{ij})^2$ between the parties, caused by either:
   (a) Change in ideological self-placements y_{ij} by party members, and/or;
   (b) Change in perceived nominee ideological placements $\bar{x}_j$ across the parties (that is, more extreme nominees).

This is a lot of moving parts!

In the interest of clarity, we proceed in stages. First, we examine the main "suspects" one at a time. In particular, we examine change in the coefficients, change in distance, and change in self-placements. Then, nomination-by-nomination, we parse the partisan gap in that nomination according to the impact of partisan affiliation versus the impact of policy evaluation. So, in the Gorsuch nomination, for example, what percentage of the measured partisan gap was due to net differences in partisan affiliations ($a_2 - a_3$) and what percentage due to differences in policy evaluations ($a_4(\bar{x}_j - y_{ij})^2$) across the parties? This query directly addresses the Realist versus Rationalist debate.

The Coefficients over Time

We begin by examining the coefficients from the regression models over time. Figure 10.11 depicts the coefficient from the nominee-by-nominee workhorse regressions, based on the imputed distance. We show only the coefficients of interest (party, distance, and uncertainty); the vertical lines depict 95% confidence intervals, while the loess lines summarize the trends in the coefficients. We follow our earlier strategy with the expected values and multiply the coefficients for party and distance in the oppose equation by -1; as a result, these coefficients should move together in the figure (the predicted coefficient for uncertainty is negative in both equations, and thus we do not multiply this coefficient by -1 in the oppose equation).

Begin with the coefficient (a_2) on membership in the president's party. The coefficient is typically positive and increases over time, suggesting increasing utility from a nominee of the same party. The coefficient (a_3) on membership in the opposing party is typically negative and becomes more negative over time. This suggests decreasing utility for a nominee of the opposite party. The net partisan effect between in-party and out-party members is $a_2 - a_3$ (that is, $a_2 + |a_3|$), so the net impact of partisanship increases over time.

The coefficient (a_4) on ideological distance is typically negative and becomes more negative over time. This indicates increasing distaste for ideologically distant nominees over time. This change thus moves in the same direction as the purely partisan affiliation effects, to increase the partisan gap.[27] Finally, the coefficient on uncertainty (a_5) is negative but changes little over time.

In sum, the weights on partisan affiliation and on ideological distance do seem to change over time, and in a way that exacerbates the partisan gap. Of course, the actual impact of ideological distance on citizen appraisals of nominees also depends on the values of the variable "ideological distance." If, in addition to weighing ideological distances more heavily, citizens also perceive bigger ideological distances to nominees across party lines, the partisan gap will grow even larger.

The Growth of Ideological Distance

In Section 10.3, we presented a wealth of evidence on how citizens perceive nominees ideologically. Then, in our regressions, we used the ideological distance between this measure and citizen's self-placement as our measure of policy evaluation. But we have not directly examined what self-placement looks like, and how it has changed. In

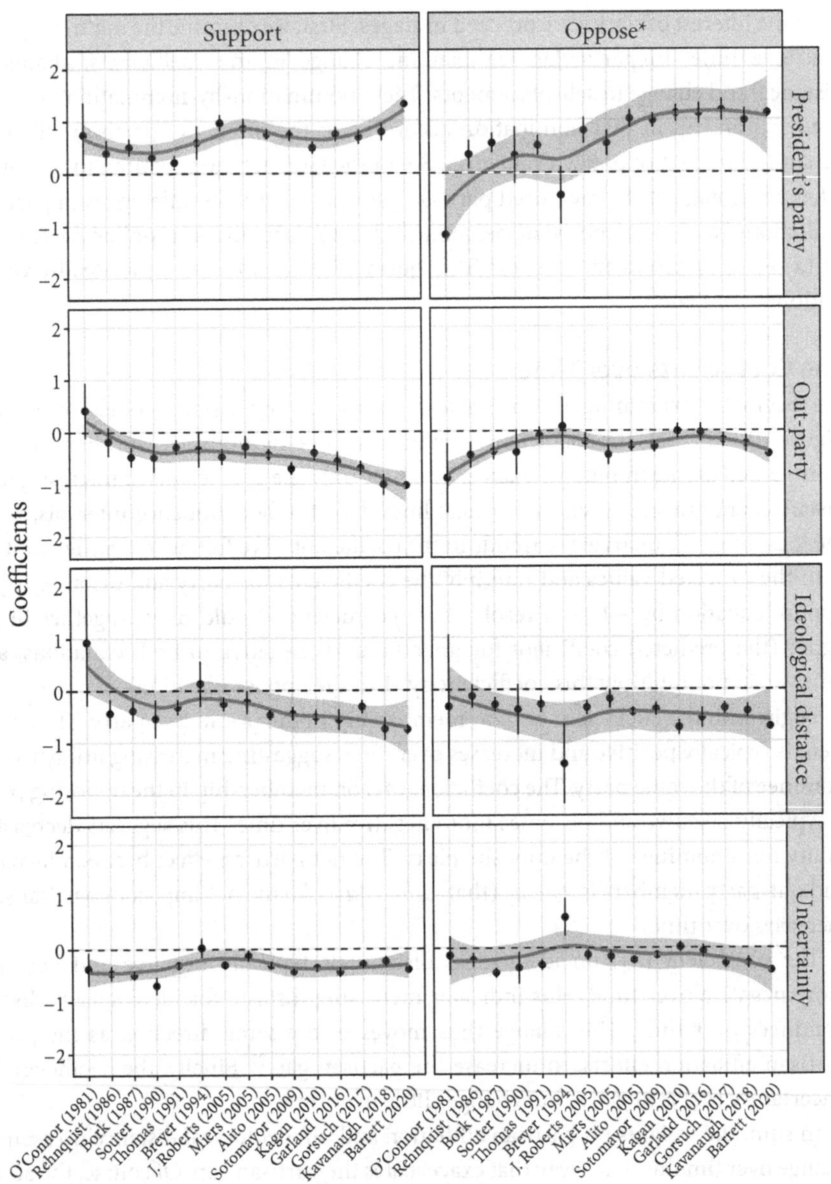

Fig. 10.11 Coefficients from the nominee-by-nominee workhorse regressions, based on imputed data. The vertical lines depict 95% confidence intervals, while the loess lines summarize the trends in the coefficients. *For President's party, Out-party, and Ideological distance, the coefficients in the oppose equation are multiplied by −1.

this section we show that, indeed, average ideological distance between citizens and nominees has increased dramatically since 1980, due mostly to changes in citizens' ideological *self-placements*.

Figure 10.12 depicts the distribution of citizen's self-placement, based on the 3-point measure of ideology. We break down responses by party in the columns, with the rows presenting separate results for each nominee (moving down chronologically). We normalize the distributions within each panel (that is, within each nominee-party pair).

The results are quite consistent with the well-known "partisan sort" documented in the American political behavior literature (and discussed briefly in Chapter 1). Within partisan identifiers, the "middle" of the ideological spectrum has been hollowed out, with Democratic identifiers becoming increasingly more liberal and Republican identifiers becoming increasingly more conservative. The changes here are quite striking. Forty years ago during the nomination of Sandra Day O'Connor, the relationship between party and ideology was rather weak; consequently, we see many moderate or conservative Democrats and many moderate Republicans in the top row of Figure 10.12. Four decades later, the 2020 nomination of Amy Coney Barrett took place before an audience of partisans whose party identity and ideological orientation were tightly linked. Few conservative Democrats and few liberal Republicans remained.

Political scientists have hotly debated the cause of the partisan sort over the past 15 years. One camp argues that the mass public has become genuinely more ideologically extreme, resulting in the ideological distributions seen in Figure 10.12. An opposing camp argues that the partisan sort is simply that—not a massive move to the wings by individuals but just a re-shuffling of party labels among people whose views have not really changed substantially.[28]

Disentangling label-shuffling from genuinely increasing ideological extremity is a Herculean empirical project, and requires data that goes well beyond what we have.[29] Fortunately, for our purposes, we can sidestep this debate. No matter what mechanism drove the patterns in Figure 10.12, the end result is the same: the average ideological distance between nominees and partisans—in particular, out-partisans—would surely have increased over time, because more out-partisans now place themselves at the wings of the ideological distribution.

Figure 10.13 shows exactly that. For each nominee with imputed ideology data, we calculated the average distance between the respondent and the nominee, by whether the respondent identified as a co-partisan, an out-partisan, or Independent. The results are crystal clear for out-partisans, with the average distance increasing greatly over time. Conversely, we see no change for Independents and little change for co-partisans.

Party and Ideology in the Partisan Gap

Partisan attachments may contribute a greater percentage to the partisan gap than in the past, based on the change in the party coefficients over time. But the contribution of ideology has changed as well—while the coefficient on distance varied somewhat,

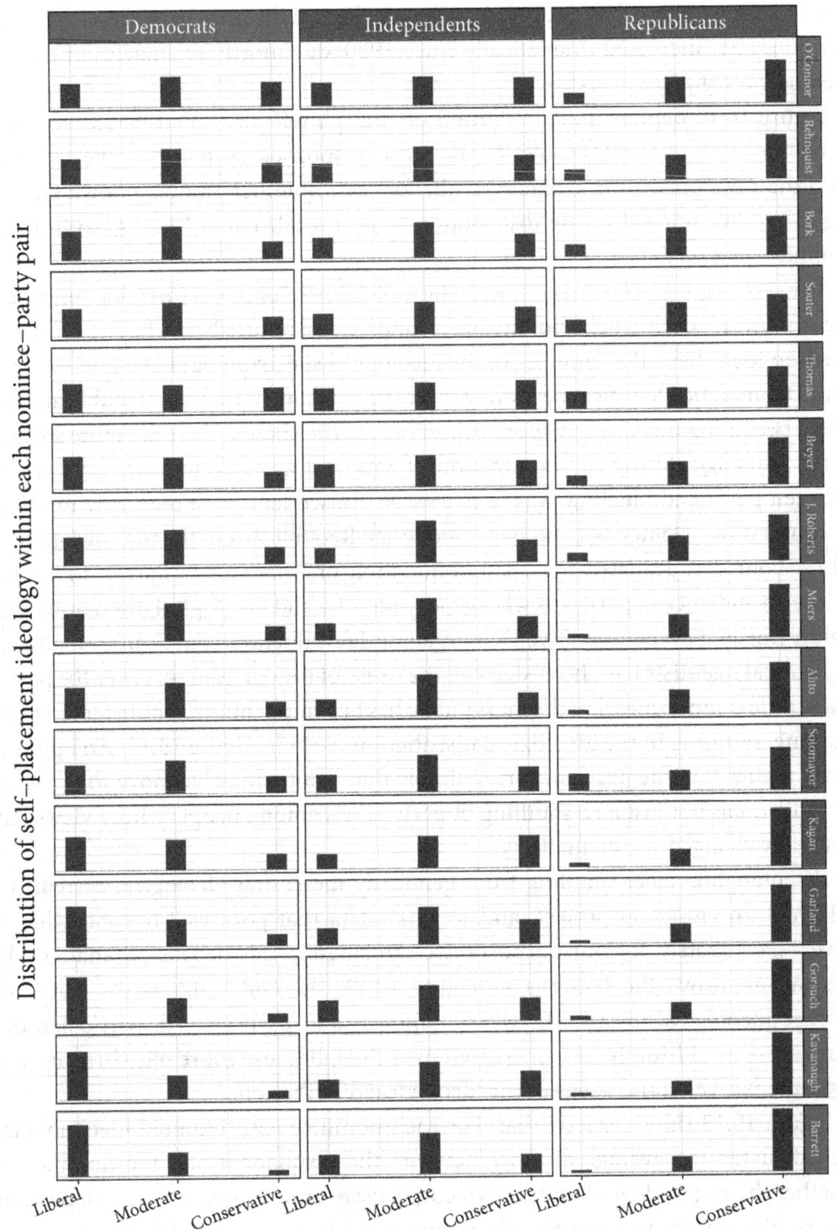

Fig. 10.12 Distribution of self-placement by nominee-party combinations, O'Connor to Barrett. Nominees in red are Republican appointees, nominees in blue are Democratic appointees.

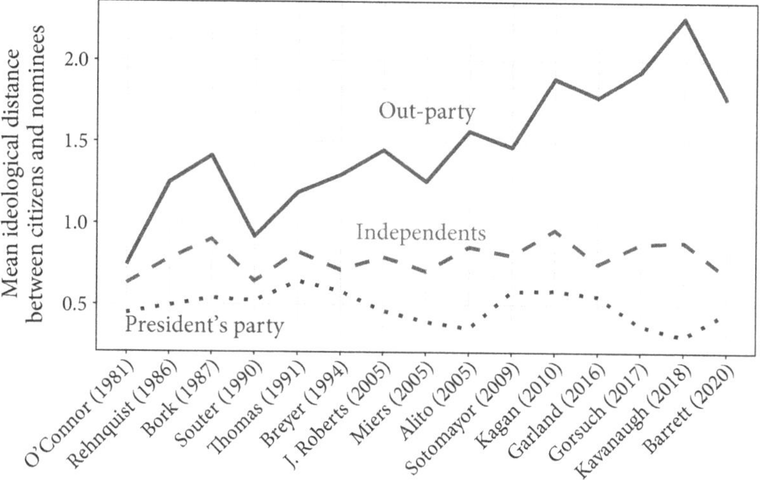

Fig. 10.13 Mean ideological distance between citizens and nominees over time, by party, based on self-placements of respondents.

the average distance between nominees and out-partisans increased dramatically. This suggests that the percentage contribution of ideology to the partisan gap would likely increase over time, even if the weights on that variable did not change. So, in any given nomination, which factor predominated, and how has this changed over time?

To understand more systematically the respective contributions of party and ideology to the partisan gap, we undertake an accounting analysis that apportions "credit" to each factor in creating the nominee-by-nominee partisan gap seen in Figure 10.10. For each nominee, we perform the following analysis. First, we begin with the actual partisan gap based on the models and data above, according to the support and oppose equations. Denote these quantities PG_{actual}. Next, we perform a counterfactual analysis in which we ask what would the gap look like if we set the president's party and out-party coefficients in the expected value calculation to zero. That is, we calculate the counterfactual partisan gap (call this PG_{CF}) using the same method as with the actual gap, but party does not enter the expected value calculation directly. This means that the partisan gap in the counterfactual analysis must, by construction, result from the different distributions of ideological distance by party.[30] For instance, returning to the Gorsuch nomination, the mean distance between citizens and the nominee (based on the 3-point quadratic distance measure) was .4 for Republicans and 2.5 for Democrats. In the counterfactual world, party cannot directly influence the size of the gap, but this sizable distance in ideology will lead to substantial differences across the partisan groups.

With the actual and counterfactual measures in hand, we can measure the relative contributions as follows. Define the party contribution $\frac{PG_{actual}-PG_{CF}}{PG_{actual}}$. The ideological contribution is simply $\frac{PG_{CF}}{PG_{actual}}$. If the partisan gap is in the expected direction

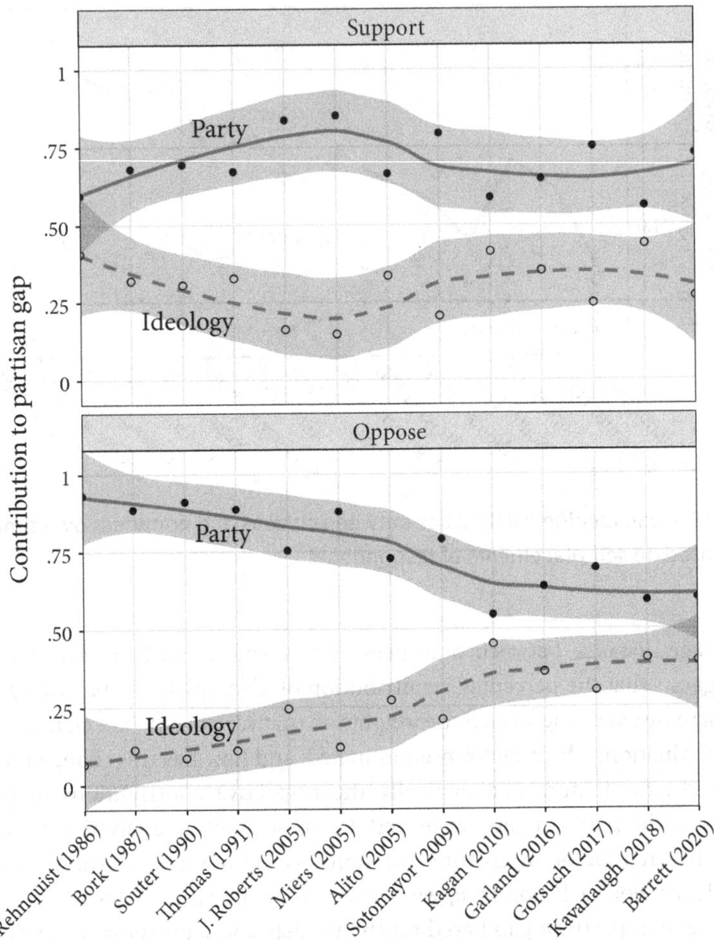

Fig. 10.14 Party versus ideological contributions to the nominee-by-nominee partisan gaps. The figure shows the percentage of the partisan gap attributable to pure partisan affiliation and to perceived ideological distance, using both the support and oppose equations.

of the president's party, then these measures will lie between 0 and 1—they are percentages.[31]

Figure 10.14 displays the percentage of the partisan gap attributable to pure partisan affiliation and to perceived ideological distance to the nominee, in each of 13 nominations, using both the support and oppose equations (the lines are loess lines, with 95% confidence intervals). The data in the figure directly address the contrasting perspectives of the Realist and Rationalist camps. Three points stand out.

First, in each nomination, *both direct partisan affiliation and policy evaluation contributed to the partisan gap*. In none of the 13 nominations was the partisan gap attributable purely to partisan identification or purely to policy evaluations. Both were important contributors to the very different responses of Democrats and Republicans to Supreme Court nominees.

Second, in all 13 nominations, *the percentage contribution of party affiliation to the partisan gap was larger than that of ideological differences.* On average, about 70% and 75% of the partisan gap was due to direct partisan affiliation (using the support and oppose equations, respectively), compared to 30% and 25% due to ideological distance, based on our measurement framework.

Third, if we focus on the oppose equation, over time the contribution to the partisan gap from ideological distance increased while that from pure partisan identification declined noticeably. (The temporal trends with respect to the support equation are less clear, but we can rule out the possibility that the partisan contribution has *increased* over time.) This finding may be quite surprising to those who frame increasing partisan gaps in this and many other arenas as "partisanship is a helluva drug." But it is completely understandable if one considers the astounding partisan sort on display in Figure 10.12. The partisan sort meant that perceived ideological distances between out-partisans and Supreme Court nominees skyrocketed, as the sort proceeded over time (see Figure 10.13). Not surprisingly, this huge increase in average ideological distance for out-partisans weighed ever more heavily in their evaluation of nominees.

10.6 Conclusion: What They Wanted and What They Got

Citizens do not select Supreme Court justices; elites do. But public opinion nonetheless matters, in two distinct ways. First, senators respond to state-level public opinion (as we will show in the next chapter). So even though citizens do not vote in a national referendum on a nominee, their perceptions and evaluations remain politically consequential. Second, if we believe that public policy—even in the form of Supreme Court appointments—should reflect the will of the people, then the public's evaluation of a nominee carries a normative punch.

From either perspective—positive or normative—the quality and thoughtfulness of public opinion matters. On the positive side, if opinion is capricious, uninformed, misinformed, or utterly dogmatic, how can citizens hope to control their representatives' behavior in a beneficial way? What can such citizens expect from their government? On the normative side, if opinion is random, ignorant, or worse, why should we accord it normative value? Why should we care if such citizens do or don't get what they say they want? On the other hand, suppose citizen opinion on Supreme Court nominees resembles Andrew Gelman's and Gary King's (1993) portrayal of opinion in presidential elections. These two scholars famously argued that public opinion in presidential elections, while volatile, ultimately becomes rather "enlightened" in the sense that it accurately reflects what citizens learned about the candidates during the campaign as well as citizens' bedrock interests based on ideology and party identification. If opinion on Supreme Court nominees is similarly "enlightened" then responsiveness to it by senators might be beneficent, and we should afford the public's expressed desires considerable normative weight.

So, what does the dense empirical work in this chapter suggest about the quality and thoughtfulness of public opinion about Supreme Court nominees? Is it enlightened or benighted, somewhat Rationalist or solidly Realist?

First, citizens perceive nominees as both partisan and ideological, two attributes that are distinguishable and separable. Strikingly, on average citizen perceptions of nominee ideology are rather accurate.

Second, on average, citizens appear to evaluate nominees using both partisan and ideological criteria. On a nomination-by-nomination basis, our estimate of the relative impacts of the two are on the order of two parts party to one part ideology, though in some recent nominations, the ratio is closer to 3:1. So, both partisanship and policy orientation have mattered for citizen evaluation of nominees, and continue to do so.

Third, the partisan and ideological evaluation of nominees results in a profound gap in evaluations between Democrats and Republicans. This partisan gap grew dramatically over time, due to a bigger partisan effect and to vastly increased ideological distances between out-party members and the nominees. A contributing factor to growing distances was the partisan sort, which resulted in liberals reliably becoming Democrats and conservatives reliably becoming Republicans.

Both Realists and Rationalists may find some satisfaction—and some dissatisfaction—in these findings. For the Rationalists, citizen response to nominees is not a pure partisan knee-jerk. Citizens rather accurately perceive nominees' ideologies, the majority of respondents are willing to place themselves on an ideological scale, and a greater distance between the nominee and the respondent is associated with lower esteem for the nominee. This looks rather "Rationalist." For the Realists, partisan affiliation does appear to alter citizen perception of nominees—in-party respondents tend to score the nominee as somewhat more moderate than do Independents, and out-party respondents tend to score the nominee as somewhat more extreme than do Independents. The effects are not huge, but they are there.[32] More crucially, our measurement and accounting framework points to a large direct impact on citizen evaluations from partisan affiliation or opposition to the nominee. We consistently estimate this effect as larger than the ideological evaluation of the nominee, though both matter.

Because today's citizens are sorted so well into the parties (or as Independents), it is hard to see how ideological distances could get much larger than they are at the time we write.[33] However, what will halt a growth in the pure partisan effect? If this effect increases substantially, citizens will increasingly view out-party nominees as unfit to serve on the U.S. Supreme Court simply by virtue of the nominee's party affiliation. Republicans will view every Democratic nominee, no matter how moderate, as anathema. We are not likely to see moderate Republican nominees like Sandra Day O'Connor or David Souter, but even if we did, Democrats with super-strong partisan responses would likely disapprove of them anyway. That world would truly contain a Realist-style populace. The analysis in this chapter shows that the actual world of nomination politics over the last 35 years was not that world, nor is it at the time we write. But it could become so.

Given the citizens we actually have—seemingly moved by purely partisan sensibilities but also sensitive to actual policy orientations—should we accord much normative weight to their expressed preferences about Supreme Court justices? Some might say, "No, it is better to allow highly motivated interest groups and those with burning ideological convictions to run the show." But we doubt that average citizens would agree, and we doubt that most students of American politics would either (but some might).

If, then, we take seriously the agency of American citizens and adopt their preferences as a normative benchmark, how should we view the nominees that our politics gave them? The theoretical framework we created in this chapter allows us to answer this question—albeit tentatively because a judgment depends heavily on theory and measurement. We present this analysis in the Appendix. To summarize the key results, we find that committed presidential co-partisans were well-served by recent nominees, but out-partisans and indeed the population as a whole suffered substantial welfare losses from nominees who were excessively extreme in their ideological orientations. Bluntly, the public wanted more moderate nominees—more O'Connors and fewer Kavanaughs.

Why didn't the public get them? As we have shown, interest groups, issue enthusiasts, and (consequently) the political parties demanded more extreme and more reliable justices, and presidents gave them what they wanted. Yet, that would not have mattered if the Senate had simply refused to confirm nominees whose ideologies put them far out of step with the average citizen. On rare occasions, such as the Bork nomination, the Senate did reject relative extremists. More often, though, the Senate confirmed them. Why did the Senate do so? The answer to that question depends on the interplay between senators' incentives and the dynamics of public opinion, a topic to which we now turn.

11
Voting in the Shadow of Accountability
Senators' Confirmation Decisions

Why do senators vote for or against Supreme Court nominees?

In Chapter 8, we described aggregate and individual patterns in Senate voting on Supreme Court nominees since 1789, with an emphasis on the 1930 to 2020 period. However, we did not really *explain* senators' vote choices. Now we attempt to do so. The core insight is simple: senators vote on Supreme Court nominees in the shadow of accountability to their constituents. The logic of accountability, in turn, explains their roll call votes.

The structure of this chapter is different from the others in Part II. In Chapters 9 and 10, we developed new theory and then applied it to data from Part I. In this chapter, we do not develop a new theory of roll call voting and electoral accountability. Instead, we draw on existing perspectives and conduct three distinct but interlinked empirical analyses. Together, the three studies go a long way to explaining the patterns in roll call voting shown in Chapter 8.

The first study examines the different incentives facing senators in low visibility versus high-visibility roll call votes. We can undertake this analysis because earlier we measured the public visibility of nominations over time. Drawing on arguments in classic studies in political science, we argue that low visibility nominations lead to "safety in numbers" voting (explained below). In contrast, high visibility nominations lead senators to weigh carefully the concerns of their constituents, which (we argue) reflect the attributes of nominees emphasized in the media, such as their quality and ideology. Straightforward empirical tests reveal the predicted patterns in roll call votes.

The second study examines the knowledge of citizens about specific roll call votes and the resulting impact on citizens' evaluations of their senators. Here we draw on empirical advances made by others but apply them to two nominations where the necessary data are available (the Kagan and Sotomayor nominations). The analysis is rather complex but again reveals strong patterns. Because of the power of the statistical techniques involved, we can conclude with some degree of confidence that when senators vote "with" their constituents, voters increase their approval of their senators, while voting "against" constituents leads to the opposite reaction. Relative to other high-profile votes, the effects of roll call votes on approval of senators in these two nominations were quite sizable, perhaps because the votes were so easy to understand.

Making the Supreme Court: The Politics of Appointments, 1930–2020. Charles M. Cameron and Jonathan P. Kastellec, Oxford University Press. © Oxford University Press 2023. DOI: 10.1093/oso/9780197680544.003.0011

The third study examines which constituents senators respond to. Because of the dramatic partisan sort discussed in Chapter 1, strong party identifiers sometimes have opinions quite different from those of the Independents who typically include the median voter in the general election. Consequently, the opinion of a senator's copartisans—critical in the primary—may differ from those of the key voters in the general election. When such "cross-pressure" occurs, to whom does the senator attend in the roll call vote? We use confirmation voting as a laboratory for examining this relatively under-studied but increasingly important phenomenon. We show strong evidence that the opinions of copartisans matter more than that of the median voter in the general election. This kind of "biased" representation helps explain the near party-line votes that have come to characterize roll call votes on Supreme Court nominees.

The following section provides a brief overview of important theoretical considerations in roll call voting and electoral accountability; we then turn to the three empirical studies. Finally, we conclude with a discussion of what the collective findings of the three investigations imply for confirmation fights going forward.

11.2 Roll Calls and Accountability: General Theoretical Considerations

A recent review of empirical studies of congressional roll call voting claims that "roll-call votes are, perhaps, the most studied decisions in the whole of political science."[1] Scholars in other subfields of the discipline might disagree, but the empirical literature on congressional roll call voting is undeniably vast. Here we focus on theoretical considerations behind the empirics.

A long tradition in the study of American politics views roll call votes through the lens of electoral accountability. In this tradition, a senator is, bluntly, an employee of citizens in the state. The senator-worker votes based on the anticipated response of the constituent-boss. Classic studies taking this perspective include Miller and Stokes (1963), Mayhew (1974), Fenno (1978), Kingdon (1989), Arnold (1990), and more recently Ansolabehere and Jones (2010) and Ansolabehere and Kuriwaki (2021). Some of these studies examine the responsiveness of representatives to their constituents' opinions, while others focus on the fate of representatives whose voting record puts them "out of step" with their districts.[2] Recent work in political economy on the "theory of political agency" (or agency theory, for short) formalizes many of the intuitions in the earlier work, sometimes with surprising results.[3]

Agency theory emphasizes two important considerations in electoral accountability. First, what do constituents really want in a representative? Second, can constituents observe the actions of representatives (here, roll call votes) and can they observe the consequence of the actions? A third topic receives some attention as well: when agents have multiple principals, to whom do they attend? These consideration all play out in roll call voting, and do so in confirmation voting in somewhat distinctive ways.

11.2.1 What Do Citizens Want in a Representative?

Citizens certainly desire senators who are hardworking, skillful, and honest. If a senator's roll call vote suggests the senator is lazy, inept, or corrupt, constituents will issue the senator a mental demerit, at least if they observe the vote. Enough demerits may warrant dismissal—i.e. a vote against the incumbent—of the senator-employee. In our view, however, citizens likely do not interpret Supreme Court confirmation votes through the lens of diligence, skill, or honesty. Rather, constituents are more likely to view such votes (if observed at all) as a test of policy congruence—whether the senator shares the preferences and values of the constituent. Prizing a representative with shared values is sensible, because constituents frequently fail to observe their representative's actions, are unable to interpret them even if observed, and may not even know their own preferences on some policy topics. But a representative who has the right values will still tend to "do the right thing" automatically (as it were). Consequently, on those roll call votes that citizens observe and actually understand, citizens are likely to use them to gauge shared or divergent values. The empirical analyses of confirmation votes that follow assume, either explicitly or implicitly, that citizens use roll call votes to evaluate policy congruence, not competence or honesty.[4]

11.2.2 What Do Citizens Observe? Actions, Consequences, and Knowledge

Some roll call votes are highly visible while others are nearly invisible. In addition, the consequences of some votes "come home to roost" in very obvious ways, for example, the 2002 vote giving President Bush the authority to go to war in Iraq. Democratic senators who voted for the ultimately unpopular war later had some explaining to do.[5] On the other hand, the consequences of other roll call votes may never become evident to the public. With few exceptions, confirmation votes probably fall into the latter category. Confirmation or rejection of a nominee has consequences for the future decisions of the court (as we discuss in Chapter 12), but rarely will constituents perceive those later consequences and then trace them back to their senator's confirmation vote. Most Supreme Court decisions are low visibility, abstruse, or even opaque. Even if a confirmed nominee brings public obloquy on himself—for example, by voting to reverse a popular landmark precedent—a long delay between the roll call vote and the controversial judicial vote may let senators escape blame for supporting the nominee.[6]

As a result, if constituents hold senators accountable for confirmation votes at all, they almost certainly do so for the *vote itself* rather than for any subsequent policy consequences. So, the main questions become whether constituents actually perceive the confirmation votes of their senators, do so correctly, and hold senators accountable for the vote on the grounds of preference congruence or incongruence. The empirical analysis below focuses on these issues.[7]

11.2.3 Accountable to Whom? Multiple Principals

Finally, members of Congress often face divergent pressures over roll call votes. A classic tension involves pressure from a highly attentive organized interest group versus the desires of rather inattentive ordinary constituents.[8] A related tension arises between the responsiveness of members of Congress to campaign contributors rather than to ordinary constituents.[9] When faced with such pressures, members of Congress often try to break the "chain of traceability" for ordinary constituents, making it hard for them to perceive or understand roll call votes and their consequences.[10]

More prominent in confirmation voting is a different variant of the multiple principals problem: cross-pressure from co-partisans and ordinary constituents, typically Independents. The importance of this type of cross-pressure reflects the extreme partisan polarization in public opinion around contemporary nominees (documented in Chapter 7), coupled with the cleaner sort of ideologues into the parties. While interest group pressure and campaign contributions may also play a role in confirmation voting, the new form of cross-pressure takes center stage in the third analysis below.

11.3 Senators' Vote Decisions: The Importance of Nominee Visibility

We start our investigation of accountability by examining how the predicates of agency theory interact with the visibility of roll call votes. Let's start with low visibility nominations. Recall from Chapters 5 and 6 that most nominations between 1930 and the mid-1960s failed to mobilize interest groups or generate much attention in the press. So far as citizens were concerned, votes on such nominees were effectively invisible. A vote one way or the other for, say, Charles Whittaker, Stanley Reed, or Frank Murphy—who but the nominee knew? Who cared?[11]

Given a likely invisible vote, one might suppose senators would feel free to vote as they pleased with no regard for their constituents (or, perhaps, just go golfing). Senators, however, do not reason this way. As Arnold (1990) emphasizes, senators must worry about the "latent public"—that is, citizens who do not perceive the vote at the time but who may become acutely aware of it subsequently. Suppose, for example, a senator votes for a nominee who, once confirmed, provokes an ethics scandal, or votes in a way that outrages the senator's constituents. Will constituents blame the senator for supporting such a nominee? We suggest that in such a situation senators seek safety in numbers. They can plausibly say, don't hold me accountable for the justice's failings, because no one knew about them—as witnessed by the fact that the president nominated him and every senator voted for him. In essence, the senator can invite citizens to use a form of "yardstick competition," employing information contained in *other* senators' voting records.[12] No one else did better and no one else could have done better, so an electoral sanction is undeserved.

This line of reasoning suggests that *invisible votes will lead to unanimous or near unanimous confirmation votes.* Of course, one cannot be sure of the true motivation of senators in such circumstances. However, if the accountability reasoning is correct, one should see a correlation between the proportion of yea votes a nominee receives and low levels of interest group mobilization and media attention, because highly consensual votes allow safety in numbers.

Confirmation votes sometimes leapt into visibility, even in the years when interest groups mobilized only opportunistically and the press typically ignored Supreme Court nominations. During that period, when a nomination did become visible and controversial, how could senators cast defensible votes? Recall two facts. First, in this period, even newspaper editorials rarely discussed nominees in ideological terms (see Chapter 6). Most citizens probably did not naturally perceive Supreme Court justices that way, although the unfortunate absence of polls in the routine nominations of this era makes this impossible to verify. However, it seems plausible that all citizens favor "high-quality" Supreme Court nominees, *ceteris paribus.* Absent a scandal, senators could defend a yea vote on quality grounds. Given a scandal, a nay vote became more explainable.

Second, interest group mobilization could cue citizens to consider nominee ideology. For example, Hoover's 1930 nominee Judge John J. Parker had voted to support so-called yellow dog contracts, which organized labor strongly opposed. In addition, as an elected official in the Jim Crow South, Parker was an avowed segregationist. When informed of these facts by organized labor and the NAACP, many union members and many African-Americans surely evaluated Parker at least partly on policy grounds. Senators from states with many union members and—outside the South—many African-Americans could explain an anti-Parker vote at least partly on those grounds. For them, a yea vote would be tougher to explain. Similarly, Southern senators from anti-union states could easily explain a yea. However, senators with pro-union but also pro-segregation constituents would have to weigh their vote carefully. In short, visible and controversial nominations sensitize constituents to nominee attributes, like quality and ideology. The logic of accountability suggests that senators should follow along in their (visible) roll call votes.

To test this conjecture, we return to the model of roll call voting introduced by Cameron, Cover, and Segal (1990) [CCS]. The logic of our test is simple: the CCS model should perform better in high-visibility nominations. Recall that the model emphasizes ideological distance and the legal qualifications of the nominee as the two main factors for predicting the likelihood of a yea vote on a nominee. Note that while the model does not really microfound why ideological distance is important for senators, one interpretation is that the senator's ideal point can be seen as a summary measure of the ideology of the constituents to whom the senator primarily attends; in this sense we can connect the CSS model to the accountability story we emphasize in this chapter.

Further recall from Chapter 8 that we showed that senators seemed to place more weight on ideology over time; a before-and-after analysis of the CCS model showed that the slope on ideological distance became steeper in the later period of our 1930–2020 time frame. That analysis shows that time matters. But *time* itself is not an explanatory variable. Here we attempt to measure changes in visibility directly and see how they map onto changes in roll call voting. To capture visibility, we rely on three broad changes discussed in earlier chapters. The first is change in media coverage; we use the total amount of coverage per nominee measure that we introduced in Chapter 6. The second is interest group activity—we use the unique number of groups that mobilized *against* the nominee (since opposition is more likely to raise the visibility of a nomination fight). The third is whether a nominee suffered a scandal or not.[13]

Figure 11.1 shows the basic relationship between aggregate voting outcomes and the three visibility measures. For each measure, the x-axis depicts the levels of

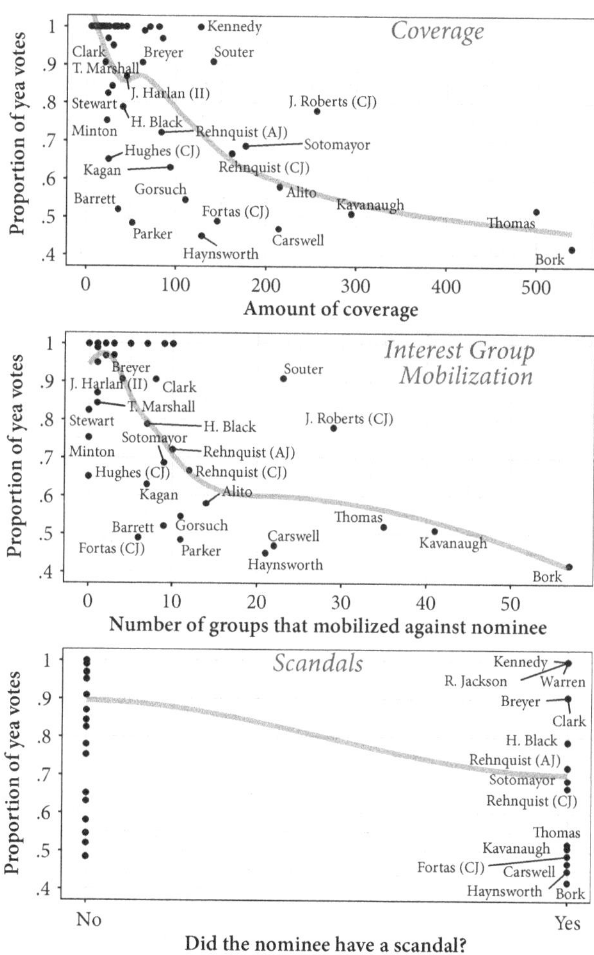

Fig. 11.1 The relationship between nomination visibility and confirmation outcomes. For each measure, the x-axis depicts the levels of visibility per nominee, while the y-axis shows the proportion of yea votes. The lines are loess lines.

Table 11.1 OLS models of individual roll call voting, 1930 to 2020. In each model, the dependent variable is individual senators' roll call votes to confirm or reject a nominee. The media coverage and interest group opposition measures are centered and divided by two standard deviations. Standard errors are clustered on the nominee. N = 4,801 for all models.

		Measure of visibility		
	Basic CCS model (1)	Media coverage (2)	Interest groups (3)	Scandal (4)
Intercept	0.72*	.76*	.76*	.61*
	−0.08	0.08	(.08)	(.16)
Senator-nominee distance	−0.55*	−0.45*	−.45*	−.38*
	(.09)	(.07)	(.07)	(.11)
Quality	.44*	.37*	.36*	.49*
	(.08)	(.09)	(.09)	(.18)
Measure of visibility (main effect)		.18	.15	.30
		(.11)	(.11)	(.19)
Distance × visibility	–	−.50*	−.51*	−.51*
		(.08)	(.08)	(.15)
Quality × visibility	–	−.06	−.01	−.16
		(.14)	(.14)	(.22)
Goodness of fit statistics				
R^2	.30	.38	.38	.34
AIC	2412	1802	1776	2102
BIC	2431	1841	1815	2141

visibility per nominee (scandal is a dichotomous variable), while the y-axis shows the proportion of yea votes they received. In each panel, there is a negative relationship between visibility and the proportion of yea votes in the Senate, as our visibility story would suggest. And, for the two continuous measures (coverage and interest group mobilization), we see that very low levels of visibility (the top-left corner) are associated with very high proportions of yeas for nominees.

Table 11.1 presents four linear probability models; the dependent variable in each is individual senators' votes to confirm or reject every nominee who reached the floor of the Senate between 1930 and 2020 (we again treat voice votes as unanimous yeas).[14] The first model only allows distance and quality to enter as predictors; in other words, it implements the basic CSS model, and confirms that both distance and quality are strong predictors of senators' votes on nominees.

Models (2), (3), and (4) implement the test of whether the CCS model works better under more visible nominations. For each measure of visibility, the models respectively allow that measure to enter as a main effect, along with interactions with distance and quality.[15] Each model tells the same story. For all three, the main effects on distance and quality are substantively unchanged from the base model. However, in all three, the distance interaction is negative and statistically significant, showing that increased distance between the senator and the nominee becomes a stronger predictor of a nay vote as visibility increases. Conversely, we find no interactive effect with quality.[16] If we take ideological distance to be the core predictor of roll call voting, then Table 11.1 confirms that its predictive effect varies strongly with nominee visibility, as our theoretical story would suggest.

As a second statistical test of this claim, Table 11.1 presents goodness-of-fit statistics for each model. The idea here is that if visibility is helping to structure roll call votes, then incorporating it into a statistical model should improve model fit. First, we can see the R^2 is higher for all three models with visibility included, compared to the base model. Second, we present the Akaike's Information Criteria (AIC) and Bayesian Information Criteria (BIC) for each model. These measures take into account that models with more parameters will generally fit the data better; lower numbers of the AIC and BIC mean better fit, after "penalizing" the model for having more parameters. We see that for all three visibility models, the AIC and BIC are lower than in the base model. Thus, overall the evidence supports the conclusion that the general increase in visibility over time went hand-in-hand with more contentious roll call votes.

11.4 Constituent Response to Roll Calls

How senators vote, anticipating constituent response, is only one half of the accountability story. The rise of visible roll call votes on Supreme Court nominations raises the possibility that voters will hold senators accountable for their votes. But do they actually do so?

In fact, Senate lore contains ominous examples of senators paying a price for "incorrect" roll call votes on nominees. Despite being virtually unknown, Carol Moseley Braun defeated incumbent Senator Alan Dixon in the Illinois Democratic primary in 1992, principally campaigning against his vote to confirm Clarence Thomas a year earlier. Similarly, Senator Arlen Specter of Pennsylvania faced a strong primary challenge leading up to the 2010 elections, with his vote against confirming Robert Bork in 1987 playing a large role in driving conservative support away from him. This challenge eventually lead Specter to switch parties in 2009.

On the broader question of how well constituents monitor their representatives, a scholarly controversy exists, similar to the "realist/rationalist" debate we evaluated in Chapter 10. The crux of the matter is *citizen knowledge*: do constituents actually know much about their representative's voting choices? Do they perceive those choices reasonably accurately? Do they then reward "good" choices and punish "bad" ones? If the answers are "no," "no," and "no," it is hard to see how accountability could play much of a role in roll call voting.

Studying those questions is difficult. First, one needs either large surveys and/or sophisticated statistical methods to measure the knowledge and preferences of citizens in House districts or states. Second, the survey questions need to examine specific roll call votes. Third, one needs a plausible "identification strategy" to untangle causality. In particular, one must account for the possibility that a constituent's evaluation of a senator's vote may reflect the constituent's overall assessment of the senator, rather than an overall assessment of the senator's votes. And, one needs to be able to account for the role of party agreement in assessment of representatives, given the changes in partisan polarization of citizens.

Early efforts to study constituent response to representative's voting behavior, while ambitious and creative, could not overcome the tremendous methodological challenges, at least in a way that today's social scientists would find credible.[17] Fortunately, contemporary political scientists have tackled each of the methodological challenges. Of particular note, political scientist Stephen Ansolabehere and co-authors created a suitable conceptual framework and implemented it using large surveys conducted over decades, with questions specifically tailored to studying roll call votes and accountability.[18] In some respects, this work represents the culmination of 60 years of inquiry by political scientists.

In this section we draw from our co-authored (2022) article with Leeann Bass and apply the Ansolabehere framework to Supreme Court confirmations. The demanding data requirements of the Ansolabehere framework mean that we can analyze only two recent nominations.[19] However, this effort is one of the few to apply the framework to Senate roll calls rather than House ones.[20]

In particular, we apply the conceptual framework set forth in Ansolabehere and Kuriwaki (2021) to the study of Supreme Court nominees. The advantage of this framework is that it allows us to account for the possibility that a citizen's evaluation of a senator's vote may be endogenous to the citizen's overall assessment of the senator. The framework also allows us to account for the role of party agreement in citizen assessment of senators, which is particularly important for more recent nominations given the rise in partisan polarization among voters both overall and on Supreme Court nominees. Finally, the framework allows us to benchmark the magnitude of the effect of voter-senator congruence on Supreme Court nominees against other high salience roll call votes.

As applied to the context of nominations, the framework has three parts:

- *Correct recall of roll call votes and senator partisanship.* Which types of voters are more likely to know how their senators voted on a nomination, as well as what party their senators belong to?
- *Does reality predict perceptions?* Does actual agreement between a voter and a senator on nominees and party predict perceived agreement on nominees and party?
- *Do perceptions affect evaluation?* Do citizens' perceptions of whether they agree with senators on nominees and party affect how citizens evaluate senators, both in terms of general approval and whether citizens vote to reelect senators?

We examined hundreds of polls in Chapter 7 that asked respondents their views on whether a given nominee should be confirmed. Applying this framework, however, requires not just this information, but also *how citizens perceive their senators to have voted on a given nominee*, as well as voter assessments of their senators. Polls that ask both type of questions are not common, but they do exist for three nominees: Clarence Thomas (1991), Sonia Sotomayor (2009), and Elena Kagan (2010).

In Bass, Cameron, and Kastellec (2022), we conducted a thorough investigation of all three nominees. The results for Thomas were somewhat ambiguous. Interested readers may consult that article; for brevity we only present the results for Sotomayor and Kagan. However, one possible reason why the evidence for accountability in the Thomas case is muddier may be timing—his nomination occurred before the parties had fully sorted, thereby complicating the public's understanding of how their senators voted. Indeed, as we discussed in Chapter 8, the main reason for Thomas' confirmation was the support of many Southern Democratic senators, whose numbers were still in the double digits. Thus, the correlation between party and voting was much weaker in the Thomas case compared to confirmations this century.[21]

To study public opinion on the Sotomayor and Kagan nominations, we use the 2009 and 2010 versions of the Cooperative Congressional Election Study [CCES].[22] We denote these the "2009 CCES" and "2010 CCES" for convenience. The surveys were conducted in the fall, a few months after the confirmations of Sotomayor and Kagan (which both occurred in August).[23]

The nominations of Sotomayor and Kagan were quite similar in terms of their political context. Both nominees were appointed by President Obama during his first two years in office, when the Senate was heavily controlled by Democrats, making their confirmations close to a sure thing from the start. Despite the relative lack of controversy, both were confirmed on near party-line votes, with Sotomayor and Kagan receiving nine and five yea votes from Republicans, respectively. Due to their overall similarity, throughout the chapter we combine the results from the 2009 and 2010 CCES polls into a single survey and present pooled analyses. There is little substantive difference in the results when we analyze Sotomayor and Kagan separately.[24]

11.4.1 Voter Recall of Senator Votes

Accountability models come in many different flavors, but a core assumption is that there is a real or potential audience for the actions of a politician. Of course, when it comes to sophistication and knowledge by the general public, reality may not accord with the logic of rational choice models.[25] A necessary condition of our accountability story is that citizens—or, at least, a sufficient number of them—can successfully monitor the votes of their senators on nominees.

We begin our analysis with voter recall of senators' votes. Beginning with voter preferences, the CCES asked respondents: "If you were in Congress, would you have voted for or against the confirmation of [Sotomayor/Kagan] to the Supreme Court?"

We code both as being either in favor of or against confirmation, with non-responses and "don't knows" coded as such. In terms of recall, the 2009 and 2010 CCES asked, respectively, "The Senate considered the appointment of Sonia Sotomayor [Elena Kagan] to the U.S. Supreme Court. Did Senator [name] vote for this appointment or against it?" These questions were repeated for the respondent's second senator.

For each survey, some respondents chose not to offer an opinion on how their senators voted. Our general strategy on how to handle such non-response is as follows. For the analysis that immediately follows in this subsection, we examine voter recall in two ways. First, we treat non-responses as being an "incorrect" recall assessment; in other words, those who do not offer a response are pooled with those who offer an incorrect response. Second, we drop non-responses, and examine recall only among those who offered an opinion. Dropping non-responses will obviously lead to higher levels of recall. But the advantage of looking at this set is that we can compare the distribution of recall to what we would observe if people were simply guessing (based on either flipping a coin or just cueing off the party of the senator). When we do that, it makes less sense to treat non-responses as incorrect, since such respondents are making an affirmative choice *not* to guess how their senator voted. In the subsequent analyses that rely on regression methods, we include non-responses; as explained shortly, such responses are directly accounted for in the measures that implement the Ansolabehere-Kuriwaki framework.

To measure respondent recall of senators' votes, we follow the example of Hutchings (2001, 852) and construct an index in the wide data—that is, one observation for each respondent—that takes on the following values:

- 0 if the respondent correctly recalled neither senator's vote.
- .5 if the respondent correctly recalled exactly one senator's vote.
- 1 if the respondent correctly recalled both senators' votes.

The top portion of Table 11.2 depicts the distribution of this index for the nominees. The first column shows the recall index when we include all respondents and code non-responses as "don't knows." We can see that recall of senators' votes on these two nominees is fairly good, with fully 46% of respondents correctly recalling both of their senators' votes. When we drop "don't knows," the picture improves quite dramatically, with only 2% correctly recalling neither senator, 10% recalling exactly one, and fully 89% recalling both correctly. To place these results in context, Ansolabehere and Jones (2010) find that on average voters are able to correctly identify about 72% of House members' votes correctly.

Of course, these raw distributions are somewhat difficult to interpret, and we might worry that many respondents are just guessing. First, note that if respondents were simply tossing a figurative coin when they respond and guessing yes or no, the null distribution of the recall index would come out to about 25% getting zero correct by chance, 50% getting one correct by chance, and 25% getting both correct. Since this null distribution is based on pure guessing, it makes sense to exclude respondents who are not willing to offer an opinion when they don't have one. When we do that, a chi-squared test easily rejects the null hypothesis that the actual distributions in the second column in Table 11.2 are not distinguishable from the pure guessing distribution.

In addition, we follow the lead of Ansolabehere and Jones (2010, 585) and note the following additional reasons why mere guessing is unlikely to explain these levels of recall. First, if responses were simply random, we would be unlikely to find any structure in the data when we model the relationship between those who perceive themselves to be in agreement with their senator and those who don't. In fact, we find a great deal of structure. Second, people might just cue on partisanship, based on either the partisanship of the roll call votes on nominees and/or of their given senator. To account for this possibility, we control for both party identification and respondent agreement with their senator (we also do this for ideology); the key results still hold. Finally, statements of correct recall and policy agreement might be endogenous to approval of a senator. To account for this, we conduct an instrumental variables analysis below, and the key results hold.[26]

Finally, in the bottom portion of Table 11.2 we also follow the lead of Ansolabehere and Jones (2010, 585) by comparing the responses of voters whose senators voted with the majority of the party and those who voted against the majority of the party. Here we switch to the long version of the data (i.e. each respondent has two observations, one for each senator), since we need to account for whether an individual senator voted for or against his or her party. In addition, since we will compare these responses to a guessing benchmark, here we only include respondents who offered

Table 11.2 Measuring voter recall of senator votes for Sotomayor and Kagan. The top portion of the table uses the wide data—one observation per respondent—to depict the distribution of the nominee-recall index, both with and without respondents who did not provide a response. The bottom part uses the long data—two observations per respondent, one for each senator—to compare the responses of voters whose senators voted with the majority of the party and those who voted against the majority of the party.

	Distribution of Index of Correct Responses	
	All respondents	**Dropping don't knows**
Recall neither	41%	2%
Recall one	14%	10%
Recall both	46%	89%
	Correct Responses by Party-Line Voting	
Percent correct (all respondents)	93%	
Percent correct when senator votes with party	94%	
Percent correct when senator votes against party	69%	

an opinion on how their senator voted. Sotomayor was confirmed by a vote of 68-31, with every Democrat voting to confirm her and all but nine Republicans voting to reject her. Kagan was confirmed by a vote of 63-37, with all but one Democrat voting to confirm and all but six Republicans voting to reject. We can see in Table 11.2 that about 93% of responses correctly identified their senators' votes on Sotomayor and Kagan. However, the results are quite different when we condition on how a senator voted relative to her party. When a senator voted with her party, voters correctly identified the vote fully 94% of the time. Conversely, that percentage drops to 69% of the time when senators vote against their party.

What is going on here? As we have seen throughout the book, by 2009, the current era of extreme party polarization was firmly in place. The growth in party sorting and polarization surely made it easier for respondents to correctly recall the votes of senators by using party as an aid. And the fact that the roll call votes for Sotomayor and Kagan were largely party-line votes made correct recall an easier task for many citizens.[27]

However, the asymmetric results in the bottom-right portion of Table 11.2 show it is *not* simply party doing the work in explaining the high levels of recall for Sotomayor and Kagan. To see this, imagine that voters simply guessed every time that senators voted in line with their party. For Sotomayor and Kagan, this means assuming all Democratic senators voted yes and all Republican senators voted no. In the Sotomayor and Kagan data, only about 4% of observations feature senators with "cross-party" votes. If respondents were simply guessing based on party, we would expect them to recall these votes correctly only about 4% of the time, since 96% of the time they would correctly align with the "straight-party" votes. Instead, the actual percentage of correct responses in these votes is about 70%. This difference provides strong evidence that most people are not simply guessing. Instead, the recall that we observe in twenty-first-century Supreme Court nominations seems quite real.

Voter Recall and Political Engagement

Examining the levels of recall is certainly worthwhile, but of perhaps even greater interest is the variation in who is, in fact, doing the recalling. From the CCES, we coded variables that capture the concept of political engagement, such as education, political knowledge, and news interest. Figure 11.2 depicts the levels of recall across each of these variables. For each panel in this figure, the y-axis depicts the mean index of recall, while the x-axis depicts the levels of the respective predictor, moving from lower levels of political engagement to higher levels. For each of the variables, higher levels of political engagement lead to higher levels of recall.

Table 11.3 presents two OLS models in which the dependent variable is the index of recall. To test the relationship between political engagement and voter recall more systematically, for each nominee we used a principal components analysis to create a single factor score that summarizes all of the variables in Figure 11.2.

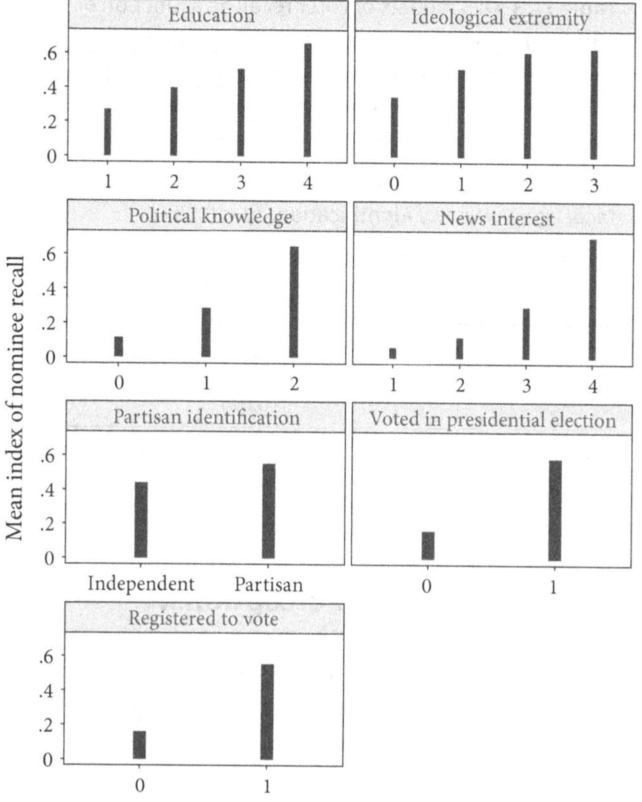

Fig. 11.2 Political engagement and voter recall of senators' votes to confirm Sotomayor and Kagan (pooling the survey data for their nominations). For each panel, the y-axis depicts the mean index of recall, while the x-axis depicts the levels of the respective predictor.

Each model contains the factor scores of engagement; we standardize the scores by centering and dividing by two standard deviations. Model (2) includes controls for education, gender, race, age, and party identification (though they are omitted from the table for clarity). In each model, the coefficient on political engagement is positive and significant. A shift of two standard deviations in engagement predicts about a 45-percentage point increase in recall for Sotomayor and Kagan.

In sum, we find that the necessary conditions for accountability with respect to voting on Supreme Court nominees do exist. Overall, voters do a decent job of identifying how their senators voted on these nominees. And, as we would expect, the ability to correctly recall correlates quite significantly with levels of political engagement among citizens.

Table 11.3 OLS models of voter recall as a function of political engagement. In each model, the dependent variable is the index of recall. Political engagement is a factor score based on a principal components analysis of the variables shown in Figure 11.2. Models (2) and (4) include, but do not display, controls for education, gender, race, age, and party identification. *$p < 0.05$.

	(1)	(2)
Political engagement	0.45*	0.39*
	(0.01)	(0.01)
Constant	0.55*	0.62*
	(0.01)	(0.04)
Controls?	No	Yes
Observations	7,311	7,311
R^2	0.24	0.29

11.4.2 Does Reality Predict Perceptions?

The next stage in our accountability analysis is to ask whether *actual* agreement on nominees predicts *perceived* agreement? In other words, does the reality of roll call voting and party agreement shape voter perceptions of roll call voting and party agreement?

To flesh out our approach for the rest of the chapter, we reproduce Figure 1 from Ansolabehere and Kuriwaki (2021) in Figure 11.3, which summarizes the relationships between actual agreement, perceived agreement, and evaluations.[28] While policy representation is important for accountability, party identification, of course, also plays a role in linking citizens and representatives. The Ansolabehere and Kuriwaki approach accounts for the importance of party by allowing the interplay of actual party agreement and perceived agreement to inform citizens' assessments of their representatives. Thus, under this conceptual framework, actual party agreement and actual issue agreement (where "issue" for our purposes means a confirmation of a Supreme Court nominee) predict perceived party and issue agreement.

Following Ansolabehere and Kuriwaki (2021), we define "perceived nominee agreement" as follows:

- +1 if a respondent's preference (based on how the respondent would have voted on the nominee) is *the same* as the respondent's perception of the senator's vote (i.e. the respondent would have voted yes (no) and perceives the senator as having voted yes (no)).
- 0 if the respondent does not have an opinion on the nominee or does not express an interest.

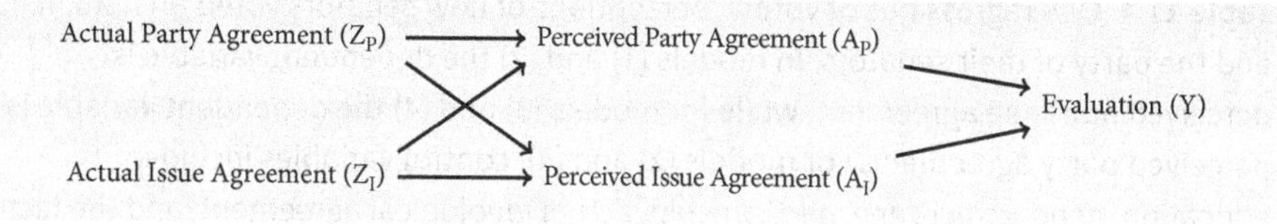

Fig. 11.3 Figure 1 from Ansolabehere and Kuriwaki (2021), which summarizes the relationships between actual agreement, perceived agreement, and evaluations.

- −1 if a respondent's preference (based on how the respondent would have voted on the nominee) is *opposite* to the respondent's perception of the senator's vote (i.e. the respondent would have voted yes (no) and perceives the senator as having voted no (yes)).

Next, we define "actual nominee agreement" in the same manner, but substitute the senator's actual vote instead of the respondent's perception of the vote. That is, +1 if the respondent's preference agrees with the senator's *actual* vote, −1 if the respondent's preference is opposite to the senator's vote, and 0 if the respondent does not have an opinion on the nominee or does not express an interest.

We code "perceived party agreement" as follows:

- +1 if the respondent identifies with the *same party* she perceives the senator to be (i.e. the respondent identifies as a Republican (Democrat) and perceives the senator as being a Republican (Democrat)).
- 0 if the respondent is an Independent or is unsure of her senator's party.
- −1 if the respondent identifies with the *opposite party* as she perceives the senator to be (i.e. the respondent identifies as a Republican (Democrat) and perceives the senator as being a Democrat (Republican)).

We define "actual party agreement" in the same manner, but substitute the senator's actual party identification instead of the respondent's perception of it.

With these measures in hand, we can now examine how well reality predicts perceptions, in terms of nominee votes and party agreement. In doing so, we note that from this point forward, we analyze the long version of the data, in which each respondent appears twice, once for each of their senators. To account for non-independence across the paired observations, we employ robust standard errors, clustered on the respondent.[29]

Finally, for models with control variables, we include demographics, party identification, and political engagement. Because ideological differences with a senator may affect perceptions, even accounting for party agreement, we follow Ansolabehere and Kuriwaki and include an "actual ideological agreement" variable that is similar in thrust to the party agreement variable.[30]

Table 11.4 OLS regressions of voters' perceptions of how senators voted on nominees and the party of their senators. In models (1) and (2) the dependent variable is perceived nominee agreement, while for models (3) and (4) the dependent variable is perceived party agreement. For models (2) and (4), control variables include: education, gender, race, age, partisanship, actual ideological agreement, and the factor score of political engagement based on the variables in Figure 11.2. *$p < 0.05$. Standard errors are clustered on respondents.

	DV: Perceived nominee agreement		DV: Perceived party agreement	
Actual nominee agreement	0.42*	0.40*	0.10*	0.08*
	(0.01)	(0.01)	(0.00)	(0.01)
Actual party agreement	0.16*	0.10*	0.70*	0.67*
	(0.01)	(0.01)	(0.00)	(0.01)
N	15,803	14,456	130,558	14,385
R^2	0.47	0.50	0.67	0.68
Control variables	No	Yes	No	Yes

Table 11.4 presents four OLS regression models. In columns (1) and (2), the dependent variable is perceived nominee agreements, while in columns (3) and (4), perceived party agreement is the dependent variable. The models in columns (1) and (3) do not include control variables; the models in columns (2) and (4) do include them, though we omit their presentation in the interest of space.

Overall, the connection between reality and perception is strong—a one-unit increase in actual agreement on their confirmation votes predicts about a 40-percentage point increase in perceived agreement with a senator. For some context, this effect size is roughly comparable to what Ansolabehere and Kuriwaki find in their study of House members (they find an average effect size of .34). In addition, and unsurprisingly, actual party agreement predicts perceived party agreement quite strongly.

Note also from Table 11.4 that for both analyses, the "cross-effect" of actual party agreement on perceived nominee agreement is much weaker than the "straight" effect of actual nominee agreement on perceived nominee agreement. Specifically, the coefficient on actual party agreement in the first two models is only .16 and .10, respectively, compared to .42 and .40 for actual nominee agreement. Thus, the results in Table 11.4 make clear that perceived nominee agreement is *not* operating directly through partisanship—actual nominee agreement (i.e. issue-based agreement) is doing most of the work.

11.4.3 Do Perceptions Affect Evaluation?

So far we have shown that the public as a whole can make sense of how their senators vote on Supreme Court nominees, and that citizens' perceptions of these votes are grounded in the actuality of senatorial decisions, particularly for Sotomayor and Kagan. Thus, the seeds for accountability are there. The final—and most difficult—piece of the puzzle is to examine whether these perceptions actually cause support for or opposition to citizens' elected representatives.

Returning to Figure 11.3 above, Ansolabehere and Kuriwaki (2021) note that one key threat to interpreting a positive correlation between perceptions and evaluation is the endogeneity (or reverse causation) of perceived agreement. "For example, a respondent might have underlying trust in the [senator], which both leads to higher job approval and also leads him to the belief that the [senator] probably agrees with him on key issues too" (Ansolabehere and Kuriwaki 2021, 4). To deal with the possibility of an unobserved confounder, Ansolabehere and Kuriwaki implement instrumental variables (IV) regressions, employing actual issue and party agreement to serve as instruments for perceived issue and party agreement. We do the same.

Before turning to the IV analysis, we begin by presenting the estimates of the reduced form relationship in Figure 11.3, which captures the relationship between *actual agreement* and voter evaluations of senators.[31] Because studies of accountability generally can only measure actual agreement (as opposed to perceptions), this relationship is the one that is usually examined in the literature. For example, Badas and Simas (2022) find a strong relationship between citizens' actual agreements with their senators' votes on the nominations of Neil Gorsuch and Brett Kavanaugh and citizens' vote choices for senators.

To study citizen evaluation, we employ two dependent variables, both of which have strengths and weaknesses. The first is citizens' vote choice for senators. Here we follow the lead of studies of accountability in the House of Representatives, which often look at whether a respondent voted for a House member in the previous election. Vote choice is probably the concept that most naturally links to theories of accountability. However, the fact that senators have six-year terms with staggered electoral cycles complicates the use of vote choice due to missing data. In 2010, fewer than a third of senators were up for re-election (after accounting for senators who either retired or were defeated in a party primary). In addition, we cannot analyze vote choice for Sotomayor, since her recall questions were asked in the 2009 CCES, a year before the 2010 Senate elections. Thus, the vote choice regressions will be relatively under-powered.

Accordingly, we follow the lead of Dancey and Sheagley (2016) and also examine voter approval of senators, based on the straightforward survey question of whether voters approve of their senators or not. We construct binary approval measures, coded 1 if the respondent either approved strongly or somewhat approved and 0 if the respondent disapproved strongly or somewhat disapproved of her senator. We construct this measure for both of the respondent's senators, meaning that all respondents across all three nominees can be included in the approval analyses.

Table 11.5 presents four OLS regressions for Sotomayor/Kagan that estimate the reduced form relationship of whether actual nominee and party agreement predict evaluations of senators. For the models in Columns (1)–(2), the dependent variable is whether the respondent approved of her senator; for the models in columns (3)

Table 11.5 OLS regression models of reduced form of actual agreement versus evaluation of senators. The dependent variable in Columns (1)–(2) is whether respondents approve of their senators, while Columns (3)–(4) employ vote choice as the dependent variable. Models with control variables include: education, gender, race, age, partisanship, and the factor score of political engagement based on the variables in Figure 11.2. *$p < 0.05$.

	Approval *Sotomayor and Kagan*		Vote choice *Kagan*	
Actual nominee agreement	0.14*	0.12*	0.13*	0.11*
	(0.00)	(0.01)	(0.01)	(0.02)
Actual party agreement	0.22*	0.17*	0.35*	0.33*
	(0.02)	(0.01)	(0.01)	(0.02)
N	120,662	13,366	17,518	1,604
R^2	0.38	0.40	0.78	0.79
Control variables	No	Yes	No	Yes

and (4), the dependent variable is vote choice. Models (1) and (3) do not include control variables, while Models (2) and (4) do include them, though we omit their presentation in the interest of space.

The results show a very strong relationship between actual agreement and citizen evaluation of senators. For approval, a one-unit increase in actual nominee agreement predicts about a 14 percentage-point increase in Model (1) and about a 12-percentage point increase in Model (2), with both measured quite precisely. The coefficients for vote choice are similar in Models (3) and (4). Again, and perhaps not surprisingly, the relationship between actual party agreement and voter assessments is quite sizable, especially for vote choice.

These reduced form estimates are important. But, as Ansolabehere and Kuriwaki note, the reduced form is incomplete, as it is silent as to *how* citizens perceive agreement with their senators and whether they act on those perceptions. Accordingly, we now return to our central question of whether perceptions of agreement causally affect voter evaluations of senators.

11.4.4 Perceptions and Voter Evaluations

Prior to using a regression framework, Table 11.6 presents a simple analysis of senator approval (we rely on approval here rather than vote choice to maximize the sample size). Specifically, it breaks down citizen approval of senators by perceived nominee and party agreement. The table is essentially a cross-tab—each cell depicts the mean level of approval among a particular combination of nominee and party agreement. The exterior row and column depict the marginal distributions, while the percentage in the bottom right-hand cell depicts the overall mean.

Table 11.6 Approval of senators by perceived nominee and party agreement, for Sotomayor and Kagan. Each cell depicts the mean level of approval among a particular combination of nominee and party agreement. The exterior row and column depict the marginal distributions, while the percentage in the bottom right-hand cell depicts the overall mean level of approval.

		Perceived party agreement			
		Agree	DK/Ind.	Disagree	Total
Perceived	Agree	90%	69%	39%	82%
nominee agreement	DK/No interest	79%	52%	32%	57%
	Disagree	54%	15%	6%	12%
	Total	83%	45%	15%	*50%*

Table 11.6 reveals a number of interesting patterns. Notice that if we condition on perceived party agreement (i.e. moving up and down the columns) moving from perceived nominee agreement to perceived disagreement is always associated with a sizable decrease in mean levels of approval. For example, among those respondents who are in party agreement, moving from perceived nominee disagreement to perceived nominee agreement predicts a shift from 54% approval to 90% approval. Similarly, among those who perceive themselves as of the opposite party as a senator, moving from perceived nominee disagreement to agreement means a shift from 6% approval to 39% approval. In addition, changes in perceived party agreement are associated with massive changes in perceived nominee agreement. For instance, among respondents who perceive they are in agreement with their senator's party, 90% support their senator. This percentage drops to 39% among respondents who perceive they are not of their senator's party.

We now turn to estimating the full relationship in Figure 11.3, in order to systematically evaluate the relationship between perceptions and evaluations. Table 11.7 presents both two-stage least squares instrumental variable regressions and OLS regressions.[32] The IV results are in the first four columns; in these models, actual nominee agreement and actual party agreement serve as instruments for perceived nominee agreement and perceived party agreement, respectively. The OLS results are in the last four columns. In Columns (1), (2), (5), and (6), the dependent variable is whether the respondent approved of her senator. In columns (3), (4), (7), and (8), the dependent variable is whether the respondent reported voting for their incumbent senator. (Recall that this measure does not exist for Sotomayor, and thus the vote choice models only include Kagan.) The odd-number models do not include control variables, while the even-number models do include them, though we omit their presentation in the interest of space.

Let's begin with the IV results. In all four models, the coefficients on perceived nominee agreement in each model are both sizable and statistically significant. For approval, a one-unit shift in perceived nominee agreement predicts about a 25 percentage point shift in approval. For vote choice, the effect sizes are smaller, but

Table 11.7 Regression models evaluating whether perceptions about nominee votes affect evaluation of senators. The first four models present instrumental variables models, while the last four models present OLS regressions. For Columns (1), (2), (5), and (6), the dependent variable is whether respondents approve of their senators on perceived nominee and party agreement. For Columns (3), (4), (7), (8), the dependent variable is whether respondents voted to re-elect their incumbent senator. Models with control variables include: education, gender, race, age, partisanship, and the factor score of political engagement. The F-statistics in the IV regressions are tests of whether actual nominee and party agreement are sufficiently strong predictors of perceived nominee and party agreement, respectively. *$p < 0.05$.

	IV Regressions				*OLS Regressions*			
	Approval		Vote choice (Kagan)		Approval		Vote choice (Kagan)	
	(1)	(2)	(3)	(4)	(5)	(6)	(7)	(8)
Perceived nominee agreement	0.25* (0.01)	0.23* (0.02)	0.14* (0.03)	0.13* (0.03)	0.19* (0.01)	0.16* (0.01)	0.16* (0.02)	0.13* (0.02)
Perceived party agreement	0.23* (0.01)	0.20* (0.01)	0.40* (0.03)	0.39* (0.03)	0.24* (0.01)	0.21* (0.01)	0.34* (0.01)	0.31* (0.02)
Control variables	No	Yes	No	Yes	No	Yes	No	Yes
N	14,166	13,129	1,670	1,574	14,473	13,129	1,671	1,574
R^2	–	–	–	–	0.41	0.44	0.73	0.75
F-stat (nominee)	5,045*	2,229*	1,700*	564*	–	–	–	–
F-stat (party)	13,148.4*	5,025*	5,951.5*	1,484*	–	–	–	–

still of substantive significance, as they are in the range of 13 percentage points. In addition, perceived nominee agreement easily passes the bar for a strong instrument. We again find significant party effects, showing that the effect of nominee perceptions is operating above the general effect of partisan alignment between citizens and senators. Next, let's turn to the OLS regressions in the last column of Table 11.7. The results for perceived nominee agreement for Sotomayor and Kagan are substantively and statistically the same as in the IV regressions.

All told then, the results from the Sotomayor and Kagan survey data strongly suggest that in the politics of today's Supreme Court nominations, voters seem to hold senators accountable for their votes on Supreme Court nominees, and that voters' assessments of senators are driven by voters' perceptions of how senators vote.

11.4.5 Comparing Nominations to Other Issues

While the results in Table 11.7 are quite informative, in a vacuum it is somewhat difficult to assess how substantively large the relationship between perceptions and assessments is. One way to benchmark the effect of perceived nominee agreement on senator approval and vote choice is to compare it to the effects seen in other high-profile votes, such as the 2009 votes on the stimulus package and the Affordable Care Act. We present this analysis in the Appendix. The upshot is that the effects for the two Supreme Court nominations are among the largest, when compared to the other roll call votes on really important policy items.

How should we think about the relative importance of votes on Supreme Court nominees in this broader context? On the one hand, the relative size of the effects for Sotomayor/Kagan is quite surprising. Recall that these were relatively low-salience and low-key nominations, whereas the ACA and the stimulus were landmark pieces of legislation that generated huge media coverage and partisan bickering. On the other hand, compared to complex legislation, Supreme Court nominations are very straightforward affairs, with outcomes that are quite stark: either the nominee is confirmed, allowing her to serve on the nation's highest court, or she is rejected, forcing the president to name another candidate. In this process, note Watson and Stookey (1995, 19): "there are no amendments, no riders and [in recent decades] no voice votes; there is no place for the senator to hide. There are no outcomes where everybody gets a little of what they want. There are only winners and losers." It seems quite plausible that this clarity allows voters to readily update their assessments of their senators based on their perceptions of how they voted on Supreme Court nominees.

11.5 Which Principal? Cross-Pressured Voting and Biased Representation

For our final investigation, we shift our perspective back to the calculus of senators. Section 11.4 established that in modern nominations, the predicates of accountability seem to hold. That means, in turn, senators should weigh public support in their home states for nominees when they cast their votes. But this still leaves open the question of *whose support* they should attend to—especially when senators are cross-pressured.

First consider the general evolution of voter preferences over time. As discussed in Chapter 10, after about 1980 or so citizens more cleanly sorted themselves into the parties by ideology. So, liberals and Democrats became one and the same, as did conservatives and Republicans. A large portion of the electorate—often comparable in size to the party blocks and sometimes larger than either—refused to affiliate with either of the two ideologically distinct parties. These Independents typically were less interested in and knowledgeable about politics, sometimes held moderate opinions, but sometimes combined liberal and conservative opinions in ways that made them uncomfortable aligning with either purist party.[33]

The partisan sort can create conditions in which representatives find themselves cross-pressured, caught between the median voter in their primary and the median voter in the general election. If one approaches this conflict in the simplest way using Downsian notions of candidate convergence, one might expect the median in the general election to triumph easily (we provide an argument to this effect shortly).

However, anomalies abound. For example, same-state senators frequently disagree, and House candidates from the same district often adopt divergent positions.[34] Studies relating summary measures of constituency preferences to summary measures of roll call voting find much apparent responsiveness to copartisans.[35]

How might partisan sorting affect senators' calculations about confirmation voting? In particular, when the preferences of the median voter in the general electorate diverge from the preferences of the median voter in the primary, to whom does the senator attend? Perhaps surprisingly, the impact of cross-pressure on roll call voting appears quite understudied.[36] Recent Supreme Court nominations provide a laboratory for studying this topic.

We do not offer a fully fleshed out theory of cross-pressured roll call voting, but some simple theoretical ideas are helpful. First, from the viewpoint of a senator, re-election involves a *compound lottery*. The primary is the first lottery; the general election is the second; and overall victory requires favorable outcomes in both. Consider Figure 11.4, which is relevant for highly visible confirmation votes. First the senator must vote either to confirm or reject. Then, the senator faces a lottery in the primary. The chances of surviving this lottery may depend on how the senator voted. Let p_1 indicate the probability of victory in the primary election given a confirm vote, while p_2 indicates the probability of victory in the primary after a reject vote. Given survival in the primary, the senator then faces the general electorate. Let π_1 indicate the senator's probability of victory in the general election given a confirm vote, and

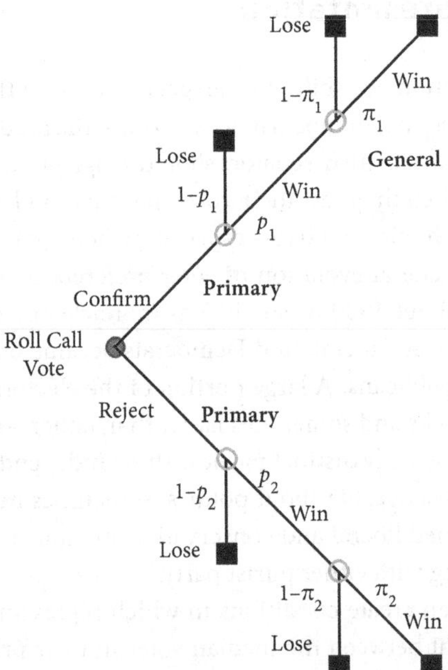

Fig. 11.4 A senator's voting calculations when the probability of being re-elected involves a compound lottery across a primary and general election. See text for details.

π_2 the probability of victory in the general election after a reject vote. The probability of ultimate victory following a confirm vote is thus $p_1\pi_1$ and that after a reject vote is $p_2\pi_2$. Clearly, a win-seeking senator should vote to confirm if and only if $p_1\pi_1 \geq p_2\pi_2$. A policy-minded senator may be willing to run higher risks but still must attend to the logic of electoral survival.

Now, suppose there is no cross-pressure, so the senator's median primary voter and the median general election voter, while not the same person, both prefer the same roll call vote, and hold the senator accountable. This situation usually requires Independents to prefer the same roll call vote as the senator's copartisans. In that case, both medians probably respond similarly to votes so $p_1 = \pi_1$ and $p_2 = \pi_2$. In that case, the senator's calculation reduces to: confirm if and only if $\pi_1 \geq \pi_2$. In words, the senator should cast the popular vote, hardly a surprising conclusion.

But suppose the senator is cross-pressured. To make matters concrete, suppose the senator's primary voters favor confirmation of the nominee while the median in the general electorate (typically an Independent) favors rejection. To the extent both sets of voters hold the senator accountable, one would suppose that $p_1 > p_2$ and $\pi_1 < \pi_2$. If so, the senator's calculation becomes confirm if and only if $\frac{p_1}{p_2} \geq \frac{\pi_2}{\pi_1}$. The left-hand side is the *copartisan differential*—the win probability in the primary after the "correct" vote relative to the win probability after the "wrong" vote. The right-hand side is the *general electorate differential*—the win probability in the general election after the "right" vote relative to the win probability in the general election after the "wrong" vote. A win-seeking senator should vote to confirm if and only if the co-partisan differential is larger than the general electorate differential.

Going further requires thinking harder about asymmetric information and the differentials. Three simple cases are informative. First, suppose the median voter in the general election doesn't notice the confirmation vote due to low interest in politics, or doesn't care enough about it to hold the senator accountable. In that case, $\pi_2 = \pi_1$ and $\frac{\pi_2}{\pi_1} = 1$. Accordingly, the primary voter, if observant of the vote, should definitely hold the senator accountable, so $p_1 > p_2$ and $\frac{p_1}{p_2} > \frac{\pi_2}{\pi_1}$, leading to a confirm vote. Thus, differential knowledge of the vote between co-partisans and Independents can be important.

Second, suppose the median voter in the general election does observe the vote and holds the senator severely accountable for it. A simple rational choice argument suggests that the primary voter should act strategically and give the senator a "pass," in other words, not hold the senator accountable for the vote. To insist on the "right" vote might lead to a loss in the general election and the election of a senator from the other party, a bad outcome for the primary voter. So, on this account, the senator should defy the wishes of the primary voters, but the primary voters should "forgive" this transgression and exact no electoral penalty in the primary.

However, what seems plausible in theory often does not occur in fact, as the actual behavior of primary voters appears strongly at odds with this account. Hall (2015), for example, shows that primary voters sometimes opt for extremist candidates; such candidates then pay a predictable price and lose in the general election. It is hard to imagine that such primary voters would deliberately forgive a deeply objectionable roll call vote by their co-partisan senator.

So, is there a third account in which primary voters insist on ideological fealty, knowing full well that it could carry a cost in the general election? We suggest the answer is yes. The intuition extends the logic of electoral "virtue signaling" to the compound lottery setting.[37] In this approach, voters are somewhat uncertain about the true preferences of the incumbent senator. By taking a costly action, the senator can credibly signal those preferences. In this sense, the electoral risk run in the general election by casting the "wrong" roll call vote is precisely the cost needed to send a credible signal to the primary electorate that the senator is a true believer and one of them. Hence, the resulting co-partisan differential would be very large. Still, a large co-partisan differential would be insufficient motivation if the roll call vote amounted to certain defeat in the general election. In addition to a large partisan differential, the general election differential must not be too large. For example, with some probability the general median voter either might not notice the vote or might not care much about the vote, evaluating the senator on other grounds such as competence in delivering pork barrel projects or supplying constituency service. Still, even if the relative size of the two differentials leads the senator to heed co-partisan opinion, defiance of the median voter is likely to carry some electoral cost in the general election. On balance, though, casting the other vote would have been even worse, leading to a likely loss in the primary. If this logic is persuasive, then one would expect to see cross-pressured senators following co-partisan opinion and then paying an electoral cost—though not certain defeat—from doing so.

Empirical Analysis of Cross-Pressured Voting

To examine the impact of cross-pressure, we rely on the data and models used in Kastellec's 2015 article with Jeffrey Lax, Michael Malecki, and Justin Phillips, "Polarizing the Electoral Connection: Partisan Representation in Supreme Court Confirmation Politics."[38] That article included every nomination through 2010 for which sufficient polling data was available to estimate support for nominees broken down by party identification of poll respondents. It uses advances in multilevel regression and post-stratification (MRP) to generate sub-constituency estimates of partisan opinion in every state using national polls, even among states with smaller numbers of respondents. We extend this dataset to include the recent nominations of Garland, Gorsuch, Kavanaugh, and Barrett.[39] Note the first nominee for which we have sufficient data is William Rehnquist's nomination to become chief justice in 1986. Thus, all of the nominations we analyze took place in the modern era.

Figure 11.5 depicts kernel density plots of our estimates of citizen support among opinion holders, broken down by Democrats, Independents, and Republicans, across states. That is, the unit of analysis is states, broken down by each type of opinion (so each density plot summarizes 50 estimates of opinion). The dots under each distribution depict the mean of that respective distribution. Vertical dashed lines

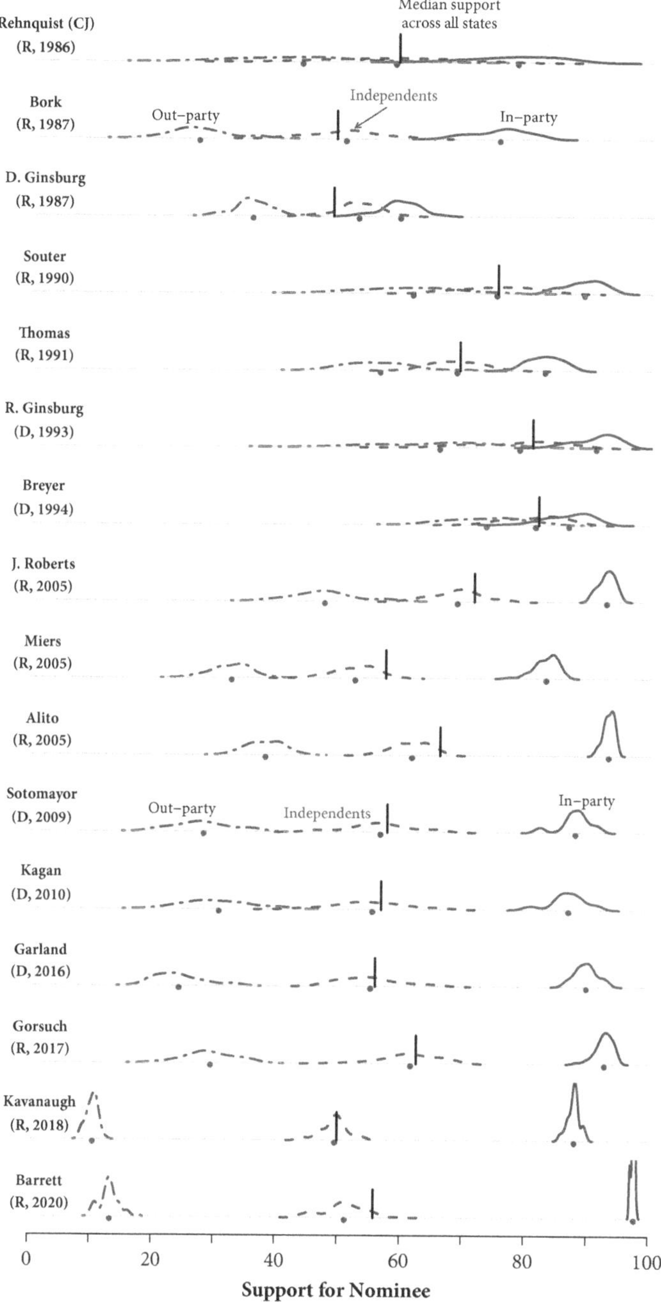

Fig. 11.5 The distribution of nominee support among Democratic identifiers, Independents, and Republican identifiers. The graph depicts kernel density plots of our estimates of support among opinion holders, broken down by members of the president's party, Independents, and members not of the president's party. (Blue means the distribution of Democratic constituencies and red Republican constituencies, with green capturing Independents.) The dots under each distribution depict the mean of that distribution. The vertical lines depict the median support across states.

depict median state-level support. Nominees are ordered chronologically. Note that support for nominees is always higher on average, and indeed very high in absolute terms, among constituents from the president's party.

Figure 11.5 also reveals that polarization—defined as the difference between median Democratic and Republican opinion—varied significantly across nominees. The nominations of Souter, Ruth Bader Ginsburg, and Breyer in the early 1990s generated little polarization and substantial overlap across constituencies. On the other hand, as demonstrated in Chapters 7 and 10, every nomination this century (beginning with Roberts) has exhibited high partisan polarization, culminating in a vast gulf in public support between Democratic and Republican constituencies for Brett Kavanaugh in 2018 and Amy Coney Barrett in 2020. Thus, Figure 11.5 shows that cross-pressure can be quite substantial.

We use regression models of roll call voting to more precisely examine the responsiveness of senators to co-partisan opinion. The key tests evaluate how the probability of a confirmation vote changes as sub-constituency opinion changes. Doing so requires careful accounting of not just nominee *support* by a particular group, but also by the *size* of that group. To that end, we employ the following predictors:

- *Supporters out of all opinion holders*: the percentage of opinion holders who support the nominee.
- *Supporters in senator's party*: the percentage of opinion holders who share their party affiliation with the senator in question *and* support the nominee.
- *Supporters who are Independents*: the percentage of opinion holders who identify with neither party *and* support the nominee.

We also fix the partisan breakdown of the opinion holder population, as follows:

- *Percentage of opinion holders in the senator's party.*
- *Percentage of opinion holders in the opposite party.*

Finally, we also control for ideological distance between the senator and the nominee, quality, and whether the senator is of the same party as the president.

Table 11.8 presents three logit models.[40] In each model the dependent variable is whether the senator voted to confirm the nominee or not. These models include all the nominees seen in Figure 11.5, except for the three who did not receive roll call votes (Douglas Ginsburg, Harriet Miers, and Merrick Garland). Each model includes varying intercepts ("random effects") for nominees in order to account for the non-independence of votes with a given nominee.

Beginning with Model (1), the "Supporters" coefficient shows the overall relationship between state-level public opinion and voting on nominees. Not surprisingly, it is positive and statistically significant. Model (2) presents the test of whether senators are more responsive to co-partisan opinion. The key coefficient, "Supporters in senator's party," captures the effect of raising support within the president's

Table 11.8 Logit models of roll call voting on nominees with estimates of public opinion broken down by partisan constituency. Random effects for nominees not shown. $^{*}p < 0.05$.

	(1)	(2)	(3)
Supporters	0.19*	0.11*	0.13*
	(0.03)	(0.04)	(0.07)
Supporters in senator's party		0.16*	0.16*
		(0.07)	(0.07)
Supporters who are Independents			−0.06
			(0.18)
Percentage in senator's party	0.05*	−0.05	−0.08
	(0.03)	(0.05)	(0.11)
Percentage in opposition party	−0.02	−0.01	−0.05
	(0.03)	(0.03)	(0.12)
Quality	0.59	.85	0.83
	(0.93)	(0.95)	(0.99)
Senator-nominee ideological distance	−5.70*	−5.70*	−5.70*
	(0.81)	(0.82)	(0.82)
Same party	2.40*	−0.50	−0.45
	(0.66)	(1.20)	(1.30)
Constant	−12.00*	−6.60*	−4.00
	(2.20)	(3.20)	(7.90)
Observations	1,291	1,291	1,291
Log Likelihood	−209	−207	−206
Akaike Inf. Crit.	435	431	433

party (compared to the combined support of Independents and supporters in the opposition party). The coefficient is positive and significant, revealing evidence of a sizable "partisan constituency effect." Finally, Model (3) adds "Supporters who are Independents," which separates out the opinion of Independents and supporters in the opposition party. Again the coefficient on "Supporters in senator's party" is positive and significant.

What is the substantive impact of co-partisan representation? To answer this, we perform a congruence analysis, measuring how often a senator's vote on a nominee matched the preferred vote of the median voter among opinion holders in his state, and how often confirmation votes matched the preferred vote of the median voter within the senator's own party, as well as that of the opposition party. We present this information in the top part of Figure 11.6 (with 95% confidence intervals depicted by the horizontal line around each estimate). We find congruence with the median voter of the entire state 73% of the time. This statistic, however, obscures a big difference in terms of partisan representation: majorities among opinion holders in the senator's own party saw their senator vote the way they preferred 90% of the time, whereas those in the opposing party saw their senator vote the preferred way only 46% of the time.

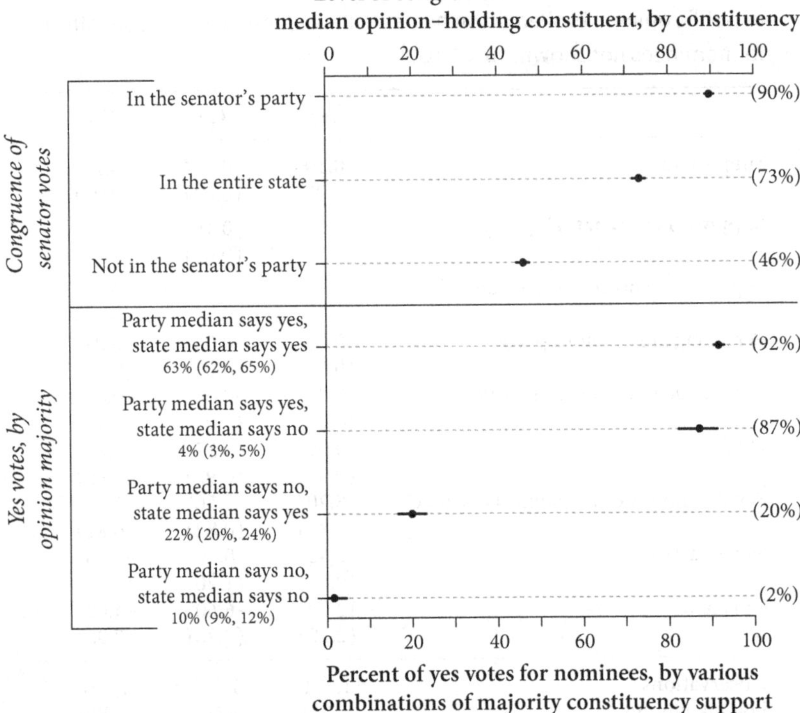

Fig. 11.6 Congruence in roll call voting on Supreme Court nominees and percent of yes votes by opinion majority across constituencies. In the top part of the graph, each point depicts the level of congruence with the median voter (among opinion holders) in the respective groups, while the numbers in parentheses denote the actual values. Horizontal lines depict 95% confidence intervals. The bottom part of the graph depicts the percent of yes votes for all the nominees according to which constituencies favor confirmation. The percentages under the labels in this part of the graph depict the proportion of observations that fall into each category.

How does a senator weigh competing constituencies when those constituencies are in conflict? Before turning to the overall evidence, consider a high-profile example of a senator who was cross-pressured: the case of Senator Susan Collins, a Republican from Maine, with respect to her vote to confirm Brett Kavanaugh in 2018. Collins faced intense pressure from both sides, given the importance of Kavanaugh's confirmation (he would replace the exiting median justice, Anthony Kennedy) and its potential impact on abortion rights, which Collins generally supported. According to the MRP estimates, 88% of Republicans in Maine supported Kavanaugh's confirmation, in line with the overall high levels of co-partisan support seen in Figure 11.5. However, opinion among Independents was split exactly 50-50 (only 11% of Maine Democrats supported Kavanaugh). With her reelection campaign imminent in 2020, Collins faced two unappealing paths: vote against Kavanaugh and face a near certain primary challenge from her right, or vote for the nominee and face a difficult general election. In the end, Collins chose the latter path. As events transpired, Collins chose wisely from an electoral standpoint. She breezed through the primary, then eked out a victory in the general election (by eight points rather than her customary margin of 20 to 30 points). Despite Collins' assurances at the time that Kavanaugh believed in *stare decisis* and would uphold *Roe v. Wade*, Kavanaugh in fact voted to overturn it in 2022. Collins then justified her pro-Kavanaugh vote to angry Mainers, saying that the nominee misled her during their 2018 pre-confirmation discussions.[41] She did not justify it as a purely rational electoral calculation in the face of a compound lottery.

Returning to the data, how do senators typically behave when they are cross-pressured like Collins was? The lower part of Figure 11.6 depicts the percent of yes votes for all nominees, according to which constituencies favored confirmation. The percentages under the labels of the left side of the graph depict the proportion of observations that occurred in each category along with the confidence intervals around that proportion. A change in whether the party median says yes versus no is far more predictive of a senator's vote than a change in whether the state median says yes versus no. Both the state median and party median favored confirmation around 63% of the time. When that happened, a senator voted yes 92% of the time. The party median favored confirmation and the state median did *not* around 4% of the time—when that rare combination happened, the percentage of confirmation votes (87%) was somewhat lower than when both constituencies agreed. That is, flipping the median voter in the state but keeping the in-party median voter constant only slightly changed the probability of a yes vote. Conversely, the state median favored confirmation in opposition to the party median 22% of the time. When that combination occurred, a yes vote followed only 20% of the time. Finally, in 10% of cases neither median favored confirmation; if so, yes votes occurred a rare 2% of the time. In short, a nominee seeking a senator's vote should much rather have the support of the median voter in the senator's party than that of the median voter in the state.

As a further comparison, suppose two baseline scenarios in which either the support of the median voter is decisive for a senator or that of the party median voter is decisive for a senator. Figure 11.7 depicts the estimated number of yes votes under these two scenarios (setting aside uncertainty), compared to the actual number of votes that each nominee received.

Figure 11.7 shows that the fate of some nominees would not vary much if they moved between "Median Voter World" and "Party Median Voter World." (The nominees are ordered in terms of the absolute value of the difference in the predicted vote outcomes between these two worlds.)

Interestingly, Kavanaugh's vote total perfectly matched both worlds; this is in part due to the fact that the nominee was sufficiently unpopular among the overall state medians in a number of states that both the co-partisan and overall opinion favored rejection for many Democratic senators. On the other hand, large gaps between the two scenarios exist for several nominees. For example, the actual vote on Barrett

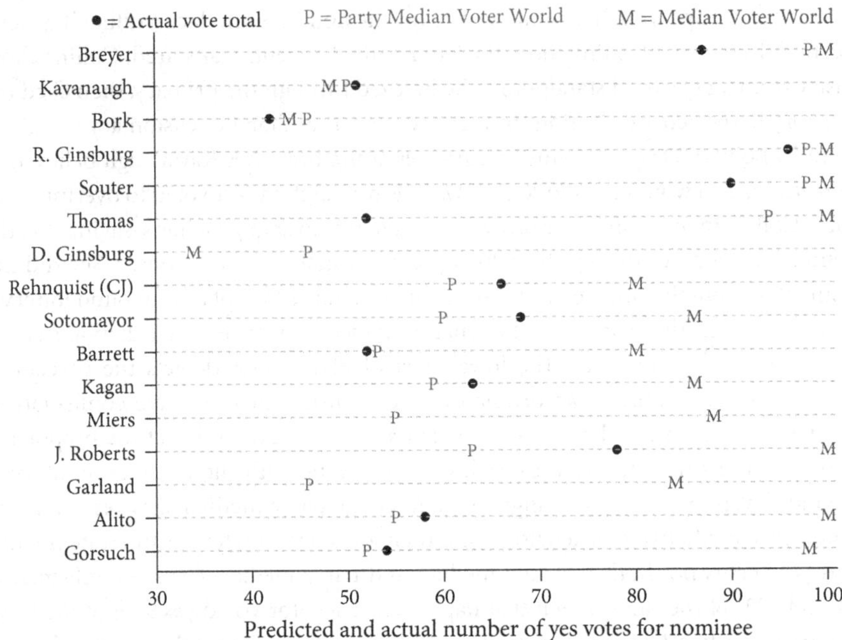

Fig. 11.7 Votes for nominees in Median Voter World and in Party Median Voter World. Each point depicts the actual number of votes each nominee received. Compared to this are the number of votes each nominee would have received if the median voter in each state (among opinion holders) controlled the senator's vote as well as the number of votes that each nominee would have received if the median voter in the senator's party controlled the senator's vote. D. Ginsburg, Miers, and Garland did not receive a floor vote, and hence do not have actual vote totals. The nominees are ordered in increasing difference between Median Voter World and Party Median Voter World.

resembled that in the "Party Median Voter World," because she was sufficiently popular among median constituencies to create a split among Democratic senators (who uniformly voted against her). Of the 13 nominees with votes, eight show strong evidence of party influence; one is a tie (Roberts); and four are ambiguous given similarities between the scenarios. Thomas is an outlier. In the Thomas case, both scenarios show easy confirmation. Yet, he was only narrowly confirmed. In the case of Miers, her vote total in the "Party Median Voter World" would have fallen below the filibuster threshold. But the vote total would have exceeded it with many votes to spare in the "Median Voter World." Thus, the tendency to follow the party median, even when the outcome for the nominee remains unchanged, drastically increases polarization in the confirmation process, by increasing the no votes of the opposition party.

In summary, in the modern period senators' confirmation votes closely aligned with public opinion. Most of the time, the state median and the party median agreed on the preferred vote, so senators faced no cross-pressure. However, in the cases where opinion diverged across the two constituencies, senators typically heeded the views of co-partisans. This empirical regularity raises pointed normative questions about representation. But in terms of explaining senatorial voting on nominees, the evidence is completely consistent with a story in which senators worry deeply about being "primaried" over Supreme Court nominations, and vote accordingly. Apparently, senators vote in the shadow of accountability—but accountability to co-partisans, not the median voter in their state.

11.6 Conclusion

In this chapter we presented a series of empirical studies designed to illuminate the electoral connection behind Senate voting on Supreme Court nominees. Collectively, the three investigations close the "circle of democratic accountability" in modern nomination politics. First, whereas in the past many nominations were sleepy affairs with low visibility, today every nomination is at least somewhat visible, and many (such as those of Clarence Thomas and Brett Kavanaugh) are extraordinarily prominent, drawing extensive media coverage and high levels of public attention. Second, the evidence from the Sotomayor and Kagan nominations (which, notably, were among the more routine confirmation fights of the twenty-first century) indicates that constituents perceive high-visibility roll call votes on Supreme Court nominees, votes which are easy to understand. Constituents then reward or punish senators for their votes. Finally, the third investigation demonstrated that senators' cast roll call votes on Supreme Court nominees in accord with constituent preferences—but with bias, as only the preferences of co-partisans count. Some loose ends remain. We cannot definitely prove that monitoring and response from engaged co-partisans cause this representation bias (though it seems likely). But whatever the micro-level mechanism, these empirical patterns have important implications for confirmation battles going forward.

What are those implications? Recall our discussion of Figure 8.4 on page 192. As shown in the figure, roll call votes on nominees are now essentially party-line affairs. By contrast, as late as the 1990s, senators displayed broad bipartisan agreement on several nominees (Souter, Ruth Bader Ginsburg, and Breyer, in particular). We argue that consensus voting, which aligns with most roll call votes in the mid-twentieth century, displayed a "safety in numbers" logic. Consensus voting offered senators readily explainable votes, should "latent publics" ever have materialized after these relatively obscure decisions.

Consensus voting broke down in the confirmation fights of the new century. As we noted in Chapter 8, John Roberts (in 2005) was the last nominee to receive a substantial number of yea votes from the out-party. Since then, no nominee has received even double-digit yea votes from the opposition party. At the same time, we showed in Chapter 7 that public opinion on Supreme Court nominees polarized dramatically by party, in contrast to earlier eras. Figure 11.5 in this chapter shows the same change in a different way. Earlier nominations display large overlap in the distribution of public opinion across party identification at the state-party level. In contrast, in the new century public opinion by party identification involves complete separation.

We argue that this pattern reflected the confluence of two distinct processes. On the one hand, liberal and conservative voters cleanly sorted themselves into the two parties. On the other, interest groups mobilized around nominations, greatly increasing their visibility to citizens, especially engaged partisans. The result was an easily understood theater of ideological conflict, played out before a captivated audience of partisan spectators. Senators' co-partisans were more than willing to hold senators accountable for their confirmation votes, and senators responded rationally to the resulting incentives. The result was party-line voting.

If this story is correct—and of course, the "if" is critical!—all the changes point in the direction of continued party-line voting in the future. A return to bipartisan roll call votes could occur, if presidents selected moderate nominees who engender less polarized evaluations in the public (we discussed this point in Chapter 10). Bipartisan votes might also transpire if interest groups declined to mobilize at every nomination, rather than trumpeting "We stand at Armageddon and we battle for the Lord!"[42] A degree of bipartisan "disarmament" might occur if Supreme Court nominations presented lower stakes than at present (we discuss reforms that might have this effect in Chapters 13 and 14). Given the realities of confirmation politics today, however, none of these possibilities seem very likely.

PART III

HOW IT MATTERS, AND WHAT THE FUTURE HOLDS

12
New Politics, New Justices, New Policies
The Courts That Politics Made

In Part I of the book we showed that the politics of Supreme Court appointments underwent a revolution between 1930 and 2020. In Part II we analyzed why the revolution took place. But we have yet to address two fundamental questions: First, *what difference did it make?* Second, *what do the current politics of appointments foretell for the future of the court*? We pursue these questions in Part III of the book. In this chapter, we begin by looking backwards, and ask how the changes in appointment politics affected the Supreme Court, the justices themselves, and the policies they made.

We proceed in five stages. First, we document how the new politics of Supreme Court appointments led to a *partisan sort* on the court: Republican justices increasingly were conservatives and Democratic justices increasingly liberals, to an extent that earlier appointees were not.[1] In fact, from the 1930s to the 1970s—and especially in the 1940s and 1950s—Republican and Democratic justices spanned the ideological spectrum, as measured by their voting behavior. But later partisan sorting led to crisp distinctions. Today, Republican and Democratic justices sort perfectly by ideology in their policy-making behavior; there is no overlap across party lines.

Second, in Section 12.3, we analyze the origins of the judicial partisan sort. We present indirect evidence that the sort was a direct consequence of the changes in presidential selection processes and goals documented in Chapters 3 and 4 and explained in Chapter 9—in particular, presidents' interest in choosing justices with greater *ex ante* policy reliability.

Third, the new politics of Supreme Court nominations also featured explicit litmus tests about specific policies, particularly for Republican nominees (as discussed in Chapter 2). In Section 12.4, we examine whether policy litmus tests work, specifically for the issues of abortion and law-and-order, for which the data is most abundant. While some methodological caveats are necessary, our analyses using two relatively strong research designs strongly suggest that policy litmus tests do indeed work. Justices who were selected under litmus tests are more likely to vote in a manner consistent with the test, compared to justices who were not.

Fourth, the judicial partisan sort affected not just the voting of individual justices but the overall makeup of the court as a whole—that is, its *ideological structure*—as we show in Section 12.5. To frame this analysis, we discuss two contending theories of judicial policy making on collegial courts. We then examine the measures

Making the Supreme Court: The Politics of Appointments, 1930–2020. Charles M. Cameron and Jonathan P. Kastellec, Oxford University Press. © Oxford University Press 2023. DOI: 10.1093/oso/9780197680544.003.0012

of ideological structure suggested by those theories. Beginning in 1970, the ideological location of the median justice moved gradually to the right, as Republican presidents made the majority of appointments to the court. In addition, throughout the 2000s and 2010s the court featured two distinct left and right ideological blocs, with a depleted center, which we call a *bimodal wing structure*. As of 2022, President Trump's appointments shifted the court to one firmly dominated by conservatives.

Finally, we examine how the changing ideological structure of the court affected Supreme Court policy. Relying on an innovative effort by Clark and Lauderdale (2010) to place majority opinions on a left-right scale, we review one policy area, search-and-seizure law. The results are consistent with both contemporary social science theory and qualitative histories of doctrine: a large liberal bloc increases the likelihood of liberal case dispositions and left-leaning majority opinions; a large conservative bloc does the opposite. Accordingly, the changing make-up of the court mattered greatly for Supreme Court policy, leading to more conservative outcomes and legal policy over time.

In sum, the impulses that drove activists and interest groups to appointment politics were well founded. The pressure they exerted on presidents led to the selection of more reliable justices, as policy litmus tests appear to have worked. In addition, the ideological distribution of the newly reliable justices altered the ideological structure of the court, which in turn changed the ideological distribution of the judicial policies they created (at least where we can measure them). In a nutshell: the new politics of Supreme Court nominations brought new types of justices, who made new courts, which then enacted new policies in a predictable and understandable way.

12.2 The Judicial Partisan Sort

In Chapter 4, we used several nominee ideology measures to document an increasingly sharp division between Democratic and Republican nominees, starting around 1970. These measures, however, all reflected perceived or imputed ideology *at the time of the nomination*. While nominee ideology is important, the key question for consequences is whether the partisanship of nominees translates into actual policy-making behavior on the court—recall the Republican motto of "No more Souters!" after Justice David Souter's policy choices frequently dismayed conservatives.

To address this issue, we examine the "judicial partisan sort," or the extent to which partisanship of the justices (based on their appointing presidents) overlaps with ideology (in terms of justices' voting behavior). More precisely, we can use an ideological scaling procedure (discussed in detail shortly) to array the justices from left to right on a sensible ideological scale. If partisanship and ideology go hand-in-hand, the justices on the left will tend to be Democratic appointees and the justices on the right will tend to be Republican appointees. But if ideology and partisanship are only loosely connected to voting behavior, the justices will be "jumbled"—some

Republicans will lie on the left and some Democrats on the right and some of both in the center.

To understand the outputs of the scaling procedure we used, some background on how the Supreme Court operates as a voting body is useful. Broadly speaking, for a given case, the court votes at three separate stages: (1) agenda setting, (2) case disposition, and (3) policy determination.

First, the court has a "discretionary docket"—it chooses which cases to hear from among the thousands appealed to it each year, allowing the court to set its own agenda. The justices select cases via voting (i.e. they cast *certiorari* votes). In theory, one could construct ideological scores for each justice based on their agenda-setting votes, but no such scale is in common use.[2]

Second, case disposition refers to which of the two sides prevails in the litigation. Above all else, courts resolve legal disputes between litigants, so every case must be definitively resolved by creating a winner and a loser. Again, the justices create this resolution by voting. These dispositional votes (sometimes called the outcome or judgment) often appear in press coverage of high-profile cases; a 5-4 vote, for example, means that five justices voted in favor of one litigant and four voted in favor of the other.[3]

Finally, policy determination differs from case disposition. Justices vote not only on the outcome (disposition) of the case, but also its rationale (policy). Unlike most courts, the Supreme Court's main job is not (simply) to resolve legal disputes but to create or modify legal policy. To do so, the justices in the majority dispositional coalition bargain among themselves over the rationale for the outcome; a designated opinion author offers a candidate majority opinion; and the justices vote by endorsing all, part or none of that opinion.[4] In other words, judicial policy is made through the final written judicial opinions, which are then announced and published. In theory, one could scale the justices using not just the dispositional votes but also the endorsement votes—that is, examining which justices join which opinions—to create ideology scores for policy determination, but to our knowledge no such scores currently exist.

Thus, political scientists have focused their scaling efforts almost exclusively on dispositional votes—we use those scores to study the judicial partisan sort.[5] In addition, we can apply several scales to policy making and the judicial partisan sort, but all correlate with one another and lead to the same conclusion. Accordingly, in this section we use the well-known "Martin-Quinn" (MQ) scores of judicial ideology, and present analyses using other scaling procedures in the Appendix.[6] While the statistical assumptions that underly the MQ scores differ somewhat from those for NOMINATE scores, they share the characteristic that under specific maintained assumptions about voting choices, MQ scores can be interpreted as similar to the "ideal points" in the standard spatial theory of voting.[7] As with NOMINATE, higher MQ scores are associated with more conservative voting patterns, and lower scores with more liberal voting. The scores are available for every justice who served beginning in the 1937 term—the scores are based on voting up to the 2019 term (which ended in June 2020).[8]

12.2.1 Detecting the Judicial Partisan Sort

Using these scores, Figure 12.1 examines the degree of partisan sorting on the court by decade from the 1930s through the 2010s.[9] In each panel in the figure, the justices who served in that decade are arranged from most liberal to most conservative, based on their average MQ scores in a given decade. That average is indicated by the

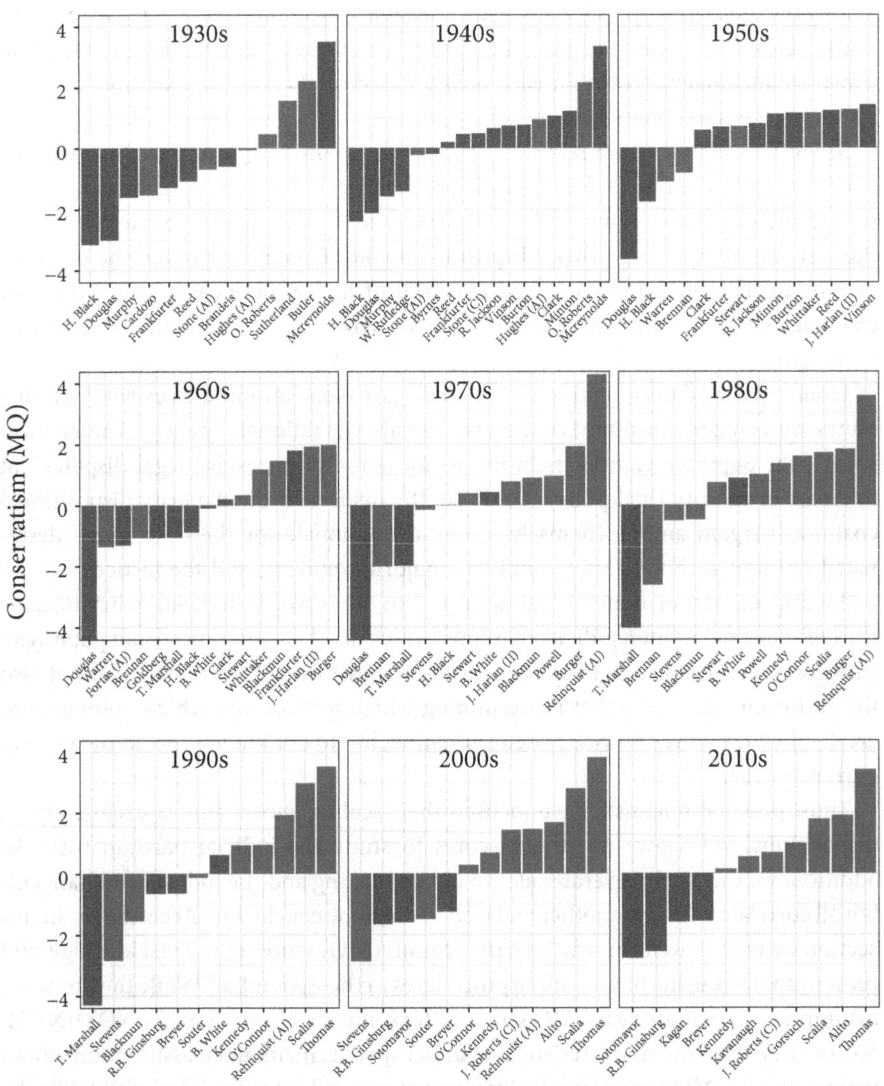

Fig. 12.1 MQ scores by justice, by decade, 1930–2020. For each panel, the bars depict the average MQ score of justices who served in that decade. The justices are sorted from most liberal to most conservative, with Democratic-appointed justices depicted with blue bars and Republican appointees with red bars.

Table 12.1 Misclassification scores and non-sorted justices by decade, based on Martin-Quinn scores. The tables list justices whose average voting does not accord with their party of appointing president.

Decade	Percent misclassified	Mis-sorted Democratic justices	Mis-sorted Republican justices
1930s	31	McReynolds	Cardozo, Hughes (AJ), Stone (AJ)
1940s	59	Burton, Clark, Frankfurter, McReynolds, Minton, Jackson, Reed, Stone (CJ), Vinson	Stone (AJ)
1950s	64	Burton, Clark, Frankfurter, Minton, Jackson, Reed, Vinson	Brennan, Warren
1960s	27	Clark, Frankfurter	Brennan, Warren
1970s	25	White	Brennan, Warren, Stevens
1980s	33	White	Blackmun, Brennan, Stevens
1990s	33	White	Blackmun, Souter, Stevens
2000s	17	—	Souter, Stevens
2010s	0	—	—

height of a justice's bar—positive scores indicate a propensity for conservative case dispositions, negative scores a propensity for liberal case dispositions. The 0 mark on the scale is a convenient baseline that corresponds to about a 50% chance of voting conservatively on case dispositions. The color of the bars indicates the party of the appointing president, red for Republicans and blue for Democrats.[10] If partisanship and ideology go together, the bars will separate cleanly by color, with blue bars on the left and red bars on the right.

Table 12.1 summarizes the information displayed in Figure 12.1 and presents a simple "misclassification" score for each decade. We calculated each justice's average MQ score by decade, classifying those with average scores greater than 0 as conservative and those with average scores less than 0 as liberal. We code a justice as misclassified if they were classified "liberal" and were appointed by a Republican president or if they were classified "conservative" and appointed by a Democratic president. The misclassification rate is the percentage of misclassified justices per decade. The table also identifies the mis-sorted justices, for each decade.

If we consider Figure 12.1 and Table 12.1 together, the emergence of the partisan sort over time is quite clear. Consider the 1930s, during which President Roosevelt and conservative justices on the court battled over the constitutionality of the New Deal. Figure 12.1 suggests that the justices in this decade were actually relatively well sorted. The misclassification score for the decade is 31%. Three justices stand out as non-sorted: the liberal Cardozo and moderately liberal Stone, both of whom had been appointed by Republican presidents (Hoover and Coolidge, respectively), and the arch-conservative Southern Democrat James McReynolds, who was appointed by Woodrow Wilson, a Democrat.

But the 1940s and 1950s were different. As we discussed in Chapter 3, once the Supreme Court accepted the New Deal, Presidents Roosevelt and Truman felt free to treat appointments as opportunities for patronage, cronyism, political reward, and tactical advantage. President Eisenhower followed that path with his appointments of Warren and Brennan. These appointments led to a series of poorly sorted courts, as shown in Figure 12.1. In the 1940s, a large bloc of moderately conservative Democrats stands out. In the 1950s, this mis-sorted bloc remained intact, and was then joined by the mis-sorted Republican appointees, Warren and Brennan. Overall, the misclassification score was 59% in the 1940s and an amazing 64% in the 1950s. Ideology and party simply did not go hand-in-hand.

As we discussed in Chapters 4 and 9, presidents increasingly took selection more seriously, prioritizing ideological screening over cronyism or political benefits that were unrelated to the court itself (as in Eisenhower's selection of Warren). The result, as seen in the Figure 12.1 panels for the 1960s to 1990s, was something of a return to the 1930s in terms of the partisan sort, with misclassification scores between 25% and 33%. The mis-sorted justices are no surprise: Warren, Brennan, Blackmun, Stevens, and Souter. Indeed, the misclassification rate fell every decade after the 1980s. The drop to 17% in the 2000s is notable, and the 2000s panel in Figure 12.1 reveals a well-sorted court, with only two mis-sorted standouts: Stevens and Souter.

The decades-long effort by presidents to build efficient screening procedures and carefully select candidates finally produced a perfectly sorted court in the 2010s. As shown in Figure 12.1, in that decade, Republican justices were all conservatives, and Democratic justices were all liberals. Presidents Trump's three appointments (Gorsuch, Kavanaugh, and Barrett) and President Biden's first appointment (Jackson) all solidified a perfectly sorted court, the implications of which we discuss below and in Chapter 13.

To be sure, the justices are not partisan robots, and individual justices will sometimes vote in unexpected ways that deviate from what the majority of their fellow liberals or conservatives do. At the same time, the current partisan differences are deep and unprecedented in the post-Civil War era. For the first time, the Supreme Court now clearly features two ideologically distinct blocs perfectly aligned with the partisan divisions on the court.[11]

12.3 What Caused the Judicial Partisan Sort?

To explain the emergence of the partisan sort, we return to the idea of policy reliability discussed in Chapter 9—the expectation that a confirmed nominee will advance the president's policy agenda on the court. There, we hypothesized that more reliable nominees will display less deviation from the president's preferences. But, we did not examine whether the justices we scored as more reliable, based on their background and career experience, actually behaved differently on the court relative to justices we rated as less reliable.

We now investigate the relationship between *ex ante* reliability, as measured by the experience and background of nominees, and *ex post* performance, as measured by justices' voting behavior once on the court. In particular, we examine whether more reliable justices vote more congruently with the preferences of their appointing president. If we can show this, then the increased emphasis on reliability likely explains the partisan sort, since it means that presidents no longer appoint justices whose voting behavior creates the mis-sorted court that we saw in earlier decades.

12.3.1 Reliability Revisited

In Chapter 9 we measured *ex ante* reliability by constructing an index for every nominee, the Policy Reliability Index (PRI), that reflects the experience and professional background of each nominee. We defined the PRI as $PRI = \sum_i \rho_i$, where ρ_i indicates the four attributes we view as conducive to policy reliability: service as a federal judge, service as an executive branch lawyer, service as a law professor, and graduation from a top law school. As we show in the Appendix, the measure displays considerable face validity. In particular, "politicos" like Hugo Black and James Byrnes score low on the measure, while nominees with extensive judicial and executive branch experience like John Roberts and Brett Kavanaugh score highest.

12.3.2 Justice-President Policy Congruence

Next, we measure congruence between presidential policies and judicial votes. To do so, we switch to the ideal points created by Michael Bailey (2007). The advantage of the Bailey scores is that they place justices and presidents (as well as members of Congress) on the same scale. To accomplish this, Bailey employs inter-institutional bridging observations—for example, a presidential statement agreeing with or criticizing a Supreme Court decision is treated like a justice's dispositional vote in the case. In a clever study, Matthew Hitt (2013) used this joint scaling to measure the alignment of a justice's actual voting behavior and the expressed policy positions of the appointing president on relevant bills and cases. We follow Hitt in using the Bailey Scores to measure president-justice congruence.

To measure congruence, we match available justices with their appointing president over the period for which Bailey scores are available: 1951 to 2020. The ideal points for justices vary by terms, and so the data for justices whose tenure began before 1951 are truncated.[12] The ideal points of presidents, by contrast, are static. To measure congruence, we calculate the absolute value of the appointing president's ideal point minus the ideal point of each justice, for each year. We then invert these scores so that higher scores mean more congruence (the maximum value of this measure is zero, which means perfect congruence).

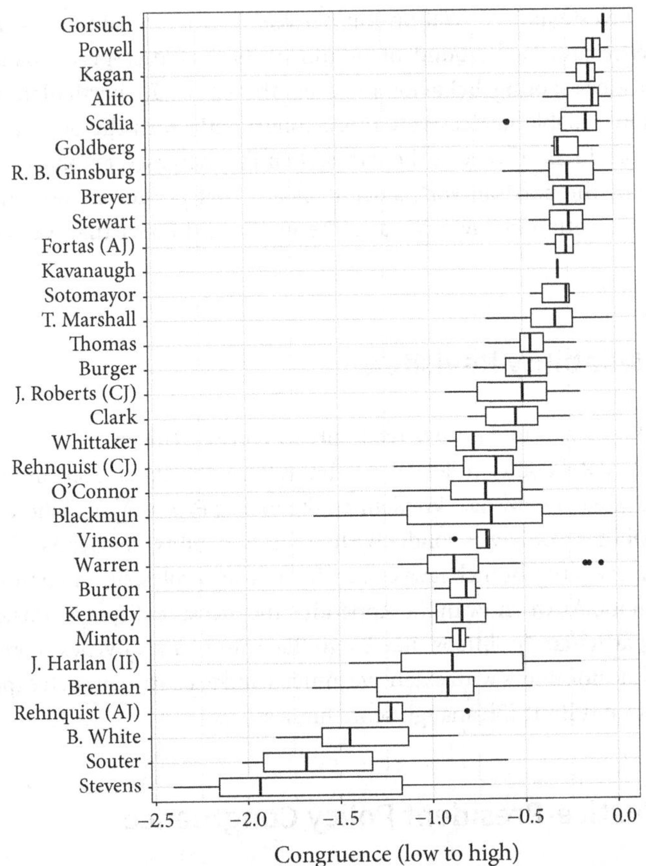

Fig. 12.2 Justice-president congruence, based on Bailey scores, 1951–2019. For each justice, the graph shows a box-and-whisker plot that depicts the distribution of congruence across their tenure. The justices are ordered from most congruent (top) to least (bottom).

Figure 12.2 presents a box-and-whisker plot that shows the distribution of congruence for each justice across their tenure on the court; the degree of variance here, of course, is affected in part by how many terms a justice appears. The plot shows fairly wide variation in congruence.

12.3.3 Congruence and Reliability Together

In his innovative study, Hitt found that justices' having either federal judicial experience or executive branch experience is correlated with higher ideological congruence with their appointing presidents.[13] These kinds of experience are folded into our PRI measure. More broadly, we can directly investigate how well higher reliability, as captured by PRI, translates into higher ideological congruence.

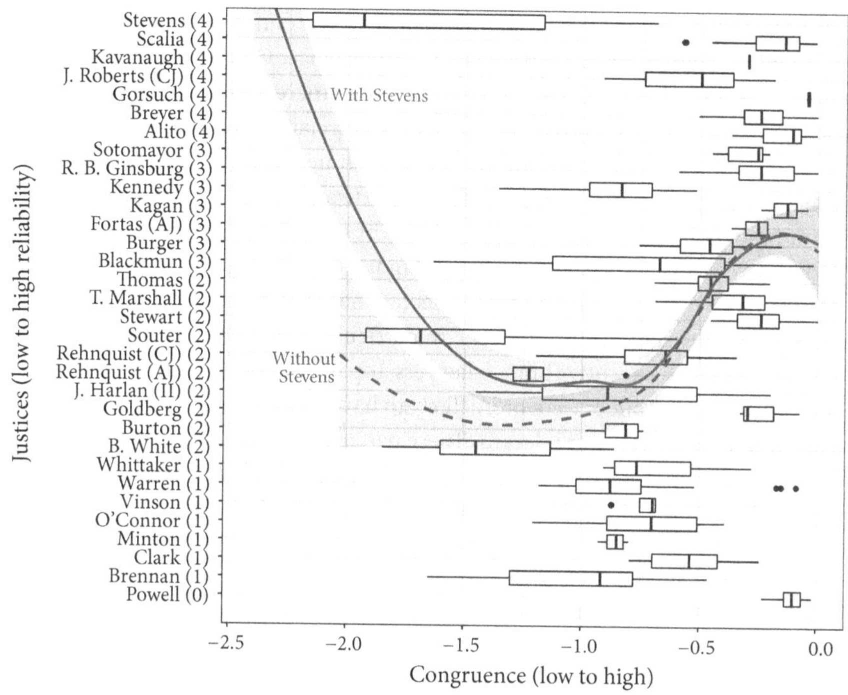

Fig. 12.3 Policy reliability and justice-president congruence, based on Bailey scores, 1951–2019.

Figure 12.3 shows the descriptive connection between the reliability index and nominee-president congruence. The vertical axis sorts justices from higher to lower reliability, with the number in parentheses indicating their score on the PRI index. For each justice, we display a box-and-whisker plot that shows the distribution of that justice's ideal points across their tenure in the data. The purple loess line depicts the general trend across the justices. If PRI accurately predicts future voting behavior, justices who tend to score higher on reliability should also tend to be more congruent with their appointing president. Instead, the solid loess in Figure 12.3 portrays a decidedly non-monotonic relationship between the two.

However, close inspection of the plot reveals that the negative slope in the left half of the graph is driven almost entirely by Justice John Paul Stevens. Stevens scores perfectly on the PRI and thus appears at the top of the vertical axis, but his voting record was quite incongruent with President Ford's ideal point, as Stevens voted increasingly more liberally over his time on the court.[14] The green loess in Figure 12.3 excludes Justice Stevens. While considerable heterogeneity in the data still remains without him, a positive relationship exists between *ex ante* reliability and policy congruence, particularly in the right half of the plot, where most of the data falls (from −1 to 0 on the congruence scale). Note here that the justices toward the top of the scale cluster toward maximum congruence (in the top-right corner).

The measure of reliability is certainly correlated with unobservable characteristics that might also predict nominee-president congruence. Given this, we cannot conclude with certainty that increased reliability caused increased congruence, and hence the partisan sort. Another possibility is that the correlation could be an artifact of the pool of nominees becoming more reliable over time. Suppose that presidents randomly selected from the pool of potential co-partisan nominees. If so, and if the pool became more reliable over time, we would then observe greater congruence over time.

However, recall from Chapter 4—see Figure 4.5 on page 94—that we showed how the eventual nominees presidents selected in recent decades were systematically different from the short-list candidates. In particular, the nominees were more likely to be federal judges, executive branch lawyers, top-law school graduates, and law professors; thus, the nominees were more likely to have all these types of experience than the candidates who were not selected. These patterns strongly suggest that presidents were not randomly selecting candidates from the pool of potential nominees, but instead deliberately searched for and selected more reliable nominees.

12.4 The Impact of Litmus Tests

While the relationship between reliability and voting on the court is informative, litmus tests provide an even cleaner way to show how presidents' search for particular types of justices produced the sort.

As we discussed in Chapter 2, the 1984 Republic party platform proclaimed policy litmus tests for Supreme Court appointees in four areas: abortion, family values, law and order, and overall conservatism. Over the next four years, President Reagan named two new justices (Scalia and Kennedy), and elevated Rehnquist to chief justice. In selecting these justices, did the Reagan Justice Department take the litmus tests seriously? In other words, did they meticulously screen appointees in terms of these specific criteria? If so, one would expect the three appointees actually to vote in accordance with the litmus tests. In this section, we present systematic evidence on the conformity of appointees to the policy demands of the appointing party.[15]

Before turning to the tests, we should clarify the underlying logic. Like our argument with respect to reliability, the idea is *not* that a litmus test exercises an independent force on a justice's voting behavior. Justices have life tenure, and shouldn't care about the motivations or incentives of the presidents who appointed them. Rather, a litmus test is a treatment applied to a *president*. Powerful groups press specific policy demands on presidents, who then use a litmus test in selecting justices to meet those demands. The posited causal effect—the president selects a justice with different policy commitments than would be the case if the litmus tests did not exist—is then revealed in the voting behavior of justices selected by treated presidents compared to those selected by non-treated presidents.

Nonetheless, as a convenient short-hand, we define a *litmus justice* as one who was appointed by a president committed to a particular policy test. For example, Justice

Powell, appointed by Richard Nixon in 1973, was a law-and-order litmus justice but not an abortion litmus justice, because in 1972 the Republican platform committed Nixon to a law-and-order litmus test but not an abortion test. Conversely, Justices Roberts and Alito, both nominated by George W. Bush in 2005, were abortion litmus justices but not law-and-order litmus justices.

12.4.1 Data

Detecting the effects of a litmus test on justice voting requires rather stringent data. First, the court must have heard a sufficient number of cases in the litmus area, in order to enable statistical analysis of votes in such cases. Second, both litmus and non-litmus justices must have cast relatively many votes on the cases, and preferably in the same cases.

Recall Figure 2.2 from Chapter 2, which showed the universe of litmus tests issued in the party platforms between 1928 and 2020. Two of these areas satisfy both criteria needed here.[16] The first is abortion, the most frequent litmus test; the second is law and order, which actually constitutes the first ever litmus test, announced by Richard Nixon and the Republican party in 1968 and 1972.[17]

For every justice, we identified whether they were appointed under an abortion test or under a law-and-order litmus test. We coded the critical variable, *litmus justice*, slightly differently for the two litmus tests. Only Republican presidents used the law-and-order litmus test, which always called for justices who would vote conservatively in criminal justice cases. Accordingly, in such cases, *litmus justice* takes the value of 1 whenever a justice was appointed under the law-and-order litmus test, and zero otherwise. In contrast, both parties have applied abortion litmus tests—but in the opposite directions. Republican litmus tests call for pro-life justices to vote in a pro-life direction, while Democratic litmus tests call for pro-choice justices to vote in a pro-choice direction. Accordingly, in abortion cases, we code *litmus justice* as 1 for a Republican justice appointed under a litmus test, -1 for a Democratic justice so appointed, and 0 otherwise (that is, for all justices not appointed under abortion litmus tests). This operationalization allows us to include both Democratic and Republican justices in a single regression framework.

Table 12.2 shows the specific justices that were appointed under one or both of the abortion and law-and-order litmus tests, along with the years in which they served on the court, and the party of their appointing presidents. Only two Democratic justices—Ginsburg and Breyer—were appointed under an abortion litmus test.[18]

We next associate cases with the appropriate litmus test. We do so using the issue/legal provision codes in the Supreme Court database, known colloquially as the "Spaeth database."[19] The unit of analysis is individual justices' votes. We code liberal dispositional votes as 0 and conservative dispositional votes as 1, based on the Spaeth coding of the underlying direction of the decision.

Table 12.2 List of justices who were subject to abortion and law-and-order litmus tests. The years show each justices' tenure on the court.

Justice	Party	Abortion	Law & Order
Burger	Republican		1969–1986
Blackmun	Republican		1970–1994
Powell	Republican		1971–1986
Rehnquist (AJ)	Republican		1971–1986
Stevens	Republican		1975–2010
O'Connor	Republican	1981–2005	1981–2005
Rehnquist (CJ)	Republican	1986–2005	1986–2005
Scalia	Republican	1986–2016	1986–2016
Kennedy	Republican	1987–2018	1987–2018
Souter	Republican	1990–2009	1990–2009
Thomas	Republican	1991–	1991–
Ginsburg	Democrat	1993–2020	
Breyer	Democrat	1994–	
J. Roberts	Republican	2005–	
Alito	Republican	2006–	
Gorsuch	Republican	2017–	2017–
Kavanaugh	Republican	2018–	2018–

Table 12.3 Litmus test logistic regressions. In each model, the dependent variable is whether the justice voted in the conservative direction, with standard errors clustered by justice. $^{*}p < .05$.

	(1)	(2)	(3)	(4)
Abortion litmus justice	1.42*	1.80*		
	(0.46)	(0.62)		
Law-and-order litmus justice			0.96*	0.91
			(0.39)	(0.56)
Intercept	−0.21	−0.42	−0.31	−0.26
	(0.40)	(0.48)	(0.30)	(0.50)
Which justices?	All	Republicans	All	Republicans
N	747	564	15,498	11,212

12.4.2 Descriptive Analysis

We begin with a simple descriptive analysis that helps illustrate the effectiveness of litmus tests. Table 12.3 presents four logistic regression models, in which the dependent variable is whether the justice voted in the conservative direction. We report two models for each litmus test; in each, we subset the data to focus on the respective issue areas. Because the first litmus test was not issued until 1968, we restrict our analyses to cases decided from the 1969 term on. For each model in this section, we cluster the standard errors by justice to account for non-independence across votes.[20]

Beginning with the abortion results, Models (1) and (2) include only abortion-related cases decided between the 1969 and 2019 terms (the court heard 59 abortion-related cases in this period). Model (1) presents a very simple test for the effectiveness of litmus tests. It includes just the indicator for *litmus justice* as a predictor—recall that this is coded such that higher values should make a justice more likely to vote in the conservative direction. Model (1) displays that pattern, as the coefficient on litmus justice is positive and statistically different from zero. (We will describe the substantive magnitude of this difference shortly.) Because most justices appointed under litmus tests were Republicans, Model (2) in Table 12.3 includes only Republican justices. The results are unchanged; indeed, the magnitude of the coefficients is even larger. All in all, the results are consistent with the hypothesis that abortion litmus tests "worked" in the sense that they led to the appointment of justices who were systematically less supportive of abortion.

Models (3) and (4) in Table 12.3 present parallel regression models for the law-and-order litmus test—overall, the court heard 1,546 such cases from 1960 to 2020. Again we see that justices appointed under a law-and-order litmus test voted more conservatively than those who were not. The coefficient on litmus justice is somewhat noisier in Model (4), which likely reflects the smaller sample size from restricting the analysis to Republican justices only.

To gauge the substantive magnitude of these differences, Figure 12.4 converts the relevant coefficients into predicted probabilities, using Model (1) in Table 12.3 for abortion and Model (4) for law and order—the latter model provides the cleanest comparison, given the absence of law and order litmus tests for Democratic justices. For each issue area, we calculate the predicted probability of voting conservatively based on whether or not a justice was appointed under a litmus test, along with 95% confidence intervals.[21]

Beginning with the abortion results, the probability of a Democratic justice appointed under a pro-choice litmus test voting conservatively is only about 19%. For justices not appointed under a litmus test, that percentage rises to about 45%. Finally, for Republican justices appointed under a pro-life litmus test, the probability of voting conservatively rises to 76%. These differences are obviously quite substantial.[22]

Turning to law and order, we only have two comparisons to make, because the law-and-order litmus test was applied only to Republican justices. But again the pattern is quite clear. For justices not appointed under that litmus test, the probability of voting conservatively is about 42%. This percentage rises to about 66% for Republicans appointed under the litmus test—again, a substantial difference.[23]

12.4.3 Two Stronger Research Designs

Although this simple descriptive analysis is suggestive, it falls short of convincingly demonstrating causality, because the regressions in Table 12.3 pool justices making decisions across many years and cases. In this subsection, we present two research

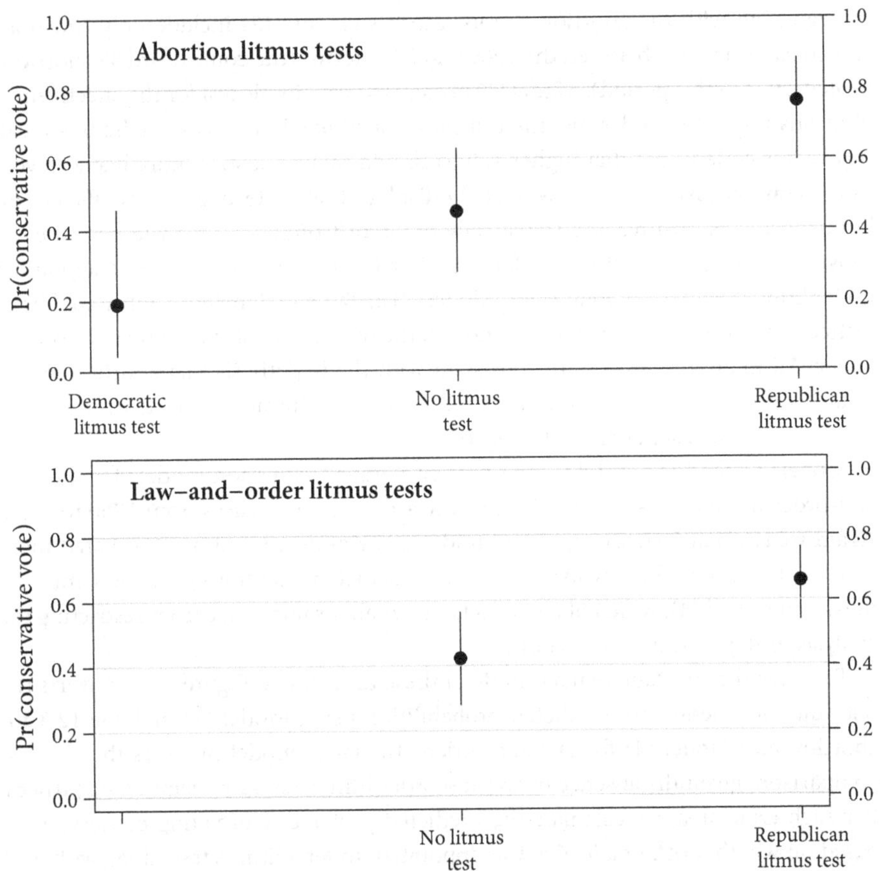

Fig. 12.4 Predicted probability of voting conservatively, by litmus test. Estimates and uncertainty based on Models (1) and (4) in Table 12.3. Vertical lines depict 95% confidence intervals.

designs that come closer to plausibly identifying the causal effect of litmus tests on justices' voting choices. Table 12.4 presents these models. For simplicity, we restrict the analysis to Republican justices.

The first design employs *case-level* fixed effects. These fixed effects account for a key source of confounding: because we examine a longer time period, both the court's membership and its agenda vary over that period, creating the possibility of omitted variable bias. Employing case-level fixed effects means that the identification of the litmus effect comes entirely from comparing litmus justices to non-litmus justices *in the same case*—neither membership nor agenda changes can affect this within-case variation. And, to the extent that certain case-level factors might induce spurious correlation between litmus tests and voting, the case-level fixed effects also account for those factors.

Table 12.4 Litmus test regressions. In each model, the dependent variable is whether the justice voted in the conservative direction, with standard errors clustered by justice. *$p < .05$.

	(1)	(2)	(3)	(4)
Abortion litmus justice	0.32* (0.08)		0.70* (0.24)	
Abortion case			−0.46 (0.32)	
Abortion case × justice			1.33* (0.47)	
Law-and-order litmus justice		0.26 (0.14)		0.62* (0.31)
Law-and-order case				0.03 (0.22)
Law-and-order case × justice				0.41 (0.26)
Intercept	0.26 (0.14)	0.49* (0.20)	0.16 (0.21)	−0.02 (0.21)
Case fixed effects	Yes	Yes	No	No
Model type	OLS	OLS	Logit	Logit
N	747	11,212	52,794	52,794

Models (1) and (2) in Table 12.4 present this analysis for abortion and law-and-order tests, respectively. Estimating such a large number of case fixed effects presents some computational hurdles, so we use OLS to estimate these models. Model (1) shows that even with the case-specific fixed effects, Republican justices who were appointed under a pro-life Republican litmus test were significantly more likely to vote in the conservative direction compared to those not appointed under an abortion test. Model (2) shows a similar positive effect in law-and-order cases, although the coefficient is estimated less precisely ($p = .09$). Still, given the demanding nature of this specification, this result provides supportive evidence for the effectiveness of law-and-order litmus tests.

A second strong research design would be a "difference-in-differences" design, combining same-unit before-and-after-treatment information with cross-unit treated/untreated information.[24] Unfortunately, such a design is impossible here, because justices are always either treated (i.e. selected by a president committed to a policy test) or untreated, so before-and-after-treatment behavior cannot be observed for the same justice. However, we can employ a "near" difference-in-differences design that, while weaker than a true difference-in-differences design, is still much stronger than the simple descriptive analysis. This approach compares how litmus justices voted in litmus area cases relative to non-litmus justices (as in the simple analysis) but also examines how both types of justices voted in *non-litmus cases*. The idea is to rule out the possibility that litmus Republican justices were somewhat more conservative than non-litmus Republican justices across the board; if so, then we would be picking up this general ideological effect and not an independent effect of the litmus tests. In other words, the causal effect of the litmus test is the *additional* amount of conservative voting beyond any baseline differences between litmus and non-litmus justices.

To implement this design, we use the following regression framework:

$$Pr(con.\ vote) = \text{logit}^{-1}(\beta_0 + \beta_1 * \text{litmus case} + \beta_2 * \text{litmus justice} + \beta_3[\text{litmus case} \times \text{litmus justice}])$$

Models (3) and (4) in Table 12.3 present these results for abortion and law-and-order litmus tests, respectively. We return to logit models, so as to generate sensible predicted probabilities. Because *litmus case* does not vary within a given case, we cannot employ case fixed effects in these models; instead we use term-level fixed effects. While the identification is not as tight compared to the models with case-level fixed effects, we still can leverage within-justice variation among justices who are broadly hearing the same set of cases in a given term.

Given the interaction term in Models (3) and (4), interpreting the coefficients is tricky. Fortunately, a graphical presentation clarifies the meaning of the results. For each model, we generated 1,000 simulations of each coefficient, and then simulated the average predicted probability of a conservative vote across every combination of litmus justice and litmus case, based on the underlying uncertainty in the parameters. Figure 12.5 depicts these estimates, along with 95% confidence intervals. For Republican litmus justices, the probability of voting conservatively in abortion cases is about 85%. For non-litmus justices, the equivalent probability drops to about 43%, a stunning difference of about 40 percentage points.

Of course, Republican justices appointed under a pro-life litmus test might also tend to vote more conservatively in all cases—not just abortion cases—compared to justices without the litmus test. The benefit of the specification in Table 12.4 is that we can benchmark the difference in abortion cases against all *other* cases. Figure 12.5A shows that abortion litmus justices indeed voted more conservatively in non-abortion cases than non-litmus justices (70% versus 54%). However, that difference is significantly smaller in magnitude—16 percentage points compared to 42. Employing the logic of a difference-in-differences design, the causal impact of the litmus test is estimated at (.85 – .43) – (.70 – .54) = .42 – .16 = 26 percentage points, a remarkably large effect. The difference between litmus and non-litmus justices in abortion cases is greater than the difference in non-abortion cases in 99% of the simulations (in other words, the 43 percentage point difference is statistically larger than the 16 percentage point difference).[25] The conclusion is again clear: the Republican Party's emphasis on appointing pro-life justices eventually paid substantial dividends.

The picture for law-and-order cases is similar, although again the differences are not quite as stark as with abortion. Republican justices appointed under a law-and-order litmus test voted conservatively in 74% of cases, compared to about 51% for non-litmus justices in such cases, or a 23 percentage point difference. For other types of cases, we see a 15-percentage point difference (64% compared to 49%).

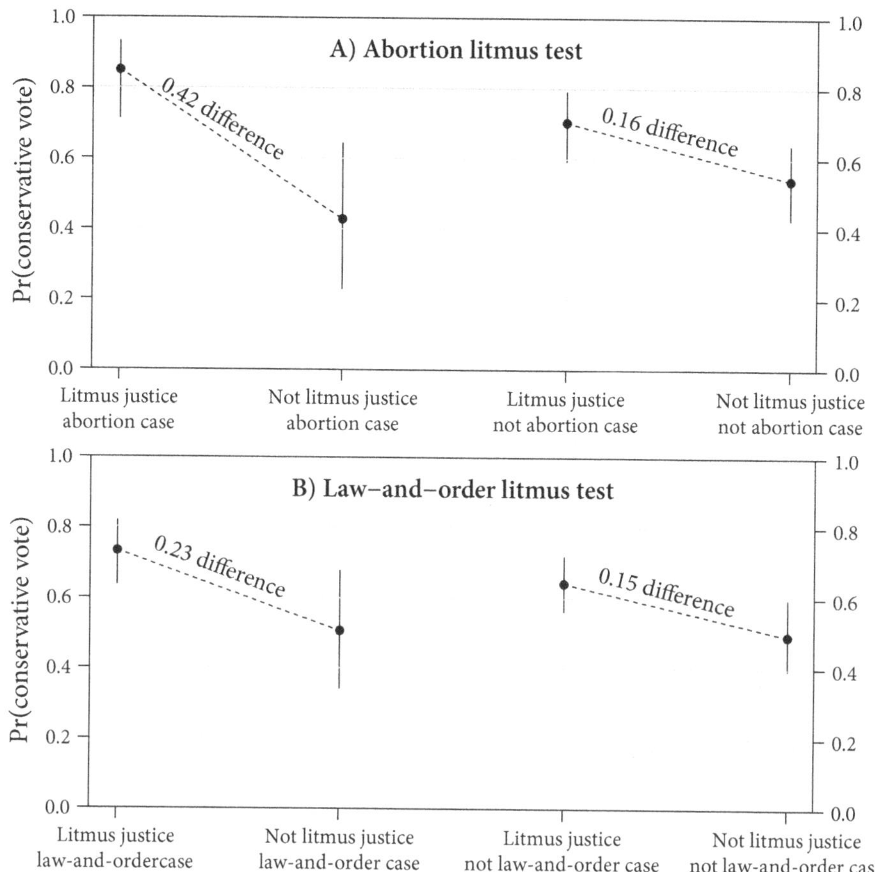

Fig. 12.5 Predicted probabilities of voting across litmus cases and justices in A) Abortion cases; and B) Law-and-order cases. The estimates are based on simulating the coefficients in Table 12.4. Vertical lines depict 95% confidence intervals.

Employing the logic of a difference-in-differences design suggests a causal effect of about (.74 – .51)–(.64 – .49) = .23 – .15 = .08 percentage points. Even though this effect is comparatively modest compared to the abortion cases, the 23-point difference between litmus and non-litmus justices in law-and-order cases is still greater than the 15-point difference in non-law-and-order cases in 93% of simulations, and is also substantively significant.

12.4.4 Summary: Do Policy Litmus Tests Work?

Do policy litmus tests work? In the two areas where enough data exist to investigate matters quantitatively, the best evidence and strongest research designs indicate that the tests did indeed work, particularly for abortion. The anti-abortion activists who worked so doggedly to change Republican judicial nominees apparently succeeded.

While the evidence for the effectiveness of the law-and-order litmus test is less dramatic, we nonetheless see a similar pattern: Republican justices appointed under the law-and-order litmus test voted more conservatively in criminal justice cases than did non-litmus justices, even taking into account the overall difference in conservative voting across litmus and non-litmus justices.

12.5 The Ideological Structure of the court

Until now, we have focused on the behavior of individual justices. Here and in the following section, we transition to collective choice—in particular, the court's definitive policies set forth in majority opinions. To begin, we introduce the concept of the court's overall make-up or *ideological structure*, which connects the justices' disparate ideologies to the court's collective policy choices.

At any given time, nine justices sit on the court, each with their own political orientation. The justices' ideologies influence their individual votes—which cases to hear, which litigant should win, and whether to join a majority opinion. But in considering what really matters with respect to the *court*—collective policy choice—individual ideologies must aggregate into some sort of "ideological structure." This structure then leads to policy content that emerges from the court's majority opinions. In thinking about the court as a policy-making institution, this policy content is ultimately what matters most, for a majority opinion obliges lower courts and the executive branch to respect the opinion's policy and enforce it with the coercive power of the state.[26] In sum, the nine ideologies aggregate into an overall ideological structure, which then affects the policy content of majority opinions. In some sense, the ideology-structure-policy linkage is the key to studying the consequences of appointment politics.

An obvious question is: what is the best measure of the court's ideological structure? This apparently simple question turns out to be quite complicated, because the best measure of ideological structure depends on one's theory of Supreme Court policy making. In the next sections, we summarize the two main theories and their associated empirical measures of the court's structure.

12.5.1 The Median Justice Approach

The Median Justice (MJ) Approach is the oldest and still the dominant approach to understanding collective choice on the Supreme Court.[27] This approach builds upon the famous "median voter theorem" (MVT) of political economy, which identifies as decisive the policy preferences of the median member of a multi-member body like an electorate, committee, or legislature—at least under certain circumstances.[28] For the Supreme Court, the MJ Approach holds that the preferences of the median justice both determine who wins and the policy content of the majority opinion.[29]

A virtue of the MJ Approach is that it cleanly identifies the best summary measure of the court's ideological structure: the ideology of the median justice, Justice 5, as expressed on a left-right scale. In the MJ Approach, the ideologies of the other justices simply do not matter, other than for determining the identity of the critical "swing" justice.

The dispositional voting scores reviewed earlier allow easy identification of the median justice in each term in the post-war period; Figure 12.6 depicts the conservatism score of the median justice from 1950 to 2020.[30] Here and for the rest of the chapter we rely on the Bailey scores to measure ideology, as the bridging mechanisms used to construct those scores makes them more suitable for dynamic comparisons of the structure of the court.[31] Figure 12.6 shows that the ideology of the median justice in the early 1950s was relatively conservative. In the mid-1950s it became more moderate, reflecting the often strange appointments of the Eisenhower years. The ideology of the court's median justice then took a dramatic liberal turn in 1962, with the appointment of Justice Goldberg to the court. This appointment established the famous late Warren Court, the high-water mark of liberalism in the court's history. But, this period was short-lived, and the median's return to conservatism in the late 1960s to early 1970s was just as dramatic as the earlier liberal shift. This rightward movement reflected the early Nixon appointees, particularly the twin nominations of Burger and Blackmun. A liberal movement occurred in the late 1970s, but a return to solid conservatism soon followed.

Figure 12.6 suggests relative stability over the next three decades with one notable exception. Given the judicial partisan sort, the court of the 2010s was highly polarized. The death of Justice Scalia in 2016 created an eight-member court, which temporarily moved the location of the median justice decidedly to the left.[32] If Merrick Garland

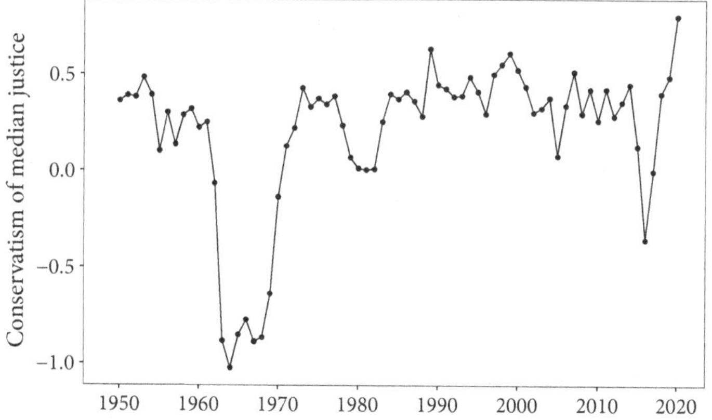

Fig. 12.6 The estimated conservatism of the median justice, 1950–2020, based on the Bailey scores. The dip in 2016 occurs because Justice Scalia's death and subsequent Senate blockade of Merrick Garland created an extended eight-member court, thereby temporarily shifting the median in the liberal direction.

had been confirmed, the location of the 2016 median would have moved even more dramatically leftward. But the successful blockade of Garland and subsequent confirmation of Neil Gorsuch returned the median to a solidly conservative position, a dramatic movement.[33] The final observation in the time series reflects the replacement of Justice Ruth Bader Ginsburg by Justice Amy Coney Barrett, establishing Justice Brett Kavanaugh as the median.[34] The ideology of the median justice as of 2020 is the most conservative in the entire time series, and is probably the most conservative since the 1930s.

12.5.2 Majority Coalition Approach

The Median Justice Approach is wonderfully simple and captures the dramatic swings of the 1960s and early 1970s. But in considering the content of majority opinions, it presents many difficulties, both logical and empirical.[35] On the empirical side, it predicts:

- Who serves with the median justice does not affect the content of the majority opinion;
- Whether the vote on the case disposition is liberal or conservative does not affect the content of the majority opinion;
- The makeup of the majority dispositional coalition likewise has no effect on the majority opinion—in other words, a unanimous dispositional vote, a 7-2 vote, and a 5-4 vote all result in the same opinion;
- Opinion authorship doesn't matter—the content of the majority opinion is the same whether it was written by Justice Scalia or Justice Stevens, for example;
- Case selection—in particular, the type of case facts a given case comprises—does not affect the content of the majority opinion.

Close observers would be puzzled by these predictions, because they seem at odds with basic observations about the court. From a theoretical perspective, the actual procedures used on the court fit very poorly with those required by the Median Voter Theorem. To be sure, the justices use pure majority rule in the binary choice of a case's disposition, so a median voter result seems natural and plausible there. But dissenting justices do not participate in crafting or endorsing the majority opinion. And justices in the majority, who do contribute to the majority opinion, do not use pure majority rule to vote over competing opinions. Given these unusual procedures, there is little reason to expect a median-voter result for majority opinion content.

Attempts to go beyond the median justice approach usually start with the procedures actually used on the court, and then attempt to develop more nuanced theories of collective choice. The details of this literature are a matter of concern mostly to specialists, and we spare the reader an exegesis.[36] Instead we focus on the most promising class of recent theories: the Majority Coalition (MC) Approach.[37] This approach tries to capture the most important of the court's actual procedures and in doing so leads to clear and arguably plausible results about opinion content.

The starting place for the MC Approach is the observation, as we noted earlier, that judicial decision making involves two distinct voting aspects—the disposition or outcome, and the policy or rationale. Crucially, dissenting from the majority disposition effectively removes a justice from the opportunity to bargain over the content of the majority opinion.[38] The majority opinion will then reflect the bargaining protocol used by the justices in the majority disposition. Different versions of the MC Approach make somewhat different assumptions about this protocol, but they all predict that hard bargaining will tend to drive the content of the majority opinion toward the center of the majority dispositional coalition, *not* the center of the court as a whole. Unanimous case dispositions can lead to a centrist opinion—because in such case the median justice of the court is also the median of the majority coalition—but cases where the court is narrowly divided on the disposition (especially 5-4 decisions) are apt to lead to opinions located toward the ideological wings of the court.

With respect to opinion content, the MC Approach sidesteps the logical and empirical difficulties of the MJ Approach.[39] But for present purposes, the key question is: from a Majority Coalition viewpoint, what is the best measure of the ideological structure of the court? Strictly speaking, the answer is: the exact distribution of all nine members, for they all matter.

We suggest a simpler and more tractable formulation: the size of liberal, moderate, and conservative blocs on the court, where blocs contain sets of ideologically compatible justices. Using this approach, one would expect a liberal bloc-dominated court like the late Warren Court to favor liberal case dispositions, and then produce quite liberal majority opinions within those liberal dispositions. The less frequent conservative dispositions would result in relatively moderate majority opinions. Conversely, a moderate-conservative oriented court would tend to produce conservative dispositions but some liberal ones as well. Then, in the conservative dispositions, members of the conservative bloc would likely write moderately conservative majority opinions joined by some moderates. In the liberal dispositions, moderates and the handful of liberals in those majorities would produce rather moderate opinions. Balanced courts would produce both types of dispositions with distinctly different majority opinions across them, but relatively rare extreme majority opinions. And so on. If these conjectures are correct, a three-bloc formulation offers a relatively simple but nonetheless nuanced characterization of the linkage between individual ideology and collective choice, as suggested by the MC Approach.

To estimate these blocs, we return to the Bailey data. We use the full distribution of ideal points for every justice from 1950 to 2019; in other words, "justice-years" are the unit of analysis. Then we divide this distribution into thirds: justices who, in a given year, fall in the bottom third are coded as being the liberal bloc, justices in the middle third are coded as being in the moderate bloc, and justices in the top third are coded as being in the conservative bloc. Because the Bailey scores are dynamic, a justice may

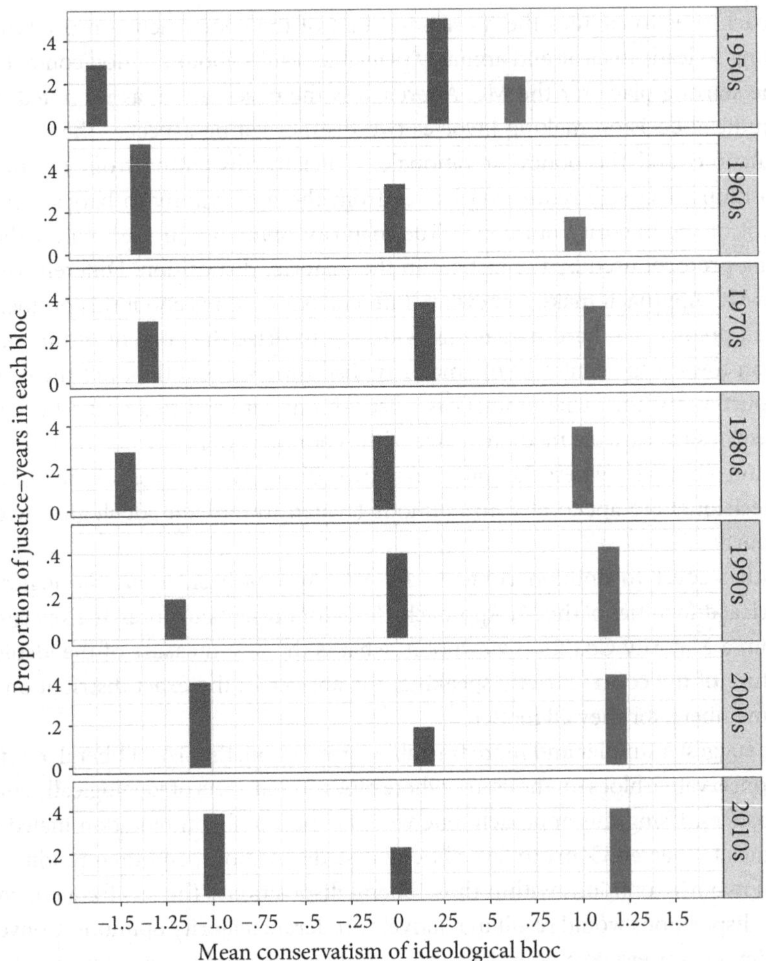

Fig. 12.7 Liberal, moderate, and conservative blocs on the court, by decade, 1950s–2010s. In each panel, the height of each bar depicts the percentages of justice-years in that bloc during a decade, while the x-axis depicts the mean ideology of the justices in each bloc. The liberal bloc is blue, the moderate bloc purple, and the conservative bloc red. The underlying scores are justice-level Bailey Scores.

appear in a different bloc in different years if their score happens to cross one of the thresholds over time.

Figure 12.7 displays liberal, moderate, and conservative blocs on the court by decade since the 1950s. For each decade, the height of the bars indicates the proportion of justice-years in each of the liberal, moderate, and conservative blocs. The x-axis indicates the mean ideology of the justices in a given bloc. For instance, in the 1950s, about 30% of justice-years fell into the liberal bloc. Of those justices, the mean of their Bailey scores was about -1.5, which is very liberal.

Figure 12.7 reveals several interesting patterns. First, periods with a one-bloc dominant structure—that is, a bloc with 5 or more members, on average—were rare. However, the 1950s saw a dominant moderate bloc, while the 1960s displayed a dominant liberal bloc. Second, the 1970s and 1980s displayed a balanced bloc structure, with each of the three blocs containing about the same number of justices, on average. Third, the 1990s displayed a bimodal moderate-conservative structure, featuring a large moderate bloc, a large conservative bloc, and a diminished liberal bloc. No period displayed the opposite bimodal structure with large moderate and liberal blocs. Fourth, the 2000s and 2010s saw the emergence of a bimodal wing structure, with large liberal and large conservative blocs but a diminished moderate bloc; here we can see the consequences of the judicial partisan sort. Fifth, the liberal bloc became less liberal over time, particularly after the 1980s. This reflected the replacement of fiery liberals like Douglas, Marshall, and Brennan with more moderate justices like Breyer and Ginsburg. Sixth, the conservative bloc became more conservative over time, with the rightward shift well established by the 1990s.

12.6 Court Structure and Collective Choice: Fourth Amendment Law

How do changes in the ideological structure of the court translate into changes in judicial policy? Answering this question quantitatively presents a thorny social science problem because measuring judicial doctrine is difficult. As a result, quantitative judicial politics has focused primarily on the analysis of dispositional votes. Although the doctrine announced in a case and the case's disposition must be compatible, relying solely on dispositional votes cannot capture the content of doctrine, which is the more consequential aspect of what the court does.

Fortunately, political scientists Benjamin Lauderdale and Tom Clark (2010) devised a clever way to estimate the ideological location of majority opinions. In particular, they use citation patterns across a set of cases to estimate which majority opinions are "closer" or "farther" from other opinions. So if one opinion cites another opinion favorably (i.e. by using it as a precedent in the writing of the current opinion), those cases are estimated as being closer in ideological space than two opinions that do not cite each other. The result is a set of estimated opinion locations that are assumed to exist in a one-dimensional ideological space.

To be sure, there exist limitations to the Clark-Lauderdale method. First, like any statistical model, it relies on certain assumptions (e.g. the meaning of an opinion does not change over time) that may not be true in reality. Second, it requires hand-coding citations, a labor-intensive procedure. Accordingly, Clark and Lauderdale estimated opinion location in only two policy areas: search and seizure, and freedom of religion. In addition, the sample size of the data—which run from 1954 to 2008—is unequal across these two areas. The Clark and Lauderdale data contains 291 search-and-seizure majority opinions, versus only 78 for freedom of religion cases. Because, as explained below, we separately consider liberal versus conservative dispositions, the freedom of religion cases quickly run into statistical power issues. So for our analyses we focus solely on the search-and-seizure cases.

The court's turn to the right in search-and-seizure law beginning in the 1970s has been well documented, both quantitatively and qualitatively.[40] But, for our purposes, no quantitative analysis has demonstrated how changes in the composition of the court map onto changes in the court's *policies* (as opposed to dispositions), to which we now turn.[41]

Figure 12.8A begins with a descriptive look at the data, examining changes in the court's dispositional voting over time. In search-and-seizure cases, a conservative disposition generally favors the state—for example, allowing evidence from a warrantless search to be used against the defendant. A liberal disposition generally favors the criminal defendant—for example, ruling evidence from a questionable search or seizure inadmissible.[42] Figure 12.8A uses a rug plot to show the incidence of conservative decisions (on the top axis) and liberal decisions (on the bottom axis). The line is a loess line that summarizes the temporal trends; it can be thought of as summarizing the probability of a conservative decision at any given point in time.

The figure illustrates the stark conservative shift in the court's dispositional voting on search-and-seizure cases over time. Around 1960, the probability of a conservative decision was only about 35%. From then, it rose steadily, peaking around 1990. Since then, it has declined slightly, but the average probability of a conservative decision was around 70% as of 2008.

What about majority opinion locations? Higher Clark-Lauderdale scores mean more conservative opinions; however, unlike with binary dispositions, the scale itself is not intuitive. To give some sense of the substantive difference in opinion locations, the majority opinion in the court's landmark liberal decision in the 1961 case of *Mapp v. Ohio*, which extended the exclusionary rule to the states, has a score of -.7. Conversely, the court's conservative opinion in the 1983 case of *Illinois v. Gates*, which greatly weakened protections for criminal defendants by adopting a new "totality of the circumstances" test for evaluating whether evidence allegedly obtained in violation of the Fourth Amendment should be excluded, has a score of 1.3.[43]

Next, Figure 12.8B depicts a year-by-year box-and-whisker plot that summarizes the distribution of opinions within each year—here we pool both liberal and conservative dispositions together. The loess line summarizes the general trend of the overall opinion locations, which tracks fairly well with the dispositional voting trends seen in Figure 12.8A—average opinion locations became more liberal in the 1960s, before becoming gradually more conservative beginning with the advent of the Burger Court in the 1970s.

Finally, Figure 12.8C breaks down opinion locations by conservative and liberal dispositions. Interestingly, the average location of majority opinions in conservative dispositions remained fairly stable between 1954 and 2008,[44] while opinions with liberal dispositions actually became slightly less liberal.

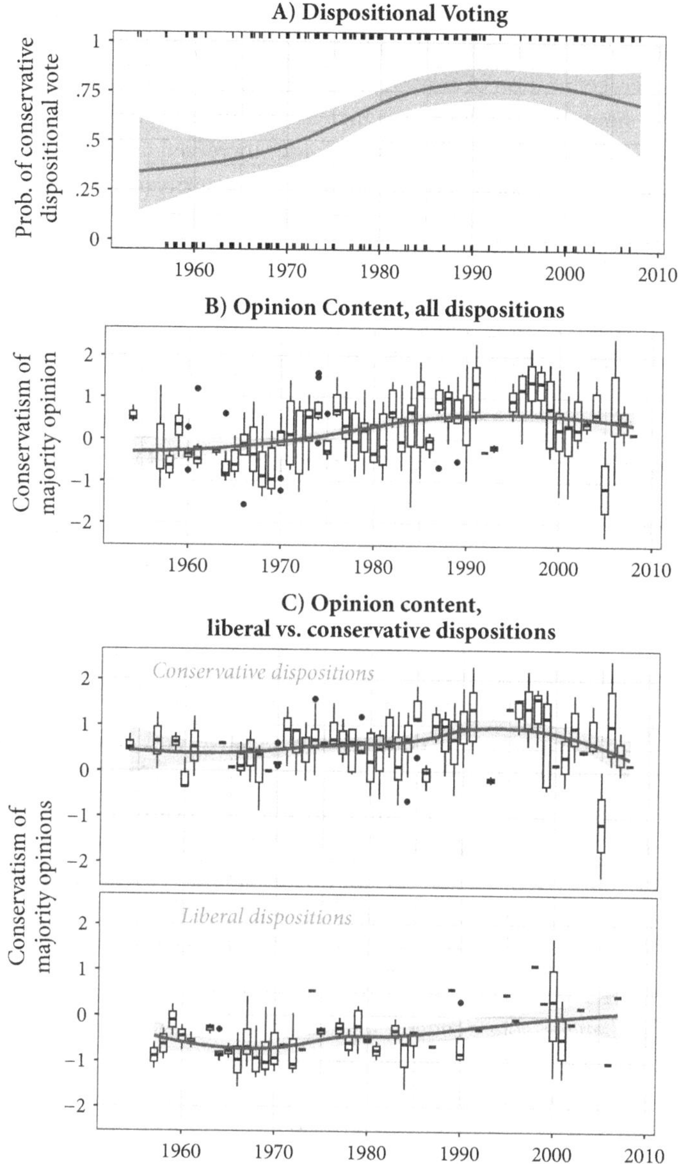

Fig. 12.8 Summarizing the court's search-and-seizure decisions, 1954–2008. A) Changes in the court's dispositional voting. The top and bottom rugs depict conservative and liberal dispositions, respectively, while the loess line summarizes the probability of a conservative decision at any given point in time. B) Changes in opinion content. The "All dispositions" panel presents a box-and-whisker plot that summarizes the distribution of opinions within each year; the loess line summarizes the general trend of the overall opinion locations. The bottom panel does the same but divides the data into conservative and liberal dispositions.

At first glance, these trends might seem inconsistent with the judicial partisan sort. But, because the court decides both cases and policy together, they actually are not. Even if the average location of conservative dispositions remained steady over time, Figure 12.8A shows that the court was increasingly likely to reach conservative dispositions, so the scope of those majority opinions increased over time. Second, since 1970, liberal justices have never enjoyed an outright majority on the court; so, in cases where the court reached the liberal disposition, at least one moderate or conservative justice had to be a member of the majority coalition, thereby constraining the ability of the liberal bloc to pull policy leftward (or even maintain the status quo). Moreover, recall from Figure 12.7 that the justices in the liberal bloc actually became more moderate over time, leading to less liberal policy in cases with liberal dispositions.[45]

12.6.1 Modeling Court Structure and Case Dispositions

We now move to a systematic analysis of the relationship between structure and outcomes. We begin by modeling the court's dispositional voting in search-and-seizure cases. Table 12.5 presents three logistic regression models; in each, the dependent variable is coded 1 if the court reached a conservative disposition, and 0 if it reached the liberal disposition.

Model (1) in Table 12.5 only includes the location of the median justice as a predictor. Not surprisingly, the coefficient is positive and significant. Model (2) includes as predictors the number of justices in the conservative bloc and the number of justices in the liberal bloc, at the time the case was heard. The omitted category is the number of justices in the moderate bloc.[46] These coefficients are as expected: increasing the number of justices in the liberal bloc decreases the likelihood of a conservative disposition, while increasing the number of justices in the conservative

Table 12.5 Disposition logistic regressions. In each model the dependent variable is coded 1 for a conservative disposition and 0 for a liberal one. * indicates significance at $p < .05$.

	(1)	(2)	(3)
Median justice	1.54*		0.23
	(0.29)		(0.58)
N. justices in liberal bloc		−0.29*	−0.25
		(0.12)	(0.16)
N. justices in conservative bloc		0.43*	0.39*
		(0.12)	(0.17)
Intercept	0.35*	0.16	0.14
	(0.13)	(0.62)	(0.62)
Observations	291	291	291
Log Likelihood	−177.00	−173.00	−173.00

bloc increases that likelihood. Finally, Model (3) is a "horse-race" regression that pits the court structure indicated by Median Justice theory against the structure suggested by the Majority Coalition viewpoint. Quite interestingly, in this model, the location of the median justice is no longer a significant predictor of dispositional voting. Conversely, the coefficient on the number of justices in the conservative bloc remains unchanged from Model (2). The coefficient on the number of justices in the liberal bloc loses statistical significance ($p = .12$), but is still negative and similar in magnitude to Model (2). All told, these results demonstrate the need for going beyond the location of the median justice when considering the relationship between the court's structure and case outcomes.

To illustrate the substantive differences implied by the model, Figure 12.9 shows the predicted probability of a conservative decision, based on Model (2) in Table 12.5 (we ignore uncertainty here for presentational clarity). In the left panel, the x-axis depicts the number of justices in the liberal bloc, going from 1 to 6.[47] Then, we vary the number of justices in the conservative bloc from 1 to 6. The individual lines show the predicted probability of a conservative decision for a given number of conservative justices; we truncate the lines where necessary to account for the fact that the number of total justices cannot exceed nine. The right plot is similar, but with conservative justices now on the x-axis and the lines varying across the number of justices in the liberal bloc.

Together, Figure 12.9 shows that altering the court's composition changes the likelihood of a conservative dispositions in two ways. (We will use the left panel to make this point but the argument is symmetric with respect to liberals and conservatives.) First, fixing the number of justices in the liberal bloc but increasing the number of conservative justices shifts the "intercept" up—that is, the baseline probability of the court reaching the conservative outcome. Second, the slope on

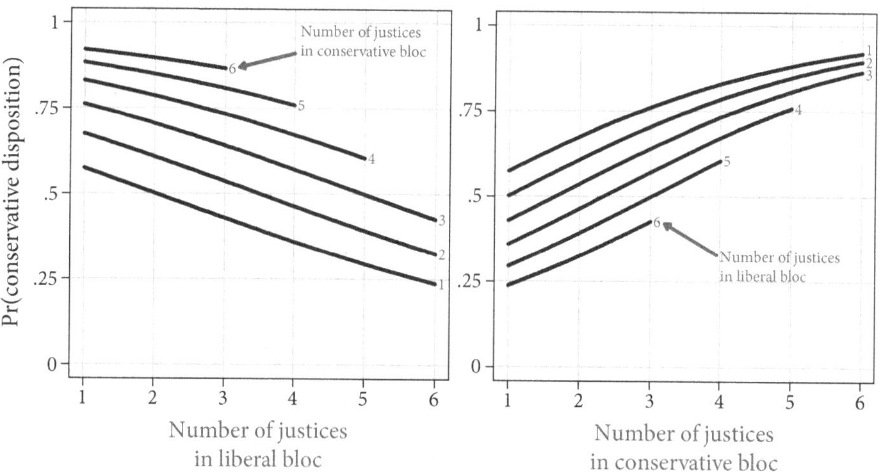

Fig. 12.9 Predicted probability of a conservative decision, sequentially varying the number of justices in the liberal and conservative blocs.

the curves is negative, meaning that adding more liberals reduces the chance of a conservative outcome, for any number of conservative justices. These graphs illustrate how the broad shift over time from a court composed predominantly of liberals and moderates to one controlled firmly by conservatives translated into conservative dispositions in search-and-seizure cases.

12.6.2 Court Structure and Majority Opinion Content

Next we analyze how changes in the structure of the court translate into changes in the content of majority opinions. Table 12.6 presents nine OLS regression models; in each, the dependent variable is the Clark-Lauderdale estimate of the majority opinion location. The nine models compromise three sets of three models, each of which are parallel in the structure of their covariates. The first three models include all dispositions, the second three include only conservative dispositions, and the final three include only liberal dispositions.

In Model (1), the sole predictor is the location of the median justice, which shows a strong and statistically significant relationship with majority opinion content. Model (2) includes only the number of justices in the liberal and conservative blocs. As with dispositions, we see the expected relationships: increasing the number of liberal justices results in majority opinions moving to the left, while increasing the number of conservatives moves them to the right. Finally, Model (3), the "horse-race" model, again shows that the location of the median justice is not a statistically significant predictor of opinion content when we account for the number of justices in the liberal and conservative blocs.

Table 12.6 OLS regressions of opinion location. * indicates significance at $p < .05$.

	All dispositions			**Conservative dispositions**			**Liberal dispositions**		
	(1)	(2)	(3)	(4)	(5)	(6)	(7)	(8)	(9)
Median justice	0.77*		0.10	0.49*		−0.02	0.37*		0.17
	(0.10)		(0.20)	(0.14)		(0.25)	(0.09)		(0.22)
N. justices in lib. bloc		−0.14*	−0.12*		−0.09	−0.09		−0.07	−0.03
		(0.04)	(0.05)		(0.05)	(0.06)		(0.05)	(0.06)
N. justices in con. bloc		0.22*	0.19*		0.15*	0.15*		0.10*	0.06
		(0.04)	(0.06)		(0.05)	(0.07)		(0.05)	(0.06)
Intercept	0.12*	−0.002	−0.01	0.52*	0.40	0.39	−0.47*	−0.49*	−0.53*
	(0.05)	(0.21)	(0.22)	(0.06)	(0.24)	(0.24)	(0.05)	(0.25)	(0.25)
Observations	289	289	289	181	181	181	108	108	108
R^2	0.18	0.21	0.22	0.06	0.10	0.10	0.13	0.13	0.14

Separating the cases into conservative dispositions, Models (4) through (6), and liberal dispositions, Models (7) through (9), shows the same basic patterns. However, some of the coefficients on the bloc are now measured imprecisely, particularly for liberal dispositions (note the sample size is much smaller, compared to conservative dispositions). Yet even here, the "horse race" models (6 and 9) for each type of disposition somewhat favors the more nuanced view of court structure rather than just the location of the median justice, as the coefficient on the location of the median justice is not statistically distinguishable from zero when we account for the overall structure of the court.

Figure 12.10 examines the substantive significance of these results in a manner similar to Figure 12.9; here we show the predicted location of majority opinions. For clarity, we break the results down into conservative and liberal dispositions; the predicted probabilities from the conservative dispositions are based on Model (5) from Table 12.6, while the predicted probabilities from the liberal dispositions are based on Model (8). We again allow both the number of liberal and conservative justices to vary (subject to the constraint that there can be no more than nine justices). Comparing the four panels in Figure 12.10 reveals the subtleties of how

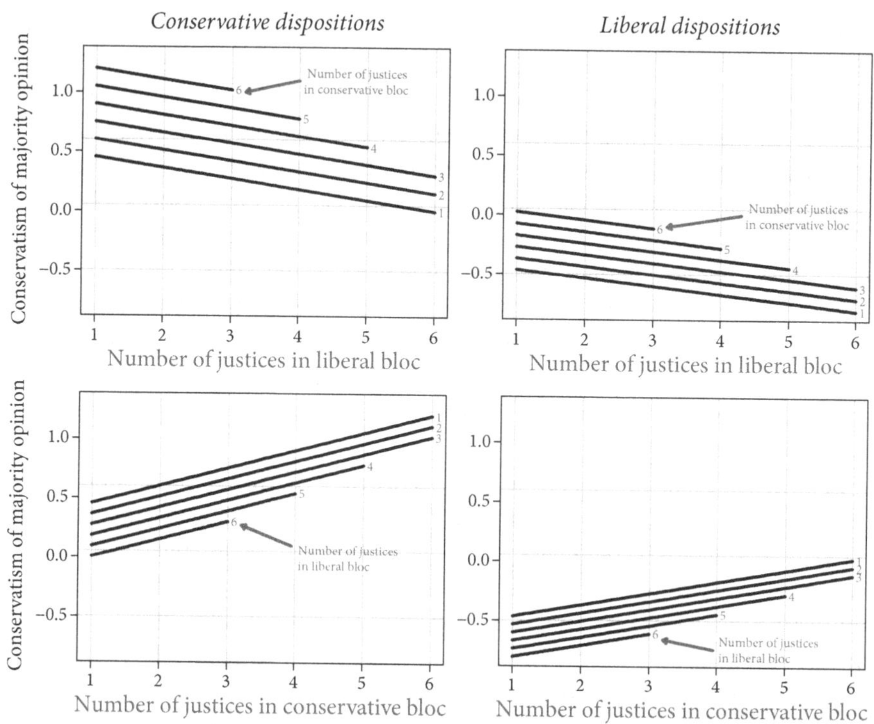

Fig. 12.10 Predicted ideological location of majority opinions in search-and-seizure cases, sequentially varying the number of justices in the liberal and conservative blocs. See text for details.

composition affects outcomes. First, we can see that policy varies greatly across liberal and conservative dispositions—note the differences in the intercept across the left and right columns. Second, even within liberal and conservative dispositions, changes in the relative composition of the ideological blocs leads to significant predicted changes in the content of the court's majority opinions.[48] Figure 12.10 makes clear that when the ideology of justices change, the doctrine follows.

12.7 Conclusion: Judicial Personnel Is Judicial Policy

"Personnel is policy." This phrase was a famous mantra of the Reagan revolutionaries who often faced hostile Washington bureaucrats. In other words, if you put the right people in the right jobs, the right policies will flow almost automatically. This insight grounds the presidential management tactic known to political scientists as "agency politicization."[49] Does the famous maxim apply to the Supreme Court? In other words, does presidential politicization of appointments work on the Supreme Court like it does with (say) the Environmental Protection Agency and the Veterans Administration? The evidence presented in this chapter suggests that the answer is yes—at least to a degree.

As shown in earlier chapters, beginning in the 1960s, presidents—especially Republican ones—worked hard and increasingly effectively to select justices who were faithful agents of an ideological orientation. This was not easy. It took decades of effort to build lower court farm teams and organize skillful White House selection operations. Then, it took years to actually staff the court with the new products of the selection machine. But hard work and persistence paid off. Justices selected for policy reliability actually voted more reliably, and those selected for specific policy views usually adhered to them when deciding cases on the court.

As a consequence, during the 2000s and 2010s, the court sorted into two distinct partisan blocs with very different ideological commitments. The judicial partisan sort hollowed out the court's ideological middle and created a new ideological structure on the court, a bimodal wing structure. A conservative dominant court finally emerged in the Trump administration.

In turn, these new courts produced new policies. While the scope of our empirical tests is limited in terms of issue areas, the results nevertheless show that judicial policy tracked the changes in the court's ideological structure. More conservative courts were more likely to produce conservative case outcomes. Even more strikingly, the policies emerging from the liberal and conservative majority dispositional coalitions reflected the makeup of the coalitions. So, as the court moved from a liberal dominant court to a bimodal wing court, liberal dispositions became less frequent, the policies from those liberal dispositional coalitions became less liberal, and policies from conservative dispositional coalitions became more conservative. A court solidly dominated by the conservative wing promises to produce a lopsided distribution of very conservative policies, a mirror-image of the liberal-dominant late Warren

Courts. Indeed, within a two-week period in June 2022, the court issued landmark opinions overruling *Roe v. Wade* and its grant of a fundamental right to an abortion, extending the individual right to carry guns in public places, and hamstringing the ability of the Environmental Protection Agency to regulate greenhouse gasses in the atmosphere.[50] In each case, at least five conservative justices voted in support of these very conservative policies, with the three liberal justices in dissent.

What are the implications from this lopsided composition for the future of the court? We turn to this question in the next chapter.

13
The Future
The Courts That Politics May Make

What does the future hold?

So far we have looked to the past, examining how Supreme Court appointment politics changed, why, and with what consequences. Now we turn our eyes to the future. Of course, no one can predict with certainty how appointment politics—and the Supreme Courts they make—will unfold over the coming years. But we can offer educated guesses. In particular, we can use computer simulations to project the probable ideological composition of the court, and how specific shifts in norms and institutions may affect that composition. The result is really a kind of social-science fiction. But by solidly grounding the underlying assumptions in historical patterns and the specific mechanisms studied in earlier chapters, we can offer plausible speculation with real bite.

This chapter proceeds as follows. The next section lays out the design choices in our simulation, which we call the Making [the] Supreme Courts (MSC) Simulator. Section 13.3 presents a core set of simulations. Unlike earlier chapters, where our data stops at 2020, in this chapter we begin with 2022 to account for Ketanji Brown Jackson's replacement of Justice Stephen Breyer. We begin with a baseline projection of the present—the court as it existed in 2022—into the future. The key result is "conservative lock-in"—in all likelihood, the existing 2022 conservative majority will persist for decades to come.

Section 13.4 examines how the events of 2016 created a historical pivot point for the court. We develop a counterfactual simulation that explores what would have happened had (1) the Senate confirmed Merrick Garland in 2016 and if (2) Hillary Rodham Clinton had defeated Donald Trump in the 2016 election. The results are dramatic: a Clinton win would likely have led to liberal majorities for many years to come. Of course, that is not what happened. Thus the 2016 election stands out as transformative for the likely future of the Supreme Court.

Next, we explore the potential consequences of plausible changes in norms or practices that would *not* require statutory or constitutional changes. First, Section 13.5 examines what would happen if the Garland blockade of 2016 becomes the norm and confirmations grind to a halt under divided party government. What are the implications for extended vacancies, and for the path of the court if the Senate map increasingly favors the Republican party?

Making the Supreme Court: The Politics of Appointments, 1930–2020. Charles M. Cameron and Jonathan P. Kastellec, Oxford University Press. © Oxford University Press 2023. DOI: 10.1093/oso/9780197680544.003.0013

Finally, Section 13.6 examines two potential institutional changes to selection and tenure. First, we perform a thought experiment to examine how the short-term trajectory of the court would have changed had the Democratic Party pursued and implemented court packing in 2021. We then examine how the introduction of term limits would affect the long-run composition of the court.

13.2 Modeling the Future: The MSC Simulator

13.2.1 The Basic Idea

The essential insight in simulating the future composition of the Supreme Court is that each seat is a *stochastic process*, a family of random variables produced by the exit-and-replacement process. A seat progresses through time, moving somewhat randomly from one "state" to another, with the transitions governed by exits from the court (via death and retirement) and entrances (via appointments). Modeling the future composition of the court means (1) conceptualizing the states, namely the ideology and age of the seat holder; (2) specifying the probabilities that govern exits and entrances and hence each seat's movement from state to state, (3) keeping track of all the seat-states as they move through time, and then (4) investigating the dynamic properties of the system as a whole. These properties include the ideology of the median justice, the size of liberal-moderate-conservative blocs, the number of justices, and the long-run tendencies of each of those variables. Because the court has nine seats (and, under court packing, possibly many more), each step becomes increasingly complex. Fortunately, a computer can perform the intricate accounting with ease, and the simulations allow us to see the behavior of the court as a whole given the underlying design choices.

The MSC Simulator examines several different scenarios in which the computer simulates every future year (extending to 2100) 1,000 times, generating various summary statistics across every analysis we perform. For linguistic clarity, we call each individual run of this procedure a "simulation," and we denote the collective scenario explored as a "policy experiment." For example, the baseline policy experiment employs 1,000 simulations, each of which contains information on the justices, and thus the court as a whole, for every year through 2100.

The following technical points are worth noting. First, under almost any reasonable set of assumptions, the *near-future composition of the court is extremely sensitive to its starting composition.* The starting court in the MSC Simulator is the actual 2022 court, which had six reliable conservatives and three reliable liberals.[1] This composition affects the composition of the court for years into the future in most of the simulations. The practical consequences are enormous.

Second, at any given time, we assume that the significance of the court's composition is *state-dependent*, not path-dependent. In other words, the court's ideological tendency is well captured by the current values of the median justice's ideology and the size of the court's ideological blocs. The prior history of these variables does not matter as such, except as the path that led to the present.[2]

Third, the details of the entrance and exit processes are extremely consequential for the court's path through time, but the processes themselves are assumed to be predictable and relatively stable; e.g. the death probability for 83-year-olds is constant. As a result, the transition probabilities from one state to another are largely time-invariant or "stationary." Furthermore, given the entrance and exit processes, it is theoretically possible for the court to move from any given state to any other state over time. For example, a court with nine conservative justices could conceivably eventually transform into a court with nine liberal justices; such a dramatic change, however, is improbable in any reasonable length of time.[3]

Together, these seemingly technical features imply a very practical consequence. The court's composition tends to a unique long-run distribution over possible compositions—i.e. ideologies of the median justice or sizes of liberal-moderate-conservative blocs.[4] To be clear, this mathematical fact does not mean that the court tends toward a *unique* ideology for the median justice. To foreshadow one key result, the baseline scenario shows that the long-run ideology of the median justice displays a bimodal distribution. So there is a smaller long-run probability of a liberal court and a larger long-run probability of a conservative court, with specific long-range probabilities.

In sum, as we present the results, the key questions are: (1) What are the implications for *the long-run distribution* of the court's composition? (2) *How fast* will the court tend to get there? and (3) *How variable* will the court's composition be in the near-term and the long-term?

13.2.2 Key Design Choices

We are not the first scholars to use computer simulations to study the path of the Supreme Court—we summarize these earlier efforts in the Appendix.[5] The first key design choice for any simulation is what method of selection to assume for Supreme Court appointments. One can imagine entirely different systems for selecting high court judges, such as those used in the American states.[6] But all existing simulations of the U.S. Supreme Court assume presidential selection with Senate confirmation, and take life-time tenure as a baseline, and we do the same.

Consequently, design choices fall into four broad categories. First, what is the initial court (the starting place) and what are the relevant characteristics of its sitting justices (e.g. their ages and ideologies)? Second, which party controls the elected branches, especially the presidency and the Senate, and how will this control be determined over time? Third, what do entering justices probably look like, in terms of ideology, conditional on control of the elected branches? Fourth, how are exits from the court due to death and retirement determined?

Table 13.1 Summary of justices on the court as of 2022, who serve as the starting justices in our simulations. The justices are ordered by year of confirmation.

Justice	Age	Year confirmed	Appointing president	NSP score	Ideological bin
Thomas	72	1991	George H.W. Bush	0.54	Conservative
Roberts	65	2005	George W. Bush	0.64	Conservative
Alito	70	2006	George W. Bush	0.65	Conservative
Sotomayor	66	2009	Obama	−0.30	Liberal
Kagan	60	2010	Obama	−0.29	Liberal
Gorsuch	53	2017	Trump	0.58	Conservative
Kavanaugh	55	2018	Trump	0.67	Conservative
Barrett	48	2020	Trump	0.45	Conservative
Jackson	51	2020	Biden	−.32	Liberal

The Initial Court

We take the initial court to be the Supreme Court as it actually existed in 2022; the nine starting justices have exactly the same ages and the same ideology scores as the 2022 justices.[7] Table 13.1 shows the 2022 court, including the names, age, year confirmed, appointing president, ideology score, and ideological bloc for each of the nine justices (the last two are discussed below). As we noted previously, the 2022 court comprised six conservatives and three liberals.[8] The table also reveals considerable variation in age among the 2022 justices.

Control of the Presidency and the Senate

One might expect the stochastic properties of party control of the U.S. presidency and the U.S. Senate to be well-studied and thoroughly understood. But this turns out not to be the case.[9] Consequently, designers of Supreme Court simulators must devise their own set of assumptions about the likelihoods of institutional control.[10]

We treat presidential party control as a simple Markov process.[11] In the 1948 to 2020 period, the historical record reveals the following transition probabilities:

- If a party controlled the White House for a single term, it had about a 78% chance of winning a second term.
- Correspondingly, if a party had been out of power for a single term, it had about a 22% chance of reclaiming the White House in the next election.
- If a party controlled the White House for two terms, it had about a 20% chance of winning a third term.
- Correspondingly, if a party had been out of power for two terms, it had about a 80% of winning the next election.

These probabilities are hardly natural laws, but instead reflect the noticeably "thermostatic" quality of public sentiment, plus learning and re-calibration by the elites who control the political parties.[12] We implement these probabilities in every simulation.

So, for example, a party in its second term of White House control has only a 20% chance of winning a third term. These assumptions allow a party to control the presidency for more than two consecutive terms, but such an occurrence is relatively rare.[13]

Second, we treat Senate control as another Markov process, but keyed to unified and divided party control. From this perspective, in each election year—presidential or midterm—the Senate is either controlled by the president's party or is not. Between 1948 and 2020, the historical probabilities of a switch in party control of the Senate during presidential election years were:

- Unified government: 38% chance of switch.
- Divided government: 18% chance of switch.

During midterm election years, the historical probabilities of a switch in party control of the Senate were:

- Unified government: 42% chance of switch.
- Divided government: 17% chance of switch.

Unfortunately, we have too few elections to accurately calculate transition probabilities separately for each party. However, as has been widely recognized, the Senate "map" has tilted noticeably in favor of the Republicans, due to the geographic distribution of party members across states. To capture this bias, in some simulations we allow an asymmetric likelihood of Senate control by Republicans.

For every simulation, we run "presidential elections" every four years and "Senate elections" every two years (i.e. in both president election and midterm years) to determine party control of the White House and the Senate. In other words, for every year in every simulation, the president is either a Democrat or a Republican, and the Senate is controlled by either the president's party or the opposition. The "election results" are draws from Bernoulli distributions, using the above transition probabilities. Institutional control of the branches varies across simulations due to the random draws.

Figure 13.1 illustrates how the simulated elections work in practice. It displays the *average* probability of a Democratic president, a Democratic Senate, and unified party government across the 1,000 simulations in the baseline scenario (discussed further below). Figure 13.1A shows how in a majority of simulations the Democrats retain the presidency in 2024. But then, on average, control tends to switch to the Republicans in 2028, reflecting the difficulty of holding the presidency for more than two terms. Notably the long-run average Democratic control of the White House eventually fluctuates around 50%, but this process takes about 40 to 50 years. Thus, over the first few decades, party control of the presidency is quite sensitive to the initial reality of Democratic control in 2022. Figure 13.1B displays a similar average for Democratic control of the Senate. Here, the impact of the initial state is much less persistent, with

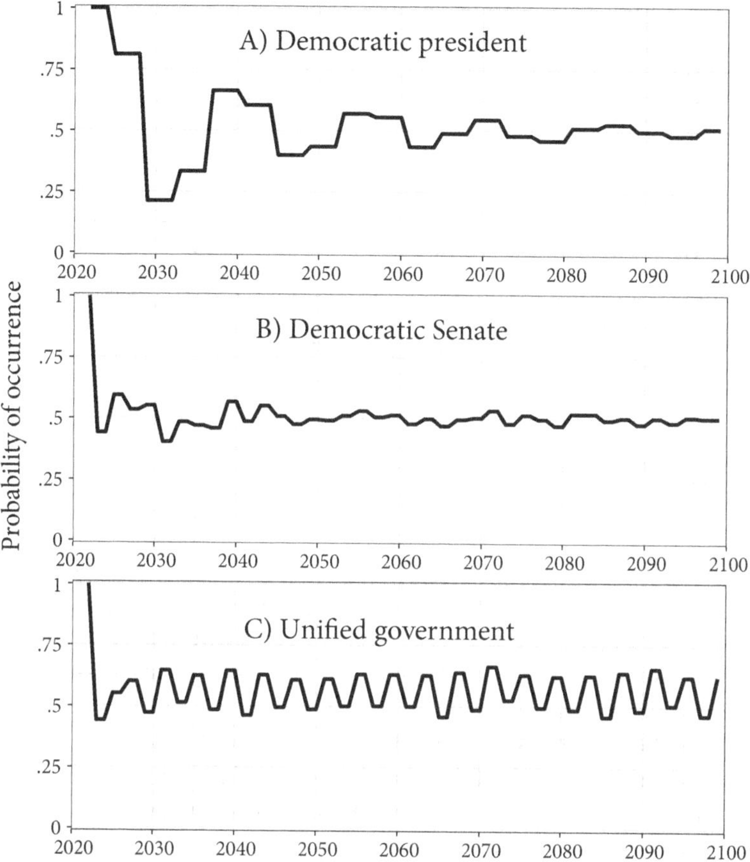

Fig. 13.1 The average probability of Democratic control of the presidency, Democratic control of the Senate, and unified government, based on our assumed transition probabilities. For each, the panels show the proportion of simulations in which the respective outcome occurs.

the average probability of Democratic control more quickly converging to about a 50% probability. Finally, Figure 13.1C indicates the average probability of unified party government. Again, the average value rather quickly converges on a long-run figure of about 55% to 60%. The relative frequency of divided party government has significant implications if the Senate confirmations become unlikely or even impossible during divided government.

13.2.3 Exits

Justices exit from the court either by retirement or death.[14] So, in every year, a simulation must account for both modes of departure.

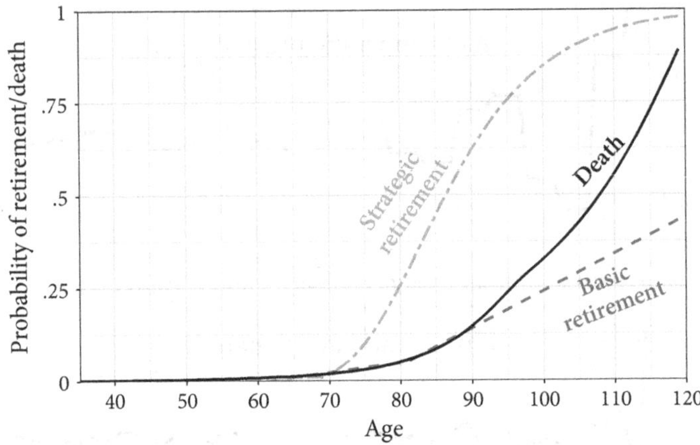

Fig. 13.2 The probability of death by age, along with the probability of "basic" and "strategic" justice retirements in our baseline simulations.

For death probabilities, we use actuarial data from the Social Security Administration.[15] For a justice of age a, we utilize the probability of dying in a given year, conditional (of course) of having lived to age a.[16] For example, the probability that an 80-year-old individual will die in the next year is about .05. This "death probability," which we denote $d(a)$, is shown in Figure 13.2.[17]

We divide the probability of retirement into two components, basic and strategic. First, we assume there is a "basic" probability (denoted $b(a)$) that a justice of a given age will choose to leave the court, either because of declining job appeal (e.g. David Souter) or because they simply believe it's time to depart. We assume this basic probability, which is also shown in Figure 13.2, is zero until age 65, then increases slowly and linearly through age 80, and more sharply after that.[18] (We graph the probabilities through age 120, but of course the actuarial tables will assert their iron logic for justices who steadfastly refuse to leave the court and end up departing "feet first."[19])

Next, we account for the possibility of strategic retirement, under which justices time their departure to coincide with favorable control of the presidency, so as to assure the selection of a comparable successor. Looking backwards, the evidence for whether Supreme Court justices have historically engaged in strategic retirements is ambiguous. Some studies find evidence that justices are more likely to retire when a president aligns with them, via party or ideology, while other studies find little evidence of strategic retirement.[20] Qualitatively, it is easy to find clear examples of strategic retirement. Justices Souter and Stevens both appeared to time their departures to allow a Democratic president to choose liberal successors (both justices, somewhat ironically, were appointed by Republican presidents), and Justice Breyer stepped down in 2022 to allow President Biden to appoint his successor. But many counter-examples also exist. Chief Justice Rehnquist, for example, declined to retire before the 2004 election despite his rapidly declining health.[21] Most notoriously, Ruth

Bader Ginsburg declined to retire when Democrats controlled both the White House and the Senate from 2009 to 2014, a decision that ultimately led to her replacement in 2020 by Amy Coney Barrett, a Trump appointee.

Despite this mixed record of strategic retirements in the past, going forward, it seems possible that more justices will opt for a strategic departure, given their strong ideological convictions and the high stakes of each appointment. Accordingly, we create a strategic retirement function that accounts for an increased tendency to retire by a justice when the current president is the same party as their appointing president. This function, denoted $s(a)$, is "turned on" when this condition holds. (In one policy experiment we show how the court's makeup would evolve in a world without strategic retirement.) The strategic retirement function, depicted in Figure 13.2, takes the value zero until age 65, increases to .01 through age 69 (conditional on a compatible president), then increases sharply after that. Thus, we assume the incentive for strategic retirement increases with a justice's age.[22]

Given these building blocks, the *total retirement probability*, $\rho(a)$ equals $b(a) + \mathbb{1} * s(a)$, where $\mathbb{1}$ is an indicator function for when the party of the justice is the same as the current president. With this probability in hand, in every year we draw the justice's retirement decision from a Bernoulli distribution; for example, if the total retirement probability is .2 in a given simulation for a given year, the justice will retire with a 20% probability and will remain on the court onto the next year with an 80% probability. Thus, the total *exit probability*, which we denote $e(a)$, equals $Pr(d(a)) + Pr(\rho(a)) * (1 - Pr(d(a)))$, where $1 - d(a)$ gives the probability that the justice does not die at the given age.

If a justice does not exit, the justice's service continues into the next year. If a justice exits, a vacancy occurs.[23]

13.2.4 Entrances: Age and Ideology

Every new justice enters the court with an assumed age and ideology. We assume entering age is distributed normally (specifically, $\mathcal{N}(52, 3)$), reflecting the likelihood that future presidents will emphasize the appointment of younger nominees in order to maximize their tenure. Recall in Chapter 4 we showed that the average age of nominees has been fairly steady over time, and tends to be in the range of 50–55 years old.

Assumptions about ideology require more thought. For the current justices, we use the NSP-measure of ideology we employed in Chapters 4 and 9; recall this measure is scaled in NOMINATE space, which runs from −1 (most liberal) to 1 (most conservative). For the baseline scenario we assume that the current era of polarization is here to stay, as is careful vetting of nominees. Thus, while variation in ideology may exist among justices in the same party, the cross-party differentiation will be large, meaning little overlap between justices appointed by Democratic presidents and those appointed by Republicans. To reflect this assumption, we assume that

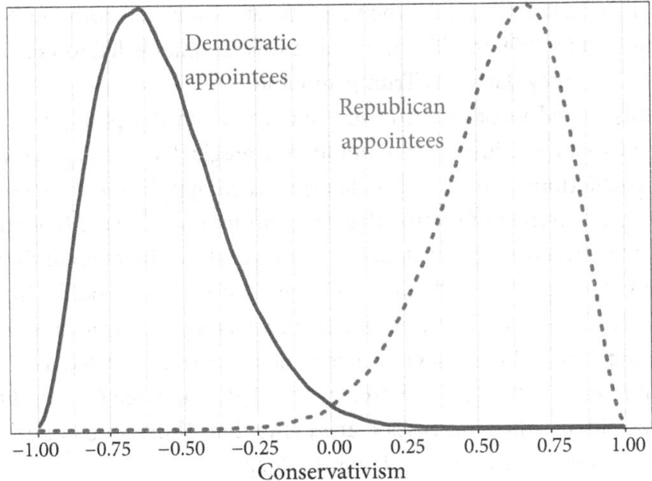

Fig. 13.3 The assumed distribution of ideology for Democratic and Republican appointees, based on our baseline assumption (a Beta distribution with shape parameters $\alpha = 3$ and $\beta = 11$).

judicial ideology is drawn from a beta distribution, with shape parameters $\alpha = 3$ and $\beta = 11$. We rescale this distribution so that it is bounded by -1 and 1 (rather than 0 and 1), and adjust the parameters so Democrats and Republicans are symmetrically distributed around zero, with Republicans more conservative and Democrats more liberal (as with NOMINATE). Figure 13.3 shows what these distributions look like for Democratic and Republican appointees. The distributions do not rule out the possibility of "moderate" justices, but most of the density lies on the "wings" of the NOMINATE space. More specifically, the means of these Beta distributions are $-.57$ and .57 for Democratic and Republican justices, respectively, while the standard deviation for each is .21.

This procedure results in a simulated ideal point for each justice. Such ideal points are not so interesting in and of themselves, given our assumptions, but as we showed in Chapter 12, changes in ideal points *on the court as a whole* in the form of medians and bloc sizes do translate into changes in judicial policy. So changes in the distribution of simulated ideal points therefore imply substantive changes in judicial policy—particularly the probability of liberal and conservative case dispositions and the ideological content of majority opinions.

Two final points about the ideology assumptions are worth noting. First, the means of these distributions produce future justices who are on average even more extreme than the 2022 justices. Whether this tendency plays out in fact is, of course, unknowable—but our interest lies in describing how the central tendencies of the court change *across* different counterfactual scenarios. Our assumptions about new justice ideology thus will not affect out cross-scenario comparisons.[24]

Second, while we assume that the initial ideology of a new justice is randomly drawn from a distribution with a mean and standard deviation, the ideology of a given justice is forever fixed by the draw. This assumption also encompasses the initial justices—we assume their ideology remains their NSP score until they exit the court. This assumption rules out the possibility of random bumps in a given justice's ideology, as well as more systematic "drift" in a liberal or conservative direction. Such possibilities can be substantively interesting, but we are primarily interested in the aggregate composition of the court, as measured by the ideology of the median justice and the size of the liberal, moderate, and conservative blocs. Consequently, we opt for the simplicity of fixed ideology (although, to be clear, the ideology of a justice in a given policy experiment will vary stochastically across simulations).

13.2.5 Summary of Policy Experiments

Table 13.2 summarizes all the policy experiments that appear in the chapter; they are listed in the first column. The table shows the variation in the key parameters and design choices made in each experiment.

13.3 The Baseline Scenario

We begin with the baseline scenario, a framework based on a continuation of current politics. Consequently, we assume polarized nomination politics, with Democratic and Republican presidents working hard to find and nominate consistently liberal and conservative justices, respectively. We also assume—for now—that confirmations occur during divided government. Of course, nothing in politics stays the same for decades! But the baseline scenario provides a useful benchmark for comparing the policy experiments.

13.3.1 The Median Justice and Bloc Sizes

To summarize the results of the baseline scenario, we first consider the year-by-year location of the court's median justice. In a given year, this location will vary somewhat across the simulations, due to randomness in the control of the presidency and the Senate, exits, and ideology of entrants. Figure 13.4 depicts histograms of the resulting distributions of the ideology of the median justice. To make the presentation manageable, we aggregate the results by decade, as we did in Chapter 12. The bins are colored from blue (more liberal) to red (more conservative).

Figure 13.4 shows that in every decade the distribution of the median justice is noticeably bimodal, with peaks in the range of [−.5, −.25] on the liberal side and [.25, .5] on the conservative side.[25] This bimodality follows from our assumptions

Table 13.2 Summary of policy experiments. If a cell is blank, that means it takes on the same value as in the baseline scenario.

Policy experiment	Starting court	Ideology	Strategic retirements	Senate control	Norms/ practices	Number of seats	Tenure
Baseline	2022 justices	Reliable ideologues ($\alpha = 3$) and ($\beta = 11$)	Standard	Historical	Standard	9	Life
No strategic retirements	–	–	None	–	–	–	–
Less predictable nominees	–	Heterogeneous nominees ($\alpha = 4$) and ($\beta = 6$)	–	–	–	–	–
2016 counterfactual	Garland + 2016 justices	–	–	–	–	–	–
No divided government confirmations	–	–	–	–	No confirmations under DG	–	–
No divided government confirmations, fixed Republican advantage	–	–	Fixed Republican advantage	Fixed Republican advantage	No confirmations under DG	–	–
No divided government confirmations, ↑ Republican advantage	–	–	Increasing Republican advantage	Increasing Republican advantage	No confirmations under DG	–	–
Democratic court packing, 2 seats	–	–	–	–	–	11	–
Democratic court packing, 4 seats	–	–	–	–	–	13	–
Democratic court packing, 6 seats	–	–	–	–	–	15	–
Tit-for-tat court packing	–	–	–	–	–	↑ over time	–
Term limits, 18 years	–	–	N/A	Irrelevant	–	–	18 years
Term limits, 9 years	–	–	N/A	Irrelevant	–	–	9 years

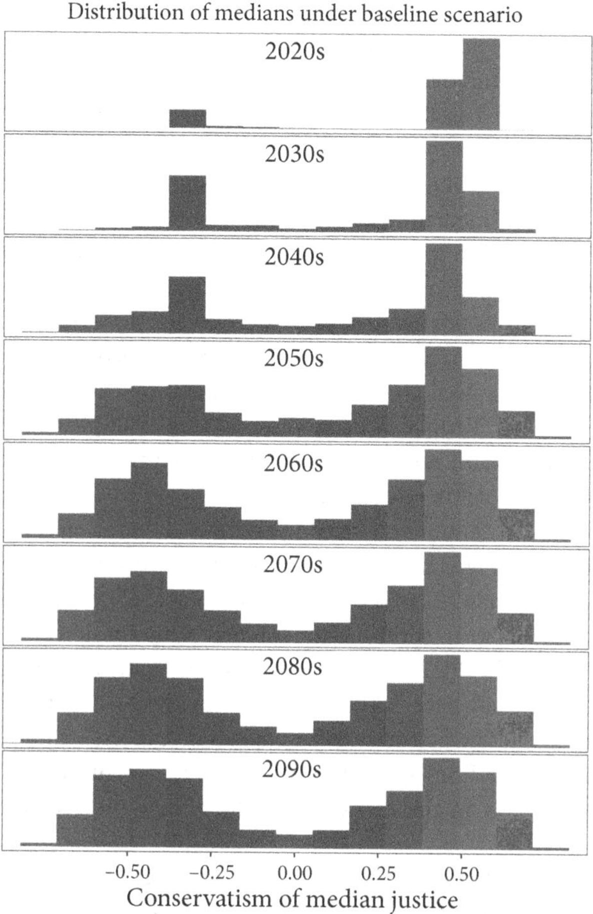

Fig. 13.4 Distribution of medians under baseline scenario, by decade. The bins are shaded from blue (liberal) to red (conservative).

about the distributions generating ideal points for new justices. One important consequence of the bimodality is that the actual median justice at any point in time is almost always either a reliable liberal or a reliable conservative; very rarely is the median justice an ideological moderate. But even with bimodal distributions, it matters which outcomes are more likely—the relative peaks of the bimodal distributions, and how they change over time, reflects the initial court, electoral outcomes in the future, and the timing of exits from the court.

In what is arguably the single most important result in the baseline scenarios, the distribution of medians in the early decades tilts heavily to the conservative side of the ideological spectrum. The conservative domination of the court as of 2022 in effect "stacks the deck" for years to come. While observers of the court might not be surprised that the court is likely to remain in conservative hands for a while, the simulations go much further than this intuition, showing a persistent conservative "bias" in the location of the median justice *through the 2050s*. It is only in the 2060s that the distribution of medians becomes roughly symmetric; by this point the long-run electoral probabilities overtake the historical realities of the early years and the results converge to our baseline assumptions, as the initial ideological skew slowly vanishes.

Of course, averages are not destiny. Figure 13.4 show that a minority of simulated courts do have liberal median justices, even in the decade of the 2020s (note the small block at about −.3 in that panel). Simulations yielding such a median typically involve Democratic presidents winning the 2024 and/or 2028 elections, combined with unusually early exits (via death or basic retirements) for several of the Republican justices. Such combinations can occur. However, the distinguished Princeton statistician J. Stuart Hunter used to admonish his students, "Remember: Rare events don't happen to me!"[26] Perhaps a string of rare events will play out and produce a liberal median justice in the not-too-distant future—but following Professor Hunter's mantra, Figure 13.4 shows that is unlikely.

A complementary and more nuanced measure of the ideological structure of the court is the size of the liberal, moderate, and conservative blocs. We place justices with ideal points less than −.2 in the liberal bloc, justices above .2 in the conservative bloc, and justices in between in the moderate bloc.[27] This division is facially plausibile and works well with the 2022 court. The three Democratic appointees (Sotomayor, Kagan, and Jackson) all have NSP scores of roughly −.3, so these cutoffs place them in the liberal bloc, which accords with qualitative assessments of their decision making.[28] The six Republican appointees on the 2022 court all have NSP scores above .4, placing them firmly in the conservative bloc. Thus, the center of the court is now empty.

Figure 13.5 displays the distribution of justice ideology by decade, by showing the proportion of justices that fall into the liberal, moderate, and conservative blocs in each decade. This picture extends the bloc analysis we performed in Chapter 12, where we showed the emergence of the polarized court over time. Consistent with the histogram of medians in Figure 13.4, Figure 13.5 shows that the average number of conservatives in the simulations exceeds the average number of liberals well into the middle of the century. Toward the middle of the century, the average size of the liberal and conservative blocs achieve parity; on average, there are four liberals and four conservatives on the court in the long-run equilibrium, with only one moderate. This composition is what the average baseline court would have—but only after many decades of a conservative majority.

13.3.2 Tenure Length and Strategic Retirements

What drives this predicted persistence of conservative control? One simple reason is the justices' longevity. Supreme Court justices now serve for extremely long periods—much longer than they used to. Figure 13.6 depicts this change in two ways.

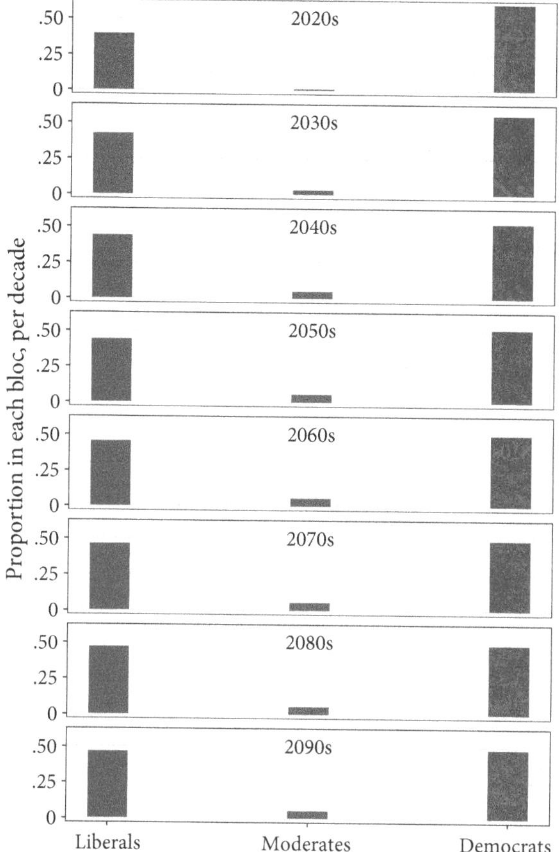

Fig. 13.5 The distribution of justice ideology by decade. The graphs show the simulated proportion of justices that fall into the liberal, moderate, and conservative blocs in each decade.

First, for each year, we calculated the average tenure of the justices on the bench at that time. Then, for each decade from the 1790s through the 2010s, we calculated the average tenure across that 10-year span. Figure 13.6A presents these results; the points show the decade-by-decade average, while the loess line summarizes the trend over time. Early on there is a "floor" effect, since the clock starts at zero for all of the initial justices in 1790. Interestingly, early in the nineteenth century, the average tenure was quite long—about 18 years in the 1820s.[29] But after this period, average tenure hovered in the 8- to 12-year range, until the 1970s. Since then, the average length of service has increased significantly. In the 2010s, the average tenure was about 16 years, compared to a low of six years in the 1940s.

Figure 13.6B cuts the data slightly differently—it shows the average tenure among the justices who *exited the court* in that decade. Here the results are even more dramatic. At the turn of the twentieth century, the average tenure of exiting justices was around 14 years. Since the 1940s, that number steadily increased, and in recent

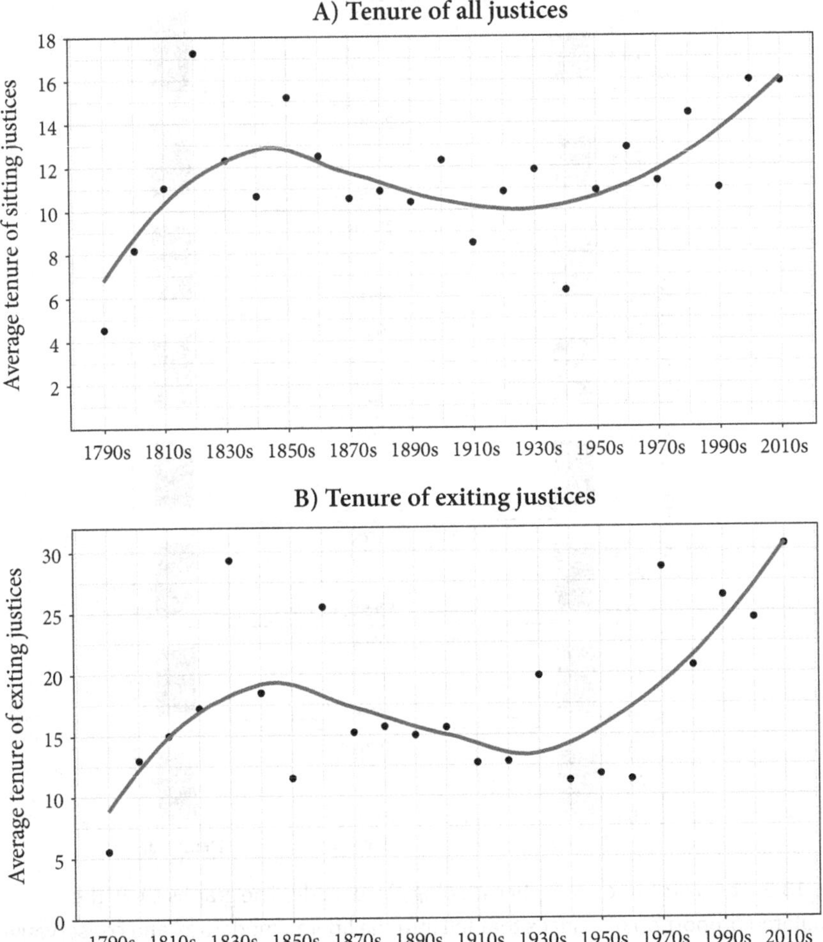

Fig. 13.6 Average Supreme Court tenure, by decade. A) The average tenure length of justices on the bench in each decade. B) The average tenure among the justices who exited the court in that decade.

decades the average tenure has approached 30 years. As we discussed earlier, this average longevity now encourages presidents to seek relatively younger nominees in order to perpetuate presidents' influence far beyond their term in office.

Strategic retirements are a second key factor in the predicted persistence of the conservative majority. Strategic retirement dampens random turnover in individual seats, so an individual seat tends to remain "in the family." As we described above, the baseline scenario incorporates a strategic retirement parameter that increases the probability of a justice retiring from the bench, conditional on their age, at moments when the current president shares their partisan affiliation. To evaluate the long-term effects of strategic retirements, we can run a policy experiment in which strategic retirements *never* occur; that is, the strategic retirement parameter is "turned off," meaning exits are only a function of "basic" retirements and death. We label this experiment *no strategic retirements.*

Figure 13.7 helps illustrate the interplay of tenure length and strategic retirements. We plot the nine justices on the court as of 2022, from most conservative to most liberal. We calculate each justices' mean year of departure, across all the simulations, for both the baseline and no strategic retirement scenario. For example, Clarence Thomas held the longest tenure of the court as of 2022, having taken the bench in 1991. In the baseline simulations, he is projected to serve on the court, on average, until about 2028, when he would be 80. In the scenario without strategic retirements, he is projected to serve an additional two years on average, until 2030.

Two important patterns emerge from Figure 13.7. First, regardless of whether the justices engage in strategic retirements, they are projected to serve for many years. This pattern is particularly true of Trump's three appointees (Gorsuch, Kavanaugh, and Barrett), as well as Justice Jackson, none of whom were older than 52 when appointed. All four are likely to serve at least through the 2040s. The other three Republican appointees are significantly older, but still all three are projected to serve at least through the majority of the 2020s. Thus, in the majority of simulations in the baseline scenario, the court remains dominated by the conservative bloc for the rest of the 2020s by virtue of the conservative justices' age and the mortality tables.

Second, under our assumptions, strategic retirement always leads to briefer tenures, since it induces justices to retire earlier under a co-partisan president than they would otherwise. If we compare the average exit year with and without strategic retirement in Figure 13.7, the difference between the two is larger for the younger justices. This reflects the fact these justices will have more opportunities over time for a strategic exit.

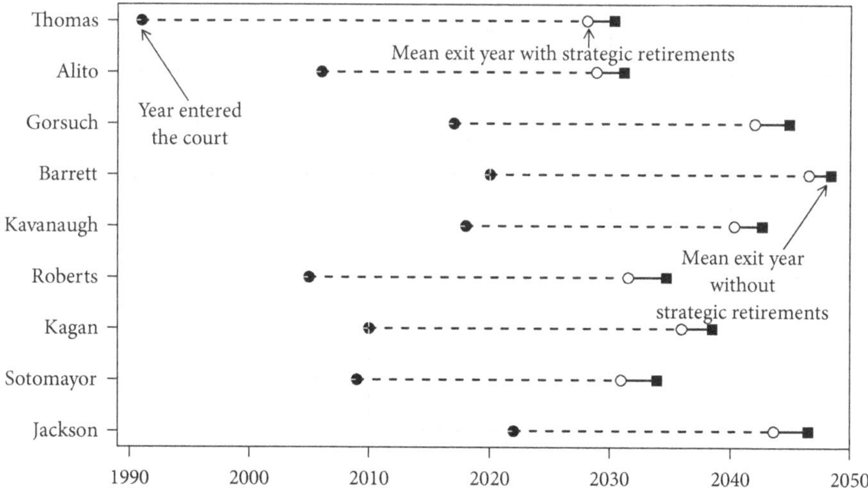

Fig. 13.7 Predicted exit year for 2022 justices, with and without strategic retirement. The justices are ordered by ideology, from conservative (top) to more liberal (bottom).

Table 13.3 Proportion of exits of 2022 justices under a co-partisan president, with and without strategic retirement.

Nominee	Without strategic retirements	With strategic retirements
Thomas	0.42	0.55
Alito	0.41	0.60
Gorsuch	0.49	0.66
Barrett	0.49	0.63
Kavanaugh	0.50	0.65
Roberts	0.47	0.64
Kagan	0.51	0.68
Sotomayor	0.56	0.71
Jackson	0.51	0.66

Because strategic retirements by definition give co-partisan presidents greater opportunity to appoint successors, such retirements tend to stabilize both the location of the median justice and the court's bloc structure. To illustrate this effect, we calculated the proportion of simulations in which each justice who was on the court in 2022 leaves under a co-partisan president, for both the baseline and no strategic retirement scenarios. Table 13.3 presents the results. Consider the scenario without strategic retirements. Due to their more advanced age, Thomas and Alito are projected to retire under a Republican president only about 40% of the time. But without strategic retirements, the justices' retirement dates are random with respect to White House control of the White House. Thus, the rest of the justices cluster around 50%, meaning that they are equally likely to retire under a Democratic or Republican president.

Conversely, under the scenario with strategic retirements, the probability of an exit under a co-partisan president is always higher. For example, both Sotomayor and Kagan are predicted to leave the court under a Democratic president about 70% of the time. To be sure, even under our assumptions, strategic retirements are hardly a guarantee of a co-partisan exit, for sometimes death intervenes (as with Justice Ginsburg) or health issues force a retirement even when a president of the opposite party is in the White House (as with Thurgood Marshall). The flip side of the Sotomayor and Kagan results is that in 30% of simulations they are replaced by Republican nominees. But, all told, the simulations demonstrate how strategic retirements help lock in the ideological status quo on the court, thus contributing to the projected long dominance of conservatives in the baseline scenario.

13.3.3 The Importance of Ideological Reliability

A final reason for the predicted conservative domination of the court for many years to come is entrant ideology. We assume future Democratic and Republican nominees will be highly ideologically reliable, and thus few justices will be moderates. In the Appendix we present the results of a policy experiment in which future nominees are less predictable than in the baseline scenario—we call this experiment "less predictable nominees." The counterfactual here is a scenario where presidents return to selecting ideologically unreliable nominees, as they did in the 1940s and 1950s. Under this (unlikely) scenario, the ideological trajectory of the court would become much more moderate compared to the baseline scenario, and much less susceptible to wild swings in the median.

If we contrast this scenario to the baseline, it is hardly surprising that reliably extreme entrants translate into more ideological polarization on the court. But the simulations help clarify how scrupulous vetting and careful selection help lock in the current conservative majority on the court. Such procedures are likely to perpetuate the conservative majority for decades.

13.4 The Transformative Election of 2016

Simulations offer a new way to appraise the transformative impact of a presidential election. The MSC Simulator allows us to alter the outcome of a single presidential election and then construct explicit counterfactual paths of the court's future composition. These alternative paths incorporate the likely subsequent trajectory of institutional control tripped off by the counterfactual election. The subsequent sequences of exits also incorporate different sets of strategic retirements, reflecting the altered future of institutional control.[30]

We use this approach to appraise the impact of the events of 2016; namely, Senate Leader Mitch McConnell's success in blocking the confirmation of Merrick Garland, followed by the shock victory of Donald Trump in the 2016 presidential election. Suppose instead McConnell had allowed a floor vote on Garland, which quite plausibly would have led to his confirmation.[31] Then, suppose Hillary Clinton had prevailed in the Electoral College, rather than just the popular vote. How might this alternative history have changed the court's future composition?

The opening part of the story is well known. President Obama's first two nominees (Sotomayor and Kagan) replaced two liberal justices (Souter and Stevens, respectively), leaving the court with either a 5-4 conservative majority, or a 4-1-4 split, depending on how one characterizes Justice Kennedy. But regardless of Kennedy's exact characterization, the appointment of Kagan in 2010 marked the first time partisanship and ideology became perfectly correlated in aggregate voting on the court, as shown in Chapter 12. The subsequent death of conservative stalwart Antonin Scalia in 2016 afforded Obama the chance to shift the court's balance rather dramatically. The analyses in Chapter 12 suggest these changes would have led to both more liberal dispositions and more liberal majority opinions and policy. McConnell's decisive action blocked these possibilities, at least in the short term. But what happened next depended on the outcome of the 2016 presidential election, and Trump's surprising victory meant that he, rather than Hillary Clinton, selected Scalia's replacement, as well as the successors to Kennedy in 2018 and Ginsburg in 2020. The result was the conservative-dominated court of the baseline scenario, as shown in Table 13.1.

How much did the events of 2016 change the future trajectory of the court? To answer the question, we developed a policy experiment that starts in 2017, but assumes confirmation of Garland, followed by a Clinton victory and a Republican Senate. Then, using the underlying assumptions of the baseline scenario, we run the simulations from that point forward, just as we did using the reality of 2022 in the baseline scenario. Of course, we can't know for sure what would have happened in a Clinton presidency. Justice Kennedy, for example, might have remained on the court in the hopes of a Republican replacement in 2021. But the simulations handle these contingencies probabilistically, just as they do in the baseline scenario.[32]

Figure 13.8 shows the results of this counterfactual analysis. For comparison purposes, the left panel reproduces Figure 13.4, the distribution of median justices

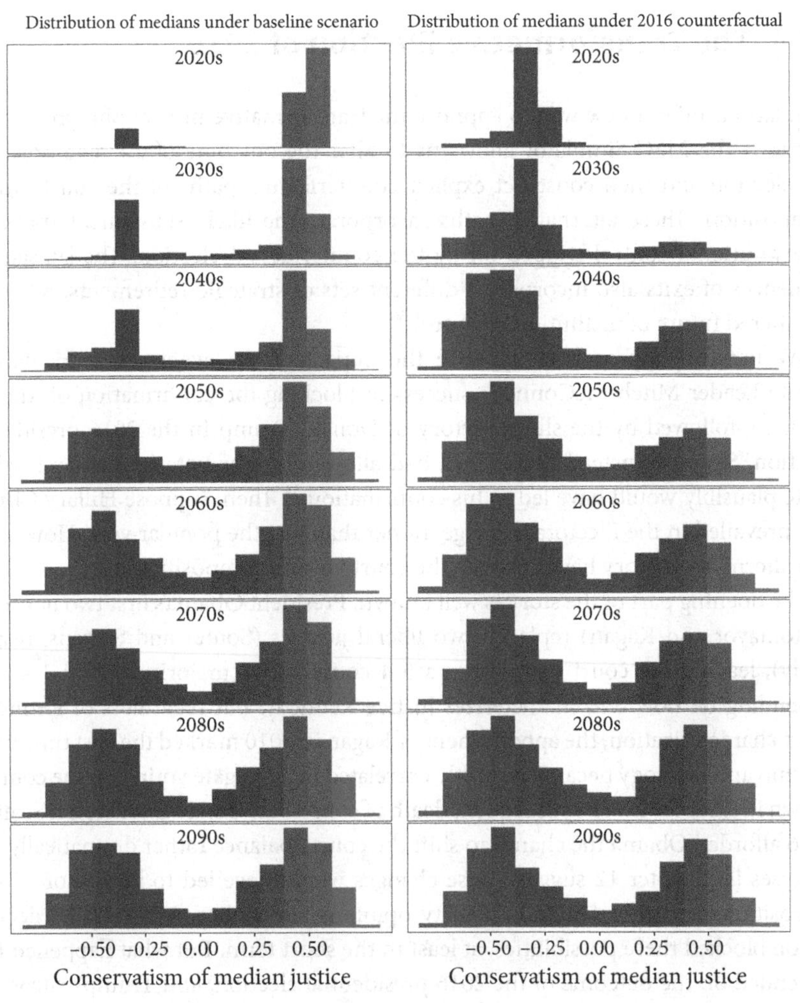

Fig. 13.8 Distribution of medians under baseline scenario and 2016 counterfactual, by decade. Bars are shaded from blue (liberal) through red (conservative).

under the baseline scenario. The right panel shows the distribution under the 2016 counterfactual. Strikingly, the two columns display nearly mirror images of one another in the early years. Under the 2016 counterfactual, the court's center is on average quite liberal, not conservative, in the majority of simulations of the 2020s. It remains so through the 2050s. At that point, the long steady-state emerges in both scenarios and two balanced wings confront one another.

The bottom line is clear: the events of 2016 were indeed a crossroads for the U.S. Supreme Court. One path led to likely liberal dominance of the court for decades. The other path led to conservative dominance over the same horizon. The road taken arose from a bold gambit in the Senate, an unlikely electoral outcome, and a string of exits from the court.

Viewing these events, liberals may well recall the words of the medieval poem *Carmina Burana*:

> I bemoan the wounds of Fortune
> with weeping eyes,
> for the gifts she made me
> she perversely takes away.

Conservatives, on the other hand, may savor the Roman philosopher Seneca's famous observation: "Luck is what happens when preparation meets opportunity."

13.5 A Plausible Future: The End of Divided Government Appointments

So far we have assumed the Senate always allows the sitting president to fill a vacant seat. The events of 2016, however, raise the possibility that a Senate controlled by the opposition will categorically refuse to confirm the president's nominee. Under this permanent "Garland scenario," a vacant seat would remain vacant until a shift in either the presidency or Senate led to unified party control.[33] To see what might happen if such blanket opposition became the norm, we developed a policy experiment that assumes no entrances on the court during president-Senate divided party government. Any vacancies that arise under divided government remain unfilled until the next occurrence of unified government (regardless of party control), for as long as the transition takes. We label this experiment, *no divided government confirmations*.

How plausible is this scenario? During the Garland blockade, partisans on both sides combed history for justifications. Republicans claimed that divided party confirmations were rare in presidential election years. Democrats called the blockade "unprecedented."[34] Both claims are somewhat contestable, but in either case this scenario goes much further than the 2016 blockade. It assumes no confirmations at any point in a president's tenure during divided party government. So a seat could remain vacant not just for a brief period, but from Inauguration Day until a president's final hours in office, and beyond. That would indeed be unprecedented and, until recently, unthinkable for the Supreme Court.

But if we look beyond the confines of Supreme Court appointment politics, a perpetual Garland scenario becomes more plausible. Take, for example, less sacrosanct independent agencies caught up in intense partisan polarization, such as the Federal Elections Commission (FEC) and the National Labor Relations Board (NLRB). The former regulates money in federal elections, while the latter sets the rules for labor-management disputes, so both agencies generate intense partisan warfare. In recent years, appointments to both agencies have often been held up during divided party government—so much so that vacancies sometimes imperil their boards' ability to reach a quorum.[35] The political logic of hold-up is transparent: the party controlling the Senate calculates that it prefers the current board—with a vacancy or even without a quorum—to a board filled by the opposition president. Presidents respond with aggressive but temporary (and sometimes dubiously legal) recess appointments.[36] The ultimate result is agency chaos, incapacity, and a diminished American government. But the brutal partisan logic trumps concerns over good governance. The scenario we explore merely transports the appointment politics of those agencies to the U.S. Supreme Court. The confluence of extreme partisan polarization with the greatest period of divided party government in American history makes this scenario far from impossible.

13.5.1 The Incredible Shrinking Supreme Court?

Under a norm of no divided government appointments, vacancies could persist for long periods, leaving the court without a full complement of nine justices. Indeed, such an event occurred in 2016–2017, when the court operated with eight members between Justice Scalia's death in February 2016 and Justice Gorsuch's confirmation in April 2017.

For each simulation under this counterfactual scenario, we calculate when a seat remains open due to divided government. Recall that in our original baseline scenarios, there are technically no "vacancies" *per se*, since justices are counted as serving for an entire year if their tenures extends to a given year, with replacements counted as entering the year after an exit. With vacancies now possible under no divided government confirmations, we count the number of seats filled in a given seat-year combination.

For the majority of the time (about 77%), the simulations predict a full nine-member court. This is because when vacancies occur, they "transition" into appointments upon the very next instance of unified government, which occur frequently in the simulations. Still, the results show that under the norm of no divided government confirmations, courts with fewer than a full complement of nine justices occur more than 20% of the time, a huge change from historical practice. Moreover, while courts with fewer than seven members would be rare, they are predicted to occur about 3%

of the time. And courts that only minimally meet the statutory quorum of six justices occur about 1% of the time. Thus, while the court would not empty out when unified government is needed to fill a vacancy, it could end up hearing cases with a bench of eight members or fewer.

13.5.2 The Senate Map: Greater Republican Advantage

Because our baseline assumption assumes symmetric election probabilities, divided government occurs on average equally under Democratic and Republican presidents; thus, having no divided government confirmations would not significantly privilege one side or the other, relative to the baseline scenarios.[37] Yet there is good reason to believe that the baseline assumption of symmetric probabilities for controlling the Senate may prove untenable in future decades, as the Senate map seems increasingly likely to favor the Republican party. This is because Democrats increasingly tend to cluster in a few large urban states, but the Constitution guarantees each state two senators. As the political scientist Jonathan Rodden (2019, 2) noted, between 1990 and 2018, Democrats won more votes than Republicans in eleven of the fifteen Senate elections, but they held a majority of seats after only six of those elections.

Indeed, this discrepancy between votes and seats became a talking point during the nominations of President Trump's three nominees. Ronald Browstein (2018), a political reporter, noted that if one assigned half of each state's population to each of its two senators, the 51 Republican senators at the time of Brett Kavanaugh's nominations represented about 143 million Americans, compared to the 182 million represented by the 49 Democratic senators.[38] Moreover, the electoral bias of the Senate is only likely to increase in the coming decades. In some sense, the Constitution destined the Senate to become a "rotten borough."[39]

To understand the potential effects of the changing Senate dynamics, we modeled bias in Senate control in two ways. First, we simulated a fixed Republican bias by increasing each of the Senate transition probabilities described above by .05 toward Republicans. Second, we simulated a linearly increasing Republican bias by multiplying the transition probabilities by .005 and adding that amount to the base probability. For both of these policy experiments, we also assume no divided government confirmations. We label these experiments *No divided government confirmations, fixed Republican advantage* and *No divided government confirmations, increasing Republican advantage*.

We examine two related quantities of interest under these scenarios. The first is how often vacancies would occur under the Republican Senate advantage. Because divided government under a Republican Senate would become more likely, as time passes, the average number of vacancies would be systematically higher under Democratic presidents than Republican ones.[40] This asymmetry in vacancies, in turn, affects the second quantity of interest—the partisan consequences for the composition of the court. Figure 13.9 shows the average location of the median justice over time,

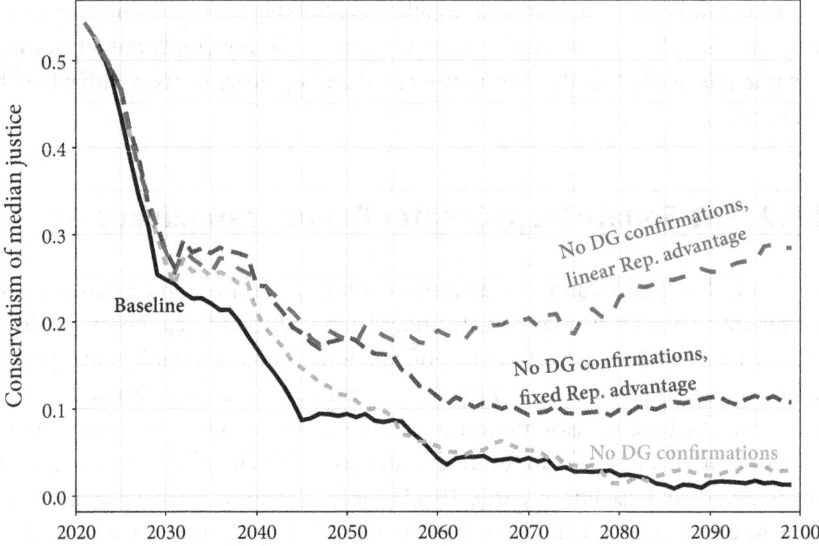

Fig. 13.9 The effect of an increasing Republican advantage in the Senate. The graph shows the average location of median justice, under the baseline scenario and the three no divided government confirmation scenarios.

under each of the three no divided government confirmation scenarios, as well as the results from the baseline scenario for reference. First, because the regular no divided government confirmation assumes symmetric Senate election probabilities, there is little difference in the average location of the median justice between the baseline scenario and the symmetric no divided government confirmation scenario; due to the timing of exits, the median under the baseline is slightly more conservative from about 2030 to 2050, but only by a substantively small amount.

The picture is quite different once we assume a Republican advantage in the Senate. Because the fixed advantage is relatively small, in addition to the fact the court is initially controlled by conservatives, little change occurs in the early decades, as seen in Figure 13.9. But in the future, after the initial court turns over, both the fixed Republican Senate advantage and especially the increasing advantage imply the likelihood of a conservative-dominated court in the majority of the simulations. Thus, the partisan advantage in vacancies translates into a substantial partisan advantage on the court.

Crucially, this effect occurs *despite* symmetric probabilities for control of the presidency. Democratic and Republican presidents would be equally likely to make a *nomination* to the court (conditional on the incidence of strategic retirements). But, the Republican bias in Senate control means that Republican presidents would be more likely to see their nominees *confirmed* under a norm of no divided government appointments. In contrast, Democratic presidents would find themselves more hamstrung in actually filling vacancies, because divided government would be much more likely to occur in their administrations than in Republican ones.

13.6 Statutory and Constitutional Reforms

Following the Garland blockade of 2016 and President Trump's subsequent appointment of three justices, the topic of reforming the Supreme Court's selection and retention institutions moved from the pages of law reviews into mainstream discussions of American politics. In this section, we examine the two most widely discussed reform proposals: court packing and term limits.

We continue the baseline assumption that presidents from both parties will appoint highly reliable ideologues, as we view a return to ideologically heterogeneous nominees (and a depolarized court) extremely unlikely. Consequently, the effects from changing formal selection institutions or tenure institutions, or both, are of great interest.

13.6.1 Court Packing

The first dramatic potential institutional change would be adding seats to the Supreme Court. The Constitution does not specify the size of the court, leaving that discretion to Congress, which also has the power to alter the size of the lower federal courts. In fact, Congress has expanded the lower courts nearly 30 times since 1789; De Figueiredo and Tiller (1996) show that Congress has been much more likely to do so during unified government than divided government, even accounting for possible caseload concerns. Unified government, of course, allows a president and Senate to work in tandem to appoint like-minded judges to the federal bench.[41]

By contrast, Congress has only rarely altered the size of the Supreme Court. Between 1789 and 1869 the number of seats on the court fluctuated between six and ten.[42] Since 1869, however, the bench has remained at nine despite the introduction of many bills that would change its size.[43] The most serious threat came in 1937, when President Roosevelt famously proposed expanding the court to break the majority's opposition to the New Deal. Roosevelt's plan proved extremely controversial even within his own party, and ultimately the Senate rejected it in a 70-20 vote.[44] Despite this humiliating legislative defeat, Roosevelt won the larger battle. First, a narrow majority on the court softened its opposition to key New Deal measures. Then, several judges retired, allowing Roosevelt to appoint an astounding nine justices in his 15 years in office.[45]

Despite Roosevelt's ultimate success, the conventional wisdom about the 1937 episode has been that court packing is a third rail in American politics. However, events in the 2010s rehabilitated the notion among some liberal activists and politicians, after the court made several rulings that seemed to advance Republican partisan interests. Among those most infuriating to liberals were the 2010 decision in *Citizens United*, prohibiting the government from restricting independent expenditures for political communications by corporations; *Shelby County v. Holder*, striking down key portions of the Voting Rights Act; and *Rucho v. Common Cause*, holding claims of partisan gerrymandering to be non-justiciable in federal courts.[46] These cases soon appeared in Democratic presidential platforms as examples of judicial perfidy (see Chapter 2). Combined with the McConnell gambit of 2016 and 2017, the pronounced tilt in the judicial playing field led some liberal politicians and advocates to call for a "hard ball" response when Democrats regained the White House. Indeed, court packing emerged as a central talking point in the 2020 Democratic primary, with several candidates expressing support for adding new seats.[47]

As it turned out, the push for court packing quickly fizzled. Democrats won control of the presidency and both chambers of Congress in the 2020 elections, but their majorities in the House and especially the Senate were razor thin, effectively precluding any radical change.[48] In addition, President Joe Biden seemed lukewarm about the idea. He came out against court packing in 2019; then, as president, appointed a bipartisan commission in 2021 to study court reform. That commission did not make a formal recommendation, as the issue of court packing divided the members.[49] The future may bring a surprising turn of fortune, but at the time we write the prospects for expanding the Supreme Court appear very dim.

Still, it is useful to examine how the court would be affected by court packing. Accordingly, we developed three policy experiments in which we assume that the court was expanded in 2021 under unified Democratic government. These experiments respectively assume an increase of two, four, or six seats, bringing the total number of justices to 11, 13, and 15, respectively. These are assumed to have taken effect in 2022, meaning the additional justices would all be Democratic appointees. Other than this, we assume everything else remains as in the baseline scenario. For now, we assume (probably unrealistically) that court packing would be a one-time event, with the size of the court forever fixed after the increase in seats. We consider tit-for-tat court packing momentarily.

Figure 13.10 shows the average ideology of the median justice under each court-packing scenario; we also show the baseline results for comparison. Not surprisingly, Democratic court packing would shift the median of the court to the left, compared to the baseline scenario of a conservative median justice.

Because the real court in 2021 had six conservatives and three liberals, allowing for either four or six new Democratic appointments would have caused immediate and lasting impact on the average location of the median, shifting it to the liberal wing of the court. But even under the scenario where only two seats would be added, it would still take several years for the average median justice to approach the centrist zero mark. Moreover, from 2030 to 2060, while the median would be liberal for most years, the deviation from zero would actually be much smaller compared to the conservative bias seen in the baseline scenario. Thus, while adding more than two seats would likely produce a dramatic and prolonged liberal court, adding only two seats would yield a more balanced court.

Of course, politics is a dynamic process, so it seems likely—in fact, virtually certain—that a Democratic expansion would provoke a Republican response. To investigate the possibility of a cycle of tit-for-tat court packing, we begin with the

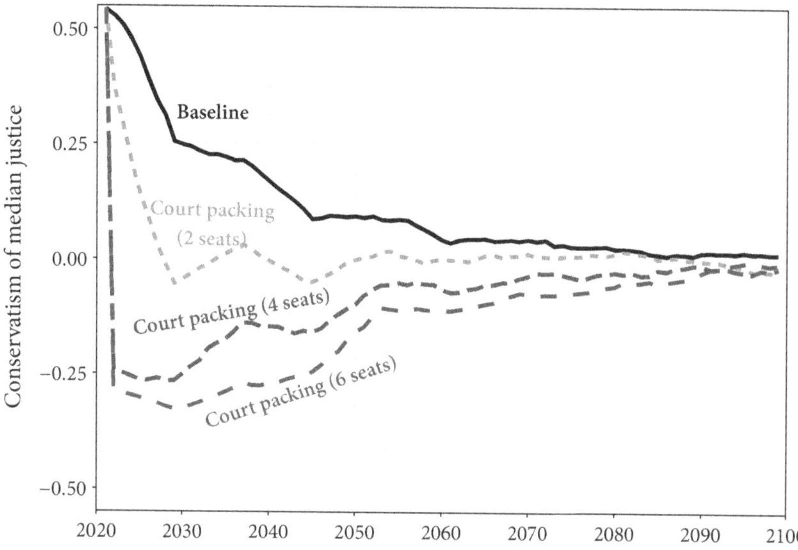

Fig. 13.10 The average location of the court's median, under the baseline scenarios and three hypothetical court packing plans implemented by Democrats in 2021.

policy experiment in which the Democrats added two seats in 2021. We then suppose that every time a new unified government occurs in which the majority party is opposite from the one that existed at the last occurrence of unified government, two additional seats are added to the court, filled by an ideological judge aligned with the sitting president (again using the baseline simulation). Because we assume court packing first occurs in 2021 under unified Democrat government, the implication is the subequent round of court packing would occur when Republicans next gain unified control of the White House and Senate.[50] In simulations where the Democrats lose the White House in 2024 and Republicans control the Senate, the tit-for-tat occurs as early as 2025–2026. This cycle continues with every switch.[51]

Modeling the composition and ideology of the court under this cycle of tit-for-tat court packing quickly becomes quite involved and computationally taxing. Instead, we pursue a simpler but important question: how many seats would the court have over this century? For every simulation, we recorded the number of seats in every year. Then, for every year we calculated the average number of seats, along with 95% confidence intervals. Figure 13.11 shows these results.[52]

The upshot is straightforward but nevertheless stark. The number of seats on the court would rise in a roughly linear fashion, reaching nearly 30 seats by the end of the century. Courts of such size are not unknown; for example, the Indian Supreme Court currently has 30 judges. But such a bulky court would be a complete departure from the American experience. The largest state supreme court has nine members, and many are as small as five. A 30-member body would resemble less a traditional American court than a legislature, requiring radical changes in procedure and operation.

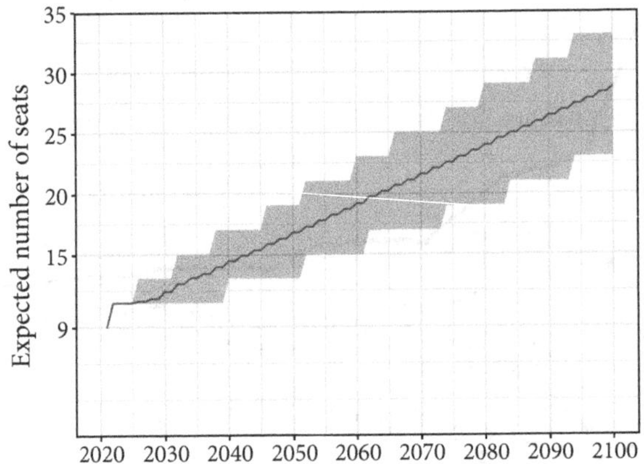

Fig. 13.11 How tit-for-tat court packing would affect the size of the court.

13.6.2 Term Limits

Court packing is and likely will remain highly contentious and bitterly partisan. There is, however, an alternative that is far less controversial, receiving endorsements from academics and politicians across the political spectrum: term limits for the justices.

Article III of the Constitution states that "the judges, both of the supreme and inferior courts, shall hold their offices during good behaviour," a clause that effectively provides Supreme Court judges with life tenure, short of impeachment. During the constitutional conventions, the institutions for selection and retention of federal judges were the subject of much debate—particularly the appointment mechanism. But the historical record suggests that there was little disagreement over the wisdom of life tenure.[53] Most famously, Alexander Hamilton argued in Federalist 78 that if "the courts of justice are to be considered as the bulwarks of a limited Constitution against legislative encroachments, this consideration will afford a strong argument for the permanent tenure of judicial offices, since nothing will contribute so much as this to that independent spirit in the judges which must be essential to the faithful performance of so arduous a duty."

Whatever the wisdom of life tenure in 1789, several modern-day realities may suggest the wisdom of a reappraisal. First, almost no other judicial system at either the state level in the United States or in other countries provides for life tenure. Yet these courts appear to function reasonably well without it.

In addition, as Calabresi and Lindgren (2005) note, many of Hamilton's empirical justifications no longer hold true today. Perhaps most prominently, the institution that Hamilton called "the least dangerous branch" now exercises sweeping authority and influence across a stunning range of policy domains. Accordingly, a somewhat greater degree of democratic accountability and responsiveness to the public may be warranted. Moreover, as we documented in Figure 13.6, the average tenure of Supreme Court justices has increased dramatically over time. Decades-long tenures substantially increase the political stakes of each appointment. Briefer tenures might dial down the heat in nominations. We return to these points in the next chapter.

Given these developments, many observers have called for an end to life tenure, replacing it either with a mandatory retirement age or, more commonly, fixed terms.[54] In addition, a number of 2020 Democratic presidential candidates either expressed outright support for term limits or openness to the idea, as have senators from both parties. Finally, a majority of the American public seems to support the idea: a poll taken in July 2018 (the month Brett Kavanaugh was nominated) found that 61% of registered voters, including 67% of Democrats and 58% of Republicans, support term limits for the justices.[55]

Still, imposing term limits presents a constitutional difficulty. Given the "good behavior" clause in Article III, such a plan would likely require a constitutional amendment, a formidable hurdle in the American system.[56] Some scholars, however, have made ingenious arguments that it is possible to implement term limits via statute, and not through the amendment process.[57] Of course, a statutory plan would inevitably end up before the Supreme Court itself; it seems unlikely that a majority on the court—and the justices on it with life tenure—would endorse a term limits statute.

These uncertainties notwithstanding, the MSC Simulator offers a way to gauge the likely impact of term limits, if they are ever implemented. Implementing term limits requires many detailed design choices about phasing in staggered terms, filling incomplete terms, and so on. The precise details of various plans to implement fixed terms differ, and the details matter. However, all the proposals share some basic features. In place of life tenure, justices would serve fixed and non-renewable terms, typically 18 years. Most proposals take 18 years as the specified term, for two practical reasons. First, the relatively long term is similar to the current status quo, so the proposal seems less radical. Second, it dovetails neatly with a nine-member court and four-year presidential terms. Staggered 18-year terms would give every president two appointments during every four-year term. Of course, just as Congress could dictate the size of the Supreme Court, so too could it set terms of any length. Lastly, while 18 years is by no means short, compared to the current justices' average tenure length, even a term of nearly two decades would reduce the chances of physical infirmity or mental incapacity impairing judicial performance.

To simulate the possible effects of term limits, we keep things simple and present two straightforward term limits policy experiments, so that we can compare the court's ideological composition under a basic term limit scheme to the other experiments we examined in this chapter.[58] The first follows most existing plans and implements 18-year terms. The second implements 9-year terms; this allows us to examine how faster turnover on the court would affect its ideological composition over time.

We describe the 18-year term experiment first. We imagine a constitutional amendment passed in 2022 and implemented in 2023, under which the sitting justices (as of 2022) are ordered by their tenure on the bench. Under the plan, the current justices would be replaced in order of seniority by their tenure on the bench. So Clarence Thomas, the longest-tenured justice, would leave in 2022, with a new justice taking over in 2023. This process would be repeated sequentially every two years, until the junior justice in 2022 (Jackson) is replaced in 2039. Thus, this design implements rolling 18-year terms.

We make several simplifying assumptions. First, for each vacancy that arises at the start of a new term, the new justice is appointed by the sitting president. The outcomes of presidential elections are still important, because they determine which party makes an appointment when a vacancy arises. This is particularly true for the phase-in period when the current justices are replaced. For example, Samuel Alito would leave the court in 2027 under this scenario, meaning the winner of the 2024 elections would choose his successor.

Second, we assume that once a seat transitions into the term limits phase, it is "assigned" to the appointing party for the duration of its 18-year term, even if the justice leaves the court before her term expires. Take Justice Thomas, for instance, who is replaced by a Democratic justice in 2023. If Thomas' replacement left the bench before their term expires in 2041, we assume they would be replaced by a Democratic justice; this process could be part of the institutional design of the amendment.[59] To be clear, this rule does not mean that a seat is assigned to the Democrats or Republicans forever; which party fills the term that expires in, say, 2037 would be determined by the outcome of the 2036 election. Accordingly, our experiment does *not* specify that a certain number of Democratic or Republican justices will be on the court at any one time, as that distribution is still determined by presidential elections. But it does mean, among other things, that sitting justices cannot strategically retire early under a co-partisan president to ensure their seat remains in the same party.

Third, we assume that all nominees are confirmed. In reality, a term limits design would have to deal with the possibility that divided government confirmations might cease, which would obviously frustrate the intended goals of term limits. One solution would be to remove the Senate's role in the confirmation process altogether. Another alternative would be to require a super-majority vote in the Senate to *reject* a nominee. Such a rule would likely not impede qualified nominees, but would prevent the president from appointing an unqualified crony or highly extreme ideologue, for example.

In the second experiment, everything is the same but instead we assume 9-year staggered terms. Presidents would have four appointments per term, beginning in 2025, and would make an appointment every year of their time in office.

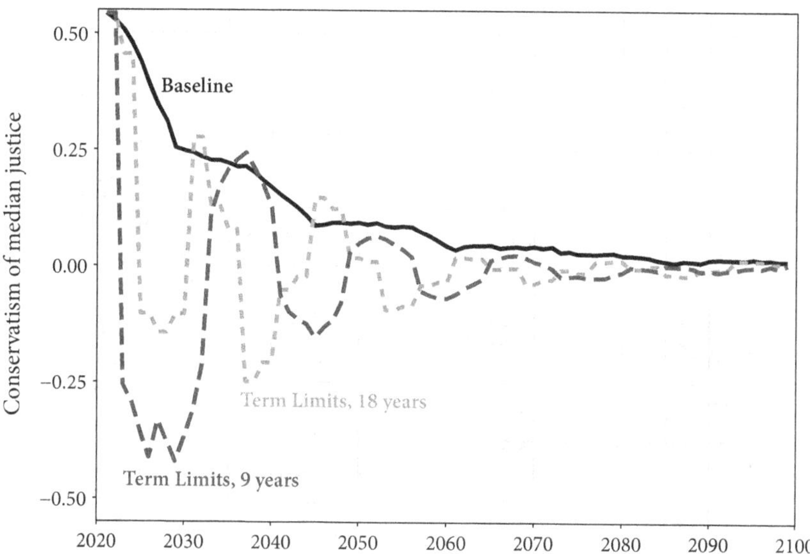

Fig. 13.12 The average location of the court's median, under the baseline scenarios and 18- and 9-year term limits.

Figure 13.12 displays the average median justice under both 18-year and 9-year term limits; we also show the results under the baseline scenario for comparison. The results are dramatic. Because the Democrats are predicted to retain control of the White House in 2024, in both the 9-year and 18-year term limits experiments, the median swings to the liberal side, especially in the 9-year scenario. Thus, a quick introduction of term limits would effectively end the conservative lock-in under the baseline scenario. The swings continue for a few decades until both term limits scenarios converge (on average) to the baseline scenario around 2060.

Importantly, this convergence might suggest that term limits produce a more moderate court. But this is not the case; Figure 13.13 shows the distribution of median justices, by decade, for both term limits scenarios. Because we assume the appointment of reliable ideologues, the more frequent turnover under both of these scenarios will produce more *balanced* courts in terms of the number of liberal and conservative justices. But at any one point in time, the court is likely to display a bimodal wing structure, with highly polarized ideological blocs. To be clear, this outcome is true in nearly all the simulations we have presented so far, due to our baseline assumptions about justice ideology. But it is important to emphasize exactly what term limits would—and would not—accomplish. This bimodality result, in turn, has implications for how we think about the "responsiveness" of the court to the tides of elections, a topic to which we turn to in the next chapter.

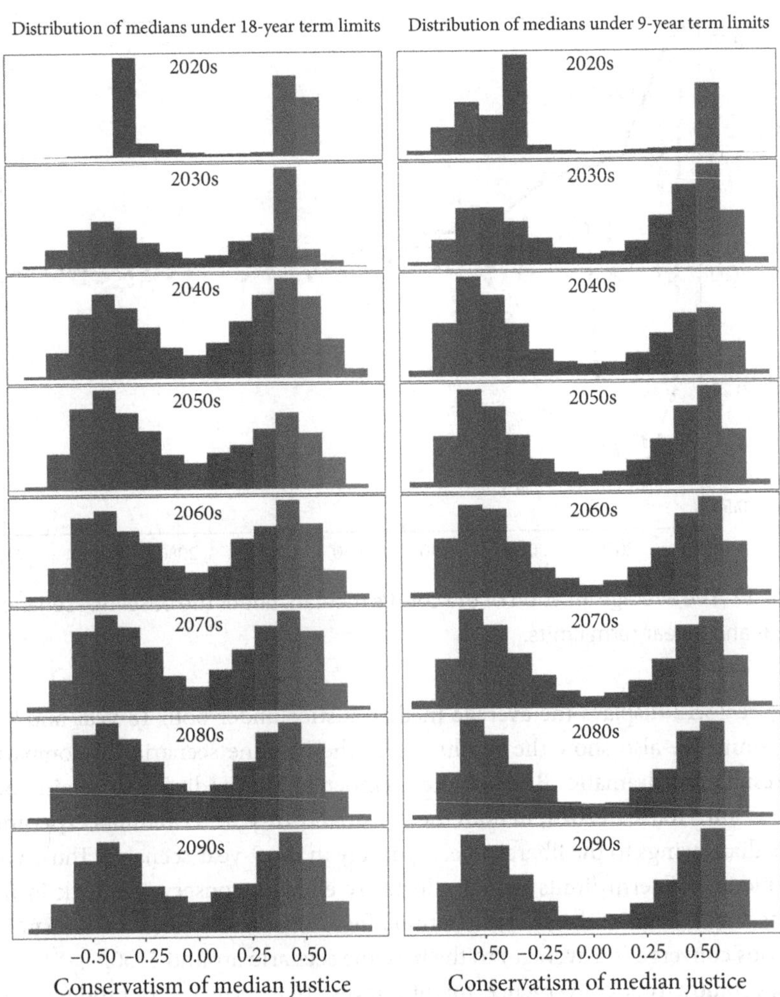

Fig. 13.13 The distribution of medians, by decades, under 18-year and 9-year limits.

13.7 Conclusion

"Never make predictions—especially about the future," Hollywood mogul Samuel Goldwyn once advised. In this chapter, we violated this undoubtedly wise injunction with impunity. To discipline our predictions about future courts, we built them on clear and explicit micro-foundations, reflecting the historical experience and arguably plausible projections.

We see one very large take-away point from the analysis and at least four subsidiary ones. The large and quite robust point is:

- The events of 2016—the Garland blockade and the election of Donald Trump—locked in place a solid conservative majority on the court. Barring a string of unlikely events, this majority will persist for several decades.

The additional points are:

1. The court is quite likely to remain polarized into two ideologically distinct blocs, with a near-empty center. As the conservative majority slowly dissipates, the median justice will probably swing regularly between the two blocs.
2. One plausible future involves the Senate refusing to confirm *any* nominees during divided government. If Supreme Court appointments come to resemble those of the NLRB and FEC, at least one seat is likely to be vacant a substantial portion of the time and, on occasion, multiple seats will sit empty.
3. Court packing seems unlikely (at least in the near future), but if implemented could produce tit-for-tat cycles of increases in the number of justices, creating a court with as many as 30 members by the end of the century.
4. Staggered term limits would prevent any long-run ideological bias in the composition of the court.

The analysis focused mainly on the ideological structure of the court itself, not the politics that will likely accompany the most probable futures. In addition, our focus has been positive, not normative. We asked only what future we are likely to see. We did not ask what future we should want and how can we get it. We turn to this task in the next chapter.

14
What Future Do We Want? Evaluating Judicial Independence

The simulations presented in Chapter 13 project future paths for the Supreme Court, under the status quo and in response to plausible changes in institutions. We stopped short, however, of *evaluating* these changes, beyond the descriptive level. We turn to evaluation in this penultimate chapter.

How to evaluate possible futures depends on one's goals and values. For example, for a dedicated partisan evaluating the projected changes is easy: does my side win or lose? But in our view, such evaluations—while inevitable in a highly partisan age—are neither interesting nor perspicacious. Is it instead possible to evaluate the possible paths for the court based on defensible first principles?

In this chapter, we develop a simple normative framework to evaluate the tradeoffs implicit in different judicial selection and retention institutions. These tradeoffs arise because different degrees of judicial independence, as embodied by lower responsiveness to election results and longer tenures on the court, create both costs and benefits to society. To gauge the tradeoffs implied in the policy experiments of the last chapter, we focus on four measurable quantities. The first is *democratic responsiveness*—the degree to which the composition of the court broadly tracks the electoral choices of the American public. The second is *judicial turnover*—the frequency with which new justices replace existing ones. The third is the frequency of *closely divided courts*—courts with compositions in which a new justice would alter the court's ideological balance. The fourth is the frequency of *out-of-step courts*—courts with a supermajority of justices appointed by one party facing unified elected branches controlled by the other party.

We examine all four quantities across the different policy experiments we presented in Chapter 13. The normative framework suggests how one might weigh the revealed tradeoffs. We stop short of making definitive recommendations, for that would simply reflect our values. But one point stands out: the current system of life tenure for highly reliable ideologues falls on the maximum side of judicial independence; indeed no other democracy endows high court judges with such job security.[1] Among the policy experiments we consider, 18-year term limits effectively reduce this independence by increasing democratic responsiveness and judicial turnover; they also would likely reduce the intensity of conflict over appointments by increasing their regularity. Whether these benefits mitigate the costs of reducing the independence of the court is a value judgment. But readers can use our framework and the simulation

Making the Supreme Court: The Politics of Appointments, 1930–2020. Charles M. Cameron and Jonathan P. Kastellec, Oxford University Press. © Oxford University Press 2023. DOI: 10.1093/oso/9780197680544.003.0014

results to probe their own values and consider the best path forward for selecting and replacing Supreme Court justices.

14.2 Constitutional Engineering

The design of high court selection and retention systems is a topic in constitutional engineering. In some sense, it resembles designing selection and retention systems for legislators, chief executives, heads of administrative agencies, the workers within those agencies, and the sub-contractors to the agencies.[2] But judicial selection and retention systems present special issues all their own.

As a practical matter, the American states display a fairly limited variety of judicial selection and retention systems. In their pathbreaking work on state high courts, Gibson and Nelson (2021, 138) array four selection mechanisms against seven retention mechanisms to create a taxonomy of 28 different designs. However, just five of the possible designs account for the majority of designs used in the states. Of these, one is the federal design; it combines selection by the chief executive with no formal retention system for appointed justices at all, effectively granting them life tenure. One might dub this the "federalist" design, since Hamilton advocated for it forcefully in Federalist 78, helping to ensure its enshrinement in the U.S. Constitution.

In fact, if we focus on state supreme courts, only three states (Massachusetts, New Hampshire, and Rhode Island) employ the federalist design of allowing the executive (i.e. the governor) to make judicial appointments that are not subject to any later retention decisions.[3] Moreover, only one of these—Rhode Island—employs the pure federalist design by awarding judges life tenure; state supreme court judges in the other two states face mandatory retirement ages. Instead, today most states select and retain judges via some form of elections.[4]

An extensive discussion of the merits of different judicial selection and retention systems is beyond the scope of this chapter.[5] But we can ask a narrower question: is there a simple modification to the federalist design for selecting and retaining Supreme Court justices that might improve its performance as benchmarked against a defensible normative standard (not short-term partisan advantage)?[6] What are the relevant considerations? We focus on responsiveness, the extent of closely balanced courts, and judicial turnover rates because these performance metrics are closely tied to the selection and retention system, are substantively important, and could be adjusted without a radical redesign of the federal judiciary.

14.2.1 Optimal Judicial Turnover: The Goldilocks Principle

Most political scientists—and most Americans—typically see democratic responsiveness and democratic accountability as good things, especially for legislators and chief executives. In contrast, when it comes to judges, many legal scholars prefer "judicial independence," which effectively means judges are neither democratically responsive nor democratically accountable. A vast scholary literature has interrogated the costs and benefits.[7]

One common defense of judicial independence is that democratically unresponsive and unaccountable judges are likely to protect the rights of minorities more vigorously than democratically responsive and accountable judges would. As an empirical proposition, however, this assertion lacks support.[8] As a logical proposition, it fails. Judges who answer to no one but themselves are free to do whatever they wish. They may support minority rights, but could just as easily could discriminate against minorities.[9] Absent judicial accountability, the crux becomes: what judicial preferences does the selection mechanism favor? Indeed, if the public as a whole increasingly supports minority welfare over time, as has been the case in the United States, one might expect judges drawn disproportionately from older cohorts to be on average less supportive of minority rights than either average citizens or a younger cohort of judges. Notably, Hamilton did not rely on the minority rights arguments in his defense of the federalist design.

In contrast, we believe that a much stronger argument for low turnover (and thus less responsiveness, in all likelihood) relies on the economic gains from a stable set of laws. A good legal system offers individuals clear economic rules that support profitable exchanges today as well as the security they need to enter into long-term relationships and projects.[10] Without that security, society risks falling into a devastating poverty trap.[11] This insight is easiest to understand with respect to common law subjects such as contracts, torts, and property law, which are not primarily the business of the Supreme Court. But it applies with nearly equal cogency to antitrust, securities regulation, constitutional rights and obligations, and administrative law, which are. To get this security, tomorrow's courts must be willing to enforce today's law. But how can the legal system credibly commit to today's law? The federalist selection and retention system offers a way: select judges who favor today's law, then retain them for a long period. Slow judicial turnover supplies the credible commitment device needed for economic prosperity. Under slow turnover, membership on the court is "sticky"—higher stickiness implies that the court's membership in a prior period (say, five or 10 years) will be a very good predictor of its membership in the current period.

But stability in the law is not an absolute good. Instead, a good legal system must also respond to changes in technology, the economy, and social relations. Otherwise, law becomes the dead hand of the past strangling the future's well-being. This argument is often sharpest concerning patent and anti-trust law, but applies to social changes arising from new technology (e.g. contraception or cryptocurrency) and new moral sentiments (e.g. same-sex marriage). New phenomena may need genuinely new thinking, not just shoehorning the novel into ill-fitting categories from the past. Younger judges, more open to new ideas and more familiar with "the felt necessities of the time," may be more adept at adapting existing law to a brave new world.[12] This argument favors more rapid judicial turnover, and thus retention

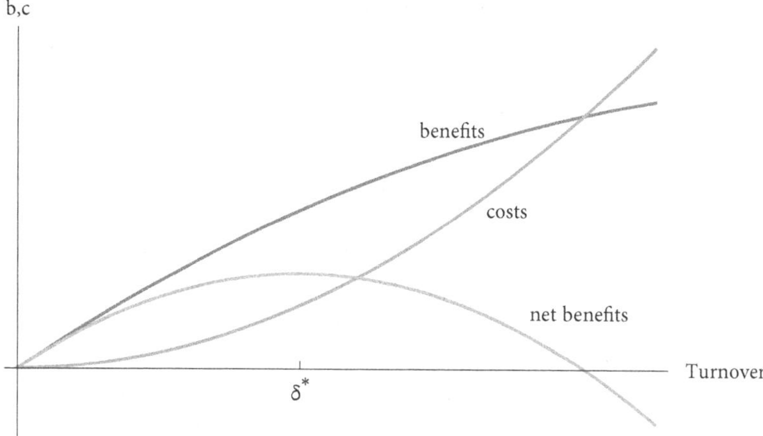

Fig. 14.1 The costs, benefits, and net benefits from varying turnover rates on the Supreme Court. The optimal level of turnover is neither too high nor too low, but just right.

mechanisms that would promote greater turnover than the status quo institutions on the Supreme Court of death and voluntary departure. A court with more turnover is less sticky—membership in years prior is less likely to predict the current composition of the court.

The reader may already intuit what we call the "Goldilocks Principle" for judicial turnover—neither too much nor too little, but just right! Figure 14.1 illustrates the basic intuition. In the figure, the horizontal axis is the rate of judicial turnover, denoted by δ; higher values correspond to more turnover and shorter tenures, and thus greater responsiveness to control of the presidency. The lowest possible rate would arise under an institutional arrangement like the federalist design, while the highest possible rate would occur with (say) complete dismissal and replacement of the court with each incoming presidential administration, as occurs with top officials in administrative agencies. The two upward sloping lines show the benefits and costs of turnover. As discussed above, an important benefit of greater judicial turnover is the greater "fit" of the law to changing social circumstances. We sketch the benefits curve as increasing but at a decreasing rate—moving from glacial turnover to a somewhat more rapid rate initially brings sizable benefits, but these benefits lessen over time.

An important cost of higher turnover is the reduced commitment power of the legal system. For example, Graber (2012) argues that the reality of polarized appointment politics portends a constitutional "yo-yo" in which doctrine swings back-and-forth wildly whenever the ideological majority of the court changes. In line with the evidence from Chapter 12 that the court now consists of two polarized blocs, Bailey and Spitzer (2017, 129–130) make a similar argument: "With a relatively empty middle on the court, small changes in membership may lead to major swings in Court. When there are few moderates, replacing a liberal justice with a conservative justice can move the court median from a moderate to strong conservative, or vice versa." Such swings between polarized blocs could jeopardize long-term projects and endeavors in society if the law becomes too unpredictable. We sketch the cost curve as low for slow turnover rates but rising rapidly as turnover becomes extremely rapid. Here, law could become so volatile and unpredictable that society slides into a poverty trap.

The third curve in Figure 14.1 is the *net benefits* curve, which captures the difference between the social benefits and social costs of turnover. The task of the constitutional engineer, in our simple framework, is to design a judicial selection and retention system that maximizes net social benefits from turnover.[13] The socially optimal level of turnover is the point labeled δ^*. As shown, this "Goldilocks Point" is not jammed against either the lowest possible turnover rate nor the highest. Of course, such extreme points could be optimal, given the shapes of the benefit and cost curves. But the figure illustrates that the Goldilocks Principle—neither too much turnover nor too little but just enough—will be optimal under many circumstances.

The shapes of the curves are not fixed. Factors like rapid technological progress will rotate the benefit curve upward; this would lead to a higher value for the optimal turnover rate, which would then favor institutions such as term limits or mandatory retirement ages that promote responsiveness and turnover. In contrast, if socially valuable projects require legal stability not just for a few years but over decades, then the cost curve rotates upward, leading to a leftward shift in the optimal turnover rate. This scenario would favor institutions that reduce responsiveness and turnover, such as lifetime appointment or a high retirement age.

14.2.2 Political Conflict, Polarization, and the Goldilocks Point

We could continue along these lines, but as political scientists we wish to turn to a factor missing from the economic efficiency-oriented framework of Figure 14.1, one that could dramatically affect the constitutional engineer's calculations: political conflict. Each turnover rate in Figure 14.1 also will be associated with a degree of political conflict, in particular, both a *frequency* and *intensity* of conflict. What factors determine the frequency and intensity of conflict associated with a turnover rate? Should we adjust the Goldilocks Point in light of likely political conflict?

In answering these questions, we return to a key argument of Chapter 1. If federal courts—like local traffic courts—made decisions with few broad-based policy consequences, then who sits on the bench would matter little, and thus selection would not engender much conflict. Turnover rates would then not link tightly to the frequency and intensity of conflict. Federal judges, of course, are not traffic court overseers but powerful policy makers. Still, suppose everyone in American society, including high court judges, agreed on judicial means and ends. If so, who sits on the Supreme Court would not matter much, vacancies would not lead to appointment battles, and turnover rates would not result in much conflict. But this supposition is quite unrealistic: federal judges are powerful actors, and politicians, organized interests, and activists on both sides now disagree intensely over means and ends and hence focus intensely on appointments. As such, conflict over court appointments becomes inevitable. In such a world, turnover rates will dramatically shape the frequency and intensity of political conflict.

The simulations in Chapter 13 showed that if control of the presidency regularly alternates between the parties, in the long run the court will feature two almost equally sized ideological blocs. At that point, one bloc may gain a transitory advantage over the other (e.g. a 5-4 majority). But soon the other bloc will have its turn, as the court shifts regularly and predictably back to 5-4 with the other side in control. And so on *ad infinitum*. If this logic is correct, then frequent turnover on the court will lead to frequent political conflict (lots of nominations) but relatively low intensity conflict because winning or losing is just a short-term affair. Today's defeat will be followed by tomorrow's victory, and vice versa. The stakes at each vacancy will be lower—though not as low as if the court were not ideologically polarized.[14]

Suppose instead the court features a low turnover rate. Appointments will occur rarely, so the frequency of conflict from appointments will be low. But because ideological lock-in will be pronounced, the stakes of each appointment will be huge, and hence the intensity of conflict would likely be larger. Moreover, because appointments would be rare events, a few strategic retirements and a fluky run of presidential control could move the court far from 5-4 configurations, and then stay there a long time. A durable court with an ideological split of 6-3, 7-2, or even greater is possible (recall the analyses in Chapter 13 suggest a lopsided conservative court through the 2050s). Now a new threat of conflict arises, one arising not from appointments *per se* but from *elections*. When the inevitable turn in the electoral tide brings a unified party government of the opposite ideological persuasion, with a real working majority in the Senate, the court will find itself the odd man out among the branches. Given the electoral outcome, the court will probably lack public support. What happens then?

In fact, we have a glimmer of the answer because we have been there before.[15] This is precisely the scenario of the Lincoln-Tawny confrontation during the Civil War and Reconstruction, and that of the Roosevelt-Hughes confrontation during the New Deal. There is only one likely outcome from such a confrontation. In a democracy, the will of the people propels forward, sometimes slowed but never stopped. A stubborn odd-man-out-court can find itself staring down an opposed public and its representatives, and the results can be devastating for the court. Congress and the president can manipulate the court's size in order to pack it, as happened during the Civil War and Reconstruction. Congress can also strip the court of its jurisdiction over controversial issues, as also occurred during Reconstruction. Public regard for the institution may plummet and take decades to restore. And, extreme policies on one side can be replaced by equally extreme policies on the other side, a fate that moderation might have avoided.[16]

If this logic is correct, then high turnover will be associated with frequent political conflict but mostly low-to-moderate intensity conflict. Low turnover, in contrast, will be associated with less frequent conflict due to less frequent appointments, but possibly higher intensity conflict at each appointment, particularly when the court is closely divided ideologically. And, even more dramatically, low turnover brings the threat of an odd-man-out court facing an angry public and unified elected branches poised to curb its power and independence.

14.2.3 Constitutional Engineering for Black Swans

Given the current electoral environment in which the two parties enjoy rough parity in national elections, it seems unlikely that the court could find itself thoroughly out-of-step with both the public and the elected branches. Such an event may fall under the category of a rare event. Rare events that carry devastating consequences have received considerable scientific and popular attention, sometimes under the rubric of "black swans."[17] Black swans are seemingly near-impossible events that actually transpire. Examples of improbable but devastating events that actually occurred include the San Francisco earthquake of 1906, the Japanese Tohoku tsunami of 2011 with the accompanying Fukushima nuclear disaster, the 2008 financial meltdown, and the 2020 Covid pandemic.

Distributions of events like this have "fat tails" and are quite different from normal distributions. Figure 14.2 illustrates by showing two fat-tailed distributions.[18] In the

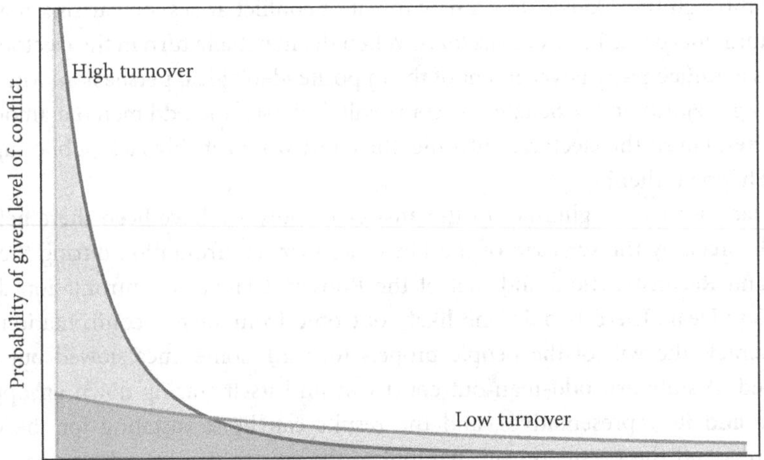

Fig. 14.2 Turnover on the court and the frequency and intensity of political conflict over appointments. With high turnover, conflict is frequent but mostly low intensity. With low turnover, conflict is less frequent but can be extremely intense—a "black swan" distribution of events.

figure, the x-axis is the intensity of political conflict, while the height of the curves shows the probability of that level of conflict. The curve labeled "high turnover" shows a distribution with a heavy left-hand tail. It features frequent low-to-moderate intensity conflict but very rare high intensity conflict of the odd-man-out variety. In contrast, the curve labeled "low turnover" displays a fat right-hand tail. This curve features infrequent conflict due to infrequent appointments but much higher probabilities of a huge odd-man-out conflict.

How should a constitutional engineer think about judicial black swans, particularly a constitutional crisis created by an odd-man-out court? Opting for a judicial selection and retention system that produces rather frequent judicial turnover produces more frequent but also smaller conflict. This path also introduces more instability in the law and possibly lower economic growth, but it also protects against "the big one"—a severely out-of-step court. In contrast, a selection and retention system that produces infrequent turnover and thus more stability in the law leads to less frequent conflict, but when appointments do occur, the conflict is more intense. Critically, this path would increase the chance of an odd-man-out crisis.

Reasonable people can reasonably disagree about which risks are better or which worse. Of course, partisan advocates myopically seek short-term political advantage and thus ignore black swan risks altogether. But *risks ignored are not risks avoided.* Engineers understand that bridges in seismically active regions should be designed not on the basis of average risks, but instead over-engineered to survive rare major earthquakes. The same principle may apply in constitutional engineering. If so, the constitutional engineer would select a judicial selection and retention system with higher rates of judicial turnover rather than the simple Goldilocks Point in Figure 14.1. On the other hand, if one dismisses black swan risks, then one would favor a design with rates of turn-over at Figure 14.1's Goldilocks point.

Because one's view of the best compromise between competing objectives depends on values about society and one's attitude toward risk, Chapter 13's simulations cannot indicate a definitive "right" answer in the responsiveness-stability tradeoff. But the simulations can provide valuable information about electoral responsiveness and ideological lock-in across the different policy experiments; let us now return to them.

14.3 Evaluating the Policy Experiments

Recall in Chapter 13 that we analyzed several policy experiments (i.e. counterfactual scenarios) to understand how different possible changes in norms and/or institutions would affect the long-term path of the Supreme Court. In that chapter, we focused on descriptively presenting the broad trends in the composition of the court across experiments. For the analyses in this chapter, we can more systemically examine the outcomes of the simulations in order to explore the tradeoffs that the different paths create. While our theoretical framework emphasizes changes in selection and retention institutions, we also include the scenarios from Chapter 13 that posit changes in norms (e.g. no divided government appointments), since these provide useful points of comparison. (We exclude the 2016 counterfactual scenario, however.)

14.3.1 Evaluating Responsiveness

The first step toward evaluating the optimal level of judicial independence is the degree to which the composition of the court is responsive to changes in the preferences of voters and their elected officials. To measure democratic responsiveness within the context of the simulations, we calculate the linkage between party control of the presidency and the ideological makeup of the court. While the Senate has the important role of "advise and consent," the mapping between party control of the White House and the court's ideological structure strikes us as the most direct gauge of the impact of the tides of democracy on the court. The idea is simple: if the public selects a Democratic president, how much, if at all, does the court move to the left? Conversely, if the public selects a Republican president, how much, if at all, does the court move to the right?[19]

To evaluate democratic responsiveness across the policy experiments, we treat each experiment as a data generating process whose output can be described and neatly summarized via simple regression models.[20] For these regressions, we use two measures of the court's ideological structure as dependent variables. The first is the estimated location of the median justice in a given year. Of course, the location of the median is a function of all the justices on the court, so a president's ability to move the median through one or two appointments is typically quite limited. The second is the proportion of justices who fall into the conservative bloc, as introduced in Chapter 12 and defined (with respect to the simulations) in Chapter 13. This measure of ideological structure, which strongly correlates with the ideological content of majority opinions, is much more sensitive to appointments. Recall we showed in Chapter 12 that bloc sizes translate into changes in judicial policy; this means that every appointment the president makes matters, even if it does not necessarily move the median.

To set up the regressions, we treat every simulation in all the policy experiments as a time series. So, for example, the baseline scenario has 1,000 time series, with an estimated median location in every year in each of the 1,000 simulations. Because presidential appointments are limited by circumstances, it makes little sense to examine the relationship between presidential control and court compositions in a year-to-year manner. Instead, for each simulation, we calculate five- and 10-year rolling averages of the proportion of years in which the president was a Republican. The five-year measure captures rather short-term responsiveness. Because by construction this measure includes fewer appointments on average, it is rather noisy. The 10-year measure, by contrast, expands the responsiveness window and captures somewhat longer term responsiveness. However, because we can begin the 10-year averages only in 2030, this measure excludes observations from the 2020s.

Table 14.1 Summary of structure of regressions

Regression label	Dependent variable	Responsiveness predictor	Lags included on right-hand side
Medians, 5 years	Location of median justice	Proportion of years in past 5 with GOP president	Median, lagged 5 years
Medians, 10 years	Location of median justice	Proportion of years in past 10 with GOP president	Median, lagged 10 years
Conservative justices, 5 years	Proportion of justices in conservative bloc	Proportion of years in past 5 with GOP president	Proportion of justices in conservative bloc, lagged 5 years
Conservative justices, 10 years	Proportion of justices in conservative bloc	Proportion of years in past 10 with GOP president	Proportion of justices in conservative bloc, lagged 10 years

Finally, in each regression, to capture the "stickiness" of membership on the court, as discussed earlier, we also include lagged values of the dependent variable. We use the same lag structure as the number of years used to calculate the rolling average of the relevant dependent variable. For example, in the regressions in which the dependent variable is the location of the median and the key predictor is the proportion of Republican presidents in the past 10 years, we also include as a predictor the location of the median lagged 10 years (i.e. the value of the median 10 years before the year under analysis). So, the regression indicates today's ideological structure as a function of the ideological structure from a decade ago, plus the proportion of Republican control of the White House during the ensuing decade. The coefficient on proportion of White House control provides the measure of the democratic responsiveness of the court's ideological structure; the coefficient on lagged structure is a measure of the inherent persistence of ideological structure—i.e. "stickiness"—within a given policy experiment.

Thus, we have four sets of regressions, the structure of which is summarized in Table 14.1. Using each set of four, we analyze each of the 11 policy experiments, running one regression for every simulation. The end product is thus four sets × 11 policy experiments × 1,000 simulations, resulting in a total of 44,000 regressions.

Figure 14.3 presents the results of four sets of regressions. For now we focus just on the responsiveness coefficients—that is, the coefficients on presidential control. (We will soon consider the results from the lagged coefficients.) Each plot presents the results from the respective sets of regressions. The points depict the median coefficient among the set of coefficients from the 1,000 regressions for a given analysis, while the horizontal lines connect the .025 percentile to the .975 percentile. Within each panel, we order the experiments by increasing responsiveness from top to bottom; this means that the order of the experiments varies across the panels.

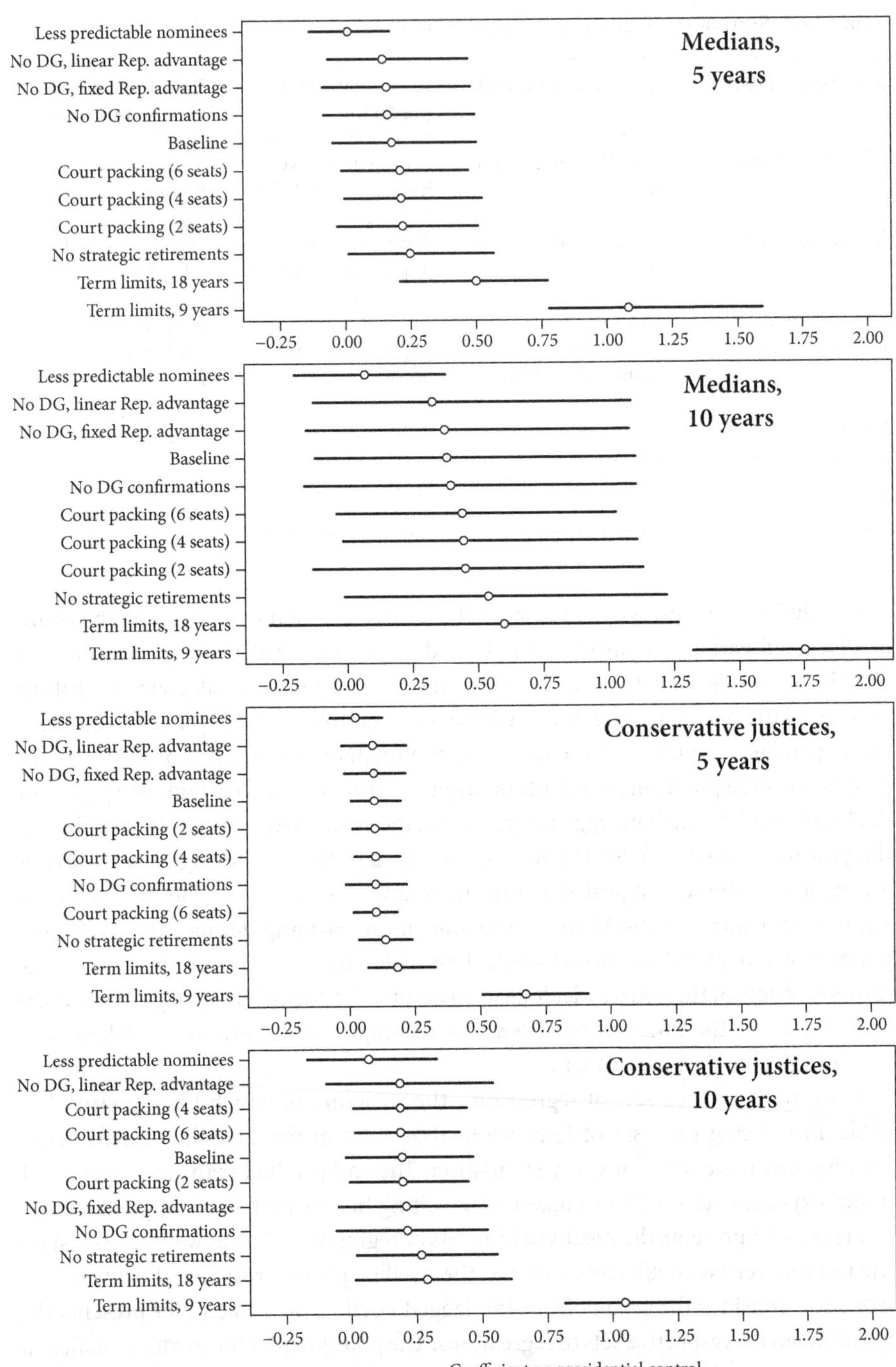

Fig. 14.3 Summary of responsiveness coefficients from regression analyses. The points depict the median coefficient while the lines connect the .025 percentile to the .975 percentile. In each panel, the experiments are ordered from least responsive (top) to most responsive (bottom).

It is important to note that the figure does *not* display traditional confidence intervals. Rather, it summarizes the spread of the responsiveness coefficients, without regard to the standard errors of the individual coefficients. Because we are working with simulated data, a frequentist approach to statistical significance is not particularly interesting, in our view. Instead, the rank ordering of the experiments by the median coefficient, along with the spread of the estimates, holds greater interest because it affords a summary descriptive comparison of the scenarios in terms of democratic responsiveness.[21]

Across the four sets of analyses, while there are some minor differences, each panel leads to the same substantive conclusions. First, *the baseline scenario generally displays low levels of democratic responsiveness.* As we have discussed throughout Chapter 13, the court's ideological makeup (especially in the initial decades after 2022) is extremely persistent under the baseline assumptions, driving down responsiveness. Perhaps surprisingly, in some of the analyses the no divided government confirmation scenarios actually display higher responsiveness on average, though the difference in the median coefficients is quite small.

Second, *the term limits experiments always score highest on responsiveness.* For 9-year terms, the coefficients on presidential control are strikingly large. This makes intuitive sense, of course. Affording a president an appointment every year allows him to quickly mold the court in his own ideological image. To give a sense of the scale here, the median coefficient on presidential control in the "Medians, 10 years analysis" is 1.75. This means that a one-unit shift in the proportion of the last decade with a Republican president would predict a 1.75 increase in the location of the median justice. A one-unit shift means zero years with a Republican to 10 years with a Republican, meaning Republican presidents would have appointed all nine justices on the court. The NOMINATE scale for medians runs from -1 to 1, so a 1.75 increase nearly covers the entire ideological spectrum. The responsiveness coefficients from 18-year terms are much smaller in magnitude but still indicate a large increase in democratic responsiveness relative to the baseline. Conversely, court packing tends to fall in the middle of the pack in terms of responsiveness.

Third, *less predictable nominees always produce the least amount of democratic responsiveness.* Under this scenario, presidents appoint nominees who are much more likely to be ideological moderates compared to the baseline assumptions. This is intuitive, because in the experiment the relationship between presidential control and nominee ideology is weak. The result is more heterogeneity in the composition of the court relative to the baseline ideology assumptions. We view this scenario as quite unlikely in the future.

Finally, *the no strategic retirements experiment always ranks third on responsiveness,* out-ranking even court packing in every analysis. This result reinforces how strategic retirements effectively frustrate a president's ability to alter the composition of the court. In a practical sense, strategic retirements remove some control over the court's composition from the hands of the people (working through presidential elections), and place a portion of it in the hands of the justices themselves.

14.3.2 The Stickiness of the Past

The responsiveness analyses tell us how closely the composition of the court tracks with changes in the party of the president. But by themselves the responsiveness coefficients ignore the stickiness of the membership of the court. This quantity is essential for understanding how the past membership of the court predicts the current composition, even after accounting for election outcomes.

Figure 14.4 extends the responsiveness analysis by comparing the responsiveness coefficients to the coefficients on the lagged median. Recall there are four sets of regressions, in which the dependent variables (location of the median justice and the proportion of conservative justices) and the length of the lagged median justice (5 and 10 years) were varied. For each set the figure depicts a scatterplot showing the relationship between the lagged coefficients (on the vertical axis) and the responsiveness coefficients (on the horizontal axis), which are based on the proportion of the past five or 10 years with a Republican president. The blue line is a linear regression line that summarizes the relationship between the two.

At a conceptual level, responsiveness and stickiness should be negatively correlated: a court where past membership better predicts current membership is one that will fluctuate less with the changing tides of presidential elections. And that is exactly what Figure 14.4 shows: a consistent negative relationship between responsiveness and stickiness, the latter measured by how strongly the lagged median predicts the current median.

While this is not so surprising, of more interest is the "tradeoff frontier" between responsiveness and stickiness across the different policy experiments. Figure 14.4 allows us to compare how the different policy experiments rank on this frontier, which is summarized by the blue line in each panel. Notably, for all four sets of analyses, 9-year term limits are an outlier, falling far on the responsiveness side of the frontier. But even 18-year term limits—which would still allow for lengthy tenures—always rank second highest on responsiveness (that is, second largest on the x-axis), showing that they do better on responsiveness than any of the other alternative experiments. In contrast, the status quo of the baseline falls much closer to the stickiness side. Thus, enhanced responsiveness apparently requires an institutional departure from life-time appointments; term limits, in particular, would shift the scale toward responsiveness.

14.3.3 Judicial Turnover

The responsiveness analysis reveals how different design features lead in a practical way to a responsiveness-stickiness tradeoff in the court's composition. This analysis implicates judicial turnover, since greater responsiveness will often require turnover to change the composition of the court. However, it is also useful to explicitly compare turnover rates across the policy experiments. This, in turn, allows us to examine the likelihood of political conflict.

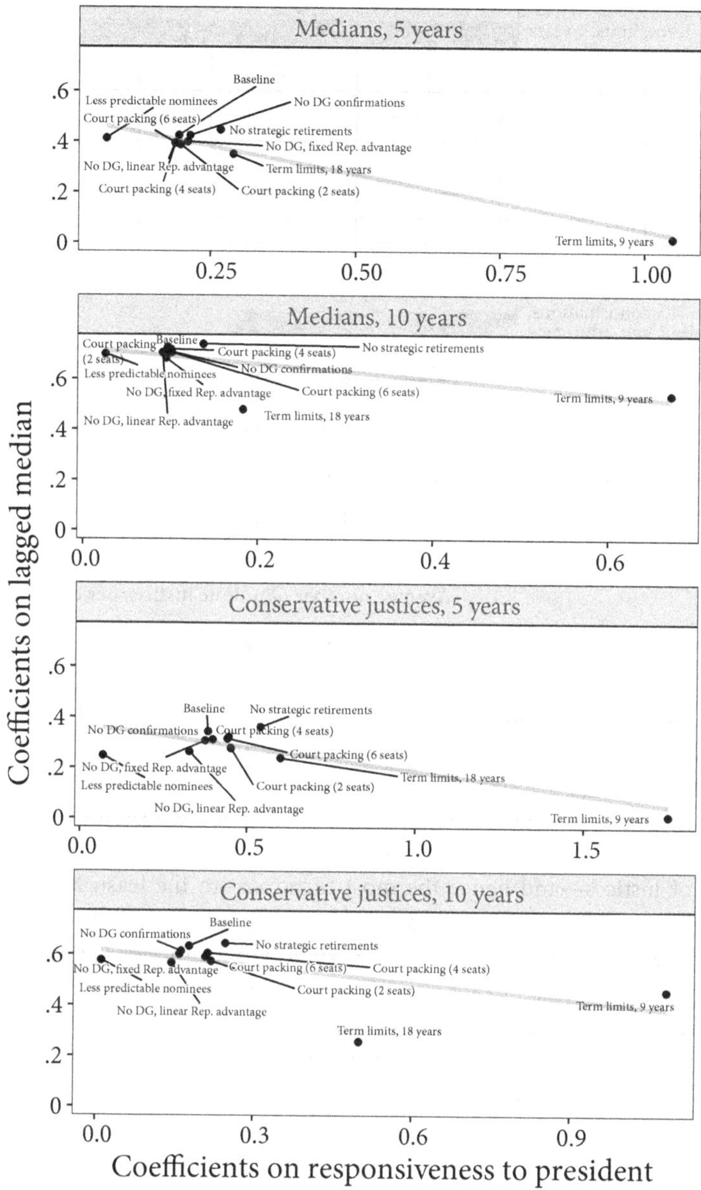

Fig. 14.4 The relationship between responsiveness and "stickiness." The y-axis depicts the coefficients on lagged membership, while the x-axis depicts the coefficients on the effect of presidential control (democratic responsiveness) on the court. Note the scale of the horizontal axes differ. The lines are OLS regression lines.

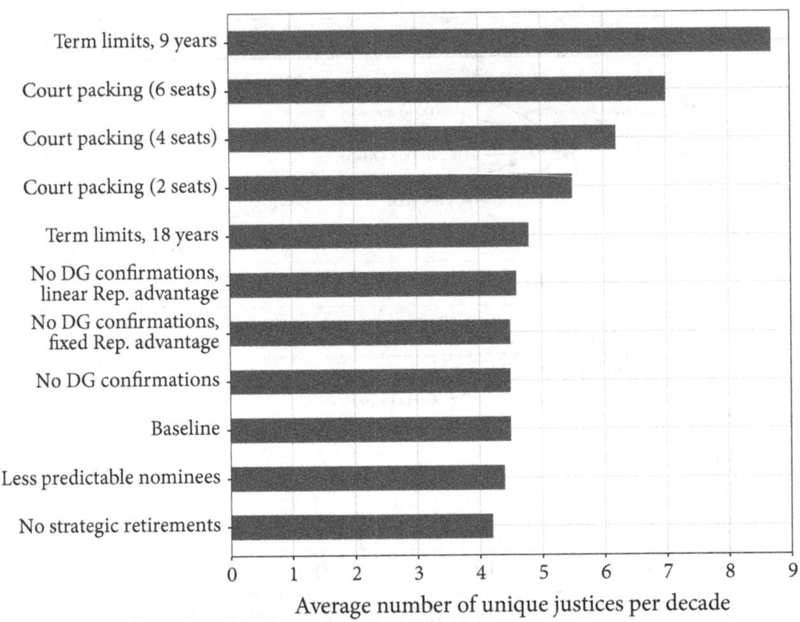

Fig. 14.5 Turnover on the future Supreme Court, by policy experiment.

First, for each policy experiment, we calculated the average number of unique justices per policy experiments, pooling across all simulations (that is, including all years). We normalize this measure by dividing by 10 years; this quantity is thus the average number of unique justices per decade. Figure 14.5 shows the results from these calculations, with the policy experiments ordered from the highest average number of justices—and hence the most turnover—to the least. Not surprisingly, term limits produce greater turnover than most of the experiments that retain life tenure; quite naturally, 9-year term limits would produce about nine unique justices every 10 years, on average. Court packing is the exception, but of course court packing by construction means more unique justices.[22]

More justices per year, of course, means a higher *frequency* of appointment conflict. But as we discussed above, a key question is not just the frequency of conflict but the *intensity* of conflict as well. Given the existence of polarized blocs of justices, frequent alteration of majorities across them will increase the frequency of conflict but likely reduce its intensity. Conversely, less frequent turnover would likely increase the intensity of conflict.

To examine variation in the frequency of conflict, for each policy experiment we calculated the proportion of simulations in which the court's partisan composition had no more than a one-seat margin; that is, either one more Democratic appointee than Republican appointees or vice versa (e.g. on a nine-member court), or an equal number in each bloc (e.g. 4-4 on an eight-member court). When such a margin prevails, the next nomination can potentially change the partisan balance of the court, depending on the partisanship of the exiting judge and the party of the president.

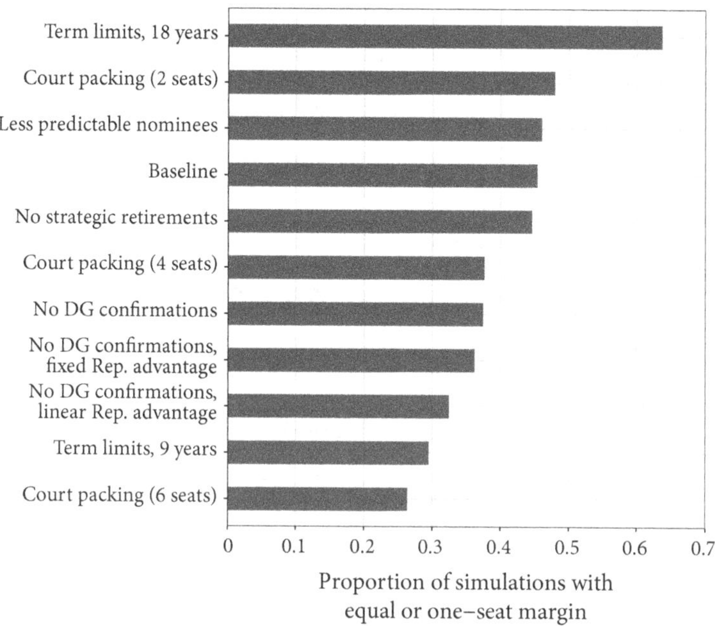

Fig. 14.6 Narrow partisan margins on the court, by policy experiment.

Figure 14.6 presents the results of this analysis. Not surprisingly, one-seat margins are maximized under 18-year term limits, because each president receives two appointments per term, and this leads on average to a balanced court. By contrast, 9-year term limits actually score low on this metric; this is because giving each president *one appointment per year* induces such rapid change in the court that the margins will typically exceed one. Likewise, adding six seats to the court would reduce the incidence of close margins, just by virtue of increasing the size of the court.

14.3.4 Political Conflicts and Out-of-Step Courts

When is the intensity of conflict likely to reach its apex? As we discussed above, the biggest threat to the court as an institution occurs when it is significantly out of step with the American public and its elected representatives. A key question then is how likely such scenarios are to occur across the policy experiments, conditional on our assumptions about election outcomes going forward.

For each policy experiment, we calculated how often one party controls at least six seats on the court and the court faces the "opposite" unified presidency and Senate—that is, at least six Republican appointees and a Democratic president and Senate, or at least six Democratic appointees and a Republican president and Senate. Obviously, these simulations are rather skeletal because they ignore control of the House and the size of the Senate majority. For the court to face a severe institutional backlash,

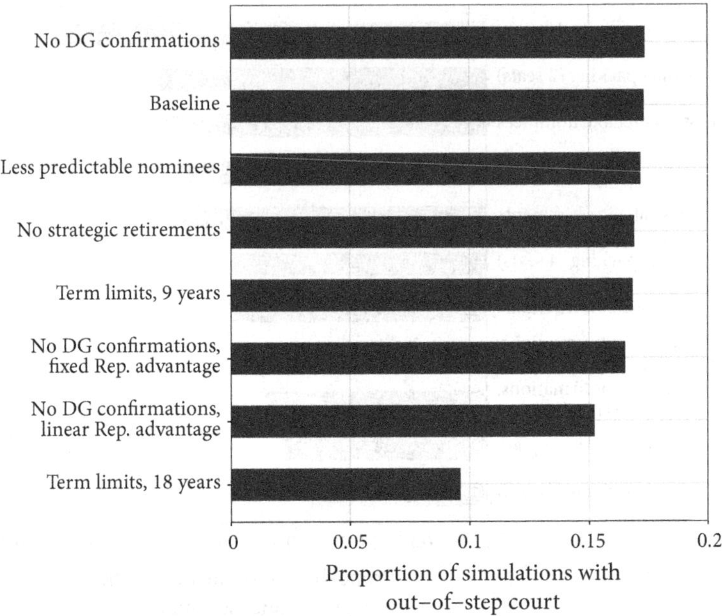

Fig. 14.7 The proportion of simulations with "out-of-step" courts, by policy experiment (court packing experiments excluded). A court is out of step if it contains at least six Democratic justices, and the president and Senate are both Republicans, or if the court contains at least 6 Republican justices and the president and Senate are both Democrats.

unified control of all three branches plus lopsided majorities in the Senate would be necessary. The knife-edge margins of the Democratic majorities in the House and Senate in 2021 and 2022, for example, would not be sufficient to allow radical interventions. Still, the simulation results are suggestive about which designs lead to a greater risk of the black swan.

Figure 14.7 shows the results. Note that we exclude the court packing experiments because, in some sense, court packing is "downstream" of being out of step. In the simulations, out-of-step courts are not really rare events, occurring upwards of 10% of the time. Although this rate is surely an exaggeration, over a long enough period truly rare events inevitably occur. But even if the levels of out-of-step courts predicted by the simulations are too high, the comparison *across* policy experiments still reveals which are more or less likely to reduce the chance of the black swan. More interestingly, the two policy experiments with the greatest likelihood of an out-of-step court are the baseline experiment and the no divided government scenario; the latter, as we argued in Chapter 13, seems quite likely to occur. The results thus suggest that the status quo of long tenures, competitive presidential elections, and more frequent strategic retirements (in all likelihood) stands the most chance of inducing an 1863- or 1937-like battle between the courts and the other branches. (Somewhat perversely, the scenario of no divided government confirmations with an increasing Republican advantage in the Senate also reduces out-of-step courts, because there would be many fewer *Democratic* majorities to be out-of-step.)

On the other side of the ledger, 18-year term limits again stand out—the frequency of out-of-step courts is lowest when presidents regularly appoint justices to fixed terms. Cumulatively, we take these results to suggest that a prudential constitutional engineer would find 18-year term limits quite attractive. In contrast, those who favor stability in the law—even at the risk of rare but very serious conflict—would find the federalist system more attractive.

14.4 Conclusion

Judicial selection and retention systems force tradeoffs between desirable but conflicting objectives. Evaluating different institutional designs requires both a normative framework and plausible measures of the magnitudes of the likely tradeoffs. We sketched a framework that acknowledges both economic and political tradeoffs in different judicial selection and retention systems. Then, we used the MSC Simulator to derive some useful indicators about the tradeoffs implicit in the policy experiments of Chapter 13. The simulations reveal that the federalist system—the status quo—skews heavily toward low electoral responsiveness, very "sticky" court compositions, less frequent but possibly more intense political conflict, and a higher probability of a major confrontation between an out-of-step court and the rest of the government. Conversely, the simulations suggest that 18-year term limits would increase electoral responsiveness, decrease the stickiness of court compositions, engender more frequent but possibly less intense political conflict, and reduce the probability of a major cross-branch confrontation.

The analyses in this chapter do not determine which future is better for the court and for the country. But we hope they are useful for readers who are interested in evaluating—or changing—the future path of appointment politics and the Supreme Court. Whatever happens in the future, the difficult questions raised by these tradeoffs result from the paths that brought us to the current politics of appointments. In the next, and final, chapter of the book, we take stock of these changes, and what we have learned from the history, theory, and empirics presented in the previous chapters.

15
Conclusion

Toward the end of his life, Francisco Goya moved into an old villa outside Madrid. There, for his eyes only, he painted a series of murals reflecting his despair after the horrors of the Napoleonic wars in Spain. These astounding works, appropriately known as his "black paintings," can be viewed today in the Prado Museum. In one of these paintings, "Duel with Cudgels," two men stand mired to the thigh in a somewhat eerie landscape. Neither tries to free himself from the clutch of the earth nor aid the other to do so. Instead, they flail at one another with clubs, in a savage and merciless attempt to beat their opponent into the ground. Neither can stop and lay down his cudgel, because to do so would cede victory to the other and bring injury or death to himself. They are doomed to vicious and never-ending strife.

And so it is today with Supreme Court appointments. Two coalitions of organized groups, activists, and elected officials struggle over every vacancy. Neither can quit lest the other prevail. But neither wants to quit. Passionate intensity fires their hearts. Both sides—rightly so, given the Supreme Court's power and discretion—view the court and its membership as a battle worth engaging whenever a vacancy occurs.

In Chapter 1, we made two strong claims about Supreme Court appointment politics. First, we claimed that understanding the origins, consequences, and trajectory

Fig. 15.1 Francisco Goya, "Duel with Cudgels," Prado Museum, Madrid.

Making the Supreme Court: The Politics of Appointments, 1930–2020. Charles M. Cameron and Jonathan P. Kastellec, Oxford University Press. © Oxford University Press 2023. DOI: 10.1093/oso/9780197680544.003.0015

of appointment politics requires a new approach to institutional analysis integrating policy making across the branches and incorporating the mass public and organized interests. We dubbed this intellectual challenge the "Pelican Problem." Second, we claimed that appointment politics offers a lens on American politics by providing a laboratory for studying in a concrete setting larger changes transforming the American separation-of-powers (SOP) system.

In this conclusion, we return to these two claims. First, by the tough standards of the Pelican Problem, how did we fare? Where did we succeed and where did we fall short in our effort to understand the real-world duel with cudgels? Second, what did we discover in the SOP laboratory? How does the peculiar politics of Supreme Court appointments illuminate big developments in American politics?

15.2 The Pelican Problem Revisited

Though inspired by a work of fiction, the Pelican Problem of Chapter 1 articulated a tough standard for understanding the politics of Supreme Court nominations. From its perspective, social scientists can claim to understand the politics of Supreme Court appointments if they can:

- Predict the likely ideology of a Supreme Court nominee chosen by any given president under a range of circumstances;
- Predict the outcome of the confirmation battle over any given nominee;
- Foresee the broad policy consequences of replacing any Supreme Court justice with a new justice; and,
- Ground each of the above predictions and forecasts in social science theory and systematic data.

We review these components, scoring successes, shortcomings, and possible directions for future research.

15.2.1 Predicting Who the President Selects

To predict the likely ideology of Supreme Court nominees, Chapter 9 presented a new theory of how presidents select long-serving political appointees, the characteristics approach. The characteristics approach views appointees as bundles of attributes, like ideology and race. A key element in the theory is presidential interest in the court, along with the president's demand for nominee ideology, policy reliability, and ascriptive characteristics like race and gender. Also important is the availability of potential nominees with desired characteristics. To forecast likely nominee characteristics in the future, one needs to forecast presidential interest in the court, presidential demand for nominee attributes, and their availability. We traced the source of presidential interest in the court and presidential demands for nominee characteristics back to the desires of organized interests within the political parties. We argued in Chapter 2 that the party platforms reflect the desires of key blocs in the parties and form a kind of accountability contract between the presidential candidate and the party power brokers. Hence, if you know what the party activists want and what they write into the "contract," you can predict what kind of nominee the president will favor, constrained by the supply of potential nominees.

This account made sense of presidential selection choices over most of a century. We believe it will continue to do so in the foreseeable future. But there is more to understand than we could tackle. A critical question is what explains the rise and fall of powerful blocs within the parties—in particular, interest groups with a distinctive agenda for the Supreme Court?[1] In our view, this is perhaps the major question that the book leaves open. Other questions are: How do the desires of activists translate into specific demands in party platforms? Overall, how influential are platform demands in shaping presidential agendas and actions—is the high responsiveness of presidents in the case of Supreme Court nominees typical or is it unusual? What happens to presidents who flout the desires of the party power brokers?

15.2.2 The Outcome of Confirmation Battles

Our approach to predicting the outcome of confirmation battles was simple: predict the roll call votes of senators. As we showed in Chapter 8, those votes varied dramatically over time—mostly unanimous yea votes in the early period became more conflictual, eventually becoming party-line votes in the later period. In Chapter 11, we analyzed these votes, stressing the importance of senators' accountability to the electorate. We did not offer new formal models of accountability in roll call voting, but our reasoning and statistical models reflect insights from political science classics as well as more recent work on the theory of political agency.[2]

To explain unanimous voting in the early era, we observed that most confirmation votes were effectively invisible to the electorate. But we argued that senators could not disregard *potential* public sentiment—for example, negative judgments if a justice was eventually revealed to be corrupt or ideologically threatening.[3] We argued that unanimous votes offered safety in numbers—a compelling rationale for yea votes in the event of problems following confirmation.

Electoral accountability became even more important in explaining visible, readily understood, and contentious votes in the later era. Here we relied on empirical investigations using new data and modern analytic techniques. We showed in Chapter 11 that, across multiple nominations, senators tended to align with the opinion of their co-partisans rather than the state's median voter. To explain this correspondence, we introduced the idea of an electoral compound lottery involving primaries and the general election. Under reasonable assumptions about voter information, greater alignment with primary voters is a rational choice for senators.

Although we applied the logic of accountability to both invisible and visible votes, the Pelican Problem also demands an explanation for the systematic shift in the visibility of confirmation votes over time. In Chapter 8 we documented the shift from the age of invisible votes to highly visible ones based on a data-driven history of media coverage of confirmation campaigns. High visibility and interest group mobilization went hand-in-hand, though the direction of causality is impossible to determine. We also reviewed all available polls on public opinion during confirmation campaigns (in Chapter 7) and explored interest group mobilization, tactics, and ideology (in Chapter 5). Despite these efforts, the social basis behind the shifting visibility of confirmation votes remains somewhat hazy.

We were able, however, to say more about what the public wanted. In Chapter 10 we devised a new way to interpret commonly asked poll questions on nominees to better infer public wishes. That investigation showed that presidential co-partisans favor the ideologically extreme nominees selected by modern presidents, but average citizens much prefer ideologically moderate nominees.[4]

The seemingly simple second demand in the Pelican Problem took us far afield, into roll call voting, electoral accountability, media coverage, public opinion, and interest group mobilization. Again, many questions remain unanswered. For example, how different are the levels of information held by presidential co-partisans versus moderate citizens (typically Independents)? The compound lottery model suggests information asymmetries affect who senators attend to. More generally, where is the border between high-visibility, readily understood roll call votes (leading to measurable accountability) and lower-visibility, more opaque ones with (presumably) much less accountability? The existing data on Supreme Court nominations simply does not allow an answer to this question but data on other issues might, by combining roll call analysis with measures of media coverage.

15.2.3 Consequences for the Court

The third demand of the Pelican Problem was to predict the policy consequences of new justices, using theory and data, a task we undertook in Chapter 12. We drew on the current frontier of theory about Supreme Court policymaking to frame a heavily empirical analysis of the justices' votes and the content of majority opinions. Although data availability constrained the generality of the findings, at least where we could measure, the evidence seems clear: the ideological location of the median justice strongly affects case outcomes—which side wins—while the size of conservative, moderate, and liberal blocs on the court strongly affects the ideological content of majority opinions—judicial policy. New appointments can alter the court both by moving the median and shifting the bloc sizes, with predictable policy consequences.

Chapter 13 took the demands for forecasts seriously, exploring possible futures for the court's composition in detail. Chapter 14 went a step farther, laying out a new normative framework for evaluating changes in norms and institutions and applying it to proposed reforms.

Again, much remains to be done. For one thing, data on the ideological content of majority opinions remains very limited. We suspect the patterns we uncovered in search-and-seizure cases exist in other policy arenas as well. But this is a conjecture. Extending the data across multiple, important policy areas would explore the generalizability of the empirical findings.

Finally, the analyses in Chapter 12 took the court as hermetically sealed from the downstream consequences of its own actions. So did the simulations. But a major lesson of the book is that the Supreme Court is quite connected to the other branches and to society at large. In the limit, the possibility of a Black Swan of a constitutional crisis across the branches (examined in Chapter 14) arises from judicial choices severely out of step with the public mood and the tides of elections.

In sum, the holistic approach to institutional analysis demanded by the Pelican Problem proved consistently challenging but frequently enlightening. We hope others embrace it as well.[5] What can be done in fiction can sometimes be done in real social science as well.

15.3 What the Lens on American Politics Revealed

Chapter 1 discussed five forces transforming American politics and governance. The five forces were (1) growth of government and the rise of the judicial state; (2) transition in interest groups from pluralism to hyper-pluralism; (3) polarization of political elites; (4) resurgence of divided party government; and (5) changes in the mass public. Let us examine each in turn and see what the appointments lens revealed.

15.3.1 Growth of Government: Schattschneider Revised

Chapter 1 documented a huge increase in the size of government and a concomitant increase in the caseload of federal courts. Well, so what? What happens when federal courts become powerful players with dramatic impacts on social relations and economic conduct? The short answer is, the expansion of power allowed new policies, the new policies created a new politics, and then *the new politics transformed the political institution itself.* Chapters 2, 9, and 12 together provide a dramatic case study in policy feedback leading to *institutional transformation.*[6]

As background, recall that the idea of policy feedback takes inspiration from E. E. Schattschneider's (1935) observation that "new policies create a new politics." So, for example, the enactment of Social Security created a powerful group of organized seniors that did not exist before, who then changed the politics of old age pensions.[7] Similarly, the enactment of legislation creating tradable pollution permits created a group of winning firms who changed the politics of acid rain by defending the new regulatory regime against its opponents.[8] Schattschneider's aphorism often rings true—but the politics of Supreme Court appointments suggests it is incomplete. The new politics created by a policy change may not just reconfigure a policy domain, it may transform the political institution that created the policy in the first place. One might call this *institutional feedback.*[9]

In Chapter 2, we saw institutional feedback at work, with the rise in policy litmus tests for Supreme Court nominees. The court's policy actions in the areas of criminal law and abortion (among others) led to a social response. Groups organized and tried to change the policies, for example, by pushing for new abortion laws in the states and by lobbying the Supreme Court as amici curiae. But the activists did more than that, at least in our view. They penetrated the political parties—especially the Republican party—which then began to specify explicit policy litmus tests for new justices.[10] Chapter 2 documented the litmus tests. In turn, presidents changed the kind of nominees they selected (studied in Chapters 4 and 9). The payoff came in the judicial revolution described in Chapter 12: the new politics of judicial appointments brought new justices, who voted differently and made new policies. The statistical analyses in the chapter indicated that the abortion and law-and-order litmus tests very likely worked. A capstone came in 2022 with the Supreme Court's stunning decision in *Dobbs v. Jackson Women's Health Organization*—all five justices who voted to overturn *Roe v. Wade* were appointed under an anti-*Roe* litmus test. In short, the appointments laboratory showed that Schattschneider's brilliant insight still holds but needs revision: New policies indeed create a new politics—and then the new politics may dramatically reshape political institutions.

15.3.2 From Pluralism to Hyper-Pluralism: The Unheavenly Chorus in a New Key

Chapter 1 also discussed the astounding growth of organized interest groups. It described a 30-fold increase in the number of organized groups in Washington, between 1929 to 2011. It documented an even bigger jump in judicial lobbyists—a 60-fold increase between 1930 and 2012. The expansion was so stunning we described it as a transition from pluralism to something new: hyper-pluralism. Chapter 5 then explored how hyper-pluralism played out in public mobilization around Supreme Court nominations. We documented an explosion in the number of mobilizers, but also huge changes in their identities and their tactics. Again, though, one can ask the "bottom line" question: what difference did the vast expansion of the groups make for anything important? The data suggest one answer, but first it is helpful to review some intellectual history.

In the 1950s and 1960s, American political scientists discovered the uncomfortable fact that political participation by organized interest groups had largely displaced political participation by individuals, at least in the halls of power.[11] In the face of this disturbing revelation, political theorists devised a new theory of American democracy, "interest group pluralism." The theory argued that interest groups actually represent individuals, so government-by-the-groups instead of government-by-the-people is perfectly fine, from a normative view. The judgment of many political scientists was perhaps best captured in an elegant apothegm by (again) E. E. Schattschneider (1960):

"The flaw in the pluralist heaven is that the heavenly chorus sings with an upper-class accent." In other words, in practice interest group pluralism delivers representation biased in favor of the wealthy.[12] Playing off Schattschneider's observation, some scholars labeled the interest group universe the "unheavenly chorus."[13]

The evidence in *Making the Supreme Court* somewhat shifts this now-standard critique of interest group pluralism. Without denying the importance of class bias in American pluralism, interest group participation in Supreme Court appointment politics highlights a different phenomenon in the age of hyper-pluralism, which is systematic *ideological* polarization. As shown in the latter part of Chapter 5, the mobilizing interest groups appear to be quite ideologically polarized; in contrast, largely missing are organized activists from the ideological center.

What happens when political participation by organized groups disproportionately reflects highly motivated, organized, and somewhat or quite extreme activist groups, with scant participation by moderates? It is unclear how many issue domains this characterization applies to beyond Supreme Court nominations, but one possibility is, the opposed extremists and their elected allies are compelled to bargain to a moderate outcome or face deadlock. In fact, one often observes this process in today's polarized Congress. There, major pieces of legislation typically pass with supermajorities and embody serious compromises. Either that, or controversial legislation fails to pass.[14] But, as shown in Chapters 8, 9, and 11, that is not what happened with Supreme Court appointments, at least in the twenty-first century. Instead, presidents nominated ideological extremists, and the Senate usually confirmed these nominees—at least, they did in the vacancies that arose during unified government.

In short, the appointments laboratory suggests that Schattschneider's characterization of the pluralist anthem may need a modification: the huge growth of groups on the left and on the right may alter the key in which the chorus sings.

15.3.3 The Polarization of Political Elites: Diffusion across the Branches

The appointments lens revealed more than polarization among the mobilizer groups. It exposed the spread of elite partisan polarization onto the Supreme Court itself. Chapter 12 examined the judicial partisan sort, in which liberal and Democrat justices become one and the same, as did conservative and Republican ones, with few remaining moderates. We attributed the judicial partisan sort to changes in who arrives on the court, in contrast to the reshuffling of individuals' party affiliations in the mass electorate's partisan sort. For example, the data in Chapters 4 and 9 reveal presidents who systematically selected the most ideologically reliable candidates from their short lists.

The Making the Supreme Court (MSC) Simulator used in Chapters 13 and 14 allowed us to explore the future of elite polarization on the court. There, the events of 2016 were decisive, exacerbated by strategic retirements by the justices. The simulation revealed that large conservative majorities are likely to persist on the court through the 2050s, barring a sequence of unusual events.

In short, the appointments laboratory revealed how elite polarization moved from one set of institutions (especially the parties and the presidency) into another, the Supreme Court. And, it provided insights into the likely durability of elite polarization in that institution, in a way that, to the best of our knowledge, has not yet been attempted for other institutions such as Congress.

15.3.4 Divided Government: New Consequences for Appointed Bodies

The data in Chapter 1 revealed that we live in the greatest age of divided party government in U.S. history. When combined with elite polarization, the results can be dramatic. Some are obvious, such as legislative gridlock. Some are explosive, such as attempts by hostile majorities in Congress to impeach and remove presidents of the opposite party. Some are subtle, such as the aggressive use of old statutes to support new forms of administrative regulation—which an ideological court may or may not allow.[15]

One development discussed and analyzed in Chapter 13 was the likely end of divided party confirmation of Supreme Court nominees. The refusal of the Senate to even consider Merrick Garland's appointment in 2016 does not "set a precedent"—future Senate majorities are free to do as they please. But it does reveal a new playbook and strategy brought about by highly polarized elites in tandem with divided party government. If there is no cost to blocking nominees during divided government, why shouldn't both parties do it? The analysis in Chapter 13 examined the likely consequences of this possible future and indicated that future Supreme Courts may regularly feature decision making by eight members rather than nine, or even fewer. While complete paralysis due to a lack of quorum seems quite unlikely, it is not outside the realm of possibility. And, with respect to appointments, a no divided government scenario would encourage justices to time their retirements not just to the party of the president, but also to Senate control, thereby increasing the stakes of every appointment even more.

Thus, the appointments lens revealed a disturbing development brought about by the combination of elite polarization and divided party government—gridlocked appointments to courts, possibly leading to both decreased government capability and more intense appointment fights.

15.3.5 The Mass Public: Partisan Bias and Rational Evaluation

Finally, Chapter 1 claimed that appointment politics offers a laboratory for studying changes in mass public opinion. To do so, we assembled the massive "megapoll" of all available public opinion polls on Supreme Court nominees since the inception of public opinion polling. There were limits on what we could learn, due to the vagaries of early polling and the peculiar questions favored by pollsters. Still, even at a straightforward level, the analyses revealed interesting patterns in who holds opinions and who does not as a consequence of media coverage, modest campaign effects from the Judiciary Committee hearings and scandals, insight into how nominee attributes (like race and gender) affect opinion, and more.

More provocatively, Chapter 10 moved beyond simple tabulations to explore a perspective rooted in modern choice theory and cognitive psychology. We called this approach the Learning-Thinking-Acting (LTA) framework. It affords a way to interpret commonly asked poll questions on nominees to better infer public wishes. The resulting analyses tried to make a contribution to the debate in political science between "realists" (who are skeptical about the ability of the public to engage in meaningful evaluation of politics) and "rationalists" (who are more optimistic). We studied partisan bias in the perception of nominees, which is clearly present but seemingly rather modest. We devised a measure of the utility gap across party identifiers in their evaluation of the same nominee. We then tried to parse the gap into separate components based on pure partisanship versus rational evaluation of ideological differences between respondents and nominees. In our accounting, in recent nominations the impact of pure partisanship was consistently larger than the impact of pure ideological evaluations, but the latter was also plainly evident in the data. One might interpret these findings as supportive of a "realistic rationalist" understanding of citizens.

Finally, Chapter 11 continued the investigation of the public, using completely different data and techniques. We showed—at least in two recent confirmations with high-quality data—that constituents updated their opinions of senators based on confirmation voting, and that the relationship between votes and approval was likely causal. This finding confirms similar scholarship on other high visibility, relatively easily understood roll call votes in the House of Representatives.[16] Those findings, plus our own, again tend to support a somewhat rationalistic understanding of citizens.

In sum, the appointments laboratory provided new, sometimes surprising, and (we hope) valuable insights into the operation of important factors shaping the new American politics.

15.4 Final Thoughts

Hand wringing and wishful dreaming will not bring a truce in the nation's duel over Supreme Court appointments. In fact, a truce is probably impossible. The Supreme Court will remain powerful. Elites will likely remain polarized. Neither side will allow presidents to return to a ramshackle and erratic selection process. Accordingly, presidents will select extremists that average citizens will find distasteful, and the court itself will remain polarized. Some of its own rulings will throw gasoline on the fire. For Supreme Court appointments, the brutal but truthful answer to Rodney King's plaintive cry, "People, can we all just get along?" is: "No, we can't."

If we can't just get along, might we at least modify the conduct of the duel? The analyses in Chapters 13 and 14 highlight two possible paths. Under the status quo of the federalist system of lifetime appointments, the blows of the dueling adversaries will be rare but heavy, occasionally devastating. The specter of an odd-man-out confrontation lurks in the background. In contrast, with staggered term limits, the blows will be more frequent but lighter, and the likelihood of an odd-man-out confrontation would probably fall. At least, this is a reasonable conjecture. Even if we are doomed to an endless duel with cudgels, members of the elected branches have the power to alter its character—but only if they choose to do so.

The distinguished political philosopher Brian Barry closed his landmark book *Political Argument* (1965) with a typically incisive and witty observation, "The end of a book of this nature marks the limits either of the author's own stamina or that which he (no doubt optimistically) attributes to his possible readers. It plainly does not mark the limits of the subject." So too, the limits of making the Supreme Court remain to be seen.

Notes

Chapter 1

1. See Shesol (2011) for an excellent history of the run-up to the court packing plan and its defeat.
2. See Robertson (1994).
3. Roosevelt would go on to make one more appointment, in 1943. His total of nine appointments was exceeded only by President George Washington, who appointed the initial justices to the court in 1789.
4. See Everett and Thrush (2016).
5. With respect to Garland's ideology, a statistical analysis by Clark, Gordon, and Giles (2016) placed him squarely in the ideological center of the D.C. circuit. See Baker and Zeleny (2010) and Ferraro (2010) on Obama's consideration of Garland in 2010.
6. See Rutkus and Bearden (2012) for a comprehensive report on Senate actions on Supreme Court nominees from 1789 to 2012. See Chafetz (2017*b*) for a qualitative historical account of how to think about "precedent" in the Senate's treatment of nominees; Chafetz also nicely places the Senate's exercise of its advice and consent powers over time within the context of legislative obstructionism in general.
7. Rappeport and Savage (2016).
8. The 2013 nuclear option also lowered the voting threshold to a simple majority for all executive appointments (e.g. cabinet appointments), other than Supreme Court justices. Importantly, manipulating Senate rules over nominations for partisan gains is not a recent innovation. Binder and Maltzman (2009, ch. 2) present evidence that the institution of "blue slips" in the Senate—through which senators can impede or even block the confirmation of nominees from their home states—came about in 1913 as a means, in part, for Senate Democrats to streamline their agendas.
9. See Cottrell and Shipan (2016). In Chapter 13, we conduct a simulation analysis to assess how much Trump's victory in 2016 affected the long-run composition of the court.
10. As we discuss in Chapter 8, the contentiousness of Supreme Court nominations has ebbed and flowed throughout American history; the middle of the nineteenth century, for example, saw many nominees either rejected or hotly debated. We show, however, that the systematic level of rancor and contention over Supreme Court nominees, as evidenced by the Garland affair, has now reached an unprecedented level.
11. The judicial preferences involved in the novel are actually historically illuminating. One of the justices targeted (Abraham Rosenberg) is a liberal lion who closely resembles Justice William Brennan, who had left the real-life Supreme Court in 1990; today, we would expect any liberal justice to be broadly pro-environment. The second targeted justice (Glenn Jensen) was thought to be a "strict constructionist" when he was appointed by a Republican president, but turned out to be quite idiosyncratic in his ideology, taking the liberal position in many areas of the law—including on the environment—and conservative positions in others. Such a justice was certainly plausible in the early

1990s; indeed, Jensen is likely modeled after Justice David Souter, who took the bench in 1990. But, as we document in several chapters in this book, real-life presidents have taken concrete steps to ensure that modern-day justices do not exhibit such ideological flexibility in their voting patterns. More recently, a Supreme Court nominee plays a farcical, if somewhat secondary, role in the 2021 comedy *Don't Look Up*. In the movie, the president (played by Meryl Streep) is caught up in a sex scandal with her nominee, a small-town sherriff with no legal experience. To distract from the scandal, the president decides to use nuclear weapons to destroy an incoming comet, whose collision with Earth would essentially end life on Earth. Suffice it to say that Streep's character is miles away from the legal genius of *The Pelican Brief*. But, like with Justice Jensen, *Don't Look Up*'s sherriff would have zero chance of being confirmed by the Senate today, even if a hapless president attempted to appoint such a nominee.

12. We expand upon the theoretical nuances of move-the-median theory and its empirical shortcomings in Chapter 9.
13. In particular, Cottrell, Shipan, and Anderson (2019) find that the location of the median justice (in terms of the court's voting behavior) moves in the direction of the president even following nominations where the president should have been constrained in his ability to move the median, given the alignment of the president, the median senator, and the status quo on the court. In Chapter 12, we show the predictive effect of the location of the median justice on the court's dispositions and majority opinions diminishes once one accounts for the ideological structure of the court in a more nuanced fashion.
14. There are numerous qualitative accounts of Supreme Court nominations over time. These range from a singular focus on particular nominees (e.g. Danelski 1964, Todd 1964) to sweeping historical coverage (Abraham 2008, Maltese 1995, Wittes 2009). In addition, there exist several excellent journalistic or "insider" accounts of particular eras of nominations or particular nominees. Greenburg (2007), for example, provides a wealth of useful background information on Republican nominees in the 1980s, 1990s, and 2000s. John Dean's (2001) play-by-play account of Richard Nixon's selection of William Rehnquist in 1971 (and Dean's role in it) is riveting. So too is Gitenstein's 1992 retelling of Robert Bork's nomination in 1987, based on his experience as chief counsel of the Senate Judiciary Committee, then chaired by Joe Biden. Finally, Mayer and Abramson (1995) offer an intensive study of Clarence Thomas' controversial nomination and confirmation.
15. On the role of war in transforming societies, see Saldin (2010) and Morris (2014).
16. For that version, see McCarty, Poole, and Rosenthal (2006) and Hacker and Pierson (2020).
17. In Chapter 2, we show that the Democratic Party has been more likely to emphasize increasing the diversity of the federal judiciary relative to the Republican Party. In Chapter 9, we show that this asymmetric interest in diversity produced a more diverse pool of judges from which Democratic presidents could draw their Supreme Court nominees, compared to Republican presidents. In Chapter 8, we show that the Supreme Court's landmark 1954 decision in *Brown v. Board of Education* injected racial considerations into nomination politics through the end of the 1960s, as seen in Southern Democrats' opposition to several nominees in the following two decades. Finally, Chapter 5 details the modern influx of identity politics groups to the cast of groups that mobilize around nominations.
18. The data come from obamawhitehouse.archives.gov/omb/budget/Historicals. As Clark (2019, 153) notes, the beginning of the twentieth century marked the period right after

the national economy was transformed from local and agrarian-based to a unified, manufacturing-intensive economy.

19. The code is revised every six years—page counts are for the titles in the Code, excluding supplements and indices.
20. Leuchtenburg (1996).
21. As Mashaw (1994) and Kalen (2015) note, the mid-twentieth century witnessed a shift from agencies making policy through administrative adjudication to rulemaking. The Federal Register only captures the latter, so just looking at changes in its size may overstate the growth of the administrative state. Nevertheless, its overall growth since the 1970s is undeniable.
22. Shapiro (1988).
23. Epp (1998).
24. See Staszak (2014) and Burbank and Farhang (2017). Also, a third reason bears brief mention. During the late twentieth century, Congress federalized parts of criminal law in order to demonstrate toughness in the so-called "war on drugs," which also served to increase federal caseloads (Alexander 2020).
25. The data comes from the Federal Judicial Center: www.fjc.gov/history/courts/caseloads-us-courts-appeals-1892-2017.
26. The data comes from Whittington (2022).
27. Throughout the book, we summarize time trends using such lines, which are called "loess lines" (short for "locally weighted smoothing"); these lines can generally be interpreted as moving averages. In the interest of presentational clarity, we usually do not display confidence intervals for these loess lines, but readers should keep in mind that there is uncertainty in the underlying trends.
28. Figure 1.6 only includes data for cases in which the court reviewed the constitutionality of federal statutes. However, through its exercise of vertical judicial review, the court has struck down many more state laws (Casper 1976, Lindquist and Corley 2013, Kastellec 2018). Including these cases (which are harder to measure) would only further highlight the court's increased power.
29. The full quotation appears in Herring (1929, 17). We borrow the verb "overrun" from Odegard (1929).
30. See Schlozman and Tierney (1986) and Schlozman, Verba, and Brady (2012).
31. The term "hyper-pluralism" is most commonly used in the political theory literature on democracy to describe a situation in which a sufficient number of comprehensive conceptions of the common good exist such that broad agreement is very difficult (see e.g. Ferrara 2014). The term has sporadically been employed in the interest group literature (see e.g. Berkman 2001, Norris 2002). Diven (2006) offers perhaps the most straightforward definition: "The theory of hyper-pluralism suggests that a large number of competing interests, and efforts by policy makers to satisfy those interests, result in complicated, piecemeal policy making that is neither efficient nor effective in achieving its multiple objectives."
32. This argument has roots in classic political science, e.g. Schattschneider (1935) ("a new policy creates a new politics") and particularly David Truman's (1951) "disturbance theory" of interest group formation. Drutman (2015) has some similarities. More broadly, our argument accords with analyses of "policy feedback" (e.g. Pierson 1993), although that literature often stresses changes in the attitudes of mass publics rather than growth

in interest groups and lobbyists (Mettler 2005). It also resonates with related arguments about policy feedback advanced by public choice-oriented scholars (e.g. Higgs 1991). We return to the theme of policy feedback in the concluding chapter.

33. These counts are based on the data collected by Box-Steffensmeier and Christenson (2012). Compared to the counts of groups, in many ways the data on judicial lobbying are even better because we can rely on detailed Supreme Court records rather than old commercial directories.
34. For example, on state regulation, see Hertel-Fernandez's (2019) study of the influence of the American Legislative Exchange Council (ALEC). On federal regulations, see Yackee (2006). On the influence of lobbying on judicial outcomes, see Collins, Jr., Corley, and Hamner (2015).
35. In Chapter 8, we describe in greater detail how to think about the concept of ideology with respect to nomination politics and what NOMINATE scores are capturing.
36. Shor and McCarty (2011).
37. DiMaggio, Evans, and Bryson (1996).
38. As we discuss in detail in Chapter 10, party polarization can arise both from politicians becoming more extreme or from the parties being better sorted; it is difficult to disentangle the two. In addition, in the middle of the twentieth century a lot of extremity fell on the "second dimension" of American politics, which was generally characterized by differences over race, which we discuss in Chapter 8—see also Poole and Rosenthal (1997).
39. Mayhew (2014).
40. Boulay and DiGaetano (1985).
41. See Wilson (1962) and McGirr (2002).
42. See Schickler (2016) and Carr, Gamm, and Phillips (2016).
43. Hall (2019).
44. Calvert (1985) and Wittman (1983) explain the underlying logic.
45. Shor and McCarty (2011).
46. On the long history of one-party Republican dominance of Kansas, see Flentje and Aistrup (2010). On the centrist Republican backlash to "the Kansas experiment"—an extreme supply-side tax cut that resulted in slashed expenditures on roads and schools—see Berman (2017).
47. At any given point, the probability is higher for any type of non-unified government; e.g. a Republican president and a Democratic House. We focus just on the Senate and presidency since the House has no role in confirmations.
48. See Mayhew (2002).
49. See Alesina and Rosenthal (1995) and Rodden (2019).
50. See Wlezien (1995) and Stimson (2018).
51. Some contemporary studies, using different data and techniques, find more "constraint"—see e.g. Fowler et al. (2022).
52. Fowler et al. (2022).
53. The question wording is: "We hear a lot of talk these days about liberals and conservatives. Here is a seven-point scale on which the political views that people might hold are arranged from extremely liberal to extremely conservative."
54. See Levendusky (2009) and additionally Fiorina, Abrams, and Pope (2006). Note, however, that political scientists are not unanimous about conversion versus sorting; see e.g. Abramowitz (2010).

55. See Iyengar and Westwood (2015).
56. As discussed in Mason (2018).
57. This is one of the major points of David Mayhew's classic 1974 book, *Congress: The Electoral Connection*.
58. As noted above, our emphasis on this change stands out from much of the literature on Supreme Court nominations. For instance, Epstein and Segal's (2005) *Advice and Consent: The Politics of Judicial Appointments* provides a comprehensive account of selection and confirmation at all levels of the federal judiciary. However, their sketch of the process (on p. 23) only posits a very narrow role for party elites and interest groups (through participation in the Senate Judiciary Committee hearings), whereas we argue that the influence of interest groups and party elites is both manifest across the process and creates feedback effects that affect both the upstream and downstream decisions of other actors.
59. From the perspective of presidential politics, Yalof (2001) provides a canonical account of how presidents from Truman to Clinton organized and undertook their selections of Supreme Court nominees. Nemacheck (2008) offers a key innovation by collecting data on individuals on the "short list" for most vacancies between 1930 and 2005. Our chapters on presidential selection and the attributes of the nominees build directly off these important studies.
60. As we discuss in more detail in Chapter 5, our arguments here align with and build upon excellent work on the role of interest groups in lower court confirmations and nominations, including Bell (2002), Scherer, Bartels, and Steigerwalt (2008), Steigerwalt (2010), and Steigerwalt, Vining, Jr., and Stricko (2013).
61. In many ways our descriptive account of media coverage of nominations dovetails quite well with the thesis in Davis' (2017) *Supreme Democracy: The End of Elitism in Supreme Court Nominations*. Davis argues that in recent decades Supreme Court nominations have transformed from "insider"-driven affairs in which presidents and senators acted mainly on their own to what are now highly visible affairs in which many different actors, including the public, play a role. However, moving beyond just the coverage itself, whereas Davis argues that this transformation represents the end of elitism, we see a substantial role in modern nomination politics for organized interests—beyond even what a cursory glance at nominations today would suggest. In our telling, the elitism of nomination politics is certainly different than it was in the early part of the twentieth century, but it has by no means disappeared.
62. Both Collins and Ringhand (2013) and Farganis and Wedeking (2014) offer excellent analyses of changes over time in the Senate Judiciary Committee's hearings on nominees. Perhaps because they are both visible and offer a range of potential data based on the back-and-forth between nominees and senators, the hearings have received an outsized degree of attention from political scientists. In addition to these books, there are also a number of published articles: see e.g. Rees III (1982), Guliuzza III, Reagan, and Barrett (1994),Williams and Baum (2006), Shapiro (2012), and Chen and Bryan (2018). Also, for more sympathetic views of the value of the hearings, see Schoenherr, Lane, and Armaly (2020) and Chafetz (2020). In Chapter 7, we show that for most nominees, the hearings have little effect on aggregate public opinion, suggesting perhaps that the hearings are over-studied relative to their importance.
63. Our arguments here about changes in Senate voting align nicely with the theory and evidence presented in Sarah Binder and Forrest Maltzman's (2009) *Advice and Dissent*.

Their book, however, focuses exclusively on appointments and confirmations to the lower federal courts, and not the Supreme Court.

64. Our arguments and evidence here dovetail nicely with that of Devins and Baum's (2019). The core argument of their book is that the current partisan polarization on the court—i.e. the fact that Democratic and Republican appointees have sorted into reliable liberal and conservative blocs—is driven by the larger polarization among elites. In broad measure we agree, and present evidence to this effect in several chapters. But whereas Devins and Baum emphasize a social-psychological explanation in which the justices' world views are shaped by interactions with like-minded elites, our posited causal mechanisms throughout the book are nearly uniformly drawn from rational choice institutionalism.
65. We discuss the academic literature on this question in detail in Chapter 13.
66. See e.g. Moe (1985) and Lewis (2008).
67. Some of these data were collected for our published papers on Supreme Court nominations. In nearly every case, however, we have backdated the relevant data to 1930 or updated the relevant data to 2020, or both. While much of our data is original, we also build on existing data collection efforts by many scholars and institutions, as we note in the acknowledgments section. The website also contains complete replication code for all the analyses that appear in the book.

Chapter 2

1. 410 U.S. 113.
2. In the years leading up to *Roe*, a few states saw their abortion laws ruled unconstitutional by state judges or lower federal court judges. However, in none of these decisions did courts establish a doctrine as far-reaching as *Roe*'s trimester framework (Kastellec 2016).
3. Luks and Salamone (2008).
4. *Dobbs v. Jackson Women's Health Organization.*
5. See Adams (1997) and Williams (2011) on public opinion on abortion over time.
6. See for example Rosenberg (1991) and Pierson (2014).
7. See Greenhouse and Siegel (2010), Lemieux (2009), and Nossiff (2001).
8. Vinovskis (1978).
9. See e.g. Adams (1997), Karol (2009), and Carmines and Woods (2002).
10. See, e.g., Moraski and Shipan (1999), Nemacheck (2008), and Epstein et al. (2006).
11. See for example Yalof (2001).
12. See for example Budge (1993).
13. Other notable studies where this issue arises include: Disalvo's (2012) use of party platforms to uncover evidence of factional influence within the parties over time; Feinstein and Schickler's (2008) use of state party platforms to trace the bifurcation on civil rights among Democratic Party activists in the North and the South between 1920 and 1968, and then the use of national party platforms to delineate the compromises between the activists; and Carr, Gamm, and Phillips' (2016) use of state party platforms as leading indicators to explore the dynamics of issue emergence on abortion and LGBT rights.
14. Schattschneider (1942, 567).
15. Duggan and Martinelli (2017) provide a review.
16. The scholarly literature on the informational limitations of American voters is vast. See Somin (2016) for a useful introduction.

17. See Bawn et al. (2012) and Noel (2013). McCarty and Schickler (2018) offer a critique of the UCLA approach.
18. Note that in addition to specifying an accountability contract, party elites may also try to select a "true believer." The selection story and the contract story are in some sense complementary. But only the contract story offers a meaningful role for the platforms.
19. This is an explicit assumption in Bawn et al. (2012).
20. See Wittman (1977) and Calvert (1985).
21. Hall (2015) provides empirical evidence of this behavior.
22. However, one can view the appointment of would-be or actual "stealth" nominees like David Souter or Harriet Miers as instances of breaking the accountability contract.
23. These documents are readily available from the American Presidency Project at the University of California at Santa Barbara (Peters and Woolley 2011).
24. In 2020, due to the Covid-19 pandemic, the Republican Party chose not to issue a new platform, and instead stated that it would simply re-ratify its 2016 platform verbatim. Accordingly, for 2020, we code the party's 2016 platform statements as also applying in 2020. Donald Trump did mention the Supreme Court once during his acceptance speech in 2020, so some of the combined platform/speeches measures we present below for the Republicans differ slightly between 2016 and 2020.
25. 347 U.S. 483
26. In practice, some statements blend into both litmus tests and ideology; for simplicity, we treat them as mutually exclusive categories.
27. See Driver (2013) on the historical importance of the Southern Manifesto.
28. While our platform data only goes back to 1928, anecdotally we can find similar reactions (and lack thereof) to other landmark controversial decisions by the court. In the 1860 party platforms, the Democratic Party implicitly praised the court's 1857 infamous decision in *Dred Scott v. Sandford* (60 U.S. 393), while the Republican platform implicitly denounced it. But neither platform invoked appointments as a means to affect policy change.
29. 558 U.S. 310.
30. 487 U.S. 735.
31. See Barnes (1999).
32. Quoted in Schmidt (2018, 424).
33. Manchester (2020).
34. Some readers may wonder whether presidents actually implement these litmus tests when selecting nominees. In Chapter 12 we show how justices appointed under litmus tests vote differently than justices who are not. Beyond that, qualitatively we can point to at least one example where failing a litmus test was consequential. Jeffrey Sutton, a judge on the U.S. Court of Appeals for the Sixth Circuit, was appointed to the bench by President George W. Bush. He quickly established a reputation as a leading conservative judge on the federal bench, and for many years he was "near the top of most short lists of potential Republican Supreme Court nominees" (Greenhouse 2014). However, his conservative *bona fides* crumbled quickly in 2011. At that time, a number of federal courts heard challenges to the Affordable Care Act ("Obamacare"), which had been enacted a year earlier along party lines, with nearly every Democratic member of Congress supporting the law, and nearly every Republican opposed. As the challenges wound their way through the courts, judicial assessment of the law split nearly evenly along partisan lines, with Republican-appointed judges voting to strike it down and Democratic-appointed judges voting to uphold it. Sutton, however, was one of the few Republican appointees to uphold the law. Half a

decade later, as Donald Trump assembled his short list of nominees to replace Justice Scalia during the 2016 campaign, Sutton's name was noticeably absent. According to Kaplan (2018, 53), "Trump had exceptional bile for Sutton, whom he labeled 'spineless,' " due to his vote to uphold the ACA. From the moment the law passed, opposition to it became a *sine qua non* for full membership in the Republican coalition, and Sutton had failed this litmus test. With one vote, his chance to become a Supreme Court justice was gone.

35. Our data begin in 1930, but if we go back farther in American history, it is not too difficult to find vivid examples of presidents with almost no interest in the policy output of the Supreme Court. Andrew Jackson, for example, in 1829 appointed the existing Postmaster General (John McClean) to the Supreme Court *so that Jackson could install a more friendly postmaster to the position* (Chafetz 2017*a*, 110). The ability of the agency to carry out Jackson's patronage goals was more important than anything the court was doing at that time, apparently.
36. See Kim (2020) on the 2020 conventions.
37. See Maag (2022) and Blanco (2022) on Biden's lower court appointments (as of early 2022).
38. Grossmann and Hopkins (2016, 3).
39. See also Teles (2008) and Southworth (2009) on the rise of the conservative legal movement.
40. On this point see the careful analyses in e.g. Shafer (1988) and Rosenfeld (2017).
41. All years except 2004 can be found on the ICPSR's website, at https://www.icpsr.umich.edu/icpsrweb/ICPSR/series/00116. The data from 2004 were provided to us by Geoff Layman, whom we thank.
42. See Miller and Jennings (1986), Miller (1988), Layman (1999), Layman et al. (2010), and Wolbrecht (2002).
43. See also Layman and Carsey (1998).
44. This trend toward polarization also occurred among members of Congress and the public at large, see Adams (1997).
45. Again the question wording differs across years. In 2004, the CDS changed the wording of the question about group membership. In addition, the proportion of missing responses is much higher than in earlier years. Accordingly, we exclude 2004 from the group analysis. See the Appendix for further details.
46. In the Appendix, we present several regression models that confirm the differences between group members and non-group members are statistically significant.
47. *Stenberg v. Carhart*, 530 U.S. 914.
48. Another way to characterize the connection between this chapter and Chapter 9 is that this chapter demonstrates changes in the *demand* for more reliable Supreme Court nominees who will vote in accordance with the parties' preferences; Chapter 9 evaluates the *supply* of such candidates and how that supply changed over time.

Chapter 3

1. Transcripts of the interviews are available at https://rbsc.princeton.edu/collections/william-o-douglas-oral-history-interviews. The quote is from Cassette 12, recorded December 18, 1962.

2. The terrific Cardozo studies are Carmen (1969) and Kaufman (1979). Fausold (1985, 92–93) is a partial exception to the sparse scholarship on the Owen Roberts selection.
3. Harding lies outside our usual time frame—and we do not have data on the short lists (described below) for his nominees—but his overall process for picking nominees is superbly documented and far too interesting not to use, so we extend the window of analysis in this chapter back to 1921.
4. Simon (1980).
5. Hess (1972).
6. Our account draws heavily upon Kramer (1990). Ford's autobiography, *A Time To Heal*, is quite terse (Ford 1979, 335), as is Brinkley (2007, 128–129), but both are consistent with the delegation story. See also Yalof (2001, 125–132).
7. Stevens' subsequent performance on the court left many conservatives unhappy, though perhaps not Ed Levi. Ford himself always regarded his sole Supreme Court pick as a tremendous success and an important part of his presidential legacy (Ford 2005).
8. Moe (2012) reviews the logic and evidence.
9. As investigated in Rudalevige (2002).
10. Our account draws primarily from chapters 1 and 8 of Greenburg (2007).
11. Greenburg (2007, ch. 11).
12. There are civil servants in the Executive Office of the President; for example, in the Office of Management and Budget. But there are virtually none in the White House itself (Walcott and Hult 1995).
13. The exceptions include the Council of Economic Advisers and the National Security Council, which have a statutory basis.
14. Classics include Moe (1985), Kernell (1986), Rudalevige (2002), Lewis (2008).
15. In addition, whereas Nemacheck relies mainly on documents in presidential libraries, trying to determine with whom presidents conferred, we rely more on synoptic histories of nominations, which arguably provide a more holistic view of the president's decisions. In our view, these two approaches are complementary, and we encourage readers to consult Nemacheck's valuable scholarship.
16. See Moe (2012, 1163), *inter alia*.
17. In a few cases presidents have clashed with their attorney general. For example, LBJ detested his inherited Attorney General Robert Kennedy, so he relied heavily on his confidante Abe Fortas for advice on legal issues (Kalman 2017, esp. ch. 1). There are other exceptions: Clinton had difficulty with Janet Reno, as did Trump with Jeff Sessions. But it does not appear that any of these conflicts made much difference for Supreme Court nominations.
18. An example is the notorious "torture memos" of the George W. Bush administration. These were legal opinions from the Office of Legal Counsel in the Justice Department, defining permissible interrogation practices in the "Global War on Terror"—see Goldsmith (2007). Other examples are the scope of executive privilege and the pardoning powers of the president, as recognized by a given administration.
19. See Drew (1995) and Yalof (2001).
20. Toobin (2017).
21. A second office in the Justice Department, the Office of Legal Policy, focuses on selection of lower federal judges. Beginning with the Carter Administration, some White House counsels involved themselves in that activity as well (see Borrelli et al. (2001) and Patterson (2000, 102)).

22. During the period in George W. Bush's administration when Vice President Cheney effectively served as "deputy president," his legal counsel (David Addington) often assumed this role (Gellman 2008, Goldsmith 2007).
23. See Strine (1995).
24. See Clayton (1992, 33–34) and Baker (1992, 188).
25. Other duties have included acting as liaison and coordinator for the Department of Justice and Department of State with the United Nations and other international organizations, managing federal-state relations, resolving intradepartmental disputes, reviewing all gifts and bequests to the United States, and considering registrants for conscientious objector status (1955 Att'y Gen. Ann. Rep. 43).
26. See the 2013 OLC Report to Congress.
27. Clayton (1992, 34).
28. Lewis (2008).
29. Rehnquist (1970, 251).
30. Gibson (2008).
31. We draw upon Jenkins (2012).
32. Epstein (2010), Brownell and Burke (1993).
33. Brownell and Burke (1993, 10–11).
34. The history of the burgeoning executive is well known and documented; Kernell (1989) is particularly helpful.
35. Kernell (1989).
36. Rosenman's (1972) delightful memoir is quite clear about this.
37. Roosevelt's string of nine nominations ended before Rosenman became Counsel. Rosenman was slightly involved in the court packing fight of 1937, mostly as a speechwriter (Rosenman 1972, ch. 9). But otherwise he appears to have played no role in judicial selection.
38. Borrelli, Hult, and Kassop (2001, 220–221), Rabkin (1995).
39. Diamond (2017).
40. Lat (2017).
41. Borrelli, Hult, and Kassop (2001, 198).
42. Toobin (2017).
43. Anderson (1968), Medved (1979). We gratefully acknowledge the assistance of the late Fred Greenstein in parsing the role of super-staffers.
44. As we discuss below, during his campaign, Donald Trump twice released short lists of candidates for the Supreme Court (Rappeport and Savage 2016, Flores and Garrett 2016).
45. Only one president seems to have concocted phony short lists for public consumption. Lyndon Johnson had no one else in mind but his good friend Abe Fortas when he nominated the super-star attorney to become associate justice in 1965 and then chief justice in 1968. And he very quickly focused on Thurgood Marshall as the best candidate for the first African-American appointee to the court (Kalman 2017). Johnson had short lists for these picks, but they were Potemkin lists; he already had selected his true nominee. (In contrast, the list of successors to Fortas following his nomination to become chief justice—which eventually resulted in the selection of Homer Thornberry—was genuine.) But for all other presidents, to the best of our knowledge, the short lists were sincere.
46. In the figure and the calculations that follow, we exclude from the analysis the nominations of Douglas Ginsburg and John Roberts to become Chief Justice. In the former

case, Nemacheck pools Ginsburg with the nomination of Kennedy; for the purposes of calculating the size of the short list, it makes sense not to treat Ginsburg as a "singleton" short list, as explained shortly. In the latter case, the circumstances of Robert's switch from an associate justice nominee to a chief justice nominee are sufficiently unusual that it makes sense to only include the short list from when he was initially selected.

47. A simple t-test of difference in means yields a p-value of 0.005.
48. Garrett and Rutkus (2010).
49. See Shipan, Allen, and Bargen (2014) for a systematic examination of what factors predict variation in search duration. One of their main findings is that presidents take longer to make nominations during periods of divided government. The regressions in their interesting article do not specifically model changes over time; like us, however, the authors note that the professionalization of the office of the president has translated into shorter durations, *ceteris paribus*.
50. Of these nominations, the Cardozo process is well documented. The Hughes and Parker nominations have received some attention, the latter primarily as an early example of interest group mobilization. The details of Owen Roberts' nomination remain obscure.
51. Mason (1956, 276).
52. Greenstein (1994).
53. This account follows Brownell's (1993) engaging autobiography.
54. Brownell's charming memoir carefully steps around the sordid parts of partisan politics, invariably casts Eisenhower in a flattering light, and downplays the political elements in judicial selection. One should read it somewhat skeptically.
55. Yalof (2001, 44–51) provides an excellent account.
56. See Biskupic (2009, 70–98) and Yalof (2001, 135–142).
57. We rely on Yalof (2001, 142–155), Jenkins (2012, 210–212), Biskupic (2009, 99–121), and Greenburg (2007, 38–46).
58. Greenburg (2007, 58) indicates that Department of Justice staffers urged senators to lobby the White House against the moderate Kennedy in favor of Ginsburg.
59. The quoted phrases come from the titles of three of Robert Bork's books (1996, 2009, 2013).
60. For the Thomas details, we rely primarily on Phelps and Winternitz (1992, 1–14), which is based on interviews with participants. See Atkinson (1999) on Marshall's exit.
61. Greenburg (2007, 167). Our account draws heavily on Drew (1995), which remains the best portrait of the Clinton White House, and to the best of our knowledge the only in-depth study of Clinton's two Supreme Court nominations. Clinton's own memoir (2005) elides far more than it reveals. Nussbaum's oral history (2002) is useful and extremely entertaining.
62. Kaplan (2018, 49).
63. Rappeport and Savage (2016), Flores and Garrett (2016).
64. Marcus (2019, 40).
65. Kaplan (2018, 63).
66. Montgomery (2019).
67. Quoted in Montgomery (2019).
68. Kaplan (2018, 57).
69. It is perhaps tempting to view the Kavanaugh nomination as an *ex ante* vetting failure by the administration. However, since Ford kept the allegations private until after Kavanaugh's nomination, there was no way for the administration to predict the emergence of the accusations.

70. In Chapter 13, we examine the long-run implications of the three appointments on the court's ideological trajectory.
71. Marimow (2019).

Chapter 4

1. John Dean (2001, 50), Nixon's White House counsel from 1970 to 1973, relays this conversation, which is drawn verbatim from the infamous taping system in the Nixon oval office. Both Dean and the taping system would play a key role in the Watergate scandal and Nixon's subsequent resignation in 1974.
2. *Swann v. Charlotte-Mecklenburg Board of Education*, 402 U.S. 1.
3. The tapes clearly reveal Nixon's commitment to specific policy litmus tests. In the same conversation he instructed Mitchell: "I want you to have a specific talk with whatever man you consider. And I have to have an absolute commitment from him on busing and integration. I really have to. Go out and tell 'em that we totally respect his right to do otherwise, but if he believes otherwise, I don't want to appoint him to the court" (Dean 2001, 51). He continues "I really want to be God damn sure though, on the criminal side and the busing issue, housing, education I just don't want to put a liberal on the court, I can't handle that" (Dean 2001, 57).
4. Nixon and Mitchell repeatedly returned to the age of possible nominees, holding age against older nominees.
5. Lyndon Johnson also surreptitiously recorded many telephone conversations. One records Johnson offering the solicitor generalship to Thurgood Marshall, while also hinting at a future appointment to the Supreme Court (The LBJ Library 2012). In another recorded conversation, Johnson schemed with Justice Abe Fortas, a close friend, to maneuver Justice Tom Clark off the court in order to create a vacancy for Marshall (DiscoverLBJ 2018).
6. See Nemacheck (2008, 84).
7. To clarify our terminology throughout this chapter and in Chapter 9, we use "candidates" generically to describe the complete set of individuals who comprise the short list, including the eventual nominees. We use "short listers" to refer to individuals on the short list who were *not* eventually nominated, while "nominees" refers to individuals actually nominated by the president. Readers should keep in mind that nominees are technically a subset of all short listers, as nominees always (by definition) emerge from the short list. "Candidates" thus describes the union of "nominees" and "short listers."
8. The measure has a degree of face validity. In addition, Nemacheck (2008) shows that the distance between the president and a candidate, as measured using the scores, predicts who the president selects from the short list. This finding adds additional confidence in the validity of the measure.
9. See Bailey (2007) on this point.
10. Of course, focusing solely on contemporary *perceptions* of nominee ideology misses the occasional disjuncture between those perceptions and later behavior, which in a few instances (such as Stevens and Souter) was dramatic. We return to this point in Chapter 12.
11. The SPR measure displays the same basic patterns as the NSP scores over time with respect to nominees. The two measures correlate at 0.84, and the SPR score reveals the same temporal trends in ideological polarization. See the Appendix for further details.

12. This data is available in the invaluable U.S. Supreme Court Justices Database (Epstein et al., 2022).
13. Notably, Nixon's cross-party appointments of Haynsworth and Carswell did not actually display ideological moderation. Rather, both nominees were Southern Democrats perceived as solid conservatives, as shown by their NSP scores in Figure 4.1. The Southern Democrats' shift into the Republican camp would contribute to the partisan sort of liberals and conservatives so characteristic of America today.
14. See Epstein, Knight, and Martin (2003) on the trend toward almost all nominees coming from the circuit courts.
15. An alternative approach would be to employ the well-known newspaper editorial measure of legal qualifications, which is often used in the roll call literature (Cameron, Cover, and Segal 1990, Epstein et al. 2006, Shipan 2008, Cameron, Kastellec, and Park 2013). While this measure is useful in this context (and, indeed, we employ it in later chapters), we do not believe it captures very well the experience and policy reliability of nominees. In particular, the measure conflates poorly qualified nominees, such as Harriet Miers, with highly qualified ones whose nomination were besmirched by some type of scandal, e.g. Douglas Ginsburg and Brett Kavanaugh. The latter clearly indicates this problem of conflation: despite being widely viewed as highly qualified due to his experience as a judge on the D.C. Circuit, Kavanaugh received an extremely low qualifications score (nearly as low as that of Harriet Miers) due primarily to the allegations of sexual misconduct levied against him. In addition, this measure does not exist for short-listers.
16. Yale, Stanford, Harvard, University of Chicago, Columbia, New York University, University of Pennsylvania, University of Michigan-Ann Arbor, UC-Berkeley, University of Virginia, Duke, Northwestern, Cornell, Georgetown, and University of Texas-Austin. These schools have almost always been in the top 14 of the U.S. News & World Report's Law School rankings since their creation in 1987, and the "top-14" designation is widely, if informally, used in the legal community—see https://en.wikipedia.org/wiki/Law_school_rankings_in_the_United_States.
17. See Babington (2005) and Luppen (2022) on the 1985 memo.
18. The coding of law school attendance before 1930 comes from the U.S. Supreme Court Justices Database; as such, it only exists for nominees, not short listers.
19. Katcher (2006).
20. Most recently, in 2020, President Trump nominated Amy Coney Barrett, a graduate of the Notre Dame Law School. Before the Barrett nomination, the last time a confirmed nominee attended a school other than Harvard, Yale, or Columbia was in 1986, when President Reagan elevated William Rehnquist (a Stanford Law School graduate) to Chief Justice. (Three failed nominees between 1986 and 2000 did not attend the Big 3: Robert Bork and Douglas Ginsburg both attended the University of Chicago Law School, while Harriet Miers received her J.D. from Southern Methodist University.)
21. We develop this argument theoretically in Chapter 9. In Chapter 12, we show how the increase in putatively reliable justices translated into more reliable voting on the Supreme Court, including in litmus test areas.
22. The patterns for short listers from 1930 to 2020 are broadly similar to all the results for nominees that we present in this section. See Ostermeier (2009) for more on the age of nominees over time.
23. We do not account for changes in life expectancy since 1789, which might affect the interpretation of these patterns. In Chapter 13 we show that while the average age of

entrance has not changed over time, the average *tenure* of Supreme Court justices has increased dramatically in recent decades.

24. Justice Gorsuch's religious affiliation is somewhat ambiguous—he was raised Catholic but attended an Episcopalian church when he lived in Colorado (Burke 2017). We code him as Catholic.
25. Among the Protestant justices, all came from "mainline" denominations, with the majority being Episcopalian or Presbyterian. At the time we write, no justice has ever been an evangelical Christian.
26. The empty boxes in the left-hand corner reflect the changing number of seats on the court over time. There have been 10 seats on the courts—the 6th and 8th seats were abolished by Congress in 1865 and 1863, respectively, to deny President Andrew Johnson the opportunity to make appointments. While the 6th seat was reestablished, the 8th seat was not; however, Congress established a 10th seat in 1863, and the court has had nine seats since 1869 (Epstein et al. 2013, 21). For simplicity, we merge the 8th and 10th seats into a single seat, and ignore the handful of years in the 1860s where the court had 10 justices.
27. See Shemtob (2012) and McCammon and Montanaro (2018).
28. The question, which comes from Gallup (2018), asks: "What is your religious preference—are you Protestant, Roman Catholic, Mormon, Jewish, Muslim, another religion or no religion?"
29. The 2022 appointment of Ketanji Brown Jackson, who is Protestant, corrected this representational imbalance slightly.
30. Daniels (1978).
31. See Prendergast (2016).
32. The dissent is from *Obergefell v. Hodges* (576 U.S. 644), in which the Supreme Court struck down state bans on same-sex marriage as unconstitutional.

Chapter 5

1. Quoted in Gitenstein (1992, 31).
2. See Stolberg and Martin (2018).
3. See Ainsworth and Maltese (1996). We summarize the Matthews nomination in n. 11 in Chapter 8.
4. See Watson (1963) and Goings (1990).
5. See Danelski (1964).
6. Beyond the Supreme Court, interest groups have been involved in lower court appointments, and in ways that strongly resemble the activities we document here. Several excellent studies of group participation in lower court appointments complement the account in this chapter; we discuss them in the Appendix. Notable are Scherer (2005), Steigerwalt (2010), and Flemming, MacLeod, and Talbert (1998). We return to this literature in the conclusion of the chapter.
7. The analyses that appear in Section 2 of this chapter are based on our 2020 article co-authored with Cody Gray and Jee-Kwang Park, "From Textbook Pluralism to Modern Hyper-Pluralism: Interest Groups and Supreme Court Nominations, 1930–2017," published in the *Journal of Law & Courts*.
8. See Bennett (1988).

9. See e.g. Tilly (2005). A recent U.S. example is Burstein (2014).
10. We omit the American Bar Association from our analysis. The ABA has been a frequent presence in nominations over our time period. However, this almost always occurs in the context of the ABA issuing its recommendations about the qualifications of the nominee. While important, this activity is qualitatively different from the mobilization goals that the other groups in our dataset pursue.
11. The AFL and CIO merged in 1955. For simplicity, we categorize involvement by either group in nominations prior to that year as falling under the AFL-CIO.
12. See e.g. Walker (1991) and Baumgartner et al. (2009).
13. The complete taxonomy appears in the Appendix.
14. See Mayer (2017) on the rise of dark money more generally and Lee (2018) on the Kavanaugh nomination. In 2021, an organization run by Leonard Leo, the former Federalist Society leader who helped shape President Trump's shortlist (as discussed in Chapter 4), received a $1.6 billion donation from a little-known donor (Vogel and Goldmacher 2022). Collecting data on interest group spending is challenging, but would shed a great deal of light on interest group tactics before and during nominations.
15. A complete list of tactics appears in the Appendix.
16. See Pertschuk and Schaetzel (1989).
17. This observation has implications for assessing empirical work based solely on interest group participation in the hearings. While this activity is undoubtedly important, to focus only on the hearings is to miss most interest group activity on Supreme Court nominations.
18. To do so, we cross-referenced our groups against the data contained both in the Washington Representatives Study (Schlozman 2010) and the Encyclopedia of Association (Bevan et al. 2013). We also employed Internet searches when necessary. We were able to find the birth years of all but three groups. A few of the repeat players also "died"—that is, they closed their doors. We also recorded this data.
19. The axis begins at 1930 to conserve space; the earliest group formation (the National Education Association) occurred in 1860.
20. The ACU is a conservative organization that sometimes lobbies Congress via public campaigns; holds an annual meeting of conservative groups, media celebrities, and potential Republican presidential candidates; and raises and distributes campaign funds. It also numerically scores congressmen on their voting, a crude approximation of Political Science's sophisticated NOMINATE scores.
21. We introduced the Washington Representatives Study in Chapter 1; see Schlozman et al. (2017).
22. The DIME scores were developed by Adam Bonica—see https://data.stanford.edu/dime. The details of the mapping between the CF scores and Hansford scores can be found in the Appendix.
23. See Epstein et al. (2006) and Cameron, Kastellec, and Park (2013).
24. The details can be found in the Appendix. The data can be thought of as a panel, with group-nominee as the unit of analysis. One modification, however, is that we only include a group in the dataset for the nominations that occur *after* their birth years and before their death years, where relevant. For example, the National Organization for Women was founded in 1966; it only enters the data for nominations after that year. This procedure leaves us with 2,987 mobilization decisions—the sample size for the regressions—that comprise 103 unique groups (some repeat players have missing data needed to create the ideology scores) across 54 nominations.

25. The measure was first developed in Segal and Cover (1989) and Cameron, Cover, and Segal (1990).
26. Specifically, we set low and high quality at the 25% and 75% percentiles of the quality measure, for all the nominees in our data.
27. Kaiser (2014), Brill (2015).
28. An outstanding case study is Libgober and Carpenter (2023).
29. See Bawn et al. (2023).

Chapter 6

1. Somewhat ironically, Marshall died on January 24, 1993—four days after President Bill Clinton, a Democrat, took the oath of office. The sad story of Marshall's departure is well told in Atkinson (1999).
2. See Berke (1991).
3. See Cochran (2014) on the viewership levels for the hearing.
4. Farganis and Wedeking (2014).
5. See Prior (2007) and Ladd (2012).
6. See e.g. Jamieson and Cappella (2008), Stroud (2011), Levendusky (2013), Gervais (2014), and Forgette (2018). The fragmentation in media has gone hand-in-hand with the rise in overall political polarization. But, as Prior (2013) explains, whether the emergence of partisan media has *increased* polarization is unclear. We return to this broad theme and its relation to changes in media coverage of Supreme Court nominees in the conclusion to this chapter.
7. To our knowledge, the only other systematic longitudinal analysis of media coverage of Supreme Court is Evans and Pearson-Merkowitz (2012), who use text analysis to analyze newspaper coverage of 10 nominations between 1981 and 2009. Their emphasis is on the discrepancy between the court's agenda and issues addressed by the media, whereas we are more interested in changes in nominee media coverage in its own right.
8. See the Appendix for a description of what constitutes a scandal, as well as a full list of nominee scandals.
9. Powe, Jr. (2000).
10. Farganis and Wedeking (2014).
11. See Pew Research Center (2010*b*), Economist (2017), and Hagey, Alpert, and Serkez (2019).
12. See Pew Research Center (2010*a*), Saad (2013), Mitchell et al. (2016), and Mitchell (2018).
13. See Pew Research Center (2007), Vavreck (2015), and Espinoza (2019).
14. See Prior (2007) and Pew Research Center (2010*a*).
15. Unfortunately, because there were no nominations to the Court between 1994 and 2005, we have no observations for the first nine years in which Fox News and MSNBC were in operation.
16. The Appendix provides more information on the sources of each type of coverage, as well as further coding details.
17. See Shipan and Shannon (2003).
18. This data was initially collected by Cameron and Park (2011) for every nominee from 1930 through Sonia Sotomayor in 2009. We extended this data through 2020; see that

paper (which also contains a theoretical account of going public on nominees) for further details.

19. See Clark (2019).
20. We exclude Owen Roberts, Byrnes, Rutledge, Burton, and Whittaker because the number of news articles about them were too few to estimate a topic model.
21. See e.g. Noack (2018).
22. For instance, if an interest group representative appeared on CNN at 4 PM to discuss the Kavanaugh nomination with Jake Tapper, then also appeared on CNN Tonight at 11 PM to talk about Kavanaugh with Don Lemon, we would record two appearances for that interest group representative on that day.
23. Sinclair (2018).
24. Cizmar (2018).
25. Editorials on Supreme Court nominees serve as the source of the widely used "Segal-Cover" (1989) scores, as well as the scores used to measure nominee qualifications that we have discussed earlier (Cameron, Cover, and Segal 1990), but few scholars have actually studied the content of editorials to understand the dynamics of nominations themselves. One interesting exception is Coyle, Fondren, and Richard (2020), who show how various friends of Louis Brandeis published editorials (among other strategies) in an effort to counter attacks against Brandeis' reputation and push his controversial nomination over the line.
26. See e.g. Kahn and Kenney (2002), Ladd and Lenz (2009), Chiang and Knight (2011), and Olson (2018).
27. See the Appendix for further details about the data collection process.
28. See the Appendix for further details on this coding.
29. The only instance in which copartisan editorial boards opposed a nominee occurred when Harriet Miers was nominated by President George W. Bush, a choice that was roundly criticized by conservatives due to Miers' lack of judicial experience, the perceived cronyism of the nomination, and her unknown views on abortion.
30. While there may be some regional differences in language, we used the *Times* to construct our dictionary because of its reputation as the nation's paper of record and its comparatively high level of attention to nominations throughout the time period under study.
31. If we break down the editorials into before and after the sexual allegations emerged against Kavanaugh in September 2018, the shift in the editorials' focus is quite clear quantitatively. Before the scandal, the ideology-to-quality ratio was .22, which would put him in line with the other twenty-first century nominees (except Miers). After the scandal hit, the ratio reversed to -.28, as editorial board writers shifted their emphasis to the allegations.
32. Of course, the liberal proclivities of the *Times*' editorial board may factor in here. However, even for the three liberal nominees between 2009 and 2016 (Sotomayor, Kagan, and Garland), ideology words outweighed quality words in the *Times*' assessment.
33. CBS Evening News debuted on July 1, 1941, under the name CBS Television News, broadcasting short news updates twice a day about developments in World War II. The regular nightly newscast debuted in 1948 and was 15 minutes long. The program extended to 30 minutes in 1963.
34. Establishing causality is very difficult because, as Prior (2013) notes, it is equally plausible that viewers who were already polarized *selected* into watching Fox News or MSNBC because they wanted to watch polarized news. Untangling causality requires randomized exposure to different media sources, and no such data exist for Supreme

Court nominations, as far as we know. However, note that the overall number of cable news watchers is still quite small, relative to all television watchers (Prior 2013, 111-112).

Chapter 7

1. Greenburg (2007, 87–107) provides a thorough recounting of the Souter selection.
2. During Souter's confirmation hearing before the Senate Judiciary Committee, Senator Howell Heflin (D-AL) said, "This committee will do a lot of peeling beneath your veneer, for you are indeed a stealth nominee" (Campbell 1990).
3. We detail the sources of our public opinion data below.
4. The Gallup Poll, founded by the pioneer George Gallup, published its first poll on October 20, 1935 (Newport 2010).
5. The tendency in the public opinion literature is to code "leaners"—respondents who first identity themselves as independents but then in a follow-up question say they lean toward one party or the other—as partisans (Keith et al. 1992). Unfortunately, many of the earlier polls do not ask a "lean" follow-up question. To maximize the number of usable and comparable polls over time, we thus do not code leaners as partisans for any of the public opinion analyses in this book, except for the accountability analyses in Chapter 11.
6. While this poll falls outside Black's nomination period, we make a one-time exception to our general rule, as this poll offers the first poll information about a Supreme Court nominee. Fifty-six percent of Americans said Black should not resign, and he successfully weathered the storm; Black would serve for nearly forty years on the court.
7. The frequency and range of public opinion polling on all subjects increased dramatically over the course of the twentieth century—see Igo (2007).
8. An implication of the distribution of polling over time is that one should be cautious in extrapolating findings from nominations with polls to nominations without polls. If a poll had been conducted on, say, Frank Murphy, Harold Burton, or Charles Whittaker, most respondents would probably have wondered who these people were. (In the no-polling era, most nominees also received voice votes in the Senate, as we document in the next chapter, another indicator of low visibility and low public interest.) On the other hand, the polls from O'Connor forward almost certainly provide a representative portrait of public opinion on Supreme Court nominees during the last 40 years or so.
9. With this downside in mind, an alternative strategy would be to use only polls taken within the same period of time toward the end of a nomination. As a robustness check, we repeated the analyses in this section using only polls taken within 30 days of the end of the nomination. This process results in roughly a third of the nominees being dropped from the subsetted data, compared to the last five polls. Nevertheless, the main results that we present here hold when we keep only polls taken in the last 30 days.
10. Note also that the last five polls data applies to both the aggregate-level and the individual-level data; because there are some polls in the former that do not appear in the latter, the polls included in the last five polls data across the different levels will be different for some nominees. The individual-level last five polls data contains about 108,000 respondents across 40 unique polls. The aggregate last five polls data comprises 90 unique polls. When we break down this data by party identification below, we are left with 60 unique polls.
11. At the left of the figure, the Black nomination lifts the loess line, but the coverage measure does not include the post-nomination period when his KKK-affiliation allegations exploded into controversy. Hence, the coverage measure is too low, given the salience

of the nomination at the time of the poll. On the right of the figure, the Kavanaugh nomination depresses the loess line, in part because the level of total coverage was so extraordinary relative to all other nominees. If one excludes the Black and Kavanaugh observations, the correlation between coverage and opinion holding increases to .59.

12. The seminal book examining variation in political knowledge is Carpini and Keeter (1996). See Mondak and Anderson (2004) and Abrajano (2015) on the gender and racial gaps in political knowledge, respectively. An outstanding recent study of public interest in politics is Prior (2019). For in-depth examinations of differences in opinion on the Clarence Thomas nomination by race and gender, see Caldeira and Smith (1996) and Hutchings (2001).
13. A concern is the distribution of polls with explicit don't know options, which may have changed over time. If so, the observed levels of non-opinions for some nominees would simply reflect variation in question wording. Unfortunately, the aggregate top-line results from Roper do not always provide full question wordings, and it is impossible to tell with certainty which questions had explicit don't know options. Using just the polls with individual-level data would result in analyzing fewer nominees. To address this concern, in the Appendix we replicate the analysis in Figure 7.5 (as well as Figure 7.6 below) using only polls in the last five polls data without an explicit don't know option (such polls are twice as numerous compared to polls with explicit don't know options). Not surprisingly, the levels of opinion holding are higher in such polls, compared to the full set of aggregate polls. However, across the nominees, the broad patterns shown in Figures 7.5 and 7.6 continue to hold in that subset of the data.
14. See Cameron, Cover, and Segal (1990), Segal, Cameron, and Cover (1992), and Epstein et al. (2006).
15. Badas and Stauffer (2018) examine the nominations of Thomas, Kagan, and Sotomayor, and find that shared descriptive identity between respondents and nominee can increase support for Supreme Court nominees when they are female and/or non-white.
16. By using the aggregate data, we implicitly weight each poll equally, regardless of sample size. An alternative strategy would be to use the individual-level data and take the mean of support by partisan group for every nominee. The cost of this strategy is that for several of the earlier nominees, we only have top-line data with information on party identification, but no individual-level data. However, if we recreate the measures of differential partisan response using the individual-level data, the substantive story remains the same, as both reveal a huge increase in the differences between co-partisan and out-party identifiers beginning in the twenty-first century.
17. Unfortunately, we have no polls with respondent party identification for the four earliest nominees with polling data (Black, Frankfurter, Fortas (CJ), and Haynsworth). So we must exclude these nominees from the analysis.
18. See Fowler (2020) for a perceptive argument about the difficulty of disentangling raw partisanship as a driver of mass behavior from policy considerations.
19. Quite interestingly, Bartels and Kramon (2021) find a similar pattern for public opinion about support for the court itself (not nominees): co-partisans of the president are much more likely to support the court, all things equal. This effect leads to dramatic changes in public opinion when partisan control of the White House switches, independent of the court's own decisions.
20. We find that five polls is the minimum necessary to conduct meaningful within-nominee analysis over time, because the polls occur over multiple months and tend to cluster around certain dates. They do not occur evenly across the campaign, unlike the "rolling

cross-sections" often used to study campaign effects during modern presidential campaigns (e.g. Erikson and Wlezien 2012).

21. Each line has a span of .75, except for Rehnquist, for whom we use 1.25 due to his smaller number of polls.
22. Focusing just on the trends masks poll-to-poll variation that exists within each nomination, but much of this variation reflects normal sampling error and variation in question wording. Accordingly, we focus on the "big picture." (Note also that there will be greater uncertainty in the within-nomination trends for nominees with fewer polls.) We present some supplementary analyses below.
23. Note that this range cuts off the nomination period of Merrick Garland. His nomination technically ended in January 2017 when the 114th Congress expired, but was effectively over by the 100-day mark (which occurred in June 2016), as Senate Republicans refused to consider his nomination.
24. In the Appendix, we present some additional fine-grained analyses for each nominee.
25. This movement is consistent with Page and Shapiro's (1992) theory of "parallel publics," which states that when opinion change occurs, it tends to occur roughly in equal measure among different groups, including partisan groups.
26. We shortly focus on the role of scandal in the Thomas and Kavanaugh nominations, which led to a second round of hearings for both. We exclude those second hearings from this analysis. In addition, both of their scandals broke within 20 days after their initial hearings. We exclude any polls from the initial hearings analysis that were taken after the scandals emerged.
27. The exact dates are as follows. Thomas, 1991: *Pre-initial hearing* 8/29–9/13; *Pre-scandal* 9/14–10/6; *Scandal emerges* 10/7–10/13; *After second hearing* 10/14–10/16. Kavanaugh, 2018: *Pre-initial hearing* 8/20–9/03; *Pre-scandal* 9/04–9/16; *Scandal emerges* 9/17–9/28; *After second hearing* 9/29–10/6.
28. Overby et al. (1992).
29. Absent panel data, it is impossible to know the exact movement of individuals, just the aggregate net movement.
30. To be sure, many of the trends for Kavanaugh are linear across the four time periods, suggesting continuity of trends rather than a scandal-induced discontinuity. We cannot know how opinion would have trended in the counterfactual absence of a scandal, but media coverage of the nomination would surely have been modest following the initial round of hearings. So a reasonable conjecture is, opinion would have stabilized in the counterfactual scenario.
31. Interested readers can find an engaging account of how they did it, penned by a key insider, in Pertschuk and Schaetzel (1989).

Chapter 8

1. This account is drawn from Maltese (1995, 26–31).
2. As Maltese (1995, 26) notes, the length of time it took news to travel in 1795 explains why Rutledge may have been willing to offer his opinion on the sensitive subject of the treaty: "The meeting took place after he had been named chief justice but before Rutledge

himself knew of the appointment, and certainly before Rutledge had formally received his commission" to the recess appointment.

3. The fact that Scalia's appointment was paired with Rehnquist's elevation contributed to his easy confirmation. Senate Democrats focused their fire on Rehnquist, based on allegations that he worked to suppress voter turnout in Arizona in the 1960s. With the spotlight on Rehnquist, who was eventually confirmed by a 65-33 vote, Scalia had an unencumbered path to confirmation.
4. See the Appendix for details on our coding of confirmation outcomes and roll call votes in this chapter.
5. This includes the initial nomination of John Roberts to become associate justice in 2005, before President George W. Bush withdrew this nomination and instead appointed Roberts to become chief justice after William Rehnquist died. The other three instances feature nominations that expired at the end of a Congress before the Senate could act; these nominees were ultimately re-nominated in the next Congress and confirmed.
6. Eight of those 127 nevertheless declined to serve on the court; the last such nominee was Roscoe Conkling in 1882. Thus, as of 2020, 119 nominations had resulted in the nominee taking the seat to which he or she was appointed. Accounting for the four chief justices who were formerly associate justices, 115 unique individuals had sat on the Supreme Court as of 2020.
7. Though it extends outside our data range, Ketanji Brown Jackson's confirmation in 2022 continued this trend, as she was approved by a 53-47 margin.
8. Before the passage of the 20th Amendment in 1933, new presidents were inaugurated in March, and thus the lame duck period was longer than it is today.
9. See Segal (1987).
10. In the Appendix we present supplemental analyses examining the relationship between timing and outcomes.
11. Matthews' story is among the more interesting in Supreme Court nomination history. As detailed in Maltese (1995, 38–44), Matthews was first nominated by President Rutherford B. Hayes in January of 1881. Matthews was an old friend of Hayes and had worked for him as a lawyer in the legal battle that ultimately led to the Compromise of 1877 and Hayes becoming president. Matthews' initial nomination immediately faced trouble, as Hayes was a lame duck president and Democrats controlled the Senate. In addition, the National Grange, a farmers' organization that worked against railroad monopolies, strongly opposed Matthews' nomination due to his work on behalf of railroads. As a result, Matthews' nomination died in the Judiciary Committee. One month later, however, Hayes' successor and fellow Republican, James Garfield, surprisingly re-nominated Matthews. In the meantime, Senate control had shifted from a Democratic majority to an even split between Democrats and Republicans. The re-nomination split the parties; many Democrats saw Matthews as a supporter of "states' rights," while many Republican senators were persuaded by the Grange's opposition. In the end, 56% of Republicans voted against Matthews, while 58% of Democrats voted to confirm—his one-vote margin of victory the closest in history.
12. Roberts himself was barely a consensus nominee, as he received support from 51% of Democratic senators. Also, while both Figures 8.3 and 8.4 exclude Merrick Garland since he did not receive a Senate vote, had a vote occurred he surely would have been a polarized nominee as well.

13. From the Oxford English Dictionary. See https://tinyurl.com/3pnc3bz4.
14. Such surveys are not impossible—Shor and McCarty (2011), for example, combine roll call votes with surveys of state legislators to conduct an ideological mapping of state legislatures. See also Adams et al. (2017) and Shor and Rogowski (2018).
15. See e.g. Clark (2019) for a thorough evaluation in changes in dimensionality of voting on the Supreme Court itself over time.
16. See Wallach (2017) for a nice review of the rise and fall of the Whig Party. As Poole and Rosenthal (1997, 5) note, by the 1850s concerns over slavery became so intense that they were eventually folded into the first dimension.
17. See Schickler (2016) on the transformation of the Democratic Party in this period.
18. The cutting lines are created by logistically regressing the probability of a yea vote on each dimension, then estimating the best separating line from the results of each logit.
19. See Maltese (1995, 68).
20. Our exclusion of Hugo Black as a nominee for which the second dimension was relevant warrants some explanation. As discussed earlier, Black's nomination was imperiled by allegations that he was a member of the Ku Klux Klan. However, racial politics did not seem to play a large role in his vote breakdown. The six Democratic senators who opposed him included two Southern Democrats and four non-Southern Democrats, while the four Republican votes (out of 14) to confirm were similarly mixed. In addition, several idiosyncratic issues were at play; namely, several senators alleged that Black was ineligible to serve on the court for complicated constitutional reasons related to the passage of a recent bill related to retirement pay for Supreme Court justices—see the *New York Times* coverage the day after Black's roll call vote at Special to the *New York Times* (1937).
21. *Smith v. Allwright* (321 U.S. 649).
22. See Murakami (2008).
23. See Peltason (1961).
24. See Abraham (2008, 206).
25. See McMahon (2011) on Nixon's goals with his appointments. More generally, the Southern strategy was an effort by Nixon and Republican political strategists to shift white Democratic voters into the Republican coalition, in part by using coded racial appeals (Maxwell and Shields 2019).
26. See Rae (1994).
27. In contrast to Thomas, Overby et al. (1992) show that Southern Democratic senators with larger African-American constituencies were *less* likely to support the nomination of Thurgood Marshall, the Court's first Black justice, a result they attribute to senators' concerns about the views of their white constituents.
28. Table 8.2 shows that John Roberts received universal support in 2005 from Southern Democrats, but as we noted above, Roberts was the last nominee to receive a significant amount of out-party support. Four months later, those same four senators would vote against Samuel Alito.
29. Formally, the model assumes senator i votes for nominee j if and only if i's utility for j is greater than a random term, that is, $u_{ij} > e_{ij}$. In some sense, the senator's role is seen as an endorsement of the nominee more than a choice between discrete alternatives. However, the random term could also be viewed as the expected value of the president's

next nominee. Utility is assumed to decrease mainly in the ideological distance between the senator and nominee, $d_{ij} = ||s_i - n_j||$, where s_i represents the ideological ideal point of the senator and n_j the ideology of the nominee in the same space. Utility can also increase or decrease in various nominee-specific factors, including interest group participation and the nominee's quality, as we discuss below. We note here that the model is not fully micro-founded, as the random utility model "black boxes" what it is exactly that senators care about when voting on Supreme Court nominees. In Chapter 11, we seek to explain changes in roll call voting by taking more seriously the individual concerns of senators—in particular, under what conditions they vote in the shadow of citizens' evaluation of senators.

30. In Cameron, Kastellec, and Park (2013) we developed a multilevel model of roll call voting that allows for senators to evaluate ideological distance in both the first and second dimension. Consistent with the analysis of roll call votes above, we found that distance in the second dimension only predicted roll call votes in the post-*Brown* period. We extend these results to 2020 in the Appendix.
31. To be sure, the estimates we use in Chapter 4 to measure nominee ideology are proxies based on president and senator ideology, so the two trends in polarization are inter-related. However, in Chapter 12 we show that estimates of *justice ideology* based on direct measures of voting (and not proxies) show the same levels of polarization.
32. Of course, using just the first dimension ignores the distance between Southern Democrats and many nominees on the second dimension, as documented above. However, such senators were almost always a numerical minority of the Democratic caucus, as Table 8.2 shows. Thus, it is fair to conclude that the general pattern in the mid-twentieth century was one of smaller differences between nominees and most senators.
33. To operationalize this variable, we use the standard editorial based-measure of legal qualifications developed in CCS. As noted in Chapter 4, a weakness of this measure is that it sometimes conflates nominees that have poorer qualifications based on their legal experience (e.g. Harriet Miers) with well-qualified nominees who suffered a scandal (e.g. Brett Kavanaugh). Still, this measure has been shown to have high predictive value in models of roll call voting.
34. While interest group mobilization occurs before senators vote, as we showed in Chapter 5, mobilization is itself endogenous to the ideology of the nominee, again complicating a causal interpretation of the relationships.
35. Public opinion will also play a key role in our explanations in Chapter 10 of changes in voting over time, and we will evaluate its role there.
36. In that analysis we also examine whether the weight that senators placed on legal qualifications varied over time.
37. While the choice of this breakpoint is arbitrary, in the Appendix we show that choosing any year between roughly 1970 and 1990 would lead to the same substantive conclusions.
38. Specifically, in calculating the predicted probabilities from the relevant logit model, we set the qualification values to the 25th percentile, 50th percentile, and 75th percentile value across all nominees.
39. Another counterfactual analysis we present in the Appendix is whether Merrick Garland would have been confirmed in 2016 had Mitch McConnell allowed his nomination to come to the floor for a vote. The answer is, probably yes.

Chapter 9

1. We first developed the theory in Cameron et al. (2019), which also supplies mathematical details, formal proofs, and explicit derivation of structural equations for estimating the parameters in the theory. Interested readers should consult that source. Here, we present a non-technical overview and focus on the empirical analyses that flow from the theory.
2. Work recognizably in this genre include Gailmard and Patty (2007), Krause, Lewis, and Douglas (2006), Lewis (2008), Hollibaugh, Jr., Horton, and Lewis (2014), Cameron and de Figueiredo (2020) and Bolton (2021).
3. The Lemieux and Stewart (1990*a*, 1990*b*) papers also constitute the first application of the famed median voter theorem to the U.S. Supreme Court, at least that we know of. Google ngrams indicate that the phrase "median justice" did not enter common usage until the early 2000s.
4. Specifically, Byron Moraski and Charles Shipan developed their own variant of MTM theory and found empirical support for its predictions about the ideology of nominees selected by presidents. More recently, Stanford political scientist Keith Krehbiel (2007) developed a different version of MTM theory and found support for its predictions about how the court should move ideologically following nominations (he also gave this class of models its name). Rohde and Shepsle (2007) presented a formal model that focused on the role of possible filibusters in an MTM game. Finally, Jo, Primo, and Sekiya (2017) developed a dynamic version of an MTM theory in which the expected outcome of a future election may affect the interplay between the president and the Senate.
5. These findings dovetail with those of Cottrell, Shipan, and Anderson (2019), who find that the location of the median justice (in terms of the court's voting behavior) moves in the direction of the president even following nominations where the president should have been constrained.
6. Almost all theoretical and quantitative research on the politics of judicial selection in general—including MTM-theories but also other work—emphasizes ideology as the key characteristic for nominees (see e.g. Moraski and Shipan 1999, Nemacheck 2008, Binder and Maltzman 2009, Bailey and Spitzer 2017, Jo, Primo, and Sekiya 2017, Bonica and Sen 2020). To be sure, there exist studies that emphasize nominee quality (see e.g. Epstein, Knight, and Martin 2003) and race and gender (see e.g Scherer 2005). But, to the best of our knowledge, the characteristics theory is the first to systematically integrate multiple characteristics using a formal theory.
7. This choice departs from the standard assumption in most models of selection that ideology is both known and fixed at the time of selection. We note two important exceptions. First, in the theory developed in Bailey and Spitzer (2017), the ideology of a nominee is uncertain, with the president and Senate knowing only the distribution of the nominee's ideal point (i.e. a symmetric range around the nominee's ideal point). This uncertainty often leads the president (and sometimes the median senator) to prefer a nominee with a more extreme ideal point, in order to "pull" the center of the court closer to their own ideal points. Our theory shares this feature, in that the president gets utility from the mean ideology of the court, which every nominee affects (as opposed to the median, which changes rarely). Second, Sen and Spaniel (2017) present a model of asymmetric information in which the president knows the nominee's ideal point with certainty but

the Senate only receives a signal, which can lead it to reject a nominee in some instances. While the characteristic theory shares the assumption that nominee ideology is uncertain, it departs from these models in that the extent of uncertainty is endogenous to the choices the president makes in selecting the nominee.

8. Some readers may believe the president values reliability or quality in and of itself. This is a minor variant on what follows and would change relatively little.
9. The rarity of diverse candidates and nominees precludes doing much more with diversity traits. One could make much finer distinctions if one applied the characteristics approach to all presidential appointees, for example.
10. This is an example of "structural" estimation of a theoretical model. The advantage is two-fold. First, the statistically estimated parameters are identical to those in the model and thus have a completely transparent interpretation. Second, one can use the estimated model to perform policy experiments that are logically compatible with the theory.
11. See Carrubba and Clark (2012) and Parameswaran, Cameron, and Kornhauser (2021) for the theoretical basis behind this claim, and Clark and Lauderdale (2010) for empirical support.
12. This is a conjecture on our part, neither a theorem nor a well-established empirical finding. If future work proves it wrong, the characteristics approach will require some modification, as applied to Supreme Court nominees.
13. The table distinguishes between the impact of exogenous variables on the ideology "buys" of conservative and liberal presidents (columns 1 and 2 in the Table). We glossed over this subtlety earlier by assuming a conservative president. The ideology scale has a zero point, with conservative "buys" being positive numbers that would move a liberal court's center in a positive (rightward) direction, while liberal "buys" are negative numbers that would move a conservative court's center in a negative (leftward) direction. This left-right scaling means that some variables affect selected ideology in opposite ways depending on the president's ideology. For example, an increase in the input price of ideology leads the president to buy less ideology (*ceteris paribus*), in terms of magnitude. For a conservative president, this means his positive buy decreases and so moves leftward toward zero—hence the predicted impact of an input price increase is negative. But for a liberal president, the higher input price means his negative buy decreases in magnitude by moving toward the right, toward zero—the predicted impact is positive in direction (though negative in magnitude). The two columns are precise about this sometimes confusing point. In the empirical analysis we interpret ideology buys in terms of their extremism so that we may gain degrees of freedom by pooling over liberal and conservative presidents.
14. See Eshbaugh-Soha and Collins, Jr. (2015).
15. This data was collected by Mattioli. For further details about this measure, see the Supplemental Appendix to Cameron, Kastellec, and Mattioli (2019), which is available at https://tinyurl.com/yv32kms4.
16. Note that normalizing the volume of rhetoric across presidents is important, because some presidents simply speak more frequently and at greater length across the board. To normalize for this variation in presidents' total rhetoric, we divide the number of voluntary policy statements about the Supreme Court by the number of total statements about any topic. Thus, the measure is the annual share of voluntary statements about the Supreme Court, as a fraction of total statements.

17. The index spikes in 2018—this is because President Trump extensively invoked the confirmation of Brent Kavanaugh in 2018 in the run-up to the midterm elections that year.
18. See the Appendix in Cameron et al. (2019) for details.
19. Since Sandra Day O'Connor's appointment in 1981, there have been only two nominees drawn from outside the Courts of Appeals: Harriet Miers and Elena Kagan. And Miers' nomination foundered in part due to her lack of judicial experience.
20. To code these variables, we used the Federal Judicial Center's biographical database (2020), which contains detailed information on every Article III judge ever appointed. For further details, see the Supplemental Appendix to Cameron et al. (2019), which is available at https://www.nowpublishers.com/article/Details/QJPS-18191. That appendix also has several additional graphs that summarize changes in the various measures we use in this chapter, such as the mean reliability of Courts of Appeals judges.
21. This metaphor has also been adopted by participants in the modern-day judicial selection battles. Nan Aron, the president of the liberal selection group the Alliance for Justice, said this in 2017 when discussing the recent success of the conservative legal movement in grooming candidates: "The Federalist Society has for years been singularly focused on building a farm team of judicial nominees who subscribe to a philosophy that is hostile to the advancement of social and economic progress in the country. Behind the scenes, during Republican Administrations, they are very engaged in identifying and recruiting for judges candidates who are ultra-conservatives" (Toobin 2017). Randy Barnett, an influential law professor and a member of the Federalist Society, agrees: "The Federalist Society is the only source of conservative and libertarian legal intellectual activity in the United States. Given that, of course Republican administrations rely on the Federalist Society as a source of talent; as a farm team" (quoted in Hollis-Brusky (2015, 154)).
22. In using this term, we recognize that judicial ideology is richer than the sheer application of partisanship to judging, and that it is overly simplistic to reduce judging on the Courts of Appeals to simply "Democratic judges" and "Republican judges," even if the party of the appointing president is a good predictor of voting behavior in many areas of the law (Sunstein, Schkade, and Ellman 2004). We thus use "co-partisan judges" as a shorthand for the much less eloquent "judges on the Courts of Appeals who were appointed by a president of the same party, or by a given president himself."
23. The last time the Courts of Appeals were expanded was in 1990. The 11 additional judgeships introduced that year brought the total number of authorized judgeships to 179, where it has remained since. (The number of active judges will always be less than this number due to vacancies.) See De Figueiredo and Tiller (1996) for a theoretical and empirical account of federal lower court expansion.
24. Of course, the logic of our theory suggests that Eisenhower may have made these appointments *because* the pool was shallow; however, as discussed in Chapter 3, qualitative accounts of Eisenhower's presidency show a lack of prioritization of the judiciary.
25. Our arguments here about the importance of the farm team are related to the arguments that Bonica and Sen (2020, ch. 5) make about the asymmetries of lawyers in the candidate pool between liberals and conservative. Bonica and Sen show that elite lawyers have skewed liberal for many decades; they then show that the probability of a conservative lawyer becoming a federal judge is much higher than a liberal lawyer, due in part to the relative scarcity of the former (though, of course, which president is doing the selecting will affect the distribution of ideology on the federal courts). Our historical data can measure such asymmetries in the candidate pool—i.e. the farm team—particularly with

respect to race and gender. However, with respect to Supreme Court appointments, we emphasize that once a farm team is sufficiently large to stock the Supreme Court once a vacancy arises, asymmetries in the rates of different types of judges to choose from across liberals and conservatives will be less important than the levels—that is, the *size* of the farm team.

26. The GHP scores are usually measured based on the Common-Space NOMINATE scores; we map the scores into DW-NOMINATE to make them comparable with the other DW-based measures that we employ. Specifically, for every senator with both a DW- and Common-Space (CS) score, we regressed their DW score on their CS score; we use the resulting constant and coefficient on the CS scores to project each judge's GHP score into DW space.
27. As with our measure of the default level of ideology, a plausible alternative would be to calculate the mean reliability levels among a president's co-partisans on the Courts of Appeals. As it turns out, all the regression results we present in Table 9.3 below are robust to using this alternative measure.
28. For all regressions in this chapter that include the full set of short listers, we employ robust standard errors that are clustered on the nomination.
29. Note that for nominees, we include the two nominations in 2005 of John Roberts—first to be associate justice and then to be chief justice—as separate observations.
30. There are years in the which the number of judges who are not white males equals zero—in such cases we add .01 to the denominator so that it does not equal zero.
31. In the Appendix we present two additional counterfactuals for ideology and policy reliability. One examines the type of nominees that President Truman would have picked between 1949 and 1952 if he faced the same cost-benefit ratio that President Obama did between 2009 and 2016. The second examines how much the early success of Roosevelt in changing the court affected his later nominations.
32. Formally, we use the `predict` command in Stata to estimate $Pr(x_j b + u_j > 0)$, where 0 is the censoring point.
33. See Toobin (2017).
34. Greenburg (2007, 233–235).
35. To do so, we modify Nixon's measure of interest in diversity. The platform-based data measure we employ indicates no Republican interest in diversity on the Supreme Court during Nixon's presidency. Yet the "private information" of the Nixon tapes (discussed in Chapter 4) plainly indicates some interest. The scale of the platform measure is 0–1; we set Nixon's interest to .33.
36. The theory also emphasizes how successfully moving the court ideologically undermines the president's later incentive to work hard to move it further. In the Appendix we present an additional simulation that shows how President Roosevelt's early nominations affected his later nominations.
37. Truman, along with some Democratic members of Congress, believed it would be inappropriate to have only one Republican appointee on the Supreme Court; in addition, Truman and Burton were good friends (Yalof 2001, 23).

Chapter 10

1. Jane Doe, along with Jim Loe and Peter Flow (who are soon to appear), are pseudonyms, but the indicated answers are real data points from the megapoll.

2. Examples include Jessee (2012), Fowler (2020), Fowler et al. (2022), and Ansolabehere and Kuriwaki (2021). Earlier efforts in this tradition include Key (1966), Fiorina (1981), and Page and Shapiro (1992).
3. See Lenz (2013).
4. See Fowler (2020) on this point. See also Bullock (2011), which uses a clever survey design to disentangle the effects of party cues and policy concerns on public opinion.
5. Figure 10.1 is not a formal directed acyclic graph (DAG) in the modern sense—see e.g. Pearl (2009) and Morgan and Winship (2015)—but instead is more in the spirit of classical path analysis. The actual theory is derived in the Appendix.
6. Inferring nominees' likely policy orientation from their partisanship is a straightforward implication of Bayesian inference in low-information settings, not unlike racial stereotyping or so-called statistical discrimination—Doleac (2021) provides a clear, non-technical overview of the literature on statistical discrimination. Among behaviorally oriented scholars, policy inferences based on partisan labels are often viewed as a kind of cognitive bias related to "projection" or motivated reasoning (Lenz 2013). It is not clear the two are observationally distinct, or even different phenomena.
7. We assume citizens have beliefs about the nominee's ideology in the Bayesian sense. So x_{ij} is a random variable with mean $\overline{x}_{ij}$ and variance $\sigma^2_{x_{ij}}$.
8. This framework is often used to study how citizens evaluate candidates in an election; see Ansolabehere and Jones (2011) for a brief review as well as Enelow and Hinich (1984).
9. The most similar paper, Bartels (1986), suggests some of the same ideas. But that paper does not actually build a theory of the survey response from the ground up. Because of our attention to "don't know" answers, also relevant is interesting work by Berinsky (1999), which employs a very different framework. Finally, with its focus on voter uncertainty about candidate policy positions, Alvarez (1998) is also a notable precursor.
10. On cognitive effort and information processing costs, see Shenhav et al. (2017) and Székely and Michael (2020).
11. The foundational paper for random utility models is McFadden (1974), with important earlier contributions by Jacob Marshak and Duncan Luce among others. Clear expositions can be found in many places, e.g. Train (2009, ch. 3), Long (1997, 155-157) and Hensher, Rose, and Greene (2015, ch. 4). Modern choice theory allows one to relax seemingly restrictive assumptions in many different ways, but space prohibits investigating every theoretically interesting possibility. We stick to the basics.
12. For Douglas Ginsburg, a larger proportion of Americans viewed him as moderate, compared to the other Republican nominees. Recall, however, that his nomination lasted only a few days—there was little time for citizens to learn much about him.
13. We exclude Douglas Ginsburg because the small sample size in his nomination precludes breaking responses down by both voter and nominee partisanship.
14. We should note that while we have thousands of observations in each model, we have only a relatively small number of unique nominees, particularly using the 5-point scale, so the results with respect to NSP (which is measured at the nominee level) should be taken with a grain of salt. Conversely, partisanship varies at the individual model, and thus affords much more variation to explore.
15. Alverez's (1998) model of candidate evaluations also features uncertainty about candidate ideology. This work exploits clever measures unavailable to us.

16. If one uses the theory as the analytical framework, failure to include the interaction term would introduce omitted variable bias. However, the coefficients are quite stable whether or not we include the interaction term in the workhorse regressions.
17. Given the interaction term, the coefficient on distance gives the main effect when uncertainty is zero, or when education is highest. Below we will show predicted probabilities based on setting uncertainty to its mean value. Note that the main effect on distance from the models is unchanged if we center distance and uncertainty at zero and then interact those centered terms.
18. The other coefficients do not change when we exclude nominee fixed effects.
19. To generate these predicted probabilities, we use the `mgen` command from Long and Freese (2014).
20. The predictive effect of distance on the don't know response is modest, but the apparent non-monotonicity is exactly what the theory predicts—a don't know answer should be more likely when the respondent is neither ideologically close nor ideologically distant from the nominee.
21. As we explain shortly, when we examine every nominee separately below, we actually impute ideological distance in order to analyze more nominees. The regression presented here uses this imputed measure to run the workhorse regressions.
22. The theory envisions that the expected values calculated from the support and oppose equations should be the same. For example, the absolute magnitude of the presidential party coefficient should be the same in both equations, with opposite signs in the support and oppose regression. In reality, this is probably far too much to ask of what is noisy observational data; indeed, in Table 10.2 we can see that many of the coefficients are in fact of somewhat different magnitudes across the support and oppose equations, even if they are all generally consistent with the theory's predictions. Accordingly, we present both measures.
23. To make this more concrete using an example, the expected value from the support equation from this regression equals $1.3 + .7 *$ pres party$-.7 *$ out-party$-.31 *$ ideological distance$-.29 *$ uncertainty (the interaction term in the workhorse regression reflects the "cost" part of the equation and is excluded). To calculate the predicted expected value among Democrats in our Gorsuch sample, we set president's party equal to zero and out-party to 1, and then use the observed values on distance and uncertainty. We can do this for every respondent to get a linear predictor, which thus gives the expected value for every respondent.
24. The strategy of conducting separate regressions across different units or time intervals has been dubbed the "secret weapon" by the statistician Andrew Gelman, as explained in this blog post: https://statmodeling.stat.columbia.edu/2005/03/07/the_secret_weap/.
25. The support and opposition equations yield quite different expected values for O'Connor; the former is far more plausible than the latter. The oppose equation is defined relative to undecideds, but there were few in that nomination, nor were there many respondents opposing confirmation. The result is a likely anomalous estimate in this instance.
26. Since our measure of differential perceptions of nominee quality is endogenous to approval of the nominee, if there are such differences and they correlate with partisanship, they will load onto the $a_2 - a_3$ differential.
27. Close inspection of Figure 10.11 reveals that the results for O'Connor and Breyer are somewhat anomalous. For both, the inverted coefficients for president's party in the oppose

equation are negative, meaning that being co-partisans was associated with being more likely to say oppose, relative to don't know. Similarly, for both, the out-party coefficients are in the wrong direction (i.e. pushing toward more support and less opposition.) Finally, for Breyer, in the support equation the distance coefficient is in the wrong direction, and in the oppose equation it is far greater in magnitude than any other nominee. The strange results for O'Connor seem to be due to the simple fact that she was equally highly liked by all partisan groups, creating some unusual patterns in the multinomial logit. For Breyer, we do not have a similar situational explanation. However, his data is based on a single poll taken very early in what was a relatively low salience nomination, so the anomalous results could just be due to sampling issues.

28. See Abramowitz (2010) for the presentation of the mass polarization camp and Fiorina (2017) for the presentation of the sorting, not polarization camp. Chapter 4 in McCarty (2019) provides an outstanding review of this literature and the debate over sorting and mass polarization.
29. In particular, one needs panel data comprising many years to track how individuals change either their ideology or their party label, or both—see e.g. Levendusky (2009, ch. 4).
30. In theory, differences could also emerge from differences in education/uncertainty by party, but in our data these distributions do not actually vary much, meaning ideology is the key driver in the counterfactual analysis.
31. As noted above in n. 27, the party coefficients for O'Connor and Breyer are anomalous and result in "reverse" partisan gaps in which the out-party has higher expected value than the president's party. Accordingly, we drop these two nominees from this analysis.
32. As we noted, this effect could result from Bayesian inference in a low information setting. But it might involve motivated reasoning as well.
33. Distances for Republicans could get larger if Democratic presidents selected nominees like William O. Douglas or Thurgood Marshall rather than Stephen Breyer or Merrick Garland.

Chapter 11

1. Theriault, Hickey, and Blass (2011, 575). Hug (2020) situates studies of roll call voting in a comparative context.
2. Other notable examples of the former include Erikson and Wright (1980) and Bartels (1991), while Canes-Wrone, Brady, and Cogan (2002) is a classic of the latter.
3. Besley (2006) is an accessible introduction. However, like most agency studies it is oriented to chief executives rather than legislators, especially American-style legislators. Few agency studies explicitly consider roll call voting; the principal exceptions that we know are an innovative paper by Snyder and Ting (2003) addressing cross-pressure from party and constituency, and Stasavage (2007), which considers the implications of public vs. private roll calls.
4. Aficionados of agency theory will recognize that these considerations lead to models of "moral hazard" and sanctioning, or to models of pure "adverse selection" and electoral selection, or to models with both moral hazard and adverse selection. For a helpful discussion, see Fearon (1999).
5. On the fallout from the Iraq war, see Reilly and Brown (2007); in particular, Hillary Clinton's vote to approve the war may have cost her the 2008 Democratic nomination,

as Barack Obama frequently invoked his opposition to the war in contrast to Clinton's support (Simon 2008). More systematically, Nyhan et al. (2012) show that many House Democrats who voted to support the Affordable Care Act in 2009 paid an electoral price in the 2010 midterm elections.

6. Situations like this give rise to "pandering" in which representatives take actions popular in the short term while discounting adverse long-term consequences. See Canes-Wrone, Herron, and Shotts (2001) and Maskin and Tirole (2004).
7. On the different implications of observable/non-observable actions versus consequences, see Fox and Weelden (2012).
8. Within political science, a foundational cite is Lowi (1964). A modern version stressing asymmetric information is Coate and Morris (1995).
9. For an introduction to a huge literature, see Grier, Grier, and Mkrtchian (2023) and accompanying references.
10. This is perhaps the central theme of Arnold (1990).
11. Binder and Maltzman (2009, 55) make a similar point in their study of lower court nominations: "so long as attention to the decisions of federal courts remained uneven across the Senate—as it did before the more forceful entry of the courts into pointed social issues in the 1960s and 1970s—few beyond the home state senators [i.e. senators of the state covered by a given judgeship] cared terribly much about the selection of new judges for the district and appellate courts."
12. On the general logic of yardstick competition, see Besley and Case (1992).
13. See the Appendix to Chapter 6 for our specific coding of which nominees suffered a scandal. As we have noted elsewhere, the standard quality measure can itself be affected by nominee scandals, as it's based on editorial assessments. With that caveat noted, here we use scandal as a supplementary measure of visibility to the media and interest group measures, and all three tell the same story.
14. In Chapter 8, we relied on multilevel logits (with varying intercepts to account for within-nominee correlation in voting) to analyze changes in roll call voting over time. Because, as will become clear, here we are interested more in goodness-of-fit measures, we use OLS models with standard errors clustered on nominees; this setup facilities our tests more easily, compared to using more complicated multilevel models. (Note all the substantive conclusions we make in the section are robust to using logit models instead of OLS.)
15. To make the regressions below more interpretable, we standardize the media coverage and interest group opposition measures by centering and dividing by two standard deviations, which makes them substantively comparable to binary predictors (Gelman 2008).
16. As we discuss in our analysis in the Appendix to Chapter 8 of the possible changing role of quality over time, teasing out such changes is complicated by the fact that quality does not vary within a given nominee, thereby reducing the effective variation across time.
17. The essential reference is Miller and Stokes (1963), which rewards study even today.
18. See Ansolabehere and Jones (2010) and Ansolabehere and Kuriwaki (2021).
19. A few studies have directly examined the link between senators' votes on Supreme Court nominees and voters' assessments of senators. Wolpert and Gimpel (1997) found that respondents' vote choices in the 1992 Senate elections were influenced by correctly recalling whether their senators voted to confirm or reject Clarence Thomas in 1991. Hutchings (2001) examined the prior question of which type of citizens were more likely to correctly identify the direction of their senators' votes on the Thomas nomination. More

recently, Badas and Simas (2022) show that voters who agreed with their senators' votes on the 2017 and 2018 nominations of Neil Gorsuch and Brett Kavanaugh, respectively, were more likely to vote in support of their senators. Our work complements and extends this existing research.

20. See also Dancey and Sheagley (2013), Dancey and Sheagley (2016), and Fortunato and Stevenson (2019).
21. In Bass, Cameron, and Kastellec (2022), we note that the circumstances of Anita Hill's allegations of sexual harassment against Thomas make it impossible to pin down any single reason for the ambiguous accountability results with respect to his nomination. The nominations of Sotomayor and Kagan were, by contrast, more routine affairs.
22. Ansolabehere (2012) and Ansolabehere (2013*a*). The "Common Content" of the CCES provides a wealth of information about respondents, including their party identification and demographic variables. The specific questions we primarily focus on, however, come from the Harvard "team" modules of the CCES in these years both of which asked respondents about their recall of their senators' votes on nominees.[17]
23. Further details about each of these polls, as well as coding choices, can be found in Bass, Cameron, and Kastellec (2022).
24. Note that the CCES samples are cross-sectional, not a panel, so the respondents do not overlap across the two years. Thus, for every nominee, each respondent is asked to evaluate the votes of their two senators. In addition, the fact that each respondent has two senators means that the data can be analyzed in its long form (one observation per respondent) or in its wide form (two observations per respondent). For each of the analyses that follows, we make clear which form we are using.
25. See e.g. Achen and Bartels (2016).
26. A full discussion of the instrumental variables analysis and its assumptions can be found in Bass, Cameron, and Kastellec (2022), along with many robustness tests and additional information on the variables used in this chapter.
27. Note that in our analyses below we account for "party agreement"—both real and perceived—between respondents and senators when we examine the link between recall and evaluations of senators.
28. As Ansolabehere and Kuriwaki note, their figure closely resembles Figure 1 in Miller and Stokes (1963).
29. Almost all of the new empirical work on accountability discussed above has focused on the relationship between voters and members of the House of Representatives. This simplifies matters since each voter has only a single representative. From a theoretical perspective, citizens' assessment of their two senators may be correlated. In the interests of simplicity, we ignore this theoretical correlation (while accounting for it empirically via the clustering), though it is certainly a worthwhile endeavor for future work.
30. Specifically, this variable is measured as the proximity between a respondent's self-reported ideology and a senator's first dimension DW-NOMINATE score. The respondent's ideology is taken from their placement on a 7-point scale ranging from "Very Liberal" to "Very Conservative," standardized to range from −1 to +1. NOMINATE scores lie between around −1 (Democrats) and +1 (Republicans). The absolute difference between the two measures is then flipped so that positive values indicate less distance; this measure ranges from −1 to +1.

31. Note that because these regressions do not incorporate perceptions, which is only asked in the modules, the sample size for the first three CCES regressions are much larger than their corresponding regressions below in Table 11.5, which do include perceptions.
32. As we discuss in Bass, Cameron, and Kastellec (2022), some readers may not be convinced that instrumental variables analysis in this context is appropriate, given the lack of a truly exogenous shock that affects treatment status. In addition, some readers might not believe the exclusion restriction has been met. For such readers, we would note that an alternative way to conceive of our design in this section is as simply one of selection on observables. The OLS models in Table 11.7 can be thought of as implementing such a design.
33. See Ahler and Broockman (2015) and Fowler et al. (2022).
34. See Bullock and Brady (1983) and Ansolabehere, Snyder, and Stewart (2001).
35. See e.g. Shapiro et al. (1990), Clinton (2006), and Lax, Phillips, and Zelizer (2019).
36. Relevant studies include Uslaner (2002) and Bishin (2009). A distinct but related literature examines the impact of open versus closed primaries on polarization of members of Congress. Notable papers include Gerber and Morton (1998), Oak (2006), and McGhee et al. (2014). Another literature examines cross-pressure between party and district. Comparative politics scholar John Carey (2008) notes that such cross-pressure is common in European parliaments with strong party discipline. In the American Congress, party leaders do not have the tools available to their European counterparts so one might expect little such cross-pressure (Cox and McCubbins 1993). Nonetheless, Snyder and Ting (2003) argue that a somewhat similar dynamic can arise in American roll call voting, due to party labels. They suggest that extremist representatives in moderate districts may vote insincerely in order to avoid electoral defeat; their paper does not consider cross-pressure between primary and general election voters.
37. See Gibbs and Cameron (2020) and Gibbs, Crosson, and Cameron (2021) on congressional virtue signaling.
38. This section essentially reproduces and extends the empirical results from that article; however, we connect the findings more generally to accountability theory and to the two other empirical investigations.
39. Full details about the data collection used to generate the MRP estimates of opinion by partisan constituencies, as well as the estimation procedures, can be found in Kastellec et al. (2015). See Hanretty (2020) for a review of MRP and Lax and Phillips (2009) for evidence of its validity in capturing state-level public opinion.
40. Kastellec et al. (2015) present an array of regression models. Some of these models incorporate the uncertainty from the opinion estimation stage. In the interests of brevity, here we present fewer models, all of which treat the opinion estimates as point estimates. Note, however, that if we run all the models employed in that article on the updated dataset, the results are statistically and substantively the same.
41. As part of her floor speech explaining her vote to confirm Kavanaugh, Collins said: "Finally, in his testimony, he noted repeatedly that *Roe* had been upheld by *Planned Parenthood v. Casey*, describing it as a precedent. When I asked him would it be sufficient to overturn a long-established precedent if five current justices believed that it was wrongly decided, he emphatically said 'no'" (Agorakis 2018). On Collins saying she was "misled" by Kavanaugh following the court's overruling of *Roe* in *Dobbs v. Jackson Women's Health Organization*, in which Kavanaugh joined the majority, see Hulse (2022).

42. In the words of Theodore Roosevelt, when bolting from the Republican party to begin his ill-fated third-party bid for the presidency.

Chapter 12

1. In using this term, we deliberately echo the title of Matt Levendusky's (2009) insightful study of the mass electorate. But we invert Levendusky's ordering, to emphasize the completely different causal mechanism: the judicial partisan sort was driven by presidential selection of co-partisans, not by party switching among sitting justices. The partisan sort on the Supreme Court is the subject of Devins and Baum (2019). Our analyses in this chapter both complement and extend Devins and Baum's research by empirically tying the emergence of the partisan sort to the increased emphasis on the Supreme Court by politicians and activists in both parties.
2. Accessing *certiorari* [cert] votes is not straight-forward, but some scholars have compiled datasets of cert votes based on the justices' private papers; see e.g. Provine (1980), Boucher, Jr and Segal (1995), and Epstein and Knight (1997). To the best of our knowledge, the only effort to scale these votes is Johnson (2018). Perry (1991) provides a classic qualitative account of cert voting.
3. Alternatively, votes can be defined by whether an opinion upholds the lower court in the case or reverses it. Some other terminology: the minority votes are called "dissents." The majority votes include both "joins" and "concurrences"; to join an opinion is to endorse it, while concurrence is an additional opinion by a justice who votes with the majority. Often times the court does not directly resolve the dispute but instead orders a lower court to rehear a case—this is called a "remand." Such a decision still counts as a disposition since it alters the status quo ante.
4. Journalistic accounts of the court or the memoirs of former clerks offer vivid accounts of bargaining—see e.g. Woodward and Armstrong (1979) and Greenhouse (2007). More scholarly accounts using the papers of the justices include Epstein and Knight (1997) and Maltzman, Spriggs, and Wahlbeck (2000). Carrubba et al. (2012) and Parameswaran, Cameron, and Kornhauser (2021) explore the incentives created by the voting rules used on the court.
5. We suspect that an analysis of either cert votes or joins would tell a similar story, but we can't say for sure.
6. As we discuss there, the different scores have various strengths and weaknesses. Since we are just using the scores to describe the partisan sort, and since all lead to the same substantive conclusion, the differences are not so important here.
7. As we discussed in Chapter 8 with respect to the ideology of members of Congress, one should keep in mind that the results of any ideal point procedures—including those of Supreme Court justices—produce summary scores of voting behavior, and not direct measures of ideology themselves. See Farnsworth (2007), Fischman and Law (2009), Ho and Quinn (2010), and Bonica and Sen (2021) for useful discussions of both what judicial ideology is (as a concept) and how to interpret various measures of judicial ideology.
8. The scores, which were originally developed in Martin and Quinn (2002), can be found at https://mqscores.lsa.umich.edu/.

9. Because the Martin-Quinn scores begin in 1937, the 1930s data only includes cases decided after that year. In the Appendix, we replicate Figure 12.1 using the Spaeth database, which includes the full decade. Adding the justices who served earlier in the decade leads to the same substantive conclusions about the court in the 1930s.
10. For every justice, we identified the party of their appointing president from Epstein et al. (2022). Two justices who were internally promoted to chief, Edward Douglass White and Harlan F. Stone, were originally appointed and then elevated by presidents of different parties. We treat their tenures as associate and chief justice separately for the purpose of identifying their party.
11. See the Appendix for visualizations of party polarization on the court going back to the 1860s, which demonstrates the emergence of this clear sorting for the first time in the post-Civil War era.
12. Because the Bailey scores start in 1951, we lack congruence scores for any justices appointed by Hoover or Franklin Roosevelt.
13. Hitt's conceptual framework bears some resemblance to the characteristics approach formalized and tested in Chapter 9.
14. The quantitative measures may not tell the whole story here. Ford was a moderate Republican and hence the Bailey measures place Stevens as quite incongruent with Ford in the later stages of Stevens' career. Yet, in 2005—well after Stevens become a reliable liberal vote on the court—Ford wrote a letter marking the thirtieth anniversary of Stevens' appointment, in which he stated, "I am prepared to allow history's judgment of my term in office to rest (if necessarily, exclusively) on my nomination 30 years ago of Justice John Paul Stevens to the U.S. Supreme Court" (Liptak 2019).
15. A small literature exists on how well the voting behavior of Supreme Court justices matches their appointing presidents' political ideology (Segal, Timpone, and Howard 2000, Cameron and Park 2009, Epstein and Posner 2016). Although some justices famously disappointed their appointing president in specific cases, appointee voting generally accords with the appointing president's ideology, especially in the years immediately after appointment. In addition, the tendency toward policy conformity has risen noticeably over time, perhaps reflecting greater care in selection. However, these studies do not test for the downstream effects of specific policy litmus tests or ideological demands contained in the party platforms and presidential acceptance speeches.
16. The litmus tests of general conservatism and liberalism were also issued in several years, but we argue that focusing on specific issue areas better reveals the effects of litmus tests.
17. The emergence of this test was due, at least in part, to the sharp increase in crime in the United States that began in the late 1960s. President Nixon and the Republican party used the rise in crime—and the resulting public turn toward punitiveness (Enns 2016)—as part of their "Southern Strategy," which "centered on employing coded race-based appeals to law-and-order and launching attacks on welfare to woo Southern and working-class white voters" (Gottschalk 2016, 148).
18. It may seem surprising that Justices Sotomayor and Kagan, appointed in 2009 and 2010, respectively, did not carry a litmus test. While the 2008 Democratic platform did state that the party "strongly and unequivocally supports *Roe v. Wade* and a woman's right to choose a safe and legal abortion," this stand was not directly linked to appointing Supreme Court justices who would uphold *Roe*. Indeed, the phrase "Supreme Court" appears only once

in the entire platform, further exhibiting the party's relative lack of policy interest in the court compared to that of the Republican party, as documented in Chapter 2.

19. The database, available at http://scdb.wustl.edu/, was first created by the pioneering political scientist Harold Spaeth, who hand-coded decades of Supreme Court cases. Specifically, we use the Justice-Centered Database, with cases organized by Issue/Legal Provision. To identify abortion cases, we select cases where the *issue* variable is coded "abortion." To identify law-and-order cases, we select cases where the *issueArea* variable is coded "Criminal Procedure."
20. For some models, the number of unique justices (i.e. clusters) is lower than the informally recommended threshold of 30-40 (Angrist and Pischke 2008, 319). The results are generally robust to an alternative strategy of using varying intercepts ("random effects") for justices, but some of the models presented below do not converge with random effects, so we choose to present models with clustered standard errors.
21. As in Chapter 9, we use the `postsim` function from the MORE_CLARIFY package (Pena 2014) to generate simulations of the coefficients.
22. The confidence intervals for the estimates are wide, but in 100% of simulations the predicted probability of voting conservatively is higher for Republican litmus justices compared to the no-litmus-test justices. The same is true when we compare non-litmus-test justices to Democratic litmus justices.
23. The predicted probability for a Republican litmus test justice is greater than the predicted probability for a non-litmus justice in 99% of simulations.
24. On this design, see Angrist and Pischke (2014, ch. 5) and Cunningham (2021, ch. 9).
25. Note in addition that all of the pairwise comparisons in Figure 12.5 are statistically different from each other.
26. Justice Brennan famously called this the "Rule of Five." As summarized by Cole (2015), this axiom states that "whatever five justices agree to, by definition, becomes law."
27. As we noted in Chapter 9, move-the-median theory as applied to nomination politics was first developed in a pair of unpublished papers by Peter Lemieux and Charles Stewart (1990*a*, 1990*b*). However, to the best of our knowledge, it was not until the 2000s that systematic attempts were made to actually estimate the location of the median justice—see e.g. Grofman and Brazill (2002) and Martin, Quinn, and Epstein (2004). While these papers did not make many theoretical claims, later papers did advance theory—e.g. Hammond, Bonneau, and Sheehan (2005), and Jacobi (2009). This emphasis on collective choice departed from earlier, behavior-oriented work that tended to focus exclusively on justice-level behavior—e.g. the "attitudinal model" of Segal and Spaeth (2002).
28. For a clear exposition of the Median Voter Theorem, see McCarty and Meirowitz (2007, 101–107).
29. As discussed in Chapter 1, the MJ Approach leads to a complete and internally consistent theory of Supreme Court appointment politics, Move-the-Median Theory. As noted in Cameron and Kastellec (2016*b*), the detailed and elaborate predictions of this elegant theory do not fare well when confronted with data about presidential selection and senatorial voting on nominees. However, this is a separate question from whether the MJ theorem helps explain *voting patterns* on the court itself; indeed, there is evidence that changes in the median justice do in fact lead to changes in how the court as a whole votes (Krehbiel 2007, Cottrell, Shipan, and Anderson 2019). We will soon examine how well changes in the median predicts voting, with an important distinction between dispositional voting and the location of the majority opinion.

30. Technically, this picture shows the median estimate among the justices on a given court, as it does not take into account uncertainty in the individual ideal points.
31. For example, Bailey (2007, 436) notes that the median justice as identified by Martin-Quinn is estimated to be as conservative in the early 1970s as it was in the early 2000s, a result that does not seem facially valid, given the ideological trajectory of the court.
32. Technically, the estimated median justice was an average of the most conservative liberal justice (Breyer) and most liberal conservative justice (Kennedy).
33. We return to events of 2016–2017 and what they meant for the ideological trajectory of the court in future years in Chapter 13.
34. The Bailey scores only run through 2019, and hence there is no data for Barrett, as of this writing. However, if we assume that Barrett is at least as conservative as Kavanaugh, which seems reasonable, then Kavanaugh is estimated as the median justice.
35. See Lax and Cameron (2007), Clark (2012), and Lax and Rader (2015) for thorough discussions of these issues.
36. See Clark (2012) for an accessible review of this literature.
37. See Carrubba and Clark (2012) and Parameswaran, Cameron, and Kornhauser (2021).
38. The logic behind this claim is that the majority's favored disposition must result from applying the policy in the majority opinion to the case in hand, and the dissenters disagree with that disposition. Hence, only those who agree with the disposition are allowed to directly craft the opinion (though justices in the majority opinion will often respond to arguments raised in dissenting opinions).
39. Importantly, the MC Approach also predicts that the preferences of the median justice should determine the outcome of the *dispositional vote*—that is, a median voter result. However, in some versions the facts of the case affect which judgment the median prefers. Case selection is thus important for both dispositions and opinion content but this topic remains at the research frontier in the MC Approach—see Sasso and Judd (2020) for a recent application.
40. See e.g. Segal (1984) and Kritzer and Richards (2005) on the quantitative side and Seo (2019) and Cohen (2021) on the qualitative side.
41. Clark and Lauderdale also use their measures of opinion location to test whether the median justice, the median of the majority coalition, or the opinion author best predicts the location of the majority opinion. This question is related, although distinct, to the one we pursue. Separately, Kastellec (2010) uses classification trees to statistically visualize how the court's search-and-seizure doctrine evolved from the 1960s to the 1980s, but this is more of a descriptive enterprise than a rigorous attempt to connect ideological structure and collective choice.
42. Clark and Lauderdale use the Spaeth database coding to code the disposition of the search-and-seizure cases in their decisions.
43. *Mapp v. Ohio* (367 U.S. 643) and *Illinois v. Gates* (462 U.S. 213).
44. The downward trend at the end of the time series is driven by 2005, where the court heard only two Fourth Amendment cases.
45. To give one concrete example of this shift that is apposite here, Justice Breyer voted very conservatively in Fourth Amendment cases, relative to other reliable members of the court's liberal bloc in the 1990s, 2000s, and 2010s (Newton 2017).
46. We cannot include all three in the same regression, since the number of justices in one bloc is a linear function of the other two.

47. Six is the maximum number of justices that appear in the liberal bloc in the Bailey data. Until 2020, there were never been more than five justices in the conservative bloc; however, in the right plot where the number of conservative justices is on the x-axis, we extend it to six to make the two plots directly comparable.
48. As a further illustration of the substantive changes in the law over the past 60 years, in the Appendix we use simulations to visualize how the content of majority of opinions changes as the composition of the court changes.
49. On agency politicization as a key tool of presidential management of the administrative state, see Moe (1985) and Lewis (2008).
50. Respectively, *Dobbs v. Jackson Women's Health Organization*, *New York State Rifle & Pistol Association Inc. v. Bruen*, and *West Virginia v. Environmental Protection Agency*.

Chapter 13

1. In the parlance of Chapter 12, it is a 3-0-6 court, or conservative-wing dominant.
2. One might argue that a long series of (say) conservative medians limits the potential doctrinal impact of a later liberal median, due to *stare decisis*. Whether horizontal *stare decisis* binds the justices is a matter of long controversy among scholars of the court. In our view, the bulk of the systematic empirical evidence suggests that prior precedents of the court act at best as a weak constraint on the justices' exercise of their policy preferences. The most forceful form of this argument can be found in Spaeth and Segal (1999) and Segal and Spaeth (2002).
3. Technically, the simulated court is an "ergodic" process—there are no "absorbing states" that forever freeze the court's composition. Tit-for-tat court packing is the one exception to this, with respect to the size of the court; the number of justices can only go up in this scenario, not down.
4. This is a consequence of the Ergodicity Theorem, in the theory of dynamic processes. See e.g. Norris (1997, section 1.10).
5. The four key contributions are Bailey and Yoon (2011), Katz and Spitzer (2014), Chilton et al. (2021*a*), and Chilton et al. (2021*b*). The Appendix discusses the many design choices in each of these papers, along with comparisons to our approach.
6. According to the National Center for State Courts, 87% of all state court judges face elections, and 39 states elect at least some of their judges (Liptak 2008). Among the states that employ judicial elections, one finds considerable institutional variation, including partisan, non-partisan, and retention elections. See Shugerman (2012) for an excellent historical review of the development of judicial elections in the American states.
7. Other simulations make somewhat different choices. For example, Chilton et al. (2021*a*) take as their starting point the 1937 court, then "re-create" the subsequent history of the court, while changing key institutional features (mainly, the implementation of term limits). Bailey and Yoon (2011) utilize a kind of ideal baseline court, with justices evenly spaced by ideology and with a given age distribution. Chilton et al. (2021*b*) start with the 2021 court, but then add four Democratic seats as an opening salvo of court packing.
8. As we explain shortly, we use the NSP score of the current justices to define their ideal points. These display some minor discrepancies with actual voting patterns among the conservatives, e.g. NSP inaccurately places Justice Thomas to the left of most of his

Republican colleagues. However, since we focus on the ideological structure of the court as a whole (as discussed in Chapter 12) and not that of individual justices, these discrepancies are inconsequential for the results.

9. There are few exceptions; see e.g. Stokes and Iversen (1962), Gans (1985), Erikson, MacKuen, and Stimson (2002), and Geruso, Spears, and Talesara (2019). Also, as usual, David Mayhew (2021) offers a penetrating take on party history.
10. For example, Bailey and Yoon (2011) assume a 50-50 chance of party control of the presidency and do not directly model control of the Senate, but instead assume it imposes some randomness on the president's choice of nominee. Chilton et al. (2021*b*) assume a simple Markov process for control of the presidency, then add a fixed 30% chance of unified control of the Senate.
11. See the Appendix for a figure illustrating the Markov transition properties.
12. See Wlezien (1995) and Erikson, MacKuen, and Stimson (2002).
13. The transition probabilities do not distinguish Democratic from Republican presidents, due to limited data. At the time we write, some observers believe the Electoral College is somewhat biased in favor of Republican presidential candidates. So, in a near dead-heat, a Republican may tend to win the Electoral College despite losing the popular vote, a so-called "inversion," as occurred in 2000 and 2016 (and nearly occurred in 2020). While the recent Republican advantage is quite real, Geruso, Spears, and Talesara (2019) show that such partisan advantage depends sensitively on the closeness of the election and precisely which states are swing states; as such, partisan advantage in the Electoral College tends to be transitory. Accordingly, we do not build such an advantage into our simulations.
14. While impeachment and removal is theoretically possible, it is not sufficiently probable to warrant simulation. While a few lower court judges have been impeached and removed by Congress, no Supreme Court justice has ever suffered this fate. (Justice Samuel Chase was impeached by the House in 1804, but was acquitted by the Senate.)
15. Specifically, we use the 2016 period life table for the Social Security area population, as provided at this url: https://tinyurl.com/6pkd5byc (last accessed November 28, 2019).
16. The SSA provides separate probabilities for males and females, but the gender differences are small enough that, for simplicity, we use the average of the two for every given age.
17. Higher socioeconomic status (SES) individuals display lower death rates than others, and of course Supreme Court justices are highly educated, high social class individuals. To account for such differences, Chilton et al. (2021*a*) use death rates for a comparable SES group, federal judges, in their backcast simulation from 1937 to 2020. Therefore, our use of standard death tables may somewhat exaggerate death probabilities. Notably, however, SES differences compress dramatically for older individuals (Angela and Lynch 2018). Consequently, the high-SES effect is likely quite small for those justices at greatest risk of mortality. In any case, using socioeconomic adjusted rates would simply result in slightly longer tenures (absent strategic retirement considerations), and would not affect the overall picture of our results.
18. This assumption inherently makes it very unlikely that a justice will exit the court very soon after joining, which accords with modern practice. However, up until the middle of the twentieth century, many justices served relatively short terms before resigning and moving to a different position (Crowe and Karpowitz 2007). James Byrne, for example,

served for just one year before resigning from the court in 1942 to lead the Office of Economic Stabilization. The last justice who left the court for a different position was Arthur Goldberg, who resigned in 1965 to become the ambassador to the United Nations. Since then, every justice has either exited the court via retirement or death.

19. We owe this colloquialism to Justice Brennan. According to Perry (2019), "As Justice William Brennan aged, inevitable questions about his retirement grew more insistent. With his Irish wit still intact, he quipped about his intention to leave the court 'feet first.'" In fact, Brennan's declining health compelled him to leave the court "head first" in 1990, seven years before he died.
20. On the side finding evidence of strategic retirements, see King (1987), Hagle (1993), and Stolzenberg and Lindgren (2010). On the other side, see Squire (1988), Brenner (1999), Zorn and Van Winkle (2000), and Peretti and Rozzi (2011).
21. President Bush's re-election nevertheless resulted in Rehnquist being replaced by a fellow Republican appointee, John Roberts, after Rehnquist died in 2005.
22. Two caveats are worth noting here. First, a more nuanced strategic retirement function would allow for justices to not only retire strategically "early," but also to postpone their retirements in the hopes that a co-partisan president takes over in a future election. Such a function would affect the specific exit date for any given justice, but would not affect our overall results, since justices would still be more likely to retire under a co-partisan president. Second, if a norm of no divided government confirmations took hold, as we examine below, justices might condition their retirement decisions on not just presidential control, but also Senate control. We leave this possibility for future research.
23. To avoid the potential issue of "double-counting," we assume that when a justice exits, if his or her replacement is "confirmed," the replacement takes the bench *in the next year*. For instance, if a Democratic justice exits in 2028 during a Democratic presidency, the new Democratic justice enters the court in 2029—this is so even if a Republican president takes office that year. However, in some scenarios explored below, we assume vacancies remain open during divided government, so in some years the court may not have a full complement of justices.
24. The "Less predictable" scenario (described below) is the one scenario where we vary the ideology of new justices, relative to the baseline assumptions.
25. The sparseness of the 2020s histogram reflects the deterministic ideal points of the justices on the initial court. Greater heterogeneity in the histograms occurs as the initial justices exit and are replaced with simulated new justices.
26. Cameron vividly recalls this classroom scene.
27. In Chapter 12, we defined the cutpoints that divided the observed distribution of all ideal points between 1950 and 2019 equally into the three bins. This allowed comparisons that highlighted the extremely different distributions of entering justices across seven decades. In contrast, the simulations employ fixed distributions for drawing justices. Accordingly, fixed cutpoints with a substantively intuitive interpretation make more sense.
28. By contrast, Justice Breyer's NSP score was only -.15. While this score was perhaps a bit too conservative for him, nearly every observer of the court would agree that he was the most moderate member of the liberal bloc between 2010—when the court sorted cleanly on partisan lines—and 2022, when he retired.
29. Three justices served lengthy terms in this era: Bushrod Washington (1799–1829), John Marshall (1801–1835), and William Johnson (1804–1834).

30. An interesting (and sometimes amusing) sub-genre of historical studies considers counterfactual histories. But rarely are these based on explicit models of underlying micro-processes. On counterfactual or "virtual" history see e.g. Ferguson (2008).
31. At the time, we used the regression models of Chapter 8 to predict the likely outcome of a floor vote. The statistical models suggested that the vote would be tight in the closely divided Senate but that Garland would ultimately gain confirmation (Cameron and Kastellec 2016*a*). We discuss this analysis in the Appendix to Chapter 8.
32. Justice Ginsburg, who died in 2020, might have retired strategically in 2017 if Clinton had won (though it's by no means certain!). But whether she would have been replaced by a Democrat depends on whether the Republican Senate would have confirmed a Clinton-initiated replacement. We investigate divided government stasis in Section 13.5.
33. The Garland scenario did not arise with any of President Trump's three nominees, nor with President Biden's nomination of Jackson in 2022, because all occurred under unified government.
34. See Chafetz (2017*b*) for a thorough evaluation of what was—and wasn't—unprecedented with respect to the Garland blockade.
35. See Lander and Greenhouse (2013) and Ackley (2020). Because the boards of the FEC and NLRB are small (five for the NLRB and six for the FEC), even a few vacancies can block a quorum. The Supreme Court's statutory quorum requirement is six.
36. For example, in *National Labor Relations Board v. Noel Canning*, 573 U.S. 513 (2014), the Supreme Court ruled that recess appointments to agencies under very short Senate recesses were unconstitutional.
37. The probability of divided government is slightly higher in the 2020s compared to later decades because the fixed reality of unified government in 2022 increases the chance of divided government following the 2022 elections. This factor translates into slightly more years with fewer than nine justices in the 2020s compared to later decades, when the transition probabilities fully kick in, but the differences are not dramatic.
38. In the end, Democratic Senator Joe Manchin of West Virginia voted to confirm Kavanaugh while Republican Senator Lisa Murkowski of Alaska opposed him, but the basic point holds.
39. This term arose in the United Kingdom to refer to a depopulated election district that nonetheless retained its original representation. See e.g. Bump (2017) on the increasing Republican bias of the Senate. One way to offset the Republican tilt would be to admit new Democrat-leaning states, e.g. Puerto Rico, the District of Columbia, and the Virgin Islands. We do not model this scenario, which we see as improbable. But the addition of new states would most likely alter future control of both the presidency and (especially) the Senate in some elections, with large implications for the court's ultimate composition.
40. See the Appendix for a visualization of how much smaller the average probability of Democratic Senate control is in the Republican advantage scenarios, compared to the baseline scenario, as well as the trends in vacancies over time.
41. Court packing has also been quite routine in the American states (Levy 2019*a*).
42. The politics in the 1860s were particularly dramatic, as outlined in Schermerhorn (2020). When President Lincoln took office in 1861, a majority of the justices were Southerners, including Chief Justice Roger B. Taney, who four years earlier had authored the court's infamous decision in *Dred Scott v. Sandford* (60 U.S. 393). While vacancies allowed Lincoln to make three appointments, the court still contained several justices who were

sympathetic to the South. In response, Congress in 1863 increased the size of the court to 10 to give President Lincoln an extra appointment. Following Lincoln's assassination in 1865, his replacement, Andrew Johnson, proved himself hostile to Reconstruction and thus was in constant battle with the Republican-controlled Congress. To thwart Johnson, Congress in 1866 passed a law stating that no Supreme Court vacancies would be filled until just seven justices remained, effectively reducing the number of seats to seven and thereby denying Johnson the ability to make new appointments. Finally, after Ulysses Grant became president in 1869, Congress increased the number of justices of Supreme Court seats back to nine, where it has remained since.

43. See Clark (2011) for a theoretical and empirical investigation of court curbing, which includes court packing.
44. See Shesol (2011) for an excellent history of the lead-up to and defeat of the court packing plan.
45. Some of the retirements were encouraged by improvements in the justices' pension plan, a deft alternative to crude court packing (Shesol 2011).
46. The citations for *Citizens United*, *Shelby County*, and *Rucho* are 558 U.S. 310 (2010), 570 U.S. 529 (2013), 139 S. Ct. 2494 (2019), respectively.
47. See e.g. Levy (2019*b*) and Millhiser (2019). Pete Buttigieg, for example, endorsed a plan (based on the proposal in Epps and Sitaraman 2019) to increase the court to 15 members, with a third of the court selected by the other 10 justices (who would be selected via the existing selection procedure). So did presidential contenders Senator Kamala Harris, Senator Elizabeth Warren, Senator Cory Booker, and Governor Steve Bullock of Montana, in various versions (Biskupic 2019, Ayesh and Perano 2019).
48. Even if every Democrat had supported court packing, which was not the case in 2021, under any plausible scenario changing the size of the Supreme Court would have necessitated eliminating the legislative filibuster. A significant number of Democrats adamantly opposed this change.
49. The final commission report is available at https://www.whitehouse.gov/wp-content/uploads/2021/12/SCOTUS-Report-Final- 12.8.21-1.pdf. See Savage (2021) on the committee's divide over the wisdom of court packing.
50. Because we do not include the House in our simulations, they may overstate the frequency under which tit-for-tat court packing occurs, since adding seats would also require the assent of the House. Nevertheless, our general point about tit-for-tat court packing would still hold, even if the overall number of seats added might be somewhat smaller.
51. Thus, we assume court packing does *not* occur when there is a shift from divided government back to the type of unified government that previously existed. For instance, if Republicans take control of the Senate in 2023 and 2024, but then Democrats retake the Senate in 2025, court packing is not implemented in 2025, since Democrats were responsible for the last expansion in 2021.
52. Chilton et al. (2021*b*) perform a very similar analysis and reach the same substantive conclusions, though our assumptions about which conditions lead to court packing differ slightly from theirs.
53. Crowe (2012, 26–28).
54. To the best of our knowledge, the earliest term limit proposal in the modern era came from Oliver (1986). In recent years, similar calls have come from DiTullio and Schochet (2004), Calabresi and Lindgren (2005), Greenhouse (2012), Chemerinsky (2013), and Klein (2018), *inter alia*.

55. See Wheeler (2018) and Washington Post (2020) on the popularity of term limits.
56. See e.g. Calabresi and Lindgren (2005).
57. See e.g. Cramton (2007).
58. Chilton et al. (2021*a*), by contrast, provide a more nuanced examination of the specifics of several different term limit proposals.
59. Many quasi-judicial agencies such as the Federal Election Commission have partisan balance requirements that establish that some proportion of commissioners on the agency must be from one party or the other (Feinstein and Hemel 2018). A term limits plan could use these statutory designs as a model.

Chapter 14

1. As Calabresi and Lindgren (2005, 819) state, "The American system of life tenure for Supreme Court Justices has been rejected by all other major democratic nations in setting up their highest constitutional courts." In addition, as we discuss below, only one American state—Rhode Island—provides judges with life tenure with no mandatory age of retirement.
2. The relevant literature is too vast to cite, but influential modern analyses focusing on elected officials include Fearon (1999), Canes-Wrone, Herron, and Shotts (2001), and Maskin and Tirole (2004). The latter contrasts elected and appointed officials and considers judges to be an archetype of an appointed, non-accountable official.
3. See ballotpedia.org/Judicial_election_methods_by_state for a list of selection methods by states. New Jersey and New York are similar to these three states, except their state supreme court judges are subject to gubernatorial re-appointment. While only these five states allow for unfettered gubernatorial appointments, several states employ "merit selection," under which the governor makes an initial appointment based on a list of candidates provided to her by a nominating commission. In addition, Gibson and Nelson (2021) note that executive appointment to fill mid-election vacancies—a sort of a "loophole" in appointment regimes—also allows governors to have a great deal of influence over state judiciaries.
4. Most states initially used the federalist design, but switched to judicial elections beginning in the mid-nineteenth century, a fascinating evolution documented in Shugerman (2012).
5. Any normative discussion must be informed by facts about how the different systems actually perform. Here, Caldarone, Canes-Wrone, and Clark (2009), Ash and MacLeod (2015), and Gibson and Nelson (2021) are quite useful.
6. With respect to partisan advantage, Hanssen (2004) presents a theory of judicial independence that investigates the optimal level of independence from the perspective of *policy makers*. The theory predicts (and the evidence supports) that politicians should favor selection and retention institutions that promote independent courts in states with higher levels of partisan competition, since the politicians in those states are more likely to be out of power—see Ramseyer (1994), Ginsburg (2003), and Stephenson (2003) for similar arguments explaining cross-national variation in judicial independence. While our search for the optimal level of judicial independence is theoretically similar to Hanssen's, our benchmark for evaluating independence is the welfare of society as a whole, not politicians more narrowly.

7. These questions are tackled from any number of standpoints in the famous debate in the legal and social science literatures on the "counter-majoritarian difficulty." This phrase, which dates to Bickel (1962), captures the potential normative problem when unelected and life-tenured judges strike down laws passed by the elected representatives of the American people. See Friedman (2009) for a thorough historical and legal examination of how much the Supreme Court has been tethered to the preferences of the American public throughout its history.
8. Several studies compare the policy decisions of judges elected under different methods, but few compare decisions of elected and appointed judges. Gibson and Nelson (2021), which does, finds few differences.
9. Indeed, several legal scholars have argued that the Supreme Court has been systematically *worse* at protecting the rights of minorities, compared to Congress. See e.g. Waldron (2006) and Bowie (2021).
10. See e.g. Weingast (1995) and Haggard, MacIntyre, and Tiede (2008).
11. A poverty trap is "a set of self-reinforcing mechanisms whereby countries start poor and remain poor: poverty begets poverty, so that current poverty is itself a direct cause of poverty in the future" (Kraay and McKenzie 2014, 127). See also Azariadis and Stachurski (2005).
12. This famous phrase comes from Oliver Wendell Holmes, Jr. (1881). See Shadmehr et al. (2022) for a theoretical model of the tension between consistency in the law and adapting to changing societal circumstances, as well as several illustrations of cases where judges confronted this tension head on.
13. Obviously, there are other desiderata as well—e.g. select and retain highly skilled and honest judges while avoiding or removing unskilled and dishonest ones. Skill and honesty could be folded into the costs and benefits of turnover without much difficulty.
14. Cameron, Kornhauser, and Parameswaran (2019) show theoretically that *stare decisis* (deference to precedent) is easiest to sustain when polarized blocs frequently and predictably alternate in holding power. The most problematic situation occurs when a large dominant bloc faces no reversal of fortune in the foreseeable future. Unfortunately, we know of few empirical studies of *stare decisis* that relate its prevalence to turnover and ideological polarization (but see Hansford and Spriggs (2018)).
15. This paragraph and the succeeding one draw on the large literature on the Supreme Court at crisis moments like 1800, the Civil War and Reconstruction, and 1937. Some relevant sources include Ackerman (2000), Ellis (1971), Hyman and Wiecek (1982), Kutler (1966), Fairman (1971), Friedman (2002), and Leuchtenburg (1996).
16. On the logic of selecting moderate, but less desirable policies, because they are more durable, see Baron (1996).
17. See Taleb (2007) for a popular account of black swans.
18. For illustrative purposes, the figure displays the probability density functions for two Pareto distributions. Insurance companies use such distributions to predict losses from earthquakes and similar events.
19. To be sure, this approach embodies a rather thin conception of democratic responsiveness, especially since the president is not elected by popular vote. Nevertheless, it presents a useful way to collectively analyze the simulations. For a classic study of democratic responsiveness across many institutions, including the Supreme Court, see Erikson, MacKuen, and Stimson (2002).

20. Within the simulation community, this approach—building a statistical "metamodel" of a simulation model—is standard. See e.g. Barton and Meckesheimer (2006).
21. The Appendix presents a table containing the median coefficient and median standard error from all 44 policy-experiment/regression combinations, along with the same for lag predictors.
22. If we also normalized by the number of *seats* on the courts, 18-year term limits would feature higher turnover than any of the court packing experiments.

Chapter 15

1. For an interesting history, see Schlozman (2015).
2. In particular, Mayhew (1974), Arnold (1990), Fenno (1978), Snyder and Ting (2003), and Besley (2006).
3. For a classic discussion of the importance in roll call votes of "latent" public opinion, see Arnold (1990).
4. The Appendix to Chapter 10 offers a welfare analysis based on the public opinion data, as parsed by the Learning-Thinking-Acting (LTA) framework. Seemingly, social welfare (based on public opinion) would be enhanced by selecting moderate rather than ideologically extreme nominees. Though surely more suggestive than definitive, this inquiry may stimulate others to use public opinion data for more ambitious normative analyses than is common.
5. In the Appendix we briefly discuss the portability of the Pelican approach as a methodology, suggesting its potential for studying Congress.
6. The literature on policy feedback is substantial; see e.g. Weir and Skocpol (1985), Pierson (1993), and Campbell (2012). Hertel-Fernandez (2020) provides a topically oriented overview. A classic study of policy feedback in judicial politics is Epp (1998), who shows how lawyers and activists help provide courts with the cases and litigants necessary to bring about social change via the law—see also Horowitz (1977). Further investigating judicial policy feedback, though difficult, would be a fruitful area of study for judicial and interest group scholars.
7. See Campbell (2003).
8. See Patashnik (2014, ch. 8).
9. Institutional feedback has some commonalities with Mettler's (2005) argument that the enactment of the GI Bill of Rights created an educated class that participated more actively in many political venues. But the links between policy, politics, and specific institutional transformation seem very clear and unusually direct in the case of Supreme Court appointment politics.
10. In Chapter 2, we presented suggestive evidence on abortion activists among delegates to the party conventions, but the exact details of activist participation and platform construction remain frustratingly hazy. The opportunity for political historians is obvious.
11. The obligatory cite is Dahl (1961). The literature rapidly became enormous, but the best contemporary empirical studies confirm the earlier findings. See e.g. Baumgartner et al. (2009).
12. For recent work adopting this perspective, see Gilens (2012) and Bartels (2016).
13. Schlozman, Verba, and Brady (2012).

14. See Mayhew (1991). Contemporary case studies of congressional law making continue to show the importance of "artful work" in building legislative coalitions—see e.g. Kaiser (2014). Finally, Lee (2009) demonstrates that Congress passes low visibility compromise legislation quite regularly.
15. For some discussion of this phenomenon, see Rothenberg (2018).
16. See Ansolabehere and Jones (2010) and Ansolabehere and Kuriwaki (2021).

Bibliography

Abraham, Henry J. 2008. *Justices, Presidents and Senators: A History of the U.S. Supreme Court Appointments from Washington to Bush II*. 5th ed. Rowman & Littlefield.

Abrajano, Marisa. 2015. "Reexamining the 'Racial Gap' in Political Knowledge." *Journal of Politics* 77(1):44–54.

Abramowitz, Alan. 2010. *The Disappearing Center: Engaged Citizens, Polarization, and American Democracy*. Yale University Press.

Achen, Christopher H. and Larry M. Bartels. 2016. *Democracy for Realists: Why Elections Do Not Produce Responsive Government*. Princeton: Princeton University Press.

Ackerman, Bruce. 2000. *We the People*, Volume 2: Transformations. Harvard University Press.

Ackley, Kate. 2020. "Senate Panel Approves Nominees to Fill All FEC Vacancies." *Roll Call*. https://www.rollcall.com/2020/12/03/senate-panel-approves-nominees-to-fill-all-fec-vacancies/.

Adams, Greg D. 1997. "Abortion: Evidence of an Issue Evolution." *American Journal of Political Science* 41(3):718–737.

Adams, James, Erik Engstrom, Danielle Joeston, Walt Stone, Jon Rogowski, and Boris Shor. 2017. "Do Moderate Voters Weigh Candidates' Ideologies? Voters' Decision Rules in the 2010 Congressional Elections." *Political Behavior* 39(1):205–227.

Agorakis, Stavros. 2018. "Read the Full Transcript of Sen. Collins's Speech Announcing She'll Vote to Confirm Brett Kavanaugh." https://www.vox.com/2018/10/5/17943276/susan-collins-speech-transcript-full-text-kavanaugh-vote.

Ahler, Douglas J. and David E. Broockman. 2015. "Does Polarization Imply Poor Representation? A New Perspective on the 'Disconnect' between Politicians and Voters." Technical report working paper, Stanford Graduate School of Business.

Ainsworth, Scott H. and John Anthony Maltese. 1996. "National Grange Influence on the Supreme Court Confirmation of Stanley Matthews." *Social Science History* 20(1):41–62.

Alesina, Alberto and Howard Rosenthal. 1995. *Partisan Politics, Divided Government, and the Economy*. Cambridge University Press.

Alexander, Michelle. 2020. *The New Jim Crow: Mass Incarceration in the Age of Colorblindness*. The New Press.

Alvarez, R. Michael. 1998. *Information and Elections*. University of Michigan Press.

Anderson, Patrick. 1968. *The Presidents' Men: White House Assistants of Franklin D. Roosevelt, Harry S. Truman, Dwight D. Eisenhower, John F. Kennedy, and Lyndon B. Johnson*. Doubleday.

Angela, M. O. and Scott M. Lynch. 2018. "Socioeconomic Status, Health, and Mortality in Aging Populations." In *Future Directions for the Demography of Aging: Proceedings of a Workshop*. National Academies Press (US).

Angrist, Joshua D. and Jörn-Steffen Pischke. 2008. *Mostly Harmless Econometrics: An Empiricist's Companion*. Princeton University Press.

Angrist, Joshua D. and Jörn-Steffen Pischke. 2014. *Mastering 'metrics: The Path from Cause to Efffect*. Princeton University Press.

Ansolabehere, Stephen. 2012. "CCES Common Content, 2010." https://doi.org/10.7910/DVN/VKKRWA.

Ansolabehere, Stephen. 2013*a*. "CCES, Common Content, 2009." https://doi.org/10.7910/DVN/KKM9UK.

Ansolabehere, Stephen. 2013*b*. "CCES, Harvard/ UCSD Module, 2010." https://doi.org/10.7910/DVN/5S8ZD1.

Ansolabehere, Stephen. 2013*c*. "CCES, Harvard/MIT Module, 2010." https://doi.org/10.7910/DVN/VALFAO.

Ansolabehere, Stephen, James M. Snyder, and Charles Stewart. 2001. "Candidate Positioning in U.S. House Elections." *American Journal of Political Science* 45(1):136–159.

Ansolabehere, Stephen and Philip Edward Jones. 2010. "Constituents' Responses to Congressional Roll-Call Voting." *American Journal of Political Science* 54(3):583–597.

Ansolabehere, Stephen and Philip Edward Jones. 2011. "Dyadic Representation." In *The Oxford Handbook of the American Congress*, ed. Eric Shickler and Frances E. Lee. Oxford University Press, pp. 293–314.

Ansolabehere, Stephen and Shiro Kuriwaki. 2021. "Congressional Representation: Accountability from the Constituent's Perspective." *American Journal of Political Science.* 66(1): 123–139.

Arnold, R. Douglas. 1990. *The Logic of Congressional Action*. Yale University Press.

Ash, Elliott and W. Bentley MacLeod. 2015. "Intrinsic Motivation in Public Service: Theory and Evidence from State Supreme Courts." *Journal of Law and Economics* 58(4):863–913.

Atkinson, David N. 1999. *Leaving the Bench: Supreme Court Justices at the End*. University Press of Kansas.

Ayesh, Rashaan and Ursula Perano. 2019. "Court Packing: Where the 2020 Candidates Stand." *Axios,* Oct. 2. https://www.axios.com/2019/04/13/court-packing-where-2020-candidates-stand.

Azariadis, Costas and John Stachurski. 2005. "Poverty Traps." In *Handbook of Economic Growth*, Vol. 1, Part A, ed. Philippe Aghion and Steven N. Durlauf. Elsevier.

Babington, Charles. 2005. "Alito Distances Himself from 1985 Memos." https://www.washingtonpost.com/archive/politics/2005/12/03/alito-distances-himself-from-1985-memos/453c2d4b-1b46-4c9d-9914-f842837d5707/.

Badas, Alex and Elizabeth Simas. 2022. "The Supreme Court as an Electoral Issue: Evidence from Three Studies." *Political Science Research and Methods*. 10(1):49–67.

Badas, Alex and Katelyn E. Stauffer. 2018. "Someone Like Me: Descriptive Representation and Support for Supreme Court Nominees." *Political Research Quarterly* 71(1):127–142.

Bailey, Michael A. 2007. "Comparable Preference Estimates across Time and Institutions for the Court, Congress, and Presidency." *American Journal of Political Science* 51(3):433–448.

Bailey, Michael A. and Albert Yoon. 2011. "'While There's a Breath in My Body': The Systemic Effects of Politically Motivated Retirement from the Supreme Court." *Journal of Theoretical Politics* 23(3):293–316.

Bailey, Michael A. and Matthew Spitzer. 2017. "Appointing Extremists." *American Law and Economics Review* 20(1):105–137.

Baker, Nancy V. 1992. *Conflicting Loyalties: Law and Politics in the Attorney General's Office, 1789–1990*. University Press of Kansas.

Baker, Peter and Jeff Zeleny. 2010. "Obama Picks Kagan, Scholar but Not Judge, for Court Seat." *New York Times,* May 10. https://www.nytimes.com/2010/05/11/us/politics/11court.html.

Barnes, Fred. 1999. "Bush and the Litmus Test." *The Weekly Standard,* June 28.

Baron, David P. 1996. "A Dynamic Theory of Collective Goods Programs." *American Political Science Review* 90(2):316–330.

Barry, Brian. 1965. *Political Argument*. Humanities Press, Inc.

Bartels, Brandon L. and Eric Kramon. 2021. "All the President's Justices? The Impact of Presidential Copartisanship on Supreme Court Job Approval." *American Journal of Political Science* 66(1):171–186.

Bartels, Larry M. 1986. "Issue Voting under Uncertainty: An Empirical Test." *American Journal of Political Science* 30:709–728.

Bartels, Larry M. 1991. "Constituency Opinion and Congressional Policy Making: The Reagan Defense Buildup." *American Political Science Review* 85(2):457–474.

Bartels, Larry M. 2016. *Unequal Democracy: The Political Economy of the New Gilded Age—Second Edition*. Princeton University Press.

Barton, Russell R. and Martin Meckesheimer. 2006. "Metamodel-Based Simulation Optimization." *Handbooks in Operations Research and Management Science* 13:535–574.

Bass, Leeann, Charles M. Cameron, and Jonathan P. Kastellec. 2022. "The Politics of Accountability in Supreme Court Nominations: Voter Recall and Assessment of Senator Votes on Nominees." *Political Science Research and Methods* 10(4):677–702.

Baumgartner, Frank R., Jeffrey M. Berry, Marie Hojnacki, David Cc. Kimball, and Beth L. Leech. 2009. *Lobbying and Policy Change: Who Wins*. University of Chicago Press.

Bawn, Kathleen, Knox Brown, Angela X. Ocampo, Jr., Shawn Patterson, John L. Ray, and John Zaller. 2023. "Groups, Parties, and Policy Demands in House Nominations." In *Accountability Reconsidered: Voters, Information, and Policymaking*, ed. Sanford Gordon Charles Cameron, Brandice Canes-Wrone, and Gregory Huber. Cambridge University Press, ch. 5.

Bawn, Kathleen, Martin Cohen, David Karol, Seth Masket, Hans Noel, and John Zaller. 2012. "A Theory of Political Parties: Groups, Policy Demands and Nominations in American Politics." *Perspectives on Politics* 10(3):571–597.

Becker, Gary S. 1965. "A Theory of the Allocation of Time." *Economic Journal* 75:493–517.

Bell, Lauren Cohen. 2002. *Warring Factions: Interest Groups, Money, and the New Politics of Senate Confirmation*. Ohio State University Press.

Bennett, David Harry. 1988. *The Party of Fear: From Nativist Movements to the New Right in American History*. UNC Press Books.

Berinsky, Adam J. 1999. "The Two Faces of Public Opinion." *American Journal of Political Science* 43(4):1209–1230.

Berke, Richard L. 1991. "Support for Thomas Inches toward Approval in Senate." *New York Times*, Oct. 4:A16. https://www.nytimes.com/1991/10/04/us/support-for-thomas-inches-toward-approval-in-senate.html.

Berkman, Michael B. 2001. "Legislative Professionalism and the Demand for Groups: The Institutional Context of Interest Population Density." *Legislative Studies Quarterly* 26(4):661–679.

Berman, Russell. 2017. "Kansas Republicans Sour on Their Tax-Cut Experiment." *The Atlantic*. https://www.theatlantic.com/politics/archive/2017/02/the-republican-blowback-against-sam-brownback-kansas/517641/.

Besley, Timothy. 2006. *Principled Agents? The Political Economy of Good Government*. Oxford University Press.

Besley, Timothy and Anne Case. 1992. "Incumbent Behavior: Vote Seeking, Tax Setting and Yardstick Competition." *American Economic Review* 85(1):25–45.

Bevan, Shaun, Frank R. Baumgartner, Erik W. Johnson, and John D. McCarthy. 2013. "Understanding Selection Bias, Time-Lags and Measurement Bias in Secondary Data Sources: Putting the Encyclopedia of Associations Database in Broader Context." *Social Science Research* 42(6):1750–1764.

Bickel, Alexander M. 1962. *The Least Dangerous Branch: The Supreme Court at the Bar of Politics*. Yale University Press.

Binder, Sarah A. and Forrest Maltzman. 2009. *Advice and Dissent: The Struggle to Shape the Federal Judiciary*. Brookings Institution Press.

Bishin, Benjamin. 2009. *Tyranny of the Minority: The Subconstituency Politics Theory of Representation*. Temple University Press.

Biskupic, Joan. 2009. *American Original: The Life and Constitution of Supreme Court Justice Antonin Scalia*. Sarah Crichton Books.

Biskupic, Joan. 2019. "Democrats Look at Packing the Supreme Court to Pack the Vote." *CNN Politics*, May 31. https://www.cnn.com/2019/05/31/politics/democrats-supreme-court-packing-politics/index.html.

Blanco, Adrian. 2022. "Biden, Who Pledged to Diversify the Supreme Court, Has Already Made Progress on Lower Court." *Washington Post*, Jan. 27. https://www.washingtonpost.com/politics/2022/01/27/federal-judge-diversity-biden/.

Bolton, Alexander. 2021. "Ideology, Unionization, and Personnel Politics in the Federal Budget Process." *Journal of Public Administration Research and Theory* 31(1):38–55.

Bonica, Adam and Maya Sen. 2020. *The Judicial Tug of War: How Lawyers, Politicians, and Ideological Incentives Shape the American Judiciary*. Cambridge University Press.

Bonica, Adam and Maya Sen. 2021. "Estimating Judicial Ideology." *Journal of Economic Perspectives* 35(1):97–118.

Bork, Robert H. 1996. *Slouching towards Gomorrah*. HarperCollins.

Bork, Robert H. 2009. *The Tempting of America*. Simon and Schuster.

Bork, Robert H. 2013. *A Country I Do Not Recognize: The Legal Assault on American Values*. Hoover Institution Press.

Borrelli, Maryanne, Karen Hult, and Nancy Kassop. 2001. "The White House Counsel's Office." *Presidential Studies Quarterly* 31(4):561–584.

Boucher Jr., Robert L. and Jeffrey A. Segal. 1995. "Supreme Court Justices as Strategic Decision Makers: Aggressive Grants and Defensive Denials on the Vinson Court." *Journal of Politics* 57(3):824–837.

Boulay, Harvey and Alan DiGaetano. 1985. "Why Did Political Machines Disappear?" *Journal of Urban History* 12(1):25–49.

Bowie, Nikolas. 2021. "Testimony before the Presidential Commission on the Supreme Court of the United States." https://www.whitehouse.gov/wp-content/uploads/2021/06/Bowie-SCOTUS-Testimony.pdf.

Box-Steffensmeier, Janet and Dino P. Christenson. 2012. "Database on Supreme Court Amicus Curiae Briefs. Version 1.0." https://amicinetworks.com/index.html.

Brenner, Saul. 1999. "The Myth That Justices Strategically Retire." *Social Science Journal* 36(3):431–439.

Brill, Steven. 2015. *America's Bitter Pill: Money, Politics, Backroom Deals, and the Fight to Fix Our Broken Healthcare System*. Random House.

Brinkley, Douglas. 2007. *Gerald R. Ford*. Macmillan.

Brownell, Herbert and John P. Burke. 1993. *Advising Ike: The Memoirs of Attorney General Herbert Brownell*. University Press of Kansas.

Brownstein, Ronald. 2018. "Small States Are Getting a Much Bigger Say in Who Gets on Supreme Court." *CNN Politics*, July 10. www.cnn.com/2018/07/10/politics/small-states-supreme-court/index.html.

Budge, Ian. 1993. "Issues, Dimensions, and Agenda Change in Postwar Democracies: Longterm Trends in Party Election Programs and Newspaper Reports in Twenty-Three Democracies." In *Agenda Formation*, ed. William Riker. University of Michigan Press, pp. 41–80.

Bullock, Charles S., III, and David W. Brady. 1983. "Party, Constituency and Roll-Call Voting in the U.S. Senate." *Legisative Studies Quarterly* 8(1):29–43.

Bullock, John G. 2011. "Elite Influence on Public Opinion in an Informed Electorate." *American Political Science Review* 105(3):496–515.

Bump, Phillip. 2017. "The Senate May Be Developing an Electoral College Issue." *Washington Post*, April 10. www.washingtonpost.com/news/politics/wp/2017/04/10/the-senate-may-be-developing-an-electoral-college-issue.

Burbank, Stephen B. and Sean Farhang. 2017. *Rights and Retrenchment*. Cambridge University Press.

Burke, Daniel. 2017. "What Is Neil Gorsuch's Religion? It's Complicated." *CNN Politics*, March 22. https://www.cnn.com/2017/03/18/politics/neil-gorsuch-religion/index.html.

Burstein, Paul. 2014. *American Public Opinion, Advocacy, and Policy in Congress*. Cambridge University Press.

Calabresi, Steven G. and James Lindgren. 2005. "Term Limits for the Supreme Court: Life Tenure Reconsidered." *Harvard Journal of Law & Public Policy* 29:769.

Caldarone, Richard P., Brandice Canes-Wrone, and Tom S. Clark. 2009. "Partisan Labels and Democratic Accountability: An Analysis of State Supreme Court Abortion Decisions." *Journal of Politics* 71(2):560–573.

Caldeira, Gregory A. and Smith, Charles E., Jr. 1996. "Campaigning for the Supreme Court: The Dynamics of Public Opinion on the Thomas Nomination." *Journal of Politics* 58(3): 655–681.

Calvert, Randall L. 1985. "Robustness of the Multidimensional Voting Model: Candidate Motivations, Uncertainty, and Convergence." *American Journal of Political Science* 29(1): 69–95.

Cameron, Charles and Jee-Kwang Park. 2009. "How Will They Vote? Predicting the Future Behavior of Supreme Court Nominees, 1937–2006." *Journal of Empirical Legal Studies* 6(3):485–511.

Cameron, Charles and Jee-Kwang Park. 2011. "Going Public When Opinion Is Contested: Evidence from Presidents' Campaigns for Supreme Court Nominees, 1930–2009." *Presidential Studies Quarterly* 41(3):442–470.

Cameron, Charles M., Albert D. Cover, and Jeffrey A. Segal. 1990. "Senate Voting on Supreme Court Nominees: A Neoinstitutional Model." *American Political Science Review* 84(2): 525–534.

Cameron, Charles M., Cody Gray, Jonathan P. Kastellec, and Jee-Kwang Park. 2020. "From Textbook Pluralism to Hyper-Pluralism: Interest Groups and Supreme Court Nominations, 1930–2017." *Journal of Law and Courts* 8(2):301–332.

Cameron, Charles M. and John M. de Figueiredo. 2020. "Quitting in Protest: Presidential Policymaking and Civil Service Response." *Quarterly Journal of Political Science* 15(4): 507–538.

Cameron, Charles and Jonathan P. Kastellec. 2016*a*. "How an Obama Supreme Court Nominee Could Win Confirmation in the Senate." *Washington Post* Feb. 17. https://www.washingtonpost.com/news/monkey-cage/wp/2016/02/17/how-an-obama-supreme-court-nominee-could-win-confirmation-in-the-senate/.

Cameron, Charles M. and Jonathan P. Kastellec. 2016*b*. "Are Supreme Court Nominations a Move-the-Median Game?" *American Political Science Review* 110(4): 778–797.

Cameron, Charles M., Jonathan P. Kastellec, and Jee-Kwang Park. 2013. "Voting for Justices: Change and Continuity in Confirmation Voting 1937–2010." *Journal of Politics* 75(2): 283–299.

Cameron, Charles M., Jonathan P. Kastellec, Lauren A. Mattioli et al. 2019. "Presidential Selection of Supreme Court Nominees: The Characteristics Approach." *Quarterly Journal of Political Science* 14(4):439–474.

Cameron, Charles M., Lewis A. Kornhauser, and Giri Parameswaran. 2019. "Stare Decisis and Judicial Logrolls: A Gains-from-Trade Model." *RAND Journal of Economics* 50(3): 505–531.

Campbell, Andrea Louise. 2003. *How Policies Make Citizens: Senior Political Activism and the American Welfare State*. Princeton University Press.

Campbell, Andrea Louise. 2012. "Policy Makes Mass Politics." *Annual Review of Political Science* 15:333–351.

Campbell, Angus, Philip E. Converse, Warren E. Miller, and Donald E. Stokes. 1960. *The American Voter*. University of Chicago Press.

Campbell, Linda B. 1990. "Souter Keeps His Counsel on Abortion." *Chicago Tribune*, Sept. 14. https://www.chicagotribune.com/news/ct-xpm-1990-09-14-9003170181-story.html.

Canes-Wrone, Brandice, David W. Brady, and John F. Cogan. 2002. "Out of Step, Out of Office: Electoral Accountability and House Members' Voting." *American Political Science Review* 96(1):127–140.

Canes-Wrone, Brandice, Michael C. Herron, and Kenneth W. Shotts. 2001. "Leadership and Pandering: A Theory of Executive Policymaking." *American Journal of Political Science* 45(3):532–550.

Carey, John M. 2008. *Legislative Voting and Accountability*. Cambridge University Press.

Carmen, Ira H. 1969. "The President, Politics and the Power of Appointment: Hoover's Nomination of Mr. Justice Cardozo." *Virginia Law Review* 55(4):616–659.

Carmines, Edward G. and James Woods. 2002. "The Role of Party Activists in the Evolution of the Abortion Issue." *Political Behavior* 24(4):361–377.

Carpini, Michael X. Delli and Scott Keeter. 1996. *What Americans Know about Politics and Why It Matters*. Yale University Press.

Carr, Matthew A., Gerald Gamm, and Justin H. Phillips. 2016. "Origins of the Culture War: Social Issues in State Party Platforms, 1960–2014." Columbia University working paper.

Carrubba, Cliff, Barry Friedman, Andrew D. Martin, and Georg Vanberg. 2012. "Who Controls the Content of Supreme Court Opinions?" *American Journal of Political Science* 56(2): 400–412.

Carrubba, Clifford J. and Tom S. Clark. 2012. "Rule Creation in a Political Hierarchy." *American Political Science Review* 106(3):622–643.

Casper, Jonathan D. 1976. "The Supreme Court and National Policy Making." *American Political Science Review* 70(1):50–63.

Caughey, Devin. 2007. "Responding to the Roosevelt Resconstruction: The South, the Supreme Court, and The New Deal Coalition." University of California-Berkeley Working Paper.

Chafetz, Josh. 2017*a*. *Congress's Constitution: Legislative Authority and the Separation of Powers*. Yale University Press.

Chafetz, Josh. 2017*b*. "Unprecedented: Judicial Confirmation Battles and the Search for a Usable Past." *Harvard Law Review* 131:96–132.

Chafetz, Josh. 2020. "Congressional Overspeech." *Fordham Law Review* 89:529.

Chemerinsky, Erwin. 2013. "Erwin Chemerinsky: Supreme Court Needs Term Limits." *The Orange County Register.*, Aug. 4. https://www.ocregister.com/2013/08/04/erwin-chemerinsky-supreme-court-needs-term-limits.

Chen, Philip G. and Amanda C. Bryan. 2018. "Judging the 'Vapid and Hollow Charade': Citizen Evaluations and the Candor of US Supreme Court Nominees." *Political Behavior* 40(2): 495–520.

Chiang, Chun-Fang and Brian Knight. 2011. "Media Bias and Influence: Evidence From Newspaper Endorsements." *Review of Economic Studies* 78(3):795–820.

Chilton, Adam, Daniel Epps, Kyle Rozema, and Maya Sen. 2021*a*. "Designing Supreme Court Term Limits." *Southern California Law Review*. 95(1):1–72.

Chilton, Adam, Daniel Epps, Kyle Rozema, and Maya Sen. 2021*b*. "The Endgame of Court-Packing." Available at SSRN: https://ssrn.com/abstract=3835502

Cizmar, Martin. 2018. "MSNBC's Rachel Maddow Explains How Brett Kavanaugh Could Be Removed from the Supreme Court and Thrown in Jail." *Raw Story*, Sept. 20. https://www.rawstory.com/2018/09/msnbcs-rachel-maddow-explains-brett-kavanaugh-removed-supreme-court-thrown-jail/.

Clark, Tom. 2012. "Bargaining and Opinion Writing in the US Supreme Court." In *New Directions in Judicial Politics*, ed. Kevin McGuire. Routledge, pp. 186–204.

Clark, Tom S. 2011. *The Limits of Judicial Independence*. Cambridge University Press.

Clark, Tom S. 2019. *The Supreme Court: An Analytic History of Constitutional Decision Making*. Cambridge University Press.

Clark, Tom S. and Benjamin Lauderdale. 2010. "Locating Supreme Court Opinions in Doctrine Space." *American Journal of Political Science*. 54(4):871–890.

Clark, Tom S., Sanford Gordon, and Michael Giles. 2016. "How Liberal Is Merrick Garland?" *Washington Post,* March 17. https://www.washingtonpost.com/news/monkey-cage/wp/2016/03/17/how-liberal-is-merrick-garland/.

Clayton, Cornell W. 1992. *The Politics of Justice: The Attorney General and the Making of Legal Policy.* Routledge.

Clinton, Bill. 2005. *My Life: The Presidential Years. Volume II.* Vintage.

Clinton, Joshua D. 2006. "Representation in Congress: Constituents and Roll Calls in the 106th House." *Journal of Politics* 68(2):397–409.

Coate, Stephen and Stephen Morris. 1995. "On the Form of Transfers to Special Interests." *Journal of Political Economy* 103(6):1210–1235.

Cochran, Amanda. 2014. "Anita Hill: Clarence Thomas Hearings 23 Years Ago Unfair." *CBS News,* March 13. https://www.cbsnews.com/news/anita-hill-clarence-thomas-hearings-23-years-ago-unfair/.

Cohen, Adam. 2021. *Supreme Inequality: The Supreme Court's Fifty-Year Battle for a More Unjust America*. Penguin Books.

Cohen, Marty, David Karol, Hans Noel, and John Zaller. 2008. *The Party Decides: Presidential Nominations Before and After Reform*. University of Chicago Press.

Cole, David. 2015. "The Power of a Supreme Court Dissent." *Washington Post,* Oct. 29. https://www.washingtonpost.com/opinions/the-power-of-a-supreme-court-dissent/2015/10/29/fbc80acc-66cb-11e5-8325-a42b5a459b1e_story.html.

Collins, Jr., Paul M., Pamela C. Corley, and Jesse Hamner. 2015. "The Influence of Amicus Curiae Briefs on U.S. Supreme Court Opinion Content." *Law & Society Review* 49(4): 917–944.

Collins, Paul M. and Lori A. Ringhand. 2013. *Supreme Court Confirmation Hearings and Constitutional Change*. Cambridge University Press.

Converse, Phillip. 1964. "The Nature of Belief Systems in Mass Publics." In *Ideology and Discontent*, ed. David Apter. Free Press.

Cottrell, David, Charles R. Shipan, and Richard J. Anderson. 2019. "The Power to Appoint: Presidential Nominations and Change on the Supreme Court." *Journal of Politics* 81(3): 1057–1068.

Cottrell, David and Charles Shipan. 2016. "If Obama Appoints Scalia's Successor, the Supreme Court Will Really Jump Leftward." *Washington Post,* Feb. 15. https://www.washingtonpost.com/news/monkey-cage/wp/2016/02/15/if-obama-appoints-scalias-successor-the-supreme-court-will-really-jump-leftward/.

Cox, Gary W. and Mathew D. McCubbins. 1993. *Legislative Leviathan: Party Government in the House*. University of California Press.

Coyle, Erin, Elisabeth Fondren, and Joby Richard. 2020. "Advocacy, Editorial Opinion, and Agenda Building: How Publicity Friends Fought for Louis D. Brandeis's 1916 Supreme Court Confirmation." *American Journalism* 37(2):165–190.

Cramton, Roger C. 2007. "Reforming the Supreme Court." *California Law Review* 95: 1313–1334.

Crowe, Justin. 2012. *Building the Judiciary: Law, Courts, and the Politics of Institutional Development*. Princeton University Press.

Crowe, Justin and Christopher F. Karpowitz. 2007. "Where Have You Gone, Sherman Minton? The Decline of the Short-Term Supreme Court Justice." *Perspectives on Politics* 5(3):425–445.

Cummings, Homer Stille. 1937. "Diary Entries." Homer Stille Cummings Papers. Special Collections, University of Virginia Library, Charlottesville.

Cunningham, Scott. 2021. *Causal Inference: The Mixtape*. Yale University Press.

Dahl, Robert A. 1961. *Who Governs?: Democracy and Power in an American City*. Yale University Press.

Dancey, Logan and Geoffrey Sheagley. 2013. "Heuristics Behaving Badly: Party Cues and Voter Knowledge." *American Journal of Political Science* 57(2):312–325.

Dancey, Logan and Geoffrey Sheagley. 2016. "Inferences Made Easy: Partisan Voting in Congress, Voter Awareness, and Senator Approval." *American Politics Research* 44(5): 844–874.

Danelski, David J. 1964. *A Supreme Court Justice Is Appointed*. Random House.

Daniels, William J. 1978. "The Geographic Factor in Appointments to the United States Supreme Court: 1789–1976." *Western Political Quarterly* 31(2):226–237.

Davis, Richard. 2017. *Supreme Democracy: The End of Elitism in Supreme Court Nominations*. Oxford University Press.

De Figueiredo, John M. and Emerson H. Tiller. 1996. "Congressional Control of the Courts: A Theoretical and Empirical Analysis of Expansion of the Federal Judiciary." *Journal of Law and Economics* 39(2):435–462.

Dean, John W. 2001. *The Rehnquist Choice: The Untold Story of the Nixon Appointment that Redefined the Supreme Court*. Free Press.

Devins, Neal and Lawrence Baum. 2019. *The Company They Keep: How Partisan Divisions Came to the Supreme Court*. Oxford University Press.

Diamond, Jeremy. 2017. "Trump White House Lawyers Up." *CNN Politics*, March 7. www.cnn.com/2017/03/07/politics/trump-white-house-counsel-office/index.html.

DiMaggio, Paul, John Evans, and Bethany Bryson. 1996. "Have American's Social Attitudes Become More Polarized?" *American Journal of Sociology* 102(3):690–755.

DiSalvo, Daniel. 2012. *Engines of Change: Party Factions in American Politics, 1868–2010*. Oxford University Press.

DiscoverLBJ. 2018. "Telephone Conversation # 10821, Sound Recording, LBJ and ABE FORTAS, 9/22/1966, 8:30AM." https://www.discoverlbj.org/item/tel-10821.

DiTullio, James E. and John B. Schochet. 2004. "Saving This Honorable Court: A Proposal to Replace Life Tenure on the Supreme Court with Staggered, Nonrenewable Eighteen-Year Terms." *Virginia Law Review* 90:1093–1149.

Diven, Polly. 2006. "A Coincidence of Interests: The Hyperpluralism of U.S. Food Aid Policy." *Foreign Policy Analysis* 2(4):361–384.

Doleac, Jennifer L. 2021. "A Review of Thomas Sowell's Discrimination and Disparities." *Journal of Economic Literature* 59(2):574–589.

Downs, Anthony. 1957. *An Economic Theory of Democracy*. Addison Wesley.

Drew, Elizabeth. 1995. *On the Edge: The Clinton Presidency*. Simon and Schuster.

Driver, Justin. 2013. "Supremacies and the Southern Manifesto." *Texas Law Review* 92: 1053–1135.

Drutman, Lee. 2015. *The Business of America Is Lobbying: How Corporations Became Politicized and Politics Became More Corporate*. Oxford University Press.

Duggan, John and César Martinelli. 2017. "The Political Economy of Dynamic Elections: Accountability, Commitment, and Responsiveness." *Journal of Economic Literature* 55(3): 916–984.

The Economist 2017. "How Leading American Newspapers Got People to Pay for news.". https://www.economist.com/business/2017/10/26/how-leading-american-newspapers-got-people-to-pay-for-news.

Ellis, Richard E. 1971. *The Jeffersonian Crisis: Courts and Politics in the Young Republic*. Oxford University Press on Demand.

Enelow, James M. and Melvin J. Hinich. 1984. *The Spatial Theory of Voting: An Introduction.* Cambridge University Press Archive.

Enns, Peter K. 2016. *Incarceration Nation.* Cambridge University Press.

Epp, Charles R. 1998. *The Rights Revolution: Lawyers, Activists, and Supreme Courts in Comparative Perspective.* University of Chicago Press.

Epps, Daniel and Ganesh Sitaraman. 2019. "How to Save the Supreme Court." *Yale Law Journal* 129: 148–206.

Epstein, Lee and Eric A. Posner. 2016. "Supreme Court Justices' Loyalty to the President." *Journal of Legal Studies* 45(2):401–436.

Epstein, Lee and Jack Knight. 1997. *The Choices Justices Make.* Sage.

Epstein, Lee, Jack Knight, and Andrew D. Martin. 2003. "The Norm of Prior Judicial Experience and Its Consequences for Career Diversity on the US Supreme Court." *California Law Review* 91(4):903–965

Epstein, Lee and Jeffrey A. Segal. 2005. *Advice and Consent: The Politics of Judicial Appointments.* Oxford University Press.

Epstein, Lee, Thomas G. Walker, Nancy Staudt, Scott Hendrickson, and Jason Roberts. 2022. *The U.S. Supreme Court Justices Database.* October 28. https://epstein.usc.edu/justicesdata.

Epstein, Lee, Rene Lindstadt, Jeffrey A. Segal, and Chad Westerland. 2006. "The Changing Dynamics of Senate Voting on Supreme Court Nominees." *Journal of Politics* 68(2): 296–307.

Epstein, Lee, Thomas G. Walker, Nancy Staudt, Scott A. Hendrickson, and Jason M. Roberts. 2013. "Codebook: U.S. Supreme Court Justices Database." https://epstein.usc.edu/justicesdata.

Erikson, Robert S. and Christopher Wlezien. 2012. *The Timeline of Presidential Elections: How Campaigns Do (and Do Not) Matter.* University of Chicago Press.

Erikson, Robert S. and Gerald C. Wright. 1980. "Policy Representation of Constituency Interests." *Political Behavior* 2(1):91–106.

Erikson, Robert S., Michael B. MacKuen, and James A. Stimson. 2002. *The Macro Polity.* Cambridge University Press.

Eshbaugh-Soha, Matthew and Paul M. Collins, Jr. 2015. "Presidential Rhetoric and Supreme Court Decisions." *Presidential Studies Quarterly* 45(4):633–652.

Espinoza, Russ. 2019. "ABC and NBC Split Network News Ratings Crown for 2018–19 TV Season." https://www.forbes.com/sites/russespinoza/2019/09/24/abc-and-nbc-split-network-news-ratings-crown-for-2018-19-tv-season/?sh=1fab23617cd9

Evans, Michael and Shanna Pearson-Merkowitz. 2012. "Perpetuating the Myth of the Culture War Court? Issue Attention in Newspaper Coverage of US Supreme Court Nominations." *American Politics Research* 40(6):1026–1066.

Everett, Burgess and Glenn Thrush. 2016. "McConnell Throws Down the Gauntlet: No Scalia Replacement under Obama." *Politico.* Feb. 13. www.politico.com/story/2016/02/mitch-mcconnell-antonin-scalia-supreme-court-nomination-219248.

Fairman, Charles. 1971. *Reconstruction and Reunion, 1864–88, Part One.* Macmillan.

Farganis, Dion and Justin Wedeking. 2014. *Supreme Court Confirmation Hearings in the US Senate: Reconsidering the Charade.* University of Michigan Press.

Farnsworth, Ward. 2007. "The Use and Limits of Martin-Quinn Scores to Assess Supreme Court Justices, with Special Attention to the Problem of Ideological Drift." *Northwestern University Law Review* 101(4):1891–1904.

Fausold, Martin L. 1985. *The Presidency of Herbert C. Hoover.* University Press of Kansas.

Fearon, James D. 1999. "Electoral Accountability and the Control of Politicians: Selecting Good Types versus Sanctioning Poor Performance." In *Democracy, Accountability, and Representation,* ed. Susan Stokes Adam Przeworski and Bernand Manin. Cambridge University Press. *Northwestern University Law Review* 101(4):1891–1904.

Federal Judicial Center. 2020. "Biographical Directory of Federal Judges." https://www.fjc.gov/history/judges/biographical-directory-article-iii-federal-judges-export.

Feinstein, Brian D. and Daniel J. Hemel. 2018. "Partisan Balance with Bite." *Columbia Law Review* 118(1):9–82.

Feinstein, Brian D. and Eric Schickler. 2008. "Platforms and Partners: The Civil Rights Realignment Reconsidered." *Studies in American Political Development* 22(1):1–31.

Fenno, Richard. 1978. *Home Style: House Members in Their Districts*. Little, Brown.

Ferguson, Niall. 2008. *Virtual History: Alternatives and Counterfactuals*. Hachette UK.

Ferrara, Alessandro. 2014. *The Democratic Horizon: Hyperpluralism and the Renewal of Political Liberalism*. Cambridge University Press.

Ferraro, Thomas. 2010. "Republican Would Back Garland for Supreme Court." *Politico*, May 6. www.reuters.com/article/us-usa-court-hatch/republican-would-back-garland-for-supreme-court-idUSTRE6456QY20100506.

Fiorina, Morris P. 1981. *Retrospective Voting in American National Elections*. Yale University Press.

Fiorina, Morris P. 2017. *Unstable Majorities: Polarization, Party Sorting, and Political Stalemate*. Hoover Press.

Fiorina, Morris P., Samuel J. Abrams, and Jeremy Pope. 2006. *Culture War?: The Myth of a Polarized America*. Longman Publishing Group.

Fischman, Joshua B. and David S. Law. 2009. "What Is Judicial Ideology, and How Should We Measure It?" *Washington University Journal of Law & Policy* 29:133.

Flemming, Roy B., Michael C. MacLeod, and Jeffery Talbert. 1998. "Witness at the Confirmations? The Appearance of Organized Interests at Senate Hearings of Federal Judicial Appointments." *Political Research Quarterly* 51(3):617–631.

Flentje, H. Edward and Joseph A. Aistrup. 2010. *Kansas Politics and Government: The Clash of Political Cultures*. University of Nebraska Press.

Flores, Reena and Major Garrett. 2016. "Donald Trump Expands List of Possible Supreme Court Picks." *CBS News*, Sept. 23. www.cbsnews.com/news/donald-trump-expands-list-of-possible-supreme-court-picks.

Ford, Gerald R. 1979. *A Time to Heal: The Autobiography of Gerald R. Ford*. Harper & Row.

Ford, Gerald R. 2005. "Letter to William Michael Treanor." http://graphics8.nytimes.com/packages/pdf/us/20100410_ford-stevens-letter.pdf. (accessed Nov. 9, 2018).

Forgette, Richard. 2018. *News Grazers: Media, Politics, and Trust in an Information Age*. CQ Press.

Fortunato, David and Randolph T. Stevenson. 2019. "Heuristics in Context." *Political Science Research and Methods* 7(2):311–330.

Fowler, Anthony. 2020. "Partisan Intoxication or Policy Voting?" *Quarterly Journal of Political Science* 15(2):141–179.

Fowler, Anthony, Seth Hill, Jeff Lewis, Chris Tausanovitch, Lynn Vavreck, and Christopher Warshaw. 2022. "Moderates." *American Political Science Review*. https://www.cambridge.org/core/journals/american-political-science-review/article/moderates/71A6A9BD7EC7A5C94F975703417F866F.

Fox, Justin and Richard Van Weelden. 2012. "Costly Transparency." *Journal of Public Economics* 96:142–150.

Friedman, Barry. 2002. "Reconstruction's Political Court: The History of the Countermajoritarian Difficulty, Part Two." *Georgetown Law Journal* 91(1):1–65.

Friedman, Barry. 2009. *The Will of the People: How Public Opinion Has Influenced The Supreme Court and Shaped the Meaning of the Constitution*. Farrar, Strauss and Giroux.

Gailmard, Sean and John W. Patty. 2007. "Slackers and Zealots: Civil Service, Policy Discretion, and Bureaucratic Expertise." *American Journal of Political Science* 51(4):873–889.

Gallup. 2018. "Religion." https://news.gallup.com/poll/1690/religion.aspx.

Gans, Daniel J. 1985. "Persistence of Party Success in American Presidential Elections." *Journal of Interdisciplinary History* 16(2):221–237.

Garrett, R. Sam and Denis Steven Rutkus. 2010. *Speed of Presidential and Senate Actions on Supreme Court Nominations, 1900–2010*. Congressional Research Service.

Gellman, Barton. 2008. *Angler: The Cheney Vice Presidency*. Penguin Books.

Gelman, Andrew. 2008. "Scaling Regression Inputs by Dividing by Two Standard Deviations." *Statistics in Medicine* 27(15):2865–2873.

Gelman, Andrew and Gary King. 1993. "Why Are American Presidential Election Campaign Polls So Variable When Votes Are So Predictable?" *British Journal of Political Science* 23(4):409–451.

Gerber, Elisabeth R. and Rebecca B. Morton. 1998. "Primary Election Systems and Representation." *Journal of Law Economics & Organization* 14(2):304–324.

Gerring, John. 2001. *Party Ideologies in America, 1828–1996*. Cambridge University Press.

Geruso, Michael, Dean Spears, and Ishaana Talesara. 2019. "Inversions in US Presidential Elections: 1836–2016." National Bureau of Economic Research working paper. https://www.nber.org/papers/w26247.pdf.

Gervais, Bryan T. 2014. "Following the News? Reception of Uncivil Partisan Media and the Use of Incivility in Political Expression." *Political Communication* 31(4):564–583.

Gibbs, Daniel and Charles M. Cameron. 2020. "Virtue Signaling: A Theory of Message Legislation." SSRN 3617960.

Gibbs, Daniel, Jesse M. Crosson, and Charles M. Cameron. 2021. "Message Legislation and the Politics of Virtue Signaling." Technical report working paper. http://www.daniel-gibbs.com/messaging.pdf.

Gibson, James L. and Michael J. Nelson. 2021. *Judging Inequality: State Supreme Courts and the Inequality Crisis*. Sage.

Gibson, Tobias T. 2008. "Office of Legal Counsel: Inner Workings and Impact." *Law & Courts: Newsletter for the Law & Courts Section of the American Political Science Association* 18(2): 7–12.

Gilens, Martin. 2012. *Affluence and Influence*. Princeton University Press.

Giles, Michael W., Virginia A. Hettinger, and Todd Peppers. 2001. "Picking Federal Judges: A Note on Policy and Partisan Selection Agendas." *Political Research Quarterly* 54: 623–641.

Ginsburg, Tom. 2003. *Judicial Review in New Democracies: Constitutional Courts in Asian Cases*. Cambridge University Press.

Gitenstein, Mark. 1992. *Matters of Principle: An Insider's Account of America's Rejection of Robert Bork's Nomination to the Supreme Court*. Simon and Schuster.

Goings, Kenneth W. 1990. *The NAACP Comes of Age: The Defeat of Judge John J. Parker*. Indiana University Press.

Goldsmith, Jack. 2007. *The Terror Presidency: Law and Judgment inside the Bush Administration*. W. W. Norton & Company.

Gorman, William M. 1980. "A Possible Procedure for Analysing Quality Differentials in the Egg Market." *Review of Economic Studies* 47(5):843–856.

Gottschalk, Marie. 2016. *Caught: The Prison State and the Lockdown of American Politics*. Princeton University Press.

Graber, Mark A. 2012. "The Coming Constitutional Yo-Yo: Elite Opinion, Polarization, and the Direction of Judicial Decision Making." *Howard Law Journal* 56:661.

Greenburg, Jan Crawford. 2007. *Supreme Conflict: The Inside Story of the Struggle for Control of the United States Supreme Court*. Penguin Books.

Greenhouse, Linda. 2007. *Becoming Justice Blackmun: Harry Blackmun's Supreme Court Journey*. Macmillan.

Greenhouse, Linda. 2012. "The 18-Year Bench: Linda Greenhouse Calls for Supreme Court Term Limits." *Slate,* June 7. https://slate.com/news-and-politics/2012/06/linda-greenhouse-calls-for-supreme-court-term-limits.html.

Greenhouse, Linda. 2014. "Judge on the Spot." *New York Times,* Nov. 26. https://www.nytimes.com/2014/11/27/opinion/judge-on-the-spot.html.

Greenhouse, Linda and Reva B. Siegel. 2010. "Before (and after) Roe v. Wade: New Questions about Backlash." *Yale Law Journal* 120:2028.

Greenstein, Fred I. 1994. *The Hidden-Hand Presidency.* Johns Hopkins University Press.

Grier, Kevin, Robin Grier, and Gor Mkrtchian. 2023. "Campaign Contributions and Roll-Call Voting in the US House of Representatives: The Case of the Sugar Industry." *American Political Science Review* 117(1):340–346.

Grofman, Bernard and Timothy J. Brazill. 2002. "Identifying the Median Justice on the Supreme Court through Multidimensional Scaling: Analysis of 'Natural Courts' 1953–1991." *Public Choice* 112(1):55–79.

Grossmann, Matt and David A. Hopkins. 2016. *Asymmetric Politics: Ideological Republicans and Group Interest Democrats.* Oxford University Press.

Guliuzza, III, Frank, Daniel J. Reagan, and David M. Barrett. 1994. "The Senate Judiciary Committee and Supreme Court Nominees: Measuring the Dynamics of Confirmation Criteria." *Journal of Politics* 56(3):773–787.

Hacker, Jacob S. and Paul Pierson. 2020. *Let Them Eat Tweets: How the Right Rules in an Age of Extreme Inequality.* Liveright Publishing.

Hagey, Keach, Lukas I. Alpert, and Yaryna Serkez. 2019. "In News Industry, a Stark Divide between Haves and Have-Nots." https://www.wsj.com/graphics/local-newspapers-stark-divide/.

Haggard, Stephan, Andrew MacIntyre, and Lydia Tiede. 2008. "The Rule of Law and Economic Development." *Annual Review of Political Science* 11:205–234.

Hagle, Timothy M. 1993. "Strategic Retirements: A Political Model of Turnover on the United States Supreme Court." *Political Behavior* 15(1):25–48.

Hall, Andrew B. 2015. "What Happens When Extremists Win Primaries?" *American Political Science Review* 109(1):18–42.

Hall, Andrew B. 2019. *Who Wants to Run?: How the Devaluing of Political Office Drives Polarization.* University of Chicago Press.

Hammond, Thomas H., Chris W. Bonneau, and Reginald S. Sheehan. 2005. *Strategic Behavior and Policy Choice on the U.S. Supreme Court.* Stanford University Press.

Hanretty, Chris. 2020. "An Introduction to Multilevel Regression and Post-Stratification for Estimating Constituency Opinion." *Political Studies Review* 18(4):630–645.

Hansford, Thomas G. and James F. Spriggs. 2018. *The Politics of Precedent on the U.S. Supreme Court.* Princeton University Press.

Hansford, Thomas G., Sarah Depaoli, and Kayla S. Canelo. 2021. "Estimating the Ideal Points of Organized Interests in Legal Policy Space." University of California-Merced working paper.

Hanssen, F. Andrew. 2004. "Is There a Politically Optimal Level of Judicial Independence?" *American Economic Review* 94(3):712–729.

Hensher, David A., John M. Rose, and William H. Greene. 2015. *Applied Choice Analysis (second edition).* Cambridge University Press.

Herring, Edward Pendleton. 1929. *Group Representation before Congress.* Johns Hopkins University Press.

Hertel-Fernandez, Alex. 2019. *State Capture: How Conservative Activists, Big Businesses, and Wealthy Donors Reshaped the American States—and the Nation.* Oxford University Press.

Hertel-Fernandez, Alexander. 2020. "How Policymakers Can Craft Measures That Endure and Build Political Power." Roosevelt Institute.

Hess, Jerry N. 1972. "Oral History Interview with Tom C. Clark." Conducted October 17, 1972, and February 8, 1973. https://www.trumanlibrary.org/oralhist/clarktc.htm (accessed Sept. 26, 2018).

Higgs, Robert. 1991. "Eighteen Problematic Propositions in the Analysis of the Growth of Government." *Review of Austrian Economics* 5(1):3–40.

Hitt, Matthew P. 2013. "Presidential Success in Supreme Court Appointments: Informational Effects and Institutional Constraints." *Presidential Studies Quarterly* 43(4):792–813.

Ho, Daniel E. and Kevin M. Quinn. 2008. "Measuring Explicit Political Positions of Media." *Quarterly Journal of Political Science* 3(4):353–377.

Ho, Daniel E. and Kevin M. Quinn. 2010. "How Not to Lie with Judicial Votes: Misconceptions, Measurement, and Models." *California Law Review* 98(3):813–876.

Hollibaugh, Jr., Gary E., Gabriel Horton, and David E. Lewis. 2014. "Presidents and Patronage." *American Journal of Political Science* 58(4):1024–1042.

Hollis-Brusky, Amanda. 2015. *Ideas with Consequences: The Federalist Society and the Conservative Counterrevolution*. Oxford University Press.

Holmes, Oliver Wendell. 1881. *The Common Law*. Little, Brown, and Co.

Horowitz, Donald L. 1977. *Courts and Social Policy*. Brookings Institution Press.

Hug, Simon. 2020. "Roll-Call Voting Behaviour in Legislatures." In *The Oxford Handbook of Political Representation in Liberal Democracies*, ed. Robert Rohrschneider and Jacques Thomassen. Oxford University Press, pp. 136–154.

Hulse, Carl. 2022. "Kavanaugh Gave Private Assurances. Collins Says He 'Misled' Her." *New York Times*, June 24.

Hutchings, Vincent L. 2001. "Political Context, Issue Salience, and Selective Attentiveness: Constituent Knowledge of the Clarence Thomas Confirmation Vote." *Journal of Politics* 63(3):846–868.

Hyman, Harold Melvin and William M. Wiecek. 1982. *Equal Justice under Law: Constitutional Development, 1835–1875*. Harpercollins.

Igo, Sarah E. 2007. *The Averaged American: Surveys, Citizens, and the Making of a Mass Public*. Harvard University Press.

Iyengar, Shanto and Sean J. Westwood. 2015. "Fear and Loathing across Party Lines: New Evidence on Group Polarization." *American Journal of Political Science* 59(3):690–707.

Jacobi, Tonja. 2009. "Competing Models of Judicial Coalition Formation and Case Outcome Determination." *Journal of Legal Analysis* 1(2):411–458.

Jamieson, Kathleen Hall and Joseph N. Cappella. 2008. *Echo Chamber: Rush Limbaugh and the Conservative Media Establishment*. Oxford University Press.

Jenkins, John A. 2012. *The Partisan: The Life of William Rehnquist*. Public Affairs.

Jessee, Stephen A. 2012. *Ideology and Spatial Voting in American Elections*. Cambridge University Press.

Jo, Jinhee, David M. Primo, and Yoji Sekiya. 2017. "Policy Dynamics and Electoral Uncertainty in the Appointments Process." *Journal of Theoretical Politics* 29(1):124–148.

Johnson, Benjamin. 2018. "The Supreme Court's Political Docket: How Ideology and the Chief Justice Control the Court's Agenda and Shape Law." *Connecticut Law Review* 50:581.

Kahn, Kim Fridkin and Patrick J. Kenney. 2002. "The Slant of the News: How Editorial Endorsements Influence Campaign Coverage and Citizens' Views of Candidates." *American Political Science Review* 96(2):381–394.

Kaiser, Robert G. 2014. *Act of Congress: How America's Essential Institution Works, and How It Doesn't*. Vintage.

Kalen, Sam. 2015. "The Death of Administrative Common Law or the Rise of the Administrative Procedure Act." *Rutgers University Law Review* 68:605.

Kalman, Laura. 2017. *The Long Reach of the Sixties: LBJ, Nixon, and the Making of the Contemporary Supreme Court*. Oxford University Press.

Kaplan, David A. 2018. *The Most Dangerous Branch: Inside the Supreme Court's Assault on the Constitution*. Crown.

Karol, David. 2009. *Party Position Change in American Politics: Coalition Management*. Cambridge University Press.

Kastellec, Jonathan P. 2010. "The Statistical Analysis of Judicial Decisions and Legal Rules with Classification Trees." *Journal of Empirical Legal Studies* 7(2):202–230.

Kastellec, Jonathan P. 2016. "Empirically Evaluating the Counter-Majoritarian Difficulty: Public Opinion, State Policy, and Judicial Decisions before Roe v. Wade." *Journal of Law & Courts* 4(1):1–42.

Kastellec, Jonathan P. 2018. "Judicial Federalism and Representation." *Journal of Law and Courts* 6(1):51–92.

Kastellec, Jonathan P., Jeffrey R. Lax, Michael Malecki, and Justin H. Phillips. 2015. "Polarizing the Electoral Connection: Partisan Representation in Supreme Court Confirmation Politics." *Journal of Politics* 77(3):787–804.

Katcher, Susan. 2006. "Legal Training in the United States: A Brief History." *Wisconsin International Law Journal* 24:335–375.

Katz, Jonathan N. and Matthew L. Spitzer. 2014. "What's Age Got to Do with It? Supreme Court Appointees and the Long Run Location of the Supreme Court Median Justice." *Arizona State Law Journal* 46:41–88.

Kaufman, Andrew L. 1979. "Cardozo's Appointment to the Supreme Court." *Cardozo Law Review* 1:23.

Keith, Bruce E., David B. Magleby, Candice J. Nelson, Elizabeth A. Orr, and Mark C. Westlye. 1992. *The Myth of the Independent Voter*. University of California Press.

Kernell, Samuel. 1986. *Going Public: New Strategies of Presidential Leadership*. CQ Press.

Kernell, Samuel. 1989. "The Evolution of the White House Staff." In *Can the Government Govern?*, ed. John E. Chubb and Paul E. Peterson. Vol. 185. Brookings Institution Press.

Key, Jr., V. O. 1942. *Politics, Parties and Pressure Groups*. Thomas Y. Crowell Company.

Key, Jr., V. O. 1966. *The Responsible Electorate: Rationality in Presidential Voting 1936–1960*. Belknap Press.

Kim, Seung Min. 2020. "Republicans Make the Courts a Feature of Their Convention; Democrats Do Not, and Liberals Are Worried." *Washington Post*, Aug. 29. https://www.washingtonpost.com/politics/trump-biden-supreme-court/2020/08/28/0f0a8158-e937-11ea-bc79-834454439a44_story.html.

King, Gary. 1987. "Presidential Appointments to the Supreme Court: Adding Systematic Explanation to Probabilistic Description." *American Politics Quarterly* 15(3):373–386.

Kingdon, John W. 1989. *Congressmen's Voting Decisions*. University of Michigan Press.

Klein, Ezra. 2018. "Ruth Bader Ginsburg and the Case for 18-Year Supreme Court Terms." *Vox*, Dec. 26. www.vox.com/policy-and-politics/2018/12/26/18155093/ruth-bader-ginsburg-supreme-court-term-limits.

Kraay, Aart and David McKenzie. 2014. "Do Poverty Traps Exist? Assessing the Evidence." *Journal of Economic Perspectives* 28(3):127–148.

Kramer, Victor H. 1990. "The Case of Justice Stevens: How to Select, Nominate and Confirm a Justice of the United States Supreme Court." *Constitutional Commentary* 7:325–340.

Krause, George A., David E. Lewis, and James W. Douglas. 2006. "Political Appointments, Civil Service Systems, and Bureaucratic Competence: Organizational Balancing and Executive Branch Revenue Forecasts in the American States." *American Journal of Political Science* 50(3):770–787.

Krehbiel, Keith. 2007. "Supreme Court Appointments as a Move-the-Median Game." *American Journal of Political Science* 51(2):231–240.

Kritzer, Herbert M. and Mark J. Richards. 2005. "The Influence of Law in the Supreme Court's Search-and-Seizure Jurisprudence." *American Politics Research* 33(1):33–55.

Kutler, Stanley I. 1966. "Reconstruction and the Supreme Court: The Numbers Game Reconsidered." *Journal of Southern History* 32(1):42–58.

Ladd, Jonathan M. 2012. *Why Americans Hate the News Media and How It Matters*. Princeton University Press.

Ladd, Jonathan McDonald and Gabriel S. Lenz. 2009. "Exploiting a Rare Communication Shift to Document the Persuasive Power of the News Media." *American Journal of Political Science* 53(2):394–410.

Lancaster, Kelvin J. 1966. "A New Approach to Consumer Theory." *Journal of Political Economy* 74(2):132–157.

Lander, Mark and Steven Greenhouse. 2013. "Vacancies and Partisan Fighting Put Labor Relations Agency in Legal Limbo." *New York Times*, July 15.

Lat, David. 2017. "Making the White House Counsel's Office Great Again." *Above the Law*, March 7. https://abovethelaw.com/2017/03/making-the-white-house-counsels-office-great-again/

Lax, Jeffrey R. and Charles M. Cameron. 2007. "Bargaining and Opinion Assignment on the U.S. Supreme Court." *Journal of Law, Economics, and Organization* 23(2):276–302.

Lax, Jeffrey R. and Justin H. Phillips. 2009. "How Should We Estimate Public Opinion in the States?" *American Journal of Political Science* 53(1):107–121.

Lax, Jeffrey R., Justin H. Phillips, and Adam Zelizer. 2019. "The Party or the Purse? Unequal Representation in the U.S. Senate." *American Political Science Review* 113(4): 917–940.

Lax, Jeffrey R. and Kelly T. Rader. 2015. "Bargaining Power in the Supreme Court: Evidence from Opinion Assignment and Vote Switching." *Journal of Politics* 77(3):648–663.

Layman, Geoffrey C. 1999. "'Culture Wars' in the American Party System: Religious and Cultural Change among Partisan Activists since 1972." *American Politics Quarterly* 27(1): 89–121.

Layman, Geoffrey C. and Thomas M. Carsey. 1998. "Why Do Party Activists Convert? An Analysis of Individual-Level Change on the Abortion Issue." *Political Research Quarterly* 51(3):723–749.

Layman, Geoffrey C., Thomas M. Carsey, John C. Green, Richard Herrera, and Rosalyn Cooperman. 2010. "Activists and Conflict Extension in American Party Politics." *American Political Science Review* 104(2):324–346.

Lee, Frances. 2009. *Beyond Ideology: Politics, Principles, and Partisanship in the U.S. Senate*. University of Chicago Press.

Lee, Michelle Ye Hee. 2018. "Liberal Activists Embrace 'Dark Money' in Supreme Court Fight." *Washington Post*, July 27.

Lemieux, Peter and Charles Stewart. 1990*a*. "Senate Confirmation of Supreme Court Nominations from Washington to Reagan." Working Papers in Political Science P-90-3, Hoover Institution, Stanford University.

Lemieux, Peter and Charles Stewart. 1990*b*. "A Theory of Supreme Court Nominations." Conference on Political Economy, Cambridge, MA.

Lemieux, Scott E. 2009. "Roe and the Politics of Backlash: Countermobilization against the Courts and Abortion Rights Claiming." College of Saint Rose working paper.

Lenz, Gabriel S. 2013. *Follow the Leader?: How Voters Respond to Politicians' Policies and Performance*. University of Chicago Press.

Leuchtenburg, William E. 1996. *The Supreme Court Reborn: The Constitutional Revolution in the Age of Roosevelt*. Oxford University Press.

Levendusky, Matthew. 2009. *The Partisan Sort: How Liberals Became Democrats and Conservatives Became Republicans*. University of Chicago Press.

Levendusky, Matthew. 2013. *How Partisan Media Polarize America*. University of Chicago Press.

Levy, Marin K. 2019*a*. "Packing and Unpacking State Courts." *William & Mary Law Review* 61:1121–1158.

Levy, Pema. 2019*b*. "How Court-Packing Went from a Fringe Idea to a Serious Democratic Proposal." *Mother Jones*, March 22. www.motherjones.com/politics/2019/03/court-packing-2020/.

Lewis, David E. 2008. *The Politics of Presidential Appointments: Political Control and Bureaucratic Performance*. Princeton University Press.

Libgober, Brian and Daniel Carpenter. 2023. "Administrative Politics with Clear Stakes and Venues: Strategic Commenting upon Federal Reserve Debit Card Regulation." In *Accountability Reconsidered: Voters, Information, and Policy-Making*, ed. Sanford Gordon Charles Cameron, Brandice Canes-Wrone, and Gregory Huber. Cambridge University Press, ch. 14.

Lindquist, Stefanie A. and Pamela C. Corley. 2013. "National Policy Preferences and Judicial Review of State Statutes at the United States Supreme Court." *Publius: The Journal of Federalism* 43(2):151–178.

Liptak, Adam. 2008. "U.S. Voting for Judges Perplexes Other Nations." *New York Times*, May 25.

Liptak, Adam. 2019. "John Paul Stevens: Canny Strategist and the 'Finest Legal Mind' Ford Could Find." *New York Times,* July 16. https://www.nytimes.com/2019/07/16/us/politics/john-paul-stevens-dies-supreme-court.html.

Long, J. Scott. 1997. *Regression Models for Categorical and Llimited Dependent Variables*. Sage.

Long, J. Scott and Jeremy Freese. 2014. *Regression Models for Categorical Dependent Variables Using Stata, Third Edition*. Stata Press.

Lowi, Theodore J. 1964. "American Business, Public Policy, Case-Studies, and Political Theory." *World Politics* 16(4):677–715.

Luks, Samantha and Michael Salamone. 2008. "Abortion." In *Public Opinion and Constitutional Controversy*, ed. Nathaniel Persily, Jack Citrin, and Patrick J. Egan. Oxford University Press, pp. 80–107.

Luppen, Luppe B. 2022. "How Do You Solve a Problem like Alito?" https://www.nycsouthpaw.com/p/how-do-you-solve-a-problem-like-alito?s=w

Maag, Brittony. 2022. "Biden Has Appointed Most Federal Judges through March 1 of a President's Second Year." *Ballotpedia News*, March 4. https://news.ballotpedia.org/2022/03/04/biden-has-appointed-most-federal-judges-through-march-1-of-a-presidents-second-year/.

Maltese, John A. 1995. *The Selling of Supreme Court Nominees*. Johns Hopkins University Press.

Maltzman, Forrest, James F. Spriggs, and Paul J. Wahlbeck. 2000. *Crafting Law on the Supreme Court: The Collegial Game*. Cambridge University Press.

Manchester, Julia. 2020. "Warren, Biden Call for Law to Protect Abortion Rights." *The Hill*, Feb. 7. https://thehill.com/homenews/campaign/482133-warren-biden-call-for-law-to-protect-abortion-rights.

Marcus, Ruth. 2019. *Supreme Ambition: Brett Kavanaugh and the Conservative Takeover*. Simon and Schuster.

Marimow, Ann E. 2019. "Two Years In, Trump's Appeals Court Confirmations at a Historic High Point." *Washington Post*, Feb. 4. www.washingtonpost.com/local/legal-issues/two-years-in-trumps-appeals-court-confirmations-at-a-historic-high-point/2019/02/03/574226e6-1a90-11e9-9ebf-c5fed1b7a081_story.html?utm_term=.ea38610a1d35

Martin, Andrew D. and Kevin M. Quinn. 2002. "Dynamic Ideal Point Estimation Via Markov Chain Monte Carlo for the U.S. Supreme Court, 1953–1999." *Political Analysis* 10(2): 134–153.

Martin, Andrew D., Kevin M. Quinn, and Lee Epstein. 2004. "The Median Justice on the United States Supreme Court." *North Carolina Law Review* 83:1275.

Mashaw, Jerry L. 1994. "Improving the Environment of Agency Rulemaking: An Essay on Management, Games, and Accountability." *Law & Contemporary Problems* 57:185.

Maskin, Eric and Jean Tirole. 2004. "The Politician and the Judge: Accountability in Government." *American Economic Review* 94(4):1034–1054.

Mason, Alpheus T. 1956. *Harlan Fiske Stone: Pillar of the Law*. The Viking Press.

Mason, Lilliana. 2018. *Uncivil Agreement: How Politics Became Our Identity*. University of Chicago Press.

Maxwell, Angie and Todd Shields. 2019. *The Long Southern Strategy: How Chasing White Voters in the South Changed American Politics*. Oxford University Press.

Mayer, Jane. 2017. *Dark Money: The Hidden History of the Billionaires behind the Rise of the Radical Right*. Anchor Books.

Mayer, Jane and Jane Abramson. 1995. *Strange Justice: The Selling of Clarence Thomas*. Plume Books.

Mayhew, David. 1974. *Congress: The Electoral Connection*. Yale University Press.

Mayhew, David R. 1991. *Divided We Govern*. Yale University Press.

Mayhew, David R. 2002. *Electoral Realignments: A Critique of an American Genre*. Yale University Press.

Mayhew, David R. 2014. *Placing Parties in American Politics: Organization, Electoral Settings, and Government Activity in the Twentieth Century*. Princeton University Press.

Mayhew, David R. 2021. "Two Centuries of Presidential Elections." *Presidential Studies Quarterly*. 52(2):393–410.

McCammon, Sarah and Domenico Montanaro. 2018. "Religion, the Supreme Court and Why It Matters." *NPR*, July 7. www.npr.org/2018/07/07/626711777/religion-the-supreme-court-and-why-it-matters.

McCarty, Nolan. 2019. *Polarization: What Everyone Needs to Know*. Oxford University Press.

McCarty, Nolan and Adam Meirowitz. 2007. *Political Game Theory: An Introduction*. Cambridge University Press.

McCarty, Nolan and Eric Schickler. 2018. "On the Theory of Parties." *Annual Review of Political Science* 21:175–193.

McCarty, Nolan, Keith Poole, and Howard Rosenthal. 2006. *Polarized America: The Dance of Ideology and Unequal Riches*. MIT Press.

McFadden, Daniel. 1974. "Conditional Logit Analysis of Qualitative Choice Behavior." In *Frontiers in Econometrics*, ed. P. Zarembka. New York Academic Press, pp. 105–142.

McGhee, Eric, Seth Masket, Boris Shor, Steven Rogers, and Nolan McCarty. 2014. "A Primary Cause of Partisanship? Nomination Systems and Legislator Ideology." *American Journal of Political Science* 58(2):337–351.

McGirr, Lisa. 2002. *Suburban Warriors: The Origins of the New American Right*. Princeton University Press.

McMahon, Kevin J. 2011. *Nixon's Court: His Challenge to Judicial Liberalism and Its Political Consequences*. University of Chicago Press.

Medved, Michael. 1979. *The Shadow Presidents: The Secret History of the Chief Executives and Their Top Aides*. Crown.

Mettler, Suzanne. 2005. *Soldiers to Citizens: The G.I. Bill and the Making of the Greatest Generation*. Oxford University Press.

Miller, Warren E. 1988. *Without Consent: Mass-Elite Linkages in Presidential Politics*. University Press of Kentucky.

Miller, Warren E. and Donald E. Stokes. 1963. "Constituency Influence in Congress." *American Political Science Review* 57(1):45–56.

Miller, Warren and M. Kent Jennings. 1986. *Parties in Transition*. Sage.

Millhiser, Ian. 2019. "Let's Think about Court-Packing." *Democracy: A Journal of Ideas*. Winter. democracyjournal.org/magazine/51/lets-think-about-court-packing-2/.

Mitchell, Amy. 2018. "Americans Still Prefer Watching to Reading the News—and Mostly Still through Television." https://www.journalism.org/2018/12/03/americans-still-prefer-watching-to-reading-the-news-and-mostly-still-through-television/.

Mitchell, Amy, Jeffrey Gottfreid, Michael Barthel, and Elisa Shearer. 2016. "Pathways to News.". https://www.journalism.org/2016/07/07/pathways-to-news/.

Moe, Terry M. 1985. "The Politicized Presidency." In *The New Direction in American Politics*, ed. John Chubb and Paul Peterson. Vol. 235. Brookings Institution Press, pp. 269–271.

Moe, Terry M. 2012. "Delegation, Control, and the Study of Public Bureaucracy." In *The Handbook of Organizational Economics*, ed. Robert Gibbons and John Roberts. Princeton University Press.

Mondak, Jeffery J. and Mary R. Anderson. 2004. "The Knowledge Gap: A Reexamination of Gender-Based Differences in Political Knowledge." *Journal of Politics* 66(2):492–512.

Montgomery, David. 2019. "Conquerors of the Courts." *Washington Post*, Jan. 2. www.washingtonpost.com/news/magazine/wp/2019/01/02/feature/conquerors-of-the-courts/?utm_term=.c7a642f1ca78.

Moraski, Byron J. and Charles R. Shipan. 1999. "The Politics of Supreme Court Nominations: A Theory of Institutional Constraints and Choices." *American Journal of Political Science* 43(4):1069–1095.

Morgan, Stephen L. and Christopher Winship. 2015. *Counterfactuals and Causal Inference*. Cambridge University Press.

Morris, Ian. 2014. *War! What Is It Good For?: Conflict and the Progress of Civilization from Primates to Robots*. Farrar, Straus and Giroux.

Murakami, Michael. 2008. "Desegregation." In *Public Opinion and Constitutional Controversy*, ed. Jack Citrin Nathaniel Persily and Patrick J. Egan. Oxford University Press, pp. 18–40.

Nemacheck, Christine L. 2008. *Strategic Selection: Presidential Nomination of Supreme Court Justices from Herbert Hoover through George W. Bush*. University of Virginia Press.

Newport, Frank. 2010. "75 Years Ago, the First Gallup Poll." *Gallup*, Oct. 20. https://news.gallup.com/opinion/polling-matters/169682/years-ago-first-gallup-poll.aspx.

Newton, Brent E. 2017. "The Supreme Court's Fourth Amendment Scorecard." *Stanford Journal of Civil Rights & Civil Liberties* 13:1–51.

Noack, Rick. 2018. "The U.S. Supreme Court Is Highly Politicized. It Doesn't Have to Be That Way." *Washington Post*, June 28. https://www.washingtonpost.com/news/worldviews/wp/2018/06/28/the-u-s-supreme-court-is-highly-politicized-it-doesnt-have-to-be-that-way/.

Noel, Hans. 2013. *Political Ideologies and Political Parties in America*. Cambridge University Press.

Norris, J. R. 1997. *Markov Chains*. Cambridge University Press.

Norris, Pippa. 2002. *The Bridging and Bonding Role of Online Communities*. Sage.

Nossiff, Rosemary. 2001. "Abortion Policy before Roe: Grassroots and Interest-Group Mobilization." *Journal of Policy History* 13(4):463–478.

Nussbaum, Bernard. 2002. "Bernard Nussbaum Oral History, White House Counsel." UVA Miller Center Presidential Oral Histories. https://millercenter.org/the-presidency/presidential-oral-histories/bernard-nussbaum-oral-history-2002

Nyhan, Brendan, Eric McGhee, John Sides, Seth Masket, and Steven Greene. 2012. "One Vote Out of Step? The Effects of Salient Roll Call Votes in the 2010 Election." *American Politics Research* 40(5):844–879.

Oak, Mandar P. 2006. "On the Role of the Primary System in Candidate Selection." *Economics & Politics* 18(2):169–190.

Odegard, Peter. 1929. "Book Review: Group Representation before Congress by E. Pendleton Herring." *American Political Science Review* 23(2):469–471.

Oliver, Philip D. 1986. "Systematic Justice: A Proposed Constitutional Amendment to Establish Fixed, Staggered Terms for Members of the United States Supreme Court." *Ohio State Law Journal* 47(4):799.

Olson, Michael P. 2018. "The Print Media and the American Party System: Evidence from the 2016 US Presidential Election." *Quarterly Journal of Political Science* 13(4):405–426.

Ostermeier, Eric. 2009. "Are Supreme Court Nominees Getting Younger?" *Smart Politics*, June 1. https://smartpolitics.lib.umn.edu/2009/06/01/are-supreme-court-nominees-get/.

Overby, L. Marvin, Beth M. Henschen, Michael H. Walsh, and Julie Strauss. 1992. "Courting Constituents? An Analysis of the Senate Confirmation Vote on Justice Clarence Thomas." *American Political Science Review* 86(4):997–1003.

Page, Benjamin I. and Robert Y. Shapiro. 1992. *The Rational Public: Fifty Years of Trends in Americans' Policy Preferences*. University of Chicago Press.

Parameswaran, Giri, Charles M. Cameron, and Lewis A. Kornhauser. 2021. "Bargaining and Strategic Voting on Appellate Courts." *American Political Science Review*. 115(3):835–850.

Patashnik, Eric M. 2014. *Reforms at Risk*. Princeton University Press.

Patterson, Bradley H. 2000. *The White House Staff: Inside the West Wing and Beyond*. Brookings Institution Press.

Pearl, Judea. 2009. *Causality*. Cambridge University Press.

Peltason, J. W. 1961. *Fifty-Eight Lonely Men: Southern Federal Judges and School Desegregation*. Harcourt Brace.

Pena, Javier Marquez. 2014. "MORE CLARIFY: Stata Module to Estimate Quantities of Interest through Simulation and Resampling Methods." https://econpapers.repec.org/software/bocbocode/s457851.htm.

Peretti, Terri and Alan Rozzi. 2011. "Modern Departures from the US Supreme Court: Party, Pensions, or Power." *Quinnipiac Law Review* 30:131.

Perry, Barbara. 2019. "There Is Precedent for Ailing Ginsburg to Remain on Supreme Court." *The Hill*, Sept. 8.

Perry, Jr., H.W. 1991. *Deciding to Decide: Agenda Setting in the United States Supreme Court*. Harvard University Press.

Pertschuk, Michael and Wendy Schaetzel. 1989. *The People Rising: The Campaign Against the Bork Nomination*. Thunder's Mouth Press.

Peters, Gerhard and John T. Woolley. 2011. "The American Presidency Project." www.presidency.ucsb.edu/index.php.

Pétry, François and Benoît Collette. 2009. "Measuring How Political Parties Keep Their Promises: A Positive Perspective from Political Science." In *Do They Walk Like They Talk?* Springer, pp. 65–80.

Pew Research Center. 2007. "Cable News vs. Network News Viewership."

Pew Research Center. 2010*a*. "Americans Spending More Time Following the News." https://www.people-press.org/2010/09/12/americans-spending-more-time-following-the-news/.

Pew Research Center. 2010*b*. "How News Happens." https://www.journalism.org/2010/01/11/how-news-happens/.

Phelps, Timothy M. and Helen Winternitz. 1992. *Capitol Games: Clarence Thomas, Anita Hill, and the Story of a Supreme Court Nomination*. Hyperion.

Pierson, Paul. 1993. "When Effect Becomes Cause: Policy Feedback and Political Change." *World Politics* 45(4):595–628.

Pierson, Paul. 2014. "Madison Upside Down: The Policy Roots of Our Polarized Politics." In *The Politics of Major Policy Reform in Postwar America*, ed. Jeffrey A. Jenkins and Sidney M. Milkis. Cambridge University Press, pp. 282–301.

Pomper, Gerald. 1967. '"If Elected, I Promise': American Party Platforms." *Midwest Journal of Political Science* 11(3):318–352.

Poole, Keith T. 2005. *Spatial Models of Parliamentary Voting*. Cambridge University Press.
Poole, Keith T. and Howard Rosenthal. 1997. *Congress: A Political-Economic History of Roll Call Voting*. Oxford University Press.
Powe, Jr., Lucas A. 2000. *The Warren Court and American Politics*. Belknap Press.
Prendergast, Curt. 2016. "Justice Kagan in Tucson: Court Doesn't Feel Political Pressure." *Arizona Tuscon Star*, Aug. 31. https://tucson.com/news/local/justice-kagan-in-tucson-court-doesnt-feel-political-pressure/article_547fcad2-737b-5352-94a8-2478fccc65e6.html
Prior, Markus. 2007. *Post-broadcast Democracy: How Media Choice Increases Inequality in Political Involvement and Polarizes Elections*. Cambridge University Press.
Prior, Markus. 2013. "Media and Political Polarization." *Annual Review of Political Science* 16:101–127.
Prior, Markus. 2019. *Hooked: How Politics Captures People's Interest*. Cambridge University Press.
Provine, Doris Marie. 1980. *Case Selection in the United States Supreme Court*. University of Chicago Press.
Rabkin, Jeremy. 1995. "White House Lawyering: Law, Ethics, and Political Judgments." In *Government Lawyers: The Federal Bureaucracy and Presidential Politics*, ed. Cornell Clayton. University Press of Kansas.
Rae, Nicol. 1994. *Southern Democrats*. Oxford University Press.
Ramseyer, J. Mark. 1994. "The Puzzling (In) Dependence of Courts: A Comparative Approach." *Journal of Legal Studies* 23(2):721–747.
Rappeport, Alan and Charlie Savage. 2016. "Donald Trump Releases List of Possible Supreme Court Picks." *New York Times*, May 18. https://www.nytimes.com/2016/05/19/us/politics/donald-trump-supreme-court-nominees.html.
Rees, III, Grover. 1982. "Questions for Supreme Court Nominees at Confirmation Hearings: Excluding the Constitution." *Georgia Law Review* 17:913.
Rehnquist, William H. 1970. "The Old Order Changeth: The Department of Justice under John Mitchell." *Arizona Law Review* 12:251.
Reilly, Daniel W. and Carrie Budoff Brown. 2007. "Half of Democratic Senators Regret Iraq Vote." *Politico*, Feb. 5. https://www.politico.com/story/2007/02/half-of-democratic-senators-regret-iraq-vote-002639.
Robertson, David. 1994. *Sly and Able: A Political Biography of James F. Byrnes*. Norton.
Rodden, Jonathan. 2019. *Why Cities Lose: The Deep Roots of the Urban-Rural Political Divide*. Basic Books.
Rohde, David W. and Kenneth A. Shepsle. 2007. "Advising and Consenting in the 60-Vote Senate: Strategic Appointments to the Supreme Court." *Journal of Politics* 69(3):664–677.
Rosenberg, Gerald N. 1991. *The Hollow Hope: Can Courts Bring About Social Change?* University of Chicago Press.
Rosenfeld, Sam. 2017. *The Polarizers: Postwar Architects of Our Partisan Era*. University of Chicago Press.
Rosenman, Samuel Irving. 1972. *Working with Roosevelt*. Harper and Sons.
Rothenberg, Lawrence S. 2018. *Policy Success in an Age of Gridlock: How the Toxic Substances Control Act Was Finally Reformed*. Cambridge University Press.
Rudalevige, Andrew. 2002. *Managing the President's Program: Presidential Leadership and Legislative Policy Formulation*. Vol. 81. Princeton University Press.
Rutkus, Denis Steven and Maureen Bearden. 2012. *Supreme Court Nominations, 1789 to the Present: Actions by the Senate, the Judiciary Committee, and the President*. Congressional Research Service.
Saad, Lydia. 2013. "TV Is Americans' Main Source of News.". https://news.gallup.com/poll/163412/americans-main-source-news.aspx.
Saldin, Robert P. 2010. *War, the American State, and Politics since 1898*. Cambridge University Press.

Sasso, Greg and Gleason Judd. 2020. "Case Selection and Supreme Court Pivots." *Political Science Research and Methods* 10(3):659–666.

Savage, Charlie. 2021. '"Court Packing' Issue Divides Commission Appointed by Biden." *New York Times*, Dec. 7. https://www.nytimes.com/2021/12/07/us/politics/supreme-court-packing-expansion.html.

Schattschneider, E. E. 1935. *Politics, Pressure and the Tariff.* New York: Prentice Hall.

Schattschneider, E. E. 1942. *Party Government: American Government in Action.* Rinehart & Company.

Schattschneider, E. E. 1960. *The Semi-Sovereign People.* Holt, Rinehart, and Winston.

Scherer, Nancy. 2005. *Scoring Points: Politicians, Activists, and the Lower Federal Court Appointment Process.* Stanford University Press.

Scherer, Nancy, Brandon L. Bartels, and Amy Steigerwalt. 2008. "Sounding the Fire Alarm: The Role of Interest Groups in the Lower Federal Court Confirmation Process." *Journal of Politics* 70(4):1026–1039.

Schermerhorn, Calvin. 2020. "Packing the Court: Lincoln and His Republicans Remade the Supreme Court to Fit Their Agenda." https://www.virginiamercury.com/2020/10/13/packing-the-court-lincoln-and-his-republicans-remade-the-supreme-court-to-fit-their-agenda/.

Schickler, Eric. 2016. *Racial Realignment: The Transformation of American Liberalism, 1932–1965.* Princeton University Press.

Schlozman, Daniel. 2015. *When Movements Anchor Parties: Electoral Alignments in American History.* Princeton University Press.

Schlozman, Kay L. 2010. "Who Sings in the Heavenly Chorus? The Shape of the Organized Interest System." In *The Oxford Handbook of American Political Parties and Interest Groups*, ed. Sandy L. Maisel and Jeffrey M. Berry. Oxford University Press, pp. 426–450.

Schlozman, Kay Lehman and John T Tierney. 1986. *Organized Interests and American Democracy.* New York: Harper and Row.

Schlozman, Kay Lehman, Sidney Verba, and Henry E. Brady. 2012. *The Unheavenly Chorus: Unequal Political Voice and the Broken Promise of American Democracy.* Princeton University Press.

Schlozman, Kay, Traci Burch, Philip Edward Jones, Hye Young You, Sidney Verba, and Henry E. Brady. 2017. "Washington Representatives Study (Organized Interests in Washington Politics)—1981, 1991, 2001, 2006, 2011. ICPSR35309-v1." Inter-university Consortium for Political and Social Research [distributor], 2014-09-15. doi.org/10.3886/ICPSR35309.v1.

Schmidt, Christopher W. 2018. "The Forgotten Issue: The Supreme Court and the 2016 Presidential Campaign." *Chicago-Kent Law Review* 93:411–452.

Schoenherr, Jessica A., Elizabeth A. Lane, and Miles T. Armaly. 2020. "The Purpose of Senatorial Grandstanding during Supreme Court Confirmation Hearings." *Journal of Law and Courts* 8(2):333–358.

Segal, Jeffrey. 1987. "Senate Confirmation of Supreme Court Justices: Partisan and Institutional Politics." *Journal of Politics* 49(4):998–1015.

Segal, Jeffrey A. 1984. "Predicting Supreme Court Cases Probabilistically: The Search and Seizure Cases, 1962–1981." *American Political Science Review* 78:891–900.

Segal, Jeffrey A. and Albert D. Cover. 1989. "Ideological Values and the Votes of U.S. Supreme Court Justices." *American Political Science Review* 83(2):557–565.

Segal, Jeffrey A., Charles M. Cameron, and Albert D. Cover. 1992. "A Spatial Model of Roll Call Voting: Senators, Constituents, Presidents and Interest Groups in Supreme Court Confirmations." *American Journal of Political Science* 36(1):96–121.

Segal, Jeffrey A. and Harold J. Spaeth. 2002. *The Supreme Court and the Attitudinal Model Revisited.* Cambridge University Press.

Segal, Jeffrey A., Richard J. Timpone, and Robert M. Howard. 2000. "Buyer Beware? Presidential Success through Supreme Court Appointments." *Political Research Quarterly* 53:557–595.

Sen, Maya and William Spaniel. 2017. "How Uncertainty about Judicial Nominees Can Distort the Confirmation Process." *Journal of Theoretical Politics* 29(1):22–47.

Seo, Sarah A. 2019. *Policing the Open Road: How Cars Transformed American Freedom*. Harvard University Press.

Shadmehr, Mehdi, Sepehr Shahshahani, Charles Cameron et al. 2022. "Coordination and Innovation in Judiciaries: Correct Law versus Consistent Law." *Quarterly Journal of Political Science* 17(1):61–89.

Shafer, Byron E. 1988. *Bifurcated Politics: Evolution and Reform in the National Party Convention*. Harvard University Press.

Shapiro, Carolyn. 2012. "Claiming Neutrality and Confessing Subjectivity in Supreme Court Confirmation Hearings." *Chicago-Kent Law Review* 88:455.

Shapiro, Catherine R., David W. Brady, Richard A. Brody, and John A. Ferejohn. 1990. "Linking Constituency Opinion and Senate Voting Scores: A Hybrid Explanation." *Legisative Studies Quarterly* 15(4):599–621.

Shapiro, Martin M. 1988. *Who Guards the Guardians?: Judicial Control of Administration*. University of Georgia Press.

Shemtob, Zachary Baron. 2012. "The Catholic and Jewish Court: Explaining the Absence of Protestants on the Nation's Highest Judicial Body." *Journal of Law and Religion* 27(2):359–396.

Shenhav, Amitai, Sebastian Musslick, Falk Lieder, Wouter Kool, Thomas L. Griffiths, Jonathan D. Cohen, and Matthew M. Botvinick. 2017. "Toward a Rational and Mechanistic Account of Mental Effort." *Annual Review of Neuroscience* 40:99–124.

Shesol, Jeff. 2011. *Supreme Power: Franklin Roosevelt vs. the Supreme Court*. W.W. Norton & Company.

Shipan, Charles R. 2008. "Partisanship, Ideology, and Senate Voting on Supreme Court Nominees." *Journal of Empirical Legal Studies* 5(1):55–76.

Shipan, Charles R., Brooke Thomas Allen, and Andrew Bargen. 2014. "Choosing When to Choose: Explaining the Duration of Presidential Supreme Court Nomination Decisions." *Congress & the Presidency* 41(1):1–24.

Shipan, Charles R. and Megan L. Shannon. 2003. "Delaying Justice(s): A Duration Analysis of Supreme Court Confirmations." *American Journal of Political Science* 47(4):654–668.

Shor, Boris and Jon C. Rogowski. 2018. "Ideology and the U.S. Congressional Vote." *Political Science Research and Methods* 6(2):323–341.

Shor, Boris and Nolan McCarty. 2011. "The Ideological Mapping of American Legislatures." *American Political Science Review* 105(3):530–551.

Shugerman, Jed Handelsman. 2012. *The People's Courts: Pursuing Judicial Independence in America*. Harvard University Press.

Simon, James F. 1980. *Independent Journey: The Life of William O. Douglas*. HarperCollins.

Simon, Roger. 2008. "Obama Beats Hillary over Head with Iraq." *Politico*, Jan. 31. https://www.politico.com/story/2008/01/obama-beats-hillary-over-head-with-iraq-008248.

Sinclair, Harriet. 2018. "Sean Hannity Claims Kavanaugh Allegations Part of 'Ugliest Smear Campaign in History.'" *Newsweek*, Sept. 27. https://www.newsweek.com/sean-hannity-claims-kavanaugh-allegations-part-ugliest-smear-campaign-history-1142044

Snow, Charles Percy. 1959. *The Two Cultures and the Scientific Revolution*. Cambridge University Press.

Snyder, James M. and Michael M. Ting. 2002. "An Informational Rationale for Political Parties." *American Journal of Political Science* 46(1):90–110.

Snyder, James M. and Michael M. Ting. 2003. "Roll Calls, Party Labels, and Elections." *Political Analysis* 11(4):419–444.

Somin, Ilya. 2016. *Democracy and Political Ignorance: Why Smaller Government Is Smarter.* Stanford University Press.

Southworth, Ann. 2009. *Lawyers of the Right: Professionalizing the Conservative Coalition.* University of Chicago Press.

Spaeth, Harold J. and Jeffrey A. Segal. 1999. *Majority Rule or Minority Will: Adherence to Precedent on the U.S. Supreme Court.* Cambridge University Press.

Special to the New York Times. 1937. "Black Confirmed by Senate 63-16; Debate Is Bitter." *New York Times*, Aug. 18. https://timesmachine.nytimes.com/timesmachine/1937/08/18/118987270.html?pageNumber=1

Squire, Peverill. 1988. "Politics and Personal Factors in Retirement from the United States Supreme Court." *Political Behavior* 10(2):180–190.

Stasavage, David. 2007. "Polarization and Publicity: Rethinking the Benefits of Deliberative Democracy." *Journal of Politics* 69(1):59–72.

Staszak, Sarah. 2014. *No Day in Court: Access to Justice and the Politics of Judicial Retrenchment.* Oxford University Press.

Steigerwalt, Amy. 2010. *Battle over the Bench: Senators, Interest Groups, and Lower Court Confirmations.* University of Virginia Press.

Steigerwalt, Amy, Richard L. Vining, Jr., and Tara W. Stricko. 2013. "Minority Representation, the Electoral Connection, and the Confirmation Vote of Sonia Sotomayor." *Justice System Journal* 34(2):189–207.

Stephenson, Matthew C. 2003. ""When the Devil Turns...": The Political Foundations of Independent Judicial Review." *Journal of Legal Studies* 32(1):59–89.

Stimson, James. 2018. *Public Opinion in America: Moods, Cycles, and Swings.* Routledge.

Stokes, Donald E. and Gudmund R. Iversen. 1962. "On the Existence of Forces Restoring Party Competition." *Public Opinion Quarterly* 26(2):159–171.

Stolberg, Sheryl Gay and Jonathan Martin. 2018. "Conservative and Liberal Groups Gird for Battle over Kavanaugh." *New York Times*, July 10.

Stolzenberg, Ross M. and James Lindgren. 2010. "Retirement and Death in Office of US Supreme Court Justices." *Demography* 47(2):269–298.

Strine, Michael. 1995. "Counsels to the President: The Rise of Organizational Competition." In *Government Lawyers: The Federal Legal Bureaucracy and Presidential Politics.* University Press of Kansas.

Stroud, Natalie Jomini. 2011. *Niche News: The Politics of News Choice.* Oxford University Press on Demand.

Sunstein, Cass R., David Schkade, and Lisa M. Ellman. 2004. "Ideological Voting on Federal Courts of Appeals: A Preliminary Investigation." *Virginia Law Review* 90:301–354.

Székely, Marcell and John Michael. 2020. "The Sense of Effort: A Cost-Benefit Theory of the Phenomenology of Mental Effort." *Review of Philosophy and Psychology* 12:889–904.

Taleb, Nassim Nicholas. 2007. *The Black Swan: The Impact of the Highly Improbable.* Vol. 2. Random House.

Teles, Steven M. 2008. *The Rise of the Conservative Legal Movement.* Princeton University Press.

The Chicago Tribune. 1932. "The U.S. Supreme Court." Feb. 21.

The Chicago Tribune. 1946. "The Supreme Court." June 8th.

The LBJ Library. 2012. "LBJ and Thurgood Marshall, 7/7/65, 1.30P." https://www.youtube.com/watch?v=Qovbu8nf53I.

Theriault, Sean, Patrick Hickey, and Abby Blass. 2011. "Roll-Call Votes." In *The Oxford Handbook of the American Congress*, ed. George C. Edwards, III, Frances E. Lee, and Eric Schickler.

Tilly, Charles. 2005. *Popular Contention in Great Britain, 1758–1834.* Routledge.

Todd, Alden L. 1964. *Justice on Trial: The Case of Louis D. Brandeis*. Vol. 321. McGraw-Hill.

Toobin, Jeffrey. 2017. "The Conservative Pipeline to the Supreme Court." *The New Yorker*, April 10th. https://www.newyorker.com/magazine/2017/04/17/the-conservative-pipeline-to-the-supreme-court.

Train, Kenneth E. 2009. *Discrete Choice Methods with Simulation*. Cambridge University Press.

Truman, David B. 1951. *The Governmental Process: Political Interests and Public Opinion*. Knopf.

Uslaner, Eric M. 2002. *The Movers and the Shirkers: Representatives and Ideologues in the Senate*. University of Michigan Press.

Vavreck, Lynn. 2015. "Why Network News Still Matters." *New York Times*, Feb. 19. https://www.nytimes.com/2015/02/19/upshot/why-network-news-still-matters.html.

Vinovskis, Maris A. 1978. "Abortion and the Presidential Election of 1976: A Multivariate Analysis of Voting Behavior." *Michigan Law Review* 77:1750.

Vogel, Kenneth P. and Shane Goldmacher. 2022. "An Unusual $1.6 Billion Donation Bolsters Conservatives." *New York Times*, Aug. 22. https://www.nytimes.com/2022/08/22/us/politics/republican-dark-money.html.

Walcott, Charles Eliot and Karen Marie Hult. 1995. *Governing the White House: From Hoover through LBJ*. University Press of Kansas.

Waldron, Jeremy. 2006. "The Core of the Case against Judicial Review." *Yale Law Journal* 115(6):1346–1406.

Walker, Jack L. 1991. *Mobilizing Interest Groups in America: Patrons, Professions, and Social Movements*. University of Michigan Press.

Wallach, Philip A. 2017. "Prospects for Partisan Realignment: Lessons from the Demise of the Whigs." Brookings Institute Press www.brookings.edu/research/prospects-for-partisan-realignment-lessons-from-the-demise-of-the-whigs/.

Washington Post. 2020. "We're Asking 2020 Democrats Where They Stand on Key Issues." *Washington Post*. www.washingtonpost.com/graphics/politics/policy-2020

Watson, George and John Stookey. 1995. *Shaping America: The Politics of Supreme Court Appointments*. HarperCollins.

Watson, Richard L. 1963. "The Defeat of Judge Parker: A Study in Pressure Groups and Politics." *Mississippi Valley Historical Review* 50(2):213–234.

Weingast, Barry R. 1995. "The Economic Role of Political Institutions: Market-Preserving Federalism and Economic Development." *Journal of Law Economics & Organization* 11:1.

Weir, Margaret and Theda Skocpol. 1985. "State Structures and the Possibilities for 'Keynesian' Responses to the Great Depression in Sweden, Britain, and the United States." In *Bringing the State Back In*, ed. Dietrich Rueschemeyer Evans, Peter and Theda Skocpol. Cambridge University Press.

Wheeler, Lydia. 2018. "Debate over Term Limits for Supreme Court Gains New LIfe." *The Hill*, Dec. 6. https://thehill.com/regulation/court-battles/419960-debate-over-term-limits-for-supreme-court-gains-new-life/.

Whittington, Keith E. 2006. "Presidents, Senates, and Failed Supreme Court Nominations." *Supreme Court Review* 2006(1):401–438.

Whittington, Keith E. 2022. "The Judicial Review of Congress Database, 1789–2022 (July 2022)." https://scholar.princeton.edu/kewhitt/judicial-review-congress-database.

Williams, Daniel K. 2011. "The GOP's Abortion Strategy: Why Pro-Choice Republicans Became Pro-Life in the 1970s." *Journal of Policy History* 23(4):513–539.

Williams, Margaret and Lawrence Baum. 2006. "Supreme Court Nominees before the Senate Judiciary Committee." *Judicature* 90:73.

Wilson, James Q. 1962. *The Amateur Democrat: Club Politics in Three Cities*. University of Chicago Press.

Wittes, Benjamin. 2009. *Confirmation Wars: Preserving Independent Courts in Angry Times*. Rowman & Littlefield.

Wittman, Donald. 1977. "Candidates with Policy Preferences: A Dynamic Model." *Journal of Economic Theory* 14(1):180–189.

Wittman, Donald. 1983. "Candidate Motivation: A Synthesis of Alternative Theories." *American Political Science Review* 77(1):142–157.

Wlezien, Christopher. 1995. "The Public as Thermostat: Dynamics of Preferences for Spending." *American Journal of Political Science* 39(4):981–1000.

Wolbrecht, Christina. 2002. "Explaining Women's Rights Realignment: Convention Delegates, 1972–1992." *Political Behavior* 24(3):237–282.

Wolpert, Robin M. and James G. Gimpel. 1997. "Information, Recall, and Accountability: The Electorate's Reponse to the Clarence Thomas Nomination." *Legislative Studies Quarterly* 22(4):535–550.

Woodward, Bob and Scott Armstrong. 1979. *The Brethren: Inside the Supreme Court*. Simon and Schuster.

Yackee, Susan Webb. 2006. "Sweet-Talking the Fourth Branch: The Influence of Interest Group Comments on Federal Agency Rulemaking." *Journal of Public Administration Research and Theory* 16(1):103–124.

Yalof, David Alistair. 2001. *Pursuit of Justices: Presidential Politics and the Selection of Supreme Court Nominees*. University of Chicago Press.

Zaller, John and Stanley Feldman. 1992. "A Simple Theory of the Survey Response: Answering Questions versus Revealing Preferences." *American Journal of Political Science* 36(3): 579–616.

Zorn, Christopher J.W. and Steven R. Van Winkle. 2000. "A Competing Risks Model of Supreme Court Vacancies, 1789–1992." *Political Behavior* 22(2):145–166.

Index

Note: Tables are indicated by a *t* and Figures are indicated by an *f*